Denver

Denver

MINING CAMP TO METROPOLIS

Stephen J. Leonard *and*
Thomas J. Noel

University Press of Colorado

Copyright © 1990 by Stephen J. Leonard and Thomas J. Noel
Published by the University Press of Colorado
P.O. Box 849
Niwot, Colorado 80544

10 9 8 7 6 5 4 3 2

The University Press of Colorado is a cooperative publishing enterprise supported, in part, by Adams State College, Colorado State University, Fort Lewis College, Mesa State College, Metropolitan State College of Denver, University of Colorado, University of Northern Colorado, University of Southern Colorado, and Western State College.

The paper used in this publication meets the minimum requirements of the American National Standard for Information Sciences—Permanence of Paper for Printed Library Materials. ANSI Z39.48–1984. ∞

Design by Carol Humphrey.

Library of Congress Cataloging-in-Publication Data

Leonard, Stephen J.
    Denver: mining camp to metropolis / Stephen J. Leonard and Thomas J. Noel. —
1st ed.
      p.   cm.
    Includes bibliographical references (p.) and index.
    ISBN: 0-87081-240-8
    1. Denver (Colo.)—History. 2. Denver Region (Colo.)—History.
I. Noel, Thomas J. (Thomas Jacob) II. Title.
F784.D457L46 1990
978.8'83—dc20
                                             90-13054
                                              CIP

To our Parents

CONTENTS

CONTENTS

MAPS

The founders of Denver builded better than they knew, for it is not likely the visions of their wildest dreams pictured anything approaching the reality that is before us now. "Denver City" was, in fact, a little frontier business enterprise in real estate.

Jerome Smiley
History of Denver, 1901

Denver, the child of 1858 gold discoveries on the South Platte River, might have died at birth except for some sharp developers. Realizing that gold lay up in the mountains, not at their base, these first Denverites began peddling town lots and supplying mountain mining towns. Ruthlessly, they crushed the Native Americans and outmanuevered rival villages such as Golden.

Broadening its horizons, the Queen City of the Plains strove to conquer the Rockies, building a railroad network to tap this vast, rugged region. By 1890, Denver had a population of 106,713 and ranked as the third-largest city west of the Missouri, behind Omaha and San Francisco. The Depression of 1893 ended the boom, but much of Denver's subsequent history followed the tracks laid in its youth.

Denver overcame its frontier rawness with twentieth-century beautification projects but remained an isolated oasis dependent on the riches of the earth, on its water supplies, and on efficient transportation. Railroads, automobiles, and, eventually, airplanes brought Denver closer to America's urban mainstream. The federal government's growing role during the Great Depression and World War II ignited a postwar boom. By the 1990s, the Mile High City had become an amorphous, automobile- addicted metropolis that blanketed more than 1,000 square miles with subdivisons, shopping centers, and smog.

Sprawling western American megalopolises now comprise many of the nation's largest metropolitan areas. Yet scholars have neglected Denver and other western cities, leaving them short on historical perspective and scholarly analysis. Previous histories of Denver, including some of our own efforts, have focused on the nineteenth century and on the City and

County of Denver. Over two-thirds of this book is devoted to the metropolis since 1900. Separate chapters cover the histories of suburban Adams, Arapahoe, Boulder, and Jefferson counties — virgin territories for professional historians. On this suburban frontier, as in the pre-1900 core city, people continue to pursue the American dream — capitalizing on nature's bounty, demanding individual freedoms and opportunities, and resisting government regulations and taxes.

Denver's past has been chronicled in terms of its power elite and the institutions they created. In retelling that tale of conquest and city building, we have also emphasized the role of previously neglected peoples, notably women, the working class, and ethnic minorities. We have wrapped the history of the metropolis around several themes, especially Denver's unusually strong and persistent dependence on mineral resources and its penchant for privatism — an emphasis on individual goals rather than on the public, common good. Unlike communities such as Salt Lake City, Denver never aspired to be a utopia, only a place to live and to make money.

Almost a century has passed since Jerome Smiley published his 978-page *History of Denver*. In updating that story, we have also endeavored to introduce new perspectives and to broaden the cast of characters involved in making a mining camp into the Rocky Mountain metropolis.

ACKNOWLEDGMENTS

Metropolitan State College of Denver and the University of Colorado at Denver supported this book in various ways. At Metropolitan State, President Thomas Brewer, Academic Vice-President James Purdue, Deans Phillip Boxer and Larry Johnson, and Professors Shirley Fredricks, Frank Nation, and Donald Wall helped, as did Mary Nation and the indispensable Karen Richardson. At CU-Denver, Vice-Chancellor for Research Fernie Baca and Dean Marvin Loflin found funding, and Professors Dick Allen, Jay Fell, Ellen Fisher, and Mark Foster read and improved portions of this work, as did Patty Limerick, Lee Scamehorn, and Hugo von Rodeck, Jr., at CU-Boulder. Dick Stevens, chair of the CU-Denver Geography Department, drew the maps. Thanks, too, to CU-Denver's June Callahan, Gerry Darr, and Lee Rozinski, who helped solve computer problems. Some CU-Denver graduate students assisted with research and manuscript reviews, including Steve Beaghler, Kathy Chamberlain, Julie Corona, Sharon Elfenbein, Peg Ekstrand, Rosemary Fetter, Barbara Goldhammer, Marcia Goldstein, Myra Kloppel, Kathy and Jim Lavender-Tehlia, Sharon Newman, Bob Olsen, Paul Turelli, Kelly Wensing, Chris Whitacre, Nancy Widmann, and Chuck Woodard.

The Denver Public Library's Western History Department offered suggestions, manuscripts, publications, and illustrations. We are deeply indebted to Eleanor Gehres and her fine staff, including Lisa Backman, Nancy Chase, Mary Daze, Britt Kaur, Augie Mastrogiuseppe, Kay Nefzger, Philip Panum, Kathey Swan, Rose Ann Taht, Lynn Taylor, Barbara Walton, and Kay Wisnia.

The other vital resource for Denver history is the Colorado Historical Society, where we are indebted to the resourceful manuscripts curator Stan Oliner, photo curator Eric Paddock, and Katherine Kane, Alice Sharp, Margaret Walsh, and David Wetzel.

Baker Business Library at Harvard, the Bancroft Library at the University of California at Berkeley, the Library of Congress and National Archives in Washington, D.C., the University of Denver Library, Rutherford Witthus of the Auraria Archives, Gene M. Gressley at the University of Wyoming, the Western Historical Collections in Norlin

Library at CU-Boulder, and Terry Ketelsen and his capable crew at the Colorado State Archives all kindly assisted our research.

Throughout the metropolis, we received invaluable assistance from governmental agencies, especially history centers, libraries, and planning offices. Particularly helpful were Bob McQuarie and the Littleton History Museum, Virginia Roberts Steele and the Aurora History Museum, Sheila Smith and the Belmar Museum in Lakewood, Lois Lindstrom, Marcetta Lutz, Francis Rizzari, Sandy Crain and Hiwan Homestead Museum, the Adams County Museum, and Lois Anderton of Boulder's heavenly Carnegie Library devoted entirely to local history.

Over the years, a great many people have reviewed and enhanced this work. Thanks to the late Louisa Arps and Margaret Jacob; to Bill Bessesen, Dick Conn, Dick Dittemore, Ruth Falkenberg, Phil Goodstein, Tom Gougeon, Ed Haley, Bill Hornby, William Leonard, Betty Miller, Sam Mamet, Louise Noel, Mary Noel, Barbara Norgren, Larry Steele, Jackson Thode, and many others. At the University Press of Colorado, we benefited from the patience, skill, and kindness of Jody Berman, Pam Ferdinand, Pete Hammond, Carol Humphrey, John Schwartz, and Judy and Luther Wilson. Vi Noel helped both authors in too many ways to mention. Your corrections and suggestions will be welcomed by either author.

S. J. Leonard and T. J. Noel
July 6, 1990

Denver

CROSSING THE PLAINS.

Part I:
Riches of the Earth, 1858–1900

Born as a mining camp, Denver became a get-and-git-out town suffering from what Mark Twain called the "Californian sudden-riches disease." When the earth's resources played out, or richer strikes occurred elsewhere, most of the footloose populace moved on. But a few Denverites persisted, perhaps out of loyalty, perhaps because of their real estate investments. These town builders dispossessed the Arapaho and Cheyenne and made Denver the railroad hub of the Rockies, spinning a spiderweb of steel to tap a vast Rocky Mountain hinterland. Fortunes from mining rushes financed a rush to respectability; the Queen City of the Plains exported pay dirt and imported culture. Palatial hotels, elegant opera houses, splendid churches, commercial blocks, schools and mansions provided at least a veneer of gentility.

Women, who saw to it that Denver became the first large city in the world to give them the vote, struggled to refine urban life. While many men relied on "Judge Lynch," some women addressed the underlying problems of disease, ignorance, poverty, and unbridled privatism. By the time the silver crash struck in 1893, Denver had emerged as the metropolis of the Rockies, the nation's twenty-sixth–largest city. Reflecting the city's Gilded Age origins, Denverites were speculative, mobile, ambitious boosters, proud of their unabashed materialism.

CHAPTER 1

Gold!

Oh the Gold! the Gold — they say
'Tis brighter than the day,
And now 'tis mine, I'm bound to shine,
And drive dull care away.

Lawrence, Kansas, *Republican*, September 2, 1858[1]

Gold! The magic metal drew thousands to Colorado in 1859. It took gold to lure them; the Pikes Peak country suffered from a terrible reputation. For half a century travelers and explorers had branded eastern Colorado a desert and damned the treacherous Rockies. In 1846 Francis Parkman had journeyed south along the Front Range from Fort Laramie to Bent's Fort on the Arkansas River. In *The Oregon Trail,* his classic portrayal of western life, he told of Colorado's "burning plains" infested with "wingless grasshoppers of the most extravagant dimensions." At Cherry Creek he dug for water in the stream's dry bed, and on its headwaters he crossed the "rough and savage glens" of the Black Forest.[2]

Parkman described a parched wasteland uninviting to Anglo-American farmers accustomed to plenty of rain. Even New Mexico's Hispanos, who knew how to scratch a living from semiarid land, stopped hundreds of miles south of Cherry Creek, checked by nature's stinginess and Indian hostility. A few visionaries, including William Gilpin, who would become Colorado's first territorial governor, argued that irrigation could turn the West into a new Garden of Eden. But easterners believed

Parkman, as earlier they had listened to explorers Zebulon M. Pike and Stephen H. Long, who warned of a great desert west of the hundredth meridian, land that Long suggested would best be left to the Native Americans.

The vast area that farmers initially spurned did attract trappers, seeking fur and freedom, solitude and Indian women. In 1816 mountain men and Native Americans traded where Bear Creek joins the the South Platte in what is now Englewood. In 1832 Louis Vasquez, a St. Louis fur trader, made a fort of cottonwood logs near the confluence of Clear Creek and the South Platte. Peter A. Sarpey, a Frenchman, built a small fort five miles north of Vasquez. Other forts — Lancaster, Lupton, Jackson, St. Vrain, and a second Fort Vasquez — dotted the South Platte between present-day Denver and Greeley.[3] Richens Lacy Wootton, who worked for William Bent in the early 1840s, regularly rode between Fort St. Vrain and Bent's Fort. The dust he raised along the Cherry Creek trail through the future site of Denver quickly settled into the plains' emptiness. Summer rendezvous and adobe forts were transitory; traffic, sporadic. Robert M. Peck, a soldier who passed through in 1857, described the South Platte valley as a "howling wilderness."[4]

Gold changed that. For centuries rumors of gold had drifted out of the Rockies. The Spanish adventurer Francisco Vásquez de Coronado had vainly searched from Mexico to Kansas in 1540 looking for fabled golden cities. In 1807, Lieutenant Pike heard of treasure in Colorado from James Purcell, a trader he met in Santa Fe. Trappers spun gilded tales, and Indian legends spoke of magical yellow bullets. Luckily for the natives, who feared that a gold rush would doom their hunting grounds, the stories were dismissed as tall tales until after 1849, when gold strikes in California captured the nation's attention.

In 1850, Lewis Ralston and other California-bound prospectors passed along the Front Range of the Rockies, panning promising streams as they went. On June 21, 1850, John Lowrey Brown recorded in his diary: "Finished crossing at two oclock. Left the Platt and traveled six miles to creek. Good water, grass, and timber. Camp 44. We called this Ralstons creek because a man of that name found gold here."[5] The discovery, which took place in present-day Arvada, was small, so they tarried only briefly, but they remembered Ralston Creek.

Seven years later soldiers commanded by Major John C. Sedgwick marched along Cherry Creek where they chanced upon seven Missourians who said they had discovered gold. Their story was verified when Fall Leaf, an Indian scouting for Sedgwick, found a few nuggets. Later, Fall

Mountains and Plains

The Cheyennes believed that in the beginning the world was covered with water. A man floating on the surface asked a duck to gather mud from the sea bottom. From this muck the man made land.

Modern geologists think that the Rocky Mountains resulted from an uplift that began around 70 million years ago. Today's peaks are the successors of the Ancestral Rockies raised 300 million years ago, and those mountains were preceded by still earlier ranges. During the eons between the erosion of the Ancestral Rockies and the birth of the present mountains, dinosaurs and other primeval creatures dwelt in the area — the 85-foot-long diplodocus, the three-horned triceratops, the squat goniopholis, and the bony-backed stegosaurus, destined for distinction as Colorado's state fossil. Near Morrison those creatures left a great deposit of fossils that paleontologist Othneil Marsh carted off to Yale University in the late 1870s.

For millions of years after the washing away of the Ancestral Rockies, the region was under water. The resultant Lyons sandstone became flagstone for Denver's sidewalks. Limestone from the shells of sea creatures provided concrete for highways and buildings. At other times swamps flourished, leaving behind carbon-rich debris that made coal and natural gas to heat homes, and oil to fuel cars.

As subterranean forces raised the present Rockies, rain and ice wore them down. Volcanoes occasionally counteracted this dissolution, their lava flows creating such features as North and South Table mountains near Golden. By 28 million years ago the eastern portions of the Colorado Rockies had been planed into tame mountains. A regional uplift changed that — the Front Range was dramatically delineated from the plains by a sharp increase in elevation. Such an abrupt demarcation made railroad building difficult, but it pleased tourists and Coloradans who have turned the mountains into their playgrounds.

Casual observers, seeing the Rockies rise majestically, assume that altitudes uniformly increase as one travels west — that Denver is higher than its eastern suburbs. Yet places as far away as Limon, 80 miles east of the Mile High City, are more than a mile high. Denver, along with its northern and southern suburbs, sits in a trough at the base of the northern Front Range. This depression causes streams that rise on high ground east and southeast of Denver, such as Cherry Creek, to flow west toward the mountains. The basin also captures the South Platte River, which, blocked by elevations rising to both the east and south of its exit from the mountains, must flow north, creating a hospitable valley. There, for more than 10,000 years, nomadic bands of early Americans hunted. There, for less than 150 years, new Americans of European, African, and Asian ancestry have built cities.

Leaf returned to Lawrence, Kansas, where he backed his reports with glittering evidence.

In the meantime, William Green Russell, a farmer and part-time prospector from the gold-mining region of northern Georgia, heard of the 1850 Ralston Creek discovery. With friends and relatives he joined other groups until, in spring 1858, the combined party numbered 104. Reaching Cherry Creek in late June, they panned along the South Platte where they found a tease of color. Theorizing that this gold dust had washed down from the mountains, Russell and five others trekked up Clear Creek. Steep slopes and a wild river convinced them that "a bird could not fly up that canyon."[6] Defeated, they returned to the plains, unaware of Clear Creek's rich gold deposits. Most of Russell's companions had become so disgusted — they were averaging less than a penny's worth of gold from each pan of gravel — that they threatened to desert him in mid-July. Russell pleaded: "Gentlemen you may all go, but I will stay if two men will stay with me."[7] A loyal dozen, including his brothers Levi and Joseph Oliver, remained.

William Green Russell, veteran of the Georgia and California goldfields, found gold in the South Platte River in summer 1858. This strike triggered the Pikes Peak Gold Rush. (Colorado Historical Society.)

The next day they found gold where Dry Creek joins the South Platte in what is now Englewood. This placer deposit temporarily yielded $10 a day per man. There, at what they called Placer Camp, the Russells entertained John Cantrell and other mountain men. Cantrell took a sack of South Platte sand to Kansas City, Missouri, where, to the delight of onlookers, he panned out a small amount of gold. Meanwhile, the Russells left Placer Camp and went north along the Front Range into Wyoming in a fruitless search for richer fields. Late in September they returned to the South Platte where they found scores of newcomers poking about in the river.

Swayed by Fall Leaf's reports, these gold seekers had left Lawrence, Kansas, in late spring 1858. For a time the Lawrence party prospected near present-day Pueblo, but hearing of the Russells' diggings on the South Platte, they had traveled north, reaching Placer Camp shortly after the Russells had departed. A mile to the north the Lawrence contingent

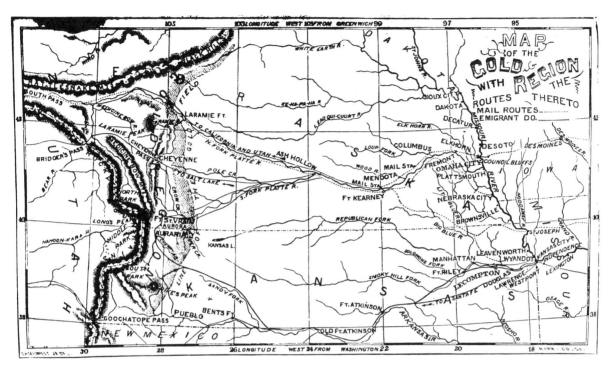

In his gold rush guidebook, William Byers steered argonauts to the Pikes Peak country via the Arkansas and South Platte river routes. Disappointed fortune seekers later threatened to lynch Byers for perpetrating a hoax. (Tom Noel Collection.)

Town founder William Larimer, in 1858, declared that Denver was "bound to be a 'great city'." In 1863, embittered by the town's flat economy and its failure to elect him mayor, he returned to Kansas. (Colorado Historical Society.)

built a dozen or so cabins, which they named Montana City. A few weeks later, on September 24, 1858, the mountain men William McGaa and John Simpson Smith, along with a handful of the Montana City miners, established another would-be metropolis, St. Charles, on the northeastern side of Cherry Creek near its juncture with the South Platte. Fearful that the winter would be harsh, most of them returned east. McGaa stayed behind, but the main task of guarding St. Charles was entrusted to one man, Charles Nichols. When the Russells returned from Wyoming they settled on the southwestern side of Cherry Creek across from the virtually empty town site of St. Charles. Soon some of the Lawrence men abandoned Montana City and united with the Russells. Others drifted in, some of them drawn by Cantrell's propaganda. On November 1, 1858, they organized the town of Auraria, naming it after the Russells' hometown in Georgia.[8]

On November 16, 1858, William H. Larimer, Jr., a veteran town promoter from Leavenworth, reached Auraria. The next day his small, well-armed party jumped the St. Charles site, telling Nichols, who had not finished his cabin, that if he objected, "a rope and a noose would be used on him."[9] McGaa shared his whisky with the interlopers; for co-operating, the furry-tongued mountain man was given town lots and honored with a street name.

James William Denver, governor of Kansas Territory, became the city's eponym. Town founders hoped that he would favor Denver City as the county seat of what was then Arapahoe County, Kansas. (Denver Public Library, Western History Department.)

Paper cities and real mining camps soon littered the area: Larimer waded across the South Platte and staked out Highland. Farther to the northwest, on Clear Creek, Arapahoe City and Golden took root. To the southeast, on Cherry Creek, Russellville rose; and south of Denver, Russell's Placer Camp attracted a few argonauts. John Pierce, one of Russell's companions, later joked that "before spring there were perhaps 20 cities in the country as large as New York, minus the wealth, population and buildings."[10]

Having ousted the St. Charles claimants, Larimer and his friends turned honest, although they were willing to overlook an occasional cabin jumping. When the journalists Horace Greeley, Albert D. Richardson, and Henry Villard visited in June 1859, they moved into the shack of an absent prospector. He suddenly appeared, said Richardson, and "apologized humbly for his intrusion."[11]

What Larimer's men did resent was theft comparable to their own: When squatters built on a vacant Denver lot, they tore down the jumpers' building. To secure its claim, the Larimer party officially organized the Denver City Town Company on November 22, 1858. Since the area was then part of Kansas Territory, they decided to name their square mile after James W. Denver, who they believed was still governor, although he had resigned a few weeks earlier. They named streets for themselves — Bassett, Wynkoop, Blake, McGaa, Larimer, Lawrence, Curtis, and Welton were all members of the town company. Other streets were given Indian names — Arapahoe, Champa, Cheyenne, Wapoola, and Wewatta.[12]

Countess Katrina Murat, one of the first to bring a woman's touch to the raw frontier crossroads, ran the El Dorado Hotel on Cherry Creek. (Colorado Historical Society.)

Soon, the rival hamlets of Auraria and Denver were vying to snare the businesses they hoped would insure prosperity. Both wanted a newspaper, so both promised town lots to editor William Newton Byers. He had arrived on April 17, 1859, and six days later published the region's first paper, the *Rocky Mountain News*. Byers located in Auraria where the second floor of Richens Wootton's saloon served as pressroom and staff living quarters. Stray bullets from the bar below disturbed sleeping printers above, so Byers laid additional flooring. To please both Auraria and Denver, the shrewd editor later moved the *News* to the dry bed of Cherry Creek — neutral ground between the puny principalities.

Land went to churches, to Masons, to Odd Fellows, and to babies. The infant Auraria Humbell received one parcel; three went to her parents. Hers was the second white birth in the Cherry Creek settlements; William Denver McGaa had been born in Auraria four months earlier, in March 1859. Baby McGaa was, however, a quarter Native American, so early chroniclers, biased against Indians, hesitated to count him. In August, John Denver Stout became Denver City's first white child.

By offering 53 lots and nine shares in the town company to the Leavenworth and Pikes Peak Express, Denver won the most important prize of all — the first stagecoach connection. Hotels and saloons wanted to be near the stage terminus, and letter-hungry citizens trooped there to pick up their mail. "It was," remembered town founder Samuel S. Curtis, "the vital move in the making of the city."[13]

Other enterprising pioneers pursued profit wherever they could. Henri Murat, a self-proclaimed count, wrote to a friend: "Gold is found everywhere," and then advised, "you can make your fortune as a shoe maker."[14] The count cut hair; the countess washed clothes. Thomas Warren, a Kentuckian, made clay pay as the town's first brick maker. He also ran a toll ferry, propelled across the South Platte by ropes, pulleys, and the river's current. "Noisy Tom" Pollock, Auraria's first blacksmith, discovered coal, which he sold for a dollar a bushel. He also found work as hangman, undertaker, and town marshal, receiving 50¢ for each person he jailed. Flexibility counted on the frontier.

Such seasoned mountain men as McGaa, Smith, Wootton, James P. Beckwourth, and Jim Baker were the new towns' old timers. Traders Beckwourth and Wootton brought welcome supplies to the isolated camps, which lacked farms, factories, and practically everything else, except dreams. Beckwourth, the son of a black slave and a white plantation overseer, first trapped in the Rockies in 1825. In the 1830s he managed Fort Vasquez, in the 1840s he helped found Fort Pueblo, in 1859 he opened a store in Auraria. Wootton, at age 42, also knew the region well. He became "Uncle Dick" to the newcomers, who respected his age, experience, and stature. Learning of the Cherry Creek excitement late in 1858, he diverted to Auraria supplies intended for the Indians. Thirsty prospectors savored his Taos Lightning, a potent whisky he served free at Christmas.[15] North of town, near the present intersection of Fifty-third and Tennyson, Baker built a toll bridge across the Vasquez Fork of the South Platte. He protested when the Vasquez Fork was renamed Clear Creek: "Cler Crik ain't cler crik. It's muddy."[16]

As 1859 dawned, the strange congregation of a few hundred men and a handful of women, housed in 75 cabins, prayed for a gold rush. Only a few thousand dollars' worth of gold dust had been washed from shallow South Platte pockets, which were quickly depleted. No veins of ore had been discovered. Yet, Luke Tierney, one of Russell's companions, predicted "by the first of June 1859 we shall have a population here of 60,000."[17]

The prophecy almost came true. Footloose farm boys and city clerks, torn from planting corn, shoeing horses, and sharpening pencils by the Depression of 1857, remembered the riches of California and headed west to the new El Dorado. Their dreams were exploited by merchants and speculators.[18] Among the hucksters were guidebook authors, many of whom touted the discoveries for the benefit of suppliers in midwestern towns. They recommended river routes: the Arkansas, the Platte, or the more dangerous Smoky Hill. They advised gold seekers to leave fancy gaiters and white Marseilles shirts at home; to take instead "three pairs of strong heavy pants, six flannel shirts, three pairs of durable boots, a coat and a military overcoat." In total, they suggested gold rush gear including oxen, wagons, and supplies costing $100 to $200 per person.[19] Such expensive advice was often ignored. Poor prospectors walked west, heedless of warnings that "to attempt to cross this desert on foot is madness — suicide — murder."[20]

Testimonials from Cherry Creek described Auraria as "surrounded by rich gold mines."[21] William Byers, who wrote about the region before he saw it, later denied that he repeated lies but did confess to including stories that were "a little bright perhaps."[22] By April 1859 the winter trickle of prospectors became a torrent. Lawrence N. Greenleaf, Colorado's first notable poet, satirized the tenderfoot:

> Upon the plains he dreamt about a nugget
> So big, it took just fourteen men to lug it;
> And waking, strove the treasure vast to seize,
> But found it was the moon behind the trees. [23]

Horace Greeley jolted westward by stagecoach to cover the rush for the *New York Tribune*. He observed that most travelers began their trek "trim and jolly" but arrived "sober as judges and as slow moving as their own weary oxen."[24] Byers estimated that as many as 150,000 argonauts set out for the Rockies, but many gave up before seeing Pikes Peak. Newspaperman Henry Villard suggested that the number was around 40,000, a guess closer to the 1860 federal census count of 34,231 in the region. At Cherry Creek the emigrants found gold scarce and prices high. Eggs sometimes fetched $2 a dozen; beans brought up to 75¢ a quart; tobacco commanded $2 a pound. Impoverished prospectors often sold their ox teams to raise money for food. That kept the price of meat low but meant that some who had come by wagon returned on foot. Hurrying home, the disgruntled "go backs" threatened to hang boosters, including Byers, and to burn Denver. An observer pitied them, "straggling across the plains in squads of dozens or scores, begging at the stations for goods to eat and a temporary shelter from the driving storms."[25]

News of rich discoveries in the mountains 40 miles west of Denver saved the town. George Jackson braved cougars and winter cold in January 1859 to prospect the northern flanks of Mount Evans. He found flake gold, but the discovery's impact was delayed because he and his friends kept the strike on Chicago Creek a secret until late April. More exciting to the eager prospectors in Denver were reports in May of John Gregory's diggings near what soon became Black Hawk: Gregory had found what no one else had — rich veins of gold.

Gold seekers who might have given up and returned east in March turned hopeful and continued west in May. The winter of 1859–1860 briefly halted the migration, until spring thawed the prairie and the emigrant flow resumed, giving Denver a census population of 4,749 by 1860, with men outnumbering women by a ratio of nearly six to one. Such precise figures, however, cloud the truth, for Denver's population continually fluctuated; the town was a revolving door, entry to, and exit from, the mountains. As an inland port on the prairie ocean's western shore, Denver emerged as supply and service center destined to outlast most of the mining centers. Fortunately, Colorado's wealth, in the mountains and on the plains, was so diverse that while individual towns rose and fell Denver survived. Gold, silver, lead, zinc, copper, vanadium, tungsten, molybdenum, oil, coal, natural gas, uranium, and oil shale would one day enrich the piedmont city. Unaware of most of these riches, the '59ers swept across the plains and marched deep into the mountains. The gold was enough for them. Yet, the wealth they sought, the gold they found, and the land they settled did not belong to them.

CHAPTER 2

Native Americans

Conquest forms the historical bedrock of the whole nation, and the American West is a pre-eminent case study in conquest and its consequences. Conquest was a literal, territorial form of economic growth.

Patricia Limerick
The Legacy of Conquest, 1987[1]

At daybreak on November 29, 1864, Colorado's Third Cavalry went hunting. Mainly young men — laborers from Denver, miners from the mountains — they had put aside picks and shovels to march out onto Colorado's eastern plains. At Sand Creek, 160 miles southeast of Denver, their commander, Colonel John Milton Chivington, halted them for a pep talk: "Men strip for action. . . . I don't tell you to kill all ages and sex[es], but look back on the plains of the Platte, where your mothers, fathers, brothers, sisters have been slain, and their blood saturating the sands of the Platte."[2]

Chivington's suggestion was sufficient; the regiment killed at will as it swept down on the nearby peaceful camp of Cheyenne and Arapaho. Old and young, women and children were indiscriminately slaughtered. A naked toddler provided a handy target as he wandered, confused, through the sand. Two troopers missed; the third did not. Captain Silas Soule, who refused to join in the butchery, later wrote to his mother, "It looked too hard for me to see little children on their knees begging for their lives, have their brains beaten out like dogs."[3]

Sketchy reports slowly reached Denver. Were over 500 Indians slain, as Chivington claimed, or was the number closer to 150, as others reported? Details did not concern the *Rocky Mountain News,* which praised the soldiers: "Among the brilliant feats of arms in Indian warfare, the recent campaigns of our Colorado volunteers, will stand in history with few rivals."[4] Unwittingly, the *News* was correct. No event in Colorado's military annals rivals the savage ferocity of the Sand

Despite accomplishments as a Methodist minister, Sunday School teacher, and military hero, John M. Chivington's reputation suffers because of his role in the Sand Creek massacre. (Tom Noel Collection.)

Creek massacre. With guns and bayonets, Chivington and his men tried to write a bloody end to the Native American era that had begun in ancient prehistory.

Artifacts found at Dent, 40 miles north of Denver, suggest that hunters occupied that area some 11,250 years ago. Similar evidence from Lamb Spring, 25 miles southeast of Denver, also indicates that the Front Range has attracted people for more than 10,000 years. These sites and other excavations have given archaeologists a glimpse of the region's early residents. From at least as early as 9000 B.C. until shortly after the 1859 gold rush, nomadic bands hunted in eastern Colorado. At first they stalked large beasts — camel, giant bison, and mammoth. As those creatures died out, hunters pursued smaller animals.[5]

In relatively modern times, around a thousand years ago, some of the natives in eastern Colorado may have planted and gathered crops. People described by archaeologists as belonging to the Dismal River culture established villages on the South Platte around A.D. 1300. Later, Apaches controlled eastern Colorado until they were ousted by Comanche and Kiowa raiders from the north. Comanches and Kiowas, in turn, were pushed southeast by other hunters, Cheyenne and Arapaho, who occupied northeastern Colorado around the year 1800. All the while, the Utes, their past shrouded in misty prehistory, dominated central and western Colorado, sometimes venturing east of the mountains in search of buffalo. Often these wanderers camped in many of the same well-watered spots that would later attract Euro-American settlers. Prehistoric artifacts and even some human remains have been found in what are now Denver suburbs — Aurora, Franktown, Hazeltine Heights, Ken Caryl

Little Raven and a band of Arapahos camped at the confluence of Cherry Creek and the South Platte River for several years after gold seekers founded Denver. He complained in vain: "It will be a very hard thing to leave the country that God gave us." (Denver Public Library, Western History Department.)

Ranch, Red Rocks, Roxborough Park, and Willowbrook.

Such deep roots did not assure the natives of uncontested ownership of the land. In 1706 Spain claimed what would become Colorado, and, later, Mexico fell heir to those claims. France also coveted Colorado, which its explorers, Pierre and Paul Mallet, entered in 1739. But neither France nor Spain and Mexico actually settled the area. The United States bought what would become northeastern Colorado — the eastern slope of the Rockies north of the Arkansas River — from France as part of the Louisiana Purchase in 1803. Nearly half a century later, after the rest of Colorado had been taken from Mexico at the end of the Mexican War (1846–1848), federal negotiators started to talk with the actual residents of the region — the Native Americans.

Sioux, Shoshones, Crows, Assiniboins, Arikaras, Arapahos, and Cheyennes by the thousands gathered at Fort Laramie on the North Platte in the late summer of 1851. Officials told them that the government did not want their land, that the U.S. Army only wished to build posts and to secure safe routes for prospectors and settlers on their way to California and Oregon. Supposedly to promote harmony among the natives, who sometimes fought over territory, agents allocated land to each group. A large tract stretching some 200 miles east from the Rocky Mountains between the Arkansas and North Platte rivers was reserved for the Arapahos and Cheyennes.[6] Those nations agreed to the Treaty of Fort Laramie, which by specifying group lands set the stage for later agreements forcing individual nations to give up more and more territory. With 27 wagon loads of gifts, the natives appeared contented. Even the land settlement, over 40,000 square miles for fewer than 10,000 Arapahos and Cheyennes, seemed reasonable. "I will go home satisfied," said Cut Hand, an Arapaho. "I will sleep sound and not have to watch my horses in the night, or be afraid for my squaws and children."[7]

For a few years the natives did sleep well. Then, minor clashes between the Cheyennes and whites gave the army an excuse to make war. Commanding over 800 men, Colonel Edwin V. Sumner and Major John

C. Sedgwick defeated the Cheyennes in 1857. Afterward, peace chiefs talked of settling down and of learning to farm. The gold seekers of 1858 and 1859 enjoyed generally peaceful passage across the plains to the Cherry Creek mining camps. William B. Parsons, author of a gold rush guidebook, praised the natives for aiding a lost prospector: "Indians will always do this unless provoked by the white man's cruelty or rapacity to do otherwise."[8]

In Denver, greenhorn prospectors mingled with hundreds of natives. The site had long been a favorite campground for the Arapahos, who relished the wild cherries that gave Cherry Creek its name. Albert Richardson, one of the first journalists to visit Denver, looked out from his cabin on a dozen Indian lodges. He saw "braves lounging on the ground wearing no clothing except a narrow strip of cloth about the hips," and "naked children playing in the hot sand" while the women were "dressing the skins of wild animals or cooking puppies for dinner."[9] Sensible gold seekers gave a party for their native landlords in January 1859. Unfortunately, such civility did not last. In April 1860, "drunken devils and bummers" attacked Indians camped near town and raped the women. "Hellish work," said the old mulatto trapper, James Beckwourth, who lamented that the natives "had been abused worse than dogs" on their own land.[10] Beckwourth asked for justice. Horace Greeley, touring the gold fields in June 1859, pled for compassion, predicting that unless the aborigines were handled as "a band of orphan children," they "will be practically extinct within the next fifty years."[11] Cheyenne elders concluded that it was useless to resist the white hordes. Sweet Medicine, a legendary Cheyenne holy man, had prophesied that the strangers would drive his people "worse than crazy."[12]

Boomers and gold seekers worried less about compassion than they did about land. They organized companies to claim town sites, and as a dodge to secure Indian titles included among the town founders the traders William McGaa and John S. Smith, both of whom had Native American wives.[13] The United States knew, however, that such ploys rested on sand. To gain clear title to farms and mines, to Denver, Golden, Central City, and Boulder, the promises made at Fort Laramie in 1851 had to be undone.

In 1860, Indian agent Albert G. Boone, grandson of the frontiersman Daniel Boone, approached the Cheyennes and Arapahos. The government sent them gifts, and Boone spent his own money to buy more. In early 1861 his investment paid off. Some of the chiefs agreed to the Treaty of Fort Wise, which gave the United States control of the Denver area and most of the rest of northeastern Colorado.[14] The flawed treaty — not all the chiefs agreed to it — was signed on February 18, 1861, just 10 days before Congress made Colorado a territory.

For the rest of 1861 and into 1862 the Cheyennes and Arapahos generally kept the peace. Jittery settlers, however, feared the natives, especially after an 1862 Sioux uprising in Minnesota. Reacting to rumors that Plains nations were uniting for war in the summer of 1863, John Evans, Colorado's second territorial governor, asked the Cheyennes to meet with him. "I set out," Evans complained, "with provisions to supply them and make them a feast, and after I got there they didn't come." Evans's emissary, Elbridge Gerry, did talk with Bull Bear, a Cheyenne warrior, who asked Gerry if Evans wanted the natives to live as white men did. Gerry said yes, to which Bull Bear, responded: "Well, you can just go back to the Governor and tell him that we are not reduced that low yet."[15]

The natives also explained that they were preparing for the autumn buffalo hunt.[16] They needed to hunt to live. Major Scott Anthony, commander of Fort Lyon on the Arkansas River, reported: "The Indians are all very destitute this season and the government will be compelled to subsist them to a great extent, or allow them to starve to death, which would probably be the easier way of disposing of them."[17] Starving young warriors sometimes raided wagon trains and stole food from farmers. In June 1864, four Arapahos went further, brutally murdering Ellen Hungate, her husband, Nathan, and their young daughters on a ranch 25 miles southeast of Denver. William Byers long remembered the Hungates' "bloated, festering bodies . . . drawn naked through the streets in an ox wagon." Denverites counted the 80 bullet holes in Nathan's corpse and looked upon the children with their heads nearly severed from their bodies.[18]

Panic swept Denver a few days later when ox drivers outside of town were mistaken for Indians. Women and children fled to two of Denver's most substantial buildings, the U.S. Branch Mint and the Army Commissary. At the commissary, sentries prepared to chop away the stairs "at the first sight of the red devils." Upstairs, ladies who had seen the Hungates' corpses described them to those who had not.[19] The scare passed, but people remained tense, ready to believe rumors. Mail was cut off in the late summer when carriers refused to cross the plains. George W. Kassler, a local businessman, wrote to his fiancée, Maria Stebbins, "The given cause was fear of Indians, but it was really a piece of strategy on the part of the mail contractor who threw up his contract and got it renewed at

double the old figures."[20]

Farmers in outlying areas were especially frightened. Mollie Sanford worried about her husband, Byron, who spent part of the summer of 1864 hauling logs from Denver to his ranch south of town. "I feel there is a great risk in his going over a lonely road 10 miles, for bands of Indians have been seen, and murders have been committed as near as that to Denver. For weeks I have hardly slept without my clothes on, ready to flee at a moment's warning." Once she considered adopting an orphan girl who had been rescued from the natives: "She saw her father butchered, and only three years old, can and does recount the whole tragedy."[21]

To control the Indians, Governor Evans, in August 1864, raised the Third Colorado Regiment commanded by John Chivington. A six-foot, four-inch tall ex–Methodist preacher noted for his "muscular Christianity," Chivington had rejected a chaplaincy for a fighting command early in the Civil War.[22] For helping defeat Confederates at the 1862 Battle of Glorieta Pass in New Mexico he was made a colonel. Now, as the

Initially friendly Arapahos turned wary as gold seekers illegally seized their land, entering Indian wars that permanently altered the United States by perpetuating the need for a standing army and fostering a legacy of conquest. (Denver Public Library, Western History Department.)

"Nits make lice," Chivington said of Native American children such as these Arapaho youngsters. (Denver Public Library, Western History Department.)

commander of the military district of Colorado he was ready to fight Indians. For over two months the Third Colorado patrolled the South Platte River — boring duty that earned them the nickname "bloodless." The threat, it seemed, had passed. Accompanied by Major Edward W. Wynkoop, Indian leaders came to Denver in September 1864 asking for peace. "What shall I do with the Third regiment, if I make peace?" a perplexed Evans asked Wynkoop.[23] Chivington dismissed the emissaries, telling them to go to Fort Lyon, where Wynkoop fed them until he was replaced by Major Scott Anthony, who withdrew their rations and suggested that they camp north of the fort on Sand Creek.

In mid-November Chivington and the Third Colorado left Denver for Fort Lyon, pausing there briefly before marching to Sand Creek. Their attack on November 29, 1864, completely surprised the waking natives. White trader John S. Smith, who was visiting the camp, tried to reason with the soldiers but hastily retreated when one yelled: "Shoot the old son of a bitch; he is no better than an Indian."[24] Assuming a mistake had been made, Chief Black Kettle raised a U.S. and a white flag. His gesture did no good. The camp scattered. Many fleet-footed young men escaped. Women, children, and the old died.

"All acquitted themselves well, and Colorado soldiers once again covered themselves with glory," reported the *Rocky Mountain News*.[25] Chivington returned a hero. He praised most of his men but condemned Captain Silas Soule for seeming "more in sympathy with those Indians than with the whites."[26] Soule was not alone in his opposition to Chivington. Wynkoop, who had pledged peace, called Chivington an "inhuman monster," a judgment shared by John Smith.[27] Not only had Smith seen the natives slaughtered; his own half-Indian son, Jack, was taken prisoner and shot in cold blood. In 1865 both the army and Congress launched inquiries. In Washington, congressmen accused Governor Evans of giving testimony marked by "prevarication and shuffling," a charge that helped lead to his removal from office. Chivington, the

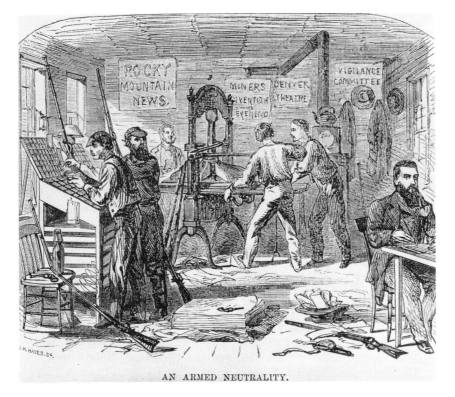

AN ARMED NEUTRALITY.

On April 23, 1859, William N. Byers began publishing the *Rocky Mountain News*, in part to help bring law and order to Colorado by scaring off "redskins" and paleface "bummers." (Denver Public Library, Western History Department.)

lawmakers said, had disgraced his uniform by ordering a "foul and dastardly massacre."[28]

Denver was placed under martial law. Soule, military commander while the army investigated, testified against Chivington, for which he earned the enmity of the colonel's partisans, one of whom shot and killed him. The Episcopal preacher Horace B. Hitchings praised the courageous captain: "He did his duty in the midst of danger, did his duty in the face of death, and fell by the assassin's hand."[29] Squiers, the soldier who shot Soule, escaped. So did Chivington. His army career was wrecked, but he went otherwise unpunished. Denver tried to forget.

Angry natives did not forget. "Now no peace," they told James Beckwourth.[30] Crossing the plains in March 1865, Clara V. Witter saw "where whole corrals made of wagons had been burned, nothing remaining but wheels and graves of the killed along the road."[31] Fighting continued in eastern Colorado until 1869 when General Eugene Carr, assisted by William "Buffalo Bill" Cody, defeated Cheyenne chief Tall Bull south of Sterling. That battle at Summit Springs proved to be the last significant clash between the army and Plains Indians in Colorado.[32]

The removal of the Arapahos and Cheyennes did not spell the end of

Native Americans in Denver. Utes from southern and western Colorado continued to frequent the city, especially in the 1870s, when payments due them under an 1868 treaty were made at the Denver Ute Agency. They posed no threat. Merchants welcomed their dollars and laughed as the once proud Utes stumbled drunk along Larimer Street. A scalp dance at Sloan's Lake in 1876 drew a large crowd including "lots of ladies prominent in church and society circles straining for a sight of the reeking scalps, which they scanned as eagerly as if they had been new bonnets."[33] Soon, white pressure for Ute territory deprived them of most of their Colorado land. Their demise in the early 1880s demonstrated that Colonel John Chivington had only done brutally and sensationally what others did with more finesse and less fanfare.[34]

Speaking of Sand Creek some 20 years after the event, John Evans unabashedly asserted, "The benefit to Colorado of that massacre, as they call it, was very great for it ridded the plains of the indians."[35] With Chivington or without him, Euro-Americans and Native Americans would have clashed. Methods might have differed without him; the results would not. The natives, slowly emerging from a hunting and gathering economy, possessed the land; the whites, speeding through the age of steam, wanted it. The newcomers' greed for gold and real estate, backed by their military muscle, cleared the way for town builders.

CHAPTER 3

Town Building

Denver is a city of four thousand people with ten or twelve streets laid out; with two hotels, a bank, a theater, half a dozen chapels, fifty gambling houses and a hundred grog shops. As you wander about these hot and dirty streets you seem to be walking in a city of demons.

William Hepworth Dixon
New America, 1867[1]

Denver's bars and brothels, where "a man's life is of no more worth than a dog's," appalled William Dixon, a touring English clergyman. Its men, he said, had many good qualities; "perseverance, generosity, enterprise," but they suffered from "frail" morals that, in his opinion, explained their aversion to marriage. He noted that up to the mid-1860s it was "quite usual for honest folks to be awakened from their sleep by the noise of exploding guns, and when daylight came to find that a dead body had been tossed from a window into the street." Still a frontier outpost, Denver frightened visitors and fell short of its founders' hopes. The Civil War, hostile Indians, isolation, fire, flood, lack of railroads, and a slow-down in Colorado's mining all retarded town building.

Respectable citizens wanted law and order. In January 1860, turkey thieves terrorized Auraria and Denver until blacksmith Thomas Pollock cracked one of the fowl-filchers' head with a rifle barrel. The others were exiled and the Turkey War ended. In July, James A. Gordon brutally murdered a popular barkeeper, John Gantz. Gordon fled to Leavenworth, where friends of Gantz caught him and beat him almost to death. Returned to Denver in chains, Gordon faced the People's Court, which decreed that he be hanged four days later — tardy justice by frontier standards. Secret tribunals acted faster. On September 2, 1860, vigilantes hanged Black Hawk, a horse thief. The next night they executed one of his partners and the following morning they shot another. Within 24 hours in December 1868, vigilantes snatched two men from the city jail and hanged them both: one from a cottonwood on Twelfth Street near Larimer; the other from the Larimer Street bridge.

Not every crime led to punishment. In frontier Denver, as elsewhere, the color of a person's skin often distorted justice. When gambler Charles Harrison shot a black man for saying that he was as good as a white man, no action was taken against Harrison. When another African-American, William J. Paine, killed Oliver Davis, also black, Paine claimed self-defense and was acquitted. In 1864 the mulatto mountain man James Beckwourth shot Paine. "Bully for Beckwourth," people said on the streets.[2]

Dueling, although losing favor in the East, retained a lease on death in the West. James Denver had dueled and killed in California; no one held it against him when it came to naming Denver after him. Hundreds of people watched the first local contest, a nonfatal encounter between Richard Whitsitt, president of the Denver City Town Company, and Thomas Warren, who operated the South Platte ferry. When Warren later challenged William Byers, the wily editor selected his own weapons — words at a safe distance: "You may murder us, but never on the so-called field of honor under the dignified name of a duel."[3] Colorado's first Territorial Legislature discouraged the slaughter by depriving both principals and their seconds of the right to vote.

Vendetta and vigilantism sprang in part from Kansas Territory's failure to enforce laws in its remote western parts. To strengthen their government, Cherry Creek pioneers created Jefferson Territory on October 24, 1859, carving it from parts of Kansas, Nebraska, New Mexico, and Utah. The territory, named in honor of President Thomas Jefferson, made Denver its capital and selected a governor and a legislature, but its authority was questioned locally, denied in Kansas, and unrecognized in Washington. The U.S. Congress mercifully killed Jefferson Territory on February 28, 1861, by forming Colorado Territory, naming it after the Colorado River.[4] Soon, courts were set up, judges selected, and laws passed. One provided up to three years in jail for "putting out eyes, slitting noses . . . or disabling tongues." Horse thieves faced a minimum of 20 years; rowdies who made a ruckus on Sunday risked $30 fines;

drunks paid for their insobriety by lugging water from Cherry Creek to fill fire barrels atop buildings.[5]

Nearly a year before Colorado Territory's creation, Denver and Auraria had ended their rivalry by consolidating. A moonlit ceremony on the Larimer Street bridge across Cherry Creek, April 6, 1860, ended the separate existence of Auraria, which had fallen behind Denver in the contest for stagecoach service and population. The gold region's first permanent settlement became west Denver, and its original name was largely forgotten.[6]

The Larimer Street bridge spanned an almost dry Cherry Creek in this 1873 view. (Colorado Historical Society.)

As pioneers put their towns together, the nation fell apart. Abraham Lincoln's election to the presidency in November 1860 caused southern states to split from the North and to form the Confederate States of America. Scarcely six weeks after Colorado became a territory, the Civil War began. In Denver, Confederates flew their flag over Wallingford and Murphy's store near Sixteenth and Larimer until Unionists attacked the rebel banner. Southerners stockpiled guns, but northern sentiment prevailed since most Denverites came from northern states. By autumn 1861 many rebels, including Denver's first mayor, John C. Moore, had returned to the South.[7]

William Gilpin, booster of the West and defender of the Union, became Colorado's first territorial governor in May 1861. "I was surrounded by professional assassins just the same as Lincoln was," he later claimed.[8] Fearing that Confederate Texans would march north to seize Rocky Mountain goldfields, Gilpin recruited the First Regiment of Colorado Volunteer Infantry, which he quartered at Camp Weld south of Denver.[9] They rushed south in February 1862 to battle Texans near Santa Fe

William Gilpin, whom President Abraham Lincoln appointed first governor of Colorado Territory, promoted the Great American Desert as a new Garden of Eden. (Tom Noel Collection.)

at Glorieta Pass. There, in March, Major John Chivington led a daring foray against the Confederate rear, destroying their supplies and forcing them to retreat.[10]

The Glorieta triumph solved only one of the problems created by the war. Intent on fighting, the divided nation lacked the capital and the interest to finance mines, build smelters, establish farms, and develop cities in Colorado. Drifters hung out in local saloons, some trying to avoid the draft; others whetting their resolve to return to the North or the South to fight. Until peace unleashed a united people's constructive energy, Denver stagnated.

Gilpin, a man of deep foresight and shallow common sense, was himself a victim of the conflict. Without securing approval from Washington, he issued $375,000 in federal promissory notes to pay for the First Colorado Volunteers. His bad checks propped up the local economy, but the Treasury Department's initial refusal to honor the unauthorized notes led, as William Byers put it, "to a war upon the governor" that forced him to resign.[11] Shrewd businessmen held onto the drafts, some of which eventually were paid.

Gilpin's successor, John Evans, reached Denver in May 1862. At 48, Evans looked back on a life many would have considered fulfilled. As a physician he had spearheaded the establishment of the Indiana Asylum for the Insane and had taught at Rush Medical College in Chicago. As a real estate developer he had helped create Evanston, a fashionable Chicago suburb named for him. As a public-spirited citizen and a dedicated Methodist he had helped found Northwestern University. Although not a close friend of Lincoln, Evans was an influential Republican. He had rejected the governorship of Washington Territory because it was too far from his Chicago business interests; Colorado suited him better. To his wife Margaret, who temporarily remained at their lakeshore home in Evanston, he wrote that he had settled in Denver, "really the only tolerable place" in the territory.[12]

Certainly, Denver surpassed Colorado City, 70 miles to the south, which enticed the Territorial Legislature into meeting there in the summer of 1862.[13] Denver also shone in comparison with Golden, nominally the territorial capital from 1862 to 1867, a prize it won by promising lawmakers free accommodations, generous libations, and firewood. Moreover, the town that welcomed Evans was starting to shed its frontier rawness. Frame houses with siding, shingle roofs, and glass windows were replacing crude log cabins, while false fronts made one-story shacks look like substantial buildings. Visiting in August 1863, John Nicolay,

St. Mary's Academy, Denver's first private school, was opened by the Sisters of Loretto and Father Joseph Machebeuf in 1864 to offer Catholics and non-Catholics education in the fine and liberal arts. (Photo by Alfred E. Rinehart, Denver Public Library.)

Lincoln's private secretary, stayed at the Planter's House, "a frame hotel built of pine, of tolerable size and for this country very well kept. . . . An excellent dinner was served."[14]

Here and there a brick building, made with soft, crumbly blocks, suggested the city to come, among them the Army Commissary at Eleventh and Larimer with its 20-inch-thick walls and the U.S. Branch Mint, misnamed since coins were not struck there, at Sixteenth and Market. A few churches also introduced civility and stability to the dusty little settlement. Almost in the country, near Fifteenth and Stout, stood the city's first Roman Catholic church, St. Mary's. More centrally located at Fourteenth and Arapahoe was Denver's first church building, built by the Southern Methodists, whose numbers dwindled at the outbreak of the Civil War. In spring 1862 Episcopalians bought the church and renamed it St. John's in the Wilderness.

Still, it took faith to see promise in the town. Most congregations wandered from temporary home to temporary home, often holding services in public halls and saloons. The Methodist church paid Henry C. Brown, one of its members, $21 a month rent for a building he had constructed in the bed of Cherry Creek. In 1865, Methodists spent $21,000 for a real church at Fourteenth and Lawrence. The Presbyterians worshipped in a small structure on Fifteenth between Lawrence and

Arapahoe. Jews, Congregationalists, and Baptists lacked permanent homes until after 1866.

Schools also languished. Owen J. Goldrick, called "the professor" because he claimed a college degree and cursed in Latin, opened a pay school in 1859, in a log cabin with a leaky roof and a sod floor on Twelfth Street between Larimer and Market, where he taught Anglo, Hispanic, and Indian students. Goldrick's short-lived school was succeeded by several other small private institutions, the principal one run by Lydia Maria Ring. Children without tuition money had to wait until late 1862 when a free school opened in rented quarters near Eleventh and Larimer. Public schools operated in temporary homes throughout the 1860s with African-American children shunted to a school in the African Methodist church from 1869 to 1873. Such overt segregation disappeared in 1873 when Denver, at last, constructed its first regular school building, the Arapahoe School between Seventeenth and Eighteenth on Arapahoe.

In the 1860s Denver City was, as the *News* put it, "so treeless, grassless, bushless" that Frederick J. Bancroft, a pioneer physician, imported dandelions to brighten the landscape.[15] Townsfolk let their pigs grovel in the garbage that filled streets and yards. "Once in a while some huge porker knocks down a child or trips up a lady," the *News* editorialized. "There is room for reform."[16] Many residents did not care. "The multitudes who made the instant cities," historian Gunther Barth has observed, "did not make instant citizens."[17] Just as gold had attracted many get-rich-quick dreamers in 1859, the difficulty of freeing pure metal from refractory ores caused many to leave in the early 1860s. In June 1864 Nathaniel P. Hill, a chemistry professor from Brown University, arrived in Denver. In a letter to his wife he complained, "I do not enjoy living in a country where every man you meet thinks it safe to carry a loaded pistol."[18] Calming his qualms, Hill stayed to build smelters that eventually would extract pure silver and gold. Meanwhile, mining slumped and so did Denver.

Things grew worse before they got better. A fire started by late-night revelers at the Cherokee House near Fifteenth and Blake on April 19, 1863, blackened the heart of the business district, causing some $250,000 in damage. Winds fanned the flames toward volunteers desperately chopping down buildings in the fire's path. Afterward, citizens recognized the folly of wooden structures and rebuilt in brick. By 1865 red brick business blocks gave the northeastern side of Cherry Creek an air of permanence lacking in Auraria, which had escaped the blaze.

Auraria's urban renewal came with the flood of May 20, 1864. Ignoring warnings from Native Americans and mountain men, settlers built ramshackle frame buildings, some of them on stilts, in the bed of Cherry Creek. They thought the creek bed safe since only twice had they seen much water in its sandy channel.[19] After several rainy days, Cherry Creek and the South Platte flooded, inundating low-lying Auraria. John Chivington braved the swollen South Platte in a flatboat to rescue William Byers's family

Barney Ford, a prominent African-American pioneer, operated a successful restaurant and hotel on Blake Street. After the 1863 fire reduced his place to ashes, Ford quickly rebuilt on the same spot. (Colorado Historical Society.)

from their ranch several miles south of town. *Rocky Mountain News* printers, sleeping at the office, escaped by grabbing a rope thrown from shore. "The water engine of death dragging its watery train of maddening waves," as Professor Goldrick described it, swept away the *News* building, the Methodist church, and the City Hall.[20] At least eight died; losses were calculated at $350,000.

Troubles continued into the summer of 1864 when Indian attacks on wagon trains, coupled with merchants' market manipulations, drove up prices. Winter brought bitter cold and, at Christmas, a violent windstorm that toppled St. Mary's 800-pound bell. Grasshoppers invaded in 1865, devouring garments drying on clotheslines and stripping the ground of vegetation. Real estate values fell from highs in 1859 and 1860 to ridiculous lows in the early and mid-1860s. Whole downtown blocks changed hands during the poker games that preoccupied the stagnant town's wheeler-dealers. In 1864, Congress granted clear titles to residents, all of whom, up to then, were technically squatters on government land. Outside the boundaries of the 960-acre Congressional Grant, speculators such as Henry Brown claimed tracts under the Homestead Act. Still, the exodus continued. From 4,749 in 1860, the town's population shrank to 3,500 in 1866.[21]

Many of the '58ers and '59ers left. The Russell brothers, who had been in and out of Denver since 1858, left permanently in 1863. William Green and Joseph Oliver joined the Confederate Army; Levi went prospecting in Montana. Uncle Dick Wootton, a Kentuckian, also may have favored the South and hence felt uncomfortable in Denver. He said that he relocated at Raton Pass on the Colorado–New Mexico border because Denver was so unstable. William Larimer, Jr., and his fellow town founder Samuel Curtis went east to command Union troops. Henri Murat and his wife moved south to Palmer Lake, where the countess lived into the twentieth century. William McGaa went north to LaPorte, sometimes visiting Denver for a drink. He died in 1867 in jail, where he had been thrown to sober up. James Beckwourth, who had left Denver for Wyoming, also died in the late 1860s on a visit to his old friends, the Crows. Mountain man Jim Baker tended a toll bridge north of town where he made pets of the prairie dogs around his adobe house. Cruel teamsters shot at the tame little rodents, which "discouraged and disgusted him with civilization."[22] He left in 1871. Others drifted away because, unlike John Evans, they did not find the place tolerable. "Damn a country," one homesick pioneer griped, "where dried apple pies are a luxury."[23]

Among the remaining faithful were stalwarts whose fortunes were so intertwined with Denver's that they fought to save the town. From time to time joined by newcomers or succeeded by their sons, they were to provide Denver with remarkably stable and able leadership for over 40 years. Homer L. Thayer's 1872 real estate map reveals that Henry Brown, William Byers, Walter Scott Cheesman, John Evans, George W. Kassler, Charles B. Kountze, David H. Moffat, and Daniel Witter all owned tracts surrounding Denver. Their futures were tied to Denver's.[24] Many of them had been born in either New York or Ohio and had lived in the Midwest before coming to Colorado. Moffat was typical. Born in New York in 1839 he had moved to Iowa in 1855 and a year later was working in an Omaha bank. He came to Denver in 1860 to sell books and newspapers. Miners, hungry for news, had paid Moffat's newsboys 25¢ a copy for the *St. Louis Democrat* and the *St. Louis Republican*.[25] In 1866, Moffat became a cashier at the First National Bank, which had been founded the year before by another New Yorker, Jerome B. Chaffee.

Moffat's friend and fellow New Yorker George Kassler also had clerked in an Omaha bank before moving to Denver where he boarded with Moffat and joined him in business. Walter Scott Cheesman, yet another New Yorker, had worked in New York City and Chicago before arriving in 1861. Charles Kountze was reared in Omaha. In 1864, at the age of 19, he had joined his brother Luther in Denver where they ran Kountze Brothers Bank, renamed the Colorado National Bank in 1866. Many of these would-be empire builders were young: Moffat, Cheesman, and Kassler were in their early 20s; Byers 30 on his arrival. Henry Brown, on the other hand, was 40. On his way to California in 1860 with his wife

DENVER: MINING CAMP TO METROPOLIS

Jane and their baby son, he had stopped in Denver because Jane, fearing Indians, had refused to go farther. Bela M. Hughes, who arrived in 1862 as president of the Holladay Overland Mail and Express Company, was another oddity among the pioneers since he was not only over 40, he was also a Southerner and a Democrat.

These experienced town builders knew how to make a city. Brown had learned carpentry in Virginia, built a sawmill in Washington Territory, farmed in California, and founded a town in Nebraska. Hughes had been a lawyer, public official, and soldier. The younger leaders were similarly well prepared. Moffat and Kassler had started their banking careers before they entered their teens. Prior to coming to Denver, Byers had hauled railroad ties, surveyed in Iowa and Oregon, and helped lay out Omaha, where he built one of the first houses. Evans had studied medicine at Philadelphia's Claremont Academy, but many of the other leaders only briefly attended school. Byers had taught himself to read and write. In Denver they pursued various businesses, humdrum compared to get-rich-quick prospecting, but profitable in the long run. Cheesman was a druggist, and Kassler first went into banking, then into stationery, then he sold insurance and eventually joined Moffat at the First National. Chaffee was one of the few who made his fortune directly from mining in the 1860s, money he used to establish Denver's First National Bank.

In 1870, census takers asked residents to estimate their wealth. Evans claimed assets of $1,450,000, a questionable figure since nearly 90 percent of it was land of unproven value. Moffat more conservatively stated his worth at $70,000, a believable fortune since in 1875 the credit agency R. G. Dun and Company judged him worthy of up to $250,000 in loans.[26] Many held government jobs — payrolls for troops and territorial officials helped sustain them and the town in the early 1860s.[27] Kassler was assistant army paymaster and later clerk in the U.S. Mint. Byers was postmaster from 1864 to 1866, and Moffat acted as territorial treasurer. Witter, whose wife Clara was the half-sister of the powerful Indiana congressman Schuyler Colfax, was the U.S. tax assessor. Anxious to please the goose who laid the golden egg of a federal job, the Witters paid $2.50 a dozen for eggs when Colfax visited in 1868 so that, as Clara explained to her children, "brother Schuyler could have his boiled egg for breakfast."[28]

From a few cabins on Cherry Creek in 1858, Denver had grown to a town of nearly 5,000 by 1860. After that, the "instant city" seemingly went dormant, like a caterpillar in a cocoon.[29] The census of 1870 showed a population of 4,759, an increase of 10 persons in 10 years. The paltry growth, however, masked real progress. During the turbulent 1860s the town edged out local rivals, established schools, churches, and a stable government, and attracted able business leaders. Spurred by self-interest, they dedicated themselves to making Denver a real city.

Gold created Denver. Conquest secured it. Location, leadership, and federal money kept it alive.[30] By the mid-1860s the Civil War was over, the Native Americans mostly subdued, law and some order established, fire and flood merely bad memories.[31] Yet the energetic empire builders could not rest. In December 1866 they learned that Union Pacific Railroad had decided to build the nation's first transcontinental line through southern Wyoming bypassing Denver. Without railroads they knew that their city and their fortunes would wither. Of all the challenges Denver was to face during the rest of the nineteenth century, none was more important to its emergence as a major Western metropolis than the building of railroads.

CHAPTER 4

A Spiderweb of Steel

A railway system [took] the energies of a generation, for it required all the new machinery to be created — capital, banks, mines, furnaces, shops, power-houses, technical knowledge, mechanical population, together with a steady remodeling of social and political habits, ideas and institutions to fit the new scale and suit the new conditions.

Henry Adams
The Education of Henry Adams, 1918[1]

Town builders knew that Denver's fate rode on rails. While harbors and river ports nourished other cities, railroads were the lifelines of settlements in the inland West. If Rocky Mountain pay dirt were to pay off, Colorado needed cheap, fast, and efficient transportation. To survive, Denver needed a railroad; to prosper it needed a spiderweb of steel.

Some 600 miles of prairie, much of it devoid of white settlers, separated Denver from the Missouri River towns of Kansas City, Leavenworth, Atchison, and Omaha. The '58ers and '59ers had come pushing wheelbarrows and handcarts, riding in farm wagons and prairie schooners. After the Leavenworth and Pike's Peak Express Company made Denver its Rocky Mountain depot, Auraria's post office and some of its hotels and saloons relocated near the stage stop at Fifteenth and Blake on the Denver side of Cherry Creek. The stage presaged the railroad in confirming Denver's dominance over rival towns, but even after regular service started, high freight rates and passenger fares in the 1860s made it difficult to supply miners and attract settlers.

Ox-drawn freight wagons, pictured at the Blake Street wholesale houses, sustained Denver during the 1860s, when cottonwoods still lined the South Platte River. (Colorado Historical Society.)

The Leavenworth and Pike's Peak Express spent $250,000 on 52 Concord stages, 1,000 mules, a 687-mile network of stations, and salaries for "sober, discreet and experienced" drivers.[2] On May 7, 1859, the first coaches — they traveled in pairs for protection — reached Denver, bringing passengers, mail, and express freight. They took out passengers, mail, and gold, sometimes returning to the States with as much as $40,000 in bullion — and a guard riding shotgun. Cherry Creekers and the mountain towns depended on wagon trains for vital supplies. In 1860, 10,000 tons of freight lumbered across the plains in three-ton wagons pulled by 10 to 12 oxen. A single wet-goods shipment to Denver, 1,600 barrels of liquor and 2,700 cases of champagne, required 80 wagons.[3]

The stage's arrival became the high point of daily life in Denver. At the sound of the rumbling vehicles drawn by four horses or mules — a ruckus that could be heard a mile away, townspeople rushed to the depot. Only high rollers — politicians, journalists, gamblers, fancy ladies, and financiers — could afford the ride, but everyone could enjoy the spectacle as passengers tumbled out and dusted themselves off. Mail was quickly taken to the post office where homesick folk waited in long lines. The stage company charged 25¢ per letter in addition to federal postage, inspiring some to read their mail, then return it as someone else's and demand a refund.

Frequent accidents, Indian raids, robberies, and heavy expenses bankrupted the Leavenworth and Pike's Peak in less than a year. Its successor, the Central Overland California and Pike's Peak Express, shortened the Leavenworth to Denver trip to six days, reduced the round-trip fare from $200 to $75, and extended service up Clear Creek Canyon. The overextended COC&PP also ran out of money, prompting employees to dub it the "Clean out of Cash and Poor Pay." It was sold at auction in 1863 to the Western stagecoach king, Ben Holladay, who put his cousin Bela Hughes in charge at Denver.

During Denver's first decade, stage lines brought passengers, mail, and express goods from the States — the Missouri River frontier towns 600 miles to the east.

Holladay and Hughes shortened the South Platte route and expanded service to mountain towns. In Denver they established a new depot at Fifteenth and McGaa. Happy with Holladay, Denverites honored him by renaming McGaa Street, Holladay Street. Two decades later, when that street became a notorious red light district, the name was changed again, at the Holladay family's request, to Market Street.[4] By then Holladay was a fading memory, although Wells Fargo, which bought him out in 1867, served railroadless parts of Colorado into the twentieth century.

Increasingly, however, stage lines faced competition. Ever since 1848 when explorer John Charles Fremont botched his attempt to chart a rail route through Colorado, surveyors had been trying to demonstrate "that neither the snow of winter nor the mountain ranges were obstacles in the way of a [rail]road."[5] William Byers assured the Union Pacific (UP) that the "hilly" land west of Denver could be crossed by rail.

Grenville M. Dodge, the chief engineer, reached a different conclusion after a surveying party encountered a September 1866 blizzard on Berthoud Pass. Heeding Dodge's advice, the UP ran its tracks across southern Wyoming where the hills were tamer, laying out Cheyenne in 1867 as the road's Rocky Mountain headquarters. Hundreds of Denverites, including Barney Ford, an ex-slave who had become a prominent innkeeper, and Edward Chase, the ace of Denver's gamblers, moved to the instant Wyoming city. It boomed as Denver dwindled, prompting the *Cheyenne Daily Leader* to crow that "Denver is too near Cheyenne to ever amount to much."[6]

Worried businessmen, including John Evans and William Byers, called a public meeting for November 13, 1867, to organize a Board of Trade. The board, a predecessor of the Chamber of Commerce, resolved

John Evans, second governor of Colorado Territory, used Chicago and Washington, D.C., connections to put Denver on the railroad map. (Tom Noel Collection.)

that if the railroads would not build to Denver, then Denver would build to the railroads. Six days later Evans, Walter Cheesman, David Moffat, and others created the Denver Pacific Railway with Bela Hughes as president. Byers warned that unless the road were built, "everybody would move away. We could not afford to pay our enormous freights.... We should break ground tomorrow."[7] Within three days the Denver Pacific sold $300,000 in stock, some shares being exchanged for promises to work on the roadbed or supply ties.

Denver declared a holiday for the ground breaking on May 18, 1868. Almost a quarter of the town's population gathered on the South Platte as kegs of beer were tapped and a band struck up "The Railroad Gallop." Two ladies guided the plow that first broke the virgin prairie, then men and mules went to work to grade a roadbed.[8] Denverites worked feverishly, knowing that Golden, 15 miles west, had already incorporated a railroad, the Colorado Central, which, like the Denver Pacific, aimed to connect with the UP's main line at Cheyenne.

Golden's chief booster, the merchant William Austin Hamilton Loveland, hoped to make his town Colorado's rail hub. Allied with the Central City lawyer Henry Moore Teller, Loveland and his Golden Crowd capitalized on the animosity to Denver shared by many smaller towns. "There is little of the Denver egotism about the Golden City folks," declared the Central City *Colorado Times*. "We can hope for advantages from Golden City that Denver in her exclusiveness would never grant."[9]

Ignoring such carping, Evans and the Denver Crowd outjockeyed Golden in the iron horse race. Working with UP allies, Evans persuaded Congress to give the Denver Pacific a land grant consisting of a 40-mile strip of alternating square-mile sections along the road's 106-mile right of way.[10] This enabled the Denver Pacific to secure loans and raise capital through land sales. Through deals with the UP, Evans got that company to lay the tracks and provide rolling stock for the Denver Pacific, but the price of outside help came high — by 1880 Evans and other local capitalists had lost control to the UP.

Evans presided over the completion of the new road on June 22, 1870. A silver spike, symbolic of railroad prosperity, also became symbolic of the improvisations that brought the iron horse to Denver. Evans had to wrap an ordinary iron spike in white paper and pretend it was silver, because the miners bringing the genuine spike from Georgetown had lingered in a saloon and pawned the precious nail to pay their bar bill.[11]

Two months after the arrival of the Denver Pacific, the Kansas Pacific became the second road to reach Denver. On August 15, 1870, a large barrel of whisky was placed on the prairie at what is now Strasburg. Five miles to the east a construction crew at Byers began laying track westward; five miles west another crew began working eastward from Bennett. The two gangs of gandy dancers set a record that day, completing 10.25 miles of track by 3:00 P.M. The workers got free drinks; Denver got a direct connection with Kansas City and St. Louis.[12]

Late in 1870 the Colorado Central finished the first stretch of its road, a narrow gauge spur connecting Golden with the standard-gauge Denver Pacific four miles north of Denver. The sulky Golden Crowd did

Denver's bonanza days began with the 1870 arrival of the Denver Pacific and the Kansas Pacific. Locomotives steamed up at the original passenger depot at Twenty-second and Wynkoop streets. (Denver Public Library, Western History Department.)

not build into Denver, hoping that their town still might become Colorado's rail hub. The financially feeble Colorado Central slowly inched north through Boulder, Berthoud, Longmont, and Fort Collins, not tying into the UP until 1877. By then Denver, with three railroads, had clearly won the soot and cinders competition. Golden did, however, win the race to the mining towns up Clear Creek Canyon. Boston capitalists financing the Colorado Central decided to save construction time and money by using three-foot-wide narrow-gauge track instead of the standard four feet, eight and a half inches. The Colorado Central's backers bought small, narrow-gauge steam locomotives previously used for filling in Boston's Back Bay, reconditioned them, and shipped them west to tackle the Rockies.

By 1872 the Colorado Central had reached Black Hawk and the mines around Central City. In 1877 the baby road puffed into Georgetown, Colorado's first silver city, 50 miles west of Denver. Seven years later, the road completed its last and most fantastic link, the Georgetown Loop. This engineering marvel used 4.7 miles of track, making three and a half complete loops to climb from Georgetown to Silver Plume. Daredevils celebrated by bicycling over the highest bridge, the Devil's Gate. Later, tourists came from all over the world to get dizzy on the Georgetown Loop.[13]

Evans, Moffat, and Cheesman also wanted to share in the mountains' wealth. They incorporated their own narrow gauge road, the Denver, South Park & Pacific Railway, in 1872. Two years and 15 miles later it reached the red sandstone outcroppings in the foothills surrounding the home and gypsum mill of a Scotsman named George M. Morrison. There, Evans established the Morrison Stone, Lime and Townsite Company, and built a hotel.[14]

The South Park line crawled on up the South Platte Canyon and over Kenosha Pass to tap South Park's goldfields before striking northwest to Breckenridge, Dillon, and Keystone. The main line ran through Fairplay and down Trout Creek to the Arkansas River, which it followed north to Leadville. In its quixotic quest for the Pacific, the South Park built the Alpine Tunnel, the first transportation bore under the Continental Divide. In 1883 the South Park ran out of steam, dying in a mountain valley north of Gunnison, 200 miles southwest of Denver.[15] Like so many of Colorado's "Pacific" railroads, the Denver, South Park & Pacific never reached the ocean. Nevertheless, it served Denver well. To feed the city's building boom, it brought Platte Valley lumber, Morrison sandstone and lime, and Gunnison County granite and coal. The South Park line also hauled Park and Summit county gold ores and Leadville's mineral riches into Denver.

Another Evans enterprise, the Denver & New Orleans Railroad, provided an outlet to the Gulf of Mexico. On the way there, the road nourished the towns of Parker, Franktown, and Elizabeth, the last named for Evans's sister-in-law, Elizabeth G. Hubbard. Within a decade the Denver & New Orleans suffered the usual fate of undercapitalized local lines and became part of the UP system, which eventually swallowed the Denver Pacific, the Kansas Pacific, the Colorado Central, and the Denver, South Park & Pacific.

The most important railroad in assuring Denver's regional dominance was the narrow gauge Denver & Rio Grande Railway (D&RG), organized in 1870 by 34-year-old William Jackson Palmer. Having supervised construction of the Kansas Pacific and having watched other roads build east to west, Palmer decided that a north-and-south line along the Front Range would be a money-maker. Palmer hoped to reach Mexico City, but the D&RG never built beyond Santa Fe, New Mexico.

The federal government gave the D&RG a 200-foot right-of-way but refused a land grant, so Palmer turned to town building to help finance construction. If existing towns refused to donate land and other incentives, the D&RG acquired property nearby for a depot and townsite. When Colorado City balked, Palmer founded nearby Colorado Springs in 1871. When Trinidad spurned him, he bypassed it for El Moro.

Although the D&RG started south, silver rushes turned two of its branches to the west. After the Leadville boom began in 1877, the road raced west to Cañon City and followed the Arkansas River to Leadville. With the rush to the San Juan Mountains, the D&RG built west over La Veta Pass, crossed the San Luis Valley, dipped into New Mexico, and then penetrated southwestern Colorado to Durango and Silverton. Palmer's road also became the first to span Colorado, linking Denver with Grand Junction.[16]

The Colorado Central, the Kansas Pacific, the D&RG, and Evans's three roads were pioneers among over a hundred different lines to lay track in Colorado. The transcontinentals that had originally ignored Denver — the Atchison, Topeka & Santa Fe; the Chicago, Rock Island & Pacific; the Chicago, Burlington & Quincy; the Missouri Pacific; and the UP — all chugged into Colorado by the 1880s. With their coming, Denver expanded its sway over Colorado and the Rocky Mountain West.

Skies darkened but the economy brightened after the Argo Smelter opened in 1878. The Argo was the first of many ore-processing giants to capitalize on Denver's railroad network. (Denver Public Library, Western History Department.)

More than any other factor, this spiderweb of steel explains Denver's nineteenth-century transformation from a mining camp to a regional metropolis. Incoming trains brought passengers and freight, making the Mile High City the hotel and business hub as well as the warehouse and distribution center of the Rockies. Outgoing trains carried the products of Denver's factories and food-processing plants to the mountains and plains. Railroads also employed thousands of Denverites to work the trains and to repair them.

Only after iron horses reached the mines did Colorado's mineral riches pay off. During the 1860s high freight costs and primitive mining and smelting methods undermined the golden promise of 1859. Refining problems were partially solved at Nathaniel Hill's Boston and Colorado smelter in Black Hawk. In 1878, Hill moved his plant to Denver at the junction of the Colorado Central and the Denver Pacific four miles north of downtown. There, he constructed the Argo Smelter, hoping that like Jason and the Argonauts of Greek mythology, he would become as rich as Croesus. Next to the Argo, competitors sprang up in the 1880s — the Omaha and Grant Smelter managed by James B. Grant and Dennis Sheedy's Globe Smelting and Refining Company. Railroads hauled ore from as far away as Montana and northern Mexico to feed smelters whose massive brick smokestacks dominated Denver's skyline. By 1890 these smelters had become the city's largest industry.[17]

The Queen City's flush times as a gold and silver center were celebrated in the grandiose Mining Exchange Building at Fifteenth and Arapahoe. (Photo by William Henry Jackson, Colorado Historical Society.)

Efficient ore processing and cheap rail transportation — as well as the discovery of Leadville and Aspen silver — caused mineral production to soar. Less than $35 million in gold and silver was produced between 1858 and 1870. Between 1881 and 1890 precious metals worth over $185 million were processed. Silver prices slid in the 1890s, but gold production soared with the Cripple Creek discoveries. Base metals also poured from the state's mines: in the 1890s over $55 million in copper, lead, and zinc was extracted. Colorado coal output, even more directly attributable to coal-burning and coal-carrying steam trains, climbed from $16,000 in 1869 to over $4 million in 1890.[18]

Railroads also sparked an agricultural boom by promoting the "Great American Desert" as a new Garden of Eden. William Byers, as land agent for the Denver Pacific, helped convince easterners, including the utopia-minded Nathan Meeker and *New York Tribune* editor Horace Greeley, that an agricultural colony north of Denver would flourish. This led to the 1870 establishment of the Union Colony, later renamed Greeley, on the Denver Pacific tracks. Not to be outdone, the Kansas Pacific set up agricultural experiment stations in eastern Colorado, and the D&RG likewise fostered settlement along its tracks. Such railroad boosterism worked. Between 1880 and 1890 the number of farmers in Colorado grew by 300 percent, and dozens of new farm and ranch towns sprouted on the eastern plains. Much of the resulting agricultural harvest flowed to Denver, which emerged as a brewing, food-processing, livestock, and flour-milling center.[19]

Arrival of the first three railroads in 1870 had an immediate impact. The *Rocky Mountain News* expanded to a nine-column format, and the First National Bank reported that its assets jumped from $457,536 to $1,538,606 that year. Denver, which had stagnated during the 1860s, grew by over 700 percent during the 1870s, reaching a population of 35,629 in 1880. To keep people coming, the railroads tirelessly advertised Colorado. The D&RG hired the photographer William Henry Jackson to produce pictures, postcards, and brochures featuring mountain scenery. The Rio Grande even created a literary department to crank out poetry and fiction, as well as travel books and brochures. Such propagandists told of mechanical monsters with "lungs of copper and breath of steam" puffing "up the steeps of the Great Divide, over the chasms deep and wide."[20] Tourism, like mining and agriculture, became big business thanks to the railroads.

By the mid-1880s a hundred trains a week snorted through Denver. Train whistles screamed and moaned all day and into the night. Hobos, new residents, tourists, health and wealth seekers arrived daily; they came in boxcars, inexpensive day coaches, and Pullman palace cars. Among the newcomers was the English sparrow. This "tramp bird," reported Denver journalist William Columbus Ferril, made its journey west by rail, nesting first at the station "in the old vines and eaves and cornices." The birds multiplied rapidly "until now the English sparrow abounds everywhere."[21]

The railroad reigned, enthroned like a king after 1881 in the majestic Union Station, the largest and busiest building in town. Its 180-foot clock tower housed a giant, electrically lit timepiece with four faces showing the correct railroad time. Within a single generation, railroads transformed a pokey frontier crossroads into an industrialized regional metropolis. Without railroads, Denver would have withered, as did many other frontier towns. With their spiderweb of steel Denverites began bragging that they had built the Queen City of the Plains.

CHAPTER 5

The Braggart City

There the great braggart city lay spread out, brown and treeless, upon the brown and treeless plain, which seemed to nourish nothing but wormwood and the Spanish bayonet.

Isabella Bird
A Lady's Life in the Rocky Mountains, 1873[1]

Roger W. Woodbury — editor, general, banker, speculator, and promoter — liked giving long speeches.[2] At the dedication of Denver's Chamber of Commerce building in 1885, he traced the human race to its origins, brought it up to date, and then spoke of Denver's almost boundless possibilities. Its climate, residents bragged, could cure "tuberculosis, anemia, overwork, and what not." Its schools outshone those in any comparable city; its water was "the best, purest and cheapest" on earth. The city's poor did not live in slums; Denver was "without cheap and unsightly shanties." Promoters admitted that people sometimes died: "Old age carries off a few each year." But, the Chamber of Commerce claimed, "the balmy climate, the pure air, the excellent sanitary conditions, endow Denverites proper with nearly perpetual youth."[3]

S. A. Gardner, a correspondent for the Peoria *Evening Call*, knew better. Visiting Denver in 1879, he observed the bodies of tuberculosis victims being quietly shipped back to their families in the East. He learned of landowners who waited for the green grass of spring to sell their normally parched farms to gullible greenhorns. He found streetcars running "two or three miles into the country," so that Denver could "keep up the appearance of vastness." He found that promoters could sugarcoat the alkali-laden dust storms that beset the city. "The air is so thin and light," they told him, "that it never does any damage." Denver even bragged of its evil, which, Gardner reported, "they rejoice in believing is like the wickedness of Paris."[4]

Gardner thought this braggadocio reflected the city's desire to keep her boarding houses and hotels full. Irish playwright Oscar Wilde, who lectured in Denver in 1882, more charitably attributed such boasting to "an earnest attempt on the part of language to keep pace with the enormous size of the country."[5] Wilde had a point. Denver had a right to brag. In the 1860s it had faced and overcome disasters. By the early 1870s when the English tourist Isabella Bird visited, the town had achieved an air of stability. Bird saw saloons frequented by "Comanche Bill," "Buffalo Bill," "Wild Bill," and "Mountain Jim." Yet, she admitted, criminals did not dangle from lampposts and the streets were as safe as Liverpool's.[6] Confident of its future, the town decided in 1874 to change its official name from Denver City to Denver. Unofficially, boosters began puffing the gawky town as the Queen City of the Plains.

By 1880 there was no doubt that Denver was a city. Its population of 35,629 made it the nation's fiftieth-largest urban center, far behind Chicago, St. Louis, and San Francisco, shy of Kansas City, but ahead of Omaha, Galveston, San Antonio, Sacramento, and Salt Lake, the only other places west of the Missouri River among the country's top 100. "She thinks she is going to be immense," Gardner wrote, "so she has laid out streets and lots enough for a hundred thousand people."[7] Such grandiose thinking proved sound. An average of 7,000 people arrived annually in the 1880s. Census takers in 1890 tallied 106,713 Denverites, one-fourth of the state's population. In a single generation the frontier crossroads had become the nation's twenty-sixth–largest city.

Railroads guaranteed Denver's survival, but the city's prosperity depended upon the regional economy. Hurt by the depression of 1873 and smitten by a grasshopper invasion in 1875, the town rebounded after 1876, primarily because of the Leadville silver bonanza. Moreover, removal of the Utes from the mineral-rich San Juans in 1873 and from most of the rest of the state by the early 1880s added more than 20,000 square miles to the Queen City's hinterland. That big economic backyard assured Denver's success. John H. Tice, visiting in the early 1870s, thought Denver would remain an isolated oasis "where no article of commercial value is or ever can be produced."[8] A dire forecast; but in 1890 the

A Vermont stonecutter, then a Kansas farmer, Horace Tabor struck it rich in his third career, becoming Colorado's premier mining man. (Colorado Historical Society.)

Chamber of Commerce reported that between 1870 and 1890 the value of locally manufactured goods had grown from $608,000 to over $40 million. Flour millers had increased their business nearly twentyfold, and the number of dwellings had risen from 1,128 to 37,500. Building permits had more than tripled, from less than $4 million in 1880 to $13 million in 1890, a record unbroken until 1922.[9]

Denver was also proud of its political preeminence. Colorado became a state in 1876 with Denver as temporary capital, an arrangement made permanent five years later. In 1868 Henry Brown had donated 10 acres of Brown's Bluff, his homestead on the hill east of Broadway, for a capitol site. When the state left the tract empty — frustrating Brown's effort to promote the area as Capitol Hill — he sued to get it back. The U.S. Supreme Court upheld Colorado's title in 1885. Construction of the capitol began in 1886; in 1894 Governor Davis Waite moved into the building, and in January 1895 the legislature convened there for the first time.

A twentyfold population increase in 20 years transformed the city. When Isabella Bird visited in 1873, the American House, a three-story hotel with a bathroom on every floor, was the finest in town. Within a decade that hostelry had been eclipsed by the five-story Windsor Hotel at Eighteenth and Larimer. Financed by English speculators, the palatial Windsor featured Brussels carpets, English china, French mirrors, and private baths. In 1892 the Windsor was overshadowed by the elegant, 10-story Brown Palace, which boasted a skylit lobby atrium the full height of the building, a bowling alley, a library, and a women's dining room.

Until Horace A.W. Tabor completed the five-story Tabor Block at Sixteenth and Larimer in 1880, Denver had largely contented itself with three-story buildings. After he was elected lieutenant governor in 1878 Tabor abandoned Leadville, the town that had made him rich. He moved to Denver bringing with him his wife Augusta, his money, and his taste for the good life. "Denver was not building as good buildings as it ought," Tabor said, "and I thought that I would do something towards setting

The Tabor Grand Opera House brought Denver architectural elegance, boosting the braggart city's rush to respectability. (Photo by William H. Jackson, Colorado Historical Society.)

them a good example."[10] After the Tabor Block, he built the five-story Tabor Grand Opera House (1881) at Sixteenth and Curtis. Its red brick exterior with white limestone trim struck some tourists as "a little gorgeous in tone in accordance with Western tastes."[11] Journalist Eugene Field, who enjoyed poking fun at Tabor, described the structure's eclectic architecture as "modified Egyptian moresque."[12] Unfazed by satire, proud citizens praised the Tabor Grand. The Opera House saloon with its glistening bar, tropical plants, and ladies' orchestra was, crowed the *Denver Republican,* "the finest bar in the United States."[13]

Tabor's buildings helped shift the city's business center away from its lower-downtown origin near Fifteenth and Blake. Completion of the Union Station (1881) at the northwest end of Seventeenth Street pleased landowners, for that street quickly became Denver's most urbane lane with the city's most exclusive private club, the Denver Club (1889) on Welton; its finest office building, the Equitable (1892) on Stout; and its best hotel, the Brown Palace (1892), on Broadway.

Tabor and others, including Henry C. Brown and Walter Cheesman, were betting that Denver

Shrewdest of the pioneer tycoons, Walter Scott Cheesman cornered the market on drinking water and played Monopoly with downtown Denver real estate. (Denver Public Library, Western History Department.)

Smelter magnate Nathaniel Hill erected this 1880s mansion on Fourteenth Street, Denver's first millionaire's row. (Tom Noel Collection.)

would grow eastward, a sensible wager considering the city's geography. The South Platte and the railroad tracks along the river's east bank retarded the development of northwest Denver. Capitol Hill, on the other hand, could be reached without crossing either the river or its bottomlands full of tracks and shacks. In 1864, Brown had built a small house on Brown's Bluff, reasoning that his elevated land with its panoramic view of the mountains would someday be valuable. He waited. In the 1870s Fourteenth Street was Denver's most fashionable neighborhood — John Evans's first home was there, as were the houses of smelter king Nathaniel Hill, banker David Moffat, and physicians Charles Denison and John Elsner. As the city's population exploded, Fourteenth Street became increasingly commercial. Storefronts were tacked onto the houses, and many of the rich rewarded Brown's patience. Banker Charles Kountze was among the first to make the move to Capitol Hill. His 40-room home on 22 lots at Sixteenth and Grant set a standard of conspicuous consumption that assured the neighborhood's quality. Brown also helped set a high tone by constructing a mansion at Seventeenth and Broadway and stocking its grounds with peacocks. He sold it a few years later to Tabor, who parked Augusta in the rambling house. Later, Tabor bought another home at 1260 Sherman, where he lived with Elizabeth McCourt Doe (Baby Doe) after she became the second Mrs. Tabor.

Cheesman, who moved to Capitol Hill in 1886, also owned upper Sixteenth Street property. When Arapahoe County, of which Denver was county seat until 1902, fell $2,000 short of the $18,000 needed to purchase a site for a courthouse at Sixteenth and Tremont, Cheesman raised the difference. On its completion in 1883 the Courthouse increased the value of Cheesman's Sixteenth Street real estate. Department stores such as McNamara's (renamed the Denver Dry Goods in 1894), Daniels and Fisher's, The Golden Eagle, The Fair, Joslins, and the May Company also favored Sixteenth, which, with the post office, the Opera House, and the County Courthouse, enjoyed heavy pedestrian traffic,[14] augmented by streetcar service.

At the Opera House thousands of curiosity seekers enjoyed the novelty of riding the elevator. At the Tabor Building they could visit another marvel — a telephone switchboard. Less than three years after Alexander Graham Bell had demonstrated the first telephone in Philadelphia in 1876, Denver had two telephone companies and 200 subscribers. The *News* called the strange device "a galvanic muttering machine" but carping did not dampen enthusiasm.[15] By 1884 it was possible to call Colorado Springs, and in 1889 Leadville was added to the system.[16] A year after the first telephone call was made in Denver the city witnessed another marvel — the introduction of incandescent lights on April 21, 1880. Just nine years earlier the Denver Gas Company had started producing illuminating gas from coal. Those who could afford it put gas lights in their homes and businesses. The streets were lit by gas on dark nights; to save fuel, boys extinguished the lamps when the moon rose. The soft gas lights lingered until 1885 when the gas company's franchise expired. Then the city shifted to incandescent streetlights reinforced with powerful, glaring arc lamps mounted on 150-foot-high towers.[17]

City building cost money. Even the fortunes of mining kings could not satisfy the demand for capital, an appetite that sometimes pushed annual interest rates to over 30 percent. As a result, Denver welcomed eastern, midwestern, and European investors. One of them, James Duff, a Scottish entrepreneur, headed the Colorado Mortgage and Investment Company, popularly known as the English Company, which channeled British funds into electric companies, real estate, and downtown hotels. Bostonians financed the Boston Building and invested in the Boston and Colorado smelter. Another smelter, the Omaha and Grant, was backed by midwestern investors and by the southerner James Grant. The Equitable Building, a Renaissance revival masterpiece designed in the shape of back-to-back Es, was a project of the Equitable Life Assurance Company of New York.

Denver's pioneer elite were joined in the 1870s and 1880s by new investors such as Duff, by successful merchants, by silver kings including Tabor and John F. Campion, by capitalists such as Dennis Sheedy, by lawyers, and by mining and refining experts. Nathaniel Hill, whose Boston and Colorado smelter made him wealthy, became publisher of the *Denver Republican* and a U.S. senator in the 1880s. Simon Guggenheim, who later dominated the state's smelting industry, also parlayed his millions into a Senate seat, as did the lawyer Edward O. Wolcott, whose riches were matched by those of his brother Henry. Senatorial laurels also eventually went to Thomas M. Patterson and Charles J. Hughes, Jr., whose legal careers rewarded them handsomely. Mining and smelting experts such as Richard Pearce and Thomas Rickard found that solving technical problems and geological secrets paid well. Irish-born James Archer, who helped bring the Kansas Pacific Railroad to Colorado, concentrated on providing services — he was the principal founder of the gas company and the first major drinking water company. Wolfe Londoner, a grocer; hardware dealer George Tritch; brewer Philip Zang; entrepreneur Henry M. Porter; department store proprietors William Cooke Daniels and William Garrett Fisher; flour millers John K. Mullen and Stephen Knight all grew in wealth during the flush 1880s.

Money mattered in a city convinced that the fit survived and that the very fit prospered. "The 'almighty dollar' is the true divinity," Isabella Bird commented, "and its worship is universal."[18] The French traveler, Jules Leclercq, observed many house fires in Denver. He was told that in bad times people torched their homes to collect the insurance. Their rationale, he said, could be found in the American maxim: "Make money, honestly if you can, but make it."[19] Money-making opportunities abounded in the rapidly growing city. Transplanted easterners wanted trees and grass, so John W. Smith built the City Ditch in 1867. Drawing water from the South Platte canyon, southwest of Littleton, the 24-mile irrigation ditch ran through present-day south Denver, creating Smith Lake in an old buffalo wallow. It then flowed north and east, providing water for side ditches that sent water down Capitol Hill into the city's center where residents diverted it to water yards. Kids frolicked in the ditches while parents fussed about their foulness.[20]

The greening of Denver with lawns, gardens, and trees on the edge of the Great American Desert proved that the City Ditch worked. The

Highline Canal was less successful. Completed 16 years after Smith's ditch, it also diverted upstream South Platte water, channeling it in an arc spanning 86 miles southeast and east of town. English investors, represented by James Duff, financed the $650,000 project, hoping that it would irrigate thousands of acres they owned. But since the waterway had a junior claim to South Platte water and could be filled only in wet years, it did not live up to its backers' expectations.[21]

Neither the City Ditch nor the Highline Canal could slake the town's thirst. Their dirty, untreated, ditch water was undrinkable. Shallow wells provided only a temporary solution since they were easily polluted, and as more were sunk, water levels fell, leaving many homes with useless wells. These dry holes were sometimes converted to privies that contaminated the remaining groundwater. Recognizing the need, William Byers and David Moffat organized the Denver Artesian Water Company in 1870, but their well three miles east of the city produced poorly, and they abandoned it. Thirteen years later, Richard R. McCormick, while drilling for coal, accidentally struck water near Seven-

Ever since the 1860s, the City Ditch has watered Denver, an oasis city averaging only 14 inches of precipitation a year. (Denver Water Deaprtment.)

50

teenth Avenue and Federal Boulevard. A water rush followed. A million and a half gallons a day flowed from artesian wells by mid-1883. Confident that its water problems were solved, voters refused to buy the company that pumped drinking water from the South Platte. By the mid-1880s pressure in the artesian wells, some of which were nearly 1,000 feet deep, fell while pumping costs rose. Finally, businessmen realized that wells alone could not supply the thirsty growing city.

James Archer, Cheesman, Moffat, and others saw not only the need for drinking water but the money to be made by providing it. Their Denver City Water Company began pumping in 1872 from the South Platte near its confluence with Cherry Creek. The arrangement did not work well: Cherry Creek entered the South Platte above the company's shallow wells, allowing pollution from the creek to seep into the pipes. Housewives fitted their faucets with strainers to catch the small fish that came squirming through, but strainers did not filter out germs. Waterborne typhoid ravaged the city in the summer of 1879. Six hundred caught the fever; 40 of them died. Mayor Richard Sopris blamed "dry weather" and "lack of rain."[22] Doctor Charles Denison disagreed. He inspected the small reservoir near the company's wells and found it polluted by offal from slop buckets and from refuse that washed in through Cherry Creek and west Denver's ditches. Denison advised people to buy water from the mountains. Others suggested drinking tea, coffee, or whisky. One *News* correspondent faced a dilemma: "If a man drinks water he imbibes wiggletails. If he drinks whisky he gets the jim-jams. Now what is a body to do?"[23] By installing sewers and by seeking purer water sources, Denver lessened the typhoid threat. In 1878 the Denver City Water Company built the half-mile–long Lake Archer along Shoshone Street between First and Eighth avenues. Burgeoning population in the 1880s forced costly expansion and spawned smaller, suburban water companies.[24]

Following Archer's death in 1882, control of the water company passed to his widow and eastern investors. Local stockholders wanted the company to expand; Mrs. Catherine Archer, who went back East, wanted to go slow. The disagreement led Moffat and Cheesman to organize the Citizens Water Company in 1889. Since the Archer company's supply had been fouled continually by the expanding city, the Citizens Water Company decided to tap pure Rocky Mountain sources. First they drew water from the mouth of South Platte canyon, 22 miles south of Denver; later they went farther up the river.

Water companies competed fiercely in the early 1890s. Rival crews battled in the streets, wielding pickaxes and flooding their competitors' trenches. For a time Citizens Water gave water away. The water war ended in 1892 when the American Water Works Company, the successor to Archer's firm, failed. Two years later its bankrupt remains combined with Citizens Water to form the Denver Union Water Company with Cheesman as president. This monopoly received an exclusive franchise to provide the Queen City's drinking water. The expanding water supply helped foster the population boom of the 1880s. The other vital internal engine of Denver's growth was its streetcar system. Entrepreneurs again smelled profit both in carrying passengers and in developing streetcar suburbs.

Streetcar Suburbs

> With the exception of the steam railways, it would seem that no institution has done so much for the upbuilding of Denver as the street railway system. [It] has enabled men of moderate means to acquire homes for themselves in pleasant places away from the business center, instead of being housed tier upon tier in congested localities as so many have to be in other cities.
>
> Jerome Smiley
> *History of Denver*, 1901[1]

In 1832, New Yorkers began using horse-drawn street railways, and other cities soon did likewise. By 1880 practically every city in the United States boasted streetcar lines. By 1900, even smaller Colorado towns, such as Aspen, Cripple Creek, Durango, and Grand Junction, had their own streetcar systems. In Denver, where the traction network developed during the 1870–1893 boom, the city spread out with its streetcars, allowing even many of the poor to live in single-family, detached homes.

Hoping to cash in on soaring real estate prices, entrepreneurs built streetcar lines ahead of development. Denver's generally flat terrain and unconstricted geography expedited rapid construction of a streetcar network. Some core neighborhoods remained more densely populated than outlying areas since some workers could not afford daily car fares, let alone suburban homes. Others simply preferred to live downtown. For their convenience, Daniel Witter built the town's first apartment house

Union Station and the Denver Horse Railroad Company at Seventeenth and Wynkoop formed the Queen City's bustling transport hub in the 1880s. (Denver Public Library, Western History Department.)

in 1875.[2] A few years later David Moffat provided luxury accommodations for the smart set at La Veta Place, 14 luxury rowhouses at West Colfax and Bannock.

Most Denverites, however, did not like close urban quarters. During the 1870s and 1880s they bought suburban homes. As residents followed streetcars out onto the prairies, the city sprawled horizontally, setting a growth pattern that the automobile would accelerate in the twentieth century. The Queen City prided itself, as journalist Richard Harding Davis reported, on having "mile after mile of separate houses . . . with a little green breathing space between."[3]

The first streetcar line, the Denver Horse Railroad Company, was constructed in 1871 by a Chicago financier, Lewis C. Ellsworth.[4] That line originated in the 600 block of Larimer Street and ran up Larimer to Sixteenth, then to its shop, carbarn, and stables on Curtis. From Sixteenth the rails turned on Champa, then shot out to the end of the line at Twenty-seventh Street. There, out in open prairie, Denverites built homes in the city's first streetcar suburb, Curtis Park. Horses initially pulled the coaches but were sometimes replaced by mules, leading Ellsworth to rename his firm the Denver City Railway Company since the word mule did not lend itself to corporate titles.

The company built its second line in 1873, starting at Fifteenth and Larimer and running northwest on Fifteenth across the railroad tracks, over the South Platte River to a dirt path — the future Federal Boulevard

Horse-drawn street railways allowed Denverites to begin suburbanizing in the 1870s. (Denver Public Library, Western History Department.)

— in largely vacant Highland. Although William Larimer had staked out Highland in 1858, it did not thrive until after the horsecar arrived.

The third line extended the Sixteenth Street tracks to Broadway and then ran south on Broadway to Cherry Creek, fostering growth in Capitol Hill, the most elegant of Denver's streetcar suburbs. The Park Avenue line, also established in 1874, took a diagonal route along Twenty-third Street from Champa to Park Avenue, spurring development in the neighborhoods of Five Points, North Capitol Hill, and City Park. By 1884 the Denver City Railway boasted 15.5 miles of track, 45 cars, 200 horses, 100 employees, and a new carbarn on Seventeenth Street opposite Union Station.[5] Disembarking railroad passengers could walk across Wynkoop Street and, for 5¢, board horsecars to many parts of the city.

Commercial and residential real estate flourished along the tracks, particularly on Sixteenth Street, which emerged as Denver's retail strip. Fifteenth Street property owners — led by Denver's elite who had been upstaged by Ellsworth and the Chicago capitalists — founded their own transit company to promote that street. In 1886, John Evans, his son William Gray Evans, William Byers, Henry Brown, Roger Woodbury, and other locals formed the Denver Tramway Company (DTC). Although the DTC never succeeded in making Fifteenth as commercially important as Sixteenth, it eventually dominated Denver's public transit.[6] The DTC secured the right to build cable or electric lines, thereby circumventing the horse/mule franchise awarded to the Denver City Railway Company. Tramway officials had had faith in electric lines since, in 1885, University of Denver physics professor Sidney H. Short had demonstrated a streetcar powered by current picked up from a slot between the rails. By July 1886, electric cars were rolling along Fifteenth, giving Denver one of the country's most technically advanced transit systems. Unfortunately, Short's line shocked animals and pedestrians who stepped on the slot during wet weather. Within a year, the $200,000 mistake was scrapped. The DTC adopted cable cars on some lines, and on others employed trolley cars, so named for the metal roof poles, capped by small wheels called trolleys that rolled along the electrified lines overhead.[7]

By 1889, New York investors controlled Ellsworth's company and restructured it as the Denver City Cable Railway Company. This firm installed underground cables similar to those in San Francisco; built a large, elegant brick power plant, carbarn, and corporate office at Eighteenth and Lawrence streets; constructed Denver's first viaduct, Larimer Street, and worked with the city to build another on Sixteenth Street.

By 1890, Denver had one of the country's more extensive cable car networks. The Welton Street line, if Smiley's *History of Denver* can be believed, was the world's longest, and the power plant at Eighteenth and Lawrence the world's largest. Within a decade all except five miles of the city's streetcar network were either cable or electric.[8]

Denver City Cable and the DTC, the two giants among at least a dozen local street railway firms, competed mightily to reach dozens of new neighborhoods, lobbying and bribing city council for streetcar franchises. Sometimes, construction crews fought to control the street. On December 10, 1889, the chief of police arrested part of the DTC's construction army to stop them from laying track illegally at night. Streetcar mania also afflicted smaller, independent city shapers. If a land developer could not coax existing transit companies to his tract, he might construct his own line to assure potential customers access to public transportation. As most Denverites could not afford a horse and buggy, public transit was essential to many moving out of the core city. To persuade the DTC to lay

By 1900, the Denver Tramway Company monopolized street-car service in the Mile High City. (Tom Noel Collection.)

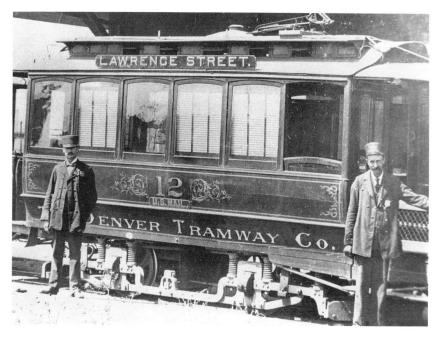

track out East Colfax Avenue to York Street and south on Broadway to Alameda Avenue, property owners paid $200,000 to the transit titans. The investment was wise, for the value of land bordering Colfax from Broadway to Milwaukee Street alone more than doubled between 1887 and 1891, rising to over $13 million.[9]

During the flush times, homes and stores popped up like dandelions along new streetcar routes. Then the Depression of 1893 shattered sub-dividers' schemes. More than 2,000 homes had been constructed in Denver in 1890; only 124 were built in 1894.[10] The city's outskirts were pockmarked by unfinished basement excavations, and abandoned subdivisions were repossessed by prairie dogs. The depression weakened rivals, enabling the DTC to seize control of 150 miles of streetcar lines by 1900, including the routes of archrival Denver City Cable, which had collapsed under a $4.3 million debt in 1898. The DTC abandoned the cable network in favor of the more reliable and flexible trolley system. Only a handful of independents survived, notably the Denver, Lakewood & Golden Railroad and a few small firms, such as Englewood's celebrated Cherrelyn Horsecar.[11]

The flight to the streetcar suburbs was hastened by the transformation of Denver's pioneer neighborhoods. Auraria, after the railroads arrived, had evolved into an industrial area pungent with the aromas of breweries, bakeries, and flour mills. Many Aurarians moved out, giving way to poorer people who needed cheap housing near factory jobs. Across Cherry Creek, Denver's rapidly expanding central business district over-ran residential blocks. As commercial buildings leapfrogged uptown, homes were converted to boarding houses and stores. Streetcar lines were laid beyond northeast Denver to industrial suburbs named for the smelters they served — Argo, Swansea, and Globeville. Immigrants swarmed into these districts, finding work in the fiery ore furnaces that became Denver's largest industry during the 1880s. Within the shadows of smelter smokestacks, blue-collar families found cheap rental units while others built their own shanties, using secondhand lumber from nearby railroad shops.[12]

Status-sensitive Denverites sought homes east and south of down-town. Some were impressed with the area around Curtis Park, Denver's first public park. Families took streetcars out Larimer, Curtis, Champa, Stout, and Welton to look at brick homes dressed in the fashionable Italianate style with flat roofs, high-ceilinged rooms, elongated windows, brick corbeling, and elegantly framed front porches. Real estate agents pointed out that Mayor Wolfe Londoner, dry goods merchant J. Jay Joslin, and former governor William Gilpin had all moved to Curtis Park. Streetcar lines out East Thirty-fourth, Thirty-first, Twenty-eighth, Twenty-second, Nineteenth, Seventeenth, Colfax, Thirteenth, Sixth, and Fourth avenues facilitated settlement of the City Park, Park Hill, and Montclair neighborhoods, where promoters offered 50-by-125-foot lots rather than the standard 25-by-125-foot city lots. Spacious yards pleased suburbanites; flower gardens, lawns, and vegetable patches enabled the bourgeois to teach their children lessons in the agrarian dream.

Park Hill, a haven for the upper crust on the high ground east of City Park, was platted in 1887 by an eccentric German, the Baron Eugene A. von Winkler. This character came to Denver after being discharged from the Prussian army, reportedly for falling off his horse. The baron pur-chased a large tract east of Colorado Boulevard, announcing that he would build a racetrack surrounded by a posh residential subdivision. His exotic plans for a racecourse did not survive his suicide, but saner devel-opers, including Denver Park Commissioner Warwick Downing, picked up the pieces of Baron von Winkler's dream and platted the finest of Park Hill's subdivisions, Downington.

A prospectus for this suburban oasis, bounded by Forest and Monaco parkways between East Colfax Avenue and Montview Boulevard,

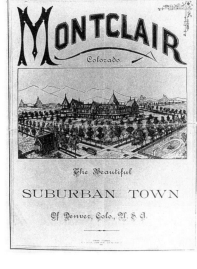

Streetcar suburbs, as this 1885 prospectus for Montclair illustrates, promoted themselves as green, spacious escapes from the core city. (Tom Noel Collection.)

claimed its parkways rivaled the "Auteil or Passy in Paris, Mayfair in London, the Ring Strasse in Vienna, Thiergarten in Berlin, Riverside Drive in New York [or] the broad avenues and 'circles' for which Washington is famous."[13] The lavish promotional brochure declared that Capitol Hill had been spoiled as a residential area by the intrusion of apartments and commercial buildings, an error that would not be repeated in "Denver's Largest Restricted Residence District." Amid Park Hill's parkways and croquet wickets, the children of Downingtown would "be free from the contaminating influence of downtown city streets" where "their delicate moral fibres are tarnished by evil associations."

Southeast of Park Hill lay Montclair, platted by the Baron Walter von Richthofen shortly before his friend Baron von Winkler laid out Park Hill. Richthofen, uncle of Manfred von Richthofen, the Red Baron of World War I aviation fame, had come to Denver in the 1870s. In 1885 he announced the grand opening of Montclair, "The Beautiful Suburban Town of Denver." At East Twelfth and Olive, Richthofen erected his own castle as a show home. Strict ordinances also guarded Montclair; where one regulation forbade the use of "common, vulgar, indecent, abusive or improper language." Despite the lure of the castle, the moral atmosphere, and Montclair's trolley connections via East Colfax and East Eighth avenues, the baron found it difficult to attract buyers.[14]

Montclair's promises of a bustling, green suburban oasis contrast sharply with the stark reality of this 1899 photograph with Aurora in the background. (Photo by Warwick Downing.)

A similar fate befell Edwin and Louise Harman, who platted their 320-acre farm on the north bank of Cherry Creek between University and Colorado boulevards as the townsite of Harman. Harman boasted a streetcar line, a town hall at East Fourth Avenue and St. Paul Street, a sandstone schoolhouse, and $75 lots. Reflecting the haphazard, spotty development of Denver's suburban fringe, neither Montclair nor Harman fully blossomed until the coming of the automobile and the post–WW II boom.

South Denver, stretching from Alameda to Yale Avenue and from Colorado Boulevard on the east to Pecos Street on the west, embraced nearly 12 square miles, making it Denver's largest streetcar suburb. In 1890 most of its 1,491 residents lived close to the streetcar lines extending south from Denver. Town promoter James A. Fleming donated his mansion as a town hall while serving as mayor. His brothers opened a lumberyard and built whole blocks of homes at a time. "It seems no more trouble for them to build a house," noted south Denver's newspaper, the *Denver Eye,* "than it is for a shoemaker to halfsole a pair of shoes."[15] Concern about the saloons, dance halls, and gambling joints clustered around Overland Park racetrack led South Denverites to incorporate in 1886 in order to crack down on vice. After the town imposed an annual $3,500 saloon license fee, the *Denver Eye,* observing that "roadhouses and saloons were all cleaned out," predicted that South Denver was "destined to be filled with the homes of our best and most prominent citizens."[16]

Broadway Terrace, on the west side of Broadway between Sixth and Ellsworth, and University Park — home of the University of Denver after 1890 — were among many communities that never became incorporated towns. The Broadway streetcar tracks reached Orchard Place (Englewood). Beyond lay the country town of Littleton, which grew up around Richard Little's Rough and Ready Flour Mill in the 1860s. Englewood and Littleton, together with Aurora, Golden, and Lakewood, formed an outer ring of suburbs tied to Denver by streetcars.

Areas east of the South Platte River were initially more accessible to the city center, but viaducts and bridges gradually opened up southwest and northwest Denver. By 1888 the streetcar suburbs of Valverde and Barnum had emerged in southwest Denver. They grew slowly, despite the promotion of circus king Phineas T. Barnum, who claimed the area had the finest climate in the world, climate that would bring even the sickest health seeker back from the edge of the grave.

North of Barnum, Villa Park with its twisting lanes gave Denverites a chance to escape from the monotonous street grid that dominated most of the city. Another unusual development pattern was the alley homes in the Snell Addition of Capitol Hill. This experiment in more densely constructed single-family housing, commemorated later as a historic district, did not catch on — homebuilders demanded larger lots. As if reacting to crowded cities elsewhere, Denverites seemed obsessed with spacious parcels with plenty of elbow room.

Northwest Denver grew rapidly after streetcar lines crossed the railroad tracks and the river via Fifteenth and Sixteenth street viaducts. Temperance advocate Horatio B. Pearce had platted the town of Highlands on his ranch in 1871. After petitioning the Territorial Legislature to incorporate his town and getting himself elected mayor, Pearce inexplicably moved to sinful Denver. His town, however, persevered, growing to over 5,000 residents in 1890, when it ranked as Colorado's sixth-largest city. Besides seven streetcar lines, there were other "secrets of Highlands' success" according to the town's report for 1891: "True to her name and nature, she stands high and sightly, where the pure air from the mountains — that God-given slayer of disease — is used first-hand by her people and swells their lungs with strength and healthfulness. [There are] no smelters, factories or emitters of smoke within her borders."[17] Highlands's virtues included sobriety: By ordinance the town declared liquor outlets "nuisances" to be discouraged by a yearly license fee of $3,000.

Northwest of Highlands, John Brisbane Walker and the British investor Doctor William Bell grew alfalfa at Berkeley Farm until the late 1880s. Then they turned their $1,000 investment into $325,000 by selling the acreage to a Kansas City syndicate that developed the town of Berkeley. With a lake, a large park, and a fledgling Jesuit college (Regis), Berkeley had much to offer prospective residents. Like Highlands it puffed its pure air and pure morals.

Denver's suburban ring included both unincorporated "additions" to the city and a dozen incorporated towns with their own officials and services. Many of these towns became financially strapped during the 1893 depression and accepted annexation to Denver as a fiscal solution. Such was the case with Barnum, Harman, Highlands, and South Denver. Creation of the City and County of Denver in 1902 brought into the city limits the towns of Berkeley, Elyria, Globeville, Montclair, and Valverde.

Although Americans of the automobile age came to think of rumbling, creaking, screeching streetcars as slow, uncomfortable, and noisy, they were a marvelous convenience to nineteenth-century Denverites. Of course, a few saw streetcars as the devil's work. Jim Baker, the old mountain man, warily boarded an electric car that he described as "the stage like thing."[18] When it moved without the help of horses, he panicked and jumped off, falling in the street. Most Denverites, however, gratefully accepted the DTC's red and yellow trolleys as a fact of life — and even of death.[19] The DTC served Denver's suburban cemetery parks,

Street crews spruce up Tremont Place in this 1898 view. Tremont led to Denver's most elegant church, Trinity Methodist, and grandest hotel, the Brown Palace. (Photo by Alex Martin, Colorado Historical Society.)

Fairmount, Riverside, and Mount Olivet, with Funeral Car A, a closed black coach with window curtains, designed to hold the casket and the bereaved. For large funerals extra cars were added, but if the mourners grieved excessively they had to pay $4 an hour for overtime.[20] On livelier occasions charter cars were rented for excursions, "Seeing Denver" tours, and even honeymoons.

Streetcars reshaped the city and the lives of its citizens. To this day their routes are identifiable by extra wide streets and older neighborhood shopping areas. By enabling people to live miles from their workplaces, streetcars rearranged urban life. In traditional "walking cities," homes, shops, amusements, and jobs had all been within easy pedestrian distance. Streetcars permitted some city dwellers to move out to the country, knowing that a 5¢ ride would whisk them into town. For the masses of Denverites, work, play, and shopping began to revolve around the routes, fares, and schedules of the DTC.

The Cook's Addition horsecar and horse trailer stand on Thirty-fourth Avenue near Colorado Boulevard. Cook's Addition to Denver, like many others, boasted its own horse railway to help coax prospective home builders out of the city. (Ed J. Haley Collection.)

Like the automobile suburbs they foreshadowed, streetcar suburbs often were sprawling and not well

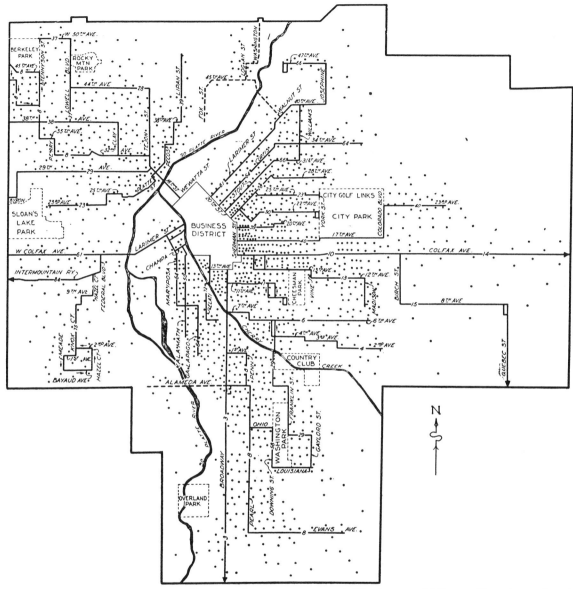

Chart 1—City and County of Denver. Street-car tracks are represented by heavy solid lines, with route numbers indicated therein; bus routes, by heavy broken lines; boundaries of parks, country club, etc., by light broken lines. Arrows on tracks at city limits signify that the lines in question extend outside the city. One dot denotes fifty families as of April 15, 1927.

When the Denver Tramway Company mapped its tracks and how the town's population clustered in 1927, Colorado's capital was still a streetcar city. (Denver Public Library, Western History Department.)

planned. Lines ran helter-skelter to where people were, or where developers hoped they would be. Property near the tracks was built up first; lots a few blocks away developed more slowly. Distant tracts with good trans-

63

portation flourished while other parcels without connections were left empty, creating a checkered cityscape.

In a 1932 "Study for Mass Transportation," the Denver Planning Commission noted that automobile passengers had come to outnumber streetcar ridership and offered an obituary for the DTC:

> Less than twenty years ago Denver boasted of a transit system that was not surpassed. In the past many lines have been built which on account of their long mileage through unsettled districts could not possibly have paid with the handicap of automobile competiton. The [Denver Tramway] company's policy was to encourage people to live away from the downtown district. This policy may have been dictated by the desire of the company to get more patronage but was partly based on its desire to aid certain real estate developments. In this way, the company has aided in building an extensive open city in which air and sunlight are everywhere available.[21]

Streetcars permitted those who could afford suburban homes the chance to escape from the saloons, brothels, crime, congestion, disease, and other pitfalls of city life. Business and professional men might tolerate and even patronize downtown dives but did not want their wives and children exposed to them. Communities such as Montclair, Park Hill, South Denver, Highlands, and Berkeley kept out undesirable uses with vice ordinances and restrictive covenants specifying minimum lot size and home construction cost. Although streetcar suburbanization enhanced the quality of life for many, it left others behind in older, crowded, less desirable neighborhoods. The streetcar allowed many Denverites to pursue private suburban dreams instead of tackling urban problems.

CHAPTER 7

Growing Pains

Children be dyin' down 'ere all the time. It all comes from these piles of dirt. . . . An' nobody comes and takes it away like they do on Capitol Hill.

Anonymous resident of Denver's Bottoms, 1890[1]

From Capitol Hill, visitors to Denver in the 1890s could survey the sprawling young city. Two dozen streetcar lines shot from downtown out to suburbs bristling with tree saplings. To the north, sulfurous smoke belched from Globeville smelter chimneys, the most prominent features on the skyline. On clear summer days the distant mountains seemed only a few miles away, but in the winter, coal smoke ruined the view and fouled the air. Worse still were the smells of overcrowded neighborhoods such as the densely packed Chinese section at Sixteenth and Wazee where a *Rocky Mountain News* reporter found overflowing outhouses and "a terrible stench." At Seventeenth and Larimer, a newsman discovered "a fleet of old shoes, cabbage leaves and potato peelings . . . vainly trying to sail upon a lake of liquid putrefaction."[2] Wags joked, "There are more flies in Denver than anywhere else in the world and they stick more."[3]

What casual observers did not see was a city overwhelmed by growth; a place largely peopled by former farmers, ex-miners, small-town and rural folk, trying to create an urban society in a nation where large cities were a recent, little-understood phenomenon. Few were born in Denver, most had lived in the city only a few years, and many were rootless transients ready to move on.[4] In pursuing their private goals many residents ignored the common good. On learning of the 1871 Chicago fire, Denver cigar merchant Amos H. Root blatantly advertised: "Horrible, Horrible all the cigars and tobacco in Chicago destroyed, but Root still has a good supply."[5] Denver was not alone in searching for order while grappling with tooth-and-claw capitalism. Cities across the land faced similar problems. Citizens wanted basic services but were unwilling to pay for them. Most failed to understand the needs of an urban society and were firm in their belief that social progress was best promoted by unrestrained competition. The fit, they believed, would survive and prosper.

During the 1860s a marshal and a few deputies maintained what order there was in Denver. As the town grew, citizens demanded better protection, so in 1874 a chief and regular force were appointed. Throughout the rest of the century, the department tried to control crime in the mushrooming metropolis, but the small band was distracted by its many other duties, ranging from capturing stray dogs to assisting injured persons. In 1887, 43 policemen served the city of 65,000, a ratio much lower than that in New York and Philadelphia. Before they bought a patrol wagon, the bluecoats either had to walk prisoners to jail, take them on the streetcar, or hire a hack. Officers once struggled for hours escorting a wet, 300-pound lady to jail. She had been found sleeping in an irrigation ditch, diverting water into the street. For such services, patrolmen — who had to provide their own uniforms — were paid $65 a month. To supplement their salaries some policemen solicited payoffs from gamblers, pimps, prostitutes, and other underworld characters.

Police chiefs came and went; morale rose and fell. Criminals often got away or, if captured, easily escaped from the old jail, a converted meat market. Occupants of that vermin-infested hole had good reason to leave. In 1884, 250 prisoners were jammed into a bull pen of 1,500 square feet, men and boys, sane and insane together. An improved jail in the basement of the new City Hall (1884) at Fourteenth and Larimer was more secure but not more comfortable; its inmates were "packed like the lower decks of a slave ship." After inspecting it in 1902, a doctor claimed to have found 3,987,237 germs including "several eastern types."[6]

The police tried to cope by adopting new methods of fighting crime. Billy clubs were issued in 1881; a few detectives were added in the early 1880s. When the first patrol wagon arrived in February 1886, Mayor Joseph E. Bates and the police force greeted it "with a flourish of handkerchiefs and wild hurrahs."[7] Efficiency was further improved the same year by the installation of telephone call boxes that hastened the reporting of

Rising crime inspired the Denver Police Department to install this steel cage at Twentieth and Larimer, allowing officers to detain drunks, toughs, and gang members until the paddy wagon arrived. (Denver Public Library, Western History Department.)

ONE OF THE FINEST!

Drinking, gambling, prostitution, and domestic abuse were among the many targets of reformers, including women who joined the crusade to cleanse the Queen City. (Colorado Historical Society.)

The New Woman Policeman "Pinches" a Brutal Husband.
—Denver Republican

crimes. In the 1890s, cages, large enough to hold three men, were placed on sidewalks to detain prisoners until the patrol wagon arrived.[8] The department refused to give officers newfangled flashlights, but it did buy two carrier pigeons to speed communications from outlying neighborhoods. Chief William H. O'Brien bought disguises for his sleuths and told them, "Go forth and catch some thieves." One detective, masquerading as a peddler, found his false whiskers too effective: He was arrested by a fellow policeman for selling without a license. Told of his officer's problem, the chief supposedly replied: "We have those disguises. . . . I paid $9 for them . . . and they must be worn if you get [thrown] in jail three times a day."[9] O'Brien's penny-pinching reflected the city's thinking. At times in the 1890s, less than $1.30 per resident per year was appropriated for the police; never was the figure above $2.

Taxpayers did not spend much on fire department protection either. Until 1881 the entire force was voluntary; the last unpaid company, the Tabor Hose, did not disband until 1885. Volunteers, or sponsors such as Horace Tabor, paid for uniforms, in which amateur firemen proudly paraded and attended balls. When they fought fires, historian Jerome Smiley recounted, "there was much confusion, uproar and wasted effort."[10] Smiley attributed the city's freedom from major blazes more to its brick and stone buildings than to its firefighters.

Health care made similarly halting progress. People tried to set up a hospital in the 1860s, but nothing much was accomplished until 1870 when Doctor John Elsner was appointed county physician. Within three

Elizabeth Byers, Margaret Gray Evans, and other charity-minded women helped the Ladies Relief Society finance this refuge for homeless children at 800 Logan Street. Built in 1876, it was demolished in 1897 to relieve the affluent Capitol Hill neighborhood of "unsightliness." (Denver Public Library, Western History Department.)

years, he completed the first building of what became Denver General Hospital. Elsner took in indigent outcasts whom he found "lying around in hen houses and barns."[11] During 1874, its first year of operation, the hospital treated 189 patients, of whom about 10 percent died. For more than a decade the county hospital doubled as a poorhouse. After 1884 paupers were sent to the Arapahoe County Poor Farm in Globeville, three miles north of downtown, where the smelter fumes were so noxious that the indigents were forced to stay inside for days at a time. At least the farm, which cost taxpayers less than $9,000 to operate in 1895, separated the poor from the acutely ill. In 1901 an insane asylum was added to the hospital. Earlier, the superintendent reported, "twenty poor unfortunates [were] crowded and huddled in quarters little better than dungeons."[12]

Private giving partially offset public stinginess. Hospitals, including Roman Catholic–supported St. Joseph's (1873) and St. Anthony's (1891), as well as the Episcopal St. Luke's (1881), set aside beds for charity cases. The city's many orphans were left in private hands until 1895, when women prodded the state to fund a home in south Denver. St. Vincent's Catholic Orphanage in north Denver housed nearly 1,500 children in 1893; the private Denver Orphans' Home sheltered 464 that

Gaming flourished in a town founded as a gamble on the gold that lured speculators armed with cards and dice as well as those with picks and pans. (Colorado Historical Society.)

year. Elizabeth Byers founded The Ladies Union Aid Society in 1860, Denver's first nonsectarian charity organization. Its limited activities were greatly supplemented by the Ladies Relief Society (1874). As the city's most important secular charity in the 1870s and 1880s, the Relief Society gave groceries and a ton of coal to needy families, supported an old ladies' home, and set up a wood yard where the able-bodied unemployed could trade labor for food and shelter. It also made home visits, operated a day nursery and kindergarten, found homes for orphans, and buried paupers. By the 1890s a dozen other charitable groups were working with down-and-outers. Besides the Ladies Relief Society, the city had a Hebrew Ladies Relief Society, a Women's Christian Temperance Union nursery, and the Newsboys and Bootblacks Home, plus a number of religious charities.

Beset by do-gooders, businessmen asked the charities to combine their appeals, leading to the 1889 creation of the Charity Organization Society headed by the Reverend Myron Reed, a Congregational minister, and Frances Wisebart Jacobs, a Jewish philanthropist. Ultimately, the society evolved into the Community Chest, a forerunner of the United Way. Solicitors promised donors that their money would be well spent. The Charity Organization's aim was, as one official put it, "to strengthen

The *Rocky Mountain News* and the Overland Stage line, keys to Denver's survival during the 1860s, shared this building on Larimer Street. The U.S. Mint, flag flying from its turret, was a a block away at Sixteenth and Market. From its new fortress, the *News* undertook a reform crusade aimed at moral survival. (Denver Public Library, Western History Department.)

the character of the weak. Nothing was to be given to the unworthy, the idle, or the drinker."[13] Told of poor Italian children who gathered watercress in the Bottoms to sell downtown, one philanthrophist remarked, "The majority of the children belong to those dagoes, who would probably [do] the same thing if they had thousands of dollars."[14]

City government proved inept at dealing with the population explosion. Politicians scrambled for office; corruption reigned; and councilmen worried less about social services than they did about patronage and power. Reformers, who only dimly grasped the reality of the changes they were witnessing, believed that society's ills could be cured by strict enforcement of liquor and gambling laws. "The offal of foreign immigration," they said, "is attempting to dictate to the moral element."[15] That dictation was obvious in the election of 1889 when Republicans nominated the cherub-faced grocer Wolfe Londoner, a pioneer of 1860, for mayor. His practical jokes had endeared him to Denverites, but his liberal attitude to drinking and gambling led reformers to back Elias Barton.[16]

On election day, some of Londoner's supporters raced from precinct to precinct in order to vote twice. Honest citizens found that their names had been used and their votes stolen by supporters of "Londoner, chaos and rum."[17] Con man Jefferson Randolph "Soapy" Smith and gunman Bat Masterson were among Londoner's partisans practicing sleight of hand at polling places. The police, who had profitable ties to the underworld, also liked the roly-poly grocer. William Byers, who complained to a policeman about illegal voting, was told: "Now, I don't see no such

Reflecting Denver's commitment to public education, the Arapahoe School, erected in 1873, was once the tallest structure in town. (Tom Noel Collection.)

thing, but if you don't go on I'll give you a taste of my club."[18] Reformers lost the first round; Londoner was declared mayor. Two years later the Colorado Supreme Court voided the fraudulent election and ordered Londoner to vacate his position. The *Rocky Mountain News* savored his removal, noting that "hizzoner" had unsuccessfully clung to his office "with a death like grip."[19]

Shenanigans in Denver gave the state, whose lawmakers were hardly pure themselves, an excuse for taking over the city's Police and Fire departments as well as the powerful Board of Public Works. Reformers demanded change, but many people accepted the corruption just as they acquiesced in the social order. In 1885 Chamber of Commerce directors agreed to bribe an army major to secure a military post — Fort Logan, south of town.[20] In politics, as in business, the spoils went to the fit. "Smartness," wrote Isabella Bird, "is the quality thought most of. The boy who gets on by cheating at his lessons is praised for being a 'smart boy'."[21]

Making smart boys and girls involved more than instruction in cheating. Denver realized that it needed schools, but during the 1860s little was accomplished. Owen Goldrick remembered that his cabin school-

This 1874 photo, taken by William G. Chamberlain from atop the Arapahoe School, shows the intersection of Seventeenth and Lawrence streets. New homes and commercial buildings sprout from the prairie. (Colorado Historical Society.)

house for 13 scholars had a flat roof, "which was a great conductor of snow and rain, much to the dripping discomfort of the dear little urchins." Five years later, Goldrick, then overseer of the town's minuscule educational system, inspected west Denver's school, a shed that sheltered 80 students. In east Denver, 70 children did "six hours daily penance in a low-roofed, broken-windowed barracks of a place."[22] Not until 1873, when the Arapahoe School was built, did the town have a first-rate school.

When Aaron Gove took charge of School District One in 1874 he faced seemingly insurmountable problems. Fortunately, Gove, an 1861 graduate of Illinois Normal University, was made of stern stuff. A Civil War hero, he had returned to his native New Hampshire in 1865 so sick with yellow fever that his father met the train with a coffin. Gove recovered and nine years later he came west. He quickly realized that two small schools, Arapahoe and Stout, with their 18 classrooms and 19 instructors, could not take care of the district's thousand pupils. "Every child," he argued, "is of importance and has the right to an education."[23] Not everyone agreed with such democratic ideals. Some supported primary education but did not approve of spending money on high schools. Some wanted the Bible read in class; others did not. Some wanted calisthenics taught; Gove did not. Some advocated manual training; Gove, who thought that students should learn in school what they could not learn outside, disagreed.

Gove adroitly met the challenge of rapid growth. Temporary buildings and half-sessions provided relief from overcrowding as he hurried to erect new buildings. In 1875 he added a tenth grade; in 1877 the city graduated its first high school class; in 1881 a separate high school was opened; and in 1885 Gove founded a night school to make real his dream of universal education. That same year, he bowed to educational innovation and allowed geography to be taught in the primary grades. In 1889 he allowed drawing to become part of the curriculum, and in 1893 compromised with manual training proponents and opened Manual Training High School. He dodged the Bible-reading issue by concluding that "discussion of the question will be unprofitable."[24]

Gove worried about Roman Catholics' antipathy to public education; Catholics objected to being taxed for public schools while they were supporting their own institutions — there were 1,775 students in six Catholic schools in 1899. Private schools such as Wolfe Hall and Jarvis Hall, both affiliated with the Episcopal church, and the Roman Catholic girls' academies, St. Mary's and Loretto, siphoned some youngsters out of the public schools; yet many of the well-to-do sent their children to public schools.[25]

Gove was fortunate that District One encompassed most of Denver east of the South Platte and north of Cherry Creek. That section included the business district and several wealthy residential areas that showered Gove's schools with substantial property tax revenue. Other districts — before 1902 the city and its suburbs were divided into 12 different school jurisdictions — were smaller and poorer and consequently lagged behind District One. West Denver trailed east Denver by seven years in graduating a high school class. When it did, in June 1884, it staged a grand event. Students carefully arranged moss to spell out the school motto "Forti et Fideli Nihil Difficile." Several orations, including "The World Is Ruled by Three Kings: Commerce, Cash and Calico," were declaimed. An ode was recited, essays read, a duet sung, a valedictory address given. Six seniors graduated in style.[26]

West Denver's high school, which shared space with elementary schools until 1893; south Denver's high school, which was housed in part of Grant School; and north Denver's high school, which occupied its own building in 1889, suffered in comparison to School District One's Denver High School, later renamed East High. Originally housed in the Arapahoe School it moved in 1881 to a separate building that, enlarged later in the 1880s, came to dominate the block between Nineteenth and Twentieth, California and Stout. To cap one of its doorway arches, officials commissioned a local sculptor, Preston Powers, to chisel a sandstone keystone using as his model the most beautiful child in the city. The six-year-old winner, selected from 5,000 contestants, looked like an angel, so East High's students became the Angels.[27]

Gove, although not a disciple of the "rule, strap and switch," did believe in discipline. "The greater half of the child's training," he said, "is cultivating and strengthening of the virtues of obedience, order, respect for the rights of others and punctuality."[28] When Edwina Fallis started first grade at Broadway School in the early 1880s, she was told to do two things: "Be good and mind the teacher." A longer list of tabus included: "Don't drink out of the cups that stand on the benches beside the water buckets. They are not clean;" and "Don't go to the water closets unless you just can't help it."[29] Edwina also found that her teacher, Miss Christine Peabody, wanted her pupils to bring a moist sponge with which to wipe their slates rather than spitting on them to do the job. Edwina survived the experience. Gove also endured, remaining as superintendent for 30 years. By 1900 he presided over a nationally recognized system of

21 schools employing over 225 teachers to educate over 14,000 pupils. Nearly 15,000 students were in other districts in the metropolitan area.

The schools had faults. Some 3,000 of District One's school-age students were not attending classes in 1900. Many left before high school. Fledgling colleges — Sacred Heart, Colorado Woman's College, and Denver University — educated only a few.[30] High school diplomas were not required for admission to Denver University's Medical School (1881), where students practiced on carcasses "as dry as leather."[31] The Gross Medical School (1887) was no better. Local legal education was even less formal, although perhaps superior to medical education; prospective lawyers learned by clerking in established attorneys' offices.

Despite their defects, the schools heralded the town's commitment to a civilized future. It was, as Gove recognized, a shaky bond. Denver, not long removed from its frontier past, was full of contradictions. When a madam opened a parlor house at Seventeenth and Welton, in a fashionable district near the Denver Club, neighbors complained to the police chief, John Farley. Farley reported to Mayor Londoner that the women had been asked to be quiet, but that since they had put a lot of money into the house he had agreed to let them stay until the first of the month, when they would move to the red light district on Holladay Street. Londoner explained to a *News* reporter that such arrangements were necessary because "in a city like Denver, we have decided that houses of prostitution are a necessary evil."[32]

"Socially and morally this place is an enigma to a stranger," commented the English tourist L. Vernon Briggs. Seeing throngs of Denverites walking south from downtown in the early afternoon of July 27, 1886, Briggs assumed that they were flocking to a ball game until he was asked if he too were "going to the hanging."[33] He followed the crowd to Broadway and Cherry Creek, where the gallows awaited Andrew Green, convicted of robbing and murdering streetcar driver Joseph Whitnah. Green, a black man, had admitted his part in robbing Whitnah but said the shooting was accidental. Undersheriff John Chivington brought the prisoner by carriage from the jail. Vendors sold popcorn, lemonade, and pictures of the condemned. Drunks waving whisky bottles staggered through the crowd of 15,000. Men took off their hats so that others, including little children who were hoisted up by their parents, could get a clear view. The choir sang "Nearer My God to Thee." At 2:30 P.M. Sheriff Frederick Cramer cut a rope attached to a 310-pound weight designed to jerk the noose up quickly. It did not work. Green slowly strangled, twitching, his palms turning blue. After 25 minutes doctors pronounced him dead. The rope was cut up for souvenirs.

The *Tribune-Republican* denounced the execution, calling it "the most depraved and disgusting exhibition witnessed in any city in the country."[34] Afterward, Denver took another step toward maturity, for Green's was the town's last legal public hanging. Such barbaric spectacles, many thought, ill served a city craving respectability.

CHAPTER 8

The Rush to Respectability

[Denverites have] a restless admiration for Eastern America, an uneasy consciousness of their inferiority to New York, Boston or Philadelphia, a dread of the ridicule of the Eastern newspapers, a desire that their children should have the advantages of an "Eastern" education.

Beatrice Webb
American Diary, 1898[1]

As Denver became a city, Denverites pursued respectability with the same vigor that prospectors sought gold. Slum lads still splashed in South Platte swimming holes, but by the late 1890s Capitol Hill's young gentlemen wore trunks and donned tops. With pretentiousness born of cowtown insecurity, they styled their germ-laden swimming pool at Thirteenth and Broadway the "Natatorium."[2] The rush to respectability had begun early. Wagon trains brought pianos for Denver's parlors, hardwood for doors, and plate glass for windows. Albert Richardson, the journalist who first visited the Cherry Creek outposts in 1859, was surprised to find on returning in 1865 "libraries and pictures, rich carpets and pianos, silver and wine."[3]

In 1872 the adolescent town entertained Alexis, Czar Alexander II's third son, who interrupted a buffalo hunt to visit Denver. Four hundred of the city's elite jammed the American House for a banquet and ball in the Russian grand duke's honor. Governor Edward McCook's wife fainted in the duke's arms; other Cinderellas were trampled by the

One of Denver's more outlandish nouveau riche, the "Unsinkable" Molly Brown became a legend immortalized by a movie, an opera, and the house museum at 1340 Pennsylvania Street. (Colorado Historical Society.)

big-footed Romanov. Enchanted by the tall young nobleman, they did not complain. They had, as compensation, souvenirs from the evening: gloves that had touched his hand; the butt of his cigar; a hair from his comb; a swatch of green velvet cut from his chair; and a tough piece of steak snatched from the ducal dinner plate.[4]

During the 1870s and 1880s, Denver grew in social graces. In 1880 the journalist Ernest Ingersoll pleased Denverites by telling them that their town was "only New York and New England and Ohio, transplanted and considerably enlivened."[5] Social prejudice, often based on race and sometimes on religion, operated in Denver as it did in the East. Rich men of humble origin lounged at the prestigious Denver Club, but wealthy Jews were barred and Catholics were not welcome. Blacks could not sit on the main floor of the Tabor Opera House, and women of all classes faced social as well as economic barriers. Within the ranks of the socially acceptable, a pecking order was gradually established. Money helped assure one's social place, but the dollar alone was not always almighty. A semblance of refinement and a regard for proper public behavior were essential.

When the wrong people blundered into the city's social world the results were predictable. Margaret Tobin Brown learned a hard lesson when she and her husband James J. came down to Denver from Leadville in 1894. Their fortune and their lavishly furnished Capitol Hill mansion normally would have gotten them into society. Maggie desperately wanted to be accepted. "Perhaps no woman in society has ever spent more time or money becoming 'civilized'," the *Denver Times* observed.[6] Unfortunately, Maggie was Irish and Roman Catholic. Her spelling was faulty, her wardrobe garish, her mother smoked a pipe. Many ladies of leisure rejected her dinner invitations and refused to invite her to their parties. Only after she had gained international attention for saving a lifeboat full of people when the *Titanic* sank in 1912 did social doyennes open their doors to her. Even Mrs. Crawford Hill asked "Molly Brown" to lunch.

Louise Sneed, a Southern belle, had married Crawford Hill, son of smelter king Nathaniel Hill, in 1895. Her background, her husband's wealth, her grand mansion at 969 Sherman, and her father-in-law's status gave her the leverage to become, as the *Who's Who in Denver Society* styled her, "the arbiter of Colorado society."[7] Her liaison with Bulkeley Wells, a dashing mining man, scandalized older socialites but made her the darling of the younger, smart set. Local butterflies badly needed a monarch since this "Aristocracy of the Parvenus" had few criteria, except money and ostentatious display, by which to measure itself.[8]

The rich reveled in their money. Roger Woodbury embellished his north Denver mansion with silver bathroom fixtures and gold-plated doorknobs. David Moffat fancied crystal chandeliers, Tiffany windows, central vacuum cleaning, tapestried walls, and electrically heated sidewalks at his home on Eighth and Grant. Dennis Sheedy, a cattleman turned banker and smelter owner, covered the walls of his sandstone fortress at 1115 Grant with sheep hide. Most of these Gilded Age grandees lived within walking distance of downtown, visibly demonstrating with their big houses on prime land that they were in command.

Some of the well-heeled also owned country homes where they stayed part of the year. Edward Wolcott's palatial Wolhurst, on the South Platte 14 miles south of Denver, was one of the most magnificent of these rural estates. Wolcott, whose wealth mirrored his success as a lawyer, politician, and investor, created his dream world on 500 acres straddling the Arapahoe–Douglas County line. The native cottonwoods did not provide a forest to his taste, so he transplanted 1,200 trees to fill his woods. He made a 17-acre lake and imported swans to swim on it. Four dozen Chinese pheasants lent an exotic touch and bred so prolifically that their progeny provided game for later generations of bird hunters throughout eastern Colorado. Wolcott, who became a U.S. senator in 1889, used his home, which grew from an original 12 rooms to 30, to entertain sumptuously national and international celebrities. The grand estate's sweetness turned sour when Wolcott's stormy marriage dramatically ended. It seemed that while Mrs. Frances Wolcott enjoyed "tea and crumpets," Edward preferred "rum and strumpets." Wolcott, renowned for his eloquence and culture, was known locally as "Edward of Navarre" because of his patronage of the Navarre, a plush house of ill repute. Wolcott left his wife in 1899 and lost his senatorship in 1901.[9] Denver

Riverside opened in 1876 as a fashionable cemetery park where pioneers could celebrate their exploits in stone. Nathan Addison Baker, a journalist and real estate developer, reputedly held horses in higher regard than humans. (Photo by Tom Noel.)

could put up with quiet scandal, but not with amorous escapades as blatant as Wolcott's.

To track who was who, caste-conscious citizens consulted social registers. The city's first *Blue Book*, published in 1892, listed over a thousand persons including members of dozens of minor clubs. Readers were informed that fashionable people used their fingers to eat pieces of small birds. A section titled "Foreign Terms Used on Menus" let the uncouth know that *calipash* was "the glutinous meat of the upper shell of the turtle" and that *calipee* was "the glutinous meat of the lower shell of the turtle."[10] Since almost anybody could learn the difference between calipash and calipee, some of the city's hoarier habitants tried to distinguish themselves from the upstarts by organizing the Society of Colorado Pioneers. At meetings members eulogized each other and screened applications from worthies who had arrived before 1861. They donated material to the Colorado State Historical Society, which was established through the efforts of Doctor Frederick Bancroft, William Byers, and others in 1879. They also encouraged early historians — William Vickers, Frank Hall, Jerome Smiley, and William Byers — by buying their massive volumes filled with flattering biographies of the empire builders. In death they continued to proclaim their precedence by inscribing "Pioneer" on their tombstones and mausoleums.[11]

Not everyone could claim pioneer status, nor were all old-timers socially acceptable. Culture, a casserole of education and taste peppered with money, was far more important than date of arrival in fixing one's social position. Some obvious roads to culture were well traveled. Wealthy young scions went east to college. Vassar, Smith, and Wellesley attracted women; Yale, Harvard, Princeton, Cornell, and Columbia suited men. Denver's Yale Alumni Club boasted over 60 members by 1898. Crawford Hill, along with many of the other graduates, belonged to the University Club but was something of a misfit, for he had attended Brown University, where his father had taught chemistry. The senior Hill was himself an oddity among the older social lions in having had a good formal education, unlike the scanty common school training of most of his peers. These men and women, many of whom could spell no better than Maggie Brown, sought culture where they could. Some collected art, some built ostentatious office buildings and homes they thought proved their good taste; some traveled.

Merchant princes such as Harold Kountze, a scion of the Colorado National Bank clan, were trained to rule in prep schools, Ivy League colleges, and private men's clubs. (Harold Kountze, Jr., Collection.)

The poet Walt Whitman viewed the South Platte Canyon southwest of Denver and wondered how Americans could think of going to Europe "when you can come here."[12] Yet, rich Denverites, like other wealthy Americans, ignored Whitman and looked for culture abroad. Margaret Gray Evans, one of the first to tour, had her Atlantic crossing eased by an invention of her husband, a sea berth designed to counteract the ship's motion. The Indian fighter Scott Anthony, his pockets bulging with real estate profits, spent several years traveling in Europe, Asia, and Africa with his family. Louise Hill did more than tour — she had herself presented to England's King Edward VII, a maneuver that assured her dominance as Denver's society queen. Denverites' admiration for things foreign was reflected in the city's architecture. Rich and poor alike favored familiar eastern and European styles rather than the Hispanic architecture of the American Southwest. Jim Baker, the mountain man, lived in an adobe house on his ranch near Fifty-third and Tennyson, but most newcomers made their cabins of cottonwood and later imported more durable pine. In fact, by prohibiting sun-dried bricks, Denver, in effect, outlawed adobe. Construction of homes and commercial buildings from kiln-fired bricks, a popular practice after the 1863 fire, gave the town the look of eastern stability it wanted.

Before the 1870s, simple commercial buildings and homes mirrored the town's smallness and its citizens' moderate means. As Denver's mothers and fathers grew wealthy, they itched to show off their riches. To please them, the city's first major architect, Robert S. Roeschlaub, abandoned pioneer plainness. His many school buildings, including Emerson (1884) at Fourteenth and Ogden, Corona (1889) at Ninth and Corona, and the monumental Denver High School (1881–1889) at Nineteenth

THE RUSH TO RESPECTABILITY

Monuments such as
Corona/Dora Moore Elementary School at Ninth and Corona in Capitol Hill flaunted new-found respectability and were major investments in building a sense of community. (Photo by Roger Whitacre.)

and California, gave Denver ornate Romanesque palaces of learning. For Denver University's campus, he designed Chamberlin Observatory (1889) and University Hall (1890). On Capitol Hill he built mansions; at its base, on Eighteenth and Broadway, he left his best work, Trinity Methodist church (1888).

Roeschlaub's contemporary, William Lang, designed St. Mark's Episcopal church (1890) at Twelfth and Lincoln, but he was better known for his houses. On Capitol Hill, he constructed pinnacled mansions and turreted town houses in romantic styles. Denverites, like other Americans, admired French chateaux, Romanesque castles, Dutch town houses, and southern plantation manors. Often, they combined disparate architectural traditions in buildings marked more by exuberance than by good taste or originality.

Ornateness and eclecticism also characterized public buildings. The Arapahoe County Courthouse at Sixteenth and Tremont, designed by the Detroit architect Elijah E. Myers, who also planned the state capitol, reflected Americans' tendency to choose Greco-Roman prototypes for civic edifices, a fashion followed in the post office (1884–1892) at Sixteenth and Arapahoe, next to the Tabor Opera House.[13] Commercial structures similarly followed eastern and midwestern trends. Some of the city's earliest skyscrapers, including Seventeenth Street's Boston (1889) and Equitable (1892) buildings, and Fifteenth Street's grandiose Mining Exchange (1891), were designed by Boston and St. Louis firms. Nevertheless, eastern forms were occasionally transformed in the West. The heavy, solid Romanesque revival architecture of Henry Hobson Richardson, the nation's leading architect of the 1880s, was modified in some Denver buildings, among them the Mining Exchange and the South Broadway Christian church (1892). There, according to architectural historian Richard Brettell, Richardsonianism was "radically active and exciting."[14]

Frank E. Edbrooke, Denver's foremost nineteenth-century architect, gave the city its best structures. Edbrooke came to Denver from Chicago in 1879 to supervise construction of the Tabor Block at Sixteenth and Larimer. He completed his last important work, the Colorado State Museum at Fourteenth and Sherman, in 1916. In the intervening years he raised the local level of taste through such buildings as the Masonic Temple (1889) at Sixteenth and Welton, Loretto Heights College (1891) at Dartmouth Avenue and Federal Boulevard, the Brown Palace Hotel (1892) at Seventeenth and Broadway, Central Presbyterian church (1892) at Seventeenth and Sherman, and the Denver Dry Goods (1894) at Sixteenth and California.[15]

Having dotted their city with showy structures, culture seekers stuffed their houses with tokens of their refinement. Treasures from their travels filled knickknack shelves and china cabinets. When their living rooms grew unlivable, they donated odd and surplus items to the Chamber of Commerce, which in the 1880s and 1890s displayed such gems as a Fiji Island headrest, an elephant hair, a thorn from Los Angeles, and a palm leaf from Cuba in a small museum the chamber housed with the Mercantile Library.

Businessmen had put their library in the Chamber of Commerce at Fourteenth and Lawrence, one of Edbrooke's edifices. In December 1885, they hired Charles Dudley, a Yale-educated librarian, at $75 a month. He carefully avoided buying literature offensive to good morals and tried to protect readers from books returned by people with infectious diseases. The Mercantile Library did not charge its borrowers, but patrons had to be sponsored by a member of the chamber. In 1889 another library, free and public, opened in the Denver High School at Nineteenth and Stout. There, librarian John Cotton Dana introduced progressive practices such as a children's library and open stacks in which borrowers could browse. At the end of the century, the Mercantile Library, renamed the City Library after it started receiving city funds in 1891, merged with the

Denver bought land for City Park in 1882, but for years leased its acres as income property. In his *History of Colorado*, Frank Hall declared: "The one fatal error for which future generations will not forgive the first was its failure to provide public parks." (Tom Noel Collection.)

school library. In 1902 it purchased an apartment row, LaVeta Place, near Colfax and Bannock and converted four of the bat- and bedbug-infested units into cramped housing for books. The same year Pittsburgh philanthropist Andrew Carnegie gave Denver $200,000 for a decent library; that plus city funds allowed construction of a new building on the LaVeta Place site. On February 15, 1910, the Denver Public Library opened its first adequate home, a $425,000 Greek temple of Turkey Creek sandstone.

Some empire builders fancied art, too. With frontier directness, one Denverite sent the dimensions of his library to a New York decorator with instructions to buy books and pictures to fill the space. Others took a more personal interest. Byers proudly displayed a painting by Albert Bierstadt; Baron Walter von Richthofen's private art gallery sported

Denver Athletic Club members have been working out in this landmark structure at 1325 Glenarm Place since 1889. Note the rooftop tennis court. (Photo by William Henry Jackson, Colorado Historical Society.)

nudes, to the dismay of proper Denverites. Junius F. Brown, a wholesale grocer who had made part of his fortune shipping whisky into Colorado in the 1860s, discovered art late in life. A reporter heralded the old man's transformation: "It was as if a wheat field suddenly burst into a bloom of roses."[16] Brown collected avidly and well; eventually, his holdings included a Millet and a Corot.

Some of the well-to-do shared their good fortune. To preserve stuffed specimens of Colorado's "furred, feathered and finned game," Doctor Bancroft, first president of the State Historical and Natural History Society, searched for exhibit space. For a time in the 1880s the organization displayed its treasures in a hotel, then at the Arapahoe County Courthouse, then at the Chamber of Commerce. In 1895 they came to rest for 20 years in the basement of the state capitol, where William C. Ferril tended and increased the collections, working so diligently that at one point he noted in his journal: "Keeping up today on quinine, rye whiskey, and two plasters on my chest and side."[17]

Ferril gathered practically everything related to Colorado, from birds to newspapers. Gradually, geological, botanical, and zoological items were deposited at the Museum of Natural History founded in 1900 to house the collection of Colorado naturalist Edwin Carter. The museum in City Park also included a small art gallery where paintings lent by Junius Brown and others were shown free — a practice that, the *Denver Times* contended, made the Denver gallery superior to Paris's Louvre. "No longer," the paper said, "is it necessary for the people of the West to journey to the effete East to view the wonderful works of the old masters."[18]

A mansion on Capitol Hill, a home in the country, a Bierstadt on the wall, a Yale degree, a pew at Trinity Methodist or at St. John's Episcopal church helped secure one's social position. Membership in an exclusive club was the final test. The most prestigious men's club was the Denver Club, founded in 1880. Its Romanesque revival house at Seventeenth and Glenarm exuded an atmosphere that induced awe: "One almost felt like taking off one's hat when one passed by," one member recalled.[19] Younger social lions fraternized at the University Club (1891) at Seventeenth and Sherman, while the sports-minded enjoyed swimming, sparring, fencing, bicycling, billiards, and Turkish baths at the Denver Athletic Club (1884) at 1325 Glenarm. In the 1890s that club's football team introduced the Ivy League novelty to Colorado and rushed to victory spurred on by the club cheer:

See, rah, see
Don't you see?
You can't beat the D.A.C.

Rac, rac, rac! Cherry and black!
D.A.C. bumblebee!
Sting! Bing! Bang! Boom!
Rah! R-r-r-r-r-r-r-r [20]

Women's clubs also helped the wealthy distinguish between the socially acceptable and the unacceptable. The Fortnightly and Monday clubs, both formed in 1881, brought cultured ladies together to hear papers on subjects ranging from "Moral Uses of Beauty" to Margaret Evans's "Prose Fiction in Europe Prior to the Renaissance."[21] Anne Evans, Margaret and John Evans's daughter, bolstered the Artists Club established in 1894, where polished women honed skills they had learned at finishing school. Whist lovers and bridge players formed social subsets, the pinnacle of which was Mrs. Crawford Hill's nine tables of whist — the "Sacred Thirty-Six."

Socialites kept tabs on each other by reading society columnists who fed the public's appetite for gossip. The cattiest of these society scribes, Mrs. Leonel Ross O'Bryan, first wrote for the *Denver Post* and then published her own weekly magazine, *Polly Pry,* which promised to "tell the truth or as much of it as a hypocritical and debilitated public can be expected to swallow." Polly's truth was often hard to take. She sneered at Maggie Brown's hairdo and ridiculed her "brown velvet gown, creepy with whole sables." Ladies with gambling fever were also pilloried: "Half the women on the hill are in debt to their eyes this very minute, and one stout and noticeable buxom matron keeps her grocers waiting until their patience is straining to the breaking point." Polly further fretted about the lack of eligible bachelors in Denver; at one point she counted only 14. "What are the poor little buds going to do?" she asked. Her solution: "Bring on your titles Mr. Englishman, bring some centuries of education and polish with them and you'll find a ready market right here in Denver."[22]

The city's need for polish was obvious to visitors conditioned by dime novels to see Denver as part of the Wild West. In the early 1890s, the Frenchman Paul de Rousiers arrived with a revolver and bullets sufficient "to make fifty of my fellow-beings bite the dust."[23] Luckily for de Rousiers's fellow beings, his cartridge box broke, scattering its contents among his socks. Even those who knew that Denver was not Dodge City found danger and excitement lurking on Market Street. On Blake Street, salesmen from Chicago and farmers from Kansas savored a taste of the town's wilder past at Ed Chase's Palace Theater, where gambling was open and the girls "were very liberal in showing their legs and bosoms."[24]

Market and Blake Street dives embarrassed Denver. So did the city's reputation as a cow town. In 1880, Ernest Ingersoll commented on Denverites' quaint custom of keeping cows — many took their cattle out of town to graze in the morning and brought them back at night. Bessy's aroma lingered through the 1890s and into the twentieth century, partly because Walter Cheesman allowed a neighbor to pasture a cow on his land at Colfax and Broadway, a sniff away from the Brown Palace Hotel.

Sidney and Beatrice Webb, prominent English socialists, visited in 1898. Beatrice was appalled. She inspected the capitol, "a pretentious half finished building," where she talked with Governor Alva Adams about state government. She found "the little man . . . too uncultivated and muddle-headed to be able to answer our questions." She went to the "unkempt and dirty" City Hall to observe a meeting of the city council, which presented "a general appearance of inefficiency." She judged local women to be "utterly empty-headed."[25] Webb was too harsh. Whatever its shortcomings, Denver had improved since the Grand Duke Alexis had visited. Perhaps Webb was jealous. She considered herself "the cleverest member of one of the cleverest families in the cleverest class of the cleverest nation of the world."[26] Yet she had to admit that Colorado's women enjoyed a right she was denied: They could vote. Cow-town Denver lacked sophistication, but when it came to women's rights it was progressive — in 1893 male Coloradans had approved women's suffrage. That triumph, however, was not secured without struggle, nor did it mask the fact that in Denver, as in the rest of the nation, women's roles and rights were narrowly defined.

CHAPTER 9

Women's Roles and Rights

Really the women did more in the early days than the men. There was so much for them to do, the sick to take care of. . . . There were so many men who could not cook and did not like other men's cooking and would insist on boarding where there was a woman.

Augusta Tabor
Interview, 1884[1]

"I know it is a great deal to ask of a woman to leave parents, home, friends, and the luxuries of life for the far west, but no one lives without hope," George Kassler wrote to his sweetheart, Maria Stebbins of Clinton, New York.[2] He wanted her to join him in Denver but he knew his chances were slim since few women were drawn to Colorado's harsh frontier. Lawrence Greenleaf versified about the scarcity of women at gold rush–era dances:

Mankind at dances 'reft of woman's charms,
Tied handkerchiefs about each other's arms.
The "knot was tied" which changed some men to
        women!
They blushed and gushed — the dances went on
        swimmin'![3]

Clara Witter, Augusta Tabor, and Mollie Sanford came west with their husbands. Most women were more prudent. Maria took a couple of

Women refined the frontier town, providing civil domestic life as suggested by this view of Margaret Gray Evans, under a portrait of her husband, with an eye on her son Evan in the Evans home at Thirteenth and Bannock. (Denver Public Library, Western History Department.)

years before saying yes to George. John Evans arrived in May 1862; his wife Margaret waited until November. Elizabeth Byers tarried for five months before joining her husband. In part, they delayed because of the difficulty of the trip. Margaret Evans spent five days and nights in the stagecoach because John decreed that they should drive straight through from Atchison, Kansas. That journey, however, was easy and fast compared to that of less-affluent women. Lydia Maria Ring, one of Denver's first schoolteachers, spent six weeks traveling from Leavenworth to Denver in 1860. When she arrived she could find no place to stay so she lived in a tent for several weeks. Emily M. Raymond's wagon train took over nine weeks to reach the Pikes Peak country from Omaha. Shortly before she entered Denver she stopped at an outlying mail station where she saw herself "in a looking glass for the first time since leaving Omaha — not that I lost much or missed it much after the first day or two."[4]

Maria Kassler's coach tipped over and, as the men worked to right it, she anxiously watched Indian camp fires in the distance. As Elizabeth Byers's coach rolled into Denver at sunrise, she felt "like the advance guard of civilization." Elizabeth, who once witnessed a murder and subsequent lynching, later wondered if she would have had the courage to stay if she had known what faced her. "Being a pioneer woman," she reminisced, "wasn't easy, but it never lacked interest."[5]

Bicycling brought liberation to many energetic women, who made it a sport and recreation for both sexes. (Photo by Charles S. Lillybridge, Colorado Historical Society.)

Maria Kassler was struck by Denver's rawness, particularly the large frog pond between Fifteenth and Sixteenth, Arapahoe and Lawrence. Clara Witter had to adjust her cooking to cope with the high altitude. Elizabeth Byers's home had a dirt floor covered with a rug that her son Frank enjoyed pulling up so he could squirm his toes in the soil underneath. Soon, however, wives of the emerging elite enjoyed pleasant homes and some leisure. Clara Witter recalled that in the 1860s ladies "would meet around from house to house and play cards" and sometimes go to the theater.[6] By the early 1870s, Margaret Evans was touring England, Elizabeth Byers was busy organizing charities, and Clara Witter was living in a "beautiful home" with "hard wood, plate glass, door knobs . . . all brought by mule from Julesburg."[7] Polishing doorknobs and washing windows was left to other women. In 1870, Margaret Evans, with two children — William Gray, age 13, and Evan, age 7 — employed a live-in

In search of sociability, women formed innumerable clubs. In 1884, Denver Cooking Club members posed with one of their concoctions. (Denver Public Library, Western History Department.)

Irish servant. The Byerses, the Witters, and the Cheesmans also hired Irish domestics. Mary Boronska, a Pole, worked for the Kasslers. A few of the wealthy, including the railroad builder William Jackson Palmer, hired African-Americans.[8]

More typical of pioneer hardships were those endured by Augusta Tabor and Mollie Sanford. By the late 1860s the Tabors were living in the back of their small store in Oro City, a mining camp near the future site of Leadville. Horace wanted their son Maxey to work; Augusta wanted the boy to go to school, so she bargained with her husband. "I told him I would go into the store and do all the boy could do."[9]

Mollie and Byron Sanford arrived in June 1860, joining "hundreds of families . . . living in wagons, tents, and shelters made of carpets and bedding." Soon they moved from the outdoor camp into a 10-by-20–foot shack that Mollie described as a mansion compared to their previous quarters. Byron went to Central City to seek work. A week after he left, Mollie confided to her diary: "I have no money. I almost feel like a lone widow — God Knows! I may be one now. Some terrible thing may have happened."[10] The Sanfords moved frequently — to Gold Hill, a booming mining camp west of Boulder, then to nearby Left Hand Gulch where they lived in a cabin "with a doorway, but no door, not even a hole for a window." Back in Denver in the late summer of 1861, Mollie gave birth to a boy while Byron was gone. The baby died: "God took him to his fold, this one pet lamb. When I first looked on his little face, he was in his coffin." Mollie soon followed her husband to Fort Lyon, where he was a lieutenant in the First Colorado Volunteers. Later, they returned to Denver and bought a ranch 10 miles south of town in present-day Little-ton. The 1864 flood washed them out, forcing them to spend the summer with other homeless families at Camp Weld. They returned to their farm in 1865 to face hordes of grasshoppers that "in a few short hours destroyed the work of weeks, and about all the hopes we had."[11]

As Denver became stable and accessible, the male-to-female imbalance declined. In 1860 there were six men to each woman, by 1890 four men to three women. In 1890, Colorado's married women outnumbered unwed females by more than 10 to 1. Only 170 women were listed as divorced that year, nearly 3,500 were widows.[12]

Even after the pioneer era, women faced many hardships. In *Solo in Tom Toms*, writer Gene Fowler recounted the life of his mother, Dora. Reared in a strict, Methodist, west Denver household, she rarely received permission to "step out." Charles Devlan, a lathe operator, recognized that the way to her heart was through her church, so he became religious.

He courted her in the parlor of her parents' home, while her mother hovered nearby. Charles and Dora were married in 1889. She was 17, he was 21. For their honeymoon they took an excursion, four hours with their friends on a chartered streetcar at a special fare of 75¢ per couple. They could afford no more. Charles made $1.25 for the 10-hour day he spent at his lathe. Unable to set up their own household, the Devlans lived with Dora's parents. By November 1889, Dora was visibly pregnant. In January, Charles, after a tiff with his mother-in-law, walked out, three months before their son Eugene was born. For four years Dora stayed with her parents; then, in 1894, she remarried. Her new husband, Frank Fowler, and her young child did not get along, so Gene Fowler, who was given his stepfather's surname, stayed with his grandparents, the Wheelers. In the first grade Gene fell in love with Helga, "a pigtailed charmer," but she spurned him. "Your parents," she told him, "are divorced."[13]

Frank Fowler had dreams. Once he envisioned making a fortune by perfecting a process to make popcorn crisper. Sometimes he sold Egg Wonder Powder, a concoction to improve bread dough. Dora helped out by taking in washing and ironing until in early 1903 she was taken suddenly ill. Her mother did not want her to have an operation; the doctor left the decision to her husband. He approved. She died at age 34 in St. Joseph's Hospital. Dora Fowler's sad story was not unusual; nor was hers one of the worst cases. She sometimes had a dollar to pay for singing lessons, and by collecting 600 soap wrappers she became the proud owner of a china soup tureen, until Gene dropped it.

Many women made ends meet by keeping chickens, doing laundry, sewing, taking in boarders. Some worked outside their homes, usually in menial jobs. The year 1880 saw 1,681 women in Denver's labor force — only 10.7 percent of all workers; by 1900 there were 12,244 — 22.4 percent of the work force. In 1900, census takers counted more than 3,000 female servants and waitresses, more than 600 nurses and midwives, and nearly the same number of laundresses. Denver also employed nearly 600 stenographers, nearly 800 sales ladies, and more than 1,200 dressmakers.

Unlike Mollie Sanford, whose husband lived long and prospered moderately, many women, particularly the widowed and the divorced, sank into poverty and oblivion. One of them, Emily French, could not escape poverty but saved herself from being forgotten by keeping a diary, a dreary tale of a woman whose husband divorced her after 31 years of marriage. Without many skills or a good education, without savings or support from her husband, she was forced to seek work, as a servant:

Women ventured into many traditionally male occupations in flexible western society. The Lady Barbers opened this shop on Fourth Avenue near Galapago Street during the 1890s. (Denver Public Library, Western History Department.)

September, Monday 29, 1890 Went at 7. I must go to some place to work, we will starve sure.

September, Tuesday 30, 1890 Oh Dear, so hard, washed all day.

October, Friday 17, 1890 [Began work for Sam and Bertha Mauck] They are nice I have $20.00 per month.

October, Saturday 18, 1890 Up at 5, built the fire, got the breakfast.

November, Saturday 1, 1890 Such a week, oh Lord, the children to take care of, she [Bertha Mauck] downtown with her husband house-hunt, he don't know what to do. I am so tired out . . . she let me sleep down stairs last night, I must rest, she sees that.

November, Sunday 9, 1890 I never combed my hair or sat down all day. I lay, for I am not feeling well enough to get up, yet I must. I come unwell last night. I am very bad of late, my age, must be. I am so glad no more babies for me. [14]

Emily French's low wages and long hours were typical. In 1888, women made an average of $6 a week and servants commonly worked 10 to 15 hours a day. To add insult, businessmen usually paid women less than they did men in comparable jobs. A woman clerk complained to the

Colorado Bureau of Labor Statistics: "A man in my place would get double the wages I do."[15] From time to time, the bureau investigated women's salaries and working conditions. A servant, who worked from 5:00 A.M. to 9:00 P.M., described her day: "I cook, wash, iron, bake, dust and sweep in a ten room house. I attend to the furnace, and carry in coal for five stoves and keep up the fires. The mistress got angry at me because I ate before I fed the dog." The Bureau found many women sewing at home: "The hum of many sewing machines can be heard in the dead hours of the night, in more than one household where some prisoner of poverty is engaged, with

Economic desperation drove some women to join the "frail sisters," "fallen angels," and "brides of the multitude" on Market Street. Belle's well-kept parlor house, spruced up for this 1885 photo, was one of two dozen whorehouses in Colorado's sin city. (Denver Public Library, Western History Department.)

drooping eyelids in her daily battle for subsistence." A stenographer earning $753.25 a year estimated that her salary let her save a little money: "about the cost of a funeral or a short spell of sickness."[16] Conditions and pay did not improve over the years. In 1914 the bureau found chambermaids working for $4 and $5 a week, head waitresses getting $10 weekly, and well-paid stenographers receiving $11 a week.

Low wages made the profits of prostitution attractive to some women and girls. The mother superior at the Roman Catholic Home of the Good Shepherd, founded in 1883 to shelter "wayward girls," reported that children as young as 10 were exploited by pimps, known as "solid men."[17] Some girls found a haven at Good Shepherd, which housed 200 in 1886. Many others eked out an existence in the tenderloin district where flashy madams such as Mattie Silks ran ritzy parlor houses, where men were "taken in and done for."[18] Cheaper sex was sold in Market Street's crude cribs where "brides of the multitude" charged only a quarter. Competition was intense. Gentlemen alleged that their hats were snatched by wanton women who would disappear inside houses of ill repute. Oscar Wilde's visit in 1882 gave the ladies a rare advertising opportunity. The playwright, they learned, loved lilies and sunflowers, so they sported the blooms. The police arrested two of them for solicitation, but a magistrate ruled that lily-liveried ladies were legal.

When a 16-year-old prostitute, Fannie Pierson, committed suicide by taking poison the newspapers wept for her, but normally the "soiled doves" were sneered at or ignored. Citizens comforted themselves with the thought that the red light district was largely confined to a well-defined section centered near Nineteenth and Market. City fathers, some of them in league with the underworld, refused to close the quarter down. Sin, they said, had been around a long time.

Many people tolerated open prostitution. They were even willing to wink at extramarital escapades, as William Byers discovered when his dalliance with Hattie Sancomb, a milliner, unraveled. Byers refused to leave his wife, Elizabeth, so Hattie tried to shoot him. She missed. To clear the air and to avoid blackmail, Byers published the melodramatic Sancomb letters in the *Rocky Mountain News*: "Oh infernal villain, if I had you here I'd plant my fingers in your eyes and tear them from their sockets," she wrote him. The ex-schoolmaster Owen Goldrick defended Byers by arguing that, while he was a "big fool," Sancomb was a "damaged article" bent on destroying a worthy pioneer. Denver eventually forgave Byers, and Elizabeth took him back.[19]

Affairs could be hidden or forgiven, but when Horace Tabor divorced his first wife, Augusta, and married Baby Doe (née Elizabeth McCourt), a beautiful, baby-faced divorcée, social leaders snubbed the new bride. Perhaps they could have forgiven her for leaving Harvey Doe after she caught him in Lizze Preston's brothel; Harvey had tried to explain that he was there looking for a business associate: "Babe came there and caught me and she did act the perfect lady and conducted herself so nicely in such a place as that. . . . Do not blame me I went in there on business of great importance to me I can assure you."[20] What many Denverites could not stomach was Tabor's abandoning Augusta, a woman who had toiled with him and for him for over 20 years. Tabor, who briefly served as a U.S. senator, wisely staged the Tabor-Doe nuptials in Washington, D.C., far from the gossips of the Rockies. Colorado's former senator, Henry Teller, attended the wedding, but Mrs. Harriet Teller refused. "I thank God," Henry Teller wrote, "he was not elected for six years; thirty days nearly killed us."[21] On returning home, the Tabors further offended their neighbors by planting their Capitol Hill mansion grounds with nude statues.

People were kinder to the doddering pioneer Henry Brown, but the cases were different. Brown, a 74-year-old widower, married Mary Mathews, a 19-year-old store clerk. "Owing to the great difference in their ages," the *Denver Times* explained, "their lives were not as pleasant as they should have been."[22] After two years they divorced. A few years later busybodies were less indulgent toward Brown's son James, who left his wife, Mary, to marry Grace Drew, an actress.

Single women faced many obstacles. Traditional attitudes about feminine roles made it difficult, if not impossible, for women to enter male-dominated professions. Edward Keating, a reporter for Nathaniel Hill's *Denver Republican*, recalled that in 1889 the paper occupied a four-story building: "There wasn't a woman from the cellar to the garret. The same pattern prevailed throughout the business world."[23] A few women breached the bastions of "the man's world." Pennsylvania-born Mary Lathrop, who came to Denver to recover from tuberculosis in 1887, left journalism to become the city's first woman attorney in 1896. In 1918 she was asked to join the American Bar Association, one of the first women to be included. She objected to being called a lady lawyer: "I'm either a lawyer or I'm not. Don't drag my being a woman into it."[24]

Doctor Justina Ford delivered an estimated 7,000 babies. She is memorialized at the Black American West Museum, which in 1989 moved into her former home at 3091 California Street. (Black American West Museum, Paul W. Stewart Collection.)

Women physicians and teachers met less resistance. Although the Colorado Medical Society refused to admit women in the 1870s, the Denver Medical Association did so in the 1880s. The 1900 census tallied more than 100 women physicians — 17 percent of all the doctors in the city. In 1902, Justina Ford jumped two hurdles when she became Denver's first black woman doctor. Teaching employed 1,027 Denver women in 1900, when they constituted nearly 80 percent of the city's educators.

Writing gave other women career options. Patience Stapleton, one of the few local authors to receive national attention in the nineteenth century, wrote short stories and novels. Gray-haired Minnie Reynolds became a familiar figure as she bicycled about Capitol Hill gathering tidbits for her society column; Ellis Meredith worked for the *News*. Polly Pry (Mrs. Leonel R. O'Bryan) enlivened the *Denver Post* before establishing her own paper, which she called *Polly Pry*. Pry stuck to gossip and avoided women's crusades. Caroline Churchill, conversely, fought for women's rights in her paper, the *Queen Bee,* "issued at anytime the editor thinks the people need it." On learning that a woman prizefighter had beaten a man, Churchill commented: "Some of these men need to have the conceit taken out of them even if it is done on a physical plane."[25]

The male conceit that barred women from many occupations also kept them from voting. George Kassler listened to the suffragette Susan B. Anthony in 1871; he admitted that she was "smart" and "gets off many good hits and truths that no one can deny," but, Kassler told his wife, "She don't know all about politics." He liked Elizabeth Cady Stanton, "a splendid looking old lady, fat as butter." Still, he wrote to Maria, "she did not convince me that I would like to see my Mae enter the political arena."[26] Most men agreed. Colorado's Constitution allowed women to vote only in school board elections, and in 1877 men rejected equal suffrage. Elizabeth and William Byers championed women's rights, but they were in the minority. Denver's Roman Catholic bishop, Joseph P. Machebeuf, blamed the agitation "on battalions of old maids disappointed in love" and on "women, who though married, wish to hold the reigns of family government."[27]

Barred from politics, some women turned to club and charity work. The Woman's Christian Temperance Union (WCTU), locally established in 1880, warred against liquor, demanded laws protecting women and children, and campaigned against vices ranging from prostitution to promiscuous expectoration. Sometimes the WCTU seemed doomed to fail, as when members tried to reform jail inmates by giving them flowers. Other programs, as historian Carolyn Stefanco has shown, made more sense. A lunch and reading room on Blake Street dished out meals for 25¢. The Women's Exchange gave women a place where they could sell cakes, aprons, and wax flowers. A day nursery, established in 1888, helped working mothers. One of the WCTU's most successful ventures, the Colorado Cottage Home, allowed unwed mothers to complete their pregnancies in peace — as free as possible from the double-standard social stigma that branded pregnant girls as loose women.[28]

Other groups similarly focused women's power and gave them an opportunity to sharpen their leadership and organizational skills. The Young Women's Christian Association opened a Denver clubhouse in 1887 and began offering recreational and social activities. It also crusaded against child labor and provided food and shelter for homeless visitors. Parson Thomas Uzzell's People's Tabernacle at Nineteenth and Blake gave leadership and preaching opportunities to such women as the

parson's mother, simply known as Mother Uzzell, to Mary Lathrop, and to Rachel Wild Peterson, whose book, *The Long Lost Rachel Wild or Seeking Diamonds in the Rough,* described her work among the poor. Other women joined literary and musical societies such as the Denver Fortnightly Club (1881), the Tuesday Musical Club (1891), the Clio (1892) and the Sphinx (1892) Clubs. There were neighborhood organizations such as the North Side Woman's Club; philanthrophic societies; political and reform associations; task-oriented groups such as the Denver Free Kindergarten Association (1890); and professional organizations including the Denver Clinical Society (1896), the Denver Council of the National Association of Women Stenographers (1898), and the Denver Women's Press Club (1898).[29]

"Denver is a city of women's clubs," the *Rocky Mountain News* observed in 1894. With condescending sexism the paper continued: "There

Carrie Nation (far right), one of many reformers to deplore the Mile High City's morals, visited the Women's Christian Temperance Union Mission to teach Denver youngsters to sing: "HO! HO! HO! Watch us Grow! When we vote saloons will go!" (Denver Public Library, Western History Department.)

THE ALBANY HOTEL ORCHESTRA
Under Direction Genevra Waters Baker
Special Program during
Mid-Day and Evening Dinner
and after Theatre

In unrefined western boomtowns, women tirelessly promoted the fine arts. This natty orchestra helped make the Albany Hotel at Seventeenth and Stout a favorite place for gentlemen. (Colorado Historical Society.)

are clubs for study of every subject with which the feminine mind has ever had to grapple." The *News* reported that since most of these groups were small, women were planning to establish the Denver Woman's Club (DWC), which would admit "all women who were able to pay the necessary fees and who possess a suitable personality for membership."[30] Among the 200 charter members were Elizabeth Byers, Margaret Evans, and the philanthropist Sarah Platt Decker, who, as the DWC's first president, pledged to make it "a power in the community."[31] With Decker's able leadership from 1894 to 1899 and a membership list that read like a "Who's Who of Denver Society," the club flourished. To feed the poor it sponsored community vegetable gardens; to educate children it organized a traveling art gallery for schools; to promote health it funded a summer baby hospital at City Park. The DWC also backed creation of a State Home for Dependent Children (1895) and enactment of a Civil Service Reform bill (1899).

By the mid-1890s the DWC knew that it would be heard at City Hall and in the state capitol because its members, unlike women in most of the rest of the United States, could vote. For that they had to thank one of the most effective women's organizations ever to operate in Colorado, the Colorado Equal Suffrage Association, founded in 1890 by six women. With headquarters in Denver, the association attracted many of the city's most able women: writers Meredith, Reynolds, and Stapleton; teacher Martha Pease; physician Mary B. Bates; and the African-American club leader, Elizabeth P. Ensley. Society ladies lent their names, and Baby Doe Tabor donated office space in the Opera House. Pressed by the women, legislators referred the suffrage question to voters in 1893. Meredith asked for outside help, but national leaders Susan B. Anthony and Lucy Stone were skeptical. "The whole case is at a disadvantage," Stone told Meredith, "for the fact there was no preparation time in advance."[32] With only $25 in their treasury, 28 local suffragettes ignored Anthony's and Stone's warnings. Ellis Meredith sought newspaper support; equal suffrage auxiliaries opened throughout the state. Labor leaders favored the proposal, as did many Republicans, including former governor John Routt, whose wife was among the suffragettes. Local Populists, members of a new national third party, also backed the women, who, like the Populists, demanded that the federal government renew purchases of silver. *Rocky Mountain News* publisher Thomas Patterson, a leading Democrat, did not like the idea of women voting, so Meredith, whose father Frederick was the paper's managing editor, used her influence to counter Patterson's opposition.

Organization, editorial support, political endorsements, and careful campaigning worked. By November 1893, 60 suffrage chapters and 10,000 Colorado women were working for "equal rights and justice for all."[33] That month Colorado's men approved women's suffrage by over 6,000 votes. In Arapahoe County, dominated by Denver and its suburbs, the vote was 8,816 for and 7,901 against. A few years earlier, Wyoming's constitution had given the ballot to women, but in Colorado, for the first time in the United States, men specifically voted for full women's suffrage. "Oh how glad I am," Anthony wrote to Meredith, "that at last we have knocked down our first state by the popular vote."[34] Until California sanctioned equal suffrage in 1911, thereby enfranchising women in San Francisco and Los Angeles, Denver was the largest city in the nation where women could vote. Anthony urged Martha Conine, one of Denver's first women legislators, to "write out every good happening and everything said by any distinguished person in favor of women suffrage and keep something of the sort floating around in the newspapers all of the time."[35] Supporters of the reform credited Colorado's women with numerous accomplishments, including ordinances restricting saloons, statutes establishing juvenile courts, and the bill that made the white and lavender-blue columbine the state flower. Enemies of women's suffrage dwelt on Denver's political corruption, charging that in 1902 women bosses had participated in election frauds that caused "Honest John" F. Shafroth to resign his congressional seat.[36] Governor Henry Buchtel once claimed that "only the dregs of womankind vote in Colorado."[37] Even Beatrice Webb faulted Denver's women for failing to attend to significant issues. Perhaps unaware of the reforms they had backed, she concluded that many club women were social climbers intent on chattering about "servants and clothes." The women's organizations, Webb judged, were primarily "mutual improvement societies; excuses for meeting at each others' houses."[38]

Naysayers aside, in gaining the ballot Denver's women had won a great victory and had accomplished what Anthony, Stone, and other national leaders had failed to do. But women had no time to relish their triumph, for they were immediately faced with problems greater than any Denver had seen since the 1860s. The optimism of the 1870s and 1880s evaporated as the price of silver plummeted. By 1893, Colorado and its Queen City were sinking into a great depression.

CHAPTER 10

The Depression of 1893

The panic hit Denver a tremendous blow, so staggering in fact, that many predicted that the city would never recover from its effects. Failures were daily in mercantile establishments, banks collapsed and industries tumbled. Bankers held nightly conferences in our effort to devise some means to avert disaster. Business was in chaos.

Dennis Sheedy
Autobiography, 1922[1]

Shortly after midnight on July 11, 1892, the People's Theater at Fifteenth and Cleveland caught fire and quickly burned. Horace Tabor, the building's owner, watched as flames leapt 50 feet into the air. Onlookers offered the silver king their condolences, which Tabor dismissed, explaining that his uninsured loss would amount to only $10,000. Observing that the building was a poor theater, he contemplated making the shell into a livery stable. Constructed hastily in the boom year of 1889, the theater had been declared unsafe three times. Inspectors condemned the roof, the walls, and the galleries. Slipshod builders failed to install a heating system; the audience kept from freezing by passing around kerosene lamps. Performers suffered. A *News* reporter recalled soprano Adelina Patti's teeth chattering "to the strains of 'Home Sweet Home'," providing an accompaniment "both novel and irritating."[2]

Like the People's Theater, Denver had been built quickly. When economic disaster struck, it hit the city almost as suddenly as the fire had consumed the theater. In both cases there had been warnings; in neither instance were they heeded. Colorado's economy was in jeopardy even before plunging silver prices precipitated collapse in mid-1893. Overbuilt and underfinanced railroads frequently steamed into bankruptcy. Ranching was declining by the 1890s because of overgrazing, hard winters, and stricter federal land laws. On the plains, sodbusters invaded the grassland, unaware that the ample rains that made their fields bountiful in the 1880s would not fall in the 1890s. Mine owners also recklessly expanded. By 1890, Colorado produced nearly 60 percent of the nation's silver. There seemed to be no end to the supply, but demand was limited. As production increased, prices first fell from $1.05 an ounce in 1890 to 83¢ in early June 1893, and then precipitously to 62¢ by late June. In the high country many silver mines shut down and laid off their workers.

The collapse stampeded many Denverites into withdrawing their savings from banks that, as a result, failed. Six shut their doors on July 18, 1893; the next day three more suspended payments, bringing mid-July closures to a dozen. Depositors who did not retrieve their money before the banks collapsed lost their savings; there was no federal insurance. David Moffat, president of the First National Bank, reputedly cashed in $2 million of his own securities and deposited the proceeds, ordering his tellers to display mountains of cash. Trusting the First National, people took their money from other banks and deposited it with Moffat.[3]

Many others, both rich and poor, did not fare as well. William Lang, the architect of many Denver mansions, turned to alcohol when his well of fees ran dry. He was killed by a train as he walked along the tracks in Illinois. His family in Denver was too poor to pay for or to attend his funeral. The once-prosperous real estate developer Henry Brown spent his declining years fighting off creditors trying to foreclose on his Brown Palace Hotel. Unable to pay his debts, John Evans lost title to the Railroad Building on Fifteenth and Larimer. Roger Woodbury sold some of his furniture to raise cash. Baron Walter von Richthofen dreamed of regaining his wealth by revamping his unsuccessful Montclair development as a health spa, a hope unrealized when appendicitis killed him in 1898.

Among the riches-to-rags crowd, Horace Tabor attracted the most attention, largely because he had such a great fall. By the early 1880s his fortune was estimated at $5 million, which he sank into mines and into Denver real estate. He spent with abandon: Baby Doe's wedding dress cost $7,000; her diamond necklace perhaps $75,000. A christening outfit for Lily, Baby Doe's first child, set Horace back $500. Their second girl, appropriately known as Silver Dollar, frolicked in the lavish Tabor mansion. That all ended when creditors turned off the lights and shut off the water. The hardware dealer George Tritch, who held the mortgage, forced the Tabors out of their home in late 1896. Samuel Johnson, a local lawyer, pitied the ex-millionaire: "His clothes became shabby and he drove about town with an old gray horse and a dilapidated buggy."[4] In desperation, Horace returned to the mountains, bought a "house" for $10, and started prospecting for a new bonanza. Augusta Tabor, who died in California in 1895, understandably left none of her half-million dollars to her unfaithful husband. Tabor's appointment in 1898 to the Denver postmastership saved him from destitution, but at $3,700 a year the job hardly restored his fortune.

Still, Tabor's salary was generous for the time. His troubles and those of much of the upper crust paled when compared with the tribulations of ordinary people who in good years made barely enough to cover their day-to-day needs. Since the unemployment spawned by mine and smelter closures created a large labor pool, employers could easily replace workers unwilling to accept pay cuts. When 200 cigar makers refused to take a 12.5 percent salary reduction in November 1893, they were locked out of their jobs. The same month Denver Consolidated Electric Company employees, facing a 10 percent cut, walked out. Throughout the summer of 1893 and into 1894, thousands of ex-miners drifted into Denver, swelling the ranks of jobless locals. Overburdened charities limited aid to those who had been in the city at least 60 days. On August 11, 1893, the People's Tabernacle announced that it could no longer feed single men, so pressing were the needs of women and children. At schools, hungry men begged for lunches meant for children.[5]

The unemployed sought work laying sewers at a dollar a day, but there were not enough public jobs to go around. A tent and shack city sprang up at Riverfront Park along the South Platte. Denver, using funds raised by the Chamber of Commerce, gave lumber and supplies to the homeless to build flatboats on which, it was hoped, they would drift away. At least two died in the attempt. Others survived and joined Jacob Coxey's army of the jobless, which marched on Washington, D.C., in a futile attempt to secure relief. By lowering the fare from Denver to the Missouri River to $6, railroads helped Denver get rid of the unemployed. Hungry men without ticket money grew so frantic that some of them forced their way on to a Union Pacific train and compelled the crew to transport them for free. Another angry mob of 450 Coxeyites abandoned their tacky boats at LaSalle, 40 miles north of Denver, and hijacked a train that they ran to Julesburg, where they were stopped by a posse.[6]

To rid itself of indigents during the 1893 depression, Denver had the homeless build boats and sail away down the South Platte to join Coxey's army in protest marches on Washington, D.C. The scheme foundered when the small craft ran aground. (Denver Public Library, Western History Department.)

In Denver the drifters sometimes turned ugly. When, in July 1893, Daniel Arata, an Italian bartender, was jailed for killing a customer who could not pay a nickel for his beer, a mob of several thousand ripped up streetcar rails, beat down the jail door and dragged Arata out, yelling "That's the dago, kill him!" Arata had one request: "Tell my mother not to cry." They hanged him and shot him, paraded his body through the streets, and hanged him again. Bloodstained souvenirs sold for 50¢; sections of the limb from which he had dangled brought a dime. Old John Chivington, then the city coroner, reported: "We find that said hanging was done by parties unknown."[7]

The only radical reformer ever to govern Colorado, Davis H. Waite attempted to purge the Queen City of its many sins. His efforts were not appreciated. Denver voters turned out in large numbers in 1894 to oust Waite after one chaotic term. (Tom Noel Collection.)

Authorities found it easier to remove unruly indigents than to solve basic economic problems. Nationally, both Republicans and Democrats agreed that it was folly for the Treasury to continue buying silver. Abandoned by the traditional political organizations, many Coloradans embraced the People's party, a short-lived third party commonly known as the Populists. In 1892, Davis Waite, a Populist newspaper editor from Aspen, was elected governor. If the federal government refused to coin silver, Waite proposed that

Denver teetered on the edge of riot and rebellion during the City Hall war in 1894, when Governor Waite's troops sought forcibly to clean out Denver's corrupt City Hall. (Denver Public Library, Western History Department.)

Colorado should mint its own money in Mexico. "Fandango Dollars" were never struck, but the governor's endorsement of the unconstitutional scheme hurt his credibility.

Although Waite favored peaceful reform, he threatened to meet violence with violence. "It is better, infinitely better," thundered the governor, "that blood should flow to the horses' bridles rather than our national liberties should be destroyed."[8] Such rhetoric frightened businessmen, among them John Evans, who were trying to get easterners to invest in Colorado. Soon Waite had another millstone to wear around his political neck — the nickname "Bloody Bridles."

Governor Waite matched his words with deeds. He hoped to clean up Denver, which he and many rural Coloradans considered a wicked place. In 1889 the State Legislature had made Denver's Fire, Police, and Public Works departments answerable to boards appointed by the governor. Early in 1894, Waite tried to remove police and fire commissioners who, he said, shielded gamblers and prostitutes. The officials, protected by policemen, firemen, and their underworld allies, barricaded themselves in the City Hall at Fourteenth and Larimer. On March 15, the impatient governor ordered state militiamen to march upon the entrenched commissioners. William Byers, president of the Chamber of Commerce, unsuccessfully tried to make peace. "Gentlemen," he said after meeting with Waite, "it is war to the knife."[9]

Waite, guarded by game wardens, stayed at his home at 1439 California. Meanwhile, inside City Hall a bomb brigade prepared to throw explosives at the militia. Outside, troopers took stock of their rifles and artillery. One officer concluded: "We can tumble that building on their heads with a dozen shots."[10] Federal intervention, late in the day, prevented the comedy from becoming tragedy. Ultimately, Colorado's Supreme Court ruled that the governor could remove the commissioners. To oust Waite, the Republicans allied with a growing national pressure group, the American Protective Association (APA), which aimed to find jobs for Protestants by firing Catholics from government positions. Some Protestants, most notably Congregational minister Myron Reed, condemned such tactics. And the Arapahoe County Republican chairman, Isaac Stevens, opposed to his party's flirtation with the APA, proposed that the bigots be "thrown into the caldron of hell."[11]

Hell had to wait. An estimated 10,000 Denverites belonged to the powerful association. Its candidate, Republican Marion Van Horn, was elected mayor in 1893. The next year it backed another winner, Albert McIntire, who defeated Waite for the governorship. Waite had hoped that his support of equal suffrage would bring him women's votes, but he was mistaken. Suffragette Ellis Meredith accused him of wrecking the Populists by trying "to build a machine for himself." She admitted that McIntire was a poor governor, but, she said, "he was a Yale man, he seemed a gentleman."[12]

Democrats, led by *Rocky Mountain News* publisher Thomas Patterson, fought the bigots. The Reverend Thomas Malone, editor of the *Colorado Catholic,* infiltrated the APA with spies. By publishing the organization's inner workings, Malone embarrassed some members and caused dissension among others. Mayor Van Horn broke from the association, explaining that he did not know its true character when he joined. In 1896, when Democrat Alva Adams was elected governor, the APA was too feeble to oppose him effectively.

APA bigotry reflected one response to the economic breakdown. Religion and charity represented another. Some turned to Parson Thomas Uzzell, whose People's Tabernacle offered immediate and practical help to the poor. Still others flocked to Francis Schlatter, a mysterious faith healer. And many listened to the Reverend Myron Reed, an able spokesman of a rising force in American Protestantism — the Social Gospel Movement, which stressed the duty of organized religion to combat economic injustice.

Denverites knew that Reed was a different kind of preacher even before the Depression of 1893. Born in Vermont in 1836, he had been a schoolteacher, a lawyer, and a soldier before becoming a minister in 1866. He came to Denver's First

Progressive social gospel cures were proposed for a depressed Denver by Myron W. Reed, the activist First Congregational church minister. (Photo by Rose T. Hopkins, Denver Public Library.)

Congregational church in 1884. After that, old-time religion was no longer the same. Reed stressed the duties of the rich and the needs of the poor: "The more helpless anything is, the more rights it has."[13] Acting on that principle, he championed many good causes. When Uzzell wanted to help the poor, Reed encouraged him; when women wanted to vote, he backed them; and when laborers called for an eight-hour working day, he supported them. In an era that had scant sympathy for Native Americans, Reed demanded justice: "Whatever the Indian of today is we made him, and he wears our shoddy blanket and eats our government steer. And we have raised Americans to kill him while he is loading his pony to go. It is a shameful, dastardly thing."[14]

Reed hoped for a bit of heaven on earth. "In the New Testament I find not only a new heaven for the dying, but a new earth for the living."[15] In defense of homeless wanderers, Reed explained: "The tramp is a product of our kind of civilization. He is a warning to us that our social system has failed." What should Denver do about the problem of overwhelming riches in the midst of overwhelming poverty? Reed had an answer: "Why not here in Denver try socialism?"[16]

Such radical ideas, coupled with Reed's support for the Populists, offended some members of his congregation, churchgoers like those described by the muckraker Upton Sinclair: the women "rustling with new silk petticoats and starched and perfumed linen" and the men "newly washed and shaved, newly groomed and gloved."[17] In support of miners

The "Fighting Parson," Thomas Uzzell, championed Denver's poor, founded the People's Tabernacle on skid row, and drove his "Gospel Wagon" around town to rescue lost souls. (Denver Public Library, Western History Department.)

striking at Cripple Creek, Reed told his flock in 1894: "Tonight my heart is with the miners at Bull Hill."[18] Since his heart was no longer with the golden-fleeced sheep on Capitol Hill, he left his church to preach at the Broadway Theater until sickness silenced him in late 1898. Ten thousand people tried to get into the theater to attend his funeral February 1, 1899. They loved him for his courage in fighting for them, for bravely arguing that "the society that permits such deadly parallels as the gorged few and the hungry many cannot last."[19]

Unlike Reed, the Reverend Thomas Uzzell was not known as a great orator. Lay-preacher Rachel Wild Peterson, who worked with him, said that "he is not much of a literati or theologian," and she admitted that "he is not apt in quotation," but she praised his ability to raise money: "He is the Prince of Solicitors and his sound has gone out from the plebian bottoms to the blue-bloods of Capitol Hill."[20] Among those he touched was Tabor, who in his affluent days agreed to buy chandeliers for Uzzell's church. "By the way, Tom," Tabor supposedly asked, "whose gonna play them chandeliers?"[21]

At the People's Tabernacle, which he took over from his brother in 1885, Uzzell needed more than melodious chandeliers. Although the 1880s were prosperous in Denver, the city still harbored many poorly paid workers who sometimes needed help. Hard times in the 1890s added to the Tabernacle's burdens. From its earliest years the organization provided services that in the twentieth century would be considered governmental responsibilities. To care for the sick, the Tabernacle organized a free dispensary; to warm the cold, it gave away clothing in winter; to cleanse the unwashed, it ran a free bathhouse. Women who wanted to learn to sew could take classes at the Tabernacle; men who were cheated of their wages could get help from Uzzell's "department of justice." Sick prostitutes received medical attention from the Tabernacle's missionaries, and homeless women were given shelter. Parson Uzzell aided thousands, but neither his work nor that of Reed substantially eased the depression. Uzzell realized his limitations. When he died in 1910 he asked that a simple inscription, "He did his level best," be chiseled on his tombstone.[22]

Uzzell and Reed died in Denver and both are buried in the city. When Francis Schlatter died and where he is buried remains as much a mystery as when and where he was born. A bearded, Christ-like figure, he came to Denver from New Mexico in the summer of 1895 as the guest of Edward Fox, a North Denver politician. Schlatter's reputation quickly grew — soon thousands of people each day were lining the 3200 block of Quivas Street to be touched by the miracle worker who stood on a wooden platform in Fox's yard. With typical Denver commercialism, vendors hawked lemonade and sold handkerchiefs with Schlatter's picture on them, but Schlatter himself refused payment. A quiet, mystical, prayerful man, he reportedly cured the blind, the disfigured, the crippled. Reed was impressed: "I seem to see a vision of the actual Christ, receiving the multitude by the sea of Galilee." In mid-November 1895 the mystic disappeared, leaving behind a note: "My mission is finished. Father takes me away. Goodbye. Francis Schlatter."[23]

Whatever good the depression may have done by causing people to attend to their souls and to the needs of others, it clearly distressed those who worshipped the almighty dollar, for it ended Denver's boom and severely retarded its growth. Historian Jerome Smiley estimated that the city's population dipped from 106,713 in 1890 to 90,000 in 1895. Although the 1900 census tallied 133,859 residents, the number showed a real growth of only around 25,000 since it reflected the city's annexation of several large suburbs including South Denver and Highlands (north Denver).

Business leaders hoped to revive the economy by boosting the city. In 1896, subscribers spent $1,700 to produce a Chamber of Commerce–sponsored booklet, "Denver Through A Camera." To their chagrin, the publisher absconded with the money they had advanced him. The Festival of Mountain and Plain, a carnival similar to New Orleans's Mardi Gras, proved to be better advertising. Established in 1895 at the urging of the Chamber of Commerce, the annual event continued until 1912. Civic leaders and their wives and daughters masqueraded as kings, queens, and princesses. Hundreds of people marched inside the block-long silver serpent, a dragonlike monster made of silver cloth. Slithering through the streets, they sang the serpent's song:

To cure depression blues, the Mile High City in 1895 launched its annual Festival of Mountain and Plain. (Denver Public Library, Western History Department.)

We spring, we sprawl,
We caper, we crawl,
With vesture of changeable hue.
We slidingly slink, as we near the brink
Of our subterranean abyss.[24]

In 1899, Wolfe Londoner, the jolly ex-mayor, led the parade of maskers, their faces blackened with burnt cork. "Every old skate for miles around," the *Denver Times* reported, "was . . . hitched to some of the worst looking rigs that could possibly be put together."[25] Everyone hoped to make money. Tourists wishing to photograph Utes had to pay for the privilege. Department stores ran specials: iron beds at Joslins for $7, jeweled matchboxes at Daniels and Fisher's for $12.50. Eddie Foy was at the Broadway Theater in *Topsy Turvy*, while at the Tabor Grand 25¢ would by a ticket to *A Milk White Flag*. Yet for all its ballyhoo, the Festival did not end the depression. The revelry merely masked Denver's doldrums. "Public spirit," Chamber of Commerce President John Campion complained in 1898, "is as dead as Lot's wife after she was turned to a pillar of salt."[26]

When Horace Tabor died on April 10, 1899, Denverites mourned the man and the passing of a flamboyant era. They wept for themselves as they filed by his casket at the capitol. Their hopes and fortunes, like his,

(Colorado Historical Society.)

had risen and fallen. Thousands stood silent as his funeral cortege passed along Seventeenth Street and down Larimer to Sacred Heart church on Twenty-eighth Street. After the services, the hearse and military escort clattered out to Mount Calvary, the Roman Catholic cemetery at Tenth Avenue and York Street, where Tabor was buried. With common sense born of the depression, onlookers talked not of raising a monument to the silver king, but of buying Baby Doe and her daughters a house.

Part II:
Riches of Diversity, 1900–1950

Economic and ethnic diversity characterized the Mile High City's middle years. After the painful lesson of the 1893 bust, the city shifted from mining and railroads to agriculture, manufacturing, and tourism. Denver achieved economic diversity but remained a financial colony, often dependent on eastern capital.

Slower growth between the 1890s and 1930s depressions enabled public officials to catch up with the chaotic, unplanned expansion of the bonanza years. Mayor Robert Speer, at once a pragmatic political boss and an idealistic progressive, transformed a drab town into a City Beautiful. He gave the city a verdant heart, a network of parkways, and neighborhood and mountain parks. Denver erected stately public buildings and expanded city services. These tremendous public improvements belatedly brought to the raw, young city a sense of community.

Denver's power elite supported municipal improvements but opposed improved working conditions. In bloody industrial warfare, they crushed unions, which never fully recovered. The New Deal, World War II, and the postwar boom made Denver a huge government-office center. Manufacturing, tourism, and recreation further boosted the Mile High City, making it a Sunbelt magnet.

CHAPTER 11

Economic Diversity

In the relentless war for commercial supremacy fought by cities, states, and nations only that community can be victorious which brings to bear upon its rivals, a well equipped and persistent army of citizens.
Meyer Friedman
President, Denver Chamber of Commerce, 1903[1]

The riches of the earth created Denver in 1858 and they helped pull it out of the Depression of 1893. Between 1900 and 1920, nearly half a billion dollars worth of gold, mostly from Cripple Creek, poured from Colorado's mines. Silver, although never regaining its nineteenth-century luster, continued to bolster the state's and Denver's economy. Coal production soared to an average of more than 13 million tons a year between 1914 and 1923. When coal declined, oil output spurted from 86,000 barrels in 1923 to 2.75 million in 1927. Bonanza oil discoveries in Wyoming, Oklahoma, and Texas also benefited Denver, which welcomed petroleum princes in the 1920s as it had silver kings in the 1880s.

Mining gave jobs to Denverites at Hendrie and Bolthoff, Stearns-Roger, and Gardner-Denver, all makers of mining machinery. Smelter men depended on mines, as did many service people: bankers and prostitutes, lawyers and saloon keepers. Civic leaders, however, had learned during the 1893 depression not to rely on mining alone. By the turn of the century they were promoting agriculture, manufacturing, and tourism to broaden the city's economy. Their drive for diversity was farsighted.

The Denver Union Stockyards promoted the livestock industry with a 10-day January stock show, the town's largest festival and an ongoing reminder that Denver is a cow town. (Denver Public Library, Western History Department.)

After 1920 mining gradually declined as Cripple Creek proved to be Colorado's largest and last El Dorado. In 1910 there were over 10,000 hard-rock miners in the state; in 1930 fewer than 3,000. In 1899, Denver's smelters, with 1,800 workers, comprised the city's largest industrial employers. Twenty years later most smelter furnaces were cold, their slag mountains spread thin as foundations for city streets.

Mining's downturn hurt individual businesses, but Denver survived. Agriculture took up part of the slack. Twenty thousand people started farming in Colorado between 1910 and 1920. Packinghouses opened; cattle sales doubled, and sheep sales increased by 600 percent between 1900 and 1920. The city's role as a processing, transportation, trade, and service center remained constant. As Colorado grew so did its capital. In 1900 there were 539,700 Coloradans, 25 percent of them Denverites. In 1940 the state counted 1,123,296 residents, 29 percent in Denver.

Manufacturing also helped balance the economy. Businesses that served local needs flourished: Millers, meat packers, brewers, bakers, and brick makers did well; but in most other areas Denver suffered from competition. The city puffed its cigar industry, which produced 8 million stogies a year in 1899, but another 52 million were imported. By 1940, when U.S. cities on the average employed 22 percent of their population in manufacturing, the Denver rate was 15 percent, making the Queen City of the Plains industrially second-rate compared to eastern and midwestern production centers.

George Kindel blamed Denver's industrial backwardness on unfair railroad freight rates. Kindel produced quality mattresses, stuffing them with clean cotton rather than with rags, carpet remnants, and old blankets as did many other manufacturers. But his eastern competitors had an

A dozen small breweries flourished in Denver until Prohibition shut their doors in 1916. The Union Brewery, whose Sixteenth Street operation embraced this outlet, merged with the Tivoli Brewery in 1901. (Denver Public Library, Western History Department.)

edge: Railroads charged them only $1 per hundred pounds to ship their mattresses to the West Coast while Kindel paid $3. John Mullen, whose Colorado Milling and Elevator Company was one of Denver's largest businesses, discovered that it cost him more to ship flour 60 miles within Colorado than from Denver to San Diego. Mullen adapted by sending flour to Japan through San Diego. Kindel, nicknamed "Freight Rates," sued the railroads, publicized their unfair charges, and as Denver's congressman from 1913 to 1915 advocated stiffer rate control laws.[2] His crusade fizzled, but even if transport charges had been lower and fairer, Denver would have suffered from its isolation and distance from large markets.

Kindel's failure confirmed what Denverites knew — that theirs was a colonial economy. Just as Boston, New York, and Philadelphia had paid tribute to London before the American Revolution, Denver found that it often danced on strings pulled in New York boardrooms. Sometimes the natives outwitted the absentee moguls — in the 1890s local owners of the Denver Tramway and the Citizens Water companies beat out rivals financed by easterners. Often, however, control slipped back to out-of-state investors. For instance, the Denver Gas and Electric Company, which became the Public Service Company of Colorado in 1923, was absorbed into the national Cities Service Company empire of energy czar Henry L. Doherty. Small businessmen begged Denver's bankers for venture capital, but normally entrepreneurs went away empty-handed since local financiers loathed risking money. And when such outsiders as the steel maker Henry J. Kaiser suggested industrial development, the bankers of Seventeenth Street allegedly responded: "Hell no, we don't want that so-and-so here."[3]

Sometimes a courageous and lucky visionary overcame the obstacles. In the 1890s, Henry Perky, using a machine he invented, began cranking out the United States's first shredded wheat at his factory at Seventeenth and Tremont. In 1910, Jesse Shwayder and his brothers opened a trunk-manufacturing company that, under the trade name Samsonite, grew into a major luggage and card table maker. Andrew McGill parlayed his design for a better fishing fly into Wright and McGill, one of the world's major fishhook manufacturers. Brothers Charles and John Gates transformed a small company making steel-studded leather tire covers — they were supposed to extend tire wear — into an important producer of rubber tires, hose, and fan belts. For decades, when Denverites wanted to show

The sugary smell of success surrounded Russell and Clara Stover, who launched their confectionery in Denver in 1923. Stover's became one of the stars of the crusade for economic diversity, attracting sweet-toothed fans across the country. (Denver Public Library, Western History Department.)

visitors a large factory, they drove them by the Gates plant, established in 1914 at 999 South Broadway.

Gates, Shwayder, and McGill were exceptional in capturing national markets; most local manufacturers achieved more modest success. Thanks to their aggressive marketing and Denver's railroad network, the Mile High City became the economic capital of the vast, ill-defined, and sparsely populated Rocky Mountain Empire. Kindel's campaign was forgotten as businessmen stopped dreaming of competing with Chicago and Pittsburgh and worked instead to outdo Pueblo and Cheyenne. Roscoe Fleming, a journalist, noted in 1946 that the power elite wanted, "perhaps unconsciously, to see the city remain small, tidy, low cost, low wage, open shop and under their control." Fleming said that they rationalized their position by arguing that Denver should be "a shrine of beauty and culture, rather than a smoky commercial town."[4]

Their vision, although self-serving, was more than an excuse for their tightfistedness. They recognized that the quality of life affected the economy. Despite smoggy winter days when coal smoke darkened the sky, Denver's usual sunshine and dryness, its cool, crisp air, and its nearby mountain playgrounds attracted tourists and their dollars. Tuberculosis sufferers also liked the rarefied atmosphere, flocking in to fill hospitals

One of Denver's most viable industries during the depressed 1890s was tending tuberculosis patients. The Reverend Frederick W. Oakes, who established an Episcopal sanatorium at West Thirty-second and Federal Boulevard, graced it with this exquisite chapel. (Tom Noel Collection.)

and boarding houses, create jobs and pump up the economy. Calculating that consumption brought more people to Denver than did gold, Fleming suggested the TB bacillus "might justly be commemorated in stone."[5] Owners of convalescent homes knew that there was money in disease. Denver Tuberculosis Society investigators in 1923 found more than 5,000 sick people living in squalor: beds only inches apart; toilets one to a floor; inadequate nursing, ventilation, and light. Proprietors of the Sunlight Home in North Denver were accused of taking kickbacks from undertakers to whom they sent corpses. Thomas Galbreath, a consumptive who wrote *Chasing the Cure in Colorado,* told of a dying man who asked his doctor and the manager of the sanatorium to stand on opposite sides of his bed. " 'Now,' he whispered, 'I can die happy — like Christ, between two thieves.' " Locals described these health seekers as "the one-lunged army" and tended to ignore their suffering. Those who could not pay for a bed sometimes died hemorrhaging in the gutters. "Because of the prevalence of consumption," Galbreath reported, "the heart of the average Denverite has become hardened toward the tubercular patient . . . human sympathy is conspicuously lacking."[6]

Many employers liked consumptives because they were willing to work for a pittance. Real estate developers cashed in on the desperate and gullible sick by selling them homes in "healthy" suburbs such as Highlands, Berkeley, or Barnum. In Montclair, Baron von Richthofen, believing that the smell of cows would restore diseased lungs, planned to house the sick above a dairy. Homes in that suburb featured open sleeping porches so the ill could breathe fresh air day and night. Other people, fearful of catching TB themselves, tried to stop the invasion of lungers, while boosters worried that Denver might become known as a city of invalids hobbling about with canes and sputum cups. In 1908, Colorado prohibited the entry of indigent, sick persons into the state. Lawmakers even considered requiring consumptives to wear a warning bell. Galbreath suggested that had the proposal been enacted, "the clatter would have been so great, the street car gongs and automobile horns could not be heard above the din."[7]

Sometimes a more caring spirit surfaced. Local Jews, nearly overwhelmed by respiratory wrecks from the ghettos of Europe and the eastern United States, led the way. In the early 1890s, Frances Jacobs helped raise $42,000 to build the Frances Jacobs Hospital. Completed in 1892 on the eve of the 1893 depression, the institution could not raise operating funds, so the building was abandoned. It remained empty, except for the rats that roamed its halls, until 1899, when it reopened as the National Jewish Hospital for Consumptives to reflect the breadth of its support and service. Fearing that it would be swamped with patients suffering from the United States' deadliest disease, National Jewish admitted only people with a good chance of recovery. Moreover, since it was nonkosher, few orthodox Jews sought care there. Instead, they flocked to the city's eastern European Jewish neighborhood flanking West Colfax. There, Jews in 1903 organized the Denver Charity Society for Consumptives, which later became the Jewish Consumptive Relief Society (JCRS). Its first seven residents lived in six tents; within 10 years 2,000 patients had been cared for at the JCRS complex on West Colfax and Pierce.[8]

Other groups followed the Jews. Episcopalians supported North Denver's Oakes Home (1894); Swedes funded National Swedish Hospital

(1908) in Englewood; in 1904, Lawrence Phipps, Sr., endowed Agnes Memorial Sanatorium, named for his mother, at Sixth and Quebec. In south Denver, Bethesda Hospital (1914) served Dutch patients; in Wheat Ridge, a western suburb, Lutherans established the Evangelical Lutheran Sanitarium (1905). Edgewater, another small town west of Denver, became home to the Craig Hospital in 1909, and in Aurora, the army used 595 acres donated by the Denver Civic and Commercial Association to house Fitzsimons Hospital, named after William Thomas Fitzsimons, the first U.S. officer killed in World War I. With 1,500 beds, Fitzsimons was larger than all the private, state, and city TB institutions in Denver combined. It attracted thousands of veterans and their families to Colorado.

Hordes of healthier people came to vacation after railroads made mass travel possible. By the late 1880s, when 20,000 visited the state, tourism had become an important industry. The poet Walt Whitman detected a "climatic magnetism of this curiously attractive region."[9] Many visitors expected to see the Wild West. Alexander Graham Bell, inventor of the telephone, reported with amazement: "I have not, since I have been here, seen a single buffalo, a single cowboy, a single Indian, and I have been in Denver six hours and I have not been shot at."[10]

Journalist William Ferril stereotyped the sightseers: Spinsters "shrivelled and well dried up"; Boston schoolmarms with "a profusion of bundles and boxes"; mashers "anxious to break the heart of the rich miner's daughter"; eastern college men "dying to kill a bear." Ferril chuckled at the "tenderfoot dude"; "with a small armament of six shooters he struts about the streets." And Ferril worried about the flatlanders' rock collecting: "The tourist campaign might well be termed a 'war on rocks'."[11]

Denverites may have agreed, but they did not say so openly. They wanted tourists to come and to spend. As auto touring became popular, Denver set up camps in parks. At City Park, Overland, and Rocky Mountain, visitors camped, showered, and square danced. The camps were closed in 1930 at the start of the Great Depression since taxpayers did not want their parks filled with poor farm families in dented pickup trucks. Still, despite hard times, middle-class and wealthy Americans continued to come. In 1941 over 3 million visited Colorado, mostly in the summer and mostly by car or train — only 7,800 arrived by air.[12]

Despite the riches of diversity — tourists; tuberculars, packinghouses and food-processing plants — the city suffered from its lack of industry, distance from large markets, and the power exercised over its destiny by eastern financiers. The careers of four men — David Moffat, Gerald

Hughes, William Gray Evans, and
Charles Boettcher — illustrate the
strengths and weaknesses of Denver's economy during the first half of
the twentieth century.

After the deaths of John Evans
in 1897, William Byers in 1903,
Henry Brown in 1906, and Walter
Cheesman in 1907, Moffat remained one of the city's few important links with its pioneer past. His
reputation and ability had brought
the First National Bank through
the Depression of 1893. By 1900,
when he turned 61, he was a multi-

David H. Moffat made and lost
fortunes in banking, mining,
and railroads. (Tom Noel Collection.)

millionaire. After work he usually stopped for an hour at the Denver Club
before returning to his mansion at 1706 Lincoln, where he settled in for
the evening unless his wife Frances pressured him into going to the
theater. It appeared that another empire builder was about to retire.
Moffat thought otherwise. In his sunset years, between 1902 and 1911, he
undertook the riskiest venture of his career — the construction of the
Denver, Northwestern & Pacific Railroad, popularly known as the Moffat
Road, from Denver to Salt Lake City. He hoped to tap coal-rich northwestern Colorado and eventually to create a major rail line by connecting
with tracks being built by Montana copper king William Clark, from Salt
Lake City to the Pacific.

The Moffat Road, expensive to construct and costly to operate,
inched through difficult terrain northwest of Denver. Along South Boulder Creek alone it required 31 tunnels. Snow-choked, 11,660-foot Rol-
lins Pass, renamed Corona for the rail station there, created a winter
barrier that often delayed trains for days. Eastern financiers Edward H.
Harriman, who controlled the Union Pacific, and George J. Gould, who
dominated the Denver & Rio Grande, feared the linkup between Moffat
and Clark. To curb Moffat, they bought out Clark, made it difficult for
Moffat to get loans, and tried to block the Denver, Northwestern &
Pacific by filing mining claims along its route. They also kept Moffat from
using the Union Station, so he built his own depot at 2101 Fifteenth
Street.

Moffat temporarily eased his credit problem by borrowing from the
First National. Who was to stop him? He was the bank's president, and he

owned 72 percent of its stock. By 1910 his railroad had not even reached Craig, in northwestern Colorado, and the First National's vaults were crammed with worthless Denver, Northwestern & Pacific IOUs. Outwardly, Moffat, who began constructing a new mansion at Eighth and Grant, appeared solvent. Bank examiners, however, were growing alarmed. To save his bank, his railroad, and himself, Moffat again tried to raise money in the East. He failed. On March 18, 1911, he died — rumor said by his own hand — in a New York hotel room. William Gray Evans brought Moffat's body home.

The newspapers initially reported that Moffat died rich, worth perhaps $25 million. Actually, he was bankrupt and so were his bank and his railroad. His friends were also in danger of bankruptcy since Moffat had used their money to finance his schemes. His associates buried him under a cheap tombstone at Fairmount, and his widow moved back to the family's old home on Lincoln, where she rented two rooms. "I'll fix myself up a bedroom there and just be happy with my memories."[13]

Within hours of Moffat's death, the First National's attorney, Gerald Hughes, had shored up the bank before its dire condition became widely known. Hughes's father, U.S. Senator Charles J. Hughes, Jr., previously the bank's lawyer and the legal brains behind many local moguls, had died in January 1911. Gerald quickly shouldered his father's responsibilities. He convinced the reclusive Leadville banker, Absolom V. Hunter, to become First National's president and to invest heavily in it. The miller John K. Mullen; the banker Mahlon D. Thatcher; Crawford Hill, and others were made directors. Their backing saved the bank, its depositors, and its shareholders. On Hunter's death in 1924, Hughes became chairman of the board at the First National, where he kept a tight rein on lending.

William Gray Evans, an investor in both the First National Bank and the Moffat Road, had reason to thank Hughes. Since the 1890s, Evans had slaved to salvage his father's declining fortune. The Denver Tramway Company, of which the younger Evans was president until 1913, eventually paid well, but the Moffat Road, in which he sank more than a quarter-million dollars, was a doomed enterprise. The Evans clan also ventured into another risky business, the Denver Union Water Company.

Historian Allen Breck, Evans's biographer, praised him for his hard work, his civic-mindedness, and his devotion to family. The tramway king's contemporaries were less kind. Gossip columnist Polly Pry described Evans as "a little, stocky man, with square shoulders and a square head," with "an expressionless, impassive sort of face, with cold gray eyes

Daniels &
Fisher,

DENVER. COLO.

WHOLESALE.

Dry Goods,

FURNISHING GOODS,

NOTIONS AND

CARPETS.

FLANNEL SHIRTS

(Our own make) and

DUCK CLOTHING,

A Specialty with us.

**Eastern Bills Duplicated,
Freight added.**

Special Inducements
offered to Contractors

RETAIL.

Dry Goods

—AND—

CARPETS.

SILKS,

Velvets, Satins,

Dress Goods,

TRIMMINGS,

SUITS, ULSTERS,

Dolmans, Shawls,

MILLINERY,

Notions, Gloves, Laces,
Hosiery, Ladies'
And Gents' Underwear,
Blankets, Linens,
Flannels, Table Damasks,
Domestics, Zephyrs,
White Goods, Fancy
Work Goods,
Handkerchiefs, Carpets,
Upholstery Goods.

Western Agents for

Butterick's Patterns.

DANIELS & FISHER,

DENVER, COLO.

BANDEAUX, CURLS, FRIZZES, PUFFS, SCOLLOPS.

William B. Daniels and William G. Fisher, who opened on Larimer Street in 1868, survived many ups and downs. May D&F Stores, as the firm was called after its 1957 sale to the May Company, survives as Colorado's best-known department store chain. (Denver Public Library, Western History Department.)

and a firm hard mouth."[14] Edward Keating, then managing editor of the *Rocky Mountain News*, saw "Napoleon Bill" as "rich, able, politically unscrupulous."[15]

Luck and fame smiled more kindly on Charles Boettcher, who made much of his early fortune selling hardware and investing in Leadville mines. Following other rich Leadvillites, he moved to Denver's Capitol Hill in 1890. A wealthy man considering retirement in 1900, he took time out to visit his native Germany, which he had left as a teenager in 1869. There he saw farmers growing sugar beets, a crop he decided to promote in Colorado. He studied German processing methods and asked his wife Fannie to discard souvenirs to make room in her suitcase for beet seed. Weary of sightseeing, Boettcher decided "that I should get back home to America and get to work."[16]

Work agreed with him; he lived until 1948, dying at age 96. As he grew older he was assisted by his son Claude Kenzie, but Charles's grasp of the state's economic direction insured that his Midas touch did not fail. When mining dominated Colorado, he made money in mining. As the economy shifted toward agriculture, he made another fortune from Great Western Sugar. He built his sugar-processing factories of high-grade cement, which led him into another profitable enterprise — the Ideal

Cement Company. In 1901 he helped organize the Western Packing Company, which sold out to Swift and Company in 1912. Boettcher deposited his money in his own bank, the original Denver National, and in the brokerage house of Boettcher, Porter, and Company. Wishing to put his eggs in many baskets, he invested in such varied Colorado businesses as the Capitol Life Insurance Company, the Public Service Company of Colorado, the National Fuse and Powder Company, the Bighorn Land and Cattle Company, and the Brown Palace Hotel. His vast empire constituted Denver's best example of economic diversification.

Hughes, Evans, and Boettcher feasted on the local and regional economy. Unlike pioneer empire builders such as John Evans, Cheesman, and Moffat, the city's second- and third-generation leaders, having suffered through the debacle of 1893 and Moffat's collapse in 1911, learned to value caution and diversification. Their fiscal conservatism, anchored in painful experience, was understandable. So was their hawk-eyed attention to politics, for they knew that what happened at City Hall affected them.

CHAPTER 12

Reformers Versus the Beast

The State of Colorado is exploited and the people robbed by a government by the Beast and for the Beast. A system of corruption that aims to pick the corruptible man for public service, and refuses the honest one an opportunity to serve, has made most of the public life and administration of public affairs in Colorado a gigantic failure, a huge oppression.

Benjamin B. Lindsey
The Beast, 1910[1]

Denver's City Hall, at Fourteenth and Larimer, was no thing of beauty. Its poorly proportioned tower, its cluttered mansard roof, and its awkward rear additions made an unsightly pile that would have been a blot on the landscape had there been any landscape to blot. Except for the sidewalk around it and a tiny plot of ground to the south, the building occupied its entire site; telephone poles took the place of trees. From its east and south windows, city workers could see and smell the filth-choked channel of Cherry Creek. Rear windows looked over the railroad yards. Jailers, who slept in the basement near the prisoners, constantly battled rats. Upstairs, city councilmen, sometimes so drunk they could not do business, doled out liquor licenses worth thousands and utilities franchises worth millions.

Denver's turn-of-the-century government, like its City Hall, was shabby, if not rotten. Until 1885 the city had been governed by a mayor

Suffragette Ellis Meredith pushed progressive reforms in Denver before going on to Washington and prominence with the U.S. capital press corps. (Colorado Historical Society.)

and a council; then it added a second legislative chamber, the Board of Supervisors. Authority was divided; responsibility hard to fix. In 1889 the State Legislature, masking its greed for political spoils as a reform measure, placed Denver's Public Works Department under commissioners appointed by the governor. Two years later the Fire and Police departments were also yanked away from the city and put under another state board. Despite these "reforms" stripping City Hall of much of its power, gambling, prostitution, and corruption continued.[2]

Disgruntled citizens demanded an end to state interference. They won home rule for the city in 1902 when voters approved Article XX of the state constitution, known as the Rush amendment after its sponsor, Denver state Senator John A. Rush. Besides giving Denver control of its own government, the measure merged the suburbs of Berkeley, Elyria, Globeville, Montclair, and Valverde into the city. The resultant 59.25 square miles became the City and County of Denver.[3] The Rush amendment specified some aspects of home rule. For example, citizens were given the right to vote on the granting of franchises. Other details were left for Denver to incorporate in its charter, a fundamental framework of government similar to a state's constitution. A charter convention, dominated by reformers, was elected in 1903. The suffragette Ellis Meredith was a member; so was the Spanish-American War hero General Irving Hale. The inclusion of the wealthy flour miller and dedicated temperance advocate John K. Mullen gave the group a powerful antiliquor voice. The convention drafted a charter providing for a strong mayor, a one-chamber city council, and nonpartisan elections. It took a shot at the city's 350 saloons by raising liquor license fees from $600 to $1,000 and by allowing neighborhoods to ban bars.[4]

Bright stars in the galaxy of social betterment included Jared Warner Mills and Ellis Meredith, veterans of the 1893 equal suffrage campaign; John Shafroth, governor (1909–1913) and U.S. senator (1913–1919);

the stockbroker James Causey; newspapermen Edward Keating, William McLeod Raine, and George Creel; Robert W. Steele of the State Supreme Court; the attorney Philip Hornbein; and Josephine Roche, the daughter of a wealthy coal company owner.[5] As important as these crusaders were, however, much of the impetus for social improvement in early twentieth-century Denver came from three ardent reformers: Thomas M. Patterson; Benjamin Barr Lindsey; and Edward Prentiss Costigan.

As a congressman and as publisher of the *Rocky Mountain News*, Thomas M. Patterson championed underdogs, including labor unions and progressive reformers. (Denver Public Library, Western History Department.)

Patterson, a native of County Carlow, Ireland, had arrived in Denver in 1872. By 1874 he was Colorado's territorial delegate to Congress, a major accomplishment for a newcomer and a Democrat in a Republican territory. After Colorado became a state, Patterson became its first member of the House of Representatives. During the 1880s he built a lucrative law practice successfully defending alleged criminals, which gave him a yearly income of $75,000. In 1890 he purchased part interest in the *Rocky Mountain News* and embarked on a new career.

Patterson stood up for the underdog. When the anti-Catholic American Protective Association grew powerful in the 1890s, Patterson, although himself a Protestant, helped squelch the bigots by campaigning against them in the *News*. In 1900, Preston John Porter, a black 16-year-old from Denver, was accused of murdering a girl near Limon. Angry farmers did not wait for the courts to act. They kidnaped the feeble-minded Porter, tied him to a stake, and slowly burned him to death, ignoring his pleas that they shoot him. For months Patterson unsuccessfully demanded the arrest of Porter's tormentors. Edward Keating, who once worked as the *News*'s managing editor, praised his former boss as "the greatest man Colorado has seen in my time."[6] Patterson was 61 in 1901, the year his selection by the State Legislature as a U.S. senator snapped the political ties between him and Robert Walter Speer. "Boss" Speer had supported Patterson's rival, Charles S. Thomas, for the Senate seat. Unable to count on Speer's Democratic party machine, Patterson worked with reform Republicans such as Costigan, and reform Democrats such as Lindsey.

Judge Ben Lindsey (far left, with moustache) was not much bigger than many of the youngsters for whom he founded Denver's famed juvenile court. (Colorado Historical Society.)

Eleven-year-old Ben Lindsey had come to Denver from his native Tennessee in 1879. For a few years his father, head telegraph operator for the Denver, South Park & Pacific Railroad, did moderately well. Then the elder Lindsey lost his job and became ill. Ben had hoped to complete Denver High School, but his family needed money so he dropped out and went to work. After his father committed suicide, Lindsey tried to kill himself, failing because his revolver misfired. Shaken by the experience, he decided "to crush the circumstances that had almost crushed me."[7] By clerking in a law office, Lindsey educated himself and in 1894 became a lawyer. Soon he was dabbling in politics, a hobby that paid off in 1898 when he backed Charles S. Thomas's successful bid for the governorship. Grateful Democrats made the 32-year-old attorney an Arapahoe County judge in 1900. Early in his career Judge Lindsey sentenced an Italian boy for stealing coal. The lad's haggard mother ran to Lindsey screaming and tearing her hair, beating her head against the wall, "as if," Lindsey remembered, "she would batter the court house down on us all and bury our injustice under the ruins."[8] Lindsey suspended the boy's sentence and investigated the case. He found the four-member family living in a two-room North Denver shack. The father, a smelter man, was unable to work because of lead poisoning. Mother, father, and their baby were freezing, so the boy stole coal. To keep such children from being treated as criminals, Lindsey worked to change the courts and the laws. By 1901 he had organized an informal juvenile court, one of the first in the country. He liked the proposed 1903 charter because it provided for a juvenile detention home.[9]

Compared to Lindsey's struggle, Edward Costigan's life had been tame and privileged. The son of a well-to-do Republican judge, Costigan, born in Virginia in 1874, completed Denver High School in 1892 and went on to Harvard. Following graduation from Harvard Law School in 1899, he returned to Denver and a partnership with his brother George. In 1901 he helped organize the Honest Election League, and the next year, as a Republican legislative candidate, he learned an unforgettable lesson as a poll watcher. Thugs attacked him as he attempted to stop fraudulent voting, and, when he complained, the police threw him out of the polling place. Charter advocates recognized Costigan's oratorical ability and asked him to speak on their behalf.

Longtime champion of reform Edward Costigan provided much of the leadership for Denver's liberals during the first third of the twentieth century. (Denver Public Library, Western History Department.)

Despite Patterson's, Lindsey's, and Costigan's efforts, the good-government charter was defeated by over 7,000 votes out of some 36,000 cast. It fared well in south Denver and Montclair, middle-class residential areas, but in lower-downtown wards, where saloons, prostitution, and gambling flourished, it was crushed. The *News* screamed about illegal voting, but the charter's defeat could not be blamed simply on ballot box stuffing. John Rush contended that "the taxeater, the thug, the gambler, the franchise grabber, the divekeeper" opposed the charter.[10] He was right. Thousands who worked for saloons, brewers, and gamblers, for the tramway, the Gas and Electric Company, the Denver Union Water Company, or at City Hall fought the charter. Thugs and franchise grabbers, barmen and bankers, dive keepers and gamblers, political hacks and grasping officials constituted a powerful force.

For nearly 20 years, Robert Walter Speer, a self-proclaimed political boss, had molded that force. He had come to Colorado in 1878 to recover from TB, which had killed his sister. The climate invigorated him, and he leapt into politics. In 1884, at age 29, he was selected city clerk by the Board of Aldermen. A year later, President Grover Cleveland appointed him Denver's postmaster. In 1891 he became a member of the three-member Fire and Police Board — a position he used to provide jobs for Democrats. His clout increased in 1901 when he became head of the Board of Public Works that controlled nearly half the city's budget. Speer got along with wardheelers and gamblers, bar keepers and brewers, corporate leaders and franchise owners. He had, according to his rival Charles S. Thomas, "an almost fulsome subservience to the managers and owners of the leading public utilities."[11]

The charter's defeat led to another convention, which drafted a document acceptable to the corporations, the brewers, and the politicians. Two months after the new charter's March 1904 adoption, Denver elected its first home-rule mayor — Robert Speer. His opponent, banker John Springer, claimed that the election was rigged but later withdrew the charge because, as J. Warner Mills alleged, William Gray Evans threatened "to crush and ruin the two Denver banking institutions with which he [Springer] was connected."[12]

Reformers had lost a battle, but they did not surrender. For the next eight years they bombarded Speer and his corporate backers. The struggle grew especially heated in 1906 when the tramway and the Denver Gas and Electric Company asked voters to approve new franchises for which the companies agreed to pay yearly fees of $50,000 and $60,000 respectively. Opponents chafed at such low payments, noting that Kansas City collected $400,000 annually from its franchise holders. By narrow margins the utilities won. Reformers questioned the outcome since many people had qualified to vote by becoming nominal taxpayers shortly before the election. Judge Lindsey investigated but was hamstrung by the refusal of witnesses to testify: Tramway president Evans left town; the Gas and Electric Company's Henry Doherty would not talk. Lindsey jailed Doherty for contempt, and the mogul slept in a hammock at night and sat on his cell floor by day since there were no chairs. Released after three days, he damned Denver for having "more sunshine and sons-of-bitches than any place in the country."[13]

Costigan argued that Lindsey had a right to investigate the election, but the Colorado Supreme Court agreed with corporate attorney Charles Hughes, Jr., and blocked Lindsey. Speer and Evans had won again. Two years later, that victory was followed by another — the reelection of Speer. Edward Keating attributed Speer's 1908 triumph to the Republicans' failure to nominate a strong opposition candidate. According to Keating, the GOP leaders sent Speer's men a slate of names with the request: "Pick the man you think you can beat and we'll nominate him."

Among Mayor Speer's many critics, these stalwarts of the Women's Christian Temperance Union could not abide his defense of more than 400 saloons in the Mile High City. (Denver Public Library, Western History Department.)

Horace Phelps, described by Keating as "certainly weak," with "no record," was chosen to oppose Speer.[14] Lindsey wrote to Jane Addams, the Chicago settlement house founder, that Evans controlled both the Democrats (Speer) and the Republicans (Phelps) and would be able to manipulate the levers of power whoever won. "I found the situation so disgusting," Lindsey told Addams, "that I took no part in the campaign."[15]

Although Lindsey found little difference between Phelps and Speer, the "church element" and the antiliquor forces found plenty. Edwin E. McLaughlin, head of Colorado's Anti-Saloon League, organized a mass meeting at which religious leaders castigated the mayor. For them the case was clear: "The forces of righteousness and lawlessness," McLaughlin wrote, "are arrayed against each other."[16] Speer had two strikes against him: He tolerated the red light district, and he favored the liquor interests. The misdeeds of his chief of police, Michael Delaney, almost caused the mayor to strike out completely. Delaney's first mistake involved Robert Fisher, a black man accused of burglary. To get a confession, Delaney kicked the defenseless Fisher in the head until, in agony, he admitted a crime he did not commit. A court threw out the confession, but since few cared about minority rights, Delaney survived until he sinned again. Although married, he had a lady friend. On seeing a visitor leave her house one evening, the jealous Delaney jumped to conclusions, seized the man, and beat him, unaware that he was an innocent plumber. Speer fired Delaney and, unhindered by the wayward lawman, won reelection.[17]

The reformers continued the good fight. Costigan investigated the red light district, where he found wine rooms: "Little girls are enticed into them, given knock out drops, ruined, and finally end in houses of ill fame."[18] The *News* demanded that the mayor crack down on the cribs where, George Creel reported, diseased women "sat for sale beside a soiled bed and a dirty washbowl."[19] Speer, who tacitly promised to protect the underworld in exchange for its votes, did nothing. "No effort," he had declared in 1904, "will be made to make a puritanical town out of a growing Western city."[20]

Lindsey, aided by journalist Harvey J. O'Higgins, trumpeted Speer's and Evans's transgressions in a series of articles, "The Beast and the Jungle," published in *Everybody's Magazine* and in book form as *The Beast*. The graft of politicians, the greed of gamblers, and the pervasive, almost hidden power of the city's corporate beast were exposed to *Everybody's* half-million subscribers.

Denver's business barons had no more love for Lindsey than he had for them. Evans tried to block Lindsey's renomination in 1904. The judge asked Walter Cheesman to intercede, but Cheesman refused, telling Lindsey that "Mr. Evans represents our interests in politics, and of course, you understand, with us politics is a matter of business."[21] O'Higgins reported that Lindsey's enemies tried "to lure him to houses of ill repute." They threatened his life. They even cut off his courtroom lights "and he has had to go to the corner drugstore at night and buy himself candles to continue his work."[22]

Lindsey, Costigan, and their supporters kept buying candles, writing, speaking, and going to court. Often, the newspapers helped them. Patterson's *News* regularly opposed Speer, while the *Denver Post* sometimes lambasted "Boss Speer" and "Napoleon Evans." The *Denver Express*, a feisty daily founded in 1906 by the California newspaper magnate Edward W. Scripps, championed clean government. Speer countered by publishing a free, city-sponsored magazine, *Municipal Facts*, a "good-news journal" of his beautification projects, of parks and sewers, of his plans for a civic center. In spite of the weekly barrage of pictures and lists of improvements provided by *Municipal Facts*, Speer's popularity waned. In 1911 he fired the county assessor, Henry J. Arnold, who had offended utility companies by suggesting that they were undertaxed. Arnold refused to vacate his office, so Speer's henchman George Collins decided to seize it. The *News* reported that Collins, afterward known as "Crowbar," broke into Arnold's office with a crowbar and threw Arnold out.[23] Such crude tactics made Arnold a hero to the reformers, who nominated him for mayor. Anticipating defeat, Speer did not seek reelection in 1912. Arnold beat both the Republican-backed nominee, Dewey C. Bailey, and the Democrat John B. Hunter, an ally of Speer. Lindsey gleefully wrote to Edward Scripps, "I do not believe in the history of municipal politics any big business bunch of city pillagers were ever so completely kicked out of politics at any election."[24]

To prevent Speer from regaining power, Lindsey, Costigan, and their friends urged Denver to adopt a commission form of government. Under this procedure, pushed as a solution to urban problems by good-government advocates nationwide, cities were to be run by elected commissioners. Individually, these managers would supervise city agencies; collectively, they would act as a city council. Strong mayors, such as Speer, would be reduced to figureheads. Arnold backed the innovation when he ran for mayor, but once in office abandoned the notion. Denver voters, on the other hand, approved of commission government in 1913. Arnold was forced out as Denver embraced a scheme that few other large cities had tried.

The experiment seemed doomed from the start. Since more than a hundred candidates vied for positions on the commission, the vote was so fragmented that those backed by Speer did well. Speer's protégé John B. Hunter became commissioner of improvements, and most of the other five commissioners had ties to Speer. Lindsey's brother Charles wrote to Ben: "From the appointments made by some of the commissioners it is becoming obvious . . . that the gang are again in harness and the corporations holding the reins."[25] The Chamber of Commerce opposed commission government; businessmen organized as the Colorado Taxpayer's Protective League criticized it.

After a three-year trial, the city abandoned the commission and restored government by mayor and council. Lindsey and Costigan not only had failed to destroy the strong-mayor system, they inadvertently had helped make it stronger. Under the 1916 charter, which grew out of the commission debacle, the new mayor gained the right to appoint the city assessor, sheriff, treasurer, clerk, and four of the nine members of the City Council. Voters spun the political wheel of fortune full circle in 1916, handing back the mayorship to Speer.

The battered progressives could do little. Some of them, like Ellis Meredith, supported Speer. Costigan's influence had waned. In 1912 he had left the Republican party to run as a Progressive for the governorship. He lost then and again in 1914, when many middle-class Coloradans turned against him because of his pro-labor views. Lindsey was in bed recovering from an operation. Patterson was fading; he died in July 1916. John C. Shaffer, who had bought the *News* in 1913, held conservative views and in 1916 backed Speer. Moreover, the reformers failed to stick together. The 1912 presidential race split them into Democratic supporters of Woodrow Wilson (Creel and Patterson) and Progressive Republican backers of Theodore Roosevelt (Lindsey and Costigan). In 1914 when Costigan ran for governor as a Progressive, his Democratic opponent was Thomas Patterson. They both were defeated by the Republican, George A. Carlson.

In spite of the setbacks, some reforms succeeded. Four of the city's wards opted to ban saloons in 1908, and in 1916 the entire state went dry. When Arnold had become mayor he had appointed journalist Creel commissioner of police. Creel turned off the red lights on Market Street in 1913. He tried to establish a rehabilitation farm for fallen women, but Arnold and the taxpayers did not like the idea. To demonstrate the health menace, Creel ordered prostitutes tested at the city hospital, where 95 of the first 144 screened were found to be diseased. Josephine Roche, a Vassar graduate with a master's degree from Columbia, assisted Arnold by working as a policewoman to clean up the district and by raising money to reunite women with their families. Although the tenderloin briefly reopened after Arnold ousted Creel, prostitution was more effectively curbed under commission government.

Judge Lindsey encouraged those measures but continued to make juvenile justice his top concern. At first, his campaign for decent treatment of young offenders was met by indifference. The police denied allegations that jailers molested incarcerated boys. Lindsey asked the governor and other leading citizens to hear the lads' stories. Shocked officials then supported Lindsey's drive for humane laws. Jailers at the state reformatory in Golden put away their shackles and, at least temporarily, stopped flogging children. New state statutes, sometimes called the Lindsey laws, forbade adults from contributing to a minor's delinquency and made parents responsible for their children's care. In time, Lindsey secured juvenile courts and a children's detention home. Between 1909 and 1913 progressive legislation poured from the state capitol as liberal

Lightning repeatedly struck the statue of Justice atop the county courthouse at Sixteenth Street and Court Place, knocking away her scales and reducing her arms to stumps. The justice dispensed by crooked Denver officials was, according to Judge Ben Lindsey's book *The Beast,* just as shocking. (Colorado Historical Society.)

Republicans and Democrats allied to pass measures that Governor Shafroth readily signed.

The powerful, although not seriously shaken, occasionally felt the reform breeze. Charles J. Hughes's death in 1911 deprived the tramway, the First National Bank, and the Denver Union Water Company of an able legal mouthpiece. Moffat's passing a few months later revealed the unsoundness both of his bank and his railroad. Distraught by Moffat's demise and Speer's defeat, Evans, who suffered a nervous breakdown in 1913, temporarily retired and went deep-sea fishing.

In 1916, Ben Lindsey wrote to Creel, who had left town, reporting that once again Denver was facing an election. Once again, Speer was running. Once again, Speer was expected to win. Once again, Lindsey was "so disgusted that I think, for a great many reasons, I will keep out of it." Yet, there was a difference. Lindsey hinted that Speer might no longer be working for the "interests." Many of the other reformers, he told Creel, believed that Speer had changed. "It is one of the strangest mix-ups we have ever had, and it only proves that Denver politics is simply beyond the understanding of anyone who hasn't lived here, or left the town."[26]

In a narrow sense, those who thought that Speer had cut his ties to Evans were wrong. In Speer's final term he helped engineer the city's purchase of the Denver Union Water Company for nearly $14 million, a price pleasing to Evans. In a broader sense, however, some of Speer's former enemies were beginning to glimpse facets of the man that later generations would see more clearly. Denver's politics were not simply polar — the forces of good versus the forces of evil. Speer, who outwardly fit the stereotype of the cigar-champing, big-city boss, was, in fact, a complex, thoughtful, innovative man; a lover of beauty, a friend of animals. As a hardheaded pragmatist, he got along with big business while pushing socialistic projects such as a city-owned bakery, coal company, and asphalt plant. Speer, too, was a reformer — a politician dedicated to efficient, powerful city government. Unlike the weak mayors of the nineteenth century, unlike the ineffective commission government, Speer got things done. Voters returned him to office in 1916 to make sure that Denver stayed on the course he had mapped out for it a decade earlier. He was determined to transform a drab, chaotic town into a City Beautiful.

CHAPTER 13

Mayor Speer's City Beautiful

The time will come when men will be judged more by their disbursements than by their accumulations. Denver has been kind to most of us
by giving to some health, to some wealth, to some happiness, and to
some a combination of all. We can pay a part of this debt by making our
city more attractive.

    Robert W. Speer
    Address to Denver Chamber of Commerce, May 24, 1909[1]

In May 1916, businessmen favoring Robert Speer's return to office staged
a rally at the City Auditorium, an ideal setting since Speer had built the
popular structure. Organizers highlighted the evening with a motion
picture, "Greater Denver," celebrating the former mayor's accomplishments. They knew that voters appreciated his beautification campaigns,
that in semiarid Denver planting a tree was as politically smart as kissing
a baby.

    Speer's commitment to the City Beautiful was more than a political
ploy. He twice traveled to Europe to study parks, parkways, and urban
design. At home he preached: "Ugly things do not please. It is much
easier to love a thing of beauty — and this applies to cities as well as to
persons and things. Fountains, statues, artistic lights, music, playgrounds,
parks, etc., make people love the place in which they live."[2] He used
Municipal Facts, the city's magazine, to publicize his programs. Old timers
read, with amazement, about parks, libraries, and museums. Until Speer
became mayor, City Hall had taken little interest in beauty and culture.

Boss Speer, like thousands of others, came to Denver as a lunger suffering from TB. Colorado's "climate cure" made a new man of the puny Pennsylvanian. (Denver Public Library, Western History Department.)

For decades, the city had grown so fast that it had struggled to pave streets and build bridges, giving little thought to aesthetics. Between 1882 and 1900, the city appropriated more than $650,000 for 11 bridges over Cherry Creek, 2 bridges over the South Platte, and 3 viaducts spanning the river and the railroad tracks. Schools took precedence over parks. Over $1.5 million was spent on school buildings in Denver's District One between 1873 and 1900.[3] Consolidation of other districts into District One in 1902 gave grade schools 21,067 pupils in 1903. The high schools — East, West, Manual, and North — counted 2,302.

Denver's first public park, Curtis Park at Thirty-first and Curtis streets, was donated by a real estate developer in 1868. Richard Sopris, mayor from 1878 to 1882 and the city's first park commissioner (1882–1891), acquired more parkland. By 1900, Denver tallied 436 acres of public parks with the three largest — City, Congress, and Washington — accounting for 90 percent of the acreage. Washington Park remained unimproved, as did Congress, where vandalized tombstones reminded picnickers of its origin as the City Cemetery.[4] City Park, with 320 acres, outshone all the others. Sopris, who purchased the land in 1882, encouraged schoolchildren to plant cottonwoods there, a practice later abandoned since many people disliked the messy, native trees. "It is not," said one forester, "the shade tree of progress."[5] By 1904 a lake had been dredged at the south end of the park, the Museum of Natural History had been built near Colorado Boulevard, and a track for buggy racing had been laid out in the northeast section. A small zoo evolved nearby — its first resident a pet bear named Billy Bryan confined to a cage as punishment for having eaten chickens.

Fledgling parks and shabby attractions did not make Denver a beautiful or a distinguished city. George W. Steevens, a British visitor, tartly commented in 1897 that the Queen City of the Plains was "more plain

than queenly."[6] Another tourist, Emma Gage, more charitably noted that the parks "are still in embryo," and she looked forward to the day when the "latent munificence" of wealthy citizens would "develop with a magnificence so lavish as to amaze the visitor."[7] That day dawned when Speer became mayor. He envisioned a new Denver, a city of grace and charm, an American Paris. For advice he looked to the Denver Art Commission, chaired by artist Henry Read, an Englishman who had come to Colorado for his health. The commission also included the hard-driving Anne Evans, influential daughter of territorial Governor John Evans and sister to the "Napoleon" of Denver's businessmen, William Gray Evans. The commission proposed, reviewed, and pushed dozens of projects: Downtown telegraph and telephone lines were buried, clearing streets of a mass of unsightly wires; poles supporting trolley lines were rebuilt to accommo-

Robert and Kate Speer had no children of their own but doubled the city's park and playgound space for all Denver's children. (Colorado Historical Society.)

142

Neoclassical architecture, exemplified by the Museum of Natural History in City Park, aspired to bring to Denver the glory that was Greece and the grandeur that was Rome. (Photo by L. C. McClure, Denver Public Library, Western History Department.)

date ornamental streetlights designed by Read; Fifteenth Street sported red and white street lamps, while Sixteenth Street became Denver's Great White Way — "a public promenade for pleasure seekers every night."[8]

Speer loved lights. In front of Union Station, the city built a Welcome Arch, 86 feet wide and 65 feet high, illuminating it with 1,294 small lights. Farther up Seventeenth, on Tremont, the Gas and Electric Company lit another arch. Even more spectacular was the illuminated fountain in City Park's south lake, which Speer dedicated the night before his reelection in 1908. The city appropriated $160,000 for street lighting in 1909, $40,000 more than it had spent on its police force 13 years earlier. Yet even the lights dimmed compared to the mayor's grander schemes: the auditorium; Cherry Creek beautification; and the Civic Center.

Denver needed an auditorium since conventioners found the city, with its nearby mountains, attractive. The National Education Association came in 1887 and 1895; the American Federation of Labor in 1894; and the biggest gathering of all, the Knights Templar, with their families some 60,000 strong, in 1892. Theaters and lodge halls could not take care of such large groups. Speer's 12,000-seat auditorium at Fourteenth and Curtis hosted its first big convention in 1908 when Democrats came to nominate William Jennings Bryan for his third run at the presidency. Apache Indians regaled the politicos with war whoops, and the city fetched mountain snow so that delegates could pelt each other with snowballs in July.

Beautifying Cherry Creek appeared, at first, to be a more fanciful project than building an auditorium, but in the long run it proved to be

To perk up a flat economy, Denver began courting conventions, honoring the 1913 Knights Templar Conclave with this knight on Champa Street. (Photo by George L. Beam, courtesy of Jackson Thode.)

144

one of Speer's greatest accomplishments. For decades people had used the creek as an open sewer, lining its banks with dumps. Jerome Smiley, in 1901, proposed banishing "the blighting blemish" altogether by diverting Cherry Creek into Sand Creek.[9] Speer realized that the bane could be a blessing. Between 1904 and 1912 he began transforming it into a walled waterway bordered by a landscaped boulevard, which the City Council named after him.

For the heart of the city, he envisioned a parklike civic center. His Art Commission, following the advice of New York planner Charles Mulford Robinson, initially wanted to make a triangular park reaching from the state capitol to the courthouse on Sixteenth and Tremont, and embracing the newly built U.S. Mint between Fourteenth Avenue and Colfax on Cherokee. Voters rejected that grand plan in 1906. The next year, New York sculptor Frederick MacMonnies suggested that land directly west of the capitol grounds be secured for the Civic Center. Elections and legal wrangling delayed matters; not until April 1912 was there money for the 13 acres. Except for the Public Library building, the tract was crowded with homes and businesses. Mayor Henry Arnold cleared the land, providing a convenient dumping ground for the tons of snow removed from streets after the 46-inch fall of early December 1913.[10] The frozen mountain melted in spring 1914, leaving an open plot that stayed empty for two years, a reminder of commission government's ineptitude.

In part, Speer's desire to complete the Civic Center brought him back to public life. On his return, construction began on the Colonnade of Civic Benefactors and the Greek Theater. By honoring donors, Speer encouraged others to give. The Cheesman-Evans family donated $100,000 for a marble pavilion memorializing Walter S. Cheesman in Congress Park, which was, consequently, renamed Cheesman Park.[11] Private money built both the Welcome Arch near Union Station and the Pioneer Monument, designed by Frederick MacMonnies, at Colfax and Broadway. Individuals graced City Park with the Richard Sopris and Joshua Monti gateways. William W. McLellan, a blacksmith, gave half his life's savings for the York Street gateway named for him. Denver's Scottish population raised $9,000 for City Park's Robert Burns statue. Banker Joseph A. Thatcher gave $100,000 for a monument by the Chicago sculptor Lorado Taft, at the north end of the City Park Esplanade. At the Esplanade's south end, near Colfax, businessman John C. Mitchell had Leo Lentelli pay tribute to pioneer miners and farmers. In 1917 alone, $275,000 was donated for beautification.

Between 1904 and 1912, Speer more than doubled park acreage.

Washington Park was extended to the south where shallow Grasmere Lake was dredged, complementing Smith Lake, the old buffalo wallow, at the park's north end. On Smith Lake, Speer built Denver's first bathing beach. He knew that it would be popular since the public bathhouse at Twentieth and Curtis, which opened in 1908, had attracted 150,000 people to its indoor pool and showers in its first year. New parks included the Sunken Gardens near Speer Boulevard and scenic Inspiration Point in north Denver. The city purchased private land in North Denver to create Sloan's Lake and Berkeley parks. At Berkeley people could swim and, for the first time, play golf on a public course. Park-goers thanked the mayor for another innovation: He removed "Keep Off the Grass" signs from park lawns. And, in a move that raised a few eyebrows, the city started allowing "spooning" in the parks. Denver, the *News* reported, wanted population. "The more young people to marry the better . . . if love-making in the parks will help it along, why then they can do all the love making in the parks they want to."[12]

Speer also recognized the need for mundane improvements. He spent nearly $10 million on streets, sidewalks, and sewers during his first two administrations. His ideas usually made sense, but sometimes he astonished his audiences. In January 1918 he told Rotarians that "animals, grain and vegetables have life, and suffer when injured the same as any of us." He reflected on the plight of celery, "torn from its home and life-supplying elements — because we did not hear its cry of anguish we gave it no thought."[13] Speer fed birds at his home and scattered grain for the sparrows that flocked to his office windowsill. Animals at City Park Zoo were freed from cramped cages and put in large enclosures. Contented wolves bred wildly, so the zoo started selling them. With its meager collection of species — beaver, badger, buffalo, deer, elk, eagles, mountain lions, and wolves — the zoo could not claim to be first-rate, but its natural habitats, which Speer promoted, brought Denver national publicity.

When the United States declared war on Germany on April 6, 1917, Speer diverted his attention from parks and went to war on the home front. Fearful that bakers would take advantage of the crisis to raise prices, he opened a city bakery that both employed and fed indigents. To control greedy coal dealers, he established a city-owned coal company. For soldiers-to-be, he set up a military training school where they could practice speaking French and fighting. Thousands from Denver volunteered, others were drafted. Many became part of the Fortieth (Rainbow) and Forty-first (Sunshine) army divisions that fought in France. Some,

Denver began building viaducts in the 1880s to bridge the river and a dangerous maze of railroad tracks. Mayor Speer managed to squeeze $546,848 from the railroads to construct the Twentieth Street Viaduct, shown here shortly after its 1911 opening. (Denver Public Library, Western History Department.)

such as Major Jerry C. Vasconcells, were lucky. Vasconcells, Denver's only WW I ace, shot down five German planes and an observation balloon. He returned a hero. Others, among them Leo T. Leyden, did not fare as well. Leyden died in France on June 15, 1918, the first Denverite to be killed in action. Lieutenant Francis Brown Lowry, an aerial photographer, suffered a similarly tragic fate when he was shot down over France in late September 1918. News of his death reached Denver on November 11, the day the war ended.[14]

Despite the war, Denver continued making improvements. The boulevards along Cherry Creek were extended, and the auditorium received a pipe organ. Work started on the Colonnade of Civic Benefactors on the south side of the new Civic Center, and funds were raised for the Voorhies Memorial on the north side. Speer began building a drive along the South Platte. The mayor's vision extended beyond the city. In May 1909 he had suggested to the Chamber of Commerce that Denver build a drive from the city into the mountains, where, he said, "the masses may spend a happy day and feel that some of the grandeur of the Rocky Mountains belongs to them."[15] Soon the publicist John Brisbane Walker and others joined the mountain parks crusade. Speer, an avid motorist, often drove into the mountains to look at prospective park sites and, in 1917, launched a campaign to build the world's highest automobile road to the top of 14,264-foot–high Mount Evans.

The City Beautiful, as Speer saw it, was more than a statue here and a fountain there. The Civic Center, for example, was designed to make government more efficient by clustering city, county, and state buildings. Landscaping made the city pleasant and provided flood control and firebreaks. Parks and playgrounds not only pleased the eye, they also promoted good health. Speer's ideal city reflected the thinking of progressive era philosophers, such as John Dewey and William James, who hoped that an improved environment would uplift the entire urban population. Although berated by reformers for being a lackey of big business, Speer was, in many respects, a champion of the poor and middle class. Denver's parks and beaches, its libraries and swimming pools, its Museum of Natural History and its zoo, were free and open to the public — although that public did not consistently include African-Americans. Denver, in Speer's vision, was not to be a city just of private places and pleasures for those who could afford them. "We can learn much from European cities," he told Denverites on his return in 1911 from inspecting 30 European cities. Those places, he observed, "operated upon the general principle that cities must be governed for the good and happiness of the masses."[16]

Many of Speer's dreams became realities; Denver eventually secured nearly 50 mountain parks, and in 1927 the Mount Evans road was finished. But Speer was destined to see only part of the heavenly city he envisioned. His office remained in the ugly, old City Hall — not until 1932 was the City and County Building completed. The elms on Speer Boulevard were still spindly, the Colonnade of Civic Benefactors only partially finished when Speer died on May 14, 1918, the victim of a cold that led to pneumonia. A year before his death, the *Denver Post* had editorialized: "Speerism has done more to debase and debauch and belittle and retard and to dwarf Denver than any other curse that has befallen us."[17] A week after his death, the *Post* praised him: "His vision was broad, his activities effective, forceful and unceasing. He was the

Mayor Speer's dream of a Civic Center — a government office park with museums, a library, and city offices — materialized two decades after his death in 1918. (Denver Public Library, Western History Department.)

creator of the 'City Beautiful'."[18] People overlooked Speer's under world friends and his kowtowing to corporations. They remembered Speer Boulevard, the parks, the auditorium, the Civic Center, and the 111,000 trees the mayor gave to residents who promised to plant and care for them. They thanked him for the greening of Denver, and because he loved beauty they forgave him for flirting with the beast.

CHAPTER 14

Denver at Leisure

Hers is a solitary grandeur and a very great isolation. . . . Denver must
and does have a keen social life. The isolation and the altitude, constantly tending to make humans nervous and unstrung, demands
amusement, self-created amusement of necessity.

Edward Hungerford
The Personality of American Cities, 1913[1]

Mayor Speer's promotion of parks, recreation, and public amusements
was particularly timely. After frenetic city building in the 1880s and
equally hectic depression days in the 1890s, the middle and upper classes
began to enjoy more leisure time. A slower economic pace following the
crash of 1893 coincided with the proliferation of labor-saving devices and
the introduction of the 40-hour week for some. People had more time for
athletics and physical fitness, for entertainment and culture. Pioneer
empire builders had boldly established banks, railroads, mining companies, and other businesses that their sons found less challenging. For
example, while Nathaniel P. Hill developed smelters, ran a newspaper,
and served in the U.S. Senate, his son Crawford built a mansion, supported his wife's role as the lioness of society, and championed the game
of golf.

Crawford Hill took to the golf greens with lawyer Henry Wolcott,
brother of U.S. Senator Edward O. Wolcott. Hill and Henry Wolcott
organized the city's first golf course at Overland Park in 1896. In 1901,
Hill and other golfers converted a 140-acre wheat field straddling Cherry

Robert W. Speer had taken great pride in making Denver's City Auditorium the nation's second largest. Citizens jammed the auditorium for Speer's funeral service. (Denver Public Library, Western History Department.)

Creek between Downing Street and University Boulevard into the Denver Country Club. Women soon joined men on the links, reaffirming the opinion of old-timers that golf was a sissy sport.[2]

The horsey set, among them Gerald Hughes's brother Lafayette, and Ira B. and Albert E. Humphreys, Jr., sons of oilman Albert E. Humphreys, played polo at the Denver Country Club. When golfers complained about the hoofprints and droppings of the polo ponies, the Humphreys brothers and Lafayette Hughes founded the Polo Club between University and Steele, Alameda and Exposition. Both the Country Club and the Polo Club attracted the elite, who early in the twentieth century started moving east from Capitol Hill into the Cheesman Park neighborhood. Many decided to live, as well as to play, in the Polo Club area, where they created new, exclusive enclaves. Movers and shakers such as Lafayette Hughes and Robert Speer settled on the north side of the Country Club. Others, among them William Gray Evans's son John, built on land at the club's southeast corner. Senator Lawrence Phipps went even farther into the country, placing his palatial Georgian mansion, Belcaro, on 10 acres southeast of the Polo Club.

Wealthy young men flocked to the Country Club and to the Denver Athletic Club (DAC). Society maidens and matrons followed. Soon, the women transformed the clubs into havens noted for card games, fine dining, and dancing. Crawford Hill's newspaper, the *Republican*, reported in 1912 that a dance fever had seized society — the turkey trot, the bunny hug, and the grizzly bear had invaded the Country Club. Dance instructor Edward Tinker had even organized a morning dance, causing busy executives to fret "as to how they are going to get downtown to the office and not miss the morning dance."[3] DAC athletes grumbled that their gym was often used for banquets and dances, and Denver Country Club golfers found that their clubhouse had become Denver's most fashionable society haunt by the 1920s.

The DAC remained loyal to manly sports. Founded in 1884, the club grew rapidly, claiming 1,000 members by 1892, when it completed its $250,000 redstone landmark at 1325 Glenarm. In 1890 the club helped addict the city to football and, in Colorado's first game, humiliated the University of Colorado Boulders, 34 to 0. The DAC continued to whip collegians until 1906, when it dropped the game after newspapers discovered that it was paying "amateurs" recruited from top collegiate teams. The resulting football gap was filled by teams fielded by the University of Denver and Golden's Colorado School of Mines.

Baseball graduated from amateur sandlot games with the appearance in 1885 of a semiprofessional team, the Denvers. Various professional, semiprofessional, and unpaid teams played at Broadway Park at Sixth and Broadway between 1893 and 1922, then switched to Merchants Park at Exposition and Broadway. The Denver Bears, as the city's pro roundballers called themselves after 1900, captured the Western League pennant in 1911, 1912, and 1913. At the bottom of the depression — 1933 — the Bears went into hibernation, not to reemerge until 1947.

Denver's bicycling days began in 1879 when merchant E. A. Richardson started selling Columbia bicycles. In a dance hall, he offered riding lessons on high-wheeled, bone-shaking machines. Only after the development of the safety bicycle and the pneumatic tire in 1894 did cycling become a craze. Denver's generally flat terrain and dry, sunny climate made it ideal for cyclists. Thousands bought two-wheelers: Clerks pedaled to work, children to school, and housewives to their shopping. The captain of the DAC's bicycle division promised businessmen that cycling would relieve their worries, improve their appetites and digestions, clear their brains, and enable them "to accomplish more work with better results."[4] Others were less enthralled. Calvary Baptist church pastor Julian L. Morrill lectured his congregation: "I call upon all good Christians and citizens, lovers of virtue, morality, common decency and patri-

William F. "Buffalo Bill" Cody boosted Denver's stock with tourists searching for the Wild West, even after his death in 1917. His tomb and museum atop Lookout Mountain still attract pilgrims. (Amon Carter Museum, Mazzulla Collection.)

otism to rise up and prevent the surrender of our Christian Sabbath to the Sunday amusement of bicycling."[5] Despite his admonition, bicycle clubs continued to compete in "century rides," 100-mile day trips.

Bicycle outings gave bird watchers a chance to see new species while the newly introduced Kodak camera allowed them the option of photographing rather than shooting birds. In the early 1900s members of the Audubon Society began substituting a Christmas bird count for traditional holiday hunting excursions, identifying over a hundred different species in the Denver area.[6]

The more bloodthirsty followed the adventures of Vice-President Theodore Roosevelt, whose 1901 Colorado hunting party bagged 14 cougars, including one, eight feet long, weighing 227 pounds. Such enthusiastic, unsupervised hunting threatened to wipe out declining species such as grizzly bears and mountain sheep. At the urging of conservationists, the Colorado Game and Fish Commission began charging $1 for a hunting license in 1903, using the revenue to regulate the sport. Beginning in 1910, the commissioners annually stocked the state's streams with millions of trout. They also promoted Colorado as a prime target for out-of-state hunters, who helped put the state among the top four in mule deer, big horn sheep, and elk kills.[7] While hunters harvested game, firms such as Colorado Tent and Awning, Redfield Gun Sight Corporation, and Wright and McGill, maker of fishing hooks and rods, reaped profits from the sporting enthusiasm.

Colorado's mountains, once regarded as obstacles, became playgrounds for hunters, hikers, campers, climbers, and skiers. Denverites founded the Colorado Mountain Club in 1912 to sponsor outings, lobby for conservation causes, and promote winter sports. Their first major victory came in 1916 with the creation of Rocky Mountain National Park north of the city. The club also supported the expansion of the Denver Mountain Parks, which grew to 20,000 acres by 1940. As early as 1914, Carl Blaurock and other club members set up a rope tow on Charles

Rilliet's Lookout Mountain ranch, taking a tire off a Model T Ford and fastening their ski tow rope to the axle. Five years later, the ski enthusiasts moved to Genesee Mountain, the first Denver Mountain Park. There, the club built a ski hut and a jump. After the Moffat Tunnel was completed in 1927, skiers took the train to the West Portal of the tunnel, where railroad construction shacks were converted into ski huts. Nearby, the Arlberg Club, founded in 1933 by monied Denverites, began grooming the ski slopes that ultimately became Winter Park.

After the invention of cable bindings (1931) and steel edges (1934), Thor Groswold opened a factory in Denver to manufacture high-quality, inexpensive, oaken skis. In 1937, the May Company, a department store that sold Groswold's skis, installed a rope tow at Berthoud Pass. The next year, Groswold and Clark Blickensderfer set up another rope tow at Loveland Pass. Across Berthoud Pass, the Winter Park ski area was made easily accessible to holidayers in 1936 when the D&RG began hauling skiers up from Denver, establishing an ongoing ski train tradition. An expanded Winter Park opened in 1941 as Colorado's first large ski area, complete with a T-bar lift. Denver was on its way to becoming America's ski capital.

Sunny days with warm "snow-eater" chinook winds regularly, if briefly, dispelled winter's grip, inspiring the *Denver Post's* masthead boast, "Climate Capital of the World." Generally mild winters encouraged Denverites to keep golf courses and tennis courts open year-round. Plentiful open space and a health-conscious population helped make outdoor recreation a major industry. Mile Highers differed from other city dwellers, according to travel writer Edward Hungerford, in that they "can build fires, cook and live in the open. A Denver society woman is as particular about her khakis as about evening frocks."[8]

For those seeking concentrated fun close to home, Elitch Gardens (1890), Manhattan Beach (1891), and Lakeside Amusement Park (1908) opened within a few miles of each other in northwest Denver. Manhattan Beach, an amusement park at Sloan's Lake, burned in 1908 and, although resurrected, languished after World War I. Lakeside, originally named White City, proved more durable. Billing itself "the Coney Island of the West," it opened at West Forty-sixth and Sheridan Boulevard. The 150-foot-high Casino Tower entrance, highlighted by 16,000 electric lights, housed a German Rathskeller and the Casino Theater. The 160-acre park, wrapped around Lake Rhoda, included a roller coaster, a ballroom, swimming pool, burro rides, ice and roller skating rinks, lawn tennis, ping

Mary Elitch, cavorting here with bruins in the bear pit, made Elitch Gardens the grand champion of Denver's amusement parks. (Denver Public Library, Western History Department.)

pong, and a miniature railroad.[9] In an effort to surpass Elitch's, investors, including the brewer Adolph Zang, spent over $750,000 on Lakeside. In 1933, during the Great Depression, the financially troubled park was purchased by Ben Krasner, whose family still operates it.

Elitch's mixed high culture with low. Besides the usual carnival attractions, Mary Elitch, who after her husband John Elitch's death presided over the park until a few years before her death in 1936, gave the city a theater, classical music, and a small zoo. Elitch's picturesque wooden theater, which opened in 1897, was destined to become the longest continually operating summer stock theater in the United States. The zoo, which included pajama-clad monkeys and an albino buffalo, did not do as well, and gradually its denizens disappeared.

Long before the formation of the Denver Symphony Orchestra in 1934, Mary Elitch recruited the Italian-born violinist, Rafaello Cavallo, to present the classics in a town not renowned for its commitment to fine music. Maestro Cavallo, who recovered from the TB that brought him to Colorado, also conducted the Denver Municipal Band and theater orchestras. Although his performances were among the city's best, he sometimes displeased critics such as the columnist Polly Pry, who complained that the *Serenade Rococo* had "been inflicted twice again upon a suffering public."[10]

Paul Whiteman, a viola player for Cavallo, attained national prominence with his big dance band. Another of the city's musical stars, George Morrison, Sr., began his career singing in African-American churches. In the 1920s he went to New York for a Columbia Records contract and the big time in Harlem clubs. Morrison continued to live in Denver, however, and opened the Morrison Club in Five Points. He also helped make other Welton Street jazz spots, such as the Rossonian Hotel Club and Benny Hooper's Ex-Serviceman's Club, legendary resorts for jazz buffs. Morrison's long career included a command performance for the king and queen of England and over 300 musical compositions before his death in 1974.[11]

While the younger generation experimented with jazz, others applauded plays, concerts, and light operas at Elitch's. Theatergoers were treated to a galaxy of stars including Denverite Douglas Fairbanks, Sr. Mary Elitch kept the public amused with the park's celebrated miniature train, its hand-carved merry-go-round, and its terrifying roller coaster. Lovers could dance at the Trocadero ballroom, and thrill seekers could watch balloon ascensions. Mary herself was a prime attraction, dashing about in a sulky pulled by her pet ostrich, cuddling bears and lions, and unsqueamishly exhibiting 30 healthy rattlesnakes. When her extravagance and generosity led to debt, John K. Mullen bought the park. He sold it to John M. Mulvihill, who allowed Mary, "The Lady of the Gardens," to reign from her cottage on the grounds. After Mulvihill died in 1930, his son-in-law and grandchildren, the Gurtler family, continued to operate Elitch's into the 1990s.

Denverites first saw moving pictures at Elitch's when Thomas A. Edison's Vitascope made its local debut. The invention proved so popular that a Vitascope Annex was added to the theater. To Mary's dismay, the "flicks" sometimes drew larger audiences than the live theater. Moving picture projectors soon found homes in other theaters, as well as in saloons and in pool halls. Venturesome shopkeepers stuck up signs, "Any Seat, Any Time 5 Cents," and converted their stores to nickelodeons where fuzzy figures cavorted in flickering light on the magic screen. By 1912 the Police Department was discouraging new applicants for the $100 annual movie house license because the city already had "55 moving picture shows and only about 12 are making expenses."[12]

Anne Evans, daughter of Governor Evans, devoted her life to enriching the culture of Colorado's cow-town capital. Largely through her efforts, the Central City Opera House became the shining example of how dying mountain mining towns might recycle their past to mine tourists. (Denver Public Library, Western History Department.)

For a time, live theater competed vigorously. Melodrama drew audiences to the Curtis, while Shakespeare attracted highbrows to the Denham. The Orpheum, which opened in 1903 at 1537 Welton, emerged as Denver's great vaudeville house. Groucho, Harpo, Chico, and Zeppo filled the place with wisecracks and slapstick, with Mother Marx coaching backstage. Will Rogers did his rope tricks there, and Sarah Bernhardt, the French tragedienne, included the theater on one of her "Farewell Tours" after her leg amputation. Curtis Street emerged as Denver's Great White Way, illuminated by 10,000 electric lights and the marquees of 13 theaters. Lights started going out after the 1929 stock market crash as stage shows increasingly surrendered to movies. With 48 theaters vying in 1930 for depression customers, some of the houses introduced "skin flicks." As an alternative, proponents of wholesome entertainment provided theaters with views of mountain parks.

Although most legitimate theaters capitulated to Hollywood, socialites Ida Kruse McFarlane and Anne Evans fought the trend by restoring the Central City Opera House, an 1878 landmark designed by Colorado's first licensed architect, Robert Roeschlaub. Central City opened its summer play festival in 1932 with Lillian Gish in *Camille*. Down in the Mile High City, the University Civic Theatre, backed by the University of Denver, kept theater alive. So did Colorado Woman's College's productions, directed by Homer L. Grout, and several small stages, such as the theater in the basement of a bungalow at 4201 Hooker.

Sensing the money to be made in movies, Harry E. Huffman, a pharmacist, opened the Bide-a-Wee movie house next to his West Colfax drugstore in 1909. He prospered and bought the Thompson theater on East Colfax, renaming it the Bluebird. During the depression Hoffman acquired one theater after another: the Tabor; the Broadway; the Orpheum; the Rialto; the Denver; and the 2,100-seat Paramount, an art deco dream designed by architect Temple Buell. On East Colfax and Race, "Mr. Movies" Huffman built the Aladdin, a pleasure dome vaguely imitating the Taj Mahal, where Denverites saw their first talking picture,

Don Juan, starring John Barrymore. In honor of the Aladdin, Huffman ornamented the hood of his Cadillac with a jinn's lamp. From the plans for the monastery in Columbia Picture's 1937 film *Lost Horizon,* Huffman built his mansion, *Shangri-La,* at Leetsdale Drive and Colorado Boulevard. The Mayan Theater at 115 Broadway aped Central American ruins, and the Isis on Curtis recalled Egyptian tombs.

Stately if occasionally flamboyant buildings, carefully tended parks and parkways, and lively theaters allowed the Queen City of the Plains to believe that she was truly regal, that her cow-town days had passed. But that delusion vanished every January beginning in 1906 when the National Western Stock Show brought farmers, ranchers, sheep, hogs, and cows to town. The 1907 event, housed in a monster tent 150-by-175 feet, included a mutant cow four feet long and less than three feet tall. By 1909 the show, with its rodeo and livestock sales, had moved into a permanent building — to the dismay of those who did not want to further fertilize the city's hayseed image.

Those who touted Denver as a cultured and a law-abiding place were also appalled at the lawlessness born of a ban on alcohol. Colorado, four years ahead of nationwide Prohibition, embarked on a great experiment: On New Year's Day 1916 the highest state went dry. The folks at Heildelberg Cafe in downtown Denver mournfully marked New Year's Eve, 1915, by singing "Last Night Was the End of the World." Some 600 saloon cats and a motley collection of tavern hounds also had cause to lament, for when the bars closed they lost their homes. Antiliquor crusaders, led by Adrianna Hungerford of the Women's Christian Temperance Union and the Reverend Arthur J. Finch of the Anti-Saloon League, rejoiced. A majority of Denverites wanted the right to drink, but sober citizens outside the city had imposed prohibition on all in a statewide 1914 vote. Hungerford and Finch soon learned that it was easier to pass a law than to enforce it. Denver tried to block the rules by asserting its right to permit the sale of liquor. Prohibitionists stopped that. Tipplers then squirmed through another escape hatch: Since they could buy alcohol for use as medicine, many became conveniently ill until late in 1918 when voters closed that loophole.

Stricter laws did not work. When Philip S. Van Cise became Denver's district attorney in 1920, he asked Police Captain August Hanebuth: "How about bootlegging, do you have much?" Hanebuth replied: "Have much! The town's full of it. You can't enforce that law. Every soft-drink parlor, pool-hall, whorehouse, hotel or resort of any kind can get it for you in five minutes."[13] North Denver gang members such as young Bruno Mauro sold bootleg liquor at the north end of the Twentieth Street viaduct where buyers could purchase $1 pints. Rich people did not have to visit the viaducts. Testifying before the Denver Grand Jury in October 1921, Judge Benjamin Lindsey spotlighted the rumored misdoings of millionaire oilman Henry Blackmer and other socialites, "with their wine parties or wild parties and their occasional orgies for which their society is so well noted."[14] Lindsey implied that Blackmer had a vault in his mansion at 975 East Seventh Avenue where he stashed the booze he had delivered by the truckload. Prohibition, Lindsey argued, had become class legislation: The rich easily evaded the rules, while the poor went to jail.

The law also hurt legitimate brewers such as Adolph Coors. To survive, Coors produced malted milk and near beer, a pale version of the real thing. Denver's largest brewery, the Zang Brewing Company, died during the dry spell, although it tried making near beer and ice cream in a futile effort to stay afloat. The vacuum was filled by smugglers and small-scale still operators. At the old Oak Leaf Dairy on the Brighton Road north of Denver, bootleggers fermented a potent concoction in a 100-gallon tank filled with grain, water, yeast, and the carcasses of mice, rats, rabbits, and cats.[15] Unsavory brews spawned unsavory characters. Many were petty crooks out to make a few bucks; some were poor people driven to extremes. "My husband couldn't find work and this was the only way I could think of to make a few dollars so we could eat," explained Millie Stowell when she was caught with 50 bottles of home-made beer.[16] Others operated on a grander scale. Pueblo's Pete Carlino tried to dominate Denver's whisky trade until he was murdered in 1931, leaving the field to local operators such as the Smaldone brothers, Roxie Stone, and Joe Roma.

Like Carlino, Roma found that crime did not always pay. He was found dead, his body riddled with 14 bullets, at his home, 3504 Vallejo Street, on February 18, 1933. Near the "little half-pint big shot of Denver gangland" lay his shattered mandolin and a music stand "overturned by a convulsive kick as a shudder of death ran through his slight body." Thus, reported Bruce Gustin of the *Denver Post,* Roma's "murderers wrote a bloody finish to his checkered career."[17] By the time he died, voters were ready to kill prohibition. On November 8, 1932, Coloradans abandoned the state dry law, with Denver voters ap proving by a margin of nearly two to one. A year later, the nation lifted the federal ban on alcohol by repealing the Eighteenth Amendment to the Constitution.

Denverites who wanted to water down the city's "gin-town" image promoted culture. By 1922 they had established a small art museum in a Capitol Hill mansion, Chappell House, at Thirteenth and Logan. Stock-broker George E. Cranmer, whose wife, Jean Chappell, had donated the museum, argued that art had value: "A ball of our Golden clay can be made into a dish worth a few cents or the same clay might be made into a porcelain worth many dollars."[18] In 1925 the city gave the museum a $3,000 budget and in 1932 provided space for some of its collections in the new City and County Building. Denverites additionally took pride in their fledgling symphony directed by Horace E. Tureman, which turned professional in 1934.[19] And they enjoyed listening to the Denver Municipal Band under Henry Everett Sachs, whose music from the bandstand at City Park complemented the ever-changing hues of the illuminated lake fountain.

Boosters could also boast about Denver's radio stations. William "Doc" Reynolds helped plug the city into its radio days with amateur broadcasts in 1919. A dentist with more passion for Marconi than for molars, Reynolds started selling wireless receivers in 1920. To entertain his customers, he established KLZ in 1922 — the city's first commercial station. Transmitting from his home at 1124 South University Boulevard, he and his wife Naomi filled the air with the sound of music: She played the piano, he tooted the saxophone, and other musicians dropped in to add variety to the programming.

KLZ attracted a rival in 1923 when KFEL began broadcasting. A more formidable foe appeared late in 1924 when General Electric's KOA went on the air. Aspiring to reach a nationwide audience, KOA built a studio and two 150-foot towers on Krameria Street between Thirteenth and Fourteenth avenues. By 1934 it had boosted its wattage to 50,000, constructed a 478-foot antenna 12 miles east of town, and built elaborate studios at 1625 California. It gave Denver a loud voice throughout the Rocky Mountain Empire and the Great Plains. With luck, radio buffs in Australia, England, and Alaska sometimes picked up KOA, which, for the 1934 dedication of its new transmitter, greeted its fans with a song:

This is station KOA
Saying hello U.S.A.
We're here to do our best
With music from the West.[20]

Sometimes, pioneer broadcasters enlivened their regular fare of music, news, and features with special offerings. In 1924, KLZ provided the first regional play-by-play coverage of a football game, describing a contest between the Universities of Denver and Colorado. The next year, a KLZ telephone hookup brought Denverites the inauguration of President Calvin Coolidge. KOA covered the blast that opened the Moffat Tunnel in 1927 by stringing over three miles of wire into the bore. A year later engineers trudged through snow to the top of Pikes Peak to broadcast back to Denver over short-wave relays and telephone lines. Less successful was KOA's attempt to transmit the commentary of a downhill skier in 1937 — the excited athlete forgot to talk.

Network programs increasingly crowded out local offerings on KOA and KLZ during the 1930s. KOA created a concert show for national syndication in the mid-1930s and produced a mystery titled "The Black Fear," featuring "authentic voodoo music just for the background of this drama which is laid in a Louisiana swamp."[21] Neither these shows nor the efforts of numerous local disc jockeys and news people, including Starr Yelland, Joe Flood, and Ray Perkins, seriously dented the popularity of national favorites such as "Amos 'n Andy," "Helen Trent," and "Duffy's Tavern." By 1948, KOA, KLZ, and KFEL had been joined by three other commercial stations — KVOD, KMYR, and KTLN — giving Denver six radio outlets. By then radio was big business. A combine including theater magnate Harry Huffman bought KLZ in 1948 for nearly a million dollars. Four years later Mayor Quigg Newton and others paid an estimated $2 million for KOA, and in 1954 KLZ was resold for $3.5 million.[22]

For intellectual fare Denverites looked to the Denver Public Library, which moved into its Civic Center quarters in 1910 and flourished under the directorships of Chalmers Hadley (1911–1924) and Malcolm G. Wyer (1924–1951). Hadley created a branch library system using $160,000 in gifts from Andrew Carnegie to build neighborhood libraries including Decker, Woodbury, Byers, Smiley, and Park Hill. Wyer did not enjoy Carnegie's munificence but found generous local supporters, particularly real estate tycoon Frederick Ross and the city's cultural grande dame, Anne Evans. Ross money established four more branch libraries, while Evans, a member of the Library Commission for over 30 years, pushed the creation of the University of Denver Library School, where Wyer became the first dean.

Anne Evans supported another of Wyer's favorite projects, the library's Western History Department. Novelist Willa Cather planted the idea by suggesting to Wyer that saving regional material should be a top priority. A sharp bargainer, Wyer bought one bankrupt book dealer's 6,000-volume collection for $3,200. When a bibliophilic businessman got in trouble with his creditors and his bibliophobic wife, Wyer paid him $7,500 for 19,000 volumes. Through such astute deals and by courting donors such as novelist William E. Barrett, who owned a massive aeronautical collection, Wyer more than doubled the library's holdings. Cataloged books alone increased from 242,388 when he arrived to 527,401 when he retired in 1951.[23]

Denverites read a lot — in 1940 the library circulated more than 1.8 million books and magazines. Local authors who gained national recognition were particularly appreciated. Some, such as Damon Runyon of *Guys and Dolls* fame, and the journalists H. Allen Smith and Gene Fowler, left Denver. Others made the city home. Barrett gained national attention in 1951 with the publication *The Left Hand of God,* and again in 1962 when his *The Lilies of the Field* was made into a movie. William McLeod Raine and Marion Castle drew on Western themes for their best-selling novels. The London-born Raine, who came to Denver to recover from TB, wrote over 70 westerns. Castle's *The Golden Fury* sold over a million copies. Another popular writer, Lenora Mattingly Weber, pleased generations of teenagers with her Beany Malone stories.

Of all Denver writers, Mary Coyle Chase became the most famous. Her play *Harvey,* winner of the Pulitzer Prize in 1945, became a staple of U.S. theater. Chase, wife of *Rocky Mountain News* city editor Robert Chase, and a *News* reporter herself, wrote her first play, *Me Third,* in 1936 for Denver's Federal Theater. Produced on Broadway as *Now You've Done It,* the whimsical production failed to please the *New York Times* and soon closed. *Harvey,* on the other hand, appealed to Americans weary of war and eager to laugh. Proud Denverites never realized that the suffocating society that drove Elwood P. Dowd into conversing with Harvey, the big, white, imaginary rabbit, was theirs.[24]

Since local tastes tended toward popular fiction, scholars and poets rarely received proper recognition. LeRoy Hafen came to the Colorado State Historical Society in 1924 as state historian and editor of the society's historical journal, *The Colorado Magazine.* In the 30 years before his 1954 retirement, Hafen wrote, co-authored, or edited over 50 books. He also wrote dozens of articles and edited hundreds of others, providing an encyclopedic coverage of much of Colorado's history.

While Hafen explored the state's past, Hannah Marie Wormington dug into archaeology. Born in Denver in 1914, Wormington attended the University of Denver, Radcliffe College, and Harvard, from which she

Elephantine promotion and unabashed sensationalism made the *Denver Post* the best-selling newspaper in what co-editors Bonfils and Tammen called "The Rocky Mountain Empire." (Denver Public Library, Western History Department.)

obtained a Ph.D. in 1954. For 31 years curator of archaeology at the Denver Museum of Natural History, she produced a classic study of prehistoric peoples titled *Ancient Man in North America.* In 1958 the American Society of Archaeologists recognized her many accomplishments by electing her its first woman president. Ruth Underhill, another pioneer woman scholar, studied under the anthropologists Ruth Benedict and Franz Boas at Columbia University in the 1930s. Her interest in Native Americans led her to write over a dozen books including the widely read *Red Man's America: A History of Indians in the United States* (1953). After retiring from the University of Denver in 1952, she wrote and lectured until shortly before she died in 1984, a week short of her hundredth birthday.

Of numerous Denver poets, Thomas Hornsby Ferril gained wide national attention. Critics, including Carl Sandburg and Bernard De Voto, acclaimed Ferril for books such as *High Passage, Westering,* and *Words for Denver.* For over half a century Ferril served bons mots to local cognoscenti. With his wife, Helen, he also edited *The Rocky Mountain Herald,* a weekly journal flaunting its 1860s origins, in which he presented his opinions, observations, and poems. The *Herald's* tiny circulation, mostly to lawyers who scanned the legal notices that supported the paper, reflected the town's shallow commitment to serious poetry. On the other hand, Gene Lindberg, who wrote homespun verse for the *Denver Post*, pleased a wide audience.

The all-time best-selling book on Denver, Gene Fowler's *Timber Line* (1933), appalled serious historians and boosters but tickled the popular fancy with an uproarious, if not always factual, account of the *Denver Post*. Many hated the *Post*, but practically everyone read it, captivated by its large headlines, red ink, photographs, and sensational stories. Other dailies pondered world affairs; the *Post* asked, in banner headlines: "Does It Hurt to Be Born?"

Since its 1859 founding, the *Rocky Mountain News* had never seen anything like the *Post*. At least two dozen dailies and many more weeklies had come and gone before 1900. Few of them were memorable. The *Denver Tribune's* claim to fame was its managing editor between 1881 and 1883, the barfly and poet Eugene Field. One of his children's poems, "Wynken, Blynken and Nod," inspired the statue that Mayor Speer placed in Washington Park. Field's small frame house, originally at 315 West Colfax, also came to rest in the park when, in 1930, Malcolm Wyer and Maggie [Molly] Brown saved it by making it a branch library.[25]

In 1884 the *Tribune* merged with the *Denver Republican* owned by Nathaniel Hill. After Senator Hill's death in 1900, his son Crawford took charge. The *Republican* voiced the conservative, antilabor sentiments of the city's elite, inspiring Judge Lindsey to call it "a corporation organ."[26] In 1913, John Shaffer, a transplanted Chicago millionaire, bought it, the *News*, and the *Times*, combining them into the *News*. The *Denver Express*, a liberal paper founded in 1906, gently competed with the *News*, but the *Denver Post*, which surpassed the *News's* circulation in 1901, was a far more dangerous adversary.

The *Post*, which took as its motto "First in Everything," prospered because its publishers knew that readers wanted entertainment: contests; giveaways; and outlandish stunts. The paper's 1925 rabbit hunt netted 120,000, half of which were given away at *Post* headquarters on Sixteenth and Champa.[27] On another occasion the *Post* captured national attention by hiring a comely lass to be a new Eve and sending her, as scantily clad as Tarzan's Jane, to lead the natural life in Rocky Mountain National Park. The paper's gossip columnist Polly Pry organized another crusade-stunt, a successful effort to have the cannibal Alfred Packer pardoned from the penitentiary where he had languished for years after having been convicted of manslaughter.[28]

Consorting with cannibals apparently did not bother Frederick Gilmer Bonfils and Harry Heye Tammen, the *Post's* publishers, whose own backgrounds occasionally turned people's stomachs. Tammen had come to Denver in 1880. Roly-poly and good-natured, he bounced from job to job — bartending, curio selling, magazine publishing — without much success until 1895, when he convinced Bonfils, a debonair Kansas Citian rumored to be a lottery con man, to put up $12,500 to buy the *Post*. The duo also dabbled in other enterprises, ranging from selling insurance to peddling coal. Tammen even persuaded Bonfils to back a circus, the Sells-Floto, which grew from a furfuraceous dog and pony show when the *Post* bought it in 1903 to one of the nation's major big tops in 1920 when Tammen's declining health forced him to sell it. The circus traveled, but it was especially dear to Denverites because it wintered in the city in Jefferson Park at Twenty-third and Eliot. There, Tammen saved money by feeding the tigers the carcasses of dead dogs and mules.

Bonfils also put profit first. He threatened merchants with exposés if they did not advertise in the the *Post*. In 1922 the paper decried questionable Wyoming oil leases granted by the federal government to the Sinclair Oil Company but the *Post* dropped its investigation after Harry F. Sinclair paid Bonfils and Tammen. When the ensuing Teapot Dome scandal drew national attention, Bonfils's shenanigans were probed by Congress and condemned by the American Society of Newspapers. *Editor and Publisher* magazine said that Denver was "living under the cloud of contemptible journalism." More-vitriolic Colorado editors called Bonfils a "hyena" and a "cootie covered rat."[29]

Tammen died in 1924, leaving several of his millions to Children's Hospital. At age 72, Bonfils was felled in 1933 by an ear infection. Samuel Johnson, a local jurist, remembered the handsome publisher as "feared and hated, with none to praise or admire his achievements, and few to mourn his passing."[30] Bonfils's daughter Helen gained control of the *Post*. She and her sister, May, despite their bitter feuding, both returned to the community in charity much of what their father had taken in greed.

John Shaffer, who languidly watched over the *News* and the *Times* from his Ken Caryl ranch 20 miles southwest of town, sold the paper in 1926 to the Scripps-Howard chain, which also controlled the anemic *Denver Express*. The three papers consolidated as the *News* in an effort to catch up with the *Post*, which had reached a circulation of 160,000 while the *News* had plummeted to 30,000. Briefly, in the mid-1930s, Scripps-Howard hoped that Helen Bonfils would sell out, but she remained faithful to the paper that under William Shepherd, editor from 1933 to 1946, piled up profits.[31]

Between 1900 and 1945, Denver made modest strides as a cultural center, took often embarrassing steps as a newspaper town, and gained national attention for its outdoor recreational opportunities. Sports, radio, clubs, and entertainment helped bring the community together. But though the mountains, the parks, the movies, and the theaters beckoned all, not everyone had the time or the money to enjoy them. Ethnic and economic cleavages divided the community and led to tension. Seeing others with leisure and wealth, many working people sought to improve their lives by organizing labor unions to agitate for better wages, hours, and working conditions.

CHAPTER 15

Working People

> We will at all times and under all conditions espouse the cause of the producing masses . . . with the object of arousing them from the lethargy into which they have sunk and which makes them willing to live in squalor, while their masters revel in the wealth stolen from labor.
>
> Western Federation of Miners
> *Miners' Magazine,* January 1900[1]

As WW I veterans came home in 1919, well-wishers, marching bands, and happy troops jammed Denver's streets. The *Post* estimated that a crowd of a 100,000, nearly 40 percent of the city's population, welcomed the returning 157th Infantry in late April. Less than two weeks later, the 168th Field Hospital paraded. Memorial Day featured a strutting pageant including aging veterans from the Spanish-American and Civil wars. In June, Lieutenant Colonel Rice W. Means led another march, and in July the 815th, an African-American outfit including 270 Denverites, arrived. Beneath their apparent joy lurked sadness and uncertainty. Over a thousand Coloradans had perished in the war. Those who returned often came home to find that someone in their family had died from Spanish influenza, which killed over 1,500 Denverites in late 1918 and early 1919. The war was over, but peace brought its own problems.

Mayor William F. Mills, Speer's successor, assured the young men: "You will be given every opportunity to emulate and excel in civic capacities your generous accomplishments as soldiers."[2] The mayor promised what he could not deliver. By 1920, when the corpses of dead

Influenza Epidemic of 1918–1919

Miranda was ill, delirious with Spanish influenza. Her landlady wanted her out. "I tell you they must come for her now, or I'll put her on the sidewalk. . . . I tell you, this is a plague, a plague, my God, and I've got a houseful of people to think about."[1]

Miranda Gay, the central character in Katherine Anne Porter's short novel, *Pale Horse, Pale Rider*, recovered. Porter, a columnist for the *Rocky Mountain News* in 1918, also survived the flu in Denver. Hundreds of others were less fortunate. Between September 1918 and June 1919, influenza and its complications, particularly pneumonia, killed over 1,500 Denverites.

Misnamed "Spanish influenza" because Spain had suffered an early attack, the flu may have originated in the United States in spring 1918. In a mutated and more dangerous form, the virus reappeared in August, striking first at East Coast military bases and then rapidly spreading to civilians.

Denver's first flu fatality, Blanche Kennedy, a University of Denver student, died September 27. Without an effective vaccine and unable to cure the disease, physicians concentrated on prevention. Initially, they advised people to cover their mouths when coughing, to wash their hands, to shun crowds. Those simple nostrums did not check the flu. With the death rate mounting, Doctor William H. Sharpley, Denver's manager of health, ordered churches, theaters, and schools to close October 6. Nine days later he also forbade outdoor gatherings. Fatalities rose for a while, then in early November they fell. On November 11, the day World War I ended, Sharpley lifted his closing and antigathering orders.

Health regulations would have been ignored that day, anyway. Thousands jammed downtown streets, shouting and yelling, trailing tin cans behind cars and bicycles to add to the din. Over 8,000 poured into the City Auditorium to sing and to listen to speeches. In the evening, theaters, many of them redecorated during their idle weeks, reopened to entertain "monster crowds." At the Strand, the sublime Ethel Barrymore starred in *Our Mrs. McChesney*. At the Broadway, vamp Theda Bara shimmied in *Salome*.

Unfortunately, the Armistice festivities triggered a second wave of sickness. Deaths skyrocketed in late November, causing Sharpley to reinstate the ban on public gatherings. He also ordered shoppers and streetcar passengers to wear gauze masks. The rules proved unpopular, especially since people were not certain that the measures would work. Theater owners objected to closing again, and many people refused to wear masks. Sharpley quickly backed down and allowed theaters and churches to reopen; a week later he revoked the mask order. The flu then ran its course, peaking during the week of December 7–14 when it killed 201. After that it declined rapidly. There was only one death on December 30, 1918.

Over 13,000 Denverites caught the disease; one in nine sufferers died. For the survivors, including Katherine Anne Porter, the war's end and escape from the flu meant rebirth: "No more war, no more plague, only the dazed silence that follows the ceasing of heavy guns; noiseless houses with the shades drawn, empty streets, the dead cold light of tomorrow. Now there would be time for everything."[2]

---

[1] Katherine Anne Porter, *Pale Horse, Pale Rider: Three Short Novels* (New York: Modern Library, 1965), p. 232.
[2] Ibid., p. 264.

doughboys began arriving for burial, luckier veterans were selling apples on street corners. Every evening, if they could spare the price of a newspaper, they could read the *Denver Post*'s front-page slogan, " 'Tis a Privilege to Live in Colorado."

The paper's publishers, Frederick Bonfils and Henry Tammen, had reason to be grateful — they were making millions. "Who does not know that money is the heart's blood of these men," reporter George Creel said of his bosses.[3] The *Post* doled out a 15¢ daily travel allowance to its reporters until Bonfils discovered that some of them were buying street-car tokens for 12.5¢ and pocketing the difference. After that, the parsimonious publishers distributed tokens. "Saving a nickel," Creel wrote of Bonfils, "bathed him in content."[4] Complaints were useless. Despite decades of organizing and agitating, wage earners at the *Post* and throughout the city had little clout. Bonfils kept his nickels; when he died in 1933 he left his wife, Belle, and his daughters, May and Helen, over $14 million. Many workers, living on less than $1,500 a year, could scarcely conceive of such a fortune — a string of dollars that would have reached from Denver to Chicago. Ordinary folks did know, however, that often they did not have enough — a realization that caused some to organize and join labor unions.

Typographers at the *Rocky Mountain News* had formed Denver's first union in April 1860. During the 1870s tailors, iron molders, stonecutters, and railroad firemen, engineers, and conductors had organized. By the late 1870s the Knights of Labor had enrolled coal miners in Boulder and Jefferson counties, and in 1882 the Denver Trades and Labor Assembly brought five local unions together. The same year, Joseph Buchanan, a printer who had come to Denver from Missouri in 1878, founded *The Labor Enquirer*, which under his editorship and that of his successor, Burnette G. Haskell, fought for workers.

Colorado's first major strike, an 1880 miners' walkout in Leadville, had failed miserably, but two successful short actions against the Union Pacific Railroad in 1884 led thousands to join Denver's unions. A failed strike against the Denver and Rio Grande Railroad the next year showed the new converts that labor's road would be rocky, but boom times in the late 1880s led to high wages for skilled workers and to increasing organization among craftsmen.

The Depression of 1893 temporarily derailed the labor movement. Employers reduced wages and laid workers off. By mid-1893, 14,000 laborers — one-fourth of the city's work force — were unemployed. The Trades and Labor Assembly fed their comrades at River Front Park and wished them Godspeed as they left the state. Many of those who stayed recognized their need for organization and for cooperation between craftsmen and common laborers. A new union, the Western Federation of Miners (WFM), which embraced skilled and unskilled workers, had by the late 1890s organized many miners and smelter men. In 1901 the WFM located its headquarters in Denver, where its ideology of solidarity influenced the Denver Trades and Labor Assembly. "All for One, One for All" proclaimed William D. "Big Bill" Haywood, the WFM's secretary-treasurer.[5]

WILLIAM D. HAYWOOD
FOR GOVERNOR

Big Bill Haywood was a star labor organizer and editor of *Miner's Magazine*. While behind bars in Idaho on trumped-up charges, he ran for governor of Colorado and received 16,015 votes. (Amon Carter Museum, Mazzulla Collection.)

Strikes, boycotts, violence, and political pressure gave labor weapons in its struggle for shorter workdays, better conditions, and fair treatment. Joseph Buchanan advised workers to avoid violence, but his weekly newspaper published the price of dynamite. After the 1885 D&RG strike failed, Buchanan promoted an ill-fated utopia in Mexico for displaced strikers. Burnette Haskell, an outspoken socialist, plotted revolution. When his plans went awry, he left Colorado to live in a cooperative colony in California. Joe Murray, a Knight of Labor, ran for Congress as a Prohibitionist, arguing that alcohol was the workingman's worst enemy. Others, seeing salvation in education, established a reading room where the proletariat could bone up on Karl Marx. To protest high rents, Denver's Union Labor party resolved "to at once purchase tents and secure ground upon which to pitch the same . . . locating our tents in a body together."[6]

Political action appealed to many unionists. In 1885 the State Legislature, swayed by labor's demands, required employers to provide seats for female clerks. Store owners dutifully put them in but then told women not to sit down on the job. Laws limiting child labor were enacted but did not stop the Overland Cotton Mills in South Denver, one of the city's largest employers, from exploiting children. The mills, which employed 240 loom operators, paid an average wage of $1.75 for an 11-hour day. At the turn of the century Judge Benjamin Lindsey charged that the mill workers "were practically slaves" and that "the children, unschooled, toiled at the machines first to liberate their parents, then to support them."[7]

Lindsey pressed for tougher laws. Yet, as late as 1910, the Colorado Bureau of Labor Statistics complained that inspectors had to rely on the young workers or their employers to obtain correct ages, "and very often one or both lied fluently." Even the bureau did not worry much about the youngsters employed in stores: "Of course it would be far better if they were in school, but if they are compelled to work they are fortunate in having such favorable surroundings."[8] In 1914, blandly overlooking the children working in sugar beet fields, it concluded: "It can safely be said that child labor does not exist in the state of Colorado."[9]

Laborers especially wanted to limit dangerous occupations to eight hours' work a day. Smelter men, who worked 12-hour shifts tending caldrons of molten metal, often demanded that their hours be reduced. Smelter owners opposed the idea. James Grant, ex-governor of Colorado and founder of the Grant smelter, spoke for the American Smelter and Refining Company (ASARCO): "The Western Federation of Miners now want eight hours. If we grant them that it will only be a question of time before they are asking for six."[10]

An eight-hour law passed by the legislature in 1899 gave workers no real relief; employers circumvented it by reducing wages. Angry workers joined the WFM and walked off their jobs in mid-June 1899. That strike failed. Then the Colorado Supreme Court further dashed workers' hopes by ruling that the law violated Colorado's constitution. A smelter man from Elyria told the Bureau of Labor Statistics: "We are slowly giving up our lives to the greed of the smelter trust that dividends may be larger. If the judges of the Supreme Court would have spent one day around the furnaces and roasters, inhaling the poison and sulfur that almost knocks one down at times, they would have understood that work in a smelter is very different from work upon a farm or in other places."[11]

Workers patiently pursued a political solution. In 1902, voters amended the state constitution to allow the legislature to mandate an eight-hour day, but lawmakers did nothing. Once again laborers confronted their bosses. Managers at the Argo Smelter placated their employees. Furnace men at the Globe and the Grant, who were making between $2.50 and $3 for 12 hours, also asked for reduced hours without reduced pay. ASARCO, which owned both plants, refused. Late in the evening of July 3, 1903, Smeltermen's Union Number 93 voted to strike. Earlier, they had heard Big Bill Haywood describe James Grant's Capitol

Hill mansion, where, Haywood reckoned, "a single piece of Grant's furniture would buy a dozen such houses and furniture" as the workers had. Haywood reminded the laborers of their children who had died and compared "the rustling silk of the wives of the smelter owners with the clatter of babies' skulls."[12]

Three hundred men marched from the Elyria town hall to the Grant smelter, where they pressed 125 workers to quit. Five untended furnaces cooled and froze. Then the strikers attacked the Globe, where they broke down fence gates and induced the night shift of 150 to walk out. Three of the Globe's seven furnaces froze. The strike dragged on — it was still nominally in effect in 1905. The Grant was permanently idled since ASARCO decided that rekindling its furnaces was not worth the cost. Its great smokestack, said Haywood, remained "a monument to the eight-hour day."[13] Production resumed at the Globe, where the police protected strikebreakers.

At every turn the WFM met strong opposition. Denver's Roman Catholic bishop, Nicholas C. Matz, told his flock to "choose between the Western Federation and your church." Haywood called Matz an "ecclesiastical parasite" and a "brazen and palpable liar." Matz saw an advantage to being in league with big business. He wrote to the New York financier J. P. Morgan: "Our timely stand in behalf of order and capitalism has had considerable to do with our successful opposition to strikes."[14] The bishop hinted that a donation would be welcome.

In April 1903, mattress manufacturer George Kindel and other business leaders organized a Citizens Alliance to fight the unions. Its president, James Craig, argued that the WFM, which rejected the moderate policies of the American Federation of Labor (AFL), was "teeming with socialists and anarchists."[15] Many agreed; WFM-inspired strikes in mining towns, particularly Cripple Creek and Telluride, had led to bloody clashes between strikers and strikebreakers.

Tension also ran high in Denver. Newspaperwoman Polly Pry vigorously opposed unions. Of Mary Harris Jones, a WFM organizer popularly known as Mother Jones, "God send us barrenness of motherhood if such as Jones be the alternative." Describing the miners as "a motley collection of filthy, ill smelling, uncouth, ignorant foreigners," Pry told of their "soup house, where they congregate three times a day to feed — no other word could describe their performance."[16] For her opinions, Pry almost paid dearly. Opening her door the evening of January 10, 1904, she was shot at by a large man in a derby hat. He missed. "I did not," Pry said, "enjoy the sensation of having the man shoot at me."[17]

Governor James H. Peabody employed the state militia to crush the Western Federation of Miners. This WFM protest poster was used as evidence in the arrest and imprisonment of union officials. (Denver Public Library, Western History Department.)

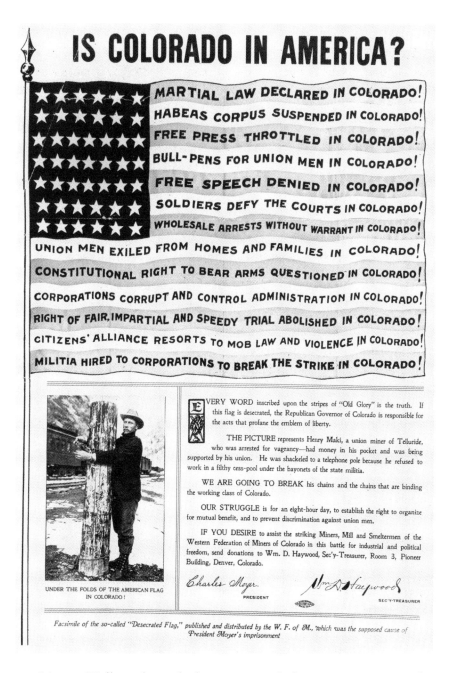

IS COLORADO IN AMERICA?

MARTIAL LAW DECLARED IN COLORADO!

HABEAS CORPUS SUSPENDED IN COLORADO!

FREE PRESS THROTTLED IN COLORADO!

BULL-PENS FOR UNION MEN IN COLORADO!

FREE SPEECH DENIED IN COLORADO!

SOLDIERS DEFY THE COURTS IN COLORADO!

WHOLESALE ARRESTS WITHOUT WARRANT IN COLORADO!

UNION MEN EXILED FROM HOMES AND FAMILIES IN COLORADO!

CONSTITUTIONAL RIGHT TO BEAR ARMS QUESTIONED IN COLORADO!

CORPORATIONS CORRUPT AND CONTROL ADMINISTRATION IN COLORADO!

RIGHT OF FAIR, IMPARTIAL AND SPEEDY TRIAL ABOLISHED IN COLORADO!

CITIZENS' ALLIANCE RESORTS TO MOB LAW AND VIOLENCE IN COLORADO!

MILITIA HIRED TO CORPORATIONS TO BREAK THE STRIKE IN COLORADO!

EVERY WORD inscribed upon the stripes of "Old Glory" is the truth. If this flag is desecrated, the Republican Governor of Colorado is responsible for the acts that profane the emblem of liberty.

THE PICTURE represents Henry Maki, a union miner of Telluride, who was arrested for vagrancy—had money in his pocket and was being supported by his union. He was shackled to a telephone pole because he refused to work in a filthy cess-pool under the bayonets of the state militia.

WE ARE GOING TO BREAK his chains and the chains that are binding the working class of Colorado.

OUR STRUGGLE is for an eight-hour day, to establish the right to organize for mutual benefit, and to prevent discrimination against union men.

IF YOU DESIRE to assist the striking Miners, Mill and Smeltermen of the Western Federation of Miners of Colorado in this battle for industrial and political freedom, send donations to Wm. D. Haywood, Sec'y-Treasurer, Room 3, Pioneer Building, Denver, Colorado.

Charles Moyer
PRESIDENT

Wm. D. Haywood
SEC'Y-TREASURER

UNDER THE FOLDS OF THE AMERICAN FLAG IN COLORADO!

Facsimile of the so-called "Desecrated Flag," published and distributed by the W. F. of M., which was the supposed cause of President Moyer's imprisonment

Merritt Walley, who picked up a seemingly lost purse in a vacant lot at Emerson and Colfax, was less fortunate. Boom! Boom! Walley was scattered about Capitol Hill by two 10-pound dynamite bombs. Alfred Horsley, better known as Harry Orchard, claimed to have done the deed. Walley, Orchard wrote, was an "innocent fellow."[18] The real target,

William H. Gabbert, chief justice of the Colorado Supreme Court, who usually walked across the lot, had taken a different route that day. Walley was Orchard's only Denver victim during summer 1905, when, Orchard alleged, he was trying to help the WFM kill its enemies. Orchard claimed that he stalked Governor James Peabody and considered murdering David Moffat. He planted an ineffective bomb at the gate of State Supreme Court Justice Luther M. Goddard's home. Barking dogs kept him from assassinating the state adjutant general, Sherman Bell. Orchard also failed to blow up a Globeville hotel filled with scab laborers. Orchard may have been lying when he implicated the WFM in his confessions, but whether he was telling the truth or not, businessmen believed that the WFM, as James Craig put it, was the "Western Federation of Murderers."[19]

Employers relaxed when they learned that on February 16, 1906, a deputy sheriff had kidnaped Haywood and dragged him off to Idaho to stand trial for plotting to kill ex-governor Frank Steunenberg, whom Orchard claimed to have dynamited. The jury did not believe Orchard's tale that WFM leaders had ordered the murder. Haywood, defended by Chicago attorney Clarence Darrow and Denver lawyer Edmund Richardson, was freed. City officials doused the lights on the Welcome Arch at Union Station when the labor leader triumphantly returned. Unchastised by the snub, Haywood continued to live at 3304 Franklin until 1917. Charged with sedition in Chicago for protesting U.S. involvement in World War I, he was convicted and sentenced to a 20-year penitentiary term that he evaded by jumping bail and fleeing to the Soviet Union. He died in Moscow in 1928. Half of his ashes were sent back to Chicago; the remainder were laid to rest in the Kremlin near Lenin's tomb.

Long before Haywood found his niche in Red Square, the WFM, which haltingly continued as the International Union of Mine, Mill, and Smelter Workers, had drifted into the left-wing backwaters of the union movement. Local unions, which had briefly embraced WFM ideals, veered to the right and allied with Samuel Gompers and the conservative American Federation of Labor, which bitterly opposed the WFM. The enactment of eight-hour legislation in 1913 further weakened militant unionism, although strife between labor and management continued in Colorado's coal-mining regions.

Wartime inflation reopened old wounds. Between 1914 and 1920 the price of food in Denver increased by 119 percent, fuel and lights went up 66 percent, and clothing costs soared 166 percent. Despite the increases,

Many struggling families raised poultry and vegetables to help make ends meet. A young chicken farmer tends her flock in the Platte River Bottoms. (Photo by Charles Lillybridge, Colorado Historical Society.)

some employers tried to reduce wages on the theory that there were plenty of unemployed ex-servicemen who would accept low pay. In 1919, Denver Tramway Company (DTC) drivers struck for three and a half days to prevent a pay cut from 48¢ to 34¢ an hour. Arbitrators later granted 58¢, a wage the company agreed to pay only until June 1, 1920. Workers countered by asking for 75¢ an hour, which the tramway refused to grant. On Sunday, August 1, 1920, employees overwhelmingly voted to strike.

The DTC was ready. It quickly turned its headquarters at Fourteenth and Arapahoe into a barracks for 175 scabs — "a bunch of thugs and toughs," said the union. The company installed showers, put in a barber's chair, and stocked a week's supply of food. John "Black Jack" Jerome, a professional union buster, imported strikebreakers, some of them University of California students, to drive the cars. Tramway general manager Frederic Hild predicted, "We won't find it difficult to

By recruiting scabs, hiring private guards, and enlisting police escorts, the Denver Tramway broke the 1920 strike of employees protesting a wage cut. (Denver Public Library, Western History Department.)

recruit as many men as we want at any time." Union leader A. H. Burt warned, "The city of Denver is going to get a taste of something it has never before witnessed."[20]

Only two streetcars ran on Monday, August 2. Denverites, few of whom owned automobiles, were forced to walk, ride bikes, or pay auto owners for rides. "This is war," declared Hild. "We are going to run cars and we are going to break the strike."[21] Gun-wielding strikebreakers shielded streetcars with wire mesh and armed them with canisters filled with soap suds to spray at strikers. Screens and suds were not sufficient. On August 5, a mob attacked a car at Fifteenth and California. Sixteen were injured in the fracas. Then the rioters laid siege to the DTC building. That evening strikers overturned four streetcars on Colfax. Strikebreakers sought sanctuary in the Immaculate Conception cathedral at Logan and Colfax. "You have punished your man," Father William Higgins assured the strikers as he rescued a battered scab, "now don't kill him."[22]

The mob also invaded the *Denver Post,* which had sided with the DTC. Tambon, Tammen's stuffed baby elephant, fell prey to the vandals, as did the paper's presses. The rioters rolled newsprint along downtown streets, making it appear that a giant had toilet-papered the city. The crowd surged south to the tramway's carbarns on Santa Fe Drive and Alaska Place, where some strikebreakers were quartered. Jerome ordered his men to fire. Four people died — one a striker, the others merely part of the throng. Shootings the next day brought the death toll to six. Fifty-two were injured.

Following declaration of martial law, federal troops enforced an uneasy peace. In November some DTC workers were rehired; others left town. Not until 1933 did they form another union. Without vacations, without overtime, they were working that year from 9 to 12 hours a day for 52¢ an hour — 6¢ less than they were making in May 1920, three months before their great strike. Their fate demonstrated labor's weakness. Even skilled workers did not do well. Carpenters considered themselves lucky to get $7 a day in 1920. Their efforts at organization reached a high-water mark that year. There were fewer carpenters' locals in Colorado in 1930 than there had been in 1920. Unionists founded a labor college in 1921 where workers could attend lectures on economics, but theory could not change the community, which remained strongly antiunion.

The depression of the 1930s further weakened labor's local position. As in 1893, work was scarce and employers cut costs by lowering wages. Samuel E. Ready, a carpenter, recalled that during those unhappy days, "my tools didn't come out of the closet for two years and a half."[23] Enfeebled unions withered; the carpenters, who cut the salary of their secretary-treasurer to $60 a year, did not meet as a state organization from 1933 to 1937, although some locals remained alive. Nationally, unions grew stronger, particularly after Congress passed the National Labor Relations Act of 1935. Colorado had tipped its hat to labor in 1933 by approving an antiinjunction law, but, as historian Ellen Slatkin has noted in her study of the Colorado State Federation of Labor, the measure was "short-lived and became a period piece of the Depression era."[24] It was weakened in 1941 when the Colorado Industrial Commission was granted the power to seek injunctions.

In Globeville, smelters declined after 1905, to be replaced by stockyards and meat-processing plants. Workers found that the big meat packers — Armour, Swift, Cudahy, and Hormel — were as opposed to unions as the smelter owners had been. Andrew Kelley, the first president of Denver's Packinghouse Union, thanked prolabor national laws, enacted in the 1930s, for forcing the companies to recognize his union. But, Kelley reported, recognition meant little since the packers frustrated labor's efforts to improve workers' pay. Kelley was blackballed from the industry.

World War II brought full employment and growth in union membership. Employers grew frightened. Colorado's legislature soothed them in

1943 by passing the Colorado Labor Peace Act. Labor lawyer Philip Hornbein joked that from the law's title one might have assumed that there was a labor war in Colorado. That was not the case. Workers were calm and generally satisfied in 1943. The Labor Peace Act attempted to make certain that workingmen would not be able to flex their developing economic muscle. Elizabeth Jameson, in her study of Colorado's carpenters, summarized the law: "Under the Act, a labor dispute could only exist between employer and employee, so it was illegal for

Working people found a friend in Miss Emily Griffith, founder of the Opportunity School, which opened in 1916. The school provided, to anyone interested, free training in English and job skills and offered several hundred other courses. (Denver Public Library, Western History Department.)

anyone else to organize, to picket, or to honor a picket line, and no jurisdictional dispute was legal."[25] By denying unions the right to engage in political activity, the act tried to destroy one of organized labor's most effective weapons. By increasing the likelihood that court injunctions would be used against strikers, the measure returned Colorado to an antiunion era reminiscent of 1900. Parts of the act were set aside by Colorado's courts, but most of it remained on the books. That law, said journalist John Gunther in *Inside USA*, "set a record in the nation for antilabor legislation."[26]

Gunther saw that Big Bill Haywood's vision of labor solidarity was only a dream in Denver. Businessmen, big and small, joined forces to squelch workers. Frederick Bonfils sometimes opposed transit king William Gray Evans, but in 1920 the DTC and the *Post* united against the unions. Small shopkeepers, government workers, and many other non-union Denverites resented union plumbers, electricians, carpenters, and, most of all, union wages.

In 1940, Denver's workers were scattered among many industries, trades, and services. The skilled and the unskilled combined grudgingly, if at all, and ethnic divisions sometimes made cooperation difficult. Before the 1920s, cheap labor could easily be imported. Even when the immigration flow dwindled, it did not immediately raise labor costs since the Great Depression insured that help could be hired for a pittance. For decades Denver had vacillated in its attitude to foreigners. Established workers feared the newcomers; businessmen liked cheap labor. In 1870, the town boasted of the 17 nationalities represented in its population. Then, needing workers, it embraced almost all comers, native or foreign. By 1920 the mood had changed. In the wake of World War I, economic stagnation, and the Russian Revolution, Denver, like much of the United States, withdrew its welcome mat.

CHAPTER 16

Ethnic Diversity

The immigrant movement started in the peasant heart of Europe. Ponderously balanced in a solid equilibrium for centuries, the old structure of an old society began to crumble at the opening of the modern era. One by one rude shocks weakened the aged foundations until some climactic blow suddenly tumbled the whole into ruins. The mighty collapse left without homes millions of helpless, bewildered people.

Oscar Handlin
The Uprooted, 1951[1]

To celebrate July 4 in 1920, thousands of Denverites thronged City Park, where they picnicked, rowed boats, and marveled at a large flag made of electric lights. Over 15,000 watched the evening pageant that featured French, Welsh, and Irish songs; Russian, Polish, and Castilian dances; Swiss yodeling, Japanese music, Scottish bagpipes, and Italian hymns. Although claiming fewer foreigners than did large eastern cities, Denver was a diverse place. The American-born dominated the city's 1920 population, constituting more than 85 percent of its 256,491 residents, of these, however, half had one or both parents born outside the country.

Denver drew its pioneers from states such as New York, Ohio, Illinois, and Missouri, places with sizable German, Irish, and English contingents. Some came seeking gold and silver, others hoped to work for the railroads or smelters. "Just off the boat" immigrants, on the other hand, often could not afford the rail fares to Denver. The filtering effect of distance might have given the city a well-off coterie of northern Euro-

Immigrants added color, texture, and exotic flavors to the Mile High City. Dagmar, Anna, and August Jensen posed amid their Danish pastries in their Capitol Hill Bakery, 2310 East Colfax Avenue. (Jody Rankin Collection.)

pean ethnics had it not been for western entrepreneurs' hunger for cheap labor. In the 1860s the Union Pacific Railroad hired Irishmen and the Central Pacific used Chinese workers. Later the Denver & Rio Grande and other Colorado railroads relied heavily on Italians. Many of these laborers gravitated to Denver; by 1890 the city tallied just over a thousand Chinese and 4,216 Irish. In the 1880s, smelters, railroad shops, and the city's booming construction industry gave jobs to Swedes, Italians, Poles, and other Eastern Europeans. Growing numbers of Japanese, Greeks, and Hispanics came in the early twentieth century, as did thousands of German-Russians who had first settled in Russia and then moved to the United States.

The larger groups were composed of subgroups that differed almost as much from one another as they did from native-born Americans. Germans were split by religious and territorial divisions. Irishmen thought of themselves as Catholics or as Protestants. Some Germans from Russia were Mennonites, some Congregationalists, others Roman Catholics. Canadians often included English, Irish, and Scottish. Until World War I shattered the Austro-Hungarian Empire, the designation "Austrian" covered a goulash of peoples: Slovakians; Slovenians; Poles; Hungarians; Serbians; and Croatians, among others. Italians identified with their hometowns or districts and found that their dialects divided them. "We could not understand one another," Mary Rossi, one of many immigrants from Potenza province in southern Italy, recalled years later.[2]

The newcomers struggled to adjust to each other and to their new surroundings. For northern Europeans who came to Colorado before 1880, the strains were lessened by the likelihood that they had lived elsewhere in North America before moving west. The Irish, English, Welsh, and Scottish could, with few exceptions, speak English, as could many Germans. Although these migrants, especially the Germans and Irish, settled near their jobs in the central city, they did not form solid ethnic neighborhoods. Instead, they cushioned the shocks of cultural change by banding together in groups both formal and informal. Local Irishmen formed an anti-English Fenian society in 1865. The same year, athletically inclined Germans established a turnverein, a unit of the international German health and social club. German singers enjoyed

181

Immigrants gathered in the saloons of their countrymen. Swiss-born Florian Spalti established this tavern at 1700 Blake Street. He sponsored many Swiss newcomers to the "Switzerland of America," including the clock maker next door. Spalti (in foreground) became Switzerland's first Colorado consul. (Colorado Historical Society.)

the Denver Männerchor. The Swiss joined the Grutli Verein; Scottish, the Caledonian Society; Welsh, the Cambrians; and the English, the Albion Club.

The foreign-born drank together in ethnic saloons. By 1900 nearly two-thirds of the city's bars were operated by immigrants. Irishmen, only 3 percent of the population, managed a tenth of the taverns. Germans not only ran dozens of groggeries but also dominated the brewing industry. The Alsatian John Good established the town's first brewery, the Rocky Mountain, in 1859. In 1901 he consolidated several concerns into the Tivoli-Union Brewery, one of Denver's largest. Good's onetime employee Philip Zang, a Bavarian, ran the most successful pre-Prohibition brewery. Adolph Coors, a Prussian, arrived in 1873 and opened a small plant. Assessed by an R. G. Dun credit appraiser in 1874 as a "practical brewer . . . of good character and habits . . . but little means," Coors ultimately outlasted two dozen local competitors.[3]

Immigrants also prayed together, often straining denominational bonds to accommodate ethnic preferences. German Methodists divided from their English brethren in 1872, making their church the first local ethnic congregation. Lutherans also split along ethnic lines. In 1878, Swedish Lutherans began worshiping at Augustana church. By 1900, Denver's 12 Lutheran churches also included Bethany Danish, Norwegian Emmanuel, and St. Paul's English. The same year, St. John's German Lutheran established the city's first Lutheran school.

Roman Catholic Germans grudgingly shared St. Elizabeth's church at Eleventh and Curtis with Irish Catholics until the Irish miller John K. Mullen built St. Leo's two blocks away and recruited an Irish priest, William O'Ryan. When Hispanics began moving into the area in the early twentieth century, the Irish consigned them to St. Leo's basement. Mullen, who delighted in building churches, donated his former homesite at Ninth and Lawrence to establish St. Cajetan's (1926) for Hispanics. That building gave Roman Catholics three large structures within a few blocks of each other. In another small area, north Denver's Roman Catholic divisions generated St. Patrick's for the Irish, Mount Carmel for the Italians, and Our Lady of Guadalupe for Hispanics.

The Scottish filled Presbyterian churches. Some Welsh joined them while others preferred Congregationalism or Methodism. English Episcopalians liked St. John's cathedral, where Dean Henry M. Hart, a cleric imported from London, maintained English traditions during his long tenure (1879–1920). After his church at Twentieth Avenue and Welton was burned by a crazed arsonist, Hart rebuilt at Fourteenth and Clarkson, pleasing Anglophiles by loosely modeling the new St. John's on the great English cathedral at Ely.

Grand churches reflected the prosperity of at least some of the immigrants. Among the British were investors and mining experts such as James Duff, Richard Pearce, and Thomas Rickard, who had the money, the expertise, and the background to assure their place in society. Germans, including the Kountze-Berger banking clan, Charles Boettcher, and hardware dealer George Tritch, made fortunes. The Irish usually did not do as well, although a few — Thomas Patterson, Dennis Sheedy, and John K. Mullen — became millionaires. The Sons of Erin did better in politics, scoring their greatest triumph in 1881 when Robert Morris defeated Tritch to become the city's first, and only, Irish-born mayor. Later immigrants faced higher hurdles. Many of them came from the east and south of Europe and could not speak English. Few had a chance to cash in on the real estate boom of the 1870s and 1880s, which favored those who held on to land homesteaded or purchased cheaply in the 1860s. Some were desperate health seekers dying of TB. Others were unskilled laborers, hoping for smelter work.

Like earlier ethnics, newcomers found companionship in associations, churches, and saloons. Polish Catholics worshiped at St. Joseph's in Globeville. Slovenians, who resented being poked by Polish ushers taking up the collection during mass, left St. Joseph's and built Holy Rosary church, half a block away. Slavs gathered to share dime buckets of beer at Joseph Prijatau's saloon near the Globe smelter. Italians found comfort and free pasta at Siro Mangini's Christopher Columbus Hall, at 2219 Larimer, where the Manginis and their 10 children lived upstairs.

Some foreigners formed compact neighborhoods. Many of the Chinese crowded "Hop Alley" between Blake and Market streets. There, newspaperman Edward Keating recalled, one could "smoke opium if you knew the right places," while the residents "ran around with pigtails which reached to their ankles."[4] Italians also lived in concentrated districts. Many initially settled in the South Platte bottomlands under the viaducts, where they could farm, gather watercress, and find driftwood for fuel. Young bachelors often lived in the rail yards, where they cooked out, slept under the stars, and waited for temporary jobs with the railroads for 40¢ a day. Mother Frances Cabrini, an Italian-American nun, reported that in Colorado "the hardest work is reserved for the Italian worker. There are few who regard him with a sympathetic eye, who care for him or remember that he has a heart and a soul: they merely look upon him as an ingenious machine for work."[5]

Joseph Mapelli, a resident of the Bottoms, took a rosier view. Seeing "all the opportunities in this country," he sent for his brothers Rodolfo, age seven, and Armando, age nine, and their cousin Salvatore Iacobucci, age 11. They spent 31 days at sea before reaching New York City, tagged for delivery to Denver, Colorado, or, as the boys pronounced it "Denvercolo." Rodolfo remembered that "no one seemed to know where that town was located in the whole U.S.A."[6] They came west by train. Since no one met them on arrival in Denver, Armando and Salvatore sat at Union Station and cried. Rodolfo wandered outside to Seventeenth Street, where he asked streetcar drivers where the Frazzinis, friends of the Mapellis, lived. "Each motorman would say 'WHAT???' I would turn and walk away. I learned to say 'what', but didn't know what it meant."[7] Finally, an Italian fruit peddler directed the boys to the Frazzinis. The next day, Joseph, who wanted his brothers to learn English properly, enrolled them in the Delgany school, where they began the long process of Americanization that, among other alterations, brought them new names — Rodolfo became Rudolph, and Armando became Herman.

They soon saw what turn-of-the-century Denver had to offer. One day they were invited to tour the Zangs' large house near the Zang Brewery. The kids were impressed: "Each room had a fireplace, bath and toilet facilities. We were all graduates of the outside back house, Forno (brick bread oven), and the Isa Box — any kind of a box that would keep a block of ice and some food, which was scarce and never allowed to spoil."[8] Hard work and an occasional lucky break brought some Italians a measure of prosperity. The Frazzinis, according to Rudolph Mapelli, gave a puppy to the Zangs, who, in thanks, gave the Frazzinis half a barrel of beer. Sold by the glass, that barrel launched the Frazzinis in the saloon business. They built a brick building in the rail yards where they established a bank, later chartered as the Italian-American Bank, with Joseph Mapelli doing "all the bookkeeping from the book in his back pocket."[9] The Italians, their fortunes improving, moved west from the Bottoms to North Denver's "Little Italy" neighborhood wrapped around Mount Carmel church at Thirty-sixth and Navajo.

Other ethnic enclaves flourished north of downtown. Smelter and packinghouse jobs drew Slavs and German-Russians to Globeville and the neighboring industrial districts of Argo, Elyria, and Swansea. Lucy Turner, an interviewer working for the Federal Writers Program, visited Globeville in 1938 to record the stories of its residents. She found that many of them had come to the United States as a result of a chain of migrations — a brother sending for a brother, a young man sending for his betrothed. In varying degrees they had been Americanized, but many old ways persisted. Some, like Mary Wysowatcky, prospered; others, like Bernice Chopyak, found the American dream elusive. The immigrant experience in Denver, as throughout the United States, proved to be a complex, kaleidoscopic interplay between individuals and societies.

Mary Wysowatcky came from Poland in 1888 to join her fiancé, John, who had migrated four years earlier. Since there were no other Poles near where she first lived she "was very homesick . . . and really cried for about three years."[10] Eventually, she moved to Globeville, where John worked for the Globe smelter. Nine children kept her busy as did summer work in the sugar beet fields, which enabled the family to buy a home at 4663 Pennsylvania. One of her sons died in World War I. Another son, Andy, was by the late 1930s attending law school at night and managing the office of District Attorney John A. Carroll by day. Compared to many of her neighbors, Mary Wysowatcky was well-off. She lived comfortably in a six-room house that, though it lacked central heating, did have a radio and a Hotpoint refrigerator, a gift from Andy.

Bernice Chopyak and her son lived in dingy rooms at the rear of the Mayflower Buffet and Beer Parlor in Globeville. She was born of Polish parents in Globeville in the late 1890s. Her father had come to the United States in 1881, believing that "money was so plentiful that you could almost pick it upon the streets." The dream never materialized. Chopyak's father worked for the Globe Smelter until the 1903 strike, after which he "did a little bit of everything." Each year the Chopyaks took their children out of school in early May, boarded up their house, and went to the sugar beet fields. There, they lived in a shack and slept on sacks filled with straw. From May to November they toiled; thinning, weeding, and finally picking beets, 12 hours hours a day, six days a week — Bernice's Roman Catholic mother would not allow Sunday work. They received $20 for each acre they tended. In a good season they could make up to $1,000. Later, Bernice worked for the National Biscuit Company, packing crackers. She married, but her husband's sickness forced her to open a beer parlor in the Polish Hall at 4837 Washington. Turner reported: "She says she really does not like the kind of life she has to live and observe in the beer parlor and she has a hard time to make it go."[11]

Turner found that most of the immigrants were hardworking people, that their houses were tidy, that they donated to the Community Chest — all badges of good citizenship. Yet, these peoples suffered economic and social discrimination. Not all Americans agreed with the Statue of Liberty's invitation: "Give me your tired, your poor, your huddled masses."

Denverites, both native and foreign, fearful of Oriental job competition, had rioted against the Chinese in 1880, destroying the laundries where many worked. The vaudeville actor Eddie Foy watched the mob on Seventeenth Street: "I saw a man climb a telegraph pole and throw a rope over a cross-arm. The crowd below began to pull, and quickly a body rose in the air, clad in a flopping black silk shirt and white trousers. It was an old, old Chinaman, seventy or eighty years of age — the only one who gave his life on that turbulent day."[12] Chinese laborers were barred from entering the United States by the Chinese Exclusion Act of 1882. In Denver, which saw its Chinese population peak at 1,002 in 1890, anti-Chinese sentiment remained strong. The Colorado Bureau of Labor Statistics fed the animosity by reporting, that same year, that the Chinese were displacing at least 1,200 "white persons" from laundry jobs, since "one Chinaman does as much work as any two men or women because he will work day and night and also Sunday."[13] Gradually, the predominantly male Chinese community withered, and by 1920 there were only 212 Chinese in the city.

In the meantime, Japanese workers recognized the United States' opportunities. By 1910, Denver tallied 585 Japanese, who, in the biased opinion of some non-Orientals, were as much a part of the "yellow peril"

A tiny Japanese community huddled around the Tri-State Buddhist church at 1942 Market Street, a reincarnation of the notorious "House of Mirrors." This youngster, whom the Buddhist temple taught to pursue "the pure and beautiful," sits on steps that led to what had been bedrooms supervised by Jennie Rogers and Mattie Silks. (Amon Carter Museum, Mazzulla Collection.)

as the Chinese. Richard E. Croskey, secretary-treasurer of the Colorado State Federation of Labor, told a mass meeting in 1908: "There must be bloodshed. It is beginning to seem that bloodshed alone will bring the Chinese and Japanese question to the attention of Congress."[14] Aware of the hatred, Japanese organizations warned members to be inside after 11:00 P.M., to talk softly, drink moderately, and to wear clean clothes.

Germans bore the brunt of the long antiliquor crusade that culminated in Colorado prohibition in 1916. U.S. entry into World War I further intensified anti-German feeling. The *Denver Post* alleged that the Kaiser's operatives were plotting to sell poisoned soap. Bill posters re-

fused to put up notices of German operas, and German language instruction was dropped from the high schools. The *Denver Herald* continued to publish in German, thanks, in part, to Mayor Speer's defense of its right to do so. Other German-oriented businesses decided to be discreet: The German National Bank became the American National; the Kaiserhof Hotel became the Kenmark.

After the war, nativists found new targets. The 1917 Russian Revolution, coupled with radical-inspired bombings in the United States, led to the Red Scare of 1919–1920. On January 3, 1920, federal agents arrested 5,000 people across the country on suspicion of radicalism. Locally, the hysteria netted a meager catch of foreign-born Communists — a housewife, a seamstress, a waiter, a stonecutter, a cook's helper. The biggest fish of all, Panagio G. Panagoupoulous, an official of the Industrial Workers of the World, was found with a trunk full of un-American literature. The *Post* foamed about the Red menace, but the *Denver Express* doubted that

Denver's Germans, the largest single foreign-born contingent until the early 1900s, lived it up until anti-German sentiment, fostered by the Prohibition crusade and two world wars, silenced such Teutonic celebrations. (Colorado Historical Society.)

188

As these Arapaho welfare workers of the 1920s attest, Native Americans continue to reside in Denver, still home to over 5,000 Native Americans. (Denver Art Museum.)

"a few thousand ignorant and foolish lunatics and degenerates are about to overthrow this government."[15]

The Red Scare passed. Still, many Denverites continued to fret. They worried about both Jews and Roman Catholics, many of whom were foreign-born. They worried about African-Americans, few of whom were immigrants but, like the immigrants, formed a group apart. Natives talked of limiting the inflow. Even some of the foreign-born thought that the United States should lock its gates. Most feared job competition; a few had special reasons. One man explained: "My wife is still in the old country; if Congress don't hurry up I am afraid she will drop in on me next summer."[16]

Most people enjoyed the ethnic entertainment at City Park, staged to celebrate Independence Day in 1920. Yet, the day before, worshipers at Grace Community church listened to Rice Means attack ungrateful immigrants: "If you do not like this country, leave it and go back to that from whence you came. If you do not do that, you may be sent back."[17] Means knew the power of prejudice — his father had been a leader of the anti-Catholic American Protective Association in the 1890s. In the 1920s, responding to their biases against African-Americans, Jews, and Catholics, some 17,000 Denverites joined the Ku Klux Klan. By 1925, thanks to the Klan, Means was elected to the U.S. Senate.

CHAPTER 17

The Ku Klux Klan

We Americans have been losing ground thru indifference or the dying out of families. We're going to regain that ground, and the klan is going to lead the way and blaze the trails.

John Galen Locke
Denver Post, August 14, 1924

Fiery crosses blazed on Denver lawns. Ward Gash, a black janitor, was ordered to leave town: "Your hide is worth less to us than it is to you."[1] Jewish attorney Ben Laska was kidnaped and beaten to stop his representing alleged bootleggers. An East High School senior was given a choice: marriage to the pregnant woman he had jilted or castration at the hands of Ku Klux Klan Grand Dragon John Galen Locke.

Klansmen savored CYANA "Catholic You Are Not an American" cigars. State legislators pondered striking at Catholics by outlawing sacramental wine. Mayor Benjamin Franklin Stapleton promised: "I will work with the Klan and for the Klan in the coming election, heart and soul."[2] By early 1925, Stapleton, Governor Clarence J. Morley, and Rice Means, one of Colorado's U.S. senators, as well as a host of lesser politicos, were Klansmen. In less than four years the organization had grown from the small Denver Doers Club, established in 1921, into what the *Post* called "the largest and the most efficiently organized political force in the state of Colorado today."[3]

Grand Dragon John Galen Locke, pictured in his office at 1345 Glenarm Place, presided over Colorado's "invisible empire." (Denver Public Library, Western History Department.)

When *Post* reporter Frances Wayne visited Dragon Locke in August 1924, at his office-lair, 1345 Glenarm, she found him jubilant over Stapleton's retention as mayor — a victory engineered by the Klan. Wayne discreetly described the short, lardy Locke, who looked more like a glittering toad than a dragon, as being "large of body and of head." She marveled at his surroundings: the flag on his outer door; the hallway lined with "swords, daggers and helmets"; the door of his inner sanctum guarded by a suit of armor.[4] Inside sat Locke, diamonds on his chubby fingers, a diamond on his watch fob, a diamond on his ample shirtfront.

Doctor Locke had not shone so brightly before he sounded the trumpet of bigotry. A New York City native, he came to Denver in 1893 and picked up a degree from the University of Denver medical school. The local medical society refused to license him, some said because he failed to keep professionally current. The Klan gave him a ladder that he

Stirred by patriotic calls to purge Denver of "un-Americanism," women donned caps and sheets in 1925 for the Kolorado KKK Ladies Auxilliary. Unlike their male counterparts in the Klan, women were not afraid to show their faces. (Denver Public Library, Western History Department.)

climbed to escape from his dungeon of obscurity. Originally established in the South after the Civil War as a means of subjugating newly freed slaves, the Klan declined in the late nineteenth century. Born again in Georgia in 1915, it spread to the North and to the West, feeding on prejudice against Jews and Catholics as well as African-Americans.

In 1920, Denver's 6,075 African-Americans comprised only 2.4 percent of the city's population of 256,491, a proportion far below that of southern cities or of northern metropolises such as New York and Chicago. Compared to the minorities massed in those places, Denver's blacks were well educated and mod-

Central Baptist, 2400 California Street, and other African-American churches were mainstays of the Five Points neighborhood. (Denver Public Library, Western History Department.)

erately prosperous. In 1920 only 222 of the city's 5,442 blacks over the age of 10 were illiterate. More than a third of Colorado's blacks owned their homes in 1920, nearly five times the New York State percentage.

Local African-Americans had long struggled for political and economic power. In the 1860s Frederick and Lewis Douglass, sons of abolitionist Frederick Douglass, successfully opposed Colorado statehood because the proposed constitution denied African-Americans the vote. Nineteenth-century businessmen such as Barney Ford, Lewis Price, and Ed Sanderlin demonstrated that frontier riches did not belong to whites alone. Ulysses Baker, a policeman from 1900 to 1932, recalled, "There would be frowns when I was forced to beat a white man, but I always attended only to duty."[5] Doctor Paul E. Spratlin served as quarantine officer. But Baker and Spratlin were exceptional. Most African-American men in 1920 were toiling as common laborers, as railroad porters, as servants, janitors, and waiters. Of the 1,200 black women employed in 1920, more than half were servants, nearly 200 were laundresses; only four were trained nurses.

The color line was everywhere. At the Tabor and other theaters, blacks were ordered to sit in the balcony. When African-American soldiers were stationed at Fort Logan south of town, nearby merchants objected. When a crime was committed, the police sometimes jailed all blacks in the vicinity. Blacks were expected to eat in black restaurants and to swim separately from whites at the Curtis Park pool, which was open to African-Americans only twice a week.

Blacks fought back. George Ross, a lawyer, and his wife, Gertie, edited the *Denver Star,* the city's oldest black newspaper, which, with other papers such as the *Colorado Statesman,* championed minority rights. In 1915 blacks and a few whites established a local of the National Association for the Advancement of Colored People (NAACP), electing George W. Gross as its first president. In 1918, Doctor Joseph H. West-brook of the NAACP convinced Red Cross officials to admit African-Americans to emergency hospitals set up to assist victims of the flu. In 1920, W. L. Darious successfully sued a white bootblack for refusing him service. Although the NAACP battled for equal rights, legal and moral pressure often proved worthless. When D. W. Griffith's film *The Birth of a Nation,* which insulted blacks, was shown in 1915, African-Americans futilely contended that it violated an ordinance outlawing "reproach upon any race."[6]

Discrimination was clearly etched on the map. Many blacks settled along Larimer and Blake streets northeast of downtown in the 1880s and 1890s. By the 1920s the black community had shifted even farther to the northeast, centering much of its commercial activity in the area known as Five Points at Twenty-sixth Avenue and Welton Street. The black residential neighborhood extended east from Five Points for about a mile, but whites in east-central Denver used custom, pressure, and restrictive real estate covenants to keep African-Americans west of Race Street.[7]

Claude DePriest, a black fireman, tested white resistance in 1920 by purchasing a home at 2649 Gaylord, two blocks east of Race. Members of the Clayton Improvement Association warned him that "if you continue to reside at your present address, you do so at your own peril."[8] Two hundred fifty angry whites called on the DePriests demanding that they move. Yet, their next-door neighbor had told the *Post,* "I'd rather have them for neighbors than some white folks."[9] The harassed DePriests decided to sell. White tempers flared again in 1921 when Walter R. Chapman, a Post Office clerk, rented at 2112 Gilpin. A white stranger told him, "If you move here your house is going to get blown up."[10] Late in the evening of July 7, 1921, a bomb blasted a hole in Chapman's front lawn and shattered his windows. He moved, and the house was occupied by another brave black, Charles E.A. Starr. It was bombed again on November 15.

Segregated neighborhoods meant segregated schools. In the mid-

1920s, over 90 percent of black elementary school children attended five grade schools in the Five Points area. Few blacks went to high school. North, East, and West counted over 1,500 students in the 1925–1926 school year; only 34 of them were black. The smallest high school, Manual Training, enrolled 88 blacks, slightly more than 10 percent of its student body. The small numbers did not stop whites from worrying about their sons and daughters socializing with their African-American class-mates. A clash, described by George Gross as "exceedingly minor," be-tween blacks and whites at a school dance in 1924 prompted School Superintendent Jesse Newlon to order segregated social events.[11] There was little chance that permanent love would bloom between the races because, until 1957, Colorado law forbade interracial marriages.

Prejudice against Jews was based not on color but on religion. Ger-man Jews, such as brothers Adolph, Frederick, and Hyman Salomon, were pioneers, but neither their wealth nor their early arrival assured them acceptance. Amy Salomon, Adolph's daughter, recalled her class-mates throwing stones at her and calling her Christ's killer. Despite such barbs, German Jews were spared the worst manifestations of anti-Semi-tism. There was no German Jewish ghetto. Temple Emanuel at Sixteenth and Pearl, completed in 1898 as a replacement for an earlier Temple Emanuel at Twenty-fourth and Curtis, was only a few blocks from St. John's Episcopal, Trinity Methodist, and Central Presbyterian, three of the city's grandest Christian churches. Some German Jews prospered. Edward Monash and Leopold Guldman owned popular department stores. Louis Anfenger did well selling insurance. Both Anfenger and smelter king Simon Guggenheim achieved political success: Anfenger was a state legislator; Guggenheim one of Colorado's U.S. senators from 1907 to 1913. Still, the Denver and the Denver Country clubs would not admit Jews, who, in turn, established their own country club, Green Gables.

Eastern European Jews suffered more. Most of them came to Denver after 1880, victims of anti-Semitism in their homelands or of TB in the eastern United States. Some settled in the old Auraria area between Cherry Creek and West Colfax, where they purchased an Episcopal chapel at Tenth and Lawrence and converted it into Shearith Israel synagogue. Others crowded into the river bottomlands whence they gradually spread out along West Colfax Avenue. On the South Platte they scratched a living by salvaging paper, rags, and all kinds of junk. Used bottles were sold for a penny or two to Jacob Zerobnick, who claimed to be "the largest bottle dealer in the West." The Radetskys

Denver's oldest and largest Jewish congregation built Temple Emanuel at Sixteenth and Pearl in 1898. (Photo by Roger Whitacre.)

bought scrap iron on Larimer Street while the Radinskys ran the Continental Junk House at Zuni and West Colfax. These recyclers helped keep the city tidy, but most people, steeped in anti-Semitism, did not appreciate the "junk men." To protect themselves from rocks thrown by Christian hoodlums, Jewish peddlers wrapped themselves with rags. In 1906 an old ragpicker was beaten and his wagon burned. A few months earlier, on Christmas 1905, a mob hurling bolts and iron bars killed two Jews who were working on the Christian holiday. The ringleaders received short sentences. Hoodlums killed two Jews a year later and, as in 1905, received light sentences.

Some German Jews fretted about the influx of the Eastern Europeans; others sacrificed to help their coreligionists. Doctor Philip Hillowitz of Temple Emanuel reminded the Germans that "the uncouth beard may hide a sage deeply versed in Talmudic lore."[12] In 1905, Louis Anfenger's daughter, Flora, demonstrated that the gulf between German and Eastern European Jews was not unbridgeable when she married Philip Hornbein, son of Samuel Hornbein, a Russian. Hornbein's career was to prove spectacular: Within 20 years he rose from clerking in his father's liquor store to become a leading attorney and staunch opponent of the Klan.

Unlike blacks and Eastern European Jews, most Roman Catholics were not easy to identify. Italians and Poles had their own neighborhoods, but the bulk of German, Irish, and native-born American Catholics blended in with the wider society. But that was no protection against

Denver's large Catholic contingent arrived on foot, by streetcar, and in Model Ts for the 1912 dedication of Immaculate Conception Cathedral at East Colfax Avenue and Logan Street. (Denver Archdiocese Archives.)

bigotry. A note, signed by the Klan, delivered to the *Denver Catholic Register* in 1922, demanded that "the Nigger and the I. W. W., the Jew," leave Denver, and declared "the Romanist is worst of all."[13] In attacking Catholics, the Klan aimed at a large target. A federal compilation published in 1916 reported 71,847 church members in Denver, of whom 28,772 were Roman Catholics. The largest Protestant denominations, Methodists (10,387), Presbyterians (6,316), Baptists (5,769), and Congregationalists (3,768), did not, even when combined, match the Catholic population. "It would be a happy day for America when she kicked every petticoated priest of Satan into the Atlantic and bid him swim home to hell," editorialized the *Square and Compass,* a Masonic publication.[14] Catholics responded by demanding that children born to religiously mixed parents be raised Catholic and by establishing an extensive school system — there were 15 Catholic schools in the city in 1920. Told that they had to march last in a 1915 patriotic parade, Catholic children retaliated by arriving early and marching first.

Rare was the Catholic, no matter how rich, who belonged to elite clubs. The 1921 *Social Record and Club Annual* did not even include multimillionaire John K. Mullen in its club section. Catholics answered such snubs by flexing their denominational muscles. Twenty thousand attended the six-hour dedication ceremony of the Cathedral of the Immaculate Conception on October 27, 1912. They gloried in their church

The Italian Village Inn on North Denver's Navajo Street changed its name to Patsy's Inn to avoid anti-Italianism. "Prohibition days were our best days," innkeeper Chubby Aiello recalled 60 years later. "We put huge barrels in the basement, not just wine, but whisky. They treated us Dagos like some people treat Mexicans now. Anything stolen, they did it. Anything wrong, it's the Dagos." (Photographs from Chubby Aiello Collection and by Roger Whitacre respectively.)

with its magnificent stained-glass windows and Carrara marble altars, its 230-foot twin spires visible for miles, for it symbolized their collective power. Klansmen considered dynamiting the cathedral, an idea Locke scotched by suggesting that Catholics would use the insurance settlement to build an even larger church.

Rather than church rubble, Locke wanted political power. To get it, he needed a large, well-disciplined organization. At first the Klan grew slowly. Organized quietly in spring 1921, it waited several months before openly announcing its existence. Mayor Dewey Bailey looked askance at the group and threatened to destroy it "if it plans to take the law into its own hands."[15] Bailey's warning went unheeded. In January 1922 the Klan accused Ward Gash of having "intimate relations with white women."[16] Before Gash left town, he complained to District Attorney Philip Van Cise, who subjected the Klan to a Grand Jury investigation. The Klan responded by threatening Van Cise with a recall election, a ploy that failed since he had wide popular support stemming from his successful war on the underworld.

In condemning the Klan, Van Cise was joined by Sidney Whipple, editor of the *Denver Express,* the Reverend Matthew Smith, editor of the *Denver Catholic Register,* Judge Benjamin Lindsey, and lawyer, Hornbein. Many others either saw the danger less clearly or, seeing it, hesitated to oppose it. Historian Robert Goldberg has pointed out that the *Rocky Mountain News* and the *Denver Times* "kept silent about the Klan issue" and that opposition from the *Denver Jewish News* and the *Colorado Statesman* was "feeble."[17] Benjamin Lindsey wrote to Samuel Untermeyer, a nationally prominent Jew, asking for campaign money in 1924. The millionaire New Yorker sent nothing. He responded that Jews were not getting involved for "they feel that the issue is at best transitory and will die of its own inequity and unAmericanism."[18] The *Denver Post* was erratic in its position. Adolph Hecker, one of Locke's strong-arm men, claimed that once, when the *Post* attacked the Klan, "Dr. Locke got in his Pierce Arrow and drove up to Bonfils' office." The dragon told the publisher, " 'Recant that story . . . or you will find the *Denver Post* the flattest place on Champa Street'."[19] The next day the *Post* praised the Klan. Unchecked, the organization grew. Rootless newcomers joined for companionship; the politically ambitious joined to get votes; merchants joined to promote business; a few of Van Cise's agents joined to spy. Feasting on bigotry, the Klan also fed on citizens' legitimate concerns about crime and corruption. Bootlegging, gambling, prostitution, and a city administration rumored to be rotten gave the hooded empire issues to exploit.

By promising law and order, Benjamin Stapleton defeated Dewey Bailey in the 1923 mayoralty election. Stapleton, a bland, bespectacled leftover from Speer's political machine, outwardly opposed the Klan, declaring that "any attempt to stir up racial prejudice or religious intolerance is contrary to our constitution and is therefore un-American."[20] Blacks, Catholics, and Jews who voted for Stapleton soon found that they had been tricked; the Klan also supported him. Once in office Stapleton rewarded Klansmen with jobs, leading Van Cise and Hornbein to demand the mayor's recall. Simultaneously, Locke grew angry because Stapleton hesitated to appoint a Klansman police chief. For a moment it appeared that Klan and anti-Klan forces would combine to oust the mayor. Then Stapleton — a politician so adroit that he would survive six elections — embraced the Klan and named their man, William J. Candlish, chief of police. Locke blessed Stapleton, and the mayor weathered the August 1924 recall vote.

The triumphant Klan then focused on the November 1924 gubernatorial and U.S. Senate races. Democrats nominated the incumbent reform governor, William E. Sweet, for a second term. Republicans, dominated by the Klan, backed a little-known district judge, Klansman Clarence Morley. Democrat Morrison Shafroth, son of ex-governor Shafroth, vied with Rice Means, the Klan's candidate, for a two-year Senate term created by the death of Samuel Nicholson. Democrat Alva B. Adams, son of ex-governor Alva Adams, ran against the millionaire Republican Lawrence Phipps, a non-Klansman who received Klan backing. "We all went down in a heap," Shafroth wrote to William Jennings Bryan, explaining to the old Democratic warhorse that "the combination of Coolidge landslide and Ku Klux Klan was too much for us."[21] Shafroth, who was focusing on Democrats, failed to note the retention of Republican congressman William N. Vaille, who had been opposed by the Klan. Nor did he mention the temporary survival of Lindsey, whose contested reelection provoked a prolonged legal wrangle. Still, in general, Shafroth was correct. The Klan, which also gained judgeships and legislative seats, appeared invincible.

Morley entered office proclaiming, "Every man under the capitol dome a klansman."[22] But not everyone agreed. Democratic state senators joined seven anti-Klan Republicans to kill almost all Klan proposals. The *Denver Catholic Register* threatened the governor with "the curse of Almighty God" if he pushed a measure to outlaw sacramental wine.[23] The antiwine bill died in committee. Efforts to destroy Lindsey's juvenile court also failed. Abolition of horseshoe inspectors and Morley's scuttling of the appropriation for Adams State Normal School in Alamosa, a spite veto to punish anti-Klansman William H. Adams, Alamosa's state senator, were among the Klan's meager victories. For his pettiness the governor's detractors titled him "Clarence the Little."[24]

Morley was not the only Klansman with problems. Both Means and Stapleton grew increasingly uncomfortable with the domineering Locke. The grand dragon erred in January 1925, when his henchmen kidnaped Keith Boehm, a 19-year-old Klansman, who had allegedly gotten Miss Mae Nash into a "delicate condition" and then refused to marry her.[25] Locke reportedly threatened Boehm with castration unless he did the honorable thing. Boehm reluctantly agreed, and Locke arranged a quick wedding in his office. The groom did not kiss the bride.

During the spring of 1925, Locke's empire began to fall apart. The

Boehm incident sullied the dragon's reputation. So did Mayor Stapleton's Good Friday raids of April 10, 1925. Using special deputies from the American Legion, the mayor bypassed the Klan-controlled Police Department to launch raids on brothels and speakeasies. The strikes unearthed corruption among the police — 12 Klan cops were suspended. A few months later Stapleton fired Chief Candlish. In May, federal officials charged Locke with income tax evasion; his refusal to produce records brought him 10 days in jail. Friends paid Locke's fine, but their support only postponed his downfall. In late June 1925, the Klan's national leader, Imperial Wizard Hiram Evans, tried to wrest control of the local Klan from Locke. Opposed locally by Stapleton and nationally by Evans, the bedraggled dragon had few choices. He resigned in mid-July and immediately organized another group, the Minute Men of America, which, although it briefly attracted 5,000 members, soon faltered.

Most Klansmen hid their robes and hoods in the recesses of their linen closets and quietly quit the Klan, although a rump organization survived into the 1930s. In early 1927, William Adams replaced Morley as governor. Charles W. Waterman, also a Klan enemy, succeeded Means in the U.S. Senate. Lindsey reported in 1927 that "the Klan is on the down grade — busted into several different parts, with the old timers fighting each other like cats and dogs and each ready to squeal on the other."[26] Morley sank back into obscurity, reemerging late in life when he was convicted of stock fraud. He served 21 months in Leavenworth Penitentiary before being paroled in late 1940. He died in 1948. Locke, always anxious to lead an organization, headed the Minute Men and on its decline created the Order of Equals, which accepted Catholics and Jews as well as Protestants. He died of a heart attack at the Brown Palace Hotel on April Fool's Day, 1935.

Stapleton rose from the Klan ashes. A native of Paintsville, Kentucky, he had come to Denver in the late 1890s. Allying with Robert Speer, he slowly rose in the Democratic party, becoming a police magistrate in 1904 and postmaster in 1915. On his election in 1923 he promised: "I have only one ambition — to make good as mayor."[27] His alliance with Locke brought him crucial support in the 1924 recall election; his abandonment of Locke saved him from the Klan rout. By quietly serving the monied men on Seventeenth Street, particularly banker Gerald Hughes, while at the same time mollifying labor, Stapleton insured that he would win again and again. His penny-pinching approach to government, his personal honesty, and his lack of flamboyance pleased most voters, who, except in 1931, kept reelecting him until 1947. Of the Klan's opponents, Philip Van Cise went on to enjoy a distinguished legal career, first as attorney for the *News* and later for the *Post*. So did Philip Hornbein, who wielded behind-the-scenes power among liberal Democrats. The Reverend Matthew Smith later became a monsignor as he built the *Catholic Register* into a large national newspaper.

The Klan burned crosses, boycotted businesses, threatened African-Americans, and pushed Catholics out of city and state jobs. It kept a 50-gallon drum of hot tar at Agnes Phipps Memorial Tuberculosis Sanatorium where, as Adolph Hecker recalled, Klansmen immersed their victims up to their necks: "It would take weeks to get that stuff off."[28] Yet, for all its bluster, the Klan claimed only one significant trophy — Judge Benjamin Barr Lindsey.

Lindsey's opposition to the Klan, together with his progressive social views, made him an easy target. In 1924 the Klan backed a Republican unknown, Royal R. Graham, for Lindsey's juvenile judge post. Lindsey campaigned hard — sometimes speaking seven times a night. Busybodies questioned his policy of interviewing young girls in his court chambers, and gossips chattered that his wife, Henrietta, had been thrown out of Baur's restaurant because she was caught smoking. "At one meeting," Lindsey reported, "wild, fanatical women like maniacs hissed in my face, 'you dirty cur.' " He asked one of them why she berated him. "With a demonical laugh she screamed, 'You are not 100% American. You are against the Klan.' "[29] In Washington, D.C., where he was a member of the U.S. Tariff Commission, Edward Costigan helped the judge raise money. Lindsey, thinking he was going to lose the election, wrote to another of his former comrades in reform, Josephine Roche, also in Washington: "I shall regret exceedingly to have the court turned over to that little crook who they have named to take it over."[30]

Lindsey won by 137 votes. Graham charged that ballot boxes were stuffed in some West Colfax Jewish precincts, bastions of Lindsey's strength. The district court upheld Lindsey's election, but in 1927 the Colorado Supreme Court ordered him to vacate his seat. Two years later, the high court disbarred him for accepting a gratuity while serving as a judge. Ironically, that action was initiated not by the Klan, but by Van Cise, who had broken with the cantankerous judge. For some of his troubles Lindsey had himself to blame. With a strong sense of his own dignity, a hunger for publicity, and a missionary zeal for reform, the judge minced few words and sidestepped few issues. He admitted that his political ally, William Sweet, was "one of the ablest governors that we have ever had." "But," he sourly poked Sweet, "I shall always know you for what you are personally — a very selfish, egotistical man."[31] Moreover, Lindsey's speeches and writings, especially *The Companionate Marriage* (1927), which advocated birth control and no-fault divorce for childless couples, alienated many who had supported his humane treatment of juvenile delinquents. Roy Howard, head of the Scripps-Howard newspaper chain, which after November 1926 controlled the *Rocky Mountain News*, understood that reformers sometimes became martyrs. "You have picked out a pretty tough job for yourself," he wrote Lindsey.[32]

The playwright George Bernard Shaw told Lindsey that someday the Klan would repent and make the bantam jurist "Lord Chief Justice, or whatever is the Denver equivalent."[33] Such was not to be. Unable to practice law in Colorado, Lindsey moved to California, where he was elected to the Los Angeles Superior Court. Although reinstated as a lawyer in Colorado in 1935, he stayed in California, dying there in 1943. Henrietta Lindsey sprinkled some of his ashes at their home in Bel Air. She secretly scattered the rest in Denver at Court House Square, then a temporary park at Sixteenth and Tremont, site of the courthouse where the kids' judge had dispensed justice for over a quarter of a century. "There is no monument to Lindsey in Denver," wrote his friend and admirer, the journalist Gene Fowler — "he needs none."[34]

There was no monument to the Klan either, unless one counts Locke's elaborate mausoleum at Fairmount Cemetery, where Klansmen reportedly burned a cross shortly after the grand dragon's demise. By the early 1930s, as the depression gripped the city, people began to forget the strange Klan interlude with its rallies on South Table Mountain, its monster parades, and its bejeweled grand dragon. New problems faced the community: jobs for the unemployed; shelter for the homeless; food for the starving.

CHAPTER 18

Depression Denver

Few people realized the seriousness of the Depression in terms of actual starvation. . . . One of Denver's leading physicians explained to me that doctors rarely stated the reason for death was actual starvation. Instead they listed one of the contributing causes. This practice helped to obscure the awful truth of suffering.

Edgar M. Wahlberg
Voices in the Darkness, 1983[1]

Three days after John Galen Locke's death, Horace Tabor rose from his grave at Calvary Cemetery. His reclusive 80-year-old widow, Baby Doe, had been found dead a few weeks earlier — her body frozen in her shack at the Matchless mine near Leadville. To reunite the Tabors, friends and relatives had Horace exhumed from the disused Calvary burying ground at Tenth Avenue and York Street. With difficulty, diggers located the silver king — vandals had stolen his marker. Without ceremony they removed the casket, still bound by the black silk braid that had tied it 36 years earlier. They took Tabor to Mount Olivet, the new Catholic cemetery west of the city, to rebury him next to Baby Doe.

Tabor's brief reappearance seemed appropriate. He had died broken by the Depression of 1893. He returned in the midst of an even greater depression. Certainly, there had been improvements in Denver since he took his leave in 1899. The population had more than doubled, rising from 133,859 in 1900 to 287,861 in 1930. The Tabor Opera House, converted to a movie theater, stood in 1935 dwarfed by more-imposing landmarks such as Daniels and Fisher's 330-foot tower (1911) at Six-teenth and Arapahoe, the Republic Building (1926) at Sixteenth and Tremont, and the Telephone Building (1929) at Fourteenth and Curtis. The old post office at Sixteenth and Arapahoe, where Tabor had been postmaster, continued to house federal offices, but people were much prouder of the new Post Office, a 1910 neoclassical temple faced with Colorado marble, at Eighteenth and Stout. Those buildings bespoke moments of prosperity, an uncertain affluence eroded in the 1920s by Colorado's faltering farms and mines. Denver's flush times had ended by the early 1930s. Few notable buildings were added to downtown in that decade, the major exceptions being the City and County Building, com-pleted in 1932, and the New Customs House (1931–1937), both built with public funds.

Tabor returned to rest with Baby Doe. He was not around on April 9, 1935, to see one of the grimier spectacles of a gloomy decade. During early April, Denver suffocated in dust-laden windstorms. On the eastern Colorado plains, in Nebraska, Kansas, and Oklahoma, black blizzards scoured parched land, creating a giant dust bowl. Cattle smothered in the fine sand; three-foot drifts covered highways and railroad tracks, stopping cars and trains. Hospital operating rooms in Denver shut down; patients under anesthesia could not breathe. On April 12 it rained — drops of thin, watery, brown mud. Denverites gave thanks and breathed easier since the shower cleared the air. They took the dust in stride, one more plague among the many that had afflicted them since 1929.

The stock market crash of October 1929, which panicked Wall Street, had little immediate impact on Denver except on Seventeenth Street, the heart of the financial district. Investors and speculators saw paper empires evaporate almost overnight. Claude Boettcher, who was traveling in the Soviet Union at the time of the debacle, returned to find much of his fortune gone. First he fired the messenger who brought him the news; then he patiently waited until stocks fell to ridiculous lows, whereupon he borrowed $2 million on his life insurance and plunged into the market to recoup his loses. Ordinary people, who rarely rode the stock exchange roller coaster, temporarily escaped unscathed. As late as 1931 the city seemed insulated from eastern distress. But, as agricultural and metals prices fell and as industry slowed, Denver found that its economy was in trouble. Between 1929 and 1932 the number of employed house-hold heads in the city fell from 87 to 68 percent. By 1933 one in every four Coloradans was out of work.

204

At the bottom of the Great Depression, the 1934 Civil Works Administration "Survey of Unfit Homes" discovered hundreds living in shacks, such as these at 3440 Kalamath, in the Platte River Bottoms. (Colorado State Archives.)

Even those with savings often found their nest eggs destroyed by bank failures. Between 1930 and 1934, 56 of Colorado's 174 state and national banks closed their doors. Fred Rosenstock, who later became a leading book and art dealer, remembered the tearful Italians who came to his office after the failure of the Italian-American Bank: "It was really pitiful. Some people lost their life savings, the result of years of hard work and frugality."[2] Charles Tribble, a moneyless artist, depended on his sister who lived on an eastern Colorado farm. "Every week she'd send me a quart of sour cream, a quart of corn, a quart of wheat. . . . This was basically what I was living on."[3]

The hungry first sought help from traditional sources, churches and private agencies. In 1930 such groups spent $87,655 to aid the poor, a figure that had quadrupled by 1932. By then, private charities were running out of money; donors were cutting back on giving. The unemployed next turned to self-help organizations. The Unemployed Citizens League, organized in June 1932, scrounged for food, shelter, and clothing.

Leaguers bartered with farmers, trading labor for tons of carrots, cabbage, and potatoes. To provide homes for evicted families, they renovated old buildings. They baked bread, mended clothes, ran soup kitchens, and repaired shoes. By September 1932 over 30,000 people were involved with the league. Members of this stopgap alliance thought the depression would soon end, but by late 1932 it was clear that they were wrong. Lacking even the pittance needed to buy shoe-repair material, the league drowned in the rising crisis.

The Reverend Edgar M. Wahlberg, pastor of Grace Methodist church, surveyed the depression years in his autobiography, *Voices in the Darkness*. He estimated that 30 self-help associations operated in the city in the early 1930s. One, which he sponsored, ran an employment agency, a shoe-repair service, a barbershop, and a food, clothing, and fuel distri-

State and city officials did little for depression-stricken unemployed and homeless, who were welcomed by the Mission of Redeeming Love, on Market Street. (Denver Public Library, Western History Department.)

bution center. Banker John Evans, grandson of territorial Governor John Evans, gave money, while his sister, Katherine Evans, helped serve lunches to children. Wahlberg made sauerkraut of surplus cabbage, giving his church the smell of a pickle factory. "Them saints ain't goin to like that," the custodian told Wahlberg.[4]

To get a close-up look at the lives of the poor, Wahlberg let his whiskers grow, dressed in old clothes, and joined the mass of homeless men living on the streets. At one soup kitchen he gagged at the smell of "a greasy, watery concoction of mangled pigs feet and lima beans." He gave his portion away. He sought shelter at the Salvation Army but was politely told they had no beds. At the City Mission, hungry men were encouraged "to be saved by the blood of Christ." Those who accepted salvation were given a ticket good for "showers, food, a bed, and break-fast."[5] Later, Wahlberg visited the Volunteers of America, who gave him good beef stew but could not provide a bed.

Bishop Frank H. Rice of the Liberal Church, Inc., ministered to the hobos who lived in rail yards and under overpasses. Rice spoke for the unworthy poor since others, he explained, attended to the "worthy poor." When Gerald Hughes declined to donate to Rice, the rebuffed bishop brazenly brayed beside the banker's door: "Oh, Lord, in Thy infinite compassion look down with mercy and forgiveness on Thy sinner Gerald Hughes! He is a good man, but he sometimes forgets. He will go home tonight to dine on roast squab under glass. Let not this luxury harden his heart to the plight of his brothers, starving tonight on the streets of Denver."[6] Hughes relented and gave $10.

City officials were less accommodating. When one of Rice's skid row parishioners starved to death, the bishop decided to stage the funeral in front of the new City and County Building. He herded his flock — bums, winos, hobos, and tramps — to the Civic Center, where they were turned away by the police. Rice then took the corpse, "fully exposed," Wahlberg recalled, "except for ragged pants and a shirt," to nearby Grace church, where the bishop damned the politicians, whom he blamed for the economic mess.[7]

Government responded slowly to the collapse. Little federal money was available until 1933. William Adams, governor from 1927 to 1933, cut spending while resisting tax increases. His fellow Democrat and successor, Edwin C. Johnson, was also a penny-pincher. Nor were depression-era mayors George Begole and Benjamin Stapleton willing to offend businessmen and property owners by raising taxes to provide jobs and relief. Officials argued that falling revenues required cutbacks to balance

Members of Denver's Visiting Nurse Association bicycled out from the Central Bank on May 31, 1934, to reach depression-era clients. (CWA photo, Colorado State Archives.)

budgets. Moreover, as Wahlberg recognized, the society was paralyzed by "a dream world of frontier civilization committed to the idea that anyone worth his salt could find something to do."[8] Taxpayer's Incorporated, a group endorsed by Claude Boettcher, theater magnate Harry Huffman, lawyer Erl Ellis, and George Cranmer, an ex-stockbroker, liked those frontier ideals and lobbied for "lower taxes through elimination of governmental waste and extravagance."[9] Campaigning for city auditor in 1933, William H. McNichols, Sr., told taxpayers: "I have long been aware of the fact that the average businessman — and home owner — has been taxed almost beyond his capacity to pay."[10]

Such frugality did not solve the problems of unemployment, homelessness, and hunger. The crisis could not be ignored. Late in 1932, Mayor Begole organized the Denver Emergency Relief Committee to distribute federal Reconstruction Finance Corporation loans and to coordinate charity work. The committee was immediately flooded with pleas for help. On Tuesday, January 3, 1933, nearly 800 families asked for aid; on Wednesday, 680 applied; on Thursday, 500 more. Relief offices opened at 8:30 A.M.; workers did not go home until 10:00 P.M. In eight days, 1,100 homeless men and boys sought shelter at the old City Hall. By early April, 11,756 families, one of every seven in the city, were receiving subsistence doles.

Desperate for space, the Emergency Committee asked the South Denver Women's Club, which was occupying the city-owned James A.

Fleming mansion at 1518 South Grant, to give up its headquarters. The ladies refused. At the Epworth Church Relief Center on Thirty-fourth and High, blacks complained about segregated facilities. At the City Charities, 650 Cherokee Street, a committee inspector found relief offices in a "dark dingy basement" tended by an "uncouth looking man" who rudely asked the visitor, "What do you want?"[11]

The Emergency Committee's chief headache was its lack of money. Although President Franklin D. Roosevelt's New Deal promised increased federal help, tightfisted state lawmakers refused to provide required matching funds, causing federal officials to withhold some money and to threaten to cut off all aid. The Twenty-ninth General Assembly, which authorized only $60,000 to match federal funds, did so little in the first half of 1933 that it became known as the "Twiddling Twenty-ninth." The State Supreme Court further frustrated relief by ruling that two modest taxes approved by the assembly were unconstitutional. A special year-end session of the legislature recessed for a two-week Christmas vacation without acting on tax increases.

Denver faced bankruptcy by the end of 1933. Running out of funds and facing a federal cutoff, the Denver Civil Works Commission (successor to the Emergency Relief Committee) met with 11 legislators on December 26, 1933. Mayor Begole told them that the city was almost broke, that it could not pay upcoming bills. One commissioner warned: "Unless the representatives of the legislature get some definite action these 40,000 people [needing help in Denver] are not going to get relief, and if no relief, what then?" He urged the legislators to "realize that it is far better and cheaper to take care of these people than for the legislature to pay soldiers." Another commissioner, Eunice Robinson, told the lawmakers that "the agencies are standing between the public and general riots."[12]

Still the legislature delayed. Federal relief administrator Harry Hopkins played his trump card by announcing that after December 31, 1933, Colorado would be denied additional aid. Starving men knew where to fix the blame. On January 3, 1934, they invaded the Colorado state capitol. Senators fled before the irate interlopers. Frank Cross, a reporter for *The Nation,* described the scene as protesters settled into the legislators' chairs: "A genuine Communist meeting followed — the first Communist meeting to be held under the dome of any state capitol in the United States."[13]

Edgar Wahlberg saw the events differently. He admitted that angry men had occupied the Senate, but he saw no Communist plot in the demonstration. At any rate, tempers cooled and the legislature reconvened. Charles Tribble recalled the mood: "This was a period very close to political explosion. . . . The left wing was getting pretty potent. . . . It was close to violence."[14] William Danks, Governor Johnson's private secretary, applied for a gun permit, explaining, "These are rather hectic days and people do things now that they would not do otherwise."[15] Lawmakers finally earmarked $2 million for relief, and, as a result, the federal government anted up half a million dollars, enough to give a family of four $5.20 in January. For once, Frank Cross suggested, the legislators ignored business lobbyists and responded to "hungry mobs."[16]

Cross overstated the ideological cohesiveness of the destitute — they wanted bread, not bolshevism. Communists, then a legal political group, although active in the local Mine, Mill, and Smelter Workers Union, gathered only 1,290 votes for their gubernatorial candidate in 1934. In 1937 they could muster only 216 registered members in all of Colorado, Wyoming, and New Mexico. Socialists did better — over 6,500 listened to their presidential candidate, Norman Thomas, when he spoke at the City Auditorium in October 1932. Nevertheless, Thomas received less than 3 percent of the city's presidential vote that year.

For political answers, many people turned to liberal Democrats, some of them formerly Progressive Republicans, such as Edward Costigan. In 1930, Costigan ran for the U.S. Senate demanding, two years before Roosevelt popularized the term, "a new deal in the black hour in which we, the people, now find ourself."[17] Costigan's effective use of radio, a medium suited to his resonant voice, coupled with his position on the issues, brought him victory.

Costigan's backers rejoiced both because he condemned "the cheer leaders of the mad race for private profit" and because his success opened doors for them.[18] Speaking in Denver in 1932, presidential candidate Franklin Roosevelt reminded Democratic stalwarts of the sweet fruits of political victory by addressing them as "future cabinet members — and not only that, but future postmasters, future judges, future district attorneys."[19] Oscar L. Chapman, Costigan's junior law partner, rode the senator's coattails into Washington, where Chapman ingratiated himself with Roosevelt's inner circle. An able, affable bureaucrat, he lasted through Roosevelt's administrations, retiring in 1952 as President Harry Truman's secretary of the interior. Costigan's protégé, Denverite Charles Brannan, became Truman's secretary of agriculture. And Paul Shriver, another of Costigan's young Turks, became director of the Works Progress Administration (WPA) in Colorado.

John Carroll, yet another Costigan backer, proved to be more durable than Shriver and more electable than Brannan or Chapman. A bright, charming Irishman, Carroll rose, like the fictional Horatio Alger, from poverty to prominence. A poor, west Denver kid, Carroll had enlisted in the army at age 16 and reenlisted after World War I because he could not find a job. He returned home in the 1920s to become a cop. Night classes at Westminster Law School brought him a law degree. In 1930 he helped direct Costigan's senatorial campaign and two years later became chairman of the local Democratic party. As a dispenser of New Deal patronage, he worked to keep Costigan in Washington. In 1936, when Costigan's ill health left New Dealers without a popular candidate, Carroll, then 35, took up the liberal banner by running for district attorney. Four years in that office plus WW II army service positioned him to become Denver's congressman (1947–1951) and eventually a U.S. senator (1957–1963).

While Chapman, Brannan, Shriver, and Carroll were newcomers to Costigan's camp, Josephine Roche was one of his oldest allies. The daughter of a wealthy coal mine operator, Roche preferred social activism to society teas. A 1908 Vassar graduate, she completed an M.A. in sociology at Columbia in 1910, after which she returned to Colorado and went to work for Judge Benjamin Lindsey as a probation officer. When Police Commissioner George Creel declared war on vice, she helped him patrol dance halls. When Costigan ran for governor of Colorado in 1914, she supported him. After her father's death in 1927 she gained control of the Rocky Mountain Fuel Company and in 1928 shocked other mine owners by naming labor leader John Lawson its vice-president. "Capital and labor," she declared, "have equal rights."[20]

In 1934, Roche — with Costigan's backing — challenged Governor Johnson in the Democratic gubernatorial primary. She faced a formidable opponent. Many Coloradans liked tall, personable, folksy Big Ed — he reminded them of their frontier past. The son of Swedish immigrants, he had grown up on a farm in Kansas. A touch of TB brought him to Colorado, where he homesteaded west of Craig in the remote northwestern corner of the state. His neighbors agreed with his contention that Colorado needed better highways, so they sent him to the legislature. Businessmen liked his conservative views. In 1930 he became lieutenant governor and in 1932 was elected governor.

Roche traveled 8,000 miles to spread her message, but it was in Denver that she garnered her strongest support. Her campaign manager, John Carroll, and his friend Andrew Wysowatcky set off firecrackers to attract 2,000 to a rally in Globeville. Poor people received Roche warmly.

She was fighting their battle by advocating a progressive state income tax that fell more heavily on the rich. Johnson looked at the economic collapse differently. He favored cutting expenses rather than raising taxes. Roche, he charged, was proposing a "fantastic setup which will use the state for an economic and political clinic."[21] Carroll, sensitive to the prejudice against women politicians, declared that "a wide-awake woman is better than a drowsy man."[22] The *Rocky Mountain News* supported Roche, while the more widely read *Denver Post* backed Johnson and worried that "radicals" would "Russianize" the country. Despite the *Post's* power, Roche won in Denver by more than 8,000 votes, but Johnson's rural strength saved him. The *Post* gloated over Big Ed's victory, which, the paper said, "halted the Red march."[23]

Johnson's triumph told the poor that they had to look to the federal government for help. Roche recognized that — she left Colorado to become assistant secretary of the Treasury, the second-highest–ranking woman in Roosevelt's administration. By early 1935 numerous federal projects were operating locally. The Reconstruction Finance Corporation (RFC) lent money to states so that they could shore up businesses and provide small doles for needy persons. Denver received $241,000 in RFC money in April 1933, a pittance compared to the need: There were over 11,000 families on relief that month. RFC also rescued the Colorado National Bank (CNB) by purchasing a million dollars' worth of its stock. Before the bailout, CNB had a good reputation, but in 1932 bank examiners told the U.S. comptroller of the currency that the bank was facing "very serious difficulties." The auditors determined that "approximately 50% of [CNB's] total loans and discounts are subject to criticism."[24] Over a million dollars in loans were poorly secured by real estate whose value had fallen far below 1929 levels. To survive, CNB swallowed its pride and accepted federal help. Individuals did the same.

During Roosevelt's first term the Federal Emergency Relief Administration (FERA) offered states relief money if they would also provide funds. Colorado's Twiddling Twenty-Ninth appropriated virtually no matching funds, but until FERA head Harry Hopkins withdrew federal dollars, FERA bore the brunt of local relief. Another Hopkins project, the Civil Works Administration, created temporary jobs until early 1934 when it ran out of money.

New Dealers did not run out of agencies. One of Roosevelt's pet projects, the Civilian Conservation Corps (CCC), marshaled young men into federal service. Living a communal life in barracks at places such as Fort Logan and Morrison, they made the outdoors accessible to Denverites by building trails and roads in the Denver Mountain Parks and the national forests. They also helped make a dream come true for George Cranmer, who had luckily liquidated his stock brokerage firm a year before the market crash. Cranmer had long been fascinated by the spectacular red rocks jutting up at the base of the mountains west of Denver. He had noticed the area's superb acoustics in 1902 when he visited there on a high school geology field trip. A quarter-century later, while traveling in Sicily, he saw the ancient, outdoor amphitheater at Taormina and envisioned a Denver counterpart. The same year, 1928, the city had added Red Rocks to its mountain parks holdings.

On his return to office in 1935, after a four-year hiatus, Benjamin F. Stapleton rewarded his campaign manager, George Cranmer, by naming him manager of parks and improvements. Cranmer grasped the opportunity to realize his Red Rocks dream. Stapleton regarded the scenic area as a giant rock garden. Cranmer, conversely, wanted to make a grand outdoor theater by leveling the boulder-strewn terrain between two massive outcroppings in order to put in seats. He convinced CCC officials to proceed quietly with plans to clear the ground. For days, workers placed dynamite charges. Then they blew up all the boulders at once — pulverizing the mayor's rock garden. When the dust settled, architect Burnham Hoyt installed the stage and seating in harmony with the natural setting, making the theater a design as well as an acoustical triumph.

The CCC and the National Youth Administration (NYA), which gave part-time jobs to college and high school students, put people on the federal payroll. Some agencies, such as the Public Works Administration, which helped construct a new sewage disposal plant, acted slowly, often becoming snarled in red tape. Others, such as the WPA, provided immediate relief, giving the jobless work repairing schools, fixing gutters, planting trees, killing rats, and filling chuckholes. Larger projects included installation of sewers, riprapping the banks of the South Platte and Cherry Creek, extending Washington Street into Adams County, building part of Buchtel Boulevard, and extending Alameda from west Denver to Red Rocks.

The WPA recognized that women and professional men needed jobs just as construction workers did. Margaret Reef, who helped Paul Shriver run Colorado's program, remembered the despair: "I would talk to a man who had been making $10,000 a year, now that was a good salary in those days . . . and that man would sit and talk to me and he would weep because he didn't know how he was going to get along — he was going to lose his home, his children were hungry. It was a ghastly thing — just

terrible."[25] For such people, WPA initiated dozens of projects. Women were hired to make clothing, stuff dolls, prepare school lunches, and run nurseries. The WPA supported weavers who repaired old textiles at the Art Museum. Researchers gathered historical data and compiled a state guidebook, *Colorado: A Guide to the Highest State*. WPA musicians gave free concerts. At the federally sponsored Baker Theater, 1447 Lawrence Street, 40 WPA players offered low-priced entertainment including Denverite Mary Coyle Chase's first play, *Me Third*. At the Baker, audiences could also watch the versatile ventriloquist George Berton, who swallowed swords and did a trained bird act.

Artists, no more employable than sword swallowers, ate because of WPA's art program. It paid them $35 a week to decorate schools and government buildings. Allen Tupper True, an 1899 graduate of Manual Training High, known for his many murals including those in the Colorado National Bank Building and in the Telephone Building, worked for the WPA. A Treasury Department grant supported Gladys Caldwell

New Deal job programs completed many City Beautiful–era goals. A 1934 Civil Works Administration crew ripraps the banks of the South Platte. (CWA photo, Colorado State Archives.)

New Deal programs benefited Denver museums, which used federal money to install and refurbish exhibits. (Colorado State Archives.)

Fisher while she chiseled two of Denver's largest statues, the mountain sheep guarding the south entrance to the downtown Post Office.

People liked the 10-ton bighorns, which closely resembled their prototypes grazing on Mount Evans. And they appreciated the Western theme of Frank Mechau's *Horses at Night,* a large mural painted under the auspices of the Public Works of Art Project for the Denver Public Library. Avant-garde art was less well received. Margaret Reef explained: "Murals had to be acceptable to a certain extent. You simply could not have them going too far out. There were some . . . who wanted to do a painting with a mouse, a key and a banana and you were supposed to know what it meant."[26] Artists could paint unorthodox pictures, but, as Charles Tribble recalled, "they just didn't get their work displayed."[27]

WPA bureaucrats walked softly, for they knew that many businessmen and politicians hated the New Deal. Governor Johnson, who saw WPA patronage in the hands of his rival, Edward Costigan, charged that "piddling around with leaf raking projects just to give politicians a job is criminal."[28] *Denver Post* drama critic Albert DeBernardi, Jr., chided the Baker Theater for encouraging "stage-struck people already employed in other lines of private industry, to throw up those jobs and take a course in acting at the expense of the taxpayers."[29] Thousands paid from 25¢ to 40¢ to see serious dramas such as Elmer Rice's *The Adding Machine* and light fare such as *The Dragon's Wishbone* at the Baker, but conservatives accused the theater of being communistic.

While the *Post* blasted the New Deal, the *Rocky Mountain News* defended it. Claude Boettcher complained to Scripps-Howard head Roy Howard: "The present editorial policy of the *News* is anything but pleasing to the business interests of Denver."[30] Howard replied that "not only the interests of the masses, but of men like you and me — call us capitalists, if you please, — will be best served by a continuance of the present Democratic administration."[31] Boettcher disagreed. At a dinner party he argued with *News* editor Forrest Davis so heatedly that, according to Davis, "I was forced to dress him down." Davis labeled Boettcher and his associates "economic royalists." The editor attributed the finan-

The Baker Federal Theater staged nearly 500 performances between 1936 and 1939. (U.S. National Archives.)

cier's bad manners partly to his being "half crocked."[32] The truth was that Boettcher and many of his friends, drunk or sober, disliked relief programs.

The debate over old-age pensions revealed the divisions between haves and have-nots. In 1936, Coloradans, spurred by attorney O. Otto Moore, amended the state's constitution to provide pensions of up to $45 a month for persons over 60. Legislators hesitated to fund the program. Not until 1944 did pensioners receive the payments. Their failure to fund pensions reflected the stance of most of Colorado's legislators during the depression. James Wickens, in his detailed study *Colorado in the Great Depression,* noted that while the poor suffered from hunger, Colorado spent much of its surplus revenue on debt reduction.

Even well-intentioned relief efforts sometimes went awry. W. J. Nixon, otherwise known as Chandu the Magician, played Bunny Rabbit in the Federal Theater's production of *The Dragon's Wishbone* and then was asked to continue at the theater. Happy to be working, he borrowed $163 for his magic show outfit, only to be fired almost immediately because of budget cuts. He wrote to the WPA in Washington, begging for a job, and, as a last resort, offered to send the bureaucrats his bag of tricks if they would pay for it. A similar problem faced 950 unpaid men working on stabilizing the Cherry Creek channel in July 1938. Less polite than

Free swimming at city parks brightened depression-era childhood. These youngsters at Curtis Park pool include a 14-year-old AAU low-board girl's champion, Viola Salazar (far right, seated). (Tom Noel Collection.)

Chandu, and with more bargaining power, they sat down on the job. One laborer told the *Rocky Mountain News* that he had not been paid for three weeks. "I have seven children. We haven't had any food for four days. I got $42.50 on my last pay day, June 26, but that's all gone now."[33]

Despite such internal snafus and considerable external opposition, the New Deal agencies did relieve suffering. Charles Tribble recalled: "It was close to violence. . . . I think the WPA program was what diverted this."[34] From mid-1935 to the end of 1937 the WPA spent $42 million in Colorado — $5 million more than the state produced in gold during the same period. Yet, all the New Deal programs could not put the nation's economy back together again. A decade after the stock market crash, thousands of Denverites were still looking for work.

But 1939 was not 1929. By 1939, the community, to some degree, had acknowledged its obligation to lend a hand to its less fortunate residents.

Even the Boettchers had grown more civic minded. In 1937, Claude Boettcher established a foundation to fund Colorado projects. "My father and I have been very successful in Colorado and we owe everything to this state," Claude reportedly admitted.[35] When voters rejected a 1938 bond issue, part of which would have funded a school for crippled children, Boettcher stepped in and more than matched federal money to build the facility. Two years later, the Boettcher Foundation paid for the Allen True murals in the state capitol rotunda depicting western water development. Frontier privatism had been struck a blow by the depression. That the government would try to provide work, however, was small consolation to dispirited East High School seniors in 1939 who ran a headline in the school newspaper: "WPA Here We Come."[36]

Uncle Sam had different plans. As Europe moved toward war, the United States strengthened its defenses. By 1937 more than 1,500 of Denver's WPA workers were remaking the Agnes Phipps Memorial Tuberculosis Sanatorium at Sixth Avenue and Quebec Street into an Army Air Corps Technical School — the beginnings of Lowry Air Base. When WPA ceased operating in 1943, Denver's high school graduates no longer worried about jobs. They knew that the military wanted them. America was at war.

CHAPTER 19

Denver Goes to War

> What do Denver children think of these planes? It must be like the
> sound of a brook to a mountain child. If it ever stopped perhaps they
> couldn't sleep.
>
> Thomas Hornsby Ferril
> *Rocky Mountain Herald,* July 24, 1943[1]

President Franklin D. Roosevelt was worried in late 1940. War raged in
Europe, Asia, and North Africa. Although the United States was at
peace with the belligerents, the country was vulnerable. By radio the
president warned Americans that "at one point between Africa and
Brazil the distance is less than the distance from Washington to Denver
— five hours for the latest type of bomber." Bombers had troubled
Americans since late 1939 when war broke out in Europe. By December
1940, Germany had conquered France and was pounding England from
the air. Roosevelt wanted the United States to help Britain: "We must be
the great arsenal of democracy."[2]

Isolated Denver, like much of the rest of the country, did not fully
support the president. In 1937 the *Denver Post* advised Uncle Sam, "If
another war is coming, let's wait for it to arrive this time instead of going
out to meet it."[3] By 1940 Mayor Benjamin Stapleton said he favored
preparedness. James Q. Newton, Sr., a prominent stockbroker, agreed
with Roosevelt but Earnest F. Barry, a creamery owner, cautioned against
aiding England, which he regarded as "a bad credit risk." The Reverend

Paul Roberts, dean of St. John's Episcopal cathedral, recalling the carnage of World War I, saw FDR's proposal as "another step along the tragic and hopeless road that some of us remember from twenty years ago."[4]

The Japanese sneak attack on Pearl Harbor, December 7, 1941, shattered isolationist sentiment. Within days the United States was

All lives, even those of Denver elementary school children such as this lad, were touched by World War II. (Tom Noel Collection.)

at war with Japan, Germany, and Italy. Describing the attack as the "act of a mad dog," the *Denver Post* editorialized, "Japan started it. The United States will finish it."[5] The *Post* could not predict how or when. Isolationism had left the nation ill prepared for war. The day Pearl Harbor was bombed, the *Post*, which had printed the day's issue before it learned of the attack, smugly captioned its pictures of homes decorated for Christmas with the headline "No Christmas blackout here."[6] Even after Pearl Harbor, citizens blithely bedecked their houses, trees, and bushes with bright lights in hopes that they might win the *Post's* annual Christmas lighting contest. As usual, the Civic Center was a garish blaze.

Such nonchalance quickly evaporated. Within a year Denverites were learning air raid rules, sewing blackout curtains, saving tin and lard, conserving gasoline and tires. Outdoor Christmas lights on homes, a tradition since 1914, were turned off. Children stopped asking Santa Claus for trikes and bikes — metal and rubber were scarce. By the end of the war in August 1945 more than 1,300 Denver-area residents had lost their lives. At home, hundreds of thousands of others saw their lives and their city transformed.

The changes had started before the war. Despite its isolationist leanings, depression-plagued Denver saw that there were money and jobs in defense industries. To induce the army to locate an air corps training center near the city, Denver floated $750,000 in bonds to purchase the Agnes Memorial Sanatorium at East Sixth Avenue and Quebec Street. To its 880 acres the city added another 960 and to seal the deal provided a bombing range of 100 square miles southeast of town. All was donated to the army, which on February 26, 1938, dedicated Lowry Air Base, naming it after Denverite Francis B. Lowry, who had been shot down over France during World War I. Six years later over

Colorado's generally clear, dry climate made Denver the choice for Army Air Corps training in aerial photography and bombardiering. This outdoor class at Lowry was dedicated to basic nomenclature. (Denver Public Library, Western History Department.)

600 buildings dotted the post where thousands of army airmen (the Air Force became an independent service in 1947) learned aerial photography, bombing techniques, and low-level flying. So rapid and massive was the buildup that Lowry soon proved inadequate. On May 18, 1942, contractors started pouring the concrete for another air facility, Buckley Field, southeast of Lowry, which was dedicated less than six weeks later on July 1, 1942. Soon Buckley's officers were making overweight youths with "mushy muscles" into tough, trained airmen.[7]

Fitzsimons Army Hospital, a relic of World War I, underwent a massive refurbishing on the eve of World War II. Its new, $3.5 million main building boasted 610 beds and some 7 million cubic feet of space, making it the largest structure in Colorado. Lowry, Buckley, and Fitzsimons generated jobs and business. They also transformed Aurora from a drowsy suburb, known for its jackrabbits and rattlesnakes, into Denver's most populous bedroom community.

Soldiers were everywhere. West of Denver, military policemen trained at Golden's Camp George West. In northeast Denver, at Thirty-

Agnes Phipps Memorial Tuberculosis Sanatorium in east Denver was reincarnated as Lowry Air Force Base in 1938. (Denver Public Library, Western History Department.)

eighth and York, the army built a great depot for medical supplies — 10 buildings encompassing 562,000 square feet. South of the city at old Fort Logan (1887), where cavalry men once paraded, army recruits learned how to type.

Spurred by patriotism and by the defense dollars flowing into the local economy, the community welcomed the GIs. United Service Organizations (USO) clubs sprang up quickly. Soon there were servicemen's centers, the largest at 1417 California, and servicewomen's centers. Reflecting the segregation that plagued the armed forces, black clubs were established in the Five Points area. Nevertheless, there was erosion of old prejudices. Sociologist Henry Hough observed in 1942 that businesses "notorious for their discrimination against minority groups are now discreet enough to make exceptions in the case of men in uniform, at least in Denver." Noting that "there has been some talk of developing a center for Spanish-speaking soldiers, patterned after the center for Negro soldiers," Hough argued that "there should be no need for such an additional center if the established community agencies are able to meet the need."[8] Despite Hough's advice, separateness continued — the African-American USO in 1944 served some 67,000 soldiers. In September 1945, a month after the war ended, citywide USO establishments provided for 75,000 guests — on September 23 alone, 5,000 used the clubs.

Individuals also made soldiers welcome. Mary Lathrop, a longtime lawyer, took servicemen by the dozen to plush restaurants such as Baur's and the Albany Hotel, where she bought them dinner. Seeing bored soldiers strolling along Colfax, firemen stopped motorists bound for the mountains and urged them to take a soldier along. Mothers, whose own sons and daughters were away at war, regularly greeted troop trains at Union Station and treated the "boys" to coffee and sandwiches at the station or at the nearby Oxford Hotel.

Rocky Mountain News columnist Molly Mayfield (pen name of Frankie Foster, wife of *News* editor Jack Foster) extended a helping hand by giving advice to lonely young men and their sweethearts. When one woman complained about a Buckley soldier, "just one gorgeous hunk of a man," who appeared indifferent to her, Molly outlined the lovesick lass's choices: "Be indifferent yourself," try the "let's be friends routine," or "let him know exactly how you feel."[9] To mock Molly's sweet advice, Lowry soldiers invented Harriet Hayfever, a columnist for the base paper, the Lowry *Rev-Meter,* who fielded questions such as "Dear Mrs. Hayfever: I am a soldier and every time I walk down the street girls whistle at me. What should I do."[10] Harriet told the harassed noncom to ignore the come-ons unless the lady whistled "The Star Spangled Banner," in which case he should stand at attention.

The army and the city, unlike Harriet Hayfever, fretted about unruly soldiers and shady ladies. Officials declared war on prostitution in July 1942 and later that month requested bars to close at midnight. In 1944 police Captain John F. O'Donnell averred that the city had "no morals problem."[11] Women called "victory girls," described by police as misguided patriots, appeared in 1943, but authorities ran most of those amateur camp followers out of town. Professional prostitutes were arrested. A 1944 inspection of 23,000 soldiers at Lowry netted only 10 cases of venereal disease.

The thousands of uniformed personnel crowding the streets and jamming Union Station, the estimated 4 million servicemen and women who passed through Denver during the war, clearly showed the community that the nation was at war. Less visible, indeed sometimes cloaked in secrecy, were the city's war industries. Few people knew exactly what was going on northeast of town at the Rocky Mountain Arsenal, established in 1942, where lethal gases and napalm bombs were made. After the war, Denverites learned that arsenal bombs had been dropped on Tokyo on March 9 and 10, 1945, burning to death 83,000 people. "In all," the

Denver Post later bragged, "69 cities were reduced to smouldering ash heaps with compliments of the Rocky Mountain Arsenal."[12]

While the press downplayed the arsenal's activities, it openly reported on the city's shipbuilding efforts. On March 5, 1942, Governor Ralph Carr and Mayor Stapleton launched Denver's first ship, dubbed the *Mountain Maid*. Actually, the craft was prefabricated parts for a navy escort vessel. Later, area firms, led by Thompson Pipe and Steel, prefabricated barges and amphibious landing craft.[13]

West of the city, at Remington's Denver Ordnance Plant, thousands of workers made ammunition, while at Cobusco Steel long-range shells were manufactured. Many Denverites knew that near the Municipal Airport over 3,000 Continental Airlines workers were modifying bombers, B-17s and B-29s, and a few fighter aircraft, to make them war-worthy. Smaller war industries, such as the Carothers-Clark egg dehydration plant, which employed 180 workers to turn 540,000 eggs a day into

George Cranmer, shown here at the 1967 unveiling of his plaque at Stapleton Airport, cleverly funneled federal funds into many public projects, from the airport to Red Rocks outdoor amphitheater. (Denver Public Library, Western History Department.)

powder, did not command as much attention as the big employers. Yet taken as a whole, the small and the large defense plants rapidly changed Denver from a city of unemployment to one with a labor shortage. War was hell on the fighting front, but on the home front it brought prosperity.[14]

Denver owed much of its good fortune to sharp-eyed local officials, particularly Manager of Parks and Improvements George Cranmer, and to the city's congressman, Lawrence Lewis. First elected on a New Deal platform in 1932, Lewis managed to keep many businessmen on his side during the 1930s. Spared serious political challengers, he lived in Washington, occasionally returning to his district where he stayed at the University Club, talked with the mayor, dined with bankers, clipped his bond coupons, and campaigned a little. In Washington the bachelor Lewis tended to duty — rarely missing a congressional roll call and almost always arriving early so he could get a front seat in the House of Representatives, which then did not assign seats. More importantly, he learned the Washington ropes and gained access to such powerful figures as Army Chief of Staff General George C. Marshall.

When, in September 1940, Lewis heard from George Cranmer that Remington (a subsidiary of DuPont Chemical) planned to build a munitions factory in the West, he asked Cranmer to fly to Washington to confer with the general. Cranmer recalled the meeting: "I never talked with a man who was more difficult to talk with than Marshall. He had completely no expression."[15] Despite Cranmer's chilly reception, DuPont liked the Denver area; it already ran a dynamite plant at Louviers, 30

miles southwest of the city. Dupont
agreed to locate the Remington facility on a 2,100-acre tract in Jefferson County, where the clay soil cut
down on dust that otherwise might
have gummed up the machines. Late
in the war, when the need for light
artillery shells declined, industrialist
Henry Kaiser took over portions of
the plant to make heavy munitions
while other parts were devoted to
producing K rations for the armed
services.

The New Deal and World War
II expanded federal involve-
ment in practically every as-
pect of urban life, including
housing. Denver's first Federal
Housing Authority project,
Country Club Gardens at
Downing and Ellsworth,
opened in 1940. (Photo by
Glenn Cuerden.)

Defense dollars changed the city fast. In the late 1930s citizens
rejoiced when the federal government announced construction of a $1.5
million prison, the Federal Correctional Institution for young men, three
miles west of Fort Logan. In 1940 they took pride in the $1.2 million
Country Club Gardens, luxury apartments at Ellsworth and Downing.
Later that year they bragged about the new Lincoln Park Housing project
at Colfax and Mariposa, initially designed to house 93 low-income families, where a six-room apartment rented for $18.75 a month. And they
boasted of the south Denver Post Office substation, an $80,000 facility at
Cedar and Broadway — a clear sign, said the *Post*, "that Denver's population is growing rapidly."[16]

By late 1941 federal expenditures of $80,000 hardly merited mention.
The mess hall at Lowry cost $266,000, and the *Post* estimated that the air
base, including planes, was worth over $40 million. The Remington
Plant, completed between ground breaking on February 17, 1941, and
dedication on October 25, cost $20 million to build and brought Reming-
ton an initial contract for more than $80 million. With a work force that
peaked at 19,500 in mid-1943, that one facility made New Deal make-
work agencies such as WPA and the Public Works Administration super-
fluous. Smaller war industries did their part to win the war and build up
the city's economy. In December 1944, Bluhill Foods at 711 South Broadway received a $77,393 contract from the army to pack 454,320 eight-
ounce cans of peanuts. A few months later Groswold Ski Company
landed an order for 33,000 snowshoes at about $10 each. Timpte built
semitrailers, Colorado Tent and Awning made parachutes, Western
States Cutlery in Boulder manufactured knives.

World War II killed the Great Depression by creating millions of new jobs and a demand for food, such as these Colorado spuds. (Amon Carter Museum, Mazzulla Collection.)

Besides benefiting directly from defense, Denver prospered because of rising demand fostered by the war. At the stockyards, livestock receipts rose above $70 million in 1941, over $10 million more than in 1940. The value of produce sold through the Denargo Market, which opened in 1939 at Twenty-ninth and Broadway, and the Wazee Market at Twelfth and Walnut rose to more than $9 million in 1941, an increase of $760,000 over the previous year. In the same period Colorado's wholesale trade grew by nearly 10 percent with Denver accounting for nearly 70 percent of the state's trade. The boom was also reflected in housing starts.

On the home front, Denver went to war with scrap drives, Victory Gardens, and morale-boosting exercises such as this War Chest of Colorado Parade. (Amon Carter Museum, Mazzulla Collection.)

In 1940 Denverites spent more than $8 million for homes, a threefold increase over 1938. In 1941, before war restrictions curtailed residential construction, more than $14 million was invested in new houses — a total not seen since 1929.

Denver liked prosperity but soon found that the war brought problems, too. Over 60,000 area residents volunteered or were drafted during the war; more than 1,300 of them did not come back. Some women volunteered: Alice Aronson, a teacher at South High School, became Denver's first WAVE in 1942. Many others remained at home to raise families and to work in war industries. Opportunity School arranged classes for women in machine shop, welding, radio maintenance, and sheet metal work. At the University of Denver women learned laboratory techniques so that they could work at the Rocky Mountain Arsenal. Jobs traditionally held by men were quickly filled by women as the draft took its toll. In 1942, the city hired nine female lifeguards, and the same year the *Denver Post* reported that a crew of women was working in south Denver repairing railroad tracks. In 1944, Fitzhugh L. Carmichael, a University of Denver professor, estimated that women held half of the 206,000 jobs in the metropolitan area. Part of this work force represented new arrivals, women who had come to Denver to be near their husbands and boyfriends in the military.

Even dogs, particularly German shepherds, perked up their ears when Uncle Sam whistled. Mickey, guard dog at the Capitol Coal Company, and Zip, Fairmount Cemetery's watchdog, both joined the army.

Compared to residents of coastal states, Denver's civilians were relatively safe from attack. Still, cautious officials organized defense councils, appointed air wardens, and recruited auxiliary police and fire fighters. On July 12, 1942, police simulated a bomb attack at Thirteenth Avenue and Josephine Street in order to test their response. A September trial of the city's big air raid siren, Paul Revere, demonstrated that Paul's soprano voice could not be heard well. Paul failed again during a test on December 14, 1942, when he "produced only a weak tone or none at all."[17]

Residents were ordered to douse lights during drills or to use blackout curtains. The Littleton Independent advised its readers: "If bombs fall near you, lie down."[18] A blackout test in mid-December 1942 brought an almost total darkening of the city. A few, however, ignored the exercise. Joseph Prechtl of 1025 Lipan left his lights blazing. When air raid wardens scolded him he switched on more. Refusing to pay a $50 fine, Prechtl went to jail.

Denver was in more danger from Lowry pilots practicing low-level flying than it was from the Germans or the Japanese. "I was in the bathroom shaving and I heard the engines falter," William K. Leonard reminisced as he remembered the tragedy of Sunday morning, September 26, 1943.[19] Moments later a B-24 Liberator with seven crewmen aboard crashed in vacant land near 2520 South Marion, a mile southwest of the University of Denver. Although the burning plane scorched five nearby houses and destroyed a garage, no civilian lives were lost. Investigators theorized that the pilot, Raymond Hansen, aimed for the open field when he realized that he was going to crash.

Journalist Thomas Hornsby Ferril speculated that children had grown so accustomed to the roar of planes that without the din they could not sleep. But Ferril never asked any toddlers. Denver historian Stephen Leonard recalled that as a child he hid in his sandbox at 2284 South Downing to get away from the dark, sinister, and noisy aircraft that skimmed the treetops in that otherwise quiet neighborhood on the city's southeastern fringe. The jitters gradually wore off. The only enemy air threat, a small one, came near the end of the war. In 1945 the Japanese, in desperation, launched 9,000 bomb-laden paper balloons, hoping that winds would carry them to North America. On March 19 one harmlessly exploded on a farm near Timnath, 70 miles north of Denver. That was as close as the city came to being bombed, and that episode frightened only a few, for it was not widely reported until after the war.[20]

For most people the daily annoyances of shortages and price controls were more vexing than the fear of being flattened by a disabled bomber. To cope with the war's dislocations, the federal government mounted a series of programs. Salvage drives netted tons of rubber, aluminum, tin, iron, fat, paper, and silk. Rationing assured that food and material would be available for the military. Since much money was being pumped into the economy while there was restricted production for civilians, the danger of inflation loomed. To prevent that, the government controlled prices. To sop up the extra cash that Americans were earning but could not spend because of price controls and rationing, the national treasury sold bonds to finance the war and to encourage citizens to save.

Denver had started recycling scrap before the United States entered the war. The Defense Council collected over 20 tons of aluminum in July 1941. People were told to "Win with Tin," so they turned in their toothpaste tubes. Kids who saved copper got free Saturday matinee admission to Harry Huffman's theaters — Huffman headed the copper drive. Courts sent their rubber doormats to the salvage heap. Cuspidors and a bank vault from the Ernest and Cranmer Building, some of the tramway's streetcar track, and metal fences were thrown on the pile. Byers Junior High School students stuffed an effigy of Adolf Hitler with 1,220 silk stockings before sending the hosiery off to war. Housewives saved fat, rags, and paper — fat was used to make paint for tanks, anti-icing fluid, and munitions; paper could be transformed into tropical helmets and bomb fins. Even costume jewelry had war uses, the *Colorado Salvage Newsletter* explained: "These items are used by our boys in the South Pacific to purchase services from the natives. Fifty-two fox holes were dug for a brooch and a pair of earrings."[21]

When salvage drives succeeded and bond sales went well, citizens reveled in their patriotism. And they took special pride in their 60,000 Victory Gardens, which yielded carrots, onions, radishes, corn, and other crops. But Denverites were less enthusiastic about mandatory restrictions, and some of them evaded rationing and price controls. From the start of the war the United States faced a critical rubber shortage; Japan dominated Southeast Asia, where most rubber was produced. In late 1942, residents were required to turn in all tires they owned in excess of five — the order brought in 190,000 tires. Gas rationing cut down on tire use and conserved fuel. Streetcar ridership boomed. The Office of Price Administration (OPA) allocated other scarce items, including shoes, butter, meat, sugar, cooking oil, and typewriters. One OPA official, his biases evident, complained about "little Mexican mothers" who begged for replacement stamps "because the baby gave them to the puppy."[22] Restaurateurs threatened to close unless they got more food. Their bluster, the OPA said, was a ploy to gain the support of downtown workers "faced with the proposition of carrying lunch or going hungry at noontime."[23]

To curb inflation, the OPA controlled many prices with 614 different regulations. Dairymen talked of striking to force the OPA to allow an increase in the price of milk. When regulators refused, the City Council taxed milk 2¢ a quart and refunded that amount to the producers — a circumvention that was later declared illegal. The agency tried to check runaway rents spawned by a severe housing shortage, a product of increasing population and the moratorium on most civilian building. Only 529 housing units were constructed in Denver in 1943. Old Capitol Hill mansions became apartment houses besieged by would-be boarders. Stores were converted to residences, and hotels overflowed with war workers and military personnel.

Motorists chafed at gasoline restrictions, and a black market soon sprang up. Drivers could have a "quickie" delivered to their homes. "A quickie," the *Rocky Mountain News* reported, was "a tideover supply of two or three gallons, at exorbitant prices, delivered in a can set behind shubbery or the ash pit as bottles of liquor once were provided."[24] Seventeen-year-old Bruce Wier confessed in 1944 that he had stolen gas ration stamps from the Golden ration office and then sold them to other students at West High. It was, Wier confessed, "a happy idea" he had to make money.[25] Investigators found that some stations had been watering their gas to stretch supplies — thereby leaving some for the black market. Richard Y. Batterton, regional OPA administrator, warned that such diversions reduced the amount of gas available to law-abiding citizens. When greedy merchants near military bases overcharged for beer and soft drinks, former district attorney John Carroll, then an attorney for OPA, vowed a crackdown on "a low form of chiseling."[26] OPA continually fought a difficult war on the home front, admitting that "only a tiny fraction of a percent of the violators of price and posting regulations ever had sanctions applied to them."[27]

Many people disliked regulators. The *Denver Post* called the old Kittredge Building, where the OPA was headquartered, the "arsenal of bureaucracy." There, claimed the newspaper, "the office boys are paid twice what soldiers, sailors and marines get."[28] The government workers provided anti-Roosevelt copy for the *Post*, but businessmen were generally pleased with the region's growing federal presence. In 1933 attorney James Grafton Rogers predicted that "the extent to which Denver holds its lead as a western center for federal bureaus may be of vast importance to its future."[29] As the government expanded during the New Deal, Denver's federal employment grew. By 1935, architect G. Meredith Musick, Sr., proclaimed that the city had gained "the undisputed title of second capital."[30] In 1936 the *Post* guessed that there were from 8,000 to 10,000 federal workers puttering away in such buildings as the Old Customs House, the New Customs House, the Telephone Building, the Post Office, and the Patterson Building. By late 1940 Denver claimed over 7,000 federal employees, not counting soldiers and WPA workers. War agencies such as the Office of War Information's radio bureau, directed by Ben Bezoff, and the regional information arm of the Office of Emergency Management, headed by journalist Gene Cervi, brought in additional employees. In 1943 the Chamber of Commerce counted 185 federal administrative offices in the Mile High City, of which 134 were regional or national in scope.

Denver sought federal workers. It was far less warm toward Japanese-Americans whose small community clustered near the Tri-State Buddhist Temple grew from 324 persons in 1940 to 2,310 in 1944. Ordered to leave the West Coast in early 1942, Japanese-Americans moved inland. Some came voluntarily; others were forced into detention camps such as the one at Amache near Grenada in southeastern Colorado. After detainees were slowly released, some gravitated to Denver. They hoped to find a haven in Colorado since Ralph Carr, the state's governor from 1939 to 1943, welcomed and defended them. Carr argued that putting U.S. citizens in concentration camps because of their race violated the Constitution and warned: "If a majority may seize a minority and place them in jails today, then every minority group regardless may expect the majority to treat them the same way."[31] Japanese-Americans soon realized that Carr did not speak for everyone; indeed he was one of the few high officials in the country openly to disagree with the federal government's manhandling of Japanese-American citizens. Ex-governor Johnson, one of Colorado's most popular politicians, said that had he been in office he would have barred Americans of Japanese descent from the state. Johnson accused Carr of failing to recognize that "the normal human reaction of our own people is hostility toward these brown men."[32]

Hostility smouldered beneath the surface, only occasionally breaking into flame. Residential segregation kept most Japanese separated from the rest of Denver. Japanese businesses were concentrated northeast of downtown at the behest of the safety manager's office, which "saw fit [to do so] because of the fear of racial prejudice."[33] In 1944 investigators for the Bureau of Public Welfare reported that Japanese were tolerated in public places "so long as they do not attend in sufficiently large groups to bring them to general attention."[34]

That same year, however, Coloradans turned down an amendment to the state constitution aimed at preventing Japanese aliens from owning land in the state. Earl Mann of Denver, then the only African-American member of Colorado's House of Representatives, urged voters to reject the measure, but in Denver it passed, by a 10,000-vote margin. *Denver Post* editor William Shepherd put a large cutout of a Japanese man with a monkey face on his desk. The paper reflected Shepherd's biases as it banged the drums of bigotry. The *Rocky Mountain News* was more tolerant, observing that "we do not try to punish Americans of German ancestry."[35] Prejudice died hard. As late as 1949, Kenneth Shibata, a Japanese-American war hero, was denied burial in Crown Hill cemetery because of his race. In 1950 another veteran, Katsuto K. Gow, found it difficult to purchase a house at 2718 Gaylord because of his ancestry.[36]

Denver sedately celebrated the end of war in Europe on May 8, 1945, with the ringing of bells and with church services. Not until Japan surrendered on August 14 did the city really rejoice. Thousands poured into downtown, honking horns, beating pans, setting off old firecrackers saved for the event. A "screaming mass of happy people" stopped trolley traffic on Sixteenth Street. Revelers swarmed over a police car at Sixteenth and California, crushing its roof. *Rocky Mountain News* reporter Sam Lusky watched as "servicemen kissed their girls and they kissed somebody else's girl and pretty soon everybody was kissing everybody else, and nobody was complaining."[37]

Beneath the joy, Lusky sensed sadness, mourning for dead fathers, sons, brothers, husbands. More than a thousand of the nearly 45,000 Denverites who either volunteered or were drafted did not return home. Adams, Arapahoe, Boulder, and Jefferson counties sent 14,000 of their citizens to war; more than 300 did not come back. Grieving parents, anxious that their sons should be buried locally, pressed for establishment of a national cemetery at Fort Logan. Kathrien Miller and veterans organizations led the fight. Miller's son, Harry, a flight engineer, was wounded while on a bombing mission over Japan in October 1944. He parachuted into China, dying later of his wounds. Peasants, thinking he was from heaven, built a shrine to him. Later, the army removed his body to Singapore and then to Hawaii. Mrs. Miller wanted him buried nearer home. John Carroll, elected to Congress from Denver in 1946, agreed with her, but cemetery owners objected to federally funded burial grounds. Harry L. Luckenbach, president of Crown Hill cemetery, explained that his association opposed the proposed cemetery, "not as cemetery men, but as taxpayers."[38] Eventually, Miller and Carroll prevailed. In November 1950, six years after he died, Harry Miller was laid to rest at Fort Logan.

The jubilation of August 14 also masked economic uncertainty. People wondered if peace heralded the return of economic hard times. Estimating that more than 14,000 workers were employed in local defense plants, Robert Harvey, director of the Defense Council, worried about layoffs: "At one fell swoop, in a day, cancellations may come and those people will be thrown out. . . .Where are you going to find jobs for returnees? The attitude of the boys is unhappy — they are restless and dissatisfied. We often hear 'what have we been fighting for?' "[39] Vera Packard told the council that women, "who have learned for the first time in their lives that they can do something real," would also be dislocated. She suggested that the city hire women to supervise delinquent children: "Such work would give them an idea that they are still doing something useful."[40]

Many of the anticipated problems did not materialize. Although millions were discharged from the military, the United States did not fully demobilize, and within a short time the country's worldwide defense commitment brought a new military buildup. Lowry remained an active post; Buckley was devoted to Naval Reserve and Colorado National Guard activities. Nor did federal agencies disband; they just became less visible as government employees moved from the Kittredge Building and other downtown offices to the vacant Remington Arms Plant, which was converted to the Denver Federal Center.

Servicemen who had found Denver hospitable during the war returned to go to school and to start families. Robert Harvey told the Defense Council that 92 percent of military men stationed in Denver wanted to come back. "With our housing problem and tragic shortages, we do not know what we are going to do with them."[41] In one sense the solution was simple. Denver built houses. In 1946, up to then a record year, permits were issued for 5,198 living units.[42] That was only the beginning as the metropolitan area awoke to the postwar world.

CHAPTER 20

The Postwar Awakening

Denver is Olympian, impassive and inert. It is probably the most self-sufficient, isolated and self-contained city in the world.

John Gunther
Inside USA, 1947[1]

World War II triggered a tremendous transformation in Denver. Massive federal spending, an influx of newcomers, and a pent-up demand for new cars and new housing unavailable during the war led to a boom that changed a drowsy provincial city into a sprawling metropolis.

Returning natives were joined by thousands of recent arrivals — many of them ex-military personnel who had fallen in love with the clean, green, and friendly Mile High City. Both natives and newcomers soon sought to modernize a town that seemed stagnant, if not backward. Ironically, this population explosion would threaten the very qualities that made Denver attractive — its small-town friendliness; clean air; mountain views; uncrowded streets, parks, and highland playgrounds. Not until the 1970s would the push for growth be reassessed. Not until the 1980s would the oil bust end the city's second great boom era.

In the late 1940s few doubted the need for change. National observers such as John Gunther were not alone in portraying Denver as a sleeping giant. Robert L. Perkin, a *Rocky Mountain News* journalist, came to a similar conclusion in 1949: "Today Denver is the reluctant capital of a region larger than most nations. It is big and beautiful, and the climate

From 2,000 feet overhead, 1956 Denver looked like a low-rise city although the recently completed Mile High Center and Denver Club Building (both right center) began a postwar eruption of skyscrapers. (Photo by Otto Roach.)

is still superb. It is also smug, sleek, and satisfied . . . contentedly disinterested in its own continuing growth, abhorrent of risk-taking, chary of progress."[2]

After the booms and busts of the 1858–1900 era, Denver's growth had slowed. Between 1900 and 1940, its population had climbed from 133,859 to 322,412. This increase far exceeded the national gain of 42 percent during the same period, but it paled in comparison to the city's spectacular growth between 1860 and 1900 when the population had skyrocketed. The first four decades of the twentieth century saw Denver slip from third among cities west of the Missouri River to fifth, behind Los Angeles, San Francisco, Houston, and Seattle. Once a booming center of speculation, Denver now played second fiddle to faster-growing

Pacific Coast towns. To make matters worse, many affluent Denverites moved or retired to snowless southern California.

Those who stayed saw only moderate change in their town. In 1946 the Daniels and Fisher's tower still dominated the city's modest skyline, as it had since 1911. The Equitable Building remained the finest office building, as it was 50 years earlier, and the Brown Palace, over a half-century old, remained the premier hotel. In both commercial and residential construction the community's conservatism was expressed in solid, classical architecture; city builders shunned the bigger, taller, and more modern. Older buildings and neighborhoods were maintained rather than demolished for redevelopment. Occasionally, an adventuresome architect such as Burnham Hoyt experimented with art deco, art moderne, or the international style, but most people preferred brick bungalows or two-story, solid, square, well-built brick structures in traditional styles. Not until after the war did ranch houses and modern commercial buildings prevail.

City fathers feared change, as did most business leaders. The Chamber of Commerce proposed in 1946 that Denver be made the nation's capital and suggested that the city be designated as the United Nation's headquarters, but that was pie-in-the-sky Babbitry that few took seriously. Spasmodic boosterism aside, Denver remained low-key, apparently disinterested in sprucing up its image. Colorado's fine beef was sold nationwide, and even in Denver, as "Kansas City cuts." In this laid-back city, visitors were perplexed by the virtually unreadable, tiny street-name signs, lettered vertically.

The Brown Palace, which John Gunther praised as "quite possibly the best hotel in the United States," was becoming a nursing home for nodding nabobs. Rather than help new restaurants get started, Denverites patronized the predictable.[3] Sunday brunch at the Oxford Hotel, dinner and dancing at the Brown Palace became habitual. Out-of-towners were treated to a glimpse of pioneer days at Zeitz's Buckhorn Exchange, where Henry H. Zeitz, belt sagging with holster and six-gun, wandered among his guests who were seated amid stuffed animals and mementos of the Old West. Denver seemed to be resting, reflecting on the past rather than betting on the future.

There were advantages to this sedentary period. Economically, the city achieved a healthy diversity as tourism, health care, government work, service jobs, and manufacturing complemented agriculture and mining. As speculation tapered off, the city had time to refine urban services. Farsighted Mayor Speer laid out parks and parkways ahead of

residential development. Both Speer and Mayor Stapleton used this era of slower growth to improve the quality of life — tripling park space, building schools and libraries, paving hundreds of miles of streets and alleys, laying sidewalks, and installing sewers.

While services caught up with growth, capitalists napped, resting on their trust funds, dividends, and income property. Slow to forget the nightmare of the Great Depression, bankers dreamed and dressed decorously. Territorial Governor John Evans, founder of a dynasty, had bet his fortune on railroads and real estate; he died cash poor. His grandson, John Evans, Sr., son of tramway king William Gray Evans, sat on the family fortune. As president of the First National Bank from 1928 to 1959, the six-foot, four-inch, trim and tidy Evans dreaded shaky speculations such as the Moffat Railroad that had driven the First National to the brink of

Henry H. Zietz, Jr. (behind bar), and Henry H. Zietz, Sr., inside their Buckhorn Exchange, 1000 Osage Street. Denverites have dined here since the 1890s, surrounded by hundreds of stuffed animals. (Denver Public Library, Western History Department.)

238

Denver's parkways, a City Beautiful–era legacy, have aged gracefully. (Photo by Tom Noel.)

bankruptcy. "At all times," Evans declared, "be ready to pay off the depositors. . . . No bank is sound unless it is completely, absolutely, and beyond all doubt in the black."[4] Evans was wary of lending more than a tenth of his bank's deposits, declaring that at the First National Bank of Denver loan-to-deposit ratio would never exceed 32 percent.

Through the Denver Clearing House Banks Association, Evans and other like-minded financiers established conservative practices for all of Denver's national banks. While prodding depositors to squirrel away their cash in savings accounts, paying, during the 1930s, between 1 and 2.5 percent, bankers reluctantly lent at 6 percent and then only to borrowers with the safest possible collateral. Christmas Club accounts bore no interest, but savers were given holiday songbooks.

Denver's second-largest bank, Colorado National, remained a family operation from its start in 1862 until 1962 when Melvin J. Roberts became president. Charles Kountze, one of four brothers who had founded the bank, had boldly invested millions in mines and railroads. His son Harold and grandnephews, Merriam and George B. Berger, Jr., took fewer chances, guarding the CNB as if it was their piggy bank. Merriam Berger reflected CNB's close-to-the-chest lending policies. "New shoes," he philosophized, "do not impress me as much as old ones well cared for."[5]

Rather than grubstake untried ventures, local financiers invested in government bonds and tended the trust funds through which the fortunes of pioneers were cautiously doled out to their children and grandchildren. Denver bankers did not bankroll the Mile High City's postwar boom, despite the fact that their assets had tripled between 1941 and 1945, when many people, unable to buy homes and cars, saved millions of dollars.[6] Capital for Denver's expansion came largely from financial centers such as New York, Chicago, Philadelphia, and Boston rather than from the money houses of Seventeenth Street. Moreover, Denver's elderly elite tried to discourage potential rivals. Henry Kaiser considered locating a postwar plant in Denver. Local business leaders, however, gave him such a cool reception that he returned "to California all covered with hoarfrost."[7]

Denver's devotion to the status quo reflected the graying of the town's old guard. In 1945, John Evans, Sr., was 60; Gerald Hughes, then the board chairman at the First National Bank, was 69, as was Claude Boettcher. Claude's father, Charles, celebrated his ninety-second birthday that year. At 70, William Shepherd also rode with the rocking-chair moguls. So did the city's 75-year-old mayor, veteran of the Spanish-American War, Benjamin Stapleton. Aging aristocrats insulated themselves in fashionable residential neighborhoods — many near Cheesman Park, the Denver Country Club, and the Polo Club grounds; a few were in newer areas such as Cherry Hills in Arapahoe County and Lakeridge Road in Jefferson County. By intermarrying, they helped keep the upper crust from crumbling. John Evans, Sr., for example, preserved his family's position by wedding Gladys Cheesman, daughter of millionaire Walter Cheesman. Their son John's first wife was Alice L. Humphreys, daughter of Ira B. Humphreys, son of oilman Albert Humphreys, Sr. Ira's brother Albert married Claude Boettcher's daughter Ruth.[8] Such inbreeding led some to think of the Denver Country Club as the Denver Cousins' Club.

Claude Boettcher well represented this graying elite and its stranglehold on Denver. A formal, formidable man given to pince-nez, he used the "royal we" in boasting, "We've been here for seventy years. We made the prairie bloom. We turned sagebrush into sugar beets."[9] Boettcher displayed a degree of noblesse oblige by setting up the Boettcher Foundation to build schools, support cultural activities, and provide scholarships. So did other wealthy families who supported worthy causes through the Denver Foundation, the A. V. Hunter Trust, the Phipps Foundation and other eleemosynary agencies.

These plutocrats, in turn, expected the city to serve their interests. The law partners Gerald Hughes and Clayton Dorsey operated in the 1930s and 1940s much as William Gray Evans did in the earlier part of the century — they made sure that the voice of big business was heeded at City Hall and in the state capitol. Dorsey was a Republican, and his father had been a U.S. senator from Arkansas; Hughes was a Democrat, his father a U.S. senator from Colorado. Later, Montgomery Dorsey, Clayton's son, admitted that the Republican-Democratic combination in his father's firm was most convenient.[10]

Publicity-shy, behind-the-scenes string pullers, almost reverently known as "the Seventeenth Street crowd," Denver's elite usually did not grub for public office themselves. Hughes was a state representative early in his career, before he assumed heavy business responsibilities. Claude Boettcher, a taskmaster at work — "Everybody sat up to their desks, there was no slovenliness in the office then" — relaxed by collecting ship models, a flotilla he anchored at the Ship Tavern in the Brown Palace — a safe harbor since he owned the hotel.[11]

E. Warren Willard, one of Boettcher's associates, recalled in 1974 how the levers of power operated in 1942. That year the U.S. Securities and Exchange Commission ordered Cities Service, a national utility combine, to divest itself of Public Service Company of Colorado.

Boettcher wanted the company to become privately owned. When the rumor spread that Denver's manager of parks and improvements, George Cranmer, might propose public ownership of Public Service, Boettcher was pressed by eastern capitalists to take action. On a Sunday morning Willard joined Boettcher at his mansion on Eighth and Logan, where they discussed the situation. Boettcher said: "I'll settle this. I'm going over to see Ben Stapleton." Told that the mayor was at church, Boettcher replied, "Well he'll be getting out right now. I'll go over and see him and I'll get this fixed." In an hour Boettcher returned: "Boys, it's all fixed. Stapleton says he's heard nothing of this and if George Cranmer has any such ideas, which he doesn't think he has, he'll see that there is nothing to it."[12]

The ease with which the powerful got their way did not mean they did not compete; often they competed in a friendly and low-key way. John Clark Mitchell II, an officer of the Denver National Bank, was married to Nancy Kountze, daughter of Harold Kountze, CNB president. The Mitchells lived with Harold, but, Mitchell claimed, they did not discuss banking at home.[13] Sometimes, divisions went deeper. In the late 1920s Gerald Hughes threw Claude Boettcher out of his office when, in Hughes's view, Boettcher tried to take advantage of the heirs of an estate Hughes was administering.[14] That rift, however, did not affect the city's direction, for whatever their personal differences, both men preferred a community free of heavy industry, free of organized labor's influence. They wanted, and got, a pretty town of parks and parkways, a city that listened to them.

Mayor Stapleton was a good listener. George Cranmer, from 1935 to 1947 manager of parks and improvements, attributed part of Stapleton's success to his having been "a police judge so he knew all the police and crooks, which is an excellent preparation for mayor."[15] First elected mayor in 1923, "interminable Ben," with the exception of 1931, was continuously reelected. Although a Democrat, Stapleton was leery of Roosevelt's New Deal. In 1944, he reported that many cities expected the national government to finance postwar reconversion, but that since Washington got its money from cities and states, he hoped "we could take care of the situation ourselves."[16] Such notions pleased Boettcher and Hughes, who also thanked frugal Ben for keeping taxes low.

Time caught up with Stapleton in 1947. Cranmer recognized that his boss was "an old man," and the Rocky Mountain News urged the mayor, then 77, to "make way for the younger generation."[17] Stapleton disagreed and ran for a fifth term. To counteract his mossback image, he went to bat

Quigg Newton's 1947 election as mayor swept the Old Guard out of City Hall and expedited the transformation of a sleepy streetcar city into a bustling automobile metropolis. (Colorado Historical Society.)

in pre-game antics as the Denver Bears opened their Western Baseball League season on May 1, 1947. Richard Milhous Nixon, a young California congressman, threw the opening pitch. Stapleton swung, missed, and fell flat on his face. A photographer snapped the old Democrat sprawling in the dust before the future Republican president. *Life Magazine* ran the photo full page with the caption, "Mayor Strikes Out."[18]

That proved to be the case in the election. Stapleton lost to a 35-year-old Yale Law School graduate, James Q. Newton, Jr. Newton went by his middle name, Quigg, even though he risked being dubbed Fig Newton after the popular fig bar. "I was lucky it didn't become 'Pig'," Newton later reflected, remembering that Stapleton had told voters not to "buy a pig in a poke."[19] Besides a memorable name, Newton boasted a pedigree acceptable to the city's first families. His grandfather Whitney had been a vice-president of Boettcher's Ideal Cement Company; his father had been a partner in the brokerage house of Boettcher and Company. Quigg had married Virginia Shafroth, granddaughter of the respected ex-governor and ex-senator John F. Shafroth. With his Yale degree, Navy service, intelligence, and good looks, Newton attracted Republican and Democratic supporters.

Among his most influential backers was Palmer Hoyt. Formerly the editor of the *Portland Oregonian*, Hoyt had been hired in 1946 to turn the nationally infamous *Denver Post* into a respectable newspaper. An ambitious man, Hoyt also planned to change Denver, and in Newton, he saw a man capable of revitalizing city government. Shrewdly, the *Post* editor let his rival, *Rocky Mountain News* editor Jack Foster, endorse Newton first. Hoyt then threw the full weight of the *Post* behind Newton. Both dailies sang the candidate's praises, the *News* in the morning, the *Post* at supper time. Both carried Newton's charges that Stapleton had added 400 employees to the city payroll to push his campaign.

Newton drew broad support. His campaign manager, William West "Bill" Grant, an attorney from the Country Club district, counted among his uncles the former governor and founder of the Omaha and Grant smelter, James Grant. Andrew Wysowatcky, a political pro from the industrial enclave of Globeville whose father had worked in the smelters, also backed Newton. Quigg won easily, receiving nearly 80,000 votes while Stapleton polled only 17,640. The retiring mayor graciously showed his successor around the City and County Building. Laying a fatherly hand on Newton, Stapleton told him, "Young man, I've left you a beautiful city."[20]

Newton had his doubts. In a symbolic gesture, he removed spittoons, telltale tokens of the odorous old order, from city offices. He brought in young Turks eager to reshape municipal government. Among them were two of his campaign strategists, public relations men Gene Cervi and Ralph Radetsky. Radetsky quickly became Newton's chief advisor. Cervi, on the other hand, broke with the mayor. The split was perhaps inevitable since Cervi was a professional gadfly who used *Cervi's Rocky Mountain Journal,* a business newspaper he edited from 1945 to his death in 1970, to irritate the city's high and mighty.

Mayor Newton enjoyed the support of liberal Democrats as well as progressive Republicans. He wielded power well, instructing his department heads to map out changes that would catapult Denver into an era of aviation, governmental professionalism, and expanded municipal services. Not since the days of Mayor Speer had the city undergone such a transformation. Denver seemed young again and in love with its new mayor. Post editor Palmer Hoyt, who maintained almost daily contact with Newton, began running a "Good News Today" column, trumpeting the plans and achievements of the administration. Newton also used the radio effectively, conducting a weekly show called "The Mayor's Mailbag."

Newton took seriously his promises to reform city hall. He hired one of his Yale classmates, Hugh Catherwood, an expert on local government, to dismantle the patronage system through which Speer and Stapleton had built their machines. Catherwood, during a 1986 interview, recalled the heady days of 1947:

> Quigg wanted me to set up a personnel system. Stapleton's system, we discovered after moving into City Hall, consisted of color coded three-by-five cards with the person's name and recommendations such as "votes the right way." As director of budget and personnel, I helped to change the old patronage system which made every job a political job. We made hiring, firing, and salary not just an arbitrary matter, based on the mayor's whims, but a merit system.[21]

The Career Service Authority, created by a 1954 amendment to the city charter, allowed the mayor to appoint cabinet heads and 50 other officials. Other jobs were protected, and procedures were initiated for hiring and firing workers. Most people regarded Career Service as a sensible step into the twentieth century. But George Cranmer, who continued to observe city government until he died in 1975 at age 91, disliked the innovation. He regarded Newton as "the worst mayor Denver ever had. . . . He put in career service and all those darn fool committees and just made it so the machinery wouldn't work."[22]

Newton also asked Catherwood to set up a full-time budget office. Catherwood recalled that under Stapleton "there was no full time budget officer, just random requests for funds from various departments. City Council never asked questions as long as their districts got stop lights, snow and garbage removal, and street pavings. I asked . . . Cranmer . . . why Denver had no printed budget. He told me that it would be disastrous if people ever found out how the city spent their money."[23]

City Council also got a housecleaning. Denver's nine council districts were redrawn to reflect the total population, not just registered voters. The traditional system had given heavier representation to wealthier, whiter neighborhoods where voter registration tended to be greater than in poorer districts. In one of those richer areas, councilman Herbert C. Dolph, D.D.S., was trapped by zealous investigators as he seemingly accepted a bribe for a liquor license. Dolph won acquittal in court, but his resignation from the council signaled the twilight of the rubber-stamp councils that marked the Speer and Stapleton administrations.

"We tried to bring modern, efficient government to Denver," Catherwood recalled. "I spent days with a stopwatch timing trash trucks in alleys. Once Mayor Newton joined me in the alley, and he decided to ask Bruce Rockwell to straighten out the Department of Sanitary Services." Rockwell reminisced in 1986, "I worked as an administrative aide until the day Quigg called me in and said, 'Bruce, we're spending $4 million a year on sanitary services and none of us can tell what goes on down there.' "[24] Rockwell discovered that the department was a patronage hotbed with 15 of the city's Democratic district captains on its payroll.

Denver General Hospital, described by Newton as "a death trap," also needed a new broom. The mayor called on Doctor Solomon Kauvar, son of Rabbi Charles E. Hillel Kauvar of Beth Ha Medrosh Hagodol congregation, to head the Health Department. Doctor Florence Sabin, famed for her research on cellular structure and an expert on public health, was also recruited to upgrade health care programs.

Thomas P. Campbell, grandson of the former *Rocky Mountain News* owner Thomas M. Patterson, was appointed manager of improvements and parks, replacing Cranmer. "It took quite a while for Campbell and the rest of us to figure out where Cranmer had squirreled away various city funds for his pet projects such as Red Rocks and Winter Park," recalled Bruce Rockwell.[25]

In a whirlwind of activity, Newton launched the reformation. Contracts and purchases were put on a competitive, open-bid basis. Proper-

Florence Sabin, the only Coloradan to be honored with a statue in the nation's capital, became the first woman professor at Johns Hopkins University and the first woman elected to life membership in the National Academy of Sciences. Born in Central Ciy, she retired to Denver, where she introduced modern public health measures. (Denver Public Library, Western History Department.)

ty taxes were reassessed along more equitable lines, and a sales tax was introduced. An updated building code was enacted; ordinances were revised and codified.

Mayor Newton wanted to go even further, to thoroughly remake city government by writing a new city charter. A charter convention of 21 members, including 4 women, debated ideas such as banning racial discrimination in hiring and establishing a civilian review board to investigate complaints against the police. Lawyer William E. Doyle pushed progressive positions, and, as Doyle remembered it, businessman "Allan Phipps was the foreleader of the conservatives."[25] Even though drafters struck out some of the more controversial proposals, such as the antidiscrimination clause, voters rejected the 1947 charter. Some of the reforms it envisioned, among them merit personnel system, were later enacted piecemeal; others, such as the civilian review board, were not.

Another defeat faced Newton when he proposed toning down the garish Christmas display at the Civic Center. That caused a public uproar, second in recent times only to the revolt provoked when the legislature tried to remove the mountains from Colorado license plates. Despite groans from a few aesthetes and atheists, Newton bowed to the majority and reinstalled a full array of Christmas figures, ranging from the Baby Jesus to Rudolph the Red-Nosed Reindeer.

Faced with updating a rapidly growing city that lacked a vision for its future, Newton quickly beefed up the planning department. The Denver Planning Commission, created in 1926, had issued ambitious and farsighted proposals since 1929, but Mayor Stapleton had rejected most of them as either too expensive or politically risky. Cranmer, when asked if he ever had a master plan, replied: "I just went from one thing to another."[26]

Newton wanted a more orderly approach. In 1949 he replaced the old, weak advisory group, which had only two paid staff members, with the Denver Planning Office, overseen by a nine-member board and headed by a professional planner. When he left office in 1955, Newton had extended his penchant for planning to the metropolitan area, creating the Intercounty Regional Planning Commission, the forerunner of the Denver Regional Council of Governments.

City planner Maxine Kurtz tackled the Civic Center, the parklike heart of the city. "Civic Center," she said in a 1986 interview, "was dreadful, not the City Beautiful ornament envisioned by Mayor Speer. It was rimmed with bars, strip joints, and even a mortuary. We fought to clean it up, ultimately getting the new, 1955 library and the Denver Art Museum located on the southwest side, and encouraged the clustering of new state office buildings on the east side."[27]

To attract developers, the Newton administration in 1952 repealed the 1908, 12-story building height limitation. Several out-of-town builders began eying high rises for the Mile High City. New Yorker William Zeckendorf sparked a postwar building boom in what he called "the town that time forgot." With the glinty eyes of a prospector, Zeckendorf assayed Denver in 1945 as "too spread out to be quaint and too ugly to be pleasant. . . . Most structures were fading five and six story brick affairs, often with cheap storefront facades. . . . Boosters told you Denver was a growing city, but the growth was in the suburbs. Denver, like so many other cities, was decentralizing so rapidly that its dry-rotted core had begun to fall in on itself."

Shaking up this sleepy, self-satisfied town became a preoccupation with the energetic Zeckendorf. He claimed that local business leaders gave him little support, "in spite of the fact that their families had been living in and off the area for generations and, therefore had the most to gain from a renaissance."[28] Despite opposition from Claude Boettcher and others, whom the Jewish New Yorker considered "politely bigoted people," Zeckendorf began collecting property. He purchased the site of the former Arapahoe County courthouse, where he built the Hilton Hotel and the May D&F department store, two ultramodern structures conceived by the internationally acclaimed architect Ieoh M. Pei. For

Zeckendorf, Pei also designed the sleek 25-story Mile High Center at Seventeenth and Broadway. This elegant glass box was the first building in Denver to exceed the height of the Daniels and Fisher tower.

Clinton and John Murchinson, Dallas oil millionaires, received a kinder reception than Zeckendorf. To the amazement of many, the old guard sold the venerable Denver Club to the Texans in 1953. They demolished the fine, red-sandstone structure and replaced it and its pleasantly landscaped lawn with a nondescript 21-story high rise, the Denver Club Building at Seventeenth and Glenarm, of which the top four floors were reserved for the Club. Tickled, the Murchinsons began erecting the $10 million, 28-story Murchinson Tower at Seventeenth and Welton. The First National Bank, seeing outsiders move so conspicuously into what the First considered its town, warily contracted a marriage with the Murchinsons. By the time the Murchinson Tower was completed in 1958 it had been renamed the First National Bank Building. John Evans, Sr., moved his bank into the skyscraper, proclaiming that the First was still on top of the town.

Careful observers, however, could see that the Denver of Speer and Stapleton, of Hughes and Dorsey, was literally passing away, as time-honored oligarchs died. Stapleton expired in 1950 at age 80. Gerald Hughes, for 32 years chairman of the First National, died in 1956; his wife Mabel, on her death, left millions of dollars to the Denver Dumb Friends League for an animal shelter. Claude Boettcher died in 1957, willing the bulk of his $16 million estate, one of the largest in Denver's history, to the Boettcher Foundation. His home became the Colorado governor's mansion. Ex-senator Lawrence Phipps smoked a cigar and drank highballs on his ninety-fifth birthday, telling friends that he wanted to live to be 100. He died a few months later, leaving his wife, Margaret, to preside over the stately Phipps mansion, which was eventually donated to the University of Denver. Evans retired from the First National in 1959, nearly 20 years before his death at age 93.

There were survivors. Evans's son, John, Jr., retained valuable chunks of downtown real estate but did not hold the power that his father once had. Asked in 1974 if he were disturbed by his family's declining role, he replied: "Not a bit. Not one bit. Not one bit."[29] Montgomery Dorsey took over as First National's board chairman in 1956, retiring in 1973. Gerald and Allan Phipps, Margaret and Lawrence Phipps's sons, remained in the public eye through their ownership, until 1981, of the Denver Broncos. Other chips off the old block turned out to be soft wood. Architect Buell sized up some of the fading families: " I know a lot of people who had a lot of money that just got awful lazy. They didn't do any work. I know an awful lot of people who went from shirtsleeves to shirtsleeves in three generations."[30]

Politically, the tired tycoons gave ground by inches. Newton modernized city government, yet he was no revolutionary. The son of a stockbroker, he knew how to get along with his father's friends. Newton's successors, William F. Nicholson (1955–1959) and Richard Batterton (1959–1963), both Republicans, also knew the power of the elite, as did the more liberally inclined Democrat Thomas G. Currigan, mayor from 1963 to 1968. Moreover, Currigan's successor, William H. McNichols, Jr. (1968–1983), seemed, at least in the eyes of his opponents, to be a Stapleton clone, the last moving part in a machine Speer began building in the 1880s. McNichols's father had been city auditor during the Stapleton regime; his brother, Stephen, had been a progressive governor. Currigan's family had been active in local politics since the 1870s. And the city's longtime congressman Byron G. Rogers (1951–1971) did some of his most effective campaigning shaking hands on Seventeenth Street. Old money and old politics counted in Denver.

That interplay, although it concentrated power in the hands of a few and led to "stand-patism" during Stapleton's sunset years, had redeeming features. The old families liked their community and took pride in it. Personally or through their foundations they donated to worthy causes — the University of Denver, the Denver Zoo, the Art Museum, Children's Hospital, Boettcher School, the Denver Public Library, the Symphony Orchestra, the Denver Museum of Natural History, to name a few. As a consequence, the boards that oversaw those organizations became the last bastions of the timeworn aristocrats. John Gunther called their largesse "conscience money," but he admitted that they provided parks and "well-kept hospitals."[31] For decades the rich put up the cash that allowed ordinary people freely to enjoy the Art Museum and the Museum of Natural History. Allan Phipps, who served as head of the Museum of Natural History, told historian David McComb in 1974 that the museum wanted to avoid charging admission. "When you start making a charge," he explained, "a lot of the people who really can benefit from the museum, low income groups, families, and so on, they are automatically shut off."[32]

There was another advantage in this concentration of money and power. A handful of people could get things done in Denver. When George Cranmer needed 15 acres near the airport in order to lure an airplane modification installation to Denver in the early 1940s, he simply asked Claude Boettcher for the land. Boettcher donated the acres, and the Continental-Denver Modification Center was built. In the mid-1970s Temple Buell pined for the good old days when business could be done easily: "Now you get these big companies coming in here and they've got big guys representing them here. But those big guys have to go back home to get their money. It's changed completely."[34]

For better or worse the old order passed. By the 1950s new money, new corporations, and new "big guys" were pouring into the city. One after another, local businesses sold out to national and international conglomerates. And by the 1950s the city of Denver was only a part of a burgeoning metropolitan area. While a handful of skyscrapers went up downtown, much more was going on in the suburban counties. In the 1950s and 1960s Denver was not growing up anywhere nearly as fast as it was growing out.

Part III:
Fragmented Metropolis, 1950–

By capitalizing on the riches of its vast hinterland and developing the talents of a diverse population and economy, Denver became the uncontested metropolis of the Rockies. Its problems came from within — from political, ethnic, and economic fragmentation. Despite the public-minded thrust of the Progressive and New Deal eras, postwar Denver remained a privatized metropolis. Its great achievements were skyscrapers, residential enclaves, shopping malls, and freeway escapes from core-city problems. While railroads and streetcars had shaped the prewar city, automobiles structured the modern metropolis. Much of old Denver was paved over with parking lots and freeways; prairies blossomed with shopping malls and subdivisions.

Boulder County, departing from the mainstream, pioneered growth management, environmental sensitivity, and the search for a higher quality of life. Adams, Arapahoe, and Jefferson counties mushroomed as ranch-house suburbs with plenty of elbowroom, perpetuating the rugged individualism and energetic capitalism of the mining camp days.

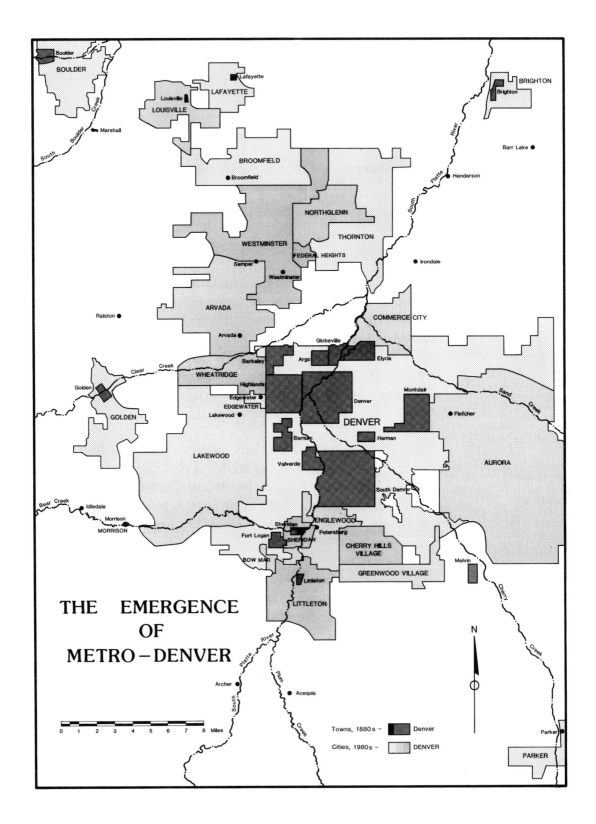

Boulder
BOULDER

Creek
South

Boulder

Marshall

Lafayette
LAFAYETTE

Louisville
LOUISVILLE

BROOMFIELD

Broomfield

BRIGHTON

Brighton

River

South

Platte

Barr Lake

Henderson

NORTHGLENN

THORNTON

WESTMINSTER

FEDERAL HEIGHTS

Semper

Westminster

Irondale

ARVADA

Ralston

Arvada

COMMERCE CITY

Golden

Clear   Creek

GOLDEN

WHEATRIDGE

Berkeley

Highlands

Edgewater

EDGEWATER

Lakewood

Globeville

Argo

Elyria

Denver

Montclair

Fletcher

DENVER

Barnum

Harman

Sand   Creek

LAKEWOOD

Valverde

AURORA

Bear Creek

Idledale

Morrison

MORRISON

South Denver

Sheridan

ENGLEWOOD

Fort Logan

SHERIDAN

Petersburg

BOW MAR

Littleton

CHERRY HILLS
VILLAGE

GREENWOOD VILLAGE

Melvin

Cherry

Creek

THE   EMERGENCE
OF
METRO – DENVER

LITTLETON

South

Platte

River

Plum

Archer

Acequia

Creek

Parker

PARKER

N

0 1 2 3 4 5 6 7 8   Miles

Towns, 1880 s – ■ Denver

Cities, 1980 s – □ DENVER

254

CHAPTER 21

Automobility

What a revolution the automobile has brought about in all our ways of life and in all our thoughts. [It] has completely altered the relation of town and country . . . making the farming districts suburbs of our cities.
Denver Post, December 31, 1916

While railroads and streetcars shaped Denver before World War II, the automobile susequently reshaped the city and its suburbs. Autos enabled Denverites to move beyond the old walking city and its streetcar suburbs into surrounding Adams, Arapahoe, Jefferson, and Boulder counties.

Cars reshaped both the cityscape and human lives. Some Denverites were conceived in cars, and many have died in them. Automobiles have made it easy to go to school, to shop, to work, and to play, anywhere in the metropolitan area, thus promoting social and economic, as well as physical, mobility. Cars became the ultimate toys of teenagers and one of their favorite sixteenth birthday requests. Middle-agers showed they had "made it" by buying a new model every year or so. Older people likewise cherished their automobiles, clinging to cars and drivers' licenses as long as possible. For both young and old, car ownership represented independence.

Automobility has been one of the United States' great adventures, not only in mass production but also in mass advertising: No down payment! Easy payment! Money-back rebates! Such ads strove to convince every American he or she could, and should, own an automobile.

After struggling with old wagon roads, as on this 1907 excursion, motorists lobbied city, county, state, and federal governments to pave the way for automobilists. (Colorado Historical Society.)

Cheap used and rental cars broadened the market. So did car theft — which replaced horse theft as a leading crime and helped distribute automobiles more equally among the haves and have-nots.[1]

Denver's automotive history began with David W. Brunton, a mining engineer and inventor of the Brunton compass. He tested several contraptions at the Mechanics Institute in Boston in 1899 before selecting a Columbia Runabout electric. Shipped west by rail, the vehicle arrived in Denver in pieces. It took Brunton a day to assemble it, and when he took his runabout for a spin, a gang of boys and newspapermen followed him. What did he feed it? How fast would it go? How could it be stopped? What kind of waste did it drop?[2] Other rich and adventuresome people bought horseless carriages. Lawrence C. Phipps, Sr., imported an $17,500 Mercedes tonneau along with a Belgian chauffeur to drive it. With a 60-horsepower engine capable of 90 miles per hour, Phipps was king of the road.[3]

Motor Vehicle Registration in Denver County

	Population	Number Registered
1900	133,859	0
1910	213,381	5,220
1920	256,491	32,604
1930	287,861	84,784
1940	322,412	109,133
1950	415,786	176,737
1960	493,887	251,757
1970	514,678	299,151
1980	492,365	340,878
1990	467,610	375,015

Note: The 1910 figures are from the *Denver Republican*, January 1, 1911. The *Colorado Year Book*, published by the State Board of Immigration and the State Planning Commission between 1918 and 1964, provides annual motor vehicle registration by county and a wealth of other information. The 1970, 1980, and 1990 figures are from the Colorado Motor Vehicle Department and include buses, cars, trucks, and motorcycles.

Denver's generally flat, dry, open terrain delighted motorists, once they donned dust coats and goggles. Cross-country driving became great sport, and the nearby mountains offered the ultimate challenge for motor machines. Although initially called "toys of the rich," automobiles became the toys and the transportation of the middle class after Henry Ford began selling Model Ts for as little as $290. By 1928, Coloradans had one car for every 4.38 residents, the nation's eighth-highest auto ownership per capita.[4] By the 1950s, even the poorest Denver household usually owned at least an old jalopy. Motor vehicle registration figures reflect the automobilization of the the Mile High City.

The number of automobile dealers in the city multiplied rapidly during the first part of the twentieth century. In 1903, the *Denver City Directory* listed 11; by 1913 there were 41, as well as auto blacksmiths, auto body builders, auto liveries, auto schools, auto suppliers, auto tire dealers, auto top dealers, and truck dealers. By 1930, Denver had 113 new car dealers, a peak later reduced by the depression and consolidation of dealerships.

Locomobiles, the first autos sold in Denver, were promoted in ads such as this in the *Denver Post* of May 1, 1900:

To accommodate the automobile, Denver was physically transformed. Corner service stations replaced homes and business blocks. (Tom Noel Collection.)

$750   LOCOMOBILE $750

The famous Steam Wagon. Cheap to Buy. Cheap to run. No noise, odor or vibration. Ready for immediate delivery. Lightest and easiest running automobile on earth. Any person can run it from one to forty miles per hour. Call on us and be convinced. Write for free Catalog. Felker Bicycle Company. State Agents. 417 16th Street.

At first, automobiles were peddled by bicycle salesmen, who kicked in free driving lessons. William B. Felker, a bicycle salesman who became Denver's first automobile dealer, soon had competition. Broadway, once a fashionable, tree-lined street, became a gasoline alley of service stations, garages, parking lots, and new- and used-car emporiums. Philip B. Short, a Broadway lot operator from the 1920s to the 1950s, recalled:

> I sold about 200 cars a year, although sales dropped to 75 a year after the crash of 1929, and most of those I had to repossess. Broadway was the new- and used-car strip in Denver. Farmers and rural people would ride the train to Denver, then walk down Broadway to drive away in a car. I sold cars to everyone, including many Negroes, most of whom had good railroad jobs. And after the sugar beet season was over, even a few Mexicans could afford used cars. Used-car dealers used to get more respect. One used-car dealer, Dick Batterton, was elected mayor of Denver in the 1950s.[5]

Competing for the horseless carriage trade, dealers courted customers in elaborate showrooms. The Cullen-Thompson Motor Company had architect Jacques Benedict design a neo-Gothic, four-story car castle at 1000 Broadway. It sported a pinnacled cornice, Gothic portals, and stained-glass windows with the Chrysler Motor Company's old logo, a winged wheel. The showroom was praised in the Denver Public Library's 1928 booklet *Art in Denver* for its architectural "conviction that beauty, of itself, gives a commercial advantage."[6]

Once, Denver aspired to compete with Detroit as an automobile manufacturing center. Robert Temple built the first local automobile, which he sold in his Temple Machine Company, 1513 Wazee Street. His 2,000-pound gasoline "road wagon" retailed for $2,000 and was described by the *Denver Post*, July 21, 1899, as having safety and emergency brakes, acetylene headlamps, and solid rubber-tired wheels turned by a heavy steel bicycle chain connected to a 10 to 12–horsepower engine. At dawn on July 21, Temple and his first customers, Mr. and Mrs. E. J. Cabler, left Denver for Colorado Springs, driving along the D&RG tracks and adjacent service roads. While Temple and Cabler took turns driving and navigating, Mrs. Cabler sat in the back "in a becoming gray Fedora, driving gloves, and a cool blue serge traveling dress." She was competing, according to the *Post* account, with the vehicle, which had "a silver leaf, gold, dark red and maroon chassis on yellow and brown wheels." The resplendent party sputtered to a stop near Palmer Lake and had to send to Colorado Springs for more gas.[7]

Between 1903 and 1953, 23 other local firms attempted to make cars for sale. Only three of them — the Baker Steam Motor Car and Manufacturing Company (1917–1924), the Colburn Automobile Company (1906–1917), and the Fritchle Automotive and Battery Company (1904–1917) — offered significant competition to the Denver branch manufacturing plants of the Ford Motor Company and the Studebaker Corporation.

Oliver Parker Fritchle, a chemical and electrical engineer, leased the 35,000-square-foot Mammoth Roller Skating Rink at East Colfax Avenue and Clarkson Street, where he manufactured an estimated 2,000 Fritchle Electrics, including Colonial Broughams, Colonial Coupes, Torpedo Runabouts, Victoria-type Broughams, roadsters, and delivery trucks. Fritchle Electrics sold for $2,000 to $3,699. Customers specified the chassis color with matching interior upholstery in either leather or mohair, with no extra charge for a monogram or coat of arms. Closed models included a dome light, flower vase, and rearview mirror; open models sported full cape tops and storm curtains. Testimonials in the 1914–1915 catalog proclaimed that after two years and 12,000 miles, the electrics were still performing well. Fritchle's 32-cell, 64-volt, 100-mile batteries were praised as superior to the more common Edison batteries. Evan Evans of Denver, son of Territorial Governor John Evans, declared that after 65,000 miles his 1908 model "runs just as well as it did the day I bought it." Fritchle Electrics became fashionable with Denver high society, including Ruth Boettcher, Mrs. J. J. Brown, John Campion, Gerald Hughes, Stephen Knight, Mrs. Genevieve Phipps, and Anna Wolcott, but improved gasoline engines and WW I material shortages forced Fritchle to close in 1917.[8]

Judge Ernest A. Colburn, a fancier of racehorses and fast cars, started the Colburn Automobile Company at Fifteenth and Colfax, where he made a $4,500 gasoline roadster capable of 72 miles per hour. By 1918, he and Denver's other automakers succumbed to out-of-town competition, including the Studebaker Brothers of South Bend, Indiana, who had been building horse-drawn wagons in the Mile High City since 1895. The brothers opened the Studebaker Colorado Vehicle Company at 1515–21 Cheyenne Place and Broadway in 1908. Six years later, they stopped making cars locally, converting their plant to an auto showroom.

With much fanfare, the Ford Motor Company opened an assembly plant on November 29, 1913, to supply Model Ts to the Rocky Mountain region. Shortly thereafter, 40 boxcars of parts arrived at the elegant Ford factory at 900 South Broadway. This four-story, 15,000-square-foot plant on a two-acre site assembled Fords until 1932. Before Henry Ford began mass-producing $950 Model Ts in 1909, few could afford automobiles.

After the price of Fords dropped to $550 in 1913, the Detroit firm sold approximately a third of the nation's cars. By the 1920s, Denverites were doing their part to meet car payments — over a sixth of the average American's take-home pay.[9] Some, unable to afford a car, simply stole one. Denver's first recorded car theft occurred on September 9, 1903, when a Franklin vanished from in front of the Boston Building on Seventeenth Street. Although owner Marcus J. Patterson had tied a leather license tag — Colorado No. 8 — to the rear axle, the car was never recovered.[10]

Wretched roads, however, did more damage than thieves, and automobilists soon began agitating for better surfaces. Ironically, bicyclists had begun the crusade for smooth roads, only to be driven off them by the growing number of motorists, as the national Good Roads Association, founded by bicyclists in 1893, became a haven for motorists as well. A Denver chapter of the association was formed in 1905 and found an ally in the Colorado Automobile Club, which 42 Denver motorists established in 1902, electing David Brunton their first president. These two clubs merged in 1908 to form the Rocky Mountain Highway Association, a predecessor of today's Rocky Mountain Motorists, the regional chapter of the American Automobile Association. The auto clubs, as well as the Denver Chamber of Commerce, began lobbying the State Legislature to pay for road building.

Lawmakers responded by establishing the Colorado Highway Commission in 1909 with an annual budget of $50,000. By the 1920s, this budget had ballooned to more than $6 million a year. The state also took advantage of the matching highway construction funds authorized by the Federal Highway Act of 1916. Such auto-oriented priorities (education received about two-thirds as much as the highway department) led the president of the State Teachers College at Greeley to declare that in Colorado million-dollar highways ran by $500 schoolhouses with $100-a-month teachers.[11]

Motorists, a small but powerful interest group, pressed public officials to spend a fourth of the state's total disbursements on roads. City funds also went into road building, which dovetailed with Mayor Speer's City Beautiful efforts to construct motorways in the city parks, tree-lined auto parkways, and scenic roads meandering through the mountain parks. Motorists and City Beautiful boosters contended that by paving the way for motorists, Coloradans could capture a fortune in tourist dollars. Arthur H. Carhart, a Denver-based U.S. Forest Service "recreation engineer," declared that auto tourism could become "Denver's greatest manufacturing plant." Carhart asserted that "Denver has the greatest play places in the country" and should develop "a systematic plan for the manufacture of recreation."[12]

Frederick Law Olmsted, Jr., commissioned by Denver to design a series of mountain parks and drives, recommended that mountain motorways be wide enough to be "safe and convenient" but "not a foot more," with "clean-cut, continuous, graceful lines." Furthermore, "the cuts as well as the fill" should be brought "to a slope of rest" to prevent "constant sliding [that] will keep the surface raw and prevent vegetation." Denver, Olmsted concluded, should build model mountain roads, unlike other "scenic" motorways responsible for "the raw, shabby, unattractive appearance of so many naturally beautiful scenes in America." In order "to bring the general public cheaply and conveniently to these parks," Olmsted urged that streetcar lines be extended to the mountain parks.[13]

Despite Olmsted's advice, mountain park design heavily favored motorists. After Genesee Park became Denver's first mountain park in 1913, Mountain Parks Superintendent Edward S. Letts prepared to "level off the top of the peak in such a manner as to accommodate a considerable number of autos." Letts reasoned that this would make the mountaintop accessible for "a large percentage of automobilists who will not get out of their machines and walk to the summit."[14]

Olmsted was appalled: "We feel very strongly that the peak should be carefully preserved in a semi-natural condition." He warned that if "the existing luxuriant cover of pine and spruce growing out of the scant soil among the ledges [is] destroyed, [it] cannot be replaced." Besides, he added, "no one would care to sit down behind the row of automobiles to enjoy life and scenery and to eat luncheon."[15] Olmsted won the battle of Mount Genesee and ultimately helped design 20 Denver Mountain Parks connected by 87.5 miles of scenic roadway. The tour began with Lookout Mountain Park and looped through a dozen others to the top of Mount Evans via "the world's highest auto road" and returned to Denver via Red Rocks Park.

Denver's mountain park and drive system, begun as a City Beautiful dream by Speer, was completed during the 1930s with the help of New Deal programs, especially the CCC and the WPA. By 1941, thousands of federal as well as city dollars had been spent to acquire land and to build roads, trails, parking areas, picnic grounds, and campgrounds in 33 Denver Mountain Parks extending over 20,897 acres. As developers moved into the foothills areas after World War II, these parks would become the centerpieces of fashionable Jefferson County suburbs.

Motor gypsies flocked like moths to Denver's free City Park auto camp, which opened in 1914. (Denver Public Library, Western History Department.)

Watching motorists stream through Denver to the mountains, some tourist-trapping townsfolk proposed "motor camps" for city parks. Travelers should at least be persuaded to make Denver the base for their forays into "them thar hills." This was hardly a new idea: Denver originated as a supply town that mined miners heading to and from the mountains.

To mine motorists, Denver opened an auto camp in 1915 at City Park. "In many cities," observed Park Commissioner Otto Thum, "automobiles are not allowed to camp inside the city limits. In Denver they are received with the greatest hospitality."[16] That summer, motor gypsies jammed City Park, where the Chamber of Commerce gave away free maps and trip logs.[17] One of the auto campers was Horace M. Albright, assistant director of the National Park Service, who noted: "The free automobile camp idea [was] first adopted by Denver, Colo., Ashland, Oreg., Cody, Wyo., and other cities near large parks. . . . It is an inspiring sight to go into a park like the beautiful City Park of Denver and see several hundred cars neatly parked in their allotted spaces and their happy owners, many of them with large families, enjoying the camp life."[18]

In 1918, the city opened another motor camp at Rocky Mountain Lake Park in northwest Denver. After that site became overcrowded, the city, in 1920, moved its motor camp to Overland Park in southwest

Denver, where the $250,000 auto camp offered free baths; laundry, reading, writing, and rest rooms; and a 24-room clubhouse, which included a billiard room, restaurant, grocery store, barbershop, and phonograph lounge. The clubhouse also featured the "finest" dance floor in Denver with "a good orchestra in a hanging bandstand, suspended like a chandelier above the center of the floor." Local youths as well as tourists flocked to Overland's "five cents a dance evenings." Summer romances apparently flourished; The Federated Churchmen of Denver condemned the dance hall at Overland Park as "Dangerous to Public Morals."[19] Accelerating auto tourism crowded Overland Park with 59,070 campers in 1923. The following year the city began charging 50¢ a night.

Colorado Highways promoted auto camping as a way to help Coloradans sell the "inexhaustible goods on their scenic shelves." "Motorists," added this highway department magazine, "were a class of people that contains prospective settlers and investors."[20] But when the Great Depression struck in 1929, auto camps were swamped by poor motor migrants, such as the Joad family portrayed in John Steinbeck's novel *The Grapes of Wrath*. Denver closed the Overland Park auto camp in 1930 and never opened another within the city limits. While auto campers had originally been upper- and middle-class motorists, they were increasingly perceived as riffraff on wheels, as poor Okies. Ragtag motor migrants of the 1930s killed the idea that automobiles were only for the rich.

After the closing of municipal auto parks, privately owned camps and motels sprang up. By 1950, 28 motels, motor courts, motor hotels, and trailer parks clustered around Overland Park on South Santa Fe Drive. Motor inns likewise proliferated on Colfax Avenue (U.S. Route 40), South Broadway, and other major traffic arteries, leading to a decline in downtown hotels. Although large new hotels have been built, small hotels by the dozens have been demolished. Of approximately 50 nineteenth-century hotels, only three — the Brown Palace, the Kenmark, and the Oxford — survive as hotels.

Boosters promoted automobility, but others had their doubts. From the start, pedestrians and horses were wary of the horseless carriage. Felker, the pioneer auto dealer, attracted the first automobile litigation, the complainant charging that Felker's horn blast caused a runaway horse mishap in 1902. Later that year, Felker was fined for racing down Fifteenth Street.[21] As speeding, thefts, and accidents mounted, Denver enacted a 1902 ordinance requiring that cars be registered and carry rear license plates "eight inches long and four inches wide," allowing "people who are run over to readily read whose vehicle it was that injured

Streetcars battled daily with cars and trucks for control of Denver streets, leading to frequent clashes, such as this crash at Sixteenth and Blake. (Tom Noel Collection.)

them."[22] The 1902 ordinance set a downtown speed limit of 8 miles per hour and 15 miles per hour elsewhere in the city. By 1906, automobile regulations filled a whole chapter of the *Denver Municipal Code*.

A 1931 *Survey of Traffic* by the Denver Planning Commission found that autos carried 215,363 Denverites daily, while only 152,991 took streetcars. Initially used for recreation, automobiles were becoming everyday transportation. The problem, planners said, was impatient people who wanted the instant, on-demand service private autos offered. "Our traffic situation is more annoying than distressing," the planners concluded, but they noted that in major U.S. cities "traffic congestion is said to be the greatest problem [whose] cost in delay to business has been estimated at millions of dollars annually."[23]

Streetcar suburbs such as Park Hill shifted to automobiles, dooming streetcar service. (Denver Public Library, Western History Department.)

Yet, Denver planners and politicians, like those in other cities, promoted automobility. Automobile suburbs were seen as a wholesome alternative to crowded, unhealthy urban living. Decentralization was clearly the preference not only of city planners but of many residents

265

moving to suburbia. As the president of the Denver Planning Commission put it: "It is easier to travel long distances to and from work, easier to build a new home amid cleaner surroundings than to put forth the effort to bring old neighborhoods up to the rising standards of American residential requirements."[24]

The costs of automobility — congestion, pollution, and aesthetic losses — were not initially evident, but one portent of problems to come, and a growing challenge for

Denver abandoned its trolley system in 1950, hastening the day when the city would be choked with cars. (Colorado Historical Society.)

city planners, was the problem of downtown parking. The Denver Planning Commission recommended that one-hour free parking downtown be changed to 15- and 30-minute free parking and that "stop and go" signs be replaced with stop lights at major intersections. The commission considered requiring off-street parking for new buildings, but not until 1946 was free parking banned on Fourteenth, Fifteenth, Sixteenth, and Seventeenth to ease downtown traffic jams.

Nelson's Corner in Edgewater fueled 1940s expeditions into suburban Jefferson County. (Tom Noel Collection.)

Saco Rienk DeBoer, Denver's preeminent city planner, warned as early as the 1920s that automobility could fragment the metropolis. (Denver Public Library, Western History Department.)

In the never-ending war on over-time parking, the city came up with its ultimate weapon — the Denver Boot. This device to immobilize cars until fines were paid was invented, patented, and first used in Denver in 1955. Frank P. Marugg, the son of a bicycle shop-keeper, learned the pattern-making trade at Manual High School. Subsequently, he invented the 12-pound steel boots and marketed them world-wide as "The One and Only Denver Boot." In Denver, the boot was being locked onto 7,000 cars a year by the 1980s, producing more than $1.3 million annually in fines and boot removal fees.[25]

Parking created more than traffic problems, according to Judge Benjamin Lindsey, who argued that automobility also had revolutionized sexual conduct. "Forty years ago," Lindsey observed in 1925,

> John Smith took Sadie Brown driving behind Old Dobbin. Dobbin ambled along, and John made love within the natural limitations prescribed by Dobbin's six miles an hour, the nearness to town and neighbors and all that. Today John makes his date with Sadie by telephone — easily, and, if he so desires, secretly. Today he sits at the wheel of a car that may be good for anything from two to eighty miles an hour. He can whisk Sadie far from all accustomed surroundings. There are roadhouses; there are long stretches of road where the solitude is complete and easy to reach; there is every inducement under the moon to irresponsible conduct.[26]

One such roadhouse, Englewood's Wayside Inn, was described in the *Rocky Mountain News*, April 23, 1909, as "the mecca for Denver motorists, and dozens of automobiles may be seen ranged outside, in the hotel yard and overflowing into the road." For the motoring crowd, the Wayside Inn offered nightly orchestral music and dancing in the Bohemian Room. Such dancing, drinking, and dating clubs surrounded by autos became a less newsworthy phenomenon in later decades.

Speakeasies of the 1920s often geared their illicit services to motorists. Many thrived as Prohibition reduced the number of liquor outlets

but enhanced the exotic appeal
of "demon rum." Thirsty scofflaws jumped in their cars to seek
out such legendary speakeasies as
the Haunted House in Globeville, the Moonlight Ranch on
Morrison Road, north Denver's
Tivoli Terrace, the Wild Horse
on Lookout Mountain, and the
Denver Motor Club in Idledale.

Drive-ins invaded Denver during the 1950s. A&W opened
this Aurora restaurant with
curbside carhops. (Kelley
Wensing Collection.)

Automobiles not only changed the way people played, but also the
way they ate. Drive-in restaurants, introduced in Texas and California
during the 1920s, first advertised in the Denver telephone book in 1930
when the Night Hawk Sandwich Shop opened at 149 Broadway: "Never
Closed — Drive-In and Curb Side Service." By 1940, hungry motorists
could resort to Baxter's Barrel at 9404 East Colfax Avenue in Aurora, the
Moon Drive-In on East Colfax in Denver, and the Humpty Dumpty
Drive Inn, 2776 Speer Boulevard, where Louis E. Ballast claimed that he
invented the cheeseburger, which he unsuccessfully tried to patent in
1932.[27] During the 1950s, drive-in dining became a nationwide craze and
by 1960 Denver had 91 such joints. Franchised drive-ins arrived in 1952
when Jerry and Ruby Anderson opened Denver's first A&W Root Beer
Stand at 8740 East Colfax.[28] In pursuit of suburban customers, the An-
dersons built another drive-in at 10660 East Colfax in Aurora. Anderson
further automobilized by purchasing an aluminum trailer to which he
added a refrigerator so he could deliver A&W cuisine to those who did
not drive to him. Anderson equipped his A&W stands with order speakers and built a third establishment at 13130 East Colfax in 1960. At the
peak of his career, Jerry Anderson employed 68 people, primarily as
carhops paid 55¢ an hour to dispense papa, mama, and baby burgers,
French fries, and root beer floats in frosted mugs from 7:00 A.M. until
midnight seven days a week.[29]

Ray A. Kroc, who transformed McDonald's into a national chain,
opened the first Denver-area outlet at 1100 South Colorado Boulevard
during the 1950s. Its spectacular success — there were 60 metro-area
McDonald's by 1990 — inspired other nationally franchised competitors,
including Burger Chef, Burger King, and Wendy's.

Drive-in entertainment flourished along with drive-in eateries. Four-
teen years after the first drive-in theater opened in Camden, New Jersey,
the East 70 Drive-In Theater was started in 1947 at 12800 East Colfax.

For the grand opening of the Centennial Drive-In in Littleton, Ralph J. Batschelet transformed the former Centennial Race Track into a "Cinemascope in the Sky," and had the film *The High and the Mighty* flown in by airplane. The North Star Drive-In at the junction of I-25 and West Eighty-fourth Avenue boasted that it had the country's largest screen and room for 1,795 cars.[30] The number of local drive-in theaters peaked around 1970 at 23. Since the 1970 heyday of the drive-in theaters, television and home videos have captured much of their former audience. Among the few 1990 survivors was the first, Aurora's East 70. Drive-in banks, drive-in liquor stores, drive-in pharmacies, and even a drive-in church have appeared in the metropolitan area.

The Mile High City's appetite for automobiles grew during World War II when production and sales were rationed. The federal Office of Price Administration (OPA), which strove to regulate car sales, reported that "50 to 75 autos were sold every day in the growing Denver black market." Denverites, an OPA official reported, were paying $300 to $400 above the legal price, indicating that they "are more willing to part with large sums for automobiles — within the law or outside it — than for anything else."[31]

Automobility speeded up after World War II — and much of the traffic headed for suburbia. As early as 1941, Denver planners noted that "suburban areas are outstripping Denver proper in rate of population growth by nearly five to one" and that the core city was developing "blighted areas that are spreading." Automobile suburbs, once seen as a solution to urban congestion, were rediagnosed as "the most sinister disease that has ever affected the welfare of large American cities."[32]

Between 1940 and the 1950s, the number of registered motor vehicles doubled in Denver. As traffic congestion grew, the old solutions — assigning another cop to a troublesome intersection, setting up another stop sign or traffic light, or passing out more tickets — did not work. To unscramble the thickening jam of autos, streetcars, and pedestrians, Mayor Quigg Newton established a Traffic Engineering Department and hired as its first head Henry A. Barnes, a former truck driver, jigsaw puzzle salesman, policeman, and traffic engineer from Flint, Michigan.[33]

Hank Barnes soon became the talk of the town. When he first proposed one-way streets to the city council, 250 irate citizens mobbed the Monday night meeting. Despite protests, Barnes began converting residential streets as well as major arteries into one-ways. To further quicken traffic flow, Barnes installed synchronized lights that would change to green as the traffic reached them. Motorists driving the speed

To unclog downtown arteries, Mayor Quigg Newton and the city's first traffic engineer, Henry Barnes, converted the downtown grid to one-way streets. (Tom Noel Collection.)

limit could go for miles without stopping for a light. Naysayers complained that these speedways only helped drivers get to the suburbs. Barnes — as usual — had an answer. He proposed that downtown Denver be included in the one-way street system, which he promised would make trips downtown faster and easier. Wary businessmen allowed experimental conversion of two downtown steets. Traffic flowed so much better that downtowners agreed to convert most of the central business district to one-ways.

Another Barnes innovation still befuddles some newcomers — traffic lights placed in the middle of the block instead of at intersections. The purpose of the midblock light, Barnes explained in his autobiography, *The Man with the Red and Green Eyes,* "is to discourage straggler cars by forming them into groups which — at the proper speed — will then move through the signal system without stopping. It's also a great help getting cross-street and pedestrian traffic through with a maximum of safety."[34]

Barnes generally sided with motorists. Trees, lawns, and sidewalks were sacrificed for street widening. His one-way streets disrupted quiet neighborhoods and, by untangling and speeding up traffic, endangered pedestrians and bicyclists. Yet he did grant walkers one major concession. "The time has come," Barnes announced after establishing one-way streets downtown, "to give the pedestrian a 30 to 70 percent chance of getting across the street alive."[35] The traffic maestro presented his scheme to Mayor Newton and his staff. They scratched their heads and said no. Barnes pleaded for a trial, promising to resign if the idea backfired. So, early one morning at Seventeenth and Stout streets, Barnes and his assistants tinkered with the traffic signals. A few winos were amazed to see all the traffic lights go red at once while new pedestrian signals all read "WALK," giving those on foot total possession of the intersection during their turn to cross. Businessmen pouring into Seventeenth Street that morning were curious yet cautious. Some went a block out of their way to avoid the newfangled signals. Only after courageous women began making the diagonal crossings, Barnes reported, did timid men follow. By the end of the day, secretaries and executives, attorneys and oilmen, derelicts and shoppers were heading for Seventeenth and Stout streets to try out "the Barnes Dance."

During his six years in Denver, Barnes installed 20,000 street signs, 375 additional traffic lights, and 62 miles of one-way streets.[36] After revolutionizing Denver's traffic, Barnes moved on to Baltimore and ultimately to New York City. There, the traffic tamer met his match. In 1968, the 61-year-old genius was found dead of a heart attack, sitting behind his desk at the Queens Traffic Control Center. *Life Magazine* called Barnes "the world's greatest traffic engineer," and the *New York Times* recalled that "his temper had been as quick as a yellow light, his wit as irreverent as a traffic-snarled truck driver's and his pipe as fuming as the back of a bus."[37]

Barnes had given Denver a relatively smooth system, yet one-ways and street widenings carried motorists only so far. For the ultimate solution Denverites looked to freeways — limited access, multi-lane, high-speed highways. Although Saco R. DeBoer, the city planner, drew freewaylike "boulevards" onto planning maps during the 1930s, none were developed until the 1940s. DeBoer's 1933 master plan called for a "circle boulevard" around Denver, a major highway to the Western Slope, and a scenic foothills road linking Boulder, Denver, and Colorado Springs.[38] Much of DeBoer's plan would become reality by the 1990s, including a belt loop interstate around Denver — I-70 piercing the mountains via the Eisenhower and Johnson tunnels, and the Peak to Peak Highway between Mount Evans and Longs Peak. But the Rampart Range Road between Cascade, west of Colorado Springs, and Sedalia, south of Denver, built as a CCC fire control road, was only a partial realization of DeBoer's Front Range foothills parkway, and West Alameda Avenue Parkway was never completed as a four-lane connection between Denver and Red Rocks Park.

While DeBoer dreamed, the hard-nosed Denver manager of improvements and parks, George Cranmer, began building. During the depression, Cranmer acquired much tax-delinquent land along the Platte River and proposed using it for what became the Valley Highway and Denver's first freeway, West Sixth Avenue. Cranmer and DeBoer had begun planning this limited-access, divided highway in the late 1930s with the help of the WPA. After the nation marched off to World War II, the Department of Defense funded construction of the freeway from Santa Fe Avenue west to the Denver Ordnance Plant at Sixth and Kipling. After the war, West Sixth Avenue became Denver's premier route into the mountains. As the major western artery it facilitated a tremendous growth in the population of Lakewood, which ballooned into the fourth largest city in Colorado.

The Denver-to-Boulder Turnpike was the second limited-access highway in the Mile High metropolis. This 17.3 mile highway was the brainchild of Professor Roderick L. Downing of the University of Colorado. He became a major proponent of a link between the university town and the state capital, taking his engineering students out to survey a modern, four-lane route. The legislature insisted that a tollbooth be installed to make users pay for the road. Begun in 1950, the turnpike was opened in 1952. It was built to freeway standards, with limited access, two 12-foot lanes in either direction, 10-foot shoulders, and a 20-foot median. By 1966, 13,774 travelers a day were paying the 25¢ toll. Heavier than expected revenues enabled the State Highway Department to demolish the tollbooths on September 14, 1967. Completion of the turnpike (U.S. Route 36) spawned growth in Westminster, Broomfield, and Boulder by cementing them into the metropolitan maze.[39]

I-25, Denver's first official interstate highway, carved a $33 million, 11.2-mile freeway through the city along the South Platte River Valley. Dubbed the Valley Highway locally, it was dedicated, after 10 years of construction, on November 23, 1958.[40] I-70, the major east-west route through Denver, was first proposed in boulevard form by DeBoer in the 1930s and again in the 1940s by Colorado Highway Department Chief Engineer Charles Vail. The staggering cost of building west of Denver through the Rockies held up construction for years, while I-80 zoomed through Wyoming and I-40 breezed through New Mexico. Coloradans once again, as in the days of the transcontinental railroad, found themselves bypassed. Governor Ed Johnson took the state's plight directly to President Dwight D. Eisenhower, who vacationed in Colorado. Johnson gave the president Colorado Fishing License No. 1 along with an elaborate presentation book that made the case for I-70. The president smiled and later helped persuade Congress to approve a 90 percent federal match for state funds.[41] Instead of building in then largely vacant Adams and Jefferson counties, I-70 sliced through several poorer neighborhoods on the northern edge of Denver, destroying many homes and bisecting blue-collar communities such as Globeville and Swansea. Some wondered, when I-70 opened in 1966, if it had been urban renewal in disguise.

The intersection of interstates 25 and 70 soon became the most congested in the Rockies. Don Martin, Colorado's first radio traffic reporter to use a helicopter, gave the intersection its popular name: the Mousetrap. "As I looked down on it," Martin recalled in a 1988 interview, "it reminded me of one of those mazes used for mice, and I called it a giant mousetrap."[42]

Trying to keep up with a million newcomers who settled in metropolitan Denver between 1945 and 1983, the state used matching federal funds to build two belt-loop freeways, I-270 and I-225, on the northeastern and southeastern outskirts. I-225 ignited explosive growth in Aurora, including the huge Aurora Mall and Town Center at East Alameda and I-225, thus helping to transform a bedroom community of commuters into an independent city. Aurora's I-225 bonanza led to a frenzy of land speculation along the beltway's proposed southwest quadrant, but freeway enthusiasts were stopped in their ruts by an environmentalist governor, Richard D. Lamm. During his 1975–1986 administration, Lamm refused to fund the southwest section.

Lamm represented a radical departure in Colorado politics. He had risen to prominence as a leader of the grass-roots uprising against hosting the 1976 International Winter Olympics. *Denver Post* columnist Tom Gavin, another of the rabble-rousers who challenged Governor John A. Love, Mayor William McNichols, Jr., and the powerful forces behind the Olympics, articulated the opposition view: "The Denver Olympics grew out of the same watch-us-grow that spawned sell Colorado programs in the past. . . . The trouble with tourists is that, having looked around, many wish to return . . . and we already have sufficient people lousing Colorado up."[43]

Dick Lamm pointed out that "everybody talks about handling the Olympics so the environment doesn't suffer, but we can't even get a land use plan adopted and can't get the billboards taken down."[44] Lamm, State Representative Bob Jackson, anti–Vietnam War activist Sam Brown, the Sierra Club, and others collected 76,000 names on a referendum petition. This led to a November 7, 1972, statewide vote in which Coloradans said

no by a three-to-two margin to any
further state funding for the Olympics. The specter of more cars, parking lots, shopping centers, and
subdivisions inspired Coloradans to
derail, for the first time, the booster
gravy train. Lamm advocated a regulated growth platform as he walked
across the state to win the governorship in 1974. Coloradans seemed determined to stop, or at least to control, growth.

C-470, stopped here to make a
connection with Ken Caryl
Avenue, paved the foothills,
which soon blossomed with subdivisions and shopping malls.
(Tom Noel Collection.)

Newspaper and television pun-
dits, radio talk-show hosts, and historians interpreted the anti-Olym-
pics vote as a turning point. But the mid-1980s crash changed that. As
unsalable homes, empty office space, bankrupt banks, and desperate real
estate speculators swamped a depressed market, Coloradans reversed
their stance. In 1989 Denver Mayor Federico Peña and Governor Roy
Romer rallied development forces, without significant opposition, to seek
the Winter Olympics again. This time a wary, once-burned Winter
Olympics Committee said no. The 1970s anti-growth crusade turned out
to be only a temporary aberration from the onward march of boosterism,
development, and lust for bigger and better airports, convention centers,
and freeways.

Sensing the change, landowners along the proposed freeways resumed their drive for highways in the 1980s. Developers and proponents
of the 26-mile southwestern belt freeway between I-25 and I-70 included
two monstrous Texas firms and Johns-Manville's spiffy subdivision, the
Ken Caryl Ranch. They and smaller landowners, accompanied by a
Chamber of Commerce chorus, blasted Lamm's decision, pointing out
that the 1968 appropriation for I-70 west of Denver had earmarked
money for I-470. Lamm had diverted those funds to other projects,
including Denver's Sixteenth Street Mall. With Lamm out of office and
Colorado in a bust during the late 1980s, suburban real estate developers
revived the dream of an outer ring of freeways. The southwest beltway,
C-470, opened in the late 1980s on the path of I-470. As Lamm had
predicted, C-470 led to a boom in Arapahoe, Douglas, and Jefferson
counties, siphoning development away from the metropolitan core to the

Freeways can be designed grace-fully to frame the landscape, as the Colorado Highway Depart-ment demonstrated with its I-70 overpass at Genesee. (Photo by Glenn Cuerden.)

periphery. Suburbanites found they could avoid downtown completely, as Highway Commissioner Flodie Anderson of Golden noted. "C-470 links suburbs without unnecessarily routing traffic through Denver. . . . We are beyond needing additional spokes on the [freeway] wheel — the hub of which is Denver."[45]

Completion of C-470 in 1990, with 13 development-spawning inter-changes, whetted appetites in the northwest corner of the metropolis, the only one without a slice of I-470. As federal funding had dried up, private developers and local governments created the W-470 Authority, com-plete with a "Beltway to the Future" logo. They proposed a 33-mile, $283 million tollway, but voters, in February 1989, rejected the plan, four to one. Afterward, Adams County and the towns of Golden and Lafayette withdrew from the W-470 Authority, but the glimmer of an interstate highway heaven kept landowners, developers, and some governmental units hopeful about reviving the plan.

On the east side, voters proved more amenable. When growth bulged beyond the I-270 and I-225 belt loops, a second, outer freeway girdle — E-470 — was proposed. When federal and state funds were not forthcoming, voters in Adams, Arapahoe, and Douglas counties agreed to fund E-470 with a $10 per license plate fee. By 1990, the prairie was being graded for a 48-mile, $480 million linkup between I-25 north and I-25 south.

With each new freeway, the Mile High City came closer to becoming a mini–Los Angeles. The metropolis sprawled over 50 miles from the western foothills to the eastern wheat fields, from Boulder in the north to Castle Rock in the south. Assured easy access into the city, many residents and newcomers suburbanized. Jobs, shops, entertainment, and even the Denver Broncos Football Club migrated to suburbia, the club moving its headquarters and training facilities from Globeville to unincorporated Arapahoe County. Freeways built to accommodate growth fostered more growth. While the core county struggled to maintain its population and its tax base, the suburban counties flourished, although to varying degrees.[46] Automobility had turned Denver inside out, transforming the streetcar and railroad city into a new metropolitan world.

CHAPTER 22

Arapahoe County

Drivers sporting Mercedes from Arapahoe County are frequently seen stopping at southeast Denver dumpsters to unload bags of trash, City Councilwoman Mary DeGroot said at a meeting Wednesday.

Rocky Mountain News, June 16, 1988

Arapahoe, Denver's wealthiest county, exemplifies suburban efforts to perpetuate the mobility, individual freedoms, property rights, and rural ideals of the Old West in new subdivisions. This commitment to privatism developed during the century of settlement before 1950, when the county consisted of a few small towns, farms, ranches, and weekend escapes from the big city. But privatism persisted as the dominant theme even after World War II, when Arapahoe emerged as an urbanized rival to the core city.

Created in 1855 as a county of Kansas Territory, Arapahoe was named for the resident Native Americans. The initial county stretched almost from the Continental Divide to the present Kansas border. As settlers arrived, other counties were formed: Boulder (1861), Jefferson (1861), Denver (1902); and Adams (1902). With the creation of the City and County of Denver, most urbanized areas were assigned to Denver, while the rural regions generally were placed in Adams and Arapahoe counties. This political division sharpened an urban versus suburban rivalry.

Before the 1950s, Arapahoe County consisted mostly of small farm-ing, ranching, and dairying communities. After World War II, however, Denver's suburbs grew into cities themselves. While Arapahoe County contained 52,125 residents in 1950, its population climbed to 391,511 in 1990. Only one out of every eight metropolitan residents lived in Arapa-hoe County in 1950; every fourth person did in 1990.

LITTLETON

Foremost of the county towns was Little's Town, or Littleton, which prided itself upon being the pioneer settlement. Founder Richard Sulli-van Little, a New Englander trained as a civil engineer, came to Denver in 1860 and prospered as a surveyor. While laying out Denver's City Ditch, Little acquired a 120-acre site of the east bank on the South Platte River, seven miles south of Denver. After building a log house and staking out another 160-acre homestead, he went back east for his wife, Angeline Harwood Little. Like her husband, she suffered from asthma and put up with frontier hardships because the salubrious Colorado cli-mate did wonders for her lungs.[1]

Along the South Platte River, Richard Little, John G. Lilley, and several others constructed the Rough and Ready Mill in 1867. Grinding both Colorado and Kansas wheat, the Rough and Ready became, accord-ing to credit appraisals of R. G. Dun Company, "the best mill in Colo-rado." Little had an "excellent reputation and [estimated worth] of $75,000 to $100,000."[2] By the 1890s, the Rough and Ready had ex-panded into a four-story, brick and stone landmark at Santa Fe Drive and Bowles Avenue.

Next to the mill, Little laid out a town, modeled after the New Hampshire village of his birth, a tidy, tree-shaded oasis with a log cabin school, St. Paul's Episcopal Church, and a cemetery. After the D&RG Railroad arrived, Little formally platted the town in 1872. The Santa Fe Railroad chugged into town a decade later and built a second depot. Both roads served as commuter lines to Denver, augmented in 1907 by the streetcars of the Denver & South Platte Railway Company. These rail links helped make Littleton what William B. Vickers in his *History of Denver* called "Denver's finest suburb."[3]

Littleton's political development epitomized the suburban suspicion of government. By 1890, this hamlet — population 1,039 — had incorpo-rated as a town in order to finance public services. Little himself refused

Wheat sacks waiting for the Santa Fe Freight to Denver reflect Littleton's origins as a flour-milling village. (Littleton Historical Museum.)

to sign the incorporation papers. He was not alone in his skepticism; nearby farmers took scant interest in nourishing what they expected to be a tax-gobbling, free-spending town hall. Such critics cited Denver's lavish expenses, corruption, and debts as evils to be avoided.

Little, who became the first postmaster in 1869, was also elected the area's first representative to the Territorial Legislature. He promoted his town as a pleasant alternative to the big, bad city to the north. Living well but unostentatiously on the profits of his mill and land sales, Little built a still-standing house at 5777 South Rapp Street. There he died in 1899.

The town mourned its founder, whose role as chief booster had already been assumed by the *Littleton Independent,* one of Colorado's longest-lived weeklies. "Now that Littleton has a newspaper," crowed the first issue, "let everyone strive to make her the most beautiful city in the Platte Valley. The time has long gone for Littleton to slumber."[4]

Edwin A. Bemis, who as a youngster worked on the paper after school, became editor and publisher in 1908. He was the son of Littleton pioneer Fred Arnold Bemis, who brought Jersey cattle to Colorado from his native Massachusetts. The elder Bemis also raised alfalfa and horses on his Brookridge Farm. Bemis and his son transplanted saplings from the banks of the South Platte to create a canopy of trees along Belleview Avenue, Littleton's northern boundary. Ed Bemis used the *Independent* to promote Littleton not only as the political and commercial center of Arapahoe County but also as the cultural oasis. Without such community movers, Littleton might not have its fine library, museum, and arts center. For Littleton, like other suburbs, had a feisty antigovernment faction that balked at taxation for basic services, not to mention cultural amenities. Some of these thrifty taxpayers objected when Littleton hired Jacques Benedict, the town's most noted architect, to design a beaux arts–style public library (1916) and town hall (1920). The latter also served as the fire department, dance hall, and first movie theater.

To help pay for such expanded services, Littletonites tried to coax businesses to the agricultural hamlet, which also touted itself as the

"Beekeeping Capital of Colorado." After the Merry Canning and Pickling Company became the lead industry in 1891, some dubbed it "Pickle Town." Others called Littleton a "cow town" after the Littleton Creamery opened in 1884. Despite its hayseed reputation, Littleton in 1902 attracted a major Denver employer, George Leyner's Engineering Works, with the promise of free land. This mining and engineering giant, reorganized as the Ingersoll-Rand Company in 1923, made Littleton its world headquarters.

The old Leyner plant at 5101 South Rio Grande Street was converted in the 1930s to the regional center for the Civilian Conservation Corps and in the 1950s to the Electron Corporation. The Coleman Motor Company of Littleton pioneered, in the 1920s, development and production of four-wheel–drive trucks and race cars. A third major employer, the Red Comet Fire Extinguisher Company, suffered the worst fire in Littleton's history in 1946. Ignoring wisecracks, Red Comet rebuilt and urged Littleton to establish a professional fire department, which it finally did in 1960.

After Colorado Highway 285 (Santa Fe Drive) became the first paved state highway in 1917, Littleton emerged as one of Denver's largest automobile suburbs. As commuters switched to cars, Littleton streetcar service was discontinued in 1926. The D&RG likewise abandoned rail passenger service, complaining that autos repeatedly crashed through the crossing gate on Main Street.

When the depression struck in 1929, it wiped out the First National Bank of Littleton and moved some hard-pressed citizens to organize the Arapahoe County Taxpayers League. The league asked all elected officials to meet with them at the Arapahoe County courthouse and insisted that all county employees take a 10 percent pay cut. All complied except county School Superintendent Minnie Q. Davis, who said that she earned her $1,800 annual salary. Angry taxpayers tossed her out in the next election.[5]

Taxpayers likewise rebelled against paying the unemployment relief tax the county added to its fees for license plates. Automobile owners, who tended to be the wealthier and more prominent citizens, frequently ignored this tax, and county commissioners failed to crack down on scofflaws. The down-and-outers found a more sympathetic hearing from Houston Waring, who followed Bemis as *Independent* editor. In his autobiography, Waring recalled that indigents "came by the newspaper for the proverbial dime, 'to get a cup of coffee and doughnut.' Many used such

Titan missiles manufactured at Martin Marietta Denver Aerospace were among the most powerful weapons in the U.S. arsenal during the cold war. (Martin Marietta Denver Aerospace.)

cash for a shot of whisky; so I gave them a card good at a Main St. cafe for a large bowl of soup, a thick hamburger and a luscious piece of pie. Each week I would pay the restaurant 15 cents for each meal provided."[6]

From 1930 until 1950, Littleton's population remained relatively stable, climbing from 2,019 to 3,378. Between the 1950s and the 1980s, however, Littleton changed from a small, sleepy, country town to the hub of a rapidly expanding suburban area. A prime reason for the skyrocketing growth was the aerospace giant Martin Marietta, which in 1959 transferred some of its activities from its home base in Baltimore, Maryland. After building a $27 million plant southwest of Littleton in Jefferson County on what had been the C. K. Verdos ranch, Martin Marietta undertook missile production programs for the Air Force, including the Titan rockets used to land astronauts on the moon. Almost overnight, Martin became Littleton's major employer. Littleton's population doubled in five years; in 1960 the *Independent* estimated that "34 percent of the Littleton homes are headed up by a breadwinner in the Martin Company."[7] Thousands of people living elsewhere in the metropolitan area also found work at Martin, where employment increased with escalating federal contacts, including 1980s projects to help build the Space Shuttle for the National Aeronautics and Space Administration (NASA), MX missiles, and commercial Titan rockets sold to British and Japanese firms to launch satellites.[8] Spin-off from Martin's multibillion dollar defense contracts bolstered the metropolitan economy but especially fueled growth in Littleton, whose space age boom launched many businesses, including the Jet Lounge and the Rocket Bar.

Another 1950s triumph for Littleton was construction of the 196,000-square-foot C. A. Norgren plant on a 30-acre site at 5400 South Delaware Street. Carl Norgren, a Swedish engineer from South Dakota, invented, in the basement of his home, the Norgren Oil Fog Lubricator for air-operated equipment, later graduating to bigger plants and other compressed-air accessories. After Carl's death in 1968, his son Neil succeeded him as president of the company and pioneered innovative employment practices, including the four-day workweek introduced in 1970.[9]

Aggressively, Littleton leaders tackled problems of the postwar boom. When part of the old downtown became seedy, Littleton created one of the first suburban urban renewal programs. Structures in the blighted area were demolished and replaced by Arapahoe Community College, a campus enclosed under one roof. This junior college, opened in 1974, geared its courses to older and part-time students and to recreational as well as vocational interests. In another enlightened move, Littleton avoided the standard solu-

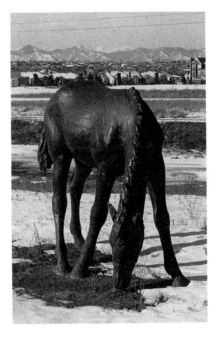

On the South Platte River Arapahoe Greenway, Susan Grant Raymond's sculpture *Coming Home* commemorates the horsey origins of what is now the Grant Ranch subdivision and Southwest Plaza. (Photo by Tom Noel.)

tion — a concrete channel — after the disastrous 1965 South Platte River Flood. Instead, the Littleton Plan of 1974 called for a 200-acre floodplain park and hike-bike path, the Arapahoe Greenway, which has attracted both recreationists and new retail and residential development. The Cooley Gravel Company, which had been mining the riverbed since the 1950s, reclaimed its 450 acres with landscaping, ponds, and wildlife wetlands, which it donated to Littleton as a city park in 1990.

"Despite incredible growth pressures, we've tried to preserve Littleton's charm in our museum and on our Main Street," observed Robert A. McQuarie, director of the Littleton Historical Museum since its 1969 founding. "We still have both the Rio Grande and Santa Fe Railroad depots, recycled as an art gallery and a meeting hall. The old town hall was converted to an arts center and the old library to a restaurant."[10]

The Littleton History Museum is the center of a 100-acre recreational and cultural complex, which includes the Edwin A. Bemis Public Library, Ketring Lake Park, Gallup Park, playgrounds, and athletic fields. Museum properties include Littleton's pioneer schoolhouse, a blacksmith shop, an ice house, and the restored Bemis farmhouse, all used for living history presentations. Symbolic of Littleton's concern for its roots is the massive cottonwood at the museum entrance, a 65-foot-high specimen 31 feet in circumference.

Littleton's origin is commemorated by the Columbine Mill (now converted to a restaurant), whose corrugated metal grain elevator crowns the skyline. Almost a century after historian Vickers called Littleton Denver's finest suburb, a July 1975 *Ladies Home Journal* survey of American suburbs joined its praise, noting that while Littleton had grown into a modern, large, prosperous suburb, it had maintained strong local government committed to recreation, culture, and historical identity. Antique Main Street remained intact, although it lost commercial dominance to such shopping centers as Cinderella City (1968), Southglenn Mall (1974), and Southwest Plaza (1983). While the city itself had only 28,503 residents in 1980, another 100,000 nearby residents relied on city services, ranging from libraries to fire protection, and used the mailing address of Littleton.

Columbine Valley, one of Littleton's poshest neighborhoods, sprang up around the Columbine Country Club during the 1960s. One of the suburban frontiersmen settling on the former Columbine Ranch across the South Platte from downtown Littleton was longtime Denver radio personality Pete Smythe. In his book, *Big-City Dropout,* Smythe captured the suburban spirit:

> The country! That was the answer. A place where a man and his family could make friends with nature; where we could look into the frank faces of a few animals for a change, instead of the same smiling masks we had been smiling at across the rims of martini glasses. . . .
>
> We bought a couple of acres on the outskirts of Denver, sold our home and built ourselves a rambling six-room, redwood ranch house, in a stand of fifty-year-old willow trees . . . I have often read of Thomas Jefferson and how he would ride about his plantation, checking his crops, his slaves, and his livestock. I don't believe he could have felt any deeper contentment than I. . . . Peg was so enthusiastic about the whole thing that she promptly had another baby.[11]

ENGLEWOOD

To the north of Littleton, Englewood neither sought nor achieved a reputation as a model suburb: Economic opportunity was the driving force behind the birthplace of the gold rush, a haven for entrepreneurs ever since.[12] Sandwiched between Littleton and Denver, it was the most populous community in Arapahoe County until Littleton's boom.

Englewood's roots extend to Placer Camp, where the Russell party first found a significant amount of gold in July 1858 and set up their short-lived diggings at the confluence of Little Dry Creek and the South Platte River. Permanent settlement did not come until 1870, when Irishman Thomas Skerritt filed a 640-acre claim on what is now downtown Englewood. Skerritt supposedly built Broadway from Denver to Englewood by locking the wheels of his wagon while driving back and forth. After he planted apple trees on the west side of Broadway between Yale Avenue and Little Dry Creek, it became known as Orchard Place.

Englewood's murky municipal beginnings lie in two country towns, Orchard Place on South Broadway and Petersburg on South Santa Fe. Of the two, Orchard Place was the tamer, noted for family amusement parks as well as raucous roadhouses. Orchard Place began to ferment after Skerritt sold 80 acres between Yale and Hampden avenues and Broadway and Santa Fe to Jacob C. Jones. Jones then sold 40 acres to Archie C. Fisk, proprietor of Fisk's Broadway Gardens, an 1880s beer garden. Other dancing, drinking, and gambling halls located nearby, inspiring a local parson to describe this forerunner of Englewood as "the next thing to hell."[13]

Hell itself, according to local bluenoses, was Petersburg. This other nucleus of modern Englewood, located along South Santa Fe Drive, stretched from Yale on the north to Belleview on the south. Peter Magnes, a congenial Swede with a Lincolnesque beard, settled in 1859 on the east bank of the Platte six miles from Denver. He erected and ran the Harvest Queen Flour Mill and experimented with growing various fruits and vegetables, including currant bushes and grape vines.[14]

Despite its innocent start, Petersburg emerged as a sin city. A two-story log tavern built in 1879 became the town's hub. For over 60 years, this notorious roadhouse thrived under various names — the Petersburg Inn, Dick's Corner, the Wayside Inn, and Pop Wyman's. Soldiers from nearby Fort Logan caroused there, as did Denverites on suburban sprees. Not far away, a ramshackle collection of saloons, blacksmith shops, and livery stables evolved over the years into a strip of bars, motels, and gas stations. Petersburg is gone today, having become a part of Englewood on the east side of South Santa Fe Avenue and a part of Sheridan on the west side. The tawdry taverns, pornography shops, and shady motels along South Santa Fe today commemorate Petersburg's sleaze.

Tom Skerritt further darkened the area's reputation by holding dog races and dog fights at his Shadyside Ranch. The notoriety of Shadyside, Petersburg, and Orchard Place inspired Jacob Jones and other reform-minded residents to incorporate the area within what are now Quincy and Yale avenues and Clarkson Street and the South Platte River. In the May 13, 1903, incorporation papers, Orchard Place was renamed Englewood — an old English word for a forested nook — apparently because some town-founders hailed from Englewood, Illinois. Jones built a home at the northwest corner of Broadway and Hampden Avenue only to see the Idlewild gambling den spring up across Broadway. He subsequently ran for mayor on a dry ticket and narrowly defeated Skerritt, whose son owned one of Englewood's many saloons. As Englewood's first mayor, Jones boosted saloon license fees and campaigned to make it the county seat, but lost the honor to Littleton in the 1904 county election.

Englewood cultivated its own commercial district on South Broadway along the route of the Cherrelyn Street Railway, a rickety wooden streetcar pulled up the hill to Quincy Avenue by a single horse. This hardworking creature rested on a rear platform as the car coasted back down Broadway to Hampden Avenue. The Cherrelyn Horse Car line had been initiated in 1884 to serve James L. Cherry's subdivision on the east side of Broadway between Quincy and Oxford avenues. James O'Brien operated a profitable sideline on his nickel fare trolley by selling photos of passengers posing with the streetcar and its horse (of six horses in service over the years, the best remembered seem to have been Quickstep, Old Dick, and Old Dobbin). These horses, unlike some of the bus drivers who would replace them, stopped automatically for waiting passengers, if local legends are accurate. Handsome, mustachioed James O'Brien was elected alderman and then mayor of Englewood. The end of the line for his famous horsecar came in 1901 when the Denver Tramway Company extended its Broadway route and sent a work car out to tow the Cherrelyn trolley to the junkyard. Englewoodites, however, rescued the car and in 1951 put it on a pedestal beside the Englewood Town Hall.

Englewood's most lavish amusement park was the Tuileries. Named for the gardens in Paris, it opened in 1907 on the former Fisk Gardens' site on the west side of Broadway between Floyd and Hampden avenues. The Tuileries had a dance pavilion, an aerodrome where aerialists and balloonists performed, a roller rink, a motorcycle racing track, a lake, baseball diamond, Oriental tea garden, and miniature train. This elaborate rival to Elitch Gardens in Denver closed in 1912, but a few years later Julian Don and Don Miller Alexander purchased it as a headquarters for Alexander Industries. The brothers used the gardens as sets for their movie company. They also manufactured and sold Eaglerock biplanes until fire killed several workers in 1928, after which Alexander

Industries moved to Colorado Springs. During the 1920s, when the Alexanders turned out several planes a day, they claimed to be the world's largest manufacturer of commercial aircraft.[15] Englewood purchased the elegant Mediterranean-style dance hall, movie studio, and airplane plant in 1931 for use as the City Hall.

After some arm twisting from the town's many carnation growers, Englewood adopted that flower as its logo in 1954, promoting itself as the "Carnation City of the World." The carnation business, the logo, and the motto all wilted in the 1970s in the heat of competition from Mexico.[16] A longer-lived Englewood institution, Swedish Medical Center, opened in 1907 at 3451 South Clarkson Street as the Swedish National Sanitarium for the Cure of Tuberculosis.

Englewood experienced steady growth after incorporation, climbing from a 1910 population of 2,983 to 7,980 in 1930, and 16,896 by 1950. During the 1920s, voters approved annexation to Denver but changed their minds in a repeat of the close, contested election. Mayor Charles Allen also sought independence from Denver's water, developing the Englewood Water Department in 1948.

In 1964, voters agreed to sell Englewood's City Park to developer Gerry Von Frellick for $1 million. On the park site between Bannock and Santa Fe, Hampden and Floyd avenues, Von Frellick built Cinderella City, which he touted as the world's largest shopping center under one roof. Soon after its March 7, 1968, opening, Cinderella City was eclipsed by even larger and shinier shopping malls elsewhere in the metropolitan region. Englewood used its $1 million to purchase seven smaller parks, hoping to silence scoffers who condemned the city for its actions.

Englewood's population had soared to 33,398 in 1960. City government also grew, moving in 1951 from the Tuileries structure to a new City Hall at 3300 South Bannock Street and again in 1965 to the remodeled C. A. Norgren plant at 3400 South Elati. Surrounding municipalities proliferated, too, and Englewood's expansion was checked by the rise of Cherry Hills Village to the east, Littleton to the south, Sheridan to the west, and Denver to the north. Locked into 3,834 acres, Englewood saw its population peak at 33,695 in 1970 and slip to 30,021 in 1980. Residential neighborhoods vary tremendously, ranging from one-bedroom shacks on unpaved streets to an enclave of millionaires, from tar-paper boxes to Arapahoe Acres, a 1950s nest of 117 low-slung, Frank Lloyd Wright–style homes.

During the 1980s, the city undertook a face-lift, inspired by civic improvements in Littleton and Denver. The old South Broadway "downtown" was dressed up with antique street lamps, trees, and trendy street furniture. Little Dry Creek was transformed into a series of waterfalls, pools, and water gardens, and a large, lavish 1985 Englewood Recreation Center. Betty Ann Dittemore, who has served Englewood as a state representative from 1967 to 1977 and as a county commissioner from 1980 to 1988, noted in 1989 that "Englewood has been slow to upgrade its downtown, but with urban renewal and tax increment financing it has started the job. Now Littleton is struggling and we've grabbed the bull by the horns and are charging ahead. Our . . . civic improvements have improved the tax base so we can provide other services, like the new rec center."[17]

GLENDALE

Glendale prided itself on fending off annexation to Denver. Subsequently, an expanding Denver completely surrounded the town bounded

Four Mile House, the oldest structure in the metropolis, has been restored as a living museum where city slickers can revive such lost arts as hewing logs. (Photos by Marcia Tate and Frank Eddy respectively.)

by East Alameda Avenue on the north and South Colorado Boulevard on the west, with a jagged southern boundary on or near East Mississippi Avenue and an even more jagged eastern line around South Forest Street.

Glendale's roots can be traced to the Four Mile House at 614 South Forest Street, a hewn log inn established in 1859 as the last stop before Denver on the Cherry Creek branch of the Smoky Hill Trail. Levi Booth, who purchased the Four Mile House after it had been heavily damaged by the 1864 Cherry Creek flood, transformed it into a 600-acre farm and ranch. Booth, a founder and grand master of the Colorado State Grange, helped construct the Glendale Grange Hall nearby in 1897.[18]

To the west of Booth's ranch, at the corner of Colorado Boulevard

and Alameda Avenue, Robert Emmett Gilmour launched the Cottage Home Dairy in 1903. When he sold the dairy in 1928, his son John Robert "Bob" Gilmour kept a half-acre and in 1929 erected a Conoco gas station at 300 South Colorado Boulevard. He put up a rooftop sign: a bobcat dressed in a tuxedo and carrying a cane over the neon messages "A Bob Cat for Service" and "Howdy Folks." Soon the gregarious Bob was pumping 4,000 gallons of gas a day, and had emerged as Glendale's town character. His son, John R. Gilmour, Jr., recalled that, to win a gas war, "My dad put up a sign: 'Free Gas.' He gave gas away all night." Old man Gilmour also gave away ashtrays, orchid pins, pens, pencils, and desk calendars in his successful courtship of motorists until a car hit him in the middle of Colorado Boulevard. Then he turned over the station to his five children, whom he had raised in the house next door.[19] "Bob Cat" and other Glendale councilmen fought annexation efforts by Denver in a series of court cases and watched Glendale become the bustling center of booming southeast Denver. The area blossomed into a glittering jungle of giant billboards and neon invitations overshadowing three dozen bars,

By the 1980s Colorado Boulevard, 50 years earlier a dirt path on the fringes of the city, had become one of Denver's busiest thoroughfares. (Photo by Glenn Cuerden.)

288

The McBroom cabin at the Littleton Museum is a cherished relic, a one-room reminder of what the good old days were really like. (Littleton Historical Museum.)

discotheques, taverns, and liquor stores. The Cottage Home and other dairies that once lined Cherry Creek succumbed to a gasoline alley of car lots, bowling alleys, fast food joints, discount stores, and other distractions for motorists on Colorado Boulevard. In 1987, John, Jr., discouraged by armed robberies of the Gilmour station, sold for $1.2 million the half-acre that had cost his granddad $98.75. The Glendale Grange Hall survives, recycled as a boutique. The Four Mile House and grounds, purchased in 1975 as a 12-acre park site by Denver, has undergone restoration and is operated by Historic Denver, Incorporated, as a farmhouse museum.

SHERIDAN

Another farm town turned suburb is Sheridan, on the western edge of Arapahoe County where Bear Creek flows into the South Platte River.

John and Isaac McBroom built the first ditch off Bear Creek and introduced the first beehive to Colorado in 1862. To the dismay of honey-loving Indians, the "white man's flies" did not survive the first winter. John, whose 1858 one-room log cabin has been moved from 3700 South Clay Street to the Jefferson County Fairgrounds, founded Sheridan in 1887, when plans were being laid to construct an army post nearby.[20] Anticipating the opening of Fort Sheridan, both the town and its principal thoroughfare, Sheridan Boulevard, were named for General Philip H. Sheridan. When the Civil War hero gave his name to a fort in the Chicago area, Denver chose as its post's eponym another Civil War commander, General John A. Logan. Soldiers flocked to Sheridan's stores, amusement centers, and Monaghan's long-lived tavern. Boosted by business from Fort Logan, Sheridan incorporated in 1890, absorbing the smaller settlements of West Petersburg, Logantown, Military Park, Fort Logan Town, and Sheridan Park. After World War II, Sheridan blossomed as a residential area, mushrooming from a 1940 population of 712 to 5,377 in 1980.

Constructed during the 1880s, when labor unions were replacing Indians as a target of federal police action, Fort Logan became useful during World War I for training rookies. (Denver Public Library, Western History Department.)

CHERRY HILLS VILLAGE

Cherry Hills Village, bordered by Denver on the north, Englewood on the west, and Littleton on the south, emerged during the 1920s and 1930s with the construction of large country homes by rich Denverites. Cherry Hills Country Club, the centerpiece of the village, claimed the finest golf course in Colorado. The horsey set of villagers incorporated in 1945 in order to create and enforce more stringent building restrictions. Within the area bounded by Hampden and Belleview avenues and Clarkson Street and what became I-25, zoning was tightened to exclude anything but single-family homes on sites of at least a half acre. From 750 residents in 1940, Cherry Hills Village grew to 5,127 in 1980, flourishing until the oil crash of the mid-1980s left it with many vacant, unsalable, million-dollar homes. Remaining residents fretted about a bizarre sort of blight — monstrous, abandoned country estates. In 1984, Cherry Hills Mayor Robert St. Clair complained that $1 million to $3 million mansions, foreclosed on after the oil bust, were being "dropped in the city's lap," ill-kept eyesores according to the mayor: "It's hard to design a house that looks well and is that big. Some people have used the word "ugly" to describe them."[21]

Perhaps this caused Cherry Hills to slip from being the country's third-wealthiest suburb to tenth place by late in the decade. Nevertheless, the authors of *Safe Places for the 80s* listed Cherry Hills Village and Columbine Valley as the places to live in metropolitan Denver. Cherry Hills was called a tranquil, rustic village, "where gravel roads are a matter of deliberate choice rather than a lack of funds. The message you get from the unpaved roads, bridle paths, and acre-plus lots is: 'This is executive country.' " Columbine Valley, whose club entrance fees climbed over $15,000 in the 1980s, likewise seemed designed to separate the very rich from the rich. Both neighborhoods, as the authors of this guide to the country's safest, most elegant communities noted, proudly claimed no murders or rapes and minuscule or zero assault, burglary, and theft rates.[22]

Arapahoe County also attracted a new retail district. When developer George MacKenzie Wallace, a transplanted New Yorker, opened the Denver Technological Center on I-25 in 1962, few guessed it would soon rival downtown Denver. Wallace had established a small engineering firm downtown in 1954. Then, as he explained it, "some goddam [ethnic slur deleted] left a scratch in my shiny new black Lincoln sedan. That's when I decided to find a place — with 14 foot wide parking spaces — where my people could have some room to work."[23] Wallace borrowed

The intersection of Denver Tech Center Boulevard and I-225 became a new center of commercial gravity during the 1980s. (Photo by Jim Krebs.)

$80,000 to buy the first 40 acres for his office and industrial park. By 1980, the Tech Center was an 827-acre office complex with square footage second only to downtown Denver. A manicured, pond-dimpled landscape meandered about sleek, modern office buildings. By using tight design guidelines and capitalizing on I-25 as the main corridor, Wallace attracted many corporate giants, including Diners Club, Hewlett-Packard, Kodak, United Airlines reservations center, and cable television companies. To serve his office park, he pushed expansion of once tiny Arapahoe County Airport. Enlarged and renamed Centennial Airport to facilitate its expansion into Douglas County, it became, during the 1970s, Colorado's busiest center for private aviation.

By 1990, the Tech Center hosted 20,000 employees working for approximately 500 firms, and Wallace was driving a $75,000 Rolls Royce and wearing emerald and diamond rings each worth $100,000.[24] The 68 office buildings boasted a 1990 vacancy rate of only 11.2 percent and lease rates as high as $17 per square foot. Although the controlling

Business executives can bypass Stapleton Airport as well as downtown Denver thanks to Arapahoe County's Centennial Airport with its winged terminal. (Photo by Tom Noel.)

interest in the center was sold in 1986 to a British firm, Wallace retained nominal control of this white-collar paradise that compares with such slick office parks as Century City in Beverly Hills. Although the Mile High City's decentralization has not been as extensive as that of cities such as Los Angeles, it has been losing not only residents but also industry, business, and service firms to the Tech Center and similar suburban office parks, such as Inverness and Greenwood Plaza.

When Denver strove to annex some of the southeast office-park area, notably Greenwood Plaza, the mayor of Greenwood Village roared: "We will fight Denver in all ways possible like Poland did when Hitler decided he needed more land. . . . We will fight until they are as bloody as a bull's hock."[25] Denver's struggle to retain dominance in a mushrooming metropolis suffered its most serious setback in 1974 with passage of the Poundstone amendment to the Colorado constitution. This amendment required Denver to gain approval not only within areas to be annexed but countywide voter approval in the county that would lose ground — effectively ending geographical growth of the City and County of Denver. Although individual developers had welcomed annexation in order to get water and other services, county commissioners and suburbanites at large resented any effort to grab their land and tax base. A primary but seldom mentioned motive behind the Poundstone amendment was fear of Denver's integrated schools with their court-mandated busing to achieve racial equality.

Freda J. Poundstone, author and champion of the amendment, typified new trends in metropolitan politics. Barely five feet tall, she packed substantial political clout. Like Poundstone, many other women have become powers to be reckoned with during the 1970s and 1980s, when female mayors, council members, county commissioners, and state legislators became common, and Denver's Patricia Schroeder became the state's most prominent, powerful, and persistent congressperson. Poundstone, the daughter of a Monterey, California, cannery operator, moved to Denver with her husband, a retired Air Force officer, after the Vietnam War. She began working for Harry Hoffman's, Denver's pioneer discount liquor store, before opening her own package liquor store in Arapahoe County. Poundstone next began lobbying on behalf of the liquor industry at the Colorado General Assembly, proving so adept at moving legislators that others sought her services. She epitomized the growing influence of political lobbyists in state and local government, where she became known as one of the most powerful personalities in Colorado. Riding the conservative political wave of the 1980s, she gained additional clout through association with brewer Joseph Coors, whose political friends included several Coloradans holding high office in the Reagan administration: Secretary of the Interior James Watt; Bureau of Land Management Director Robert Burford and his wife Anne Gorsuch, regional administrator of the Environmental Protection Agency.

GREENWOOD VILLAGE

In 1986, Poundstone was elected mayor of Greenwood Village, one of the newest and wealthiest Arapahoe County enclaves. Incorporated in 1950, Greenwood Village is bordered by Cherry Hills on the north, Littleton on the west, and Aurora on the east. It includes much of the Tech Center and Greenwood Plaza, an even flashier office park adorned with a sculpture garden containing works of Henry Moore and Red Grooms's *Brooklyn Bridge* set amid neo-renaissance office towers, and the Fiddler's Green outdoor amphitheater. In the heart of Greenwood, Harlequin Plaza features large black and white marble tiles and a design drawn from Pablo Picasso's portraits of Harlequins. As both mayor of Greenwood Village and a powerful statewide political broker, Poundstone became a political champion of privatism. "I'm perceived as ultra-conservative," she once declared, "but really, I'm a believer in individual rights."[26]

Such rugged individuals have brought to Arapahoe County not only booming office parks and lavish residential enclaves, but busted agricultural hopes. This long, skinny county stretches halfway to Kansas, and the eastern end of its 60 miles contains as many dead towns as live ones. Since 1900, Melvin, Peoria, and Salem have bit the dust; Byers, Deer Trail, and Strasburg hang on. The county's endangered agricultural roots have been perpetuated in one patch of grasslands set aside in the 1970s as the Plains Conservation Center. Visitors are packed aboard a hay wagon to tour a house, blacksmith shop, and one-room schoolhouse — all made of sod. On this 2,000-acre preserve maintained by the East Arapahoe Soil Conservation District, blue grama and buffalo grass flourish once again, and antelope and prairie dogs thrive as they did in the 1850s, when Arapahoe County was created.

Roxborough State Park, a 760-acre preserve of spectacular red-sandstone monoliths, became a battleground during the 1970s after surrounding subdivisions chained the road into this public park and posted it: "No Trespassing. Private Property. Trespassers will be Prosecuted!" (Photo by Tom Noel.)

Since the 1950s, the county has become the economic pacesetter in the metropolitan area, attracting many high-tech industries, including Electron, Honeywell, Jeppesen Sanderson, Marathon Oil, Martin Marietta, C.A. Norgren, and several giant cable television companies. Urban services and planning, though, have not kept up with the explosive growth transforming rural areas. While Wallace's dream of building a private mass transit corridor from downtown Denver to the Tech Center ran aground, automobile traffic jammed major arteries — Hampden, Quincy, Belleview, Arapahoe, and County Line. Despite traffic congestion, many suburban residents opposed the road widening necessary to accommodate the shopping centers, office parks, and services that followed them to suburbia. Arapahoe County residents have been more willing to pay for first-rate schools, however, and the Cherry Creek School District, for instance, leads the state in teacher salaries and per capita expenditures on students.

HIGHLANDS RANCH

Arapahoe County, since its 1902 restructuring, has been the principal suburban frontier for the metropolitan area. During the 1980s, however, development reached the Douglas County line. Construction of the I-470 beltway, just south of County Line Road, cemented Arapahoe

County's new urbanized role, putting it on the city side of the newest superhighway. Now, dreamers and developers are pushing to the countryside of the new I-470 beltway into Douglas County.

Completion of I-25 in the 1960s and of I-470 during the 1980s opened Douglas County to suburbanization. The Lawrence C. Phipps II Highlands Ranch at South Broadway and County Line Road was purchased by Mission Viejo of California, a subsidiary of the Phillip Morris Companies. This conglomerate, which also markets Kraft cheese, Miller beer, Jello, Marlboro cigarettes, and Maxwell House coffee, promoted Highlands Ranch as Colorado's finest and most carefully planned community, a suburban utopia born after Phipps's death in 1976. Marvin Davis, Colorado's premier oil tycoon before he moved to California in 1987, bought the 22,000-acre ranch for $13.5 million, then sold it two years later to Mission Viejo for twice that sum, leaving the Phipps children wrangling over lost millions in a bitter lawsuit. Despite the oil bust of 1983, Highlands Ranch continued to attract homeowners, selling 682 homes in 1987 — 11 percent of all new homes sold in the six metropolitan counties.[27] By 1990, Highlands Ranch had marketed almost 5,000 homes, populated by more than 10,000 residents, replacing Castle Rock, the county seat, as the largest town in Douglas County.

Thus did metro-Denver's sprawling suburbs continue to invade outlying rural regions. Between 1970 and 1990, Douglas County's population soared from 8,407 to 60,391. By 2100, developers expect that Douglas County will have a larger population than Denver. Frank Walker, vice-president of the posh Castle Pines development south of Highlands Ranch, predicted that Douglas County in the 1990s will evolve from "a bedroom community for Denver and the Tech Center [to] an employment center of its own."[28]

Not everyone was tickled with the proliferation of suburbia. Castle Rock Mayor George Kennedy noted that "growth comes but the revenue needed to provide services lags behind"; and Suzy McDanal, a county commissioner, warned that "Douglas County continues to give growth its own free rein, rather than take the leadership to coordinate and direct the growth in the county's best interest. With the footprint that has already been laid, there's a very good chance you'll see a strip city from Denver to Colorado Springs."

CHAPTER 23

Jefferson County

> Saturday night there was a meeting at our house. Men came from all the ranches west of us — halfway to the mountains. . . . At first, everybody was trying to talk at once, and someone said the only way they could ever keep water coming down the ditch in dry spells was to put men with high-powered rifles up on the hills, and shoot hell out of any so-and-so that went tampering with a ditch.
>
> Ralph Moody
> *Little Britches*, 1950[1]

Moody's best-selling novel depicted water wars, one well-spring of local squabbles that eroded a sense of community in the county named for Thomas Jefferson, where privatized enclaves have resisted incorporation and other local efforts to shoulder governmental tasks. Bumpy geography as well as politics characterizes the county, which ranges from the heavily suburbanized South Platte River bottoms to tiny highland hamlets, from Colorado's fourth-largest city to the Lost Creek Wilderness Area. It embraces both public-spirited Arvada with its ambitious cultural complex and the large, affluent, unincorporated city of Evergreen, which has shunned local governmental functions other than fire, police, recreation, and water.

Jefferson County boasts the first documented gold discovery in the metropolitan area, an 1850 placer on Ralston Creek. Its name commemorates Jefferson Territory, the 1859 experiment in self-government. Never recognized by the federal government, Jefferson Territory proved unpopular when it tried to levy a $1 poll tax. Protestors declared that the tax collector "will get a far greater display of bullets than dollars."[2] Although Jefferson Territory soon passed into oblivion, hostility to government and taxes persists.

Dinosaur tracks discovered along West Alameda Avenue Parkway in Jefferson County indicate it was a prehistoric thoroughfare (Martin Lockley Collection).

GOLDEN

Jefferson, one of Colorado's 17 original counties, made Golden its county seat. That town was named for Tom Golden, who first settled in 1858 where an old trail crossed Vasquez (Clear) Creek. Initially, the town competed with nearby Apex, Arapahoe City, Bradford City, Golden Gate, and Mount Vernon, all of which contested Golden's county government. They organized the rival District of Mount Vernon and Ni-wot County during the early 1860s. All these early rivals became ghosts, but Golden, with backing from the Boston Company, thrived to vie with Denver.[3]

George West, a writer for the *Boston Transcript,* served as president of the Boston Company party that founded Golden City in June 1859. West built the Boston Company Trading Post on the north bank of Clear Creek on what would become Golden's main street, Washington Avenue. He tirelessly promoted Golden City as "the right location, where the canyons flattened out into the plains. Travelers and supplies bound for the diggings are forced to use the canyons as highways and our town is right at the crossroads."[4] In 1859, West founded the *Western Mountaineer,* a short-lived newspaper followed by *The Colorado Transcript,* which was published by his descendants and in-laws. West used his gazettes to promote Golden's hopes of becoming the capital of Colorado Territory, working with William Loveland, another Massachusetts man. Together they persuaded territorial legislators to make Golden the capital in 1862, seducing the lawmakers with free use of Loveland's store as a meeting hall, free firewood, and $10-a-week rooms. "Everything is being prepared for a right good time when the legislature meets," the press observed. "Cheney [Golden's popular saloon keeper] is putting up more ice and importing more whiskey."[5]

Golden lost the territorial government to Denver in 1867 but aspired to be the rail capital after Loveland founded the territory's first

The Colorado School of Mines in Golden had trouble with truants — its students often dropped out to join mining rushes. (Colorado Historical Society.)

railroad, the Colorado Central, in 1865. To survey a line from Golden up Clear Creek Canyon to Central City and Georgetown, Loveland engaged Edward L. Berthoud, a Swiss engineer who also was Golden's mayor.[6] After Berthoud, Loveland, West, and the Golden Crowd lost the railroad race with Denver, they focused on attracting the state engineering college. Loveland helped persuade the legislature to establish the Colorado School of Mines (CSM) in 1874 and purchase a small, Episcopal boys' boarding school, Jarvis Hall, as its home. As president of the Board of Trustees, Loveland reported in 1876 that the college was in "a flourishing condition," and that, with the exception of one paid professor, all faculty "have given their services gratuitously."[7] Among the volunteer "professors" was West, who taught military science, and Berthoud, who taught botany.

The school did not construct its own building until 1880; it did not award its first diploma until three years later. Not until 1893, when the state gave it $20,000, did Mines begin to attract a credentialed professorate. The rowdy, male student body became notorious for its frequent strikes, harassment of faculty, and low graduation rate — many students dropped out to work in mining without benefit of a diploma. This did not prevent the *Transcript* from dubbing the school "the world's foremost college of mineral engineering," a claim made by CSM to this day. Jefferson County's other state school, the State Industrial School, founded in 1881, grew much faster. This reform school in Golden had 147 captive pupils by 1890 and 180 inmates a century later when it was known as the Lookout Mountain School.[8]

Despite the efforts of Loveland, Berthoud, and West, the town stagnated after reaching a peak population of approximately 3,000 during the late 1870s. Golden lost residents until World War II brought a resurgence that quadrupled its population between 1940 and 1980, when it reached 12,237.

While Golden faded early as a railroad, mining, and smelting center, it ultimately became Colorado's brew city. Adolph Coors, an orphan who immigrated to New York in 1868 to avoid service in the Prussian army, toiled in an Illinois brewery and a Denver bottling works before he and a partner opened a brewery in a former Golden tannery in 1873. In 1880, Coors bought out his partner and with his brother William opened a bottling works. Tipplers could sample Coors lager in a beer garden amid the cottonwood grove beside Clear Creek. The firm survived Prohibition by making malted milk, near-beer, pottery, and, most notably, porcelain. When World War I cut off the supply of laboratory porcelain, then made exclusively in Germany, Coors took up the trade and became the world's major producer of chemical porcelain. Porcelain continued to be a company product even after Repeal, when Coors became Colorado's number-one brewery.

During the 1960s, Coors jumped from twelfth to fourth place in suds sales. Good times flowed until 1977 when AFL-CIO Brewery Workers Local 366 struck, complaining of paternalistic practices and lie detector tests. Although Coors broke the strike, labor and liberal groups conducted a long and damaging boycott. Joe Coors, grandson of Adolph, attracted national notoriety for bankrolling conservative causes and candidates, including Ronald Reagan. The private, cautious nature of the Coors family may be traced to tragedies: the death of Adolph Coors, Sr., in a fall from a Virginia Beach hotel window, and the kidnaping and murder of Adolph Coors III in 1960. Adolph Coors, Jr., ran the brewery after his father's death, then turned over control to his surviving sons, William and Joseph. Joe's sons, Joseph, Jr., Jeffrey, and Peter, took over operations in the 1980s and focused more on beer and less on politics. They negotiated an agreement with the AFL-CIO to end the boycott and in 1989 began negotiating the purchase of the Stroh Brewery of Detroit, the nation's third-largest. Coors now has 10,000 employees in Golden

Monumental public art of the City Beautiful period included this proposal for Buffalo Bill's tomb on Lookout Mountain, a Denver Mountain Park. After the scout and showman crossed the Great Divide in 1917, Mayor Speer and the *Denver Post* collaborated to make Cody's grave and museum a tourist shrine. (Amon Carter Museum, Mazzulla Collection.)

alone, manufacturing Colorado's best-known product.

While Coors flourished, Golden remained a small town that cherished its folksy Main Street Welcome Arch, inscribed:

> HOWDY FOLKS!
> WELCOME TO GOLDEN
> WHERE THE WEST LIVES!

To retain its small-town flavor, Golden passed a preservation ordinance in 1983 to designate local sites and districts such as the Twelfth Street residential neighborhood. A private group, the Golden Landmarks Board, kept the Astor House from being razed in 1972, converting it to a museum. Loveland's Hall, which housed county government until the courthouse was built in 1877, has been refurbished as the Mercantile Restaurant. The Ace High Bar (formerly the Golden Opera House), the Coors Building, the Foothills Art Center (formerly the Presbyterian church), H. J. Foss & Company, Stewart's Grocery, and other venerable institutions line a picturesque main street that remains the community hub.[9]

Tourists flock to Golden for free Coors Brewery tours and tastings, to see the Buffalo Bill Grave and Museum on nearby Lookout Mountain, and to inspect the Colorado Railroad Museum. There, founding curator Robert W. Richardson delights rail fans with thousands of artifacts, extensive exhibits, research materials, and steam train excursions.[10] The city's Pioneer Museum, operated by the Daughters of the American Revolution, and its public library are tucked into the City Hall complex. A large recreation center was opened in 1961, and Golden still owns and operates its 1874 city cemetery.[11] On the south side of town, massive, ultramodern county office buildings were constructed during the 1980s.

Golden's small-town charm is due in part to its geography; it is protected from urban sprawl by the Front Range rising abruptly to the west in Lookout Mountain and Mount Zion. On its eastern flank, North and South Table mountains block Denver's suburban sprawl. Townsfolk have fought efforts to mine gravel in and around the town and to erect high rises, a laid-back attitude epitomized by *The Golden Transcript*. "The editor just wanted to put a fence around the town," recalled veteran reporter Virginia Weigand in 1975. "At one point, we who worked on the *Transcript* were told not to sell any more subscriptions. The editor thought we had enough, and didn't want us to get too big."[12]

LAKEWOOD

While Golden remained small, Lakewood emerged as Jefferson County's giant, housing more than a third of its 450,000 residents by 1990.[13] Colorado's fourth-largest city has a municipal seal proclaiming "Unity, Prosperity, Progress," with two hands clasped in harmony — a logo belying the long, bitter, and ongoing battle to make a community of reluctant citizens.

Lakewood was platted in 1889 by William Loveland, the ubiquitous pioneer who moved there from Golden to be closer to Denver after he acquired the *Rocky Mountain News* in 1878. With the state's leading newspaper, he hoped to boost his political career. A Democrat in a Republican state, he ran, unsuccessfully, for governor and for the U.S. Senate. His new town did better, attracting farmers, a grange hall, and a few merchants along its West Colfax Avenue main street. The town started to grow after the Denver, Lakewood & Golden Railroad was established in 1891 but then suffered setbacks — the crash of 1893, and the 1894 passing of city father Loveland, who died in his home at West Colfax Avenue and Harlan Street.[14]

Lakewood and the surrounding communities it ultimately absorbed — Alameda, Bancroft, Bear Creek, Green Mountain, and Mountair — flourished with dairies, farms, orchards, ranches, and one of the country's largest chicken and egg operations, Mile High Poultry Farms. Health care became the other major business after Doctor Charles D. Spivak opened the Jewish Consumptive Relief Society (JCRS). Starting in 1904 as a small tent colony, JCRS evolved into a major TB sanatorium and research center. Renamed the American Medical Center in 1954, the 105-acre site harbored 34 buildings of various ages, styles, and functions. Part of the grounds were developed in 1957 as the $20 million JCRS Shopping Center on West Colfax Avenue, but the well-preserved core campus complex survives as a center for general medicine and research with its synagogue now converted to a museum.[15]

During the 1940s, Lakewood's pastoral nature changed rapidly. On the eve of World War II, the federal government bought the Hayden

The Texas Pavillion and cottages of the Jewish Consumptive Relief Society, on West Colfax in Lakewood became a haven for the "one-lunged army." (University of Denver, Center for Judaic Studies.)

Ranch, which stretched from West Sixth to Alameda, from Kipling to Union streets. Ground breaking began in 1940 for the Denver Ordnance Plant with Remington Arms, Kaiser Industries, and General Foods as contractors. The $35 million plant was guarded by two concrete watchtowers and 15 miles of high, barbed wire–topped fences that did not keep out coyotes looking for the turkeys once raised thereabouts. During the war, 20,000 people worked at the plant, and West Sixth Avenue was redesigned as Colorado's first freeway to provide ready access. After peace came in 1945 the plant became the Denver Federal Center, one of the largest concentrations of federal workers outside Washington.[16] By 1990, the Federal Center housed 30 agencies and some 8,000 employees, of whom only 317 can be accommodated in a bomb and fallout shelter to keep government humming in a post–nuclear war world.

As many federal workers sought homes nearby, the old Green Mountain firing range was subdivided for houses and shopping centers that now climb into the foothills. Country estates such as those of Doctor Frederick Bancroft, May Bonfils, Margaret and J. J. Brown, Jacob Downing, and Governor James Grant were reborn as homesites and retail plazas.[17] During the 1960s Lakewood mushroomed into a community of more than 90,000 but continued to rely on the county commissioners and county services. The need for better police and fire protection, schools and libraries, streets and traffic coordination, and more water and sewers became acute. Moreover, the lack of the services made Lakewood a prime target of Denver annexation attempts. For 80 years, the community strung out along West Colfax Avenue had drifted along as a ward of Jefferson County. Indeed, no one knew exactly what Lakewood was, since it had no definite boundaries. Individuals identified with their neighborhoods, which ranged from shantytowns on dirt roads to carefully planned communities such as The Glens, a 1920s residential park built by Cyrus Creighton. The Glens' curvilinear streets, parklike setting, and core community center were laid out by Colorado's premier landscape architect, Saco DeBoer, as an 80-acre "park for happy homes." Developers marketed The Glens, located on West Colfax between Estes and Garrison streets, and other subdivisions as distinctive, small enclaves rather than as parts of Lakewood.

A larger sense of community was promoted by the Lakewood Grange, whose Friday night galas featured the Lakewood Brothers singing such local favorites as "Chick, Chick, Chicken."[18] Longtime Welcome Wagon hostess Norma Morris became Lakewood's best-known representative. The town also took pride in the Westernaires, a snappy, pearl-button posse of cowboys and cowgirls. Founded in 1949 for Jefferson County youth between the ages of 9 and 18, the Westernaires teach horsemanship and military precision to youngsters who then go forth in show teams as Lakewood's Ambassadors of Goodwill.[19]

Goodwill proved hard to find when the question of incorporation arose. A 1947 effort was killed when a hastily organized Taxpayers Protective Alliance persuaded 28 petition signers to go to court and ask that their names be removed. Following that fracas, the *Jefferson County Republican* observed that the "Lakewood incorporation battle" rivaled the "water, range fence and sheep v. cattle feuds in the Old West."[20] Not until 1955, when the Denver Water Board drew its "blue line" to exclude new water taps for Lakewood, did folks reconsider. In a 1956 vote, residents said no to "Ridgewood" (a consolidation of Wheat Ridge and Lakewood) by a margin of five to one, but rumors of planned Denver annexations kept the incorporation drive alive, leading to a 1961 vote, another resounding NO!

In 1969, a coalition spearheaded by school board member James J. Richey, an executive for Proctor & Gamble, gained support from various chambers of commerce, the Jefferson County Board of Realtors, the League of Women Voters, and others who formed Citizens for the Incorporation of Lakewood. This time, Wheat Ridgers, who had voted heavily against annexation, were excluded. The incorportion group stressed positive goals, but fear of annexation by Denver probably decided the election; voter turnout was also prompted by another bugaboo, the notorious "garage gorilla" who repeatedly beat and raped Lakewood women, stirring demands for the stronger law enforcement promised by incorporation proponents.

On June 24, 1969, voters, by a two-to-one margin, approved incorporation. The initial name of the new community, Jefferson City, was soon changed to Lakewood, with skeptics proposing alternatives such as Tax Bug, Taxhaven, Taxedo Junction, and Turkey Town.[21]

The newborn city stretched from Sheridan Boulevard to Youngfield Street between Thirty-second and Quincy, encompassing 31.5 square miles and 97,743 residents. Richey, the first mayor, recalled 20 years later: "Our first city council meeting took place less than 24 hours after the election (in a grade school, with some members having difficulty fitting into the . . . seats). . . . It was a little "scary" to recall that the day after the election we had the responsibility to govern a city of 90 thousand plus, and we didn't have a telephone, a paper clip, a wastebasket."[22] Richey expressed high hopes for planning, parks, and improved municipal services but could do little until the city's powers were spelled out in a charter. This led to new battles, with "aginers" repeatedly defeating proposals. Opponents groused that a charter would mean taxes and a land-use commission "that was merely a disguised planning commission."[23] Not until 1983 did Lakewood gain a home-rule charter, after quelling a secession effort in south Lakewood.

Wadsworth Boulevard, expanded during the 1950s to reach the Martin Marietta Plant, emerged as the new main street. The old West Colfax Avenue strip retained such relics as the Bugs Bunny Motel and the Lakewood Bar and Grill, a fount of Italian food and spirits since the 1940s. Another popular, undesignated Colfax landmark was Lane's Tavern, an ancient shack where Benny Lane has been serving dirt-cheap "platters" filled with six-ounce beer glasses since 1936. More pleasing to local boosters is the White Fence Farm, a manicured farm turned into a restaurant, gardens, barnyard zoo, and haven for rural Americana at 6263 West Jewell Avenue. Erected in 1948 by Lucas Wilson, it is still run by his family, with the slogan "We're Bringing the Country Back to the City." Chickens, a million of which have been eaten at this busy restaurant, are conspicuously absent. Underneath its oversized U.S. flag, White Fence Farm flaunts pride, patriotism, and apple pie, as well as preening pet peacocks.

Colorado's most reluctant city has also taken some steps to engender community pride, launching a Lakewood on Parade day in 1976. Red Rocks Community College opened in 1969 on West Sixth Avenue; all classrooms, offices, and support facilities are under one roof in a sprawling brick and concrete complex on a generous site. By 1988, Red Rocks boasted a woman president, 65 full-time faculty, 200 part-time teachers, and 5,600 students.

Another community asset is the Belmar Museum and Park on May Bonfils Stanton's estate at the corner of West Alameda and South Wadsworth. The 750-acre grounds, with a $1 million, Carrara marble mansion modeled on the Petit Trianon at Versailles, was built by Stanton with her *Denver Post* inheritance. At Belmar, May declared, "the 20th century does not exist." She slept in a bed once owned by Marie Antoinette, sat in a crested chair that had supported Queen Victoria, and owned a piano played by Frédéric Chopin.[24]

After her death at Belmar in 1962, the mansion was demolished. Where formal gardens, lily ponds, and game parks once stood, development began in 1964 with the construction of Villa Italia Shopping Center, housing subdivisions, a huge apartment and condominium complex, and the Iron Gate Office Park. Appalled by these developments, May's husband, Charles E. Stanton, gave $10,000 to Lakewood to plan a civic center, museum, park, and arts complex on what was left of the Belmar grounds. "Money for the arts," Stanton declared, "actually generates further revenues upon which the city's vitality depends. More importantly, it helps to develop a liveable urban environment and higher quality of life."[25] With such encouragement, Lakewood master-planned what remained of the estate for civic and cultural uses, including a city hall, the Bonfils-Stanton Main Branch of the Jefferson County Library, the 126-acre Belmar Park, a projected arts complex, and Lakewood's Historical Belmar Village and Museum. Museum Director Sheila Smith said proudly in 1989:

We have grown from a tiny museum in the old calf barn to a complex of nine structures ranging from the 1869 Ralston schoolhouse to a 1930s-style ranch house, Hallack-Webber House. These are only two of over 100 historic structures in Lakewood we hope to place on the National Register. We've already landmarked the Stone House, an outstanding, vernacular river-rock residence from the 1860s restored at Bear Creek and Estes Street. Our other National Register site is the Peterson Farmhouse, relocated on the Belmar grounds. We have an ideal location here in the center of Lakewood, from which to try to lift the community's historical consciousness. The city passed a special Signs of Significance ordinance to protect signs such as the 36-foot-high cowboy cook and palomino horse on top of Davies Chuck Wagon Diner on West Colfax. That diner is a 46-ton, stainless steel structure moved here June 12, 1957, by rail from the New Jersey manufacturer.[26]

Since 1985, the city has tried to instill awareness and pride with a free publication sent to residents, *Looking at Lakewood*. It surveys what has become a city of 45 square miles, stretching from C-470 to Sheridan Boulevard between West Twenty-sixth and Thirty-second avenues on the north and Hampden and Bowles avenues on the south. The city has spent much time wrestling with a maze of special districts for water, sewage, fire, and other services. To this day Lakewood has no consolidated fire department, while its Water and Sewer Department coordinates 25 districts. This city of over 130,000 is emerging from a stormy adolescence and is just beginning to take an active interest in metropolitan affairs.

ARVADA

In contrast to Lakewood, Arvada has achieved a sense of community, a historical consciousness, and a civic pride that make it a suburban pacesetter. Arvada traces its origins to the 1850 gold strike on Ralston Creek, but settlement did not come until after the 1859 gold rush. Benjamin Franklin Wadsworth staked out the town on Ralston Creek near its junction with Clear Creek in 1870, donating land to establish the Arvada Methodist church; helping organize a public school; constructing the Wadsworth water ditch; and converting part of his home to the post office. His wife, Mary Ann Wadsworth, named the town for her sister's husband, Hiram Arvada Haskin. The name derives from that of the biblical figure Arva, leader of the Arvadites who settled in what is today Lebanon.[27] Wadsworth strove to incorporate his nine-block town in 1887, but not until 1904 did residents vote to do so. Wadsworth did not live to see this — he was killed in a Denver runaway horse accident in 1893 — but the incorporation plat named Wadsworth Boulevard in his honor.

Located eight miles northwest of Denver, Arvada housed fewer than 100 residents during the early 1900s. Then it began to flourish as an agricultural center, a role puffed by the *Arvada Enterprise*, a weekly begun in 1908. Enterprise enlivened Arvadans — they built the area's first water tank, a town hall, a public school, a public library, and even assembled a municipal band. The Arvada Women's Club talked the town into municipal garbage collection and sidewalk rubbish bins in 1929. Townsfolk organized the Annual Harvest Festival in 1925 to celebrate completion of the first paved road and the agricultural riches of the Clear Creek valley. Over the years this fall gala has featured contests in ladies' slipper kicking, boys' wheelbarrow racing, tall-tale telling, grape spitting, egg throwing, and spelling bees, not to mention pretty kitty and ugly dog competitions.

Eugene E. Benjamin enhanced Arvada's role as a farm hub in 1925 by opening the Arvada Flour Mill, which crowned the skyline and touted the town in sacks branded Arva-Pride.[28] Hoping to make the town shine brighter, the Chamber of Commerce erected a large, electric ARVADA on the water tank. Arvada installed the county's first traffic light in 1941, when its population had reached 1,500. Infuriated by this blatant government interference, some motorists "came to a complete stop as they had done at the previous stop sign, then continued on through, regardless of the color of the light."[29]

Unlike many country towns, Arvada anticipated growth, hiring planner Saco R. DeBoer in 1919. He designed McIlvoy Park on Grandview Avenue, where Clemency McIlvoy had donated the three-acre family homesite provided intoxicating liquors were banned perpetually on the premises. DeBoer continued to plan for Arvada until shortly before his death in 1974. To enhance its parks, Arvada established the county's first recreation district in 1955 — the North Jeffco Metropolitan Recreation and Park District — which sprinkled the city with playgrounds, three recreation centers, five swimming pools, an ice arena, 40 tennis courts, bowling lanes, and a golf course.

Arvadans set up one of the first planning commissions in the metropolitan area in 1929, enacted zoning codes as early as the 1930s, and deepened wells and constructed additional water storage tanks during the 1950s. The Arvada Water Department bought raw water from Denver to treat, store, and sell. Accepting its role as part of a burgeoning metropolis, Arvada reconciled its street names and numbering system with Denver's in 1949. A year earlier, Arvada annexed land and platted subdivisions, beginning a landslide of development. Even during the boom, Arvadans emphasized residential rather than commercial or industrial development. When entrepreneurs proposed a major retail complex, the city expressed skepticism, and the Lakeside Shopping Center was constructed just south of its borders.[30] Arvada's progressive mayor, veterinarian Gail H. Gilbert, worked with the University of Denver departments of architecture, geography, and planning to protect what he called "a city of homes."

Arvada was the largest, fastest-growing community in Jefferson County until Lakewood's 1969 incorporation. Realizing that his town's phenomenal growth was not unique, Mayor Gilbert proposed that the state establish a Department of Urban Affairs,[31] a far sighted suggestion lost on state officials. While state and county offered little help, Arvada drew up its own comprehensive plan in 1964. Since homeowners paid over 90 percent of the city's taxes, Arvada strove to enhance its quality of life to keep the affluent from moving to bigger, posher homes in newer foothills communities such as Evergreen, Genesee, Indian Hills, Ken Caryl Ranch, and Lookout Mountain. As the high tide of suburban development swept through the town and beyond, Arvadans determined to make their city distinctive.

In an extraordinary step, Arvadans in 1973 approved a $7 million bond issue to create not only parks and open space, but also the Arvada Center for the Arts and Humanities. The center opened in 1976 in a grassy south-facing hillside park — a spacious brick complex housing a 2,000-seat amphitheater, a 500-seat theater, and 1,500 square feet of gallery space, as well as studios and meeting halls. This center outshines any other Denver suburban arts and humanities showcase, presenting many nationally prominent artists and exhibitions. Nor did Arvada forget its old downtown. In 1959, the town formed an urban renewal board to revive Olde Town Arvada. This project provided landscaping, design review, façade facelifts, and publicity for such veteran businesses as Fred's Arvada Tavern, the Arvada Stationery Store, Dimmer's Bakery, the First National Bank, and the antique shops in old houses along Grandview. Olde Town Arvada sparked a reincarnation of Clear Creek Valley Grange Hall Number 4, one of the oldest in the state, as the Festival Playhouse. The sign on the town's water tower was repainted to read "Olde Town Arvada" and spotlit at night to publicize the renaissance.

Arvada's historical consciousness was awakened by people such as Lois Lindstrom, a first-grade teacher. In 1972, she became the founding president of the Arvada Historical Society, which had enlisted 800 members by 1973. When the society proposed a museum and cultural center, Lindstrom found herself chairing the Arvada Cultural Center Committee that spearheaded the bond issue campaign. Next, she tackled acquisition of the Arvada Flour Mill, which she, her husband, and volunteers restored as a museum and home for the society.

The city, whose boundaries had not changed since its 1904 incorporation, grew by leaps and bounds after 1940. Surveying the town from her office at the Arvada Cemetery in 1985, old-timer Mary Jo Thompson recalled: "All this over here was in cherry trees when I came . . . And then, here come the houses and you go to sleep one night, get up the next morning and there'd be ten [new homes] staring you in the face."[32]

Between 1940 and the 1990s, Arvada's population zoomed from 1,482 to more than 100,000.[33] The nine-block farm town blossomed into a city of 13,873 acres.[33] Arvada has ambitious plans for the 1990s, hoping to annex another 21,000 acres, extending the city limits from Sheridan Boulevard on the east to Colorado Highway 93 on the west between, roughly, West Fifty-second and Eighty-eighth avenues. Although now Colorado's sixth-largest city, Arvada has retained a distinctive personality; a 1983 survey showed it had the highest percentage of Colorado natives among Denver's suburbs, a high rate of citizen involvement, and a low crime rate. A sense of place has been promoted by activists such as Lindstrom. "Some people care about the place where they live, and some people don't," she noted. "But we let them know that Arvada isn't just some place a developer put up."[34]

WHEAT RIDGE

South of Arvada, Wheat Ridge sits atop the south bank of Clear Creek, where farmers grew superior wheat. During the nineteenth century, Wheat Ridge became a community with Colorado's first grange hall, a church, school, post office, Lutheran Sanitarium, and country stores and vegetable stands along West Thirty-eighth Avenue. Among the pioneers taking advantage of Clear Creek and the Rocky Mountain Ditch was William W. Wilmore, who opened Wilmore Nurseries at Thirty-eighth and Wadsworth in 1884. Wilmore recalled years later that an early grist mill on Clear Creek and "wonderful wheat production . . . as high as 60 bushels per acre" gave the town its name.[35] He championed the pioneer Methodist congregation, organized in 1874, and, with other prohibitionists, kept Wheat Ridge a dry and godly place until the 1950s.

George W. Olinger, another Wheat Ridge fixture, built his mansion at Twenty-ninth and Wadsworth, then planted Crown Hill Cemetery across the boulevard. This suburban city of the dead with its Tower of Memories

Wheat Ridge pioneer William W. Wilmore worked with the Women's Christian Temperance Union to keep the town saloonless. (Denver Public Library, Western History Department.)

crowned Olinger's chain of mortuaries, which came to include his own mansion. To remind all Denverites of the inevitable, and of opportunities to purchase cemetery real estate, a gigantic electric cross was installed in 1958 on Mount Lindo. This novel piece of outdoor advertising above Olinger's tomb is visible from many parts of the metropolis. Despite complaints that it is an illegally large advertisement and tasteless, if not offensive, Jefferson County has protected the 398-foot-high electric cross as a landmark.

Olinger also established cities for the living, building, with other capitalists, housing throughout the metropolitan area, ranging from the affluent Indian Hills estates to Olinger Gardens in Wheat Ridge. The Gardens, a 1920 workingman's subdivision, offered six-room houses on standard-sized lots for around $2,000. Thanks to such affordable suburban homes, Wheat Ridge became a town of 1,094 by 1940. During the flush 1950s, ranches, farms, and even the lovely Rose Acres Gardens at 6230 West Twenty-sixth were subdivided. By 1969, when Wheat Ridge incorporated, it had a population of almost 30,000.

Unlike Arvada and Lakewood, Wheat Ridge has remained a stable, semirural community bounded approximately by Sheridan Boulevard and Yougfield Street between West Fifty-second and Twenty-sixth avenues. A series of city parks linked by a greenway adorns Clear Creek. The Wheat Ridge Historical Society uses the park at 5610 Robb Street for its Sod

High in the foothills of Jefferson County, Evergreen's main street was dusted by spring and fall cattle drives. (Colorado Historical Society.)

House and the Johnson-Colehan Log Cabin. The City of Wheat Ridge has restored the James W. Richards farmhouse at 5349 West Twenty-seventh as a museum, meeting place, and park.

EVERGREEN

The affluent foothills community of Evergreen epitomizes the suburban dream. Although now a sizable city, it remains an unincorporated, vaguely defined area with municipal services confined to fire, recreation, sanitation, and water districts, all of which have different boundaries. This picturesque, forested community of homes selling for as much as $16 million is a land of private driveways and NO TRESSPASSING signs.[36] Its tale began in 1859 when Thomas C. Bergen, an Illinois farmer, settled in nearby Bergen Park. Hoping to find gold, Bergen wound up raising cattle and felling timber. He served as one of Jefferson County's first commissioners and, although he listed his occupation as farmer, apparently he and his wife spent much of their time boarding tourists. The Bergens' daughter, and son-in-law, Amos F. Post, opened a trading post on what became Evergreen's main street (Colorado Highway 74). Other pioneers included a French farmer, Julius Dedisse, who homesteaded in 1869, and rancher D. P. Wilmot, whose wife named the hamlet for its thick evergreen blanket of fir, pine, and spruce trees. Post's store and the cluster of cabins earned a post office in 1876, and by 1890 the census taker counted 308 residents. By then, Evergreen had already become a summer tourist

Evergreen, where snow falls as late as June and as early as September, became a cool summer retreat for Denverites. (Colorado Historical Society.)

town. Robert Stewart's still-standing 1871 hotel was reinforced by Troutdale and Brookvale, resorts served by the stage line from the railhead in Morrison.

Ponderosa-clad hills, jubilant creeks, and cool, crisp mountain air made Evergreen a popular summering spot for prominent Denverites, beginning with Governor John Evans in 1868. Narrowly spared subdivision 120 years later, the 6,000-acre Evans spread has been preserved as a few ranches, a state wildlife area, and open space. The Cranmers, Dodges, Gateses, Phippses, Wilfleys, and other wealthy clans followed the Evanses to Bear Creek Canyon, building summer cottages of rustic slab wood, local granite, and river rock.

The masses also discovered Evergreen after the City of Denver transformed the hamlet at the junction of Bear and Cub creeks into a recreation center. Denver acquired the 420-acre Dedisse property on Bear

Creek, converting it to a park, where Evergreen Dam was constructed in 1927. The lake became a haven for outdoorspeople, especially devotees of fishing and ice skating. The nearby Troutdale Hotel and Realty Company gave Denver additional acreage on the condition that the city build and maintain an 18-hole golf course. Evergreen's greenbelt was thickened between 1915 and 1938 by Denver Mountain Parks' acquisition of 3,000 more acres. Jefferson County Open Space further insulated Evergreen with the 1,140-acre Means Meadow Park.

In 1940, 483 residents called Evergreen their home and twice that many summered there. An early effort at local government came in 1925 with the Mountain Parks Protective Agency. It patrolled private property until 1974, when the Jefferson County Sheriff's Department took over. After paratyphoid broke out and frightened away tourists, Evergreen created a sanitation district in 1949. Otherwise, the town was a legal fiction, an orphan dependent on Jefferson County. Although DeBoer produced a 1927 town plan, not until 1986 did Evergreeners accept a master plan.

Hiwan Homestead, one of Colorado's best examples of rustic vernacular log architecture, is now a nifty museum in Evergreen. (Photo by Tom Noel.)

A relic of the 1920s and restored in the 1980s, Tiny Town remains just that. (Photo by Tom Noel.)

The artsy-craftsy set, commuters, and retirees who flocked to Evergreen rejected incorporation twice at the polls but voted in 1969 to form the Evergreen Metropolitan Recreation and Park District. This district promoted a sense of community, arts, crafts, music, and drama, as well as

315

constructing the Evergreen recreation center; and managed Evergreen Lake for Denver Mountain Parks as well as Alderfer Ranch and Kittredge Park for Jefferson County Open Space. Evergreen's most intriguing land-mark, Hiwan Homestead, almost became the real estate office for the Hiwan Ranch subdivision. In the nick of time, the Jefferson County Open Space Department purchased this fanciful log house in 1974 for use as a museum.

Evergreen's population zoomed from 2,321 in 1970 to an estimated 16,000 in the 1990s, yet it remained an official noncity, a bastion of privatism where fantasies of rugged, colorful individualism are acted out each year at the Hiwan Homestead's Mountain Man Rendezvous. As Evergreen activists Barbara and Gene Sternberg have pointed out:

> In all fairness it must be said that if residents of Evergreen . . . truly wanted to be responsible for their own future, they could have shoul-dered the burdens of time and cost involved in incorporating a city.

With the subdividing of the Ken Caryl Ranch in the 1970s, suburbia leaped over the hog-backs and began climbing into the foothills. (Photo by Tom Noel.)

Red Rocks, a spectacular outdoor theater carved out of the red-sandstone foothills as a Denver Mountain Park, has delighted Easter sunrise churchgoers, classical music fans, and rock and rollers with its varied performances. (Denver Public Library, Western History Department.)

Paradoxically, the more subdivisions that were added . . . the less possible a solution by incorporation because of the dilution of the sense of community and the sheer size and spread of developed areas.[37]

Addressing Evergreen's preoccupation with the good life now rather than preparation for the future, the Sternbergs observed that "As a reflection of community values it is striking that adult golfers are integrated into the core of Hiwan, walking through lovingly tended greens and pine groves, while the [school and playground for] children are spun off at the edge of the community; much of their allotted acreage is covered with gravel."[38]

The small foothills town of Morrison offers a contrast to Evergreen. Although closer to Denver and lying in the path of development, Morrison has remained a village of around 500 residents, using a National Register Historic District designation to help preserve its small-town ambience. Other mountain towns — Buffalo Creek, Idledale, Indian Hills, Kittredge, Pine, and Tiny Town — have remained relatively small, while Conifer, like Evergreen, has grown tremendously. Founded in the 1860s as Bradford Junction, Conifer remained a tiny crossroads until recent decades, when strip shopping malls and subdivisions sprouted in what is still an unincorporated, unofficial community.

Jefferson rapidly evolved into the most populous suburban county, jumping from a 1960 population of 127,452 to over 500,000 in the 1990s, when it expects to become more populous than even Denver County. Wheat fields, ranches, and foothills where deer and elk once roamed became housing tracts, a transition that left the county short of open space except for the considerable acreage of Denver Mountain Parks, including Jefferson County's most popular attractions — Buffalo Bill's Grave and Museum on Lookout Mountain and Red Rocks outdoor

Not only homeowners but industry, including this huge international headquarters built for Johns-Manville, have taken to the Jefferson County foothills. (Photo by Nick Wheeler.)

amphitheater. Although owned and maintained by Denver, the parks primarily accommodate Jefferson County residents. The open space crunch led environmentalists to organize PLAN JEFFCO in 1971 and to persuade voters a year later to approve a half-percent county sales tax to acquire open space.[39]

PLAN JEFFCO continued to watchdog the Open Space Department, pushing a successful 1980 vote to expand the department's role to construction, maintenance, and management of park facilities. This permitted construction of a sports complex at Clements Park and camping facilities at White Ranch and Reynolds Park. Open Space's half percent sales tax had raised $75 million by 1990 and purchased more than 17,000 acres. A third of the revenue went to incorporated cities while the other two-thirds bought land in unincorporated areas. "Although Boulder County gets more attention," Open Space Department Public Information Specialist Teresa Ford reported in 1989, "we have acquired about as much land. And we have become a national, award-winning model of how to develop parks in a conservative county."[40]

ROCKY FLATS

Jefferson County commissioners went along with the Open Space program but ignored the county's most noxious nightmare — the Rocky Flats Nuclear Weapons Plant. Indeed, the commissioners not only ignored the message but fired the messenger. When Jefferson County Health Department Director Doctor Carl J. Johnson published studies linking plutonium from Rocky Flats to increased infant mortality and incidence of cancer, he was forced to resign in 1981.[41]

The Atomic Energy Commission built the $45 million Rocky Flats facility on a rock-strewn, barren plateau. Nearly everyone cheered; this was the most expensive industrial complex ever built in Colorado and a boon to the economy. An army of 2,800 construction workers completed the top-secret project in 1953; the Dow Chemical Company was selected to operate the plant, which makes and periodically inspects and reconditions plutonium triggers for nuclear weapons. By the 1980s, Rocky Flats employed 6,000 workers in a 100-building compound with an annual payroll of $250 million and annual purchases of another $180 million.[42]

A fire and explosion on September 11, 1957, raised fears that plutonium had been released into the air, but the worst accident at Rocky Flats started on Sunday, May 11, 1969. A briquet of scrap plutonium spontane-

ously ignited, and flames spread rapidly through Building 776. It took
two years and $45 million to clean
up this radioactive blaze, one of the
most expensive industrial fires in
history.[43] Government officals and
Dow International denied that air
and groundwater contamination was

At the Rocky Flats Lounge,
workers at the gigantic plutonium plant across the highway
can drown out fears of radioactive contamination. (Photo by
Tom Noel.)

a serious problem. Indeed, Dow and its successor, Rockwell International,
were repeatedly given lavish performance bonuses by the plant owner
since 1973, the U.S. Department of Energy. Yet, Johnson's scientific
evidence, as well as rising protests from antiwar and antinuclear groups,
persuaded Governor Richard Lamm and U.S. Representative Timothy
Wirth to appoint a task force to investigate.

The Lamm-Wirth Task Force on Rocky Flats, in its final report of
October 1975, pointed out health hazards and recommended that the
Flats be converted to nontoxic uses. Not only workers at Rocky Flats but
people living downwind in Arvada, Westminster, Wheat Ridge, and
northwest Denver had been exposed to plutonium, which reportedly
caused a 6 to 16 percent higher than normal cancer incidence between
1969 and 1971.[44] Although experts argued about the degree of danger,
most conceded that the facility sat in a bad place — 16 miles upwind of
the largest population center in the Rockies. Concerned citizens began
protesting at the plant in 1970, and demonstrations soon became an
annual rite of spring for thousands who encircled Rocky Flats in a hand-
holding human chain. Protestors included one of America's best-known
living poets, Allen Ginsberg, who noted that plutonium was named for
Pluto, Greek god of death and the underworld. For Rocky Flats, the
bearded, beatnik bard composed his "Plutonium Ode" to "set this verse
prophetic on your mausoleum walls to seal you up Eternally with Diamond Truth! O doomed Plutonium."[45]

Ginsberg's curse had been forgotten by June 6, 1989, when 75 Federal
Bureau of Investigation and Environmental Protection Agency sleuths
staged a secret, sunrise raid. These snoopers found that Rocky Flats had
been illegally storing and incinerating radioactive waste.[46] A few months
later, Rockwell was replaced by EG&G, a Massachusetts-based conglomerate. Department of Energy Secretary James Watkins toured the plant
with the new managers, promising to take "whatever action is appropriate to ensure the protection of public health and safety."[47] It is a promise

Coloradans have heard before.

Many are not sure whether Rocky Flats really is dangerous, despite the warnings from Johnson and the Colorado Medical Society, as well as numerous suits and damage settlement awards. The resignation and even bemused apathy of many citizens was reflected in bumper stickers sold across Highway 93 from the plant at the Rocky Flats Lounge: "Keep Rocky Flats Safe, Move Denver."

The proposed W-470 interstate highway along the western, undeveloped edge of Rocky Flats suggested that development was coming, plutonium or not. Land on the eastern and southern boundary of the four-square-mile weapons plant is targeted for 1990s annexation and development by Arvada. Not even plutonium stopped the annexation wars, with Arvada and Lakewood adopting parcels of unincorporated Jefferson County. Smaller neighbors of these giants, the incorporated enclaves of Edgewater, Lakeside, and Mountain View jealously guarded their independence.

Jefferson County in 1980 had a higher per capita income and educational level than the state average, and a population that was 96.9 percent white or Hispanic.[48] The county schools, one of the few consolidated county services, excelled and showed a willingness to experiment with open and year-round classes. Created in 1950 with the consolidation of 39 smaller districts, Jefferson County School District R-1 is now the largest in Colorado and the twenty-seventh largest in the nation.[49]

Such a large governmental entity proved an irresistible target for county conservatives. Among other complaints, they found fault with the superintendent of schools and with housing the school district offices in the "posh" Denver West Office Park. In the November 7, 1989, elections, a record 32 percent of registered voters turned out to fire a double-barreled blast. By shooting down both a bond issue and a property tax increase, both of which were to aid the school district, the electorate forced the schools to lay off personnel. Voters, especially the elderly and childless, refused to invest in the county's future, in its more than 75,000 public school students.

Although Jefferson County will be the most populous county in the metropolitan area by the year 2000, it retains suburban notions of small, limited government, of automobility, economic segregation, political fragmentation, and privatism. "Jefferson County just has a more western mentality, live-and-let live, more neighborly," as commissioner Marjorie E. "Bunny" Clement put it in 1990: "One of the things with the growth that I find sad as cities grow and become more urbanized is that there are those people in the city that don't want anything to do with the rural aspect. They want to zone out animals."[50]

Affluent residents of semiautonomous subdivisions have demonstrated a marked preference for ranch houses with multicar garages, if not stables and horses. Despite intensive urbanization and the specter of Pluto at Rocky Flats, Jefferson County has fancied itself a cozy, rural haven, exemplifying urbanist Lewis Mumford's definition of suburbia as "an asylum for the preservation of illusion."

Frontier-era fantasies drew both tourists and settlers into Jefferson County, which boasted the Tepees at Evergreen and The Fort of Morrison, a recreation of Bent's Fort offering "Food and Drink of the Old West." (Photos from the Paul and Donna McEncroe Collection and the Denver Public Library, Western History Department respectively.)

CHAPTER 24

Boulder County

The main lookout of citizens is not how to make money as quickly as possible so as to go somewhere else to enjoy life, but how to get as much satisfaction out of life as they can in a very agreeable locality.

Frederick Law Olmsted, Jr.
The Improvement of Boulder, Colorado, 1910

By controlling the explosive growth that overwhelmed other Front Range cities after World War II, Boulder became one of the more livable places in the metropolis. Besides capitalizing on its role as an educational center, the university town developed cultural and recreational amenities. By protecting its spectacular natural setting, respecting its older neighborhoods, and restoring its quaint main street as a pedestrian shopping mall, the town used its past to cushion residents against the shock of rapid suburbanization.

Critics of the "People's Republic of Boulder" argued that its strict building and land use regulations would scare away business, yet the city's planning paid both public and private dividends. Between 1960 and 1980, people and businesses flocked in, doubling the population to 76,685. The 1980s crash hurt Boulder less than most other places in the region; US West, the communications giant, selected it for its $42.5 million regional Center for Advanced Technologies Research. Not only corporate giants sought out the foothills town: Chamber of Commerce

Visitors to Boulder's Columbia Cemetery, the pioneer bone-yard, can enjoy the town's well-protected views and foothills. (Carnegie Branch Library for Local History, Boulder Historical Society Collection.)

General Manager Kay Benson Ryan boasted that Boulder is "one of the best small business havens in the Western United States."[1]

Businesspeople, like residents, appreciated a stable, attractive setting, and Boulder became a model of growth management during the 1970s, enacting a 1 percent sales tax, 40 percent of which helped to pay for a $45 million greenbelt. This 17,300-acre carpet insulated Boulder against creeping suburbanism. The town also limited motor vehicle noise to 80 decibels, building heights to 55 feet, and population growth. The growth control scheme — sometimes dubbed the Danish Plan for its major champion, Councilman Paul Danish — limited new housing permits to 2 percent each year, and was based on a Petaluma, California, plan upheld by the U.S. Supreme Court.[2] Boulder, according to the American Society of Planning Officials, ranked among the top 13 communities in the nation for effectively controlling growth. Even Denver's planning director conceded, "Boulder is not only the best planned city in Colorado, it's a national pacesetter."[3]

Ironically, this town renowned for planning originated in a plan gone awry. Town founder Captain Thomas A. Aikins and 10 other gold seekers struck out in 1858 for the Cherry Creek diggings. Traveling along the South Platte River trail, they camped at Fort St. Vrain. There, as Aikins later recounted, "I mounted the walls of the old fort, and with field-glass could see that the mountains looked right for gold, and the valleys looked

Eldora, one of many mining towns on upper Boulder Creek, gussied up for this 1898 Main Street portrait. (Photo by J. B. Sturtevant, American Heritage Center, University of Wyoming.)

rich for grazing."[4] Bewitched by those mountains and valleys, Aikins followed the St. Vrain River westward to its confluence with another stream. Naming Boulder Creek for its many large rocks, Aikins followed it "till we pitched tents under the red rocks at the mouth of Boulder Canyon." From this October 17, 1858, base camp Captain Aikins and his sidekicks prospected South, Middle, and North Boulder creeks, then tested tributary streams such as Four Mile and Left Hand. Gold was first discovered at Gold Hill, later at Eldora, Jamestown, Magnolia, Nederland, Sunshine, and Ward. These mining camps soon became towns, but

Chief Niwot, or Left Hand, who often encamped with his Arapaho bands on Boulder Creek, welcomed gold-seeking palefaces in fall 1858. (Denver Art Museum.)

Aikins's settlement remained the supply hub. For him, as for many who came after him, Boulder County's valleys were as magnetic as its mountains. Delighted with the rich soil at the base of the foothills and the abundance of antelope, elk, mountain sheep, and mule deer, Aikins settled on the plains.

Arapahos, led by Chief Niwot (Left Hand), also favored Boulder Valley, where they had hunted for decades. Niwot surprised Aikins by welcoming him in passable English and sharing a dream: Boulder Creek would swell to a flood, drowning all the Arapahos but sparing the whites. Although Niwot allegedly refused gold nuggets, he fancied cigars and let the white men stay for what they promised would be only one winter.[5]

After the palefaces staked out claims and built cabins, the Arapahos called the newcomers *niatha*, meaning skillful, clever, spiderlike. Chief Niwot restrained Manywhips and other aggressive young braves who yearned to drive away the whites, but his peacekeeping only postponed tragedy. Niwot and many of his people did not survive the slaughter at Sand Creek. Boulder's Company D, led by Captain David H. Nichols and including Thomas Aikins, took part in this massacre of old men, women, and children.

Even before this bloody solution to "the Indian problem," Aikins and others founded Boulder City on February 10, 1859. They platted a two-mile-long town in the mouth of Boulder Canyon, offering 4,000 home-sites at $1,000 each. These lots, measuring 50-by-140 feet, were larger than the 25-by-125-foot parcels standard in Denver and elsewhere.[6] The community's early interest in elbowroom was reflected in the inital town plat's generous assignment of almost half the site to roads, alleys, parks, and public space. Resisting pressure to reduce the price or size of town lots, Boulder early displayed cautious land use. Not everyone agreed. Amos Bixby, a boomer and editor of the *Boulder Valley News*, in 1880 wrote disparagingly of this decision:

> Early in the affairs of the Town Company, two parties arose — one in favor of holding the lots high, in order to make a "big thing" for themselves; the other in favor of giving away alternate lots to those who would build on them, or doing most anything to induce population and capital. Unfortunately, the high-priced party prevailed, but the lots were not taken at $1,000 each. . . . It was the hope and reasonable expectation, of the advocates of the liberal policy, to have centered here the men of money and enterprise . . . and thus to have made Boulder what Denver afterward became, the leading town of the territory.[7]

Nonetheless, the town survived because of its diversified industries and resources. Flour, gold, and lumber mills made Boulder City a supply center for farmers and miners. Boulder County abounded in the riches of the earth. Forming the northeastern tip of Colorado's mineral belt, it has been among the state's top producers of coal, copper, crude oil, feldspar,

At Nederland's Town Hall, a modern-day mountain man relaxes with the town weekly, *The Mountain-Ear.* (Photo by Tom Noel.)

gold, lead, nickel, and silver, as well as the leading source of tungsten.[8] Colorado's second major silver strike was on upper Boulder Creek at Caribou. Erie, Lafayette, Louisville, Marshall, and Superior blossomed as coal towns, while Lyons produced vast amounts of rosy Lyons formation sandstone, a favorite building material.

Valmont Butte, five miles east of Boulder at the junction of North and South Boulder creeks, yielded basalt used for cobblestone. Valmont, where Aikins settled down to farm until his death in 1876, also emerged as an agricultural center, rivaling Boulder as the county's most populous and prosperous village. By kidnaping the hand press of the *Valmont Bulletin,* the county's first newspaper, Boulderites silenced their rival. Subsequently, the *Boulder Daily Camera,* published for three generations by the Paddock family, became the county's principal gazette.[9]

Gold and silver mining played out by 1900, but tungsten was found up Boulder Creek at Nederland. This hard, ductile metal, used to strengthen steel, became precious during World War I. Nederland boomed once again, producing 80 percent of the nation's tungsten. The market crashed after the war, and Nederland shrank to a tiny town that turned to mining tourists.

Other riches of the earth gushed forth from the plains, where the first Boulder County oil well was drilled in 1901. Within a decade, production was averaging roughly 30,000 barrels a year. Like booms in gold, silver,

and tungsten, the oil bonanza ultimately fizzled. Coal, mined since the
1860s, proved to be the county's
most dependable mineral resource
until the last mine closed in 1973.
Notwithstanding booster claims
that Boulder County was a bottom-
less mineral chest, one boom after
another busted.[10]

After living on the third floor
of Old Main in the early days,
University of Colorado
presidents graduated to this
presidential palace. (Colorado
Historical Society.)

In the long run Boulder found more wealth in mining minds than in
minding mines. Professor Owen J. Goldrick opened the territory's first
school, a makeshift affair in a rented hovel in Denver, but Boulderites
built the first schoolhouse in 1860. During the political scramble for
territorial institutions, Boulder lost the capitol to Denver and the penitentiary to Cañon City, and settled for third prize — the state university.
At that time, as the folklore has it, Colorado's town boosters preferred the
penitentiary: Prisoners could be hired out as cheap labor, whereas faculty
and students were thought of as a rather strange and unproductive lot.
The school was little more than a joke to the legislature in Denver.
Indeed, when the bill to create a university was introduced in 1861,
lawmakers facetiously nominated presidents Abraham Lincoln and Jefferson Davis to its board of trustees.[11] After years of debate, the legislature
begrudgingly appropriated $15,000 with the proviso that Boulder citizens
match that amount. They did and celebrated ground breaking for Old
Main on July 27, 1875. Colorado's statehood the following year seemed to
be a blessing: The national government required the state to set aside 72
sections of land "for the use and support of a state university."[12] Thus
reassured, the university opened its doors to 44 students in fall 1877.

Stingy legislators shortchanged federal support by placing poor, un-
wanted tracts in the university trust fund, lands that by 1885 were
earning only $239 a year in leases. Furthermore, the lawmakers appeased
rival towns aspiring to be the "Athens of the West" by opening other
underfunded colleges at Golden (1874), Fort Collins (1879), and Greeley
(1889). The University of Colorado's (CU) first president, Joseph Sewall,
moved into the third floor of Old Main with his family. He and Boulder
School Principal Justin E. Dow were the only regular faculty members.
Sewall, after resigning in frustration in 1886, summed up his experiences:
"Ten years of my life were mostly filled with sadness, disappointment and
sorrow. . . . I tried to be hopeful, but it was bitter work."[13]

Consistent use of pink-toned local Lyons sandstone, red-tile roofs, and architectural elements borrowed from the hill towns of northern Italy lend serenity to the Boulder campus of the University of Colorado. (Photo by J. Martin Natvig.)

CU survived because of local donations of land, money, and labor. Townsfolk gave the 45-acre hilltop site and sent high school students to the struggling "university" to pad enrollments. During the presidencies of Horace M. Hale and James H. Baker, CU evolved from a glorified high school into a university of 1,200 students with a $300,000 operating budget. By the time Baker retired in 1914, CU had a medical school (1883), a law school (1892), an engineering school (1893), a football team (1899), a college of education (1908), a college of commerce (1908), a graduate school (1909) and a Denver Extension Division (1912).

Despite these gains, lawmakers continued fiscally to starve President Baker. He considered closing the school in 1899 after five years without any funding from the legislature. When the General Assembly crowned Denver's $2,798,389.53 state capitol with a gold dome, Baker protested that it cost more than the whole university plant.[14] The scrawny school finally gained respectability during the 1919–1939 presidency of George Norlin, who had joined the faculty as a professor of Greek in 1899. It was Norlin who engaged Philadelphia architect Charles Klauder to give the campus uniform buildings — red-tile roofs atop rusticated Lyons-sandstone structures — and a Tuscan style borrowed from the hill towns of northern Italy. Klauder's master plan, implemented by local architects such as Glen Huntington, has been generally followed to this day, making the campus Colorado's best example of attractive, consistent architectural planning.

The university is not the town's only educational endeavor. The Boulder Chautauqua, started in 1898 by Texas teachers looking for a cool summer retreat, has been restored and revived. Among more-recent alternative schools are the Naropa Institute with its Jack Kerouac School of Disembodied Poetics, the East-West Center/Family Arts Institute, the Eckankar Boulder Satsang Society, the Neuro-Linguistic Programming Center, the Hakomi Institute, the Nyingma Institute of Colorado (Tibetan Buddhism, transcendental meditation, yoga), the Boulder School of Massage Therapy ("the country's second oldest massage school"), the Rolf Institute, the Shining Mountain Waldorf School, three Montessori schools, and the Boulder Free School, whose 1989 catalog offerings included: "Grateful Dead Theory: How has the music expanded your horizons, been a signpost to new space, shown you the ripple in still water and influenced your life in general?"

Metro residents seeking such enlightenment have had easy access to Boulder since the 1870s, when railroads tied the town to Denver's spiderweb of steel. The Denver & Boulder Valley Railroad, the Colorado Central, the Union Pacific, and the Colorado & Southern all connected Denver to Boulder, which also operated its own streetcar system, the Boulder Street Railway Company, from 1899 until 1931.

LONGMONT

Railroads likewise nurtured Longmont, Boulder County's second-largest city. In some ways, such as its utopian origins and its municipally owned power plant, Longmont has out-Bouldered Boulder. Founded in 1871, the town named for Longs Peak blossomed as a rural haven planted by the Chicago Colorado Colony. These idealists from the Windy City offered settlers of "industry, temperance, and morality" $155 memberships entitling them to three town lots and outlying farmsteads.[15] Several hundred colonists created a model town with communal irrigation ditches and tree-lined streets of tidy homes, schools, and churches. Longmont absorbed the older, adjacent village of Burlington and by 1900 had a population of 2,201. During the twentieth century, the pastoral hamlet grew into a city housing a Great Western beet sugar plant, the Kuner-Empson Cannery, and the state's largest turkey farm. Since the 1960s, Longmont has become home of the Federal Aviation Agency's Rocky Mountain Air Traffic Control Center and several high-tech and publishing operations. These industries helped push the population from 11,487 in 1960 to an estimated 50,000 in 1990.

Longmont has taken a lively interest in historic preservation. The town's Landmark Designation Commission completed an inventory classifying 515 local historic structures. The original east- and west-side residential neighborhoods were placed on the National Register of Historic Places, along with the Dickens Opera House, Longmont College, the old firehouse, and the Kuner-Empson Cannery, which was transformed into apartments.

To keep ahead of bustling Longmont and other rivals, Boulderites launched a hometown railroad, the Colorado & Northwestern, in 1897. Besides serving mining regions, the Colorado & Northwestern touted itself as an excursion line along "The Switzerland Trail," climbing Four Mile Canyon to Sunset. From there one branch went to Ward, another to the resort towns of Eldorado Springs, Eldora, and Nederland.

Boulder County's greatest transit system — the Denver & Interurban (D&I) Railroad — was a mile-a-minute, pollution-free electric line, opened July 23, 1908. Boarding one of 16 daily trains, passengers paid 50¢ for roomy seats in mahogany-paneled steel coaches with leather seats. This Denver-based subsidiary of the Chicago, Burlington & Quincy linked Boulder, Broomfield, Denver, Eldorado Springs, Lafayette, Louisville, Marshall, and Superior. "Boulder," the *Denver Post* declared on July 24, 1908, "is now a suburb of Denver." The D&I transported students, shoppers, working people, and tourists. Wary of Denver's tentacles, Boulderites forced concessions from the line before allowing it to run down Pearl Street and through the university campus. Boulder required the D&I to pay street-paving and franchise taxes and to stop at any corner where passengers wanted on or off.[16]

Completion of the Denver-Boulder Turnpike in 1952 led to the sprouting of subdivisions in Broomfield, developed by the Turnpike Land Company controlled by such Denver high rollers as Aksel Nielsen. (Tom Noel Collection.)

BROOMFIELD

Midway between Boulder and Denver on the D&I lay Broomfield, a hamlet of rustics noted for their broom corn. Broomfield traces its beginnings to Henry and Sarah Church, who in 1864 started ranching at what is now 104th Avenue and Old Wadsworth Boulevard. The Churches also maintained a stage-stop nucleus of a little town. Church's, as the settlement was first called, caught the eye of Adolph Zang, a Denver beer baron. In 1879, Zang bought much of the surrounding land and started raising French Percheron horses, fruit trees, and berries on his 4,000-acre Elmwood Stock Farm. Elmwood and adjacent cornfields caught the attention of developers after the interurban train began service. They began puffing new subdivisions "within 20 minutes ride of Denver" and $125 homesites "double the size of a city lot and large enough to keep a cow, chickens and have a garden."[17]

Despite such promotions, the area remained sparsely settled as late as 1950, when Broomfield had only 176 residents. The 1952 completion of the Boulder Turnpike — with the tollgate interchange at Broomfield — changed that. In 1955, the Turnpike Land Company was formed by Kenton C. Ensor, president of K. C. Construction Company; Roger Knight, president of the Denver U.S. National Bank; Aksel Nielsen, president of the Title Guaranty Company; and John Sullivan of Bosworth Sullivan, a brokerage house. This quartet of capitalists, who fathered many metropolitan subdivisions, bought a site from the Zang Investment Company for what they promised would be a model, planned "bedroom community."[18] Nielsen, a Danish immigrant with a fourth-grade education who became one of Colorado's most powerful developers, hardly saw eye to eye with Boulder's slow-growth policies, as he recalled 30 years later:

> Broomfield was our most spectacular deal. We turned that old Zang Ranch into a city. We held on to the land, added sewer, water, utilities and then called in the builder. That's the secret. Hold on to the land as long as you can. Denver is surrounded by wide open spaces where I never tried to shape development. I just gave people what they wanted. I like the growth pattern here — you've got to have the ups and downs or you have a planned economy.[19]

Broomfield blossomed. By 1960 its 4,535 residents spilled over the Boulder County line into adjacent Adams and Jefferson counties. By 1990 it had become a city of almost 30,000 and little remained of the broom corn village, save the old Zang's Spur grain elevator and the railroad depot, which has been relocated and rehabilitated as the Broomfield Historical Society Museum.

LOUISVILLE

Wildfire growth northward brought the Broomfield city limits to within a few farmsteads of Louisville, which was expanding southward. Louis Nawatny, for whom Louisville was named, first found coal there in 1877.

After the railroad steamed in the following year and built a depot, Nawatny was joined by some of his fellow Poles and by Italians eager to work the coal mines. By 1920 the town boasted a population of 1,799 and the Colacci clan's Blue Parrot Cafe, a still-popular pasta and Chianti restaurant.

Labor wars and declining coal production caused Louisville to stagnate between the 1920s and 1960s. For several decades the town sustained itself on bootlegging and Italian restaurants, serving Boulderites, who banned liquor in 1907 and did not approve liquor by the drink until 1967. Not only Louisville taverns profited from Boulder's sober, slow-growth policies: People unable to find housing in Boulder frequently settled five miles southeast in Louisville, where the population climbed to 5,593 by 1980. Although the town's last coal mine closed in 1954, residents celebrated their heritage in 1976 by placing in front of City Hall a statue of a miner clutching his pick and lunch pail.[20]

LAFAYETTE

As Louisville sprawled, it bumped into Lafayette, another coal town in the northeast corner of Boulder County. Lafayette had been founded by Mary Elizabeth Miller, who named the town for her husband. Lafayette Miller died at age 38 leaving Mary with six children, a sad story that grew rosier when the Millers found a 14-foot coal seam on their spread. During the 1890s, Mary established the Bank of Lafayette and became, locals claimed, the nation's first lady bank president.

Lafayette's rich coal mines brought flush times, but owners shared little of the wealth with the workers, who toiled more than eight hours a day for as little as $3. Workers dreamed the union dream but lost the "long strike" of 1910–1915 and did not walk out en masse again until 1927. Many worked just over the Weld County line at the Columbine Mine in the misnamed community of Serene. When mine owners brought in scabs, strikers picketed the Columbine. Owners retaliated by hiring private guards, who on November 21, 1927, fired on strikers, killing 6 and wounding 60.

Lafayette has slowly recovered from its labor wars and mine closings to become a city of some 10,000. To help remind newcomers of the town's past, Ruthene Rodwick began displaying miners' hats and tools in her tiny grocery store, where she gave tours for schoolchildren and visitors. In 1975, at the age of 68, she turned over her grocery shelves to mining

This frame house, moved to Lafayette's Simpson Street Historic District from the Gladstone Coal Mine a mile north of town, became the Lafayette Miner's Museum in 1980. (Photo by Tom Noel.)

memorabilia commemorating the town's sooty, bloody history. And in the 1980s, she gave her collection to what has become the Lafayette Miners Museum. The museum, the restored Mary Miller House, the company store, the miners' boarding house, and other frugal frame buildings on Simpson Street have earned a place on the National Register of Historic Places as relics reflecting the lives of coal miners. When Lafayette wanted to honor its fallen heroes in the late 1980s, the Colorado Historical Society balked at endorsing their marker for the Columbine Mine Strike victims, calling it too controversial and divisive. But the Industrial Workers of the World, who had organized the 1927 strike, sent Carlos Córtez, a Chicago poet and labor activist, to sprinkle some of the sacred ashes of Joe Hill, the union organizer and martyr, on the graves of the strike victims. Their obscure graves were adorned with a marble tombstone reading: "Lest We Forget Six Union Miners were killed at the Columbine Mine fighting for a Living Wage and a Measure of Human Dignity."[21]

BOULDER

While coal mining became only a memory, new bedroom communities sprouted along the Boulder Turnpike, which had attracted surprisingly little opposition in Boulder; local bankers embraced it as "the magic carpet ride to progress." Few foresaw how fast traffic would accelerate. The turnpike soon paid for itself, enabling the state highway department to close the tollbooth in 1967 — 13 years ahead of schedule. As its boosters hoped, the road brought new business to Boulder. For years the Western States Cutlery Company had been the only major manufacturing plant, but in 1949 the Esquire-Coronet Magazine Subscription Service selected Boulder as its national headquarters. Reorganized as Neodata in 1963, this subscription and mailing operation employed 1,200 in 1989. Ball Brothers, the old Muncie, Indiana, fruit jar firm, moved its Aerospace and Research Division to Boulder in 1957. With 3,000 on the payroll, Ball became one of the county's largest employers. The International Business Machine Corporation (IBM) opened its huge plant in northeast Boulder in 1965 and emerged as the county's largest private employer with over 5,000 employees.[22]

Federal installations flocked in. Rocky Flats, opened just south of the Boulder County line in 1951, mushroomed into a massive plant dispensing many county paychecks. The National Oceanic and Atmospheric Administration and the National Telecommunications and Information Agency also joined the rush. In 1950, Boulder offered 217 acres to attract the National Bureau of Standards, which rejected 26 other cities to select the university town as its headquarters. The Chamber of Commerce helped persuade the city to overlook greenbelt and blue-line laws and donate a 530-acre Table Mesa site for the National Center for Atmospheric Research (NCAR). Walter Orr Roberts, the director of NCAR, became the town's celebrity scientist, a guru of the space age who calculated the orbit of the Soviet Union's 1957 Sputnik. As early as the 1970s, Roberts warned that acid rain, ozone depletion, and global warming were becoming earth-threatening problems. Roberts also demonstrated architectural acumen by collaborating with architect I. M. Pei to create a home for NCAR inspired by the Indian pueblos of New Mexico. The spectacular NCAR structure borrowed its pink-red color from the adjacent Flatirons by mixing local aggregates with the cement.

While the university's research facilities helped attract high-tech industry, its relatively affluent students encouraged "new age" businesses. None of the hippie capitalists did better than Mo Siegel, who at age 21 founded Celestial Seasonings in 1971. Siegel gathered wild herbs for his teas while his wife sewed the tea bags by hand. They marketed their colorfully packaged teas with brand names such as Grandma's Tummy Mint, Morning Thunder, Sleepytime, and Red Zinger, which caught the fancy of the flourishing health food market. Thirteen years after incorporating his "bags-to-riches" firm, Siegel sold out to Kraft for a reported $27 million. When Lipton Tea targeted the Kraft subsidiary for a takeover in 1987, employees bought Celestial, enlarging the nation's largest herbal tea company plant on a 51-acre complex at the corner of Red Zinger Way and Sleepytime Lane.[23]

Other off-beat businesses flourished: Big Sur Waterbeds; Boulder Futon Company; Leanin' Tree Western Greeting Cards; Mountain High Frozen Yogurt; Time Out Hot Tubs; the Tropi-Tan Salon; and White Wave Tofu. Mental and spiritual consumer goods were also produced. The University Press of Colorado found competitors in the Johnson, Pruett, and Westview publishing houses. Spiritually minded Boulderites sustained Boulder Beer, a plethora of New Age religious cults, a Buddhist Temple, and the medieval-style cloister of the Walburga Benedictine nuns.

Boulder County's ultimate boom-bust-boom saga began in the Aristocrat Steak House, a Broadway favorite for its huge six-egg omelets and large, juicy steaks — where several IBM employees met to concoct the Storage Technology Corporation (STC), a computer data storage and retrieval firm. Jesse Aweida, a Palestinian with an engineering degree from Swarthmore, and several other IBM malcontents formed Storage Tek in 1969. STC became Colorado's fastest-growing company during the 1970s, with sales skyrocketing to over a billion dollars a year by 1982, when it was the nation's tenth-largest computer company. The crash came in 1984, when the firm lost over half a billion dollars, declared bankruptcy, and laid off 4,000 workers. STC seemed to be recovering by 1988 when it posted profits of $44 million and reemerged as a major employer.[24]

The business boom was matched by a growth spurt at the university. Following World War II, CU overflowed with thousands of GI Bill students, for whom hundreds of trailer homes were brought to town. Despite the creation of rival state universities during the 1970s at what had been colleges in Greeley and Pueblo, and expansion of Colorado State University, the Boulder campus thrived, leading the legislature to cap enrollment in 1971 at around 20,000 students. During the 1960s and 1970s, some old-timers complained that another 20,000 hippies, street people, panhandlers, and dope fiends overran the town.

Proliferating subdivisions, traffic, and smog sparked a grass-roots movement reinforced by the national environmental awakening of the 1960s. Crusaders rediscovered a local open space tradition: Boulder Mountain Parks, the pioneer effort to preserve the town's natural fringe, had been founded in 1898. This was 14 years before Denver established its mountain parks, an idea subsequently adopted by Colorado Springs, Trinidad, and other communities. For its first mountain park, Boulder bought the 80-acre Chautauqua site in 1898. Afterward, the federal government contributed Boulder, Flagstaff, and Green Mountain parks, while private citizens donated Gregory Canyon, Boulder Falls, and Fourth of July Campground above Eldora.

Following its 1903 formation, the Boulder Improvement Association had persuaded the City Council to limit the size of the city and vigorously acquire parkland. Frederick Law Olmsted, Jr., the nation's leading landscape architect, commissioned in 1908 to plan the city and its parks, designed park systems all across the country after an apprenticeship with his father, the creator of New York's Central Park and San Francisco's Golden Gate Park. In his Boulder report, Olmsted suggested regulating traffic flow, planting street trees, establishing "sewage farms" for recycling waste, and attacking the "billboard nuisance." He advised Boulderites to build a "city of homes" and to beware of any manufacturing plant with "the slightest drawback in the way of noise, dirt, disorder, or annoyance." Olmsted further warned against greedy entrepreneurs "taking from all for the sake of a few." He proposed a floodplain park along Boulder Creek and an "urban forest" in the surrounding foothills.[25] Olmsted's suggestions, with some refinements by later planners, most notably Saco De-Boer and Trafton Bean, became a community goal, although critics charged that Olmsted and his disciples were "a definite minority who do not wish to see dinner pails and overalls on the streets of Boulder."[26]

While the city tightly regulated industry, it indulged wildlife. An estimated 400 mule deer run free within the city limits, munching vegetation, stopping motor vehicles (which kill about 120 deer a year in Boulder County), and otherwise testing environmental commitments. The city stocks Boulder Creek with catch-and-release trout and has built an underground Fish Observatory near the Clarion Harvest House Hotel. Such efforts brought to town some of the wildlife of upper Boulder Creek, which tumbles from the Continental Divide through the Indian Peak Wilderness, Roosevelt National Forest, and Boulder Mountain Parks. These nature preserves, along with the southeast corner of Rocky Mountain National Park, greenbelt the western, mountainous half of Boulder County. Samuel Bowles, a Massachusetts newspaperman, described in 1869 the scenery that still charms tourists: "Everywhere about us, where the snow and the rocks left space, were the greenest of grass, the bluest of harebells, the reddest of painter's brush, the yellowest of sunflowers and buttercups. All, with the brightest of sun and bluest of sky, made [me] feel still that no spot in all our travel is more sacred to beauty than this of our noon camp on Boulder [Creek]."[27]

Boulder's Parks and Recreation Department epitomized the city's underwriting of "the good life." During the 1980s, when many other communities were privatizing recreation, Boulder offered classes in everything from horseback riding to pottery making, from dancing to sailing; staged fireside lectures, sponsored the Boulder Arts School; and produced summer concerts, plays, and dances. The department maintained not only swimming pools, but a nude swimming hole, Coot Lake, until its conversion, after considerable observation and debate, to a wildlife wetlands.[28]

Boulder environmentalists are among the nation's most aggressive. PLAN (People's League for Action Now) Boulder County was established in 1959. Dismissed by developers as just another zany cult, PLAN persuaded the city to draw a blue line eliminating water-pipe extensions into the foothills above 5,870 feet. PURE (People United to Reclaim the Environment) was formed in 1969 as another grass-roots effort to insulate the town with a greenbelt, while also campaigning for zero population growth. Although many of these pressure groups were short-lived, new ones continually sprang up. In 1989, Boulder welcomed the Greens, an international environmental party founded in Germany in 1979. The Boulder Greens were an offshoot of the Eco-Feminists, a local discussion group founded in 1989 by two psychotherapists to arrest the "denigration of women and destruction of nature . . . inherent in the constructs of patriarchal society."[29]

The town sponsored Eco-Cycle, one of the country's first and most successful solid waste recycling programs. This weekly curbside pickup of cans, glass, autumn leaves, and newspapers has achieved 60 percent participation since its inception in 1977.[30] When Boulder received a national environmental award, Mayor Ruth Correll declined to accept because the ceremony was in a state that had not ratified the national equal rights amendment.[31]

Boulder has embraced not only pacesetting environmental laws, but also adventuresome health and welfare programs. It became the first community in Colorado to open an abortion clinic, a people's clinic, a public methadone program, and to provide free needles for drug-addicted AIDS victims. The limits of liberalism have been tested in Boulder — and were reached in 1974. After Mayor Penfield Tate, an African-American, and Councilman Tim Fuller sponsored a city ordinance banning job

Boulder's Chatauqua Park, a haven founded by Texas schoolmarms, is now restored as an intellectual retreat and safeguarded as a National Register Historic District. (Carnegie Branch Library for Local History, Boulder Historical Society Collection.)

discrimination based on sexual preference, Fuller was recalled and Tate narrowly survived a recall vote. Even many Boulderites balked at affirming gay rights: They rescinded the human rights ordinance in a referendum vote.[32]

Boulder's eccentricities have not escaped national attention. A July 28, 1980, *Newsweek* article, "Where the Hip Meet to Trip," proclaimed that "Boulder boasts some of the toughest environmental statutes and loosest enforcement of drug laws in the United States." *Newsweek* concluded that "laid back too far can eventually lead to strung out." Despite such predictions, Boulder had a relatively low crime rate.[33] The city's open-minded approach to law enforcement attracted the attention of the National Institute for Corrections, who moved their headquarters there in 1977. Although accused of lax law enforcement, Boulder's vigilant Environmental Police, in green and white Chevrolets, enforce noise, snow, trash, and weed removal ordinances. They ticket smoking chimneys on high-pollution days, smoking cars, and, in public places, smoking people. Bike path police in blue serve as pedaling peacekeepers among bicyclists, runners, and strollers.

While protecting its fringes, Boulder turned to its aging core. A Historic Preservation Code passed in 1974 established the Landmarks Preservation Advisory Board to designate landmark structures and districts. By 1990, 40 buildings had been designated, along with three historic districts: Chautauqua Park; Floral Park; and Mapleton Hill. Boulder's Pearl Street was reincarnated as a pedestrian mall and Boulder Creek reborn as a greenway. In 1988, Boulder rewarded owners of historic structures by waiving sales taxes on building materials used for preservation of certified landmarks.[34]

Neighborhoods were also safeguarded by a strict sign code and a 55-foot building-height ordinance, as well as a 1982 Solar Access ordinance. Older areas were protected further by tight zoning and creating the installation of curvilinear streets, and neckdowns (expanded pedestrian space) at intersections. Rather than pander to motorists, Boulder concentrated on alternative transportation, sponsoring its own bus system in addition to supporting the Regional Transportation District. Typically, Boulder built bike paths instead of widening streets. The sports-minded town also emerged during the 1980s as an international center for cycling and running. In 1975, Mo Siegel, president of Celestial Seasonings and an avid cyclist, launched the annual Red Zinger bicycle race. It grew into a three-week, 2,000-mile race, subsequently sponsored by Coors, which drew teams from all over the world. Frank Shorter, the first American to win the International Olympics marathon, brought his gold medal to Boulder and became chief guru and shoe salesman of Boulder's running cult. The Bolder Boulder, a 10-kilometer race, attracted 20,000 entrants by the late 1980s. The wackiest celebration of alternative transportation, the Kinetics Festival, occurs each May at the Boulder Reservoir featuring homemade, human-powered vehicles competing in a race across both land and water.

Lycra-, spandex-, and nylon-clad runners, bicylists, hikers, and rock climbers abound. The town boasts a dozen health clubs, some with walls simulating rock faces for climbing practice, and the Flatirons and Eldorado Canyon often are crawling with climbers. Colorado's premier sports town consumes vast quantities of mineral water, sprouts, and tofu — Boulder's Alfalfa's Market sold 1,000 pounds of tofu a week during the late 1980s, 770 pounds more than Alfalfa's Littleton store.[35]

While Boulder focused on proper diets, exercise, and alternative transportation, it became a motorists' nightmare with some of the worst traffic congestion in the metropolis. Boulderites, one veteran bicyclist charged, "drive their cars to nearby meetings to discuss ways to reduce auto traffic."[36] Although some questioned the Boulderites' dedication to healthful, active, non–car-dependent life, the town's commitment to growth management has been obvious. After Boulder braked its boom, towns on the county's eastern prairie flourished. Concerned that a population explosion was merely being relocated, Boulder officials persuaded surrounding rural areas to join in creation of the Boulder Valley Comprehensive Plan, a 1978 intergovernmental agreement. Subsequently, county commissioners downzoned 25,340 acres so that 155,488 of the county's 750,000 acres were shielded from suburbanization by agricultural zoning. Another 10,961 acres were designated as open space.[37]

While Boulder grew from a 1970 population of 66,870 to approximately 86,000 in 1990, the county population zoomed from 102,602 to roughly 220,000. Beyond Boulder's blue lines and greenbelts, unchecked expansion of other communities triggered annexation wars. Superior contested Louisville's proposed 1,100-acre annexation for industrial projects and a 600-acre dump. Superior's City Manager Laura Belsten announced a 47-acre counterannexation designed "to stop them from coming over on our side of the [Boulder] turnpike." Lafayette's many annexations tripled its size between 1978 and 1988. Lafayette Planning Director Brent Bean justified land grabbing by pointing to Broomfield's 3,000-acre annexation near Lafayette and declaring, "If we didn't do it, then [Broomfield or Louisville] would have done it." Even the isolated foothills town of Lyons annexed nearby flatlands to prevent "rustling" by Longmont.[38]

Boulder County Land Use Director Ed Tepe blamed the annex-and-develop disease on Colorado's loose annexation laws, on the abolition of the state's planning commission during the 1960s, and on the national disease of automobility. Other towns did not always share Boulder's interest in growth management. In 1989, they outvoted Boulderites to defeat a county open space sales tax. Pro-development champions charged that growth controllers were creating an upper-class enclave where housing was prohibitively expensive for low-incomers.

At 5,354 feet, Boulder has imagined itself closer to heaven than the rest of the metropolitan area, flaunting its elevation in meters on the city limits signs. Boulderites have not settled for being just another suburb in a sprawling metropolis. Sheltered in its green valley, Boulder has pursued an elevated quality of life and even tried to insulate itself from nuclear holocaust by outlawing atomic weapons within the city limits.

Boulder has been able to chart an independent course in part because it has controlled its own water supply ever since the 1870s creation of the Boulder Water Department. After purchasing the Arapahoe Glacier from the federal government in 1928, Boulder has boasted cool, clear drinking water from Colorado's largest glacier.[39] The town doubled its supply during the 1940s by participating in the Colorado–Big Thompson diversion project, which tunneled under Rocky Mountain National Park. This infuriated Olmsted, who joined a national crusade to stop the project, as a "subordination of National Park values,"[40] but by such means, Boulder escaped the tentacles of the Denver Water Department.

The principal factor behind the Boulder phenomenon lies in the town's history, which reveals a pattern of extraordinary effort to govern the boom-and-bust cycles that have crippled or killed many Colorado towns. From the beginning, Boulder accepted slower growth by charging more for larger lots. The University of Colorado provided faculty and student views and votes that curbed pro-development forces. Boulder's interest in regulated growth did not begin during the 1960s and 1970s. It has been a persistent theme, evident in the initial 1858 town plat, in the 1903 Civic Improvement Association, and in the city's early development of mountain parks.

Finally, this community took seriously Olmsted's comprehensive 1910 plan instructing Boulderites to focus on the fundamental question: "What physical improvements within the reach of the city will help to make it increasingly convenient, agreeable and generally satisfactory as a place in which to live and work?"[41] Boulderites named a city park for Olmsted and reprinted his master plan in 1967 with a new preface acknowledging that the struggle is ongoing: "If planning is to be successful in protecting Boulder's attributes, plans must be carried out — not just proposed."

CHAPTER 25

Adams County

All too often histories of Colorado have dwelt on the history of Denver and the mining camps with maybe a few cowboys thrown in, overlooking the contribution of Adams County and other agricultural areas. . . .

Albin Walker
Adams County, 1977

Adams County has epitomized suburban privatism. Property owners have shaped development with minimal guidance from cities, towns, and the county in this agrarian-minded haven for small businesses, farmers, and robust ethnic communities.

As recently as 1968, the population of unincorporated areas (81,435) almost equaled that of incorporated communities (81,620).[1] Unincorporated places include Goat Hill, a sidewalkless, sewerless neighborhood of poor farmers whose informal community center was a Penitente *morada* on West Sixty-fifth Place. After the crude morada was replaced by Our Lady of Visitation church, which consisted of retired trolley cars resting on cinder blocks, parishioners supported their church by raffling off farm animals — until a non-Catholic won a Catholic porker. Although their trolley car church always welcomed them, Goat Hill residents were not always welcome elsewhere, especially when they wanted to chill out at the nearby Hyland Hills community swimming pool, Water World.[2]

Dupont, Eastlake, Henderson, Irondale, Retreat Park, and Welby are, like Goat Hill, unincorporated. So were Box Elder, Manila, Scranton, and Shamrock, which have become ghosts, while Strasburg survived and Bennett and Watkins boomed as part of the suburban frontier. Many of these towns figured that incorporation would lead only to higher taxes. Adams County understood. Both local and county officials have been reluctant to govern: The county decided in 1979 not to regulate gravel quarrying despite popular protest and concerns that one pit would destroy a historic fur trade site.[3]

County government has been loose ever since 1902, when Adams was carved from Arapahoe County and named for Governor Alva Adams. Since then it has become the industrial and agricultural muscle of the metropolis. Wildcat entrepreneurs fancied its skimpy regulations and pliable officials. Residents resisted restrictions and killed a proposed 1961 metrowide sales tax to fund a Metropolitan Capital Improvements District. Arapahoe, Denver, and Jefferson County voters approved, but not Adams, which ultimately persuaded the Colorado Supreme Court to rule against this attempt at regional cooperation.

Adams County has the highest crime, poverty, and unemployment rates in the metropolitan area. Crime has been difficult to control, especially because county sheriffs, district attorneys, and other officials have been charged in recent decades with conflict of interest, jury tampering, malfeasance, sexual harassment, and other sins that have led to resignations and sometimes convictions. In 1987 the county administrator was arrested for shoplifting. Ten years earlier the planning director was forced to resign after soliciting campaign contributions from persons doing business with his department. The county treasurer was convicted of five counts of embezzlement, while the superintendent of the largest school district was charged with theft. Adams County commissioners strove to brighten the county's image with a new logo, only to be blasted by citizens for extravagance. To improve its reputation, the county in 1985 hired a public information officer, but she soon resigned, discouraged by the county's persistent political squabbles.[4]

Adams has been a dumping ground for whatever other communities did not want — a dog track, feed lots, hog farms, junkyards, massage parlors, and the Metropolitan Denver Sewage Disposal District treatment plant; mobile home courts, oil refineries, rendering plants, striptease bars, and sand and gravel quarries. In 1988, after Denverites complained of noise, air pollution, and congestion at Stapleton International Airport, Adams County welcomed a new airport. State, county, and local officials persuaded Adams voters to allow Denver to annex the necessary land. Adams residents reckoned that the airport would make their county the metropolitan transportation hub, with attendant hotels, motels, restaurants, convention facilities, and jobs galore. This space age dream appealed to Adams County — a chunk of the High Plains 18 miles wide and 72 miles long, stretching eastward halfway to Kansas. Upon its November 15, 1902, creation the county extended all the way to Kansas, but in 1903 the eastern half was divided between Washington and Yuma counties.

BRIGHTON

Adams's rural orientation is reflected in its county seat — bucolic Brighton, which sprang up in 1870 at the junction of the Denver Pacific and the Denver & Boulder Valley railways. Initially named Hughes Station for Bela M. Hughes, president of the Denver Pacific, the town consisted of a frame depot, telegraph station, section house, and a few farms and ranches. Then Daniel F. Carmichael began buying lots; he platted a town in 1881, which his wife named for her hometown in New York, Brighton Beach. Carmichael not only founded the town, he also turned his mansion into the first courthouse and donated land to any congregation willing to build a church.[5]

During the 1880s Brighton prospered, gaining a creamery, the Fulton Irrigation Ditch, a newspaper, and incorporation. Main Street basked in the shade of Carmichael's $30,000, three-story opera house, the Kuner-Empson Cannery, and the Great Western Sugar Company plant. This well-organized community of approximately 400 residents out-campaigned Fletcher (now Aurora) and Harris (now Westminster) to become the county seat by a 14-vote margin in 1904.

Brighton emerged as one of Colorado's first agribusiness centers. Germans from Russia did much of the stoop labor until around 1900, when Naochi "Harry" Hokasono began supplying Great Western and other employers with cheap Japanese labor. During the 1920s, the Japanese Association of Brighton formed to protect their interests, insisting that sharecroppers should give no more than a fourth of their profits to landlords. Many saved money to buy their own land, then sent to Japan for "picture brides." Both brides and grooms hoped their partner bore some resemblance to the photographs used by matchmakers; both toiled in the fields, along with their children. Fearing the loss of their native language and culture, the Japanese opened their own school in 1927.

Brighton, the Adams County
seat, seen here in a January 22,
1910, L. C. McClure photo, remains an agricultural hub.
(Amon Carter Museum,
Mazzulla Collection.)

During World War II, they proved their loyalty by volunteering for
military service, often joining the army's highly decorated, casualty-
ridden 442nd Battalion. Slowly, the patriotism, hard work, and model
citizenship of the Japanese eroded prejudice. With the growing assimilation of the second generation *nisei*, the Japanese American Association
sold its school and used the proceeds to donate a six-acre park to the city.[6]

As Japanese and Germans bought and tended their own land, sugar
beet growers began importing Mexican and Mexican-American workers.
During World War I and the 1920s, hundreds of Hispanics moved into
the Brighton area. By 1929, an estimated 9,000 Spanish-speaking migrants had become year-round residents in metro-Denver — many in
Adams County.[7] To this day, several thousand Spanish-surnamed people
summer in Adams County migrant labor camps, where wages and conditions remain primitive.[8] Improvements have been blocked by the Colorado General Assembly. Representative Walter Younglund, longtime
chairman of the House Agricultural Committee, once argued that employers should not be required to provide field toilets, wisecracking that

migrant laborers would not know how to operate them. Younglund, who boasted that the leather peanut pouch on his desk was a trophy carved from an Indian woman at the Sand Creek Massacre, was not noted for his sensitivity to minorities. He persuaded the legislature to flush the 1986 toilet bill.[9]

Brighton's once-mighty Great Western Beet Sugar Company refinery closed in 1977, after 60 years as the town's major industry. (Photo by Tom Noel.)

Colorado's legislature has not taken significant action on migrant labor since 1971, when the legislative council found that "in spite of various programs and services the seasonal farm laborers, by and large, still suffer from low wages, substandard housing, poor education, and lack of adequate health services."[10] A medical study in the same report found that migrant children had an abnormally high infant mortality rate: 63 per 1,000. Surviving youngsters often suffered from malnutrition, skin disorders, upper respiratory tract infections, and measles. One of the few agencies to care for migrant workers during the 1980s, the State Health Department, established Salud Family Health Centers in Brighton and Commerce City.[11] Although Adams County was spending half its budget for welfare programs, little went to migrants.[12] To help overcome Anglo apprehension and promote the assimilation of Mexican-American migrants, Joe R. Doran and Elfrán Durán started a Brighton Chapter of the Good American Organization. Since the 1960s, Hispanics have been politically active in Brighton, electing a Hispanic mayor, councilpersons, school board members, and a community relations supervisor.[13]

Between 1950 and 1990, Brighton grew from a town of 4,336 to a city of almost 15,000. The county grew even faster, from 40,234 in 1950 to almost 200,000 by 1990. Despite this tremendous increase — primarily in Northglenn, Thornton, and Westminster — the county has been tardy in creating greenbelts and greenways except for the Adams County Greenway, a hike-bike-horse trail on Clear Creek and the South Platte River. Adams has converted the Denver Poor Farm to the 1,150-acre Regional Park where the Adams County Historical Society opened a museum on the site of the county's first non-Indian settlement — Henderson's Island.

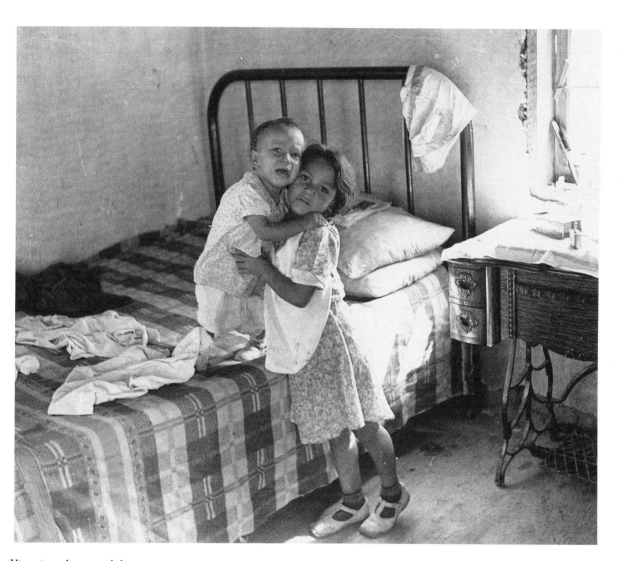

Hispanic workers provided much of the muscle to harvest Colorado's sugar beets. In 1938, this six-year-old girl took care of her baby brother as their mother "work[ed] outside somewhere." (Photo by Allison, Farm Security Administration, U.S. Library of Congress.)

HENDERSON

Back in 1858, Jack D. Henderson started a ranch and a roadhouse that evolved into a town, complete by the 1890s with a grange hall, hotel, general store, blacksmith shop, church, and cemetery. Around 1900, Denver bought Henderson's spread at the junction of Old Brighton Road and East 124th Avenue and converted it to a poor farm, locally derided as a "pest house." The indigent and diseased placed there were asked to support themselves by farming. Denver closed the poor farm in 1952, but Henderson lived on as a commercial crossroads, profiled in the December 28, 1970, *Adams County Standard* as a community of

> about 500 people, two up-to-date schools, Henderson and Hazeltine; three garages: Johnson's Garage and Cafe, Lopez and Amigos Garage, and Dave's Auto Parts; Ed Stuffert's well drilling; Grosshans' General Grocery Store; Jack Speer, the barber; Al Trunkenboltz Appliances and Campers and Suttons' Trailer Court. Other businesses in the area are Robert Larrabee's flour mill; Healthway; John Sweetman's hay dealership; Adams blacksmith shop; M & G feed yards; Brighton Egg Plant; American Fertilizer and Chemical Co.; Schnell Produce; Bromley Machine Co.; and Manhart Liquor Store.

This country town became a regional recreational and governmental center after the county bought the 360-acre poor farm for $176,000 in 1959. Transformed into the Adams County Regional Park, it sports a golf course, rodeo and race grounds, nature preserve, fishing ponds, and mobile-home hookups, as well as the Adams County History Museum. The county established nine other parks embracing a total of 108 acres. To boost the puny parks, the Adams County Trails and Open Space Foundation formed in the 1980s. The foundation's goals for the 1990s include completion of the Clear Creek and Platte River greenways and new trails along the O'Brien Canal and Sand Creek.[14]

The county's major recreational lure is Barr Lake State Park. Built in the 1880s as an irrigation reservoir and sewage disposal site for Denver, Barr Lake aspired to be a tourist oasis. Barr City, named, as is the lake, for a Burlington Railroad civil engineer, attracted few residents or tourists. In 1977 the 2,500-acre site was converted to Barr Lake State Park, noted for its water birds, bald and golden eagles, and fishing.

AURORA

Three-fourths of Adams County's largest city, Aurora, now lies in Arapahoe County, but its origins lie in Fletcher, a rival of Brighton for the Adams County seat. Donald K. Fletcher, a Denver real estate tycoon, founded Fletcher in 1891 but fled the scene after the 1893 Crash. He left residents with bond payments for nonexistent water; irate settlers renamed the town Aurora. Despite marketing in Denver newspapers as

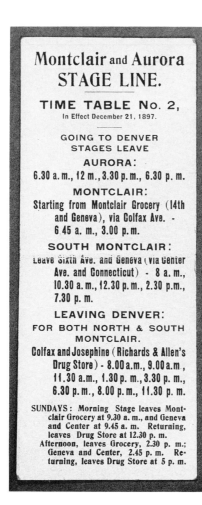

The Montclair and Aurora Stage Line introduced Denverites to the once sleepy east-side suburb that has become Colorado's third largest city. (Tom Noel Collection.)

Montclair and Aurora STAGE LINE.

TIME TABLE No. 2,
In Effect December 21, 1897.

GOING TO DENVER
STAGES LEAVE
AURORA:
6.30 a. m., 12 m., 3.30 p. m., 6.30 p. m.
MONTCLAIR:
Starting from Montclair Grocery (14th and Geneva), via Colfax Ave. -
6 45 a. m., 3.00 p. m.
SOUTH MONTCLAIR:
Leave Sixth Ave. and Geneva (via Center Ave. and Connecticut) - 8 a. m.,
10.30 a. m., 12.30 p. m., 2.30 p. m.,
7.30 p. m.

LEAVING DENVER:
FOR BOTH NORTH & SOUTH
MONTCLAIR.
Colfax and Josephine (Richards & Allen's Drug Store) - 8.00 a.m., 9.00 a.m,
11.30 a.m., 1.30 p. m., 3.30 p. m.
6.30 p. m., 8.00 p. m., 11.30 p. m.

SUNDAYS: Morning Stage leaves Montclair Grocery at 9.30 a. m., and Geneva and Center at 9.45 a. m. Returning, leaves Drug Store at 12.30 p. m. Afternoon, leaves Grocery, 2.30 p. m.; Geneva and Center, 2.45 p. m. Returning, leaves Drug Store at 5 p. m.

"The Most Popular Subdivision Ever Placed on the Market," Aurora grew slowly, reaching a population of 202 by 1900 and not incorporating until 1903.[15]

Aurora remained small and sleepy until World War II, although the opening of Fitzsimons Army Hospital and the Denver Municipal Airport helped boost the population to 2,295 in 1930. The awakening began with the establishment of Lowry Air Base, Buckley Field, and the Rocky Mountain Arsenal.

Colorado's sunny, clear air made Lowry the choice for training army air corpsmen in aerial photography and bombardiering. After 1947, when the Air Force was weaned from the army, it continued to use Lowry as a major training center. During the 1950s Lowry served as a summer White House for President Eisenhower, and from 1955 to 1958 it was the first home of the U.S. Air Force Academy, pending completion of the Colorado Springs campus. Lowry continued to employ approximately 10,000 military and civilian personnel in the 1990s, annually lubricating Colorado's sputtering economy with an estimated $400 million in payroll and local purchases. The base's importance in the development of aerial photography, aviation science, and spacecraft is commemorated in the exhibits of the Lowry Heritage Museum.[16]

Buckley Air National Guard Base, which opened in 1942 as an air base and bombing range, has become the home of the Colorado Air Guard.

A fourth major federal installation located in Adams County is the Rocky Mountain Arsenal. The toxic wastes oozing out of the now-defunct chemical weapons and pesticide plant make it Adams County's number-one problem, and what has been called "the most polluted place in America."[17] In 1940, the idea of a chemical weapons plant delighted

Fitzsimons Army Hospital, named for the first U.S. Army physician killed in World War I, opened in 1920 in Aurora. The main hospital, then said to be Colorado's largest structure, opened four days before the bombing of Pearl Harbor. (Tom Noel Collection.)

all concerned. General Charles S. Shadle, commander at the arsenal from 1945 to 1947, recalled years later how the 27-square-mile site was selected in 1940:

> I helped pick the site after Colorado Senators Eugene Millikin and Big Ed Johnson and Denver Chamber of Commerce officials showed us what was then an asparagus patch near the end of the High Line Canal. We prepared there to retaliate if the Nazis ever used chemical warfare first. After the war I asked a German general why they didn't use chemicals. "That would have been suicide," he told me, "you were so much better prepared."[18]

The Army Chemical Corps spent an estimated $62 million to buy the land between Quebec Street and Buckley Road, from East Fifty-sixth to East Eighty-eighth, and to construct a plant producing chemical and incendiary weapons by the end of 1942. During the war the arsenal employed 3,000 military and civilians. They made mustard and nerve gas, napalm, and white phosphorus bombs as well as other chemical weapons. Except for the napalm and phosphorus bombs dropped on Japan, most of these weapons were stored at the arsenal and never used.[19]

After World War II, the army leased parts of the facility to the Shell Oil Company, which made 14 insecticides there. The army continued to

The Lowry Air Base crew aboard this B-36 bomber had a terrific 1955 view of Aurora's Del Mar Circle, East Colfax Avenue, and Hoffman Heights. (Tom Noel Collection.)

use parts of the plant, particularly during the Korean and Vietnam wars. The arsenal also produced Aerozine-50, a rocket fuel that powered Titan missiles used for military tests and space explorations. Rachel Carson's 1962 best-seller, *Silent Spring,* focused national attention on the arsenal, claiming that its toxins "poison wells, sicken humans and livestock, and damage crops — an extraordinary episode that may easily be the first of many like it."[20] As early as 1950, dead ducks were found floating on the arsenal's cooling ponds. In 1953 Shell and the army discovered that hazardous liquids had eaten through sewer lines to seep into the soil and groundwater, so they began dumping their chemical garbage into huge trenches. This contaminated nearby fields, a fiasco ending with the army's awarding $250,000 for crop damage. Then officials devised a new solution — digging a well to bury the arsenal's poisons more than 12,000 feet underground. This scheme created a new nightmare. A series of earthquakes, measuring as high as 4.2 on the Richter scale, began rattling the metropolitan area. Geologists blamed the tremors on the pumping of an estimated 175 tons of waste into the bowels of the earth.[21]

During the 1970s, public concern mounted, especially after the army allowed more than 10,000 Boy Scouts to hold their annual Jamboree at the arsenal. In 1975 the Colorado State Health Department sued the army and Shell for polluting wells. The response was installation of a $10.7 million filtration system. Nevertheless, toxic wastes continued to taint the South Platte watershed and nearby wells. Complaints continued even after the army spent $23.1 million to clean up drinking water. Public and congressional opposition scuttled the army's plan to dump excess and obsolete chemical weapons into the ocean. Subsequently, the army began disposing of noxious chemicals at the arsenal in what it called "the largest single undertaking of this nature ever conducted in the history of the United States Army."[22]

In 1981 the army finally stopped dumping at the arsenal, and Shell shut its plant in 1982. Lawsuits continued. The State of Colorado sued the military, which in turn sued Shell, which sued its 250 insurance companies for the cleanup, priced by state officials as high as $5 billion.[23]

Putting the best possible face on "the most poisoned place on earth," Adams County commissioners asked federal officials in 1975 to convert it to a national park. Twelve years later, Colorado Governor Roy Romer seconded the park idea, proposing that the $105 million facility be dismantled and its polluted site be transformed into a "Central Park of the West." During the 1990s, surrounding land seemed destined for intense development; the arsenal's eastern flank would be girded by Highway E-470 and the new Denver International Airport.

This projected buildup has led Denver's U.S. Representative Patricia Schroeder and others to argue for a Rocky Mountain Arsenal wildlife preserve. Toward that end, the U.S. Fish and Wildlife Service began conducting arsenal tours during the 1980s, treating nature lovers to views of the bald and golden eagles wintering there, to glimpses of both western mule deer and eastern white-tailed deer, and to close encounters with raccoons and great horned owls. Not to be seen were ground-burrowing prairie dogs: They were exterminated before they could pass poisons in the food chain on to predatory red foxes, hawks, and eagles. "Only the center third of the arsenal site is badly contaminated," explained a Fish and Wildlife agent. "We're trying to expose as many people as possible to the wildlife here so they can help us pressure Uncle Sam not to just sell or give away the land. It would make an absolutely fabulous wildlife area!"[24]

Jobs at the arsenal, Buckley, Fitzsimons, and Lowry, as well as at Stapleton Airport, triggered a population explosion in Aurora. Growth was further spurred by the 1949 decision of the Aurora City Council to establish its own water department rather than rely on Denver's, whose

The bizarre landmarks known as the giant's golf-balls — Buckley Air Field's radar towers — are reminders of Denver's tremendously lucrative military presence. (Photo by Glenn Cuerden.)

restrictive polices choked Aurora's growth. With the 1967 completion of the Homestake Water Project, a joint venture with Colorado Springs, Aurora gained an adequate water supply.[25] Between 1950 and 1960, the population quadrupled to 48,548, and by 1980 Aurora had become the state's third-largest city, with 158,588 residents.

Aurora ballooned in area as well, after starting an aggressive annexation program in 1956 when it annexed Hoffman Heights, a 1,705-home subdivision built around Del Mar Circle on what had been the Cottonwood Ranch. Sam Hoffman's successful subdivision was followed by others, such as Heather Ridge, Mission Viejo, Morris Heights, Pheasant Run, San Francisco, Sunstone, Tollgate, Village East, and Wind Creek. Aurora's invasion of the prairies led to growing complaints about rattlesnakes. Residents besieged the City Council with demands that the snakes be removed from irrigation ditches, weedy patches, and open fields. A biologist from the state's wildlife department testified that suburbanites should give the rattlers time to move out, but, until the economic slump of the mid-1980s abruptly halted Aurora's growth, developers moved faster than the snakes.[26]

Pricey Aurora subdivisions such as Antelope, Chaparral, Chenango, Churchill, and Saddle Rock Ranch attracted the affluent, including

members of the Denver Broncos Football Club. Since nearly all the new developments were south of Colfax Avenue, the town's population center shifted away from the East Colfax commercial strip. Havana Street, the eastern boundary of Lowry Air Force Base, became Aurora's new main street. Buckingham Square Shopping Center opened on South Havana in 1972, only to be eclipsed four years later by the Aurora Mall, which claimed to be Colorado's largest shopping center when it opened at East Alameda Avenue and I-225.

Aurora officials joined the move south and east. The first city center had been just north of Colfax on Emporia Street in a complex housing the city administration, Fire and Police departments, and the library. Following the shopping centers that served as Aurora's hubs, the city fathers moved to Buckingham Square Shopping Mall. After Aurora Mall opened, the city shifted its offices once again to what it declared would be a permanent city center. Grandiose plans for a lavish civic center collapsed during the mid-1980s, but Aurora used the vast municipal tract

Aurora's civic pride soared in 1989 with the completion of the domed, $21 million Aurora Justice Center at 15000 East Alameda Avenue. (Rocky Mountain Prestress, Inc.)

north of Aurora Mall to build a library, police headquarters, a farm-fresh produce emporium — the Aurora Public Market — and a neoclassical, $21 million Justice Center. The last is crowned by a 65-foot-high, 72-foot-wide dome that opens into wide east windows catching the morning sun, thus honoring Aurora, goddess of the dawn.

Rising Aurora found a champion in Dennis Champine, a Havana Street used-car salesman. While on the City Council, he once commanded attention by slugging a fellow councilman. The outspoken, handsome Champine was elected mayor in 1979 and during his eight years in office talked about bringing big-league baseball and convention centers to Aurora. He challenged Denver officials to a softball game and joked that the losers "have to annex Commerce City."[27] A charismatic leader, Champine promoted Aurora's transformation from a suburb to an ambitious city that annexed everything in sight. By the 1990s, the boundaries stretched southward into Douglas County as far as Lincoln Avenue, northward into Adams County as far as Eighty-eighth Avenue, and from Havana and Yosemite streets on the west to Watkins Road on the east. "We're now a city of about 100 square miles," City Manager James R. Griesemer reported in 1989, "but we've worked out future annexations, from the Weld County line to Douglas County, that will make Aurora a city of 200 square miles"[28] — the largest city in Colorado.

With the new Denver International Airport, Aurora anticipates a boom in the 1990s. This time, instead of sprawling south as it has since the 1950s, Aurora's growth would swing back northward into Adams County. In the far southeastern corner of the city, the Aurora Water Department created a reservoir at the junction of Coal and Senac creeks. Besides providing water, Aurora Reservoir is a recreation area larger than Cherry Creek Reservoir, the state park that had served as Aurora's principal playground. The $41 million, 820-acre Aurora Reservoir on the former Lowry Bombing range opened in 1991 with beaches, a marina, stocked fishing, a 10-mile bike track, and two golf courses. Aurora's Parks and Recreation Department further expanded by buying faltering private country clubs — Spring Hill in 1973, Meadow Hills in 1977 — and reopening them to the public.

While most of Aurora blossomed, the old core city — the retail strip along East Colfax Avenue — struggled. As whites moved out, African- and Asian-Americans moved in, transforming the main street into a colorful alternative to suburbia's shopping malls. A concentration of Korean businesses made East Colfax Avenue the metropolitan area's

Korean economic center. By the 1990s, several thousand blacks lived in the same north-of-Colfax area where the 1930 census taker had found all 11 of the town's African-Americans.

By the 1980s, Aurora was looking forward to the day when it would eclipse Denver. "I could see us having a twin-city relationship like Minneapolis–St. Paul," Aurora City Councilman Paul Tauer declared in 1984, "with Aurora in the role of Minneapolis and Denver playing St. Paul."[29] Three years later, Tauer, a high school history teacher, was elected mayor when Dennis Champine retired to devote his time to the Colorado Rangers, a fledgling International Hockey League team.

New cities such as Aurora, theorized city manager Griesemer, should not try to mimic places that, like Denver, had urbanized a hundred years ago. Griesemer envisioned Aurora as a series of "activity centers," where, "if the economic, social, and technological forces shaping our city today don't encourage the creation of a downtown, you'd be wasting a lot of effort to build one."[30]

Aurora's subdivided communities of condominiums, townhomes, and ranch houses have struggled for identity. The quest for community roots led to the establishment of the Aurora Historical Commission in 1970. The commission opened the Aurora History Museum in 1979 and established the Aurora Historical Preservation Commission, which has designated a dozen landmarks, including several of the funky neon signs along East Colfax. The Gully Homestead and the DeLaney Round Barn were restored as historical attractions, while the old Fox Theater was converted to the Aurora Fox Arts Center. Virginia Steele, founding curator of the Aurora History Museum, remarked in 1989 that

> during the 1970s Aurora grew by 111 percent — the fastest growth in the United States for any city over 100,000. With slower growth in the 1980s — we're at about 232,000 now — it's been easier to create a historical consciousness and a sense of place. The city has made a commitment by giving the museum its old — if 1978 can be called old — courthouse for our new home, where the Aurora History Museum will reopen in 1991, Aurora's centennial. City Council has appropriated a significant amount of money to help us survey historic and archaeological sites in the newly annexed areas. It takes time. But we have as great a sense of community and heritage as Denver did at the turn of the century when it had just finished a spurt of growth and rapid annexations.[31]

WESTMINSTER

Westminster, the second-largest city in Adams County, traces its origins
to Westminster University, a Presbyterian school founded in 1892. This
"Princeton of the West" stood on Crown Point, the highest hill in the
county. Nearby, the town's pioneer settler, Pleasant DeSpain, Sr., had
built a sod house and homesteaded in 1870 at West Seventy-sixth Avenue and Lowell Boulevard. The DeSpain Irrigation Ditch, the Farmers
High Line Canal, and a water tower on Lowell helped attract other
settlers. Among them was Edward Bowles, whose house at 3924 West
Seventy-second Avenue has been restored as the museum of the Westminster Historical Society.[32]

With its elevated site and majestic, red-sandstone university building
designed by Stanford White, the prominent New York architect, the
town had high hopes. After incorporation in 1911 Westminster floated a
$28,000 bond issue to establish its own water department. As population
climbed from 235 in 1920 to 1,686 in 1950, the town also dug more

artesian wells. With the postwar boom, Westminster evolved from a country town to a city of 50,211 by 1980, and its wells were running dry. What scarce water was available was often tainted by inadequately treated sewage from upstream users along Clear Creek. Diving into the metropolitan scramble for water rights, Westminster acquired Standley Lake and built a water treatment plant and a 4.5 million gallon tank. Officials also undertook to eliminate Westminster's ubiquitous outhouses by passing an ordinance requiring anyone within 300 feet of a sewer main to pay for an attachment.[33]

Many Italians and Hispanics from northwest Denver moved into Westminster's inexpensive tract housing. In this down-to-earth suburb with its many backyard gardens and truck farms, Fred Ward was an exception. Ward, a sensationally successful auto salesman who made the Hudson Hornet a best-seller in Denver, bought a 160-acre estate at West 120th and Tejon. When wheeler-dealer Ward landed in prison in 1951 for double-mortgaging Hudsons, his estate was subdivided by the Loup Miller Development Company as The Ranch, an enclave of custom luxury homes in the $100,000 to $300,000 range.[34]

Completion of the Boulder Turnpike, which ultimately had two Westminster exits, made that town one of Denver's most accessible suburbs. Land not rearranged by turnpike builders was subdivided as the Apple Blossom subdivision, where the developer promised to leave one tree of the old orchard on each lot — or replace it with a new apple tree. Westminster's boom was not shared by its university. In 1915 the trustees had converted it to an all-male operation, only to lose many students during World War I. The college closed in 1917 but was resurrected in the 1920s as Belleview College, a kindergarten through twelfth-grade school and seminary for the Pillar of Fire Church.

The town platted in 1890 between West Seventy-second and Eightieth avenues and Lowell Boulevard and Raleigh Street mushroomed by 1980 into Colorado's tenth-largest city. Almost a thousand new homes a year popped up in Westminster during the flush 1970s and early 1980s.[35] By 1990 it stretched from West 156th Avenue on the north to West Sixty-eighth on the south, between Alkire Road and I-25 on the east. Westminster strove for distinction by building an $8 million, monumental municipal center with an expansive courtyard and a 136-foot-high clock tower. The tower is an architectural allusion to London's Big Ben, City Manager Bill Christopher explained: "We pondered long and hard about an identity feature. Although our tower is less than half as high, its bells outnumber Big Ben's 14 to 1."[36]

At 6425 Brighton Boulevard in Commerce City, the Hiawatha Saloon, dehydrated by Prohibition, became the Model Garage and Tourists Rooms. After this 1929 snapshot was taken, the old saloon was recycled again as Eason's Machine Shop. (M. Verne Eason Collection.)

COMMERCE CITY

Commerce City has never trod the primrose path taken by more euphemistically named suburbs. Rather, it has been a center of agribusiness and industry, with unpretentious working-class neighborhoods. German hog farmers first settled along Sand Creek, feeding their pigs Denver's garbage and then feeding the hogs back to Denver. Italian and Japanese truck gardeners also lived and labored along Sand Creek around its confluence

Commerce City's crowning landmarks and a major source of its distinctive aroma are the mighty oil refineries that fuel the metropolis. (Photo by Stephen J. Leonard.)

with the South Platte River. This well-watered bottomland also attracted dairies such as Fairview Farm, Morning Sun Farm, and White Star.

The area was incorporated as Commerce Town in 1952 when a 14-year-old boy allegedly mounted his horse and galloped around like Paul Revere, warning that Denverites were coming to annex the area. About 300 alarmed townsfolk met at the McCoy Caterpillar Showroom to voice overwhelming support for incorporation.[37] Alfred Krough, a hog farmer, was elected the first mayor. Commerce Town consolidated Adams City (platted in 1903 in hopes of capturing the Adams County seat), Commerce Town, Rose Hill, and, later, Derby. The new town was bounded approximately by the South Platte River on the west and Quebec Street on the east between Fifty-second and Seventy-second avenues. The community's three railroads, many highways, and proximity to Stapleton Airport attracted farm implement and trucking firms, oil refineries, steel supply companies, grain elevators, and mills. While some communities raised their noses, Commerce City went to the dogs — welcoming the Mile High Kennel Club track.

Commerce Town, which soon promoted itself to Commerce City, evolved from an agricultural to an industrial hub. Once it led Colorado's hog production; then farms gave way to Stapleton Industrial Park. Truck gardens succumbed to the refineries of the Asamera, Conoco, King Resources, Perry, and Tenneco oil companies. Refinery fragrances soon overpowered those of feed lots and slaughterhouses. With a 1990 population of almost 20,000, the city has fought hard to counter its image as the armpit of the metropolis, preferring to be known as "Denver's no-nonsense industrial suburb."[38]

In recent years Commerce City attempted a face lift with a $3.5 million recreation center, new parks, senior centers, and more than $20 million in streets, curbs, and gutters.[39] The city boasts a budget surplus and lower taxes than many surrounding communities, Mayor David Busby noted in 1989. His predecessor, Harold Kite, added that another of the good things was that "the residents aren't really aware of the community's poor image outside of its boundaries."[40]

NORTHGLENN

Northglenn, directly northwest of Commerce City, first crystallized, like many other suburbs, around a grange hall. Riverdale Grange Hall Number 187 housed not only grange meetings but also civic, social, and religious gatherings. The grange hall and a few surrounding farmsteads prevailed until the 1950s, when Perl-Mack, a Denver land company and subdivision developer formed by the Perlmutter family and Samuel Primack, began buying up ranches. In 1959, Perl-Mack opened show homes in "The Most Perfectly Planned Community in America," as North Glenn called itself. The North Glenn Mall opened in 1968, and in 1969 the city incorporated to build municipal services with a 2 percent sales tax. In 1970 the name was changed from North Glenn to

Northglenn, and four years later the city unveiled its logo and a flag featuring mountains and evergreen trees, both of which were in short supply in the raw prairie suburb. Belatedly, the Post Office opened a Northglenn station in 1976, and the Mountain States Telephone Company was persuaded to drop the 10¢ long distance charge for Denver calls north of 104th Avenue. For the opening of the Northglenn civic office gardens, garden club activist Eleanor Wyatt composed "Our Glenn" to the tune of "Five Foot Two":

> Now we've built a City for show
> Then everybody loved our Glenn.
> With a City our size
> We must realize
> That we have to learn to harmonize
> and everybody loves our Glenn
> With dreams so large
> Ahead we charge. . . .[41]

Songs of harmony did not sway voters to appreciate city government and services. Water provoked the loudest controversy. Originally, water was provided by the neighboring town of Thornton, which planned to use its liquid tentacles to annex Northglenn, a scheme thwarted by a 1969 Colorado Supreme Court decision. To escape dependence on Thornton, Northglenn established its own water department, which became a near-disastrous drain on the town's budget, forcing Northglenn to do what it had promised it would never do — enact a property tax. Besides the 1983 property tax, the city began charging for garbage collection, triggering protest meetings and unsuccessful efforts to recall the mayor and city council. Things did not go as well as they might in the "best planned community of North America," with its anthem promoting love and community-mindedness. Yet Northglenn somehow managed to provide parks, recreation, libraries, and water for one of Colorado's newest cities, which boasted more than 30,000 residents on its thirtieth birthday in 1989.

THORNTON

Colorado governor Dan Thornton and Hollywood actress Jane Russell presided at the 1953 grand opening of Thornton. The maestro behind

Colorado's newest city, developer Sam Hoffman, named his subdivision after the governor and had the actress decorate its first two show homes. Curvaceous Russell Boulevard was named in honor of the raven-haired, shapely starlet. By 1960, the $8,000 to $11,000 brick homes had been snapped up by 11,353 residents.[42]

Thornton's neighborhoods offered affordable housing, including several mobile home parks such as Valley View Estates. Rosie Horst, who raised three children in Valley View, declared, "The one thing I resent is people calling it a trailer park. This is my home and it's just as good as anybody else's." In the day of mobile homes with three bedrooms, large kitchens, and fireplace dens, trailer homes have been upgraded to mobile homes or, even better, manufactured homes — the proper term according to LeMoyne Brown of the Colorado Manufactured Housing Association.[43]

"The City of Planned Progress" responded to apprehension about its proliferating low-income neighborhoods in 1980 by requiring design review and a minimum size of 1,000 square feet for all new single-family homes. Developers wanting to build smaller and multifamily units to accommodate first-time home owners blasted Thornton's belated effort to become exclusive. In 1983 the city dropped its restrictions, to the relief of developers, including an official of Bill Wall Homes, who noted: "Thornton was literally trying to legislate quality home building. They were difficult to work with. Now, everyone is working together to make Thornton grow."[44] By 1990 Thornton housed 60,000 people and stretched roughly as far north as 136th Avenue and as far south as Seventy-fourth Avenue, between Holly and Zuni streets. Although Northglenn eluded Thornton's aggressive annexation ambitions, Thornton's 1990s agenda includes annexations northward to the Weld County line, which would add another 20 square miles to this ambitious boomtown.[45]

Thornton gained its water supply, the Northwest Utilities Company, and constructed the elaborate Columbine Water Treatment Plant, which sold water to neighboring communities. To pump up its prestige, the town spanned I-25 with Thornton Parkway and sanctioned the grandiose Thornton Town Center Mall. This $80 million, 1989 project combined a 100,000-square-foot recreation area, a 244,000-square-foot Biggs "hypermarket" selling everything from chocolate eclairs to snow tires, and 100 smaller shops. A grand entry arch and skylighted arcade welcomed shoppers from throughout the metropolitan area.[46]

Thornton and Northglenn's wrangling is symptomatic of Adams County's shortcomings. Its communities have competed more often than they have cooperated, despite many common problems. Northglenn and Thornton spent much of their short lives squabbling over water, building two systems when one would have been cheaper and more practical. Wasteful water wars have left both cities with low bond ratings and expensive water. Annexation wars preoccupied not only Northglenn and Thornton but also many other communities, until a 1988 pact whereby many Adams County entities agreed to negotiate annexation spheres.[47]

The failure to plan and regulate has left Adams County short of effective zoning, green space, and preservation laws. Only a handful of designated landmarks grace the county, notably Brighton's Depot Restaurant, Westminster College and Bowles House Museum, and Aurora's locally designated properties. The lack of a preserved heritage has deepened the problems of community pride, according to Professor Hugo von Rodeck of the Adams County Historical Society. Rodeck, former director of the University of Colorado Museum, Northglenn charter commissioner, and longtime resident, observed, "We have a population here popping in from everywhere. They have no common heritage and we must promote one."[48]

Adams has the lowest median income in the five-county metropolis, according to the 1980 census — $7,259. It also has, in some areas, affordable housing and a lower cost of living, which has attracted many young families, including minorities, pursuing the dream of home ownership. By 1990 an estimated 50,000 Spanish-surnamed individuals formed almost a quarter of the county's population. The African-American population of north Aurora likewise was growing by leaps and bounds.

Competition, coupled with minimal county effort to equalize economic and social conditions, led to considerable disparity among communities. Federal Heights, in western Adams County, with many mobile homes, had 9.1 percent of its population living in poverty in 1980, while east Westminster's rate was 5 percent.[49] Developed in 1968 by flying enthusiasts, Van Aire's $200,000 to $500,000 homes feature garages that accommodate small airplanes, with driveway access to the small private airport at the enclave's heart.

Adams County remains a live-and-let-live community, where individuals and local governments prize their independence and privatism. With a huge new airport complex on the horizon, the county is looking away from its earthy past to the future.

CHAPTER 26

Ethnic Relations

Unless this country, its institutions, and its people face the fundamental problem which is racism, we're not going to change things.

A. Edgar Benton
Rocky Mountain News, September 30, 1970

On an August afternoon in 1932, Denver's African-Americans tried to change things. Aided, the newspapers said, by Communists, 150 blacks, intent on integrating Washington Park's bathing beach, gathered east of Smith Lake in south Denver, an overwhelmingly white section of the city. Parks Manager Walter Lowry urged them to leave: "You never before tried to use this beach." Safety Manager Carl Milliken warned, "if you go into the lake you will be acting at your own peril." The blacks responded, "We're citizens, have your cops protect us."[1]

They then went swimming. Whites quickly left the water, armed themselves with sticks and stones, and advanced on the newcomers who fled toward the trucks that had brought them. When two trucks would not start, the blacks were pursued and beaten as nearly a thousand onlookers watched. The police arrested 17 people — 10 African-Americans and 7 whites who had encouraged the blacks to assert their rights.

The *Denver Post* drew a moral from the riot — "The Communist menace in this country is underestimated by many people" — and warned that "agitators can foment riots and cause other disturbances resulting in human injury and property damage."[2] African-Americans

Whites enjoyed Washington Park's bathing beach, but African-Americans were driven away when they tried to swim there in 1932. (Denver Public Library, Western History Department.)

also learned from the confrontation. They had not been violent. The worst the *News* could charge one of them with was hurling a "vile epithet."[3] Yet they were arrested while their attackers went free. Still in the shadow of its Klan days of the 1920s, Denver was not ready to guarantee liberty and justice for all.

Eight years later Hattie McDaniel, who spent some of her early years in Denver, won an Academy Award for her 1939 role in the film *Gone with the Wind,* becoming the first black to be so recognized. Her stereotype "mammy" character pleased Denverites who took pride in her Oscar, but, as the Washington Park riot had demonstrated, African-Americans were expected to stay in their places and play assigned roles. When, in 1941, blacks asked to be hired to help build the Denver Ordnance Plant, Paul Shriver, director of Colorado's Work Progress Administration, told them that "Negroes and Mexicans have one chance out of a thousand [to be employed]." Jerome Biffle learned a similar lesson about prejudice in the mid-1940s when he was told that he and other African-Americans at

Mayor Quigg Newton, who made the first systematic effort to survey and improve the life of ethnic minorities, meets here in 1947 with the city's Committee on Human Relations. (Denver Public Library, Western History Department.)

East High could belong only to the Letterman's Club. He made the most of his talent by winning the 1952 Olympic gold medal in the broad jump; that gained him fame at home but did not assure him total acceptance, for, in 1952 as in 1932, Denver, like other U.S. cities, suffered from racism.[4]

World War II brought full employment, and ample jobs meant wider opportunities for African- and Hispanic-Americans. The city's black population almost doubled during the 1940s, rising from 7,836 in 1940 to 15,059 in 1950, when African-Americans comprised 2 percent of the city's population. Hispanic numbers similarly increased. Sensitive to these changes, Mayor Quigg Newton in 1947 commissioned a task force to study minorities. The committee reported that many people discriminated against "Negroes, Spanish-Americans, Japanese, and Jews." City department heads gave lip service to equality but rarely hired minorities. Only one Hispanic and two blacks were on the police force; Japanese applicants were told that they could not meet the height requirement. Charged with brutality, the Police Department lamely rationalized: "We don't want to give [minorities] the idea that we are babying or coddling them."[5]

The mayor's task force also found hospitals that would not admit blacks; restaurants that would not serve Jews, let alone blacks; realtors who would not sell to blacks. Statistics from the early 1940s showed that 88 percent of the city's Spanish-Americans lived in substandard housing, as did 45 percent of its African-Americans. The committee concluded that "64,000 men, women and children — Negro, Spanish, Japanese and Jewish — [are] forced to live behind the barbed wire of prejudice."[6]

Yashitaka Tamai, pastor of the Tri-State Buddhist temple since 1931, was memorialized by Sakura Square's high-rise housing for the elderly, Tamai Towers. (*Denver Post.*)

The Japanese community, centered around the Tri-State Buddhist Temple at 1947 Lawrence Street, shrank from its WWII peak population, estimated as high as 5,000, to 2,500 in 1950. Unobtrusive and quiet, most Japanese kept a low profile. Those who came to citywide attention had such obvious talent that other Denverites learned to respect them. Bill Hosokawa, reporter and eventually editor for the *Denver Post,* joined the paper in 1946. Later he wrote the definitive account of that newspaper as well as a history of second-generation Japanese in the United States, *Nisei: The Quiet Americans.* Larry Tajiri, the *Post*'s drama critic, delighted theatergoers. And lawyer Minoru Yasui, head of the Commission on Community Relations from 1967 to 1983, promoted Japanese-American solidarity, while reminding the larger community of the injustices inflicted on loyal Japanese-Americans during World War II.

Anti-Japanese sentiment ebbed as the nisei emerged as a small, proud segment within the larger community. When lower downtown was redeveloped in the early 1970s, the Japanese built Sakura Square, a high-rise apartment and shopping complex between Nineteenth and Twentieth, Larimer and Lawrence. The site already contained the Tri-State Buddhist church, successor to the Buddhist Church of Denver founded in 1916.[7] In Sakura Square's serene garden they placed a memorial to Governor Ralph Carr, who had championed their rights in 1942.

In the postwar years, Jews, like the Japanese, cut away much of the barbed wire of prejudice that had long surrounded them. Attorney Philip Hornbein, Sr., described the 1920s Ku Klux Klan surge in Denver as a "small fire in the forest, which fills the sky with smoke."[8] As the air cleared, many gentiles came to respect the Jewish community. Rabbis, including Charles Kauvar of Beth Ha Medrosh Hagodol (the Great House of Learning synagogue), William S. Friedman of Temple Emanuel, and Manuel Laderman of the Hebrew Educational Alliance, participated in numerous civic projects. Jewish entrepreneurs built businesses that provided jobs for thousands. Jesse Shwayder and his brothers, for example, made Samsonite Luggage internationally known and gave the city one of its anchor industries. Abraham B. Hirschfeld went from near rags to riches making A. B. Hirschfeld Press one of the West's largest printing houses.

Jews shared the fruits of their labor with the wider community. National Jewish Hospital gradually shifted its focus from curing TB to treating a variety of lung diseases. In west Denver the Jewish Consumptive Relief Society adopted a new name, the American Medical Center, and a new mission — the cure of cancer. Shortly after World War II the Jewish community built yet another hospital, naming it after Major General Maurice Rose, a Denver native killed in 1944 as he led his troops into Germany.

The location of General Rose Hospital at Tenth Avenue and Clermont Street in east Denver bespoke the migration of many Jews away from the central city and from neighborhoods bordering West Colfax, where as late as 1947 over 40 percent of the city's 16,000 Jews lived. Four years later only a third of them still resided there. Many had moved to the Hilltop area, a developing residential district between Sixth and Alameda avenues extending east from Colorado Boulevard toward Quebec Street. There Jews built new synagogues and a commodious community center.

Even in their comfortable new neighborhood, Jewish citizens sometimes had to walk on the smoldering embers of the Klan years. The Reverend Kenneth Goff, a right-wing Christian, fanned anti-Semitic sentiment by arguing that "Communism is a modern version of the Jewish world state."[9] Jewish physicians were long barred from the staffs of some hospitals, and even the most prominent Jews were denied membership in such social bastions as the Denver Club. It was not until the late 1960s that Doctor Abraham Kauvar, head of Denver's Department of Health and Hospitals, and brother of an earlier director, Doctor Solomon Kauvar, was asked to join the Denver Club. Kauvar pondered the step. "I said, 'Fine, but I don't want to be the first one.' "[10] Assured that he would be the second Jewish member, Kauvar joined and eventually became president. When Alan Berg, a Jewish talk-show host, was gunned down by out-of-state neo-Nazis in 1984, Denverites were incensed at his murder. But four years later, vandals reminded Jews of the Holocaust by emblazoning swastikas on the Hebrew Educational Alliance at 1555 Stuart Street.

While overt anti-Semitism sometimes boiled after World War II, old quarrels between Roman Catholics and Protestants gradually cooled. In the 1950s some Protestants questioned John Carroll's fitness for the U.S.

Denver's rich Hebrew heritage includes the home of the late Israeli prime minister Golda Meir, originally in west Denver's Little Israel neighborhood. Threatened with demolition, the house was moved on September 25, 1988, to Ninth Street Park on the Auraria campus, where it was restored. (Rosemary Fetter Collection.)

Senate; his wife Dorothy was a Catholic. Bigots likewise tried to use Bert Keating's faith against him in 1955 when he ran for mayor. Denverites in general, however, did not seem to be swayed by such tactics. In 1956 they sent Carroll to the Senate and helped elect Stephen L. R. McNichols, a Catholic, governor of Colorado. In the 1960s and 1970s two Catholics, Thomas Currigan and William McNichols, Jr., won the city's mayorship. In January 1973 a Catholic nun, Helen Weber, was made director of the Colorado Council of Churches educational ministries. Later that year the Catholic Archdiocese of Denver, under the ecumenical leadership of Archbishop James V. Casey, joined the council, thereby formalizing smoother relations between Catholics and Protestants.

Some walls crumbled, but other barriers based on skin color remained. Achieving harmony among African-Americans, Hispanics, and the heterogeneous dominant group imprecisely known as Anglos became one of the city's principal postwar tasks, a challenge that made building roads, schools, and hospitals seem simple by comparison. Louis Sidman, director of the Anti-Defamation League, recognized the problem in 1948 when he told citizens that "the habits and morals of a basically conservative community cannot change quickly."[11] Mayor Newton's committee exposed the city's sins, but his administration moved cautiously. The charter proposed in his first term left out a proposed antidiscrimination clause; later Newton put a small splint on fractured racial relations by establishing the Commission on Human Relations with Helen Peterson, part Sioux, as its first director.[12]

During the 1947 election Newton chided Stapleton for failing to hire black policemen. In response, Stapleton quickly added two blacks to the force. By 1954 there was a black on the Library Commission, a black assistant district attorney, and two black state legislators. There were a few black policemen, but no black detectives. In 1955, Newton's last year as mayor, all of the city's black firemen were still assigned to Station Three at 2500 Washington near Five Points, an intersection of three streets at Twenty-sixth and Welton, the hub of the African-American neighborhood. Lee Casey, city editor of the *Rocky Mountain News*, editorialized in 1949: "The Negro should insist upon his rights and do so now. Those who are not Negroes should likewise insist that these basic rights be observed, and right now."[13] The *Denver Post,* edited after 1945 by Palmer Hoyt, stopped using racial designations except in crime stories and started putting African-Americans' pictures on the front and society pages. In 1950, Hoyt hired George Brown as the *Post*'s first black reporter.

Brown tested local racial waters in 1951 by attempting to swim at Lakeside Amusement Park's pool, which refused to admit him. The manager explained, "We have a tough element out here — they might

Although better off than blacks in some other cities, many Denver African-Americans lived in substandard housing such as this Five Points shack. (Denver Housing Authority.)

Denver's blacks have found great strength in their churches. The Reverend Wendell T. Liggins, pastor at Zion Baptist since 1937, said in 1987, "My dream is to see integrated churches." (Photo by Tom Noel.)

throw rocks at you."[14] At Sportland, the Young Men's Christian Association pool on Thirty-first and Madison, Brown was ordered to keep out — a restriction that puzzled him since he was young, a man, and a Christian. Brown found motels more accommodating, but of the 25 where he attempted to register, five would not have him. At the Blue-Vue, one of the many motels lining South Santa Fe, he was told, "I know that God loves you as much as he loves me, but I'm sorry." The manager of the Crestview Trailer camp at 5525 Federal Boulevard was even harsher: "We don't have restrictions on pets, but we have to draw the line on Negroes."[15] Restaurants were more open than motels, but 2 of the 40 eateries Brown visited told him that he would have to eat in the kitchen.

In 1952, Isaac Jones, a reporter for the *Baltimore Afro-American,* praised Denver for its progress in integrating public accommodations. Jones also found that blacks had secured at least a few good jobs. Many African-Americans in 1950 still did menial work, but some had moved up. Federal employment at the Air Force Finance Center at Thirty-eighth and York attracted some blacks to Denver. The Yellow Cab Company hired African-American drivers, as did the tramway. The public schools employed black teachers, and a few schools were racially mixed. Jones concluded that in Denver, "fair play reigns" and "the color line does not exist."[16]

He overstated the case. Colorado's capital seemed advanced compared to places in the South where blacks were prevented from attending white schools, eating at white restaurants, and drinking from white drinking fountains, but, Denver was far from being an integrated city. Residential segregation insured that most blacks and whites would live apart. In 1952 blacks remained concentrated in the Five Points area, although some had moved toward City Park. East of York Street between Seventeenth and Twenty-sixth avenues, City Park and the City Park Golf Course provided a milewide buffer between the expanding black neighborhood and affluent sections of Park Hill east of Colorado Boulevard.[17]

From residential segregation much else flowed. Since practically all of the city's African-Americans lived in northeast Denver, there was little likelihood that a black would be seen in a restaurant, a theater, or a park in south Denver, although sometimes the black amateur baseball team, the White Elephants, played at Merchants Park at West Exposition Avenue and South Broadway. South Denverites might sometimes encounter a black at City Park, or at Union Station since many African-Americans worked for the railroads, but usually white Denverites clung to their white world.

Mayor Newton knew that the Five Points neighborhood, its 13,500 inhabitants crammed into small homes or sharing large, old homes cut up into apartments, had become dangerously overcrowded by the late 1940s. In 1949 he pleaded with residents of northeast Park Hill, a new area of moderately priced homes, to allow blacks into the Cavalier subdivision, 48 houses near Thirty-fifth and Dahlia. "Negroes," he said, "are holed up in a small area which is getting worse and worse. . . . They are victims of an unwritten law. Sooner or later there must be a breaking through."[18]

Many whites wanted the breakthrough to come later. For decades they relied on restrictive covenants in property deeds to keep minorities out of many areas. After 1948, when the U.S. Supreme Court made such clauses legally unenforceable, defenders of white neighborhoods relied on custom, on the reluctance of banks to lend to blacks, and on real estate agents' unwillingness to show homes in white areas to blacks. "I can't sell you this house," a salesman explained to George Brown in 1954. "I have no objections myself. I really wish I could sell it to you, but I'd lose my broker's license if I did."[19] Such informal stratagems became more difficult to use after 1959, when Colorado toughened its antidiscrimination laws, and after 1965, when the state strengthened its fair-housing statutes in response to the national civil rights movement.

Neighborhood change, when it came, was largely determined by the geography of northeast Denver and by the fact that blacks, many of them relatively well-paid government and railroad employees, had the money to move east from Five Points toward Park Hill. Northern portions of lower downtown and deteriorating neighborhoods bordering the South Platte River did not attract many blacks and were left to poorer people, many of them Hispanic.[20] In the early 1950s a few blacks moved east of York, north of Twenty-sixth Avenue. White flight followed. By 1963 neighborhoods between York and Colorado Boulevard north from Twenty-sixth to Thirty-eighth Avenue had become largely black. Overcrowding, however, continued since the African-American population more than doubled in the 1950s, reaching 30,251 in 1960.

As blacks moved east of Colorado Boulevard in the early 1960s some Park Hill residents moved out, especially those living in moderately priced homes north of Thirty-second Avenue. Other whites, particularly those residing south of Twenty-sixth Avenue, in large, expensive homes, decided to stay. By obtaining R-0 zoning for much of Park Hill, a designation that prevented homes from being subdivided into apartments, residents sought to make their neighborhood economically, if not racially, exclusive. Then, in July 1965 the Park Hill Action Committee (PHAC), made up of blacks and whites, called for an open city — one in which blacks would be welcome to live anywhere. PHAC advised whites to stay in Park Hill and to welcome black newcomers. It also urged other white neighborhoods to join in the process of residential integration. Noting that Colorado's 1965 fair housing law opened options for African-Americans, the committee warned that unless blacks dispersed, Park Hill would become overwhelming black.[21] To some degree PHAC's efforts succeeded. Many whites stayed in parts of Park Hill; others, attracted by large houses at bargain prices, moved in. Park Hill prided itself on its relatively smooth integration, but the picture was not perfect. By the early 1970s, its northeast section was heavily African-American, its northern parts largely African-American, while its neighborhoods south of Twenty-third Avenue remained predominantly Caucasian.

"Negroes are permitted to buy houses in Park Hill, at least north of 26th," *Post* reporter Charles Roos wrote in 1963, "but they encounter great difficulty elsewhere in the Denver area." Roos noted that in letting blacks buy east of Colorado Boulevard the community was following a policy of allowing "Negroes to extend their ghetto when it becomes physically necessary, but not to allow them to disperse."[22] Blacks who crossed the color line found themselves the objects of curiosity, if not mistreatment. In 1962 Tracy Smith and his family moved to the northwestern suburb of Northglenn. On their first day there hundreds of people cruised by their house — "mostly they just stopped, parked and gaped at us."[23] The Willis L. Gilbert family, at 1434 South Fillmore, got along well with their neighbors, but in August 1965 someone burned a cross on Gilbert's front lawn.[24]

Custom, economics, and ethnocentricity proved powerful barriers against integration. In 1970 the metropolitan area counted 50,191 blacks, of whom 94 percent were in Denver, mainly in north central and northeast sections. The development of Montbello, a tract of moderately priced homes northeast of Stapleton Airport in the late 1960s and early 1970s, provided blacks and others a modern, integrated, and affordable residential area. In the 1970s, protected by antidiscrimination laws, more blacks settled outside the city limits, but predominantly black neighborhoods persisted, whether within Denver or in other counties. In northwest Aurora, for example, many African-Americans resided south of Stapleton Airport. Those living north of Colfax were listed by census takers as citizens of Adams County; those south of Colfax as residents of Arapahoe County. That African-American concentration in a few Aurora census tracts gave Adams and Arapahoe counties black contingents constituting between 2 and 3 percent of their total populations, but it did not indicate significant residential integration. In 1980 Jefferson and Boulder counties tallied black proportions under 1 percent. That year 76 percent of the metropolitan area's 77,779 African-Americans still lived in Denver.

Residential segregation insured that schools would also be segregated. Doctor Kenneth Oberholtzer, school superintendent between 1947 and 1967, explained in 1964 that School District One had no color line, that educational segregation was due to housing patterns. However, the 1960 opening of Barrett Elementary, with nearly 90 percent black students, at Twenty-ninth and Jackson, smacked of deliberate segregation since Barrett drained blacks from Park Hill schools east of Colorado Boulevard. One third-grader at Park Hill Elementary, in 1960, later recalled that after Barrett opened, Park Hill "suddenly became lily white."[25]

Integrationists saw Barrett as a blatant example of racism. It was not an isolated case. Apparently to accommodate whites in areas that were becoming black, the schools permitted parents in those neighborhoods either to enrol their children in the local school or to send them elsewhere. That escape hatch was closed after a school became largely black so that there was not much chance that blacks would attend white schools. When white schools became crowded, students were bused to

Rachel Noel, distressed when her daughter was ordered to leave "white" Park Hill Elementary for "black" Barrett School, ran for the Denver School Board, where she became a champion of integrated schools. (Denver Public Library, Wetern History Department.)

other schools. If a black school exceeded capacity, temporary classrooms were built.

When her daughter was removed from Park Hill Elementary and sent to Barrett, Rachel Noel became angry. She found that at Barrett her daughter relearned in the fifth grade what she had been taught at Park Hill in the fourth. In 1965, Noel, a sociologist with a master's degree from Fiske University, became the first black school board member.[26] In May 1968, shortly after the assassination of civil rights leader Martin Luther King, Noel and another board member, attorney A. Edgar Benton, persuaded the board to order formulation of a school desegregation plan.[27] Some students volunteered to be bused in early 1969. Hundreds of blacks decided to attend white schools, many of them modern facilities with generous budgets. Only 74 whites shifted to predominantly black Manual High. The board then decided on additional busing. School chief Robert D. Gilberts envisioned voluntary and mandatory busing of some 5,000 students in autumn 1969.

That proposal, especially forced busing, distressed many parents. The angry majority spoke loudly on May 20, 1969, defeating prointegration board candidates Benton and Monte Pascoe, who had urged voters to recognize, as the *Denver Post* had in early 1969, that "there are too many children who are dying, educationally, everyday in the segregated schools of Denver."[28] Few listened. After the election Calvin Trillin reported in the *The New Yorker* that in Denver "Doing the Right Thing Isn't Always Easy."[29] But undoing integration seemed easy since the district had not started large-scale busing. New board members Frank Southworth and James Perrill joined other anti-busers to scuttle Gilberts's plan on June 9, 1969.

Stymied by the board, integrationists quickly turned to the courts. Wilfred C. Keyes, a black resident of Park Hill, and seven others sued the schools, claiming that their children had been denied their constitutional rights.[30] Federal District Judge William Doyle, a Denver native and a graduate of West High, agreed with some of the arguments made by Keyes's attorneys, Gordon Greiner and Craig Barnes. For autumn 1969, Doyle ordered busing for nearly 3,000 students, about 3 percent of the district's enrollment of 96,000. In March 1970, Doyle held that segregation had come about more as a result "of neighborhood housing patterns" than of "positive law or as a result of official action;" but, since this de facto school apartheid led to unequal education, Doyle said it violated the equal protection mandate of the U.S. Constitution's Fourteenth Amendment.[31] As a cure he prescribed the desegregation of 17 schools and ordered the integration of teaching and administrative staffs.

The school board's antibusing majority did not like the ruling. In September 1970, A. Edgar Benton ruefully observed that "at Byers Junior High, where I have two daughters, nothing is being done to make [integration] work."[32] Southworth charged that Doyle's order would "completely destroy the Denver public schools."[33]

Judge Doyle's initial order turned out to be only a first, small step. Appeals took the case to the U.S. Supreme Court, which in 1973 ruled that in gerrymandering Park Hill enrollments, the Denver School Board had "created a prima facie case of segregative purpose." The justices also said that unless the board could show that Park Hill schools were isolated from the rest of the district and hence had a reason for operating differently, Denver would have to "desegregate the entire system 'root and branch'."[34] In December 1973, Doyle decided that Park Hill was geographically part of School District One — that there was no valid reason to treat the area differently. In April 1974 he ordered rearrangement of school boundaries, creation of paired schools between which students would be bused for part of the day, and the busing of an estimated 6,000 students in addition to the 5,000 already being bused to achieve integration.

Doyle recognized that busing was an awkward tool and tried to minimize it. Many parents, however, could not stomach even limited busing. Some grumbled and talked of organizing an alternate school system. Some moved to the suburbs; others put their children in private institutions. Public school enrollment peaked in 1970 at 97,781 students; in 1971 the total dropped to 94,338, and in 1972 the number was 91,616. The April 1974 court order bred even greater paranoia. Up to then the busing burden had fallen mainly on blacks who were transported into white areas. Voicing his fears in late 1973, school superintendent Louis J. Kishkunas remarked: "What really scares me is that we will have to transport whites into black dominated schools."[35]

Superintendents frequently resigned and school board meetings became battlegrounds, the furor often spilling over into the schools. In February 1974 the antibusing Citizens Association for Neighborhood Schools (CANS) urged students to boycott classes. More than 50 percent did so. At John F. Kennedy High School in southwest Denver only 161 students out of 1,585 attended. Naomi Bradford vowed that she and others would disobey the court order even "if our husbands are put into jail for it."[36] Nolan Winsett, president of CANS, called the ruling "tyrannical" and urged the board to appeal, a step they agreed to in May 1974.

Benton warned "that unless this country, its institutions, and its people face the fundamental problem which is racism, we're not going to change things." And he accused the board of thwarting progress: "The system has used its personal resources, its financial resources, and its resources for educating the community in a negative way by making all its efforts to fight the thing in court."[37] Integrationists criticized the board for spending millions of dollars in a futile effort to free the system from court control.[38] They suggested that riots, such as the one at George Washington High School in September 1970, might have been avoided had the board tried to make integration work. Court supervision, they argued, improved educational opportunities for blacks and Hispanics and broadened Anglos' horizons. Magnet schools such as Knight Academy in south-central Denver drew praise for educational excellence. By 1985 all except three of the city's schools had achieved or were approaching integration guidelines.

Antibusers contended that court orders did little good, that social segregation remained. At Kennedy High School in 1981 only one of the 130 students attending the junior prom was black. Historian Phil Goodstein noted: "The real problem that haunted [Denver Public Schools] throughout this epic was the internal segregation of the schools. White parents had no desire to see their kids go to school where racial riots were brewing right beneath the surface."[39] White fears led to white flight. That, coupled with the aging of the core city's white population, brought about declining enrollments. There were some 30,000 fewer students in the public schools in 1980 than in 1970. Moreover, by 1983 the white percentage had dropped to 40 from 54, 10 years earlier. Some whites moved and newcomers with children often decided to locate in the suburbs rather than in the central city. Generally opposed to busing, most of these suburbanites supported the 1974 Poundstone amendment to the state's constitution, which severely limited Denver's and its schools' ability to expand through annexation.[40]

The anger sparked by busing spread beyond courtrooms and school cafeterias. Doyle's 1969 ruling apparently triggered the February 1970 dynamiting of 46 school vehicles. Twenty-three buses were destroyed and 15 were damaged in a parking lot at 2800 West Seventh Avenue. On East Seventh Avenue Parkway, Doyle's house was bombed. "We thought the furnace had exploded," his wife Helen recalled.[41] Afterward, federal marshals watched over the jurist. Lawmen also protected School Superintendent Howard Johnson, who ran the troubled system from 1970 to 1973. He needed guarding, for the school district's headquarters were bombed. So was Keyes's home; he was dazed by a deadly device filled with metal bearings. Violence afflicted both sides — antibuser Perrill's house was fire-bombed, and in October 1973 school board member Robert Crider, also a busing opponent, opened a package bomb that had been mailed to him. Police Captain Robert Shaughnessy, who helped disarm the device, observed that if the three sticks of dynamite had exploded, Crider "would be dead and his house would be lying on top of him."[42]

The integration controversy spread from school contests into general elections. In 1970, Democrat Craig Barnes, proponent of integration and opponent of the Vietnam War, eked out a 30-vote primary victory over veteran congressman Byron Rogers. That fracturing of the city's Democrats demonstrated the divisive power of the war and busing, a division made even clearer in the November general election when Republican Mike McKevitt defeated Barnes and broke 25 years of Democratic dominance in Denver's congressional district.[43]

The debate would not die. In the 1971 mayor's race, Democrat Dale Tooley challenged incumbent William H. McNichols, Jr. The *Rocky Mountain News* explained that "the McNichols team is trying to link Tooley with the 'ultra-liberal' philosophies of Craig Barnes and pro-busing advocates."[44] McNichols won. Similarly, Congresswoman Pat Schroeder, who by reuniting most Democrats in 1972 managed to unseat McKevitt, was targeted in 1974 as probusing by her Republican opponent, Frank Southworth. Schroeder, a sagacious strategist with support from senior citizens, women, and minorities, survived the furor.

Her success proved that there was more to local politics in the 1970s than busing. Smoke from the integration fight obscured a gradual, but eventually dramatic, change in the core city's racial and political climate. In 1951 Denver had no black city councilmen and only two black legislators, Republican Earl Mann and Democrat Elvin Caldwell. By the mid-1970s George Brown, who had also served as a state senator, had been elected Colorado's lieutenant governor; there was one black coun-

Patricia Scott Schroeder, Denver's U.S. representative since 1972, has been a battler for women's and children's rights, environmental causes, defense budget pruning, and civil rights. (Photo by Jim Richardson, *Denver Post*.)

cilman — Caldwell; a black school board member — Omar Blair; and several black legislators. By 1990 Denver boasted an African-American district attorney, Norman Early, who had been appointed to replace Tooley in 1983 and had won election in his own right in 1984 with nearly 70 percent of the vote. Wellington Webb, an ex-legislator, had become city auditor, and ex-councilman Bill Roberts had been appointed Denver's manager of public works, making him also the deputy mayor. Two blacks, Hiawatha Davis and Allegra "Happy" Haynes, sat on the City Council, and there was a black school board member, Ed Gardner, as well as three Denver African-American legislators.

Not only did the number of black officials increase, but the character of African-American leadership and the nature of black expectations also changed. Although sensitive to injustice, blacks had often been stymied by widespread racism. In June 1915, Clarence Holmes, a student at Washington, D.C.'s Howard University, wrote to Oswald Garrison Villard, president of the National Association for the Advancement of Colored People (NAACP), telling him that Denver "must have a branch [of the association] and we must have it soon."[45] By the end of the year Denver did have a chapter, under the presidency of George Gross. As the principal voice defending blacks in the 1920s and 1930s the NAACP fought the Ku Klux Klan and opposed theater and swimming pool segregation. But the NAACP discovered, as did the youths who tried to swim at Washington Park in 1932, that progress was slow and white backlash powerful.

In the 1940s black and white members of Denver's Committee on Racial Equality (CORE) picketed theaters and sat in at restaurants that refused to serve African-Americans. James Atkins, in *Human Relations in Colorado: 1858–1959*, credited the NAACP with pursuing the resulting cases through the courts and praised Carle Whitehead, who organized the local affiliate of the American Civil Liberties Union (ACLU) in 1932. After its founding in 1947, the Denver chapter of the National Urban League pushed for better jobs for blacks. In 1953 the May Company on

Sixteenth Street hired a black cashier, and in 1954 Safeway employed an African-American checker.

To former state Representative Earl Mann those victories appeared marvelous. In 1959, he recalled that when he was released from Fitzsimons Hospital in 1919 blacks could not use city golf courses, had only one tennis court available to them at City Park, and had to sit in the "buzzard's nest," as the balconies in movie theaters were called. As Mann saw it, amazing progress had been made: "Today gone are those restraints. In our public schools 118 Negro teachers; 15 Negro policemen; Negroes in both branches of our State Assembly; a Negro municipal judge."[46]

Elvin Caldwell, who in 1956 became the first black to sit on the City Council, also recognized the limits of the possible. His popular Rossonian Lounge and Grill in the heart of Five Points, where he practiced old-fashioned ward politics, served him well. Aware both of local conservatism and of the growing civil rights movement, Caldwell adroitly maintained his power. African-American activists wanted him to move faster and accused him of having "a moral fiber not unlike that of soggy shredded wheat cereal."[47] Caldwell did not like militants any more than they liked him. Charging that his life had been threatened by the Black Panthers, a black-power organization, he wrote to Police Chief George Seaton in 1969: "So far as I am personally concerned I won't be satisfied until every Black Panther is run out of Denver." He continued, "I feel very strongly that any time a person calls a police officer a pig he should be arrested immediately."[48]

Caldwell's law and order stance pleased whites and was quietly endorsed by many older blacks who disliked violence. Other African-Americans, most of them young, wanted change, and, spurred by the national civil rights movement, they wanted it fast. Lewis Rhone voiced their rage when he told an East High School gathering, "We have never seen any people get their freedom non-violently. There is no such thing as a non-violent revolution."[49]

Denver had hoped that it would be spared riots such as had engulfed the Watts section of Los Angeles in 1965. After all, many of Denver's African-Americans were better off economically and educationally than blacks in other large cities, and Denver's black population was small in comparison to its nonblack populace. But such hopes proved illusory as tensions mounted in the late 1960s. The killing of "Skijump" Cook, a black man, by a white off-duty policeman in July 1967 spurred militants to ask: "How long are these white men going to be allowed to walk our streets and kill us off and walk again?"[50] The Black Panthers, organized in

Brothers Lauren (left) and Clarke Watson (right) battled against racial injustice by helping to form Denver's Black Panthers. (Photo by Dick Davis, *Rocky Mountain News*.)

1967, demanded change. Initially led by Lauren Watson, a 27-year-old journalist, the Panthers proposed arming blacks to protect their community against the police. The Panthers' tactics included a visit to the Colorado State Senate visitors' gallery, where Watson and others, clad in black motorcycle jackets and black berets, peered through black sunglasses at the nervous senators.

Lawmakers had reason to be frightened. Violence at the Dahlia Shopping Center on Thirty-fourth and Dahlia in the mid-1960s foreshadowed clashes to come. After the 1968 assassination of Doctor Martin Luther King, some blacks took to the streets. Although the newspapers minimized the unrest of April 1968, many people knew that there had been school riots, attacks on teachers and police, looting on Colfax. Years later, the *Rocky Mountain News* summarized the police log for the three days following Doctor King's death: 52 fires; 100 vehicles damaged; 19 stores looted. It was not Watts, but it was not what Denver wanted. The mayhem of the late 1960s spilled over into the 1970s and the 1980s, becoming so common that it often went unnoticed unless, as in the 1990s, it took on especially sinister overtones as gangs fought over turf and drugs.[51]

Responsible blacks condemned violence, but few were willing to wait for slow change. Some continued to support such moderates as Caldwell, who remained on the City Council until 1980, when he resigned to

Reflecting smoother race relations in the 1980s, "Daddy" Bruce Randolph became a citywide hero for his lavish generosity. Over many years, Daddy Bruce has offered thousands of the poor a free meal on Thanksgiving. (Photo by Roger Whitacre.)

become manager of safety, the first black to serve in the mayor's cabinet. Others admired Arie Taylor's sharp tongue. Described by the *Chicago Sun Times* as "a large, fierce, black woman," Taylor in 1972 became the first black woman of any size or temperament to sit in the State Legislature. There the ex–cab driver and former Air Force sergeant loudly battled for minority and women's rights. "I think," she said, "you should come in with a bang and let them know you're here."[52]

Taylor got attention, but she could not work miracles. To mark the twentieth anniversary of Doctor Martin Luther King's death, the *Rocky Mountain News* in 1988 studied the city's African-American community. It found that King's dream was tarnished; that racism still festered; that housing discrimination persisted; that economic progress fell short of black hopes. In the northeast quadrant of the city, Thirty-second Avenue was renamed Martin Luther King Boulevard and Thirty-fourth was re-christened Bruce Randolph Avenue to honor the generous barbecue baron "Daddy" Bruce. Such gestures, however, were marred by a touch of civic schizophrenia: In the northwest section of town those avenues retained their old names.

Denver was not unique. The whole nation made profound racial readjustments after World War II, and success was often measured in terms of steps made rather than in goals reached. Achieving mile-high harmony was complicated since, as the Supreme Court pointed out, Denver was tri- rather than bi-ethnic. After World War II, besides re-thinking the relationship between its blacks and whites, the city had to adjust to its burgeoning Hispanic population.

CHAPTER 27

Fractured City

If blood is going to flow, then let
It flow all over town. If gas is going
To be used then let it be used all over
Town. If pigs are going to run wild
Then let them run wild all over town.
And if we're going to be
Disrupted and violated then let
This whole . . . town be
Disrupted and violated.
    Sign in Columbus (La Raza) Park, reproduced in *El Gallo*, July 1973

Shortly after midnight on March 17, 1973, policeman Steven Snyder traded shots with Luís Martínez in the alley near Sixteenth and Downing behind the Crusade for Justice, an organization dedicated to Chicano power. Snyder, wounded in the side and leg, shot Martínez in the head, killing him. Policewoman Carol Hogue, Snyder's partner, radioed for help. When other cops arrived they were fired on from nearby apartments. Three of the four officers ordered to search 1547 Downing retreated, wounded. Minutes later the second story of the building exploded — perhaps from dynamite stored within; perhaps, as Crusade partisans suggested, as the result of a police grenade. Before dawn medics counted one dead, Luís Martínez, and 16 hurt, a dozen of them police officers.[1]

Rodolfo "Corky" Gonzales, the Crusade's charismatic leader, pro-claimed Martínez, who had taught dance at the Crusade's school, a hero and a martyr. The Crusade declared 1973 "El Año de Luís 'Junior' Martínez," and *El Gallo,* Gonzales's cocky newspaper, wished him fare-well: "Adiós Hermano! No has muerto. VENCEREMOS!!!!!!"[2]

The *Rocky Mountain News* saw the confrontation differently, report-ing that "investigation shows no police wrongs in shoot-out."[3] Listening to the gunfire that night, District Attorney Dale Tooley recalled his army days, "It did something to the pit of your stomach to hear it in your own city."[4]

Although shocked by the St. Patrick's Day blowout, Denver was prepared for violence. By 1973 bombings were nothing new; clashes between police and minorities had become routine. Summer after sum-mer, Chicanos fought police at Columbus Park, the tattered turf at Thirty-eighth and Osage that Chicanos insisted on calling La Raza Park while the city clung to the old name. Well-armed riot police won the battles, but not the war — Columbus ceased being a family park. Churn-ing in their helicopter over Chicano neighborhoods, police ferreted out midnight miscreants, but many citizens detested the department's high-tech crime stoppers. *Cervi's Rocky Mountain Journal* fired an editorial at the noisy bird "begging to be hated," and *Cervi's* marveled at Mayor William H. McNichols, Jr., who claimed that there was little racial tension between elements in the community — "theirs or ours."[5]

Denver, a fractured city of "theirs or ours," suffered from divisions old and poorly understood, deep and difficult to heal. Black-white tensions fueled by the busing controversy were only part of the racial divisions that plagued the city. In deciding the Keyes case, the U.S. Supreme Court observed that with 66 percent of its school population Anglo, 20 percent Hispano, and 14 percent black, Denver was a tri-ethnic city, but in lumping all nonblacks and non-Hispanics together in a category called "Anglo," the high court overlooked Denver's ethnic complexity.[6] Al-though more than 90 percent of the metropolitan area's 1,227,612 resi-dents in 1970 were born in the United States, many were of non-Anglo lineage — Germans, Irish, Italians, Swedes, Poles, Greeks, Chinese, Japanese, and others. Their communities, although declining, still per-sisted. Italian restaurants in north Denver, Dutch churches in south Denver, the Slovenian Hall in Globeville, and the German Turnverein east of downtown all testified to the city's ethnic heritage. So did the 1970 federal census, which listed 54,000 metropolitan residents with

German as their mother tongue, the second-largest foreign-language group in the area, topped only by the 89,851 Spanish speakers. Italian came in third with 11,634. Over 7,000 French speakers were tallied, more than 6,000 Swedish, over 5,000 Yiddish, nearly 5,000 Polish, 3,218 Norwegian, 2,477 Greek, and 2,432 Czech.[7]

Hispanics, living in old neighborhoods flanking the South Platte, vied with blacks, Italians, Poles, and other Eastern Europeans for housing, political power, jobs, and educational opportunities. In assessing the city's schools the Supreme Court concluded, "Negroes and Hispanos in Denver suffer identical discrimination in treatment when compared with the treatment afforded Anglo students."[8] Hispanics complained about old school buildings, structures with a character that fell out of favor in the 1950s and 1960s as school functionaries built low-slung brick boxes. Hispanics also objected to those teachers and administrators who ignored Hispanic heritage. But few Hispanic leaders saw busing as an answer. Instead, they hoped to maintain their neighborhood schools, believing that by sticking together they could improve their lot.

Improvement was needed. Although a few Hispanics were among Denver's pioneers, most gold seekers, as well as settlers who came between 1860 and 1900, hailed from the eastern and midwestern United States. That Colorado had once belonged to Spain, that part of it later belonged to Mexico, that Hispanic settlements in southern Colorado predated the founding of Denver, mattered little to Yankee newcomers. Promises of respect for their culture in the Treaty of Guadalupe-Hidalgo that ended the Mexican War did not protect Hispanos in New Mexico and southern Colorado from being reduced to second-class citizens. Some scratched out a living farming and sheep grazing; some toiled in coal mines; others worked for the railroads. Some traveled to eastern and northern Colorado to slave in the sugar beet fields, which after 1900 provided a harvest as bitter to stoop laborers as it was sweet to landowners and sugar processors. Growers wanted cheap labor. German-Russians, Japanese, Koreans, Hispanics born in the United States, and Mexican nationals, among others, hoed, topped, and picked beets. The backbreaking labor paid poorly; as late as 1949 the average annual income for migrant workers was $800.

Many seasonal workers stayed in northern Colorado, settling in towns such as Brighton and Fort Lupton north of Denver. Others balanced seasonal farm jobs with winter work in the coal-mining centers of Lafayette and Louisville. Many gravitated to Denver, which offered them employment and an opportunity to live in their own communities. There

Governor Edwin Johnson stationed state troopers on the Colorado border in 1936 to keep out Hispanic migrants. (Photo by Arthur Rothstein, Farm Security Administration, U.S. Library of Congress.)

they could send their children to school and their ill to a hospital. James Michener, in his novel *Centennial,* described these dispossessed newcomers, "off to a wretched corner by themselves, living in hovels, . . . quiet people who arranged a world that gave them dignity and a kind of rude repose."[9] Michener recognized that good could have come from the juxtaposition of cultures. "A marvelous symbiosis of English and Spanish cultures might have evolved in these decades if it had been encouraged or even permitted to flourish." But, he lamented, "there was almost no Anglo who could even comprehend that such a thing was possible, so the two races lived apart in deepening suspicion."[10]

Before 1930 it was easy for most people to overlook the city's small Hispanic community. The 1910 *City Directory* listed only 12 persons with the common Hispanic surnames of Gonzales, López, and Martínez. By 1920 there were 113 with those names, by 1930 over 300, by 1940 over 600, and in 1950 over 1,100. That year the Denver Area Welfare Council guessed that there were between 30,000 and 45,000 Spanish-Americans

in Denver. The 1960 federal census gave a more exact picture, recording 43,147 Spanish-Americans in the city. By 1970 the number had risen to 86,345 and by 1980 to 91,937. Since the city's total population changed little between 1960 and 1980, the dramatic increase in Hispanic numbers meant more than a doubling of the Hispanic percentage of the total population, from less than 9 percent in 1960 to over 18 percent in 1980. In the metropolitan area outside the central city Hispanic population also increased, rising from 52,583 in 1970 to 81,425 in 1980, but since total suburban population burgeoned in the same period the percentage of Hispanics living in the suburbs declined slightly.

Although most Hispanics were native-born U.S. citizens, many had close connections with Mexico. Like other ethnic groups — Protestant and Catholic Irish, German and Eastern European Jews — Hispanics were divided among themselves. Some stressed their southwestern heritage, which dates back to sixteenth-century New Mexico. Others emphasized their Mexican-Indian origins. In the 1960s, as blacks rejected the designation Negro, factions within the Hispanic community also argued about names. Many disliked terms such as *Mexican-American* and *Spanish-American*, but they did not agree on new nomenclature. Wrestling with the problem, one Denverite wrote:

Farmers wanting cheap stoop labor made little distinction between Hispano Coloradans and Mexican migrant labor. Both groups flocked to metro-Denver. (Photo by Arthur Rothstein, Farm Security Administration, U.S. Library of Congress.)

My father's family . . . came to the Americas from San Lucar de
Barrameda, Spain with Oñate in 1598. They also came from Galicia,
Santiago de Compostella, Portugal, France, Flanders, and Greece. My
mother's people were also from Spain. My mother's grandfather was full
blooded Navajo Indian, my father's grandmother was full blooded
Cheyenne Indian, his grandfather was second generation Comanche,
and his other grandmother was third generation Apache. You tell me,
am I Chicano?[11]

Some, mainly those with roots in New Mexico and Colorado, wanted to
be called Hispanos. Others, usually those of Mexican-Indian background,
preferred to be called Chicanos.[12] Such distinctions were not apparent to
the wider society until the late 1960s. Before then most Denverites
grouped all "Mexicans" together, using the term Spanish-American as
the polite designation. Often, however, politeness was disregarded.

Hispanics, like African-Americans, faced walls of prejudice and barriers of bigotry. Historian Donald Wall, who grew up in Brighton, later
recalled that the town's movie theater made Spanish-Americans sit in
the balcony. Sociologist Paul Taylor talked to one Colorado farmer in the
1920s who spoke of a "plantation like relationship" existing between him
and his Mexican laborers; another grower told Taylor: "A Mexican is the
best damn dog any white man ever had."[13]

During the depression, Governor Johnson proposed shipping Mexican nationals back to Mexico. The *Englewood Monitor* praised Johnson
and advocated "placing those who refuse [to go] in concentration camps
where they will be fed and housed, but not pampered."[14] Aware of this
bigotry, *Rocky Mountain News* editor Jack Foster reminded his readers in
1945 "of the brown faces lying silent in the white snows of Belgium."[15]

Returning Hispanic servicemen discovered that their patriotism did
not guarantee them equality or respect. In 1946 the *Western Voice*, a
publication backed by the Reverend Harvey Springer of Englewood,
praised congressional sleuths who were looking into "red activities
among the Spanish-speaking." The anti-Catholic, anti-Semitic, anti-
Communist paper noted that congressmen were especially interested in
"that phase of the agitation that has led local peons to go about at night
attacking white people walking alone."[16] Such anti-Hispanic attitudes
led to economic discrimination. Mayor Newton's 1947 Committee on
Human Relations surveyed 189 businesses and found that 80 "employed
no Spanish-Americans." One employer told committee investigators that
"Negroes and Spanish have a slight mental inferiority." An employment

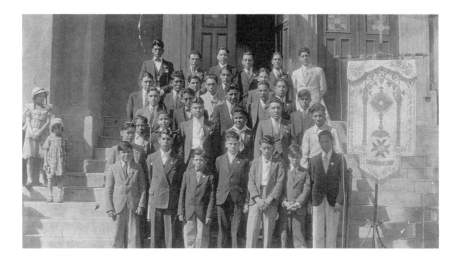

St. Cajetan's Church at Ninth and Lawrence served the Hispanic community with a school, credit union, and health clinic. (Magdalena Pérez Collection.)

agency reported that "Spanish and Negro applicants are hired only for domestic work," and a large airline admitted doing "selective hiring," with the result that "our personnel is almost totally Anglo-American."[17]

A 1950 study, "The Spanish-American Population of Denver," conducted by the Denver Area Welfare Council, revealed that the average Spanish-American family made only $1,840 a year. Black families earned $1,930 and whites made over $3,000. The council estimated that 60 percent of Hispanics lived in substandard housing, 90 percent did not complete high school, 50 percent sought help from social welfare agencies; that they occupied 30 percent of all public housing and constituted over a third of the city's jail inmates; that their infant mortality rate was six times greater than that for residents of more affluent areas.

There were rays of hope. In places, Hispanic communities were taking root and flowering. Between 1940 and 1950 Hispanic home ownership rose from 10 to 50 percent. Two Roman Catholic churches, St. Cajetan's (1926) at Ninth and Lawrence and Our Lady of Guadalupe (1936) at Thirty-sixth Avenue and Kalamath Street, provided Spanish-speaking priests and a sense of community to the predominantly Catholic Hispanic population. Small businesses catering to the Hispanic market also sprang up. In 1947 a stroll along Larimer Street north of Twenty-first Avenue would take one past the Juárez Lounge, the El Paso del Norte and Mexico City restaurants, La Estrella, La Rosita, La Barca, and Casa Blanca Cafes, the Valencia and Coronado hotels, the Mexico Theater, Juliansito Pool Hall, Progreso Grocery, Medico Dental Building, Lucero's Dress Shop, and the El Charro Inn — all in a single block. At the Mexico

Mexican food and music enlivens Denver's nightlife, as at this fiesta at La Casa de Manuel, a Larimer Street cafe open since 1955. Despite a 90-day demolition lease on the cafe, Manuel Silva has made La Casa one of the city's most popular and long-lived cantinas. (Photo by Roger Whitacre.)

Theater, 2118 Larimer, Spanish speakers enjoyed Mexican movies, and on KMYR they could listen for half an hour a day to Francisco "Paco" Sánchez's Spanish radio show.

The sheer size of the Hispanic community gave it some political clout. In 1943 James Fresques, a Republican, was elected councilman from District Eight. As a child he had toiled picking crops; later he became a pharmacist. By 1945 he was president of the City Council, the first Hispanic to hold that position. In the 1950s he served as an assistant to both Mayors Nicholson and Batterton before being placed in charge of the Denver Housing Authority.

In the heart of Denver's Little Mexico, Margarita García tempts passersby with South of the Border treats at La Popular, 2012 Larimer. (Photo by Roger Whitacre.)

Fresques's success coincided with rising Hispanic aspirations. Roger Baldwin, national head of the American Civil Liberties Union, observed in 1950 that "Spanish-Americans are the largest unorganized minority in the United States."[18] Local Hispanics wanted to change that. In the late 1940s and throughout the 1950s they set up organizations such as the GI Forum, the League of Latin American Citizens, the Colorado Latin American Conference, and the Latin American Education Foundation. When Lino López of the Denver Commission on Community Relations compiled his *Colorado Latin American Personalities* in 1959, he found dozens of success stories among Hispanics: Attorney Bert A. Gallegos was serving in the state legislature; Bernard Valdez was managing the city's 615-unit Sun Valley

John F. Kennedy (left) with U.S. Senator John A. Carroll. Denver's Democrats got a boost from Kennedy's 1960 presidential campaign. (Auraria Archives, John A. Carroll Collection.)

Housing project; Paco Sánchez had left KMYR to establish his own Spanish-language station, KFSC; Lawyer John F. Sánchez had landed a job in the district attorney's office; Tony Lovato, who had picked beets as a kid, had become vice-president of Colorado's AFL-CIO.

Individual achievements, however, did not solve the problems of most Hispanics. Metropolitan State College sociologist Daniel Valdez noted in 1969: "We are about ten years behind Negroes . . . and we must catch up." Catching up was not easy. Attorney Ronald N. Pacheco went to the heart of the matter: "Well, we can assimilate if we've got the finances. That's easy. But what about the Mexican on the other end — the poor one?"[19] Divisions among Hispanics made unified action difficult. Some agreed with attorney Roger Cisneros when he argued for assimilation: "It is incumbent upon the Spanish-American to operate under the rules imposed by the majority."[20] Others, inspired by the black civil rights movement and by César Chávez's struggle to unionize California farm workers, grew increasingly militant. Some, including Roman Catholic priests Peter García and Craig Hart, tried to shame their church into paying more attention to its Hispanic parishioners. Others, such as Elizabeth and Waldo Benevídez and Richard Castro, promoted grass-roots neighborhood organizations.

Among these champions of the "Mexican on the other end," Corky Gonzales captured a large share of the public's attention. Born in Denver in 1928, the son of migrant workers, he attended nine schools before graduating from West High. A skilled boxer, young Gonzales won national and international amateur championships before turning professional. By the mid-1950s, his boxing days over, he was pursuing a political

The Denver Police Department, which had barely recovered from the Burglars in Blue Scandal of the early 1960s, took another beating during racial unrest in the later 1960s and the 1970s. (Denver Public Library, Western History Department.)

career that faltered when Elvin Caldwell beat him in the 1955 City Council race in District Eight. Later, he became a Democratic district captain, and in 1960 he helped gather Hispanic votes for presidential candidate John F. Kennedy. By 1964 Gonzales was directing the local Neighborhood Youth Corps, a federal program designed to give work to poor kids.

A year later Gonzales took on an even more arduous task — the chairmanship of Denver's faction-ridden War on Poverty program. "I think highly of Corky. He's done a magnificent job with the Neighborhood Youth Corps," said Mayor Thomas Currigan, who endorsed Gonzales's selection to the poverty post.[21] "I'm an agitator and a trouble-maker. . . . They didn't buy me when they put me in this job," Gonzales told the *Rocky Mountain News*.[22] Yet despite his rhetoric, he continued to work within the system that had worked for him. From picking sugar beets to professional boxing; from Corky's Corner Restaurant and Corky's Gym to a bail bond business; from a Democratic captaincy to the directorship of the Neighborhood Youth Corps, Gonzales had followed the highway to success often traveled by ethnic entrepreneurs.

That ended in 1966. Facing accusations that he discriminated against blacks in the Youth Corps program, Gonzales was forced out by Currigan. Within weeks of his exit, Gonzales declared that he and his supporters were launching a Crusade for Justice. The Crusade fought on many fronts. In 1967 Gonzales ran for mayor. Some saw the move as a vengeful attempt to sink Currigan by taking enough Democratic votes from him to bring victory to the Republican candidate, Don Nicholson. Others viewed the contest as the natural outgrowth of rising Chicano political expectations. Without much money and with a platform calling for a civilian review board for police, a city employees' union, and a city income tax, Gonzales had no hope of being elected. Moreover, a rival Hispanic group, the New Hispano party, siphoned support from Gonzales by nominating James García for mayor.

Currigan had little to fear. During his first term he had brought a measure of peace to the scandal-ridden police department by appointing

Harold Dill, a career cop, chief. Currigan convinced voters to support a convention center and to replace the run-down Denver General Hospital. By using the convention center appropriations to match federal funds, Currigan secured millions in urban renewal money for the Skyline Project that transformed downtown. Both the *Post* and the *News* supported him in 1967. Houston "Hoot" Gibson, a conservative Democratic city councilman, opposed both Currigan and urban renewal, but neither his nor Gonzales's candidacy shook Currigan. He defeated all challengers, including Republican Don Nicholson, without a runoff. Gonzales received only 4,179 votes.

What the Crusade lacked in numbers, it made up for in rhetoric and strategy. Gonzales made his headquarters in the former Calvary Baptist church, an imposing structure at Sixteenth Avenue and Downing Street, where he edited a newspaper, *El Gallo,* and ran a school, Escuela Tlatelolco, to teach Chicano culture. With energy reminiscent of his boxing days he kept punching at the political and social establishment. In May 1968, Gonzales hauled Currigan into court for violating a city charter prohibition against spending more than $1,000 on a mayoral campaign.[23] A month later Gonzales and other protesters marched on police headquarters. In November the Crusade called for the creation of neighborhood school boards and demanded that schools teach Chicano heritage. Clashes continued in 1969. A three-day student walkout at West High led to riots and Gonzales's arrest. That summer, young crusaders, protesting conditions at Lincoln Park pool in central Denver, stormed southeast Denver's Eisenhower pool, scaling the fence and capturing the lifeguard. At Columbus (La Raza) Park Chicanos grew angry at "gringos who sat in the sun all day trying to get brown," so, as *El Gallo* put it, "200 youths surprised 9 gringos who were lying around, kicked their ass, and told them to get out of our community."[24]

In 1970 Gonzales and other activists established Colorado's La Raza Unida, a political party calling for land reform and justice for farm workers and condemning the war in Vietnam. Salvatore Carpio, La Raza's nominee for Congress, polled fewer than 6,000 votes. La Raza Unida tried to focus Chicano power and to publicize the problems faced by the poor. Its weak showing reflected, in part, growing apprehension about the Crusade. Many moderate Hispanics disagreed with the Crusade's tactics and rejected the organization's anti–Vietnam War stance. Some remained Democrats; some did not vote. Others found political expression through organizations such as the West Side Coalition, which tried to stop the construction of the Auraria Higher Education Complex, a proj-

Despite the 1980s economic doldrums, young and idealistic Mayor Federico Peña orchestrated city-building and beautifying efforts reminiscent of the Speer era.

ect that destroyed a Chicano neighborhood in old west Denver.

Moderates also rejected the lawlessness of young Chicanos. Unruly youths attacked Hispanic leaders in the summer of 1973 at the James Q. Newton, Sr., Center at 4438 Navajo Street. Refused admission to the building, the juveniles broke car windows and hit school board member Bernard Valdez with a dust mop. Far more serious was the 1973 shooting of Richard Castro, a director of the West Side Coalition, by a Crusade partisan. *El Gallo* ran a picture of the bleeding Castro, with the warning: "If you can't do anything for the movement, don't do anything against it or it may cost you your life."[25]

Such militance cost the Crusade its life. The good that it did — education for dropouts and its constant war on drugs — could not wash away the belief, increasingly shared by both Hispanics and non-Hispanics, that the Crusade was a radical and dangerous organization.[26] Castro survived to win five terms in the Colorado House of Representatives before being appointed head of Denver's Agency for Human Rights and Community Relations and gaining a seat on the school board. Sal Carpio became a respected member of the city council. And other Hispanic leaders, including Councilman Sam Sandos and state Representative Federico Peña, made their mark in politics. In the meantime the Crusade crumbled.[27]

By the late 1970s, to the city's relief, differences of opinion were largely being dealt with in voting booths and council chambers rather than in the streets. Hot political contests, of which there were many between Quigg Newton's retirement in 1955 and Federico Peña's narrow victories in the late 1980s, also revealed that Denver was a fractured city, but debates over persons and issues at least offered a chance for civil discourse and the possibility of nonviolent solutions.

Newton's decision not to seek a third term in 1955 brought three hopefuls into that year's race. Ernest Marranzino, a north Denver Italian, had served on the City Council. Bert Keating had been an election commissioner, state legislator, and Denver district attorney. William Nicholson, the lone Republican in the theoretically nonpartisan race,

Gays "came out of the closet" during the 1970s, emerging as a political force that helped to overthrow the Old Guard and elect Federico Peña and Congresswoman Pat Schroeder. (Photo by Glenn Cuerden.)

had served as a Colorado state senator. Marranzino's third-place finish in May suggested that Italian politicians lacked a sufficiently large constituency to win citywide elections. In the June runoff, bigots urged voters to reject Keating because he was a Roman Catholic. Nicholson condemned this vestige of the city's Ku Klux Klan past and won by a narrow margin.[28]

In 1959, as in 1955, personalities seemed more important than issues. Most Democrats supported labor leader and ex-councilman George Cavender. Although in north Denver, Italian Democrats backed Roland "Sonny" Mapelli, he was eliminated in the May election. In June the Republican candidate, Richard Batterton, formerly Mayor Nicholson's manager of public works, defeated Cavender. The late 1950s were good years for Republicans, who capitalized on the city's prosperity and on the affection people had for President Dwight Eisenhower, who frequently visited the city with his wife, Mamie, a Denver native. By 1963 things had changed. Eisenhower was no longer president, and Mayor Batterton was stewing in a massive police scandal. Democratic mayoral candidate Thomas G. Currigan, once an aide to Quigg Newton and after 1955 city auditor, stirred the pot, knowing that voters did not like the smell.

The police scandal that came to a boil during Batterton's administration had been long simmering and long covered up. In 1946, District Attorney James T. Burke accused cops of committing crimes ranging "from murder to petty larceny."[29] Mayor Benjamin Stapleton's manager of

Denver's St. Patrick's Day Parade is one of the country's largest and a chance for all ethnic groups to march and celebrate together. (Photo by Tom Noel.)

safety, Robert J. Kirschwing, promised that the problems were being solved. Grand Jury indictments of 17 officers failed to bring convictions, and Stapleton's friends accused Burke of political grandstanding.[30] In 1949 the resignation and subsequent suicide of the respected, reform-minded police chief John O'Donnell might have triggered scrutiny of the department, but seemingly no one wanted to delve too deeply.

Clearly there were problems in 1953 when Bobbie G. Whaley joined the force. In his training class he and other rookies were told not to accept graft: "Remember this, men — don't take graft! You'll see some of the older men taking handouts, but don't take graft."[31] Whaley soon found that cops were taking more than graft. At first he kept his eyes shut when others stole; in time he became an adept burglar himself. Cops, it seemed, would steal almost anything — meat, dresses, appliances. A number of them specialized in safecracking. Asked why he and his friends did not try armed robbery, Whaley explained: "Why take a chance on somebody getting hurt when you can make ten times as much money with perfect cover as a safecracker."³² Whaley, who once interrupted a burglary of his own to arrest civilian thieves, later pondered the process whereby potentially good officers devolve into really bad cops. "A lot of things entered into it: A breakdown in discipline, lack of leadership, complacency and stupidity on the part of the brass, low pay, some detectives who could not find their shoes if they took them off."³³

The conviction of a policeman for burglarizing the Pink Lady Tavern at 519 Eighteenth Street in late 1954 might have alerted supervisory officers. If it did, they did little about it. Nor did they listen to the 1956 warnings of an honest cop, Captain Tom Branch, who told Mayor Nicholson of command problems in the department. For his truthfulness, Branch, a 15-year veteran, was made to walk a dangerous beat in Five Points. Two years later, cops suspected of stealing meat were allowed to resign. The next year, the Arapahoe County district attorney, Martin Miller, warned Denver that dishonest deputy sheriffs in his county probably had connections with dishonest officers in Denver. Still, nothing was done.

When, in 1960, Officer John D. Bates, suffering from a bad conscience, told his superiors that he had apprehended a cop-thief and then let him go, Bates's bosses suggested that he see a psychiatrist. The psychiatrist, in turn, concluded that Bates was telling the truth. Upset with the slowness of an internal inquiry, Bates went to *Rocky Mountain News* reporter Al Nakkula, whose paper pressed for a full investigation. Batterton and his safety manager, John Schooley, minimized the problem. "In any group of 750 people," the mayor contended, "you are likely to turn up a bad apple or two."³⁴

By 1961 the rotten apples were filling bushel baskets. In December 1960 one cop admitted 18 burglaries; eight officers were arrested in January 1961; in July the Adams County sheriff, Bob Roberts, was caught as he and ex–Denver cops cracked a supermarket safe in Commerce City. That led Batterton to ask for state help in dealing with crime that extended into the suburbs. On one day in September 1961, 22 officers suspected of crimes were indicted. Eventually, 61 persons, 54 of them Denver policemen, were tried, and many of them were sent to jail. Although often they were allowed to plead guilty to only one count of burglary, some had committed numerous heists. Bobbie Whaley, for example, was tagged with 43 burglaries. He stashed thousands in cash behind paneling in his recreation room and eventually laundered his money by investing it in a car wash. With perhaps a million dollars in ill-gotten gains to their discredit, the burglars in blue made Denver the United States' crooked-cop capital.

The sordid police drama played out slowly into 1962, making Batterton appear ineffectual and giving Currigan political ammunition. But the ex-auditor's victory was not certain; another Democrat, attorney William Grant, Jr., a respected member of wealthy pioneer clans, entered the race and threatened to split the Democrats. Both the *Post* and the *News* endorsed Grant to no avail. Currigan's grass-roots organization knocked Grant out in May, and in June, Currigan beat Batterton by 15,000 votes.

Younger Democrats, such as lawyer Dale Tooley, appreciated Currigan's leadership, which, although it failed to satisfy African-American and Chicano militants, seemed progressive compared to the scandal-plagued Batterton era. Tooley, born in Denver in 1933, had by the late 1960s gained the chairmanship of the city's Democratic party. When Currigan decided in 1968 to abandon his poorly paid mayor's post for a vice-presidency at Continental Airlines, Tooley supporters hoped to make their man mayor by having him appointed manager of public works, the post from which Denver's mayor is selected if the incumbent dies or resigns. The reality, however, eluded them, since William H. McNichols, Jr., Currigan's manager of public works, refused to step aside.

McNichol's father, a conservative Democrat, had been city auditor during the Begole, Stapleton, and Newton administrations; his brother Stephen was twice elected governor of Colorado. Supposedly fearful that Stephen McNichols would enter the 1963 mayor's race, Currigan reputedly agreed that in return for Steve's staying out, Currigan would name William McNichols, Jr., manager of public works. When Currigan resigned in December 1968, McNichols became mayor, thereby setting the stage for more than a decade of bitter rivalry with Tooley.

As was the case in most of the city's post–WW II mayoralty races, the 1971 election became a three-way contest with one Republican contender, State Senator Joe Shoemaker, and two Democratic candidates, McNichols and Tooley. The May election was close, with Shoemaker taking 29 percent of the vote, McNichols 33, and Tooley 34 percent. After Shoemaker's elimination, some voters shifted to McNichols, giving him a 1,739-vote edge over Tooley in June.

Tooley then looked elsewhere. In 1972 he defeated Jarvis Seccombe for the office of district attorney. Tooley's 10 years as DA were to be filled with notable trials and run-of-the-mill cases — 200,000 in all — but he still wanted to be mayor. In 1975 he again ran against McNichols and again beat the mayor in the May election only to have victory evaporate in the June runoff. Four years later, attorney Felicia Muftic challenged

McNichols. Riding the crest of a booming economy, the mayor easily won a third term without a runoff. It was going to be his last term, said the 69-year-old McNichols.[35]

Tooley patiently waited in his modest office in the West Side Court Building at Colfax and Speer, anticipating the day when McNichols would gracefully bow out of his suite in the City and County Building half a mile away. In 1982, Tooley resigned his post to seek, once again, the mayor's job. Abandoning any idea he may have had of retiring, McNichols, vigorous at 73, announced for a fourth term. Voters, it seemed, were to face another déjà vu election. Everyone, however, was in for a surprise.

Denver had changed during the 1970s. The downtown of the early 1960s, much of it the faded monuments of previous booms, had been replaced by a nondescript skyscraper metropolis by the early 1980s. Washington Park, once the domain of automobiles, toddlers, and flower lovers, was by the 1980s carpeted with cyclists, joggers, and volleyball enthusiasts. In City Park, where once the municipal band played Sousa and little tykes in sailor suits ate jelly beans, rock music blared and dope changed hands. At Cheesman Park, the erstwhile sanctuary of dowagers, wading children, and the *Denver Post*'s summer musicals, gays and straights argued over territory. And Swiss steak, a Saturday night delight of the 1950s, slowly slid from the culinary scene as young, well-heeled professionals explored strange gastronomical worlds ranging from fried ducks' feet to alligator steaks.

The extent of political change was less apparent. McNichols's victories had maintained the power of an old guard of Democrats allied with Republicans. Black and Chicano militants had gradually grown hoarse and by the early 1980s had seemingly lost their voices altogether. Tooley often pointed out McNichols's connections with the airlines and with Seventeenth Street's bankers, but Tooley's years as DA had tarnished his once liberal image. Newcomers to the city, lacking a sense of local political history, saw little difference between the old mayor and his middle-aged opponent. But there had been profound political shifts. In 1972, 32-year-old attorney Pat Schroeder's victorious bid for the U.S. House demonstrated the increasing power of women, the breakdown of old political alliances, and the growing liberal bent of many voters. Her success also helped open doors to other women. In 1975, Cathy Donohue and Cathy Reynolds became the first women elected to the City Council.[36] Fifteen years later women held a majority on the 13-member council.

In the 1970s Hispanics also found that their growing numbers, cou-pled with old-fashioned precinct work, could bring victory. As their suns rose, the stars of Italian politicos, long dominant in the skies of north Denver, set. From 1933 to 1970, Mike Pomponio, although he rarely held public office, ruled northwest Denver's Democrats, delivering their votes, listening to their complaints, getting them city jobs. On Pomponio's death in 1973 *Rocky Mountain News* columnist Tom Gavin concluded: "The old order passeth."[37]

That it would pass was already clear in 1970 when the City Council increased the number of council districts from 9 to 11 and rearranged boundaries. By creating District Eleven in northeast Denver, the council made possible greater black representation. A new District Nine, which ran from the city's northern boundary south along the South Platte, contained so many Hispanics that they would likely be able to elect a councilperson, thereby gaining representation they had lacked since the mid-1950s. Moreover, in west-central Denver a reconstituted District Three offered Hispanics the chance to secure a second council slot. The new arrangement did not immediately help. In 1971, celebrating a last Italian hurrah, Eugene DiManna defeated Peter García, ex-priest turned social activist, for the District Nine seat. Sam Sandos, of Greek-Mexican ancestry, ran that year in District Three, but was beaten by J. Ivanhoe Rosenberg.

By 1975 things had changed. DiManna's victory brought him head-aches as Hispanics continually complained that he failed to represent them. They tried to recall him, a move he fought in the courts until February 1975, when he was forced to face Sal Carpio in a special election. DiManna won. And in the regular council election in May 1975 he gained more votes than Carpio largely because remnants of the Cru-sade for Justice, angry at Carpio for being too moderate, backed Ernest Vigil. Finally, in the June runoff Carpio edged DiManna, thus ending 40 years of Italian dominance in District Nine.[38] Sandos was victorious in District Three, giving Hispanics two council seats, their first since Fresques had left in 1955. In 1979 Carpio ran without opposition; Sandos won by a landslide.[39]

Besides picking up council positions, Hispanics also gained greater power in the State Legislature. In the late 1960s Roger Cisneros sat in the state Senate and "Paco" Sanchez held a House seat. In 1971, Betty Benevídez took a place in the House, as did Reuben Valdez. General Assembly doors opened even wider in the mid-1970s as Castro and Pauline Baca-Barragan of Thornton won positions. Majority Democrats in the lower house elected Valdez speaker of the House for the 1975–1977 term. By 1977 there were two Hispanic state senators from Denver, Don and Paul Sandoval, and four metropolitan-area representatives — Baca-Barragan, Castro, Laura M. DeHerrera, and Valdez.

Given their success in council and legislative districts, Hispanics looked to larger political fields. Valdez unsuccessfully aimed at the lieutenant governorship in 1978. By the early 1980s Carpio was considering running for mayor but decided that the time was not right for a Hispanic candidate. State Representative Federico Peña, although less experienced in city affairs than Carpio, was bolder and luckier. Some old-timers considered his 1983 mayoral candidacy as merely symbolic since Peña was a newcomer without the hallowed connections of either Tooley or McNichols, both native Denverites. Born in Laredo, Texas, in 1947, Peña had arrived in Denver in 1973. For a time he worked for the Mexican American Legal Defense Fund and later practiced law privately. In 1979 he began four years in the State Legislature, where in his second term he became leader of the minority Democrats.

Photogenic and energetic, the 36-year-old Peña gave voters the chance to support a fresh face. Those who discounted his candidacy failed to see that the voters had changed. Many were black or Hispanic; Peña appealed to them. Some were newcomers; Peña appealed to them. Many had previously been disinterested in politics; Peña persuaded them to register to vote. Young people liked him; so did the gay community, which appreciated his commitment to individual rights. Unencumbered by a radical past, moderate in tone, he did not frighten middle-of-the-road voters. Indeed, Peña offered business interests a picture-perfect candidate, one with whom they could get along, one whose ethnic ties and image bespoke electability. His managers adroitly capitalized on his strengths by casting both Tooley and McNichols as stale politicians; a piece of campaign strategy that worked.

McNichols, his administration floundering and laboring under the cloud of the city's failure to rapidly clean up the 25-inch snowfall of December 24, 1982, was buried under a Tooley-Peña avalanche in the May 17, 1983, election. "The people who think I can make it snow also think I can take it away. I can't do either," McNichols lamented.[40] Repeating Benjamin Stapleton's 1947 debacle, the mayor ran third, getting fewer than 26,000 votes. Peña, who had asked voters to "imagine a great city," led the pack; Tooley trailed by nearly 8,000. Tooley did better in June, but Peña won by 4,400 votes. The ex–district attorney graciously conceded. "By then," he recalled, "I had become pretty good at making concession speeches."[41]

Stricken by cancer, Tooley died in April 1985. Among his accomplishments he counted 10 successful years as DA, his push for disclosure of campaign finances, and his initiation of administrative reforms. He also felt good about the tone of his campaign. Commenting on his 1983 race against Peña, Tooley noted, "We had succeeded in conducting a massive campaign without once bringing in race as an issue and without using any of the tactics of the kind the McNichols campaign had successfully used in 1971."[42]

"This city is a great thing, really, and whoever gets it I'm sure will take good care of it," McNichols remarked as he left office.[43] At first, tending the city seemed simple. Then both Peña's and the community's high spirits faded as declining oil prices, like a pin pricking an over-inflated balloon, let the air out of the local economy. Economic discontent spilled into politics. In 1987 Peña faced seven rivals in his bid for a second term. Republicans backed wealthy attorney Donald Bain, a political neophyte from an old family. City Auditor Mike Licht also wanted to be mayor, as did former mayor Currigan. McNichols endorsed Dennis Gallagher, a northside politician whose care for his constituency had brought him two years in the state House of Representatives followed by three terms in the state Senate. Bain beat Peña in the May election, with Gallagher taking third place, but Peña turned the tables in June, winning by 3,026 votes out of the 156,322 cast. In his concession speech Bain said, "Let's keep Denver a great city. Let's make Denver an even greater city."[44]

Rhetoric masked reality. Talking about a great city was easy; making one was difficult. Old divisions festered, largely unspoken, largely ignored. Clarke Watson, brother of the 1960s black activist Lauren, ran for mayor in 1987 without much attention or much support. Hispanics took pride in Peña's victories, but their poverty and excessive school drop-out rates persisted.[45] Race still counted in elections — not only among so-called Anglos, but also among African-Americans and Hispanics. In many Hispanic and black areas Peña beat Bain by six to one and greater margins. Bain outdistanced Peña in more-affluent and whiter neighborhoods, but even there Peña usually received a fair number of votes, indicating that whites were more likely to support him than African-Americans or Hispanics were to back Bain. Similarly, Democrat Wellington Webb, the victorious candidate for auditor, did exceedingly well in black areas and also picked up many votes from white neighborhoods. His white opponent, Bill Schroeder, drew few black votes.[46]

Among the new faces down-
town are East Indian nuns, missionary followers of Mother
Theresa of Calcutta. In 1990
they moved into the old Cathedral Convent at 1840 Grant to
work with AIDS patients, the
homeless, and other victims of
the fragmented city. (Photo by
James Baca.)

Those fractures, although deep, were brushed aside in the late 1980s
as Denver concentrated on its economic woes. Twice before, in the 1890s
and the 1930s, it had suffered a similarly rapid decline. In the 1970s and
1980s history seemingly repeated itself as one of the city's best decades
was followed by one of its worst. The economic roller coaster had to be
taken seriously, for more than elections and bond issues, more than riots
and rhetoric, economic shifts determined the course of the metropolitan
area in the 1970s and 1980s.

CHAPTER 28

An Economic Roller Coaster

The rich are getting richer, the poor getting fewer, population is up, sales are up, income is up, new jobs are being created like crazy and the only thing going down appears to be unemployment. Business is so good, people are starting to worry. "How long will all this last?" they ask. What's next? Where are we now? Where have we been?

Denver Business World, November 6, 1978

With machine gun rapidity newspaper headlines in October 1973 rattled Denverites with disturbing reports. On October 10, U.S. Vice-President Spiro Agnew resigned. Ten days later, President Nixon, mired in the Watergate scandal, fired Archibald Cox, the special prosecutor investigating the case. On October 28, Denver school board member Robert Crider "narrowly escaped death" from a package bomb.[1] In the meantime, in retaliation for U.S. support of Israel, Arab states embargoed oil shipments. As the valves were shut oil prices rose.

Nixon resigned and Agnew faded from memory, but the energy crisis remained. For most of the nation, mounting petroleum prices forced economic belt tightening. Colorado also had reason to worry. Its 1972 petroleum production lagged behind its consumption by 18.9 million barrels, and its natural gas output fell 162 billion cubic feet below its use. Soon Denverites faced gasoline shortages and higher prices. But, for the city's economy as a whole the crunch proved to be a blessing, for it added oil to a boom that had begun during World War II. When the bubble burst in the 1980s, Denverites blamed their sick economy on the ailing oil industry, an overly simple diagnosis that failed to recognize that oil only partially explained their city's wild roller coaster ride.

Denver's boom was well under way by the early 1970s as thousands of people, attracted by climate, scenery, recreation, and economic opportunities, poured in each year. Between 1940 and 1950 the metropolitan population jumped from 384,372 to 563,832. The 1950s saw an increase of more than 350,000, and between 1960 and 1980 another 700,000 people became Denverites. The suburbs accounted for most of the growth. The City and County of Denver went from 322,412 people in 1940 to 493,887 in 1960. Then, since the city hesitated to annex territory for which costly water and services would have to be provided, growth slowed. Some land was added, such as the 3,000-acre Miller Ranch northeast of Stapleton Airport that became the Montbello subdivision. Other patches of prairie annexed to the southwest and southeast of the city quickly sprouted with upper middle-class homes. Denver's population peaked at 514,678 in 1970, then fell to 492,365 in 1980. Combined with the decline were other troublesome shifts. Those remaining in the central city tended to be older and poorer. Moreover, more residents meant more air and water pollution. Traffic jams, inadequate public services, and overflowing dumps constantly warned citizens that gains brought pains.[2]

Prosperous Denverites ignored such unpleasant realities as the roller coaster sped upward, its ascent only intermittently interrupted by steep dips. In 1965 and 1966, for example, fewer than 6,000 building permits for single-family homes were issued in the metropolitan area, but in 1973 some 19,000 permits were written. Then the number fell until 1977, when it rebounded to above 20,000. Multifamily construction was even more volatile. In 1972 some 25,000 permits were issued; three years later fewer than 1,000 were recorded.[3]

Sometimes, developers had only to announce building plans in order to sell homes; Jordon Perlmutter and Sam Primack of Perl-Mack Enterprises sold 59 yet-to-be-built houses in a single day in 1954. Soon, Perl-Mack was constructing residences by the thousands and developing whole communities such as Northglenn and Southglenn. By 1978 the company had built 21,000 houses, and the demand remained so strong that prices continued to climb. Northglenn homes, which originally sold for from $12,000 to $24,000, fetched more than $60,000 by the late 1970s. Resale prices rose more than 10 percent a year; a residence that sold for $37,190 in 1975 cost $85,242 in 1981. Many people settled for smaller lots or moved into condominiums. Only 647 condos were sold in

By 1960 Denver boasted a few skyscrapers to match its mountains. (Colorado Historical Society.)

1975, but six years later more than 3,000 were marketed at a per unit price more than $22,000 below that of detached houses.[4]

Commercial real estate also boomed. In 1950, downtown Denver contained slightly more than 1.2 million square feet of prime space, much of it in venerable landmarks such as the Boston and the Equitable buildings. By the late 1970s developers had finished or were completing projects slated to give downtown nearly 10 million square feet of space by 1981. The tallest of the new towers, the 1.2 million-square-foot, 56-story Republic Plaza (1983) between Sixteenth and Seventeenth on Tremont, boasted almost as much prime space as did all of downtown in 1950.

The construction frenzy of the 1970s and early 1980s remade the skyline that had started to change in the early 1950s when the Murchinson

The Denver Urban Renewal Authority demolished much of downtown's silver-and-gold–age structures of brick and stone. (Denver Public Library, Western History Department.)

brothers built the Denver Club Building (1954) and William Zeckendorf constructed the Mile High Center. The 28-story First National Bank Building (1958) at Seventeenth and Welton, the 22-story Hilton Hotel (1960) at Sixteenth and Court, the 27-story Western Federal Savings Building (1962) at Seventeenth and California, the 31-story Security Life Building (1964) at Sixteenth and Glenarm, and the 42-story Brooks Towers (1967) at Fifteenth and Arapahoe let visitors to Denver know in the 1960s that they were not in Cheyenne or Salt Lake City. Few of the later skyscrapers, with the exception of 1999 Broadway, could be favor-

Temporary parking lots and partially finished high rises gave Denver a constant under-construction look during the 1970s. (Photo by Tom Noel.)

ably compared with I. M. Pei's Mile High Center, which was dwarfed in the early 1980s by the United Bank's 697-foot cash register–shaped shrine to money. Still, the city took pride in its new downtown.

With few exceptions it was a new downtown and for that the Denver Urban Renewal Authority (DURA) and its director, J. Robert Cameron, took much of the credit or, as some would have it, the blame. Established in 1958, DURA's first redevelopment embraced the Avondale district near Federal and Colfax. The next year the agency demolished a stretch along Blake Street north of downtown. Other moderately sized renewals followed until 1968, when the Skyline Urban Renewal Project began remaking central downtown. DURA razed most buildings in the 113-acre Skyline district, a 27-block tract stretching from Cherry Creek on the south to Twentieth Street on the north between Curtis and Larimer. A stretch of Larimer Street recycled as Larimer Square evaded the destruction, as did the Daniels and Fisher tower, long a symbol of Denver. A few buildings found new uses: The Denver City Cable Railway Building at Eighteenth and Lawrence became the Old Spaghetti Factory, and next door the Dunn Shoe and Leather Company reemerged as offices. Normally, however, DURA simply knocked buildings down or blew them up. Preservationists howled, but there was no stopping DURA as it bulldozed the ground for the Tabor Center, Prudential Plaza, Sakura Square, Denver National Bank Plaza, the Denver Center for the Performing Arts, and more than a dozen other major developments.[5] To the south of Skyline, DURA seized 169 acres that became the Auraria Higher Education Complex.[6] The uptown part of downtown prospered without DURA. There, economic pressures killed old and middle-aged structures that were replaced with taller and shinier edifices.

These flashy monoliths, which made the core city look impressive, hid a truth. Beginning in the 1950s businesses decentralized, and downtown's power declined. Previously, it had had no serious rivals. The

Denver emerged as a national center for oil, coal, and solar energy in the 1970s. Downtown became the nesting place of the construction crane. (Photo by Glenn Cuerden.)

commercial hubs of Arvada, Aurora, Englewood, and Littleton were pale compared to Sixteenth Street, as were the miles of small businesses that flanked Colfax, Broadway, Santa Fe, and Federal. Nor was downtown threatened by neighborhood business districts that had cropped up along tramway lines, brick blocks housing drugstores, butchers, bakeries, variety stores, bars; small and sometimes medium-sized groceries such as Piggly Wigglies and Miller's Markets, King Soopers, and Safeways; barber shops, family theaters, cleaners, and other "mom and pop" establishments with mom and pop and their kids sometimes living upstairs or at the back of the shop. Downtown did not worry about these minnows, nor did it stew about errant tuna such as Montgomery Ward, which swam out of the

In the 1920s, Temple "Sandy" Buell began his 60-year career as a Denver architect and developer. (Ken Fuller Collection.)

mainstream, building a big store at 555 South Broadway. The May Company, Joslin's, Neusteter's, Gano-Downs, Cottrell's, the Denver Dry Goods, Daniels and Fisher, all were downtown. Tramway tracks and most bus lines converged there; people went downtown to bank, consult their lawyers, and lunch at the Denver Dry's Tea Room. They ate ice cream at Baur's, dined at elegant restaurants such as the Blue Parrot, and saw their doctors and dentists in the Republic, the Majestic, and the Metropolitan buildings.

By 1980 the central city was collecting less sales tax than were suburban shopping centers and was losing office tenants to suburban office parks. Its Sixteenth Street Mall (1982) attracted shoppers, and skyscrapers towered above its streets, but they could not revive its glory years of nearly absolute dominance.

Thousands of train travelers had once used Union Station as their door to Denver; airline passengers deplaned at Stapleton and scattered to hotels throughout the metropolitan area, or they rented cars and drove straight into the mountains to ski. By 1989 only seven of the region's 25 principal hotels and motels remained downtown.[7] Moreover, downtown failed to adjust to huge numbers of automobiles. Even people who lived in the central city often found it easier to eat, drink, shop, and park in shopping malls than to cope with downtown's traffic, meters, and parking garages. The changes occurred gradually, but two milestones stand out — the 1955 completion of Temple Buell's Cherry Creek Shopping Center and the 1962 birth of George Wallace's Denver Tech Center.

Architect Temple Buell, a TB victim, came from Chicago to Colorado in 1923 to recover his health. He decided to settle in Denver rather than in Colorado Springs because he judged the larger city would have more buildings. He guessed correctly and over the next half-century added many structures to the city — the Paramount Theater, Mullen Home for Nurses, and many schools including Kennedy and Lincoln high schools. More significant, however, was his grasp of Denver's future. In 1925 he bought 49 acres for $25,000 at the intersection of First and

University. With the Denver Country Club to the west and the Polo Club to the south, his land appeared to be well situated, but since there was not much use for it Buell leased it to the city for a dump.

Buell later recalled a conversation he had in the 1940s with J. C. Nichols, a Kansas City developer. Nichols told Buell that "cities will not grow like onions . . . they will grow like grapes."[8] That prophetic insight, which sociologists later called multiple-nuclei theory, correctly predicted the shape of post–WW II U.S. cities with their scattered commercial and office districts. Buell capitalized on the idea. While other developers graded land for houses, he built the Cherry Creek Shopping Center in the early 1950s, confident that the newly constructed Cherry Creek Dam southeast of the city would protect his buildings from floods. Sears moved its vacuum cleaners and jeans from downtown, and the more upscale Denver Dry Goods opened a large branch store in 1953. Following the lead of Kansas City, where the first shopping center, Garden Place, had been built in the 1930s, Buell clustered his buildings around a landscaped mall and provided acres of adjacent parking. Soon, bigger and better malls cropped up to compete for shoppers' dollars. Lakeside (1956) boasted 777,000 square feet, and Lakewood's Villa Italia (1977) with 1.25 million square feet and Englewood's Cinderella City (1968) with 1.3 million square feet both outshone Lakeside. Eventually, they all bowed to the mightiest mall of all, Southwest Plaza (1983) in Littleton, which reckoned nearly 1.5 million square feet.[9]

By the 1980s Buell recognized that Cherry Creek needed redevelopment — a project completed several months after his death, at age 94, in 1990. Although he failed to see his dream remade, he saw his ideas materialize as shopping centers restructured the metropolis. And he had the additional satisfaction of accurately predicting that much of the city's commercial development would proceed in a southeasterly direction. By 1988 there were 10.3 million square feet of office space in 171 buildings in the Cherry Creek–Glendale sector, which, combined with Southeast Suburban's 19.6 million square feet, clearly outdid the core city's 24.3 million square feet.

George Wallace dreamed a similar dream and enjoyed a similar success. Wallace, a transplanted New Yorker, established an engineering firm in Denver in 1954. Like Buell, he reasoned that the city would grow to the southeast, and he, too, saw traffic congestion downtown as a reason to move. In 1962 he purchased 40 acres of farmland bordering I-25 some 15 miles southeast of downtown. "All I wanted to do was have room for parking spaces," he explained.[10] By 1975 his plot been transformed into

The Denver Tech Center inspired nearby developments including The Triad at I-25 and Orchard Road. (Photo by Jim Krebs.)

nearly 800 carefully planned acres with 27 buildings. Looking two decades into the future, Wallace dreamed of a total investment of a billion dollars. A burst of construction in the late 1970s and early 1980s saw many of his plans materialize. At times in the mid-1980s the 255 buildings in the Southeast Suburban area, many of them in or near the Tech Center, were leasing more office space than was downtown.

Although core city chauvinists hated the shopping centers and feared the office parks, metropolitan real estate as a whole flourished from 1950 to 1980. So did local banks and savings institutions that financed much of the expansion. Rejecting the conservatism of earlier financiers, bankers took off their hats, loosened their ties, and jumped on the roller coaster. Neil Roberts, head of United Bank in 1979, observed that in the 1930s "it would have taken an almost total consortium of all the banks in Denver to lend anyone a million dollars." That, he claimed, had changed: "Banking in Denver can serve its client's needs."[11]

Part of the shift reflected the passing of an earlier, more cautious generation of financiers, men such as Gerald Hughes and John Evans, Sr., of the First National Bank. In 1955, a year before Hughes died, the First National had $203,546,215 on deposit, of which 35 percent was lent out. In 1980 the bank lent nearly 68 percent of its $1.3 billion. Bankers at the old banks grew more flexible to meet the challenges posed by people who, like Elwood Brooks of the Central Bank, believed in giving customers direct bank loans.[12] Savings and loans competed for deposits, as did innovative institutions such as The Women's Bank, founded in 1978, which had attracted $12 million in deposits by mid-1979. Even more meteoric was the rise of Michael R. Wise's Silverado Savings, which doubled its loans from $51 million to $105 million between 1982 and 1983. In response, traditional banks tried new strategies; for example, Colorado National's national bank card system. United Bank's President Neil Roberts explained: "Machines are sometimes nicer than the occasional surly teller . . . and are more accurate."[13]

Stockbrokers also strayed from conservative paths. Such established firms as Boettcher and Company, Bosworth-Sullivan (which became Dain, Bosworth in 1978), and Hanifen Imhoff added staff. Newer operations, such as Blinder, Robinson, and Company, enjoyed the fruits of underwritings and a hot penny stock market. In 1981 alone 96 companies raised $361 million through initial public-stock offerings handled by Colorado brokers. Meyer Blinder's crew worked so diligently that Blinder soon knew what a glorious thing it was to be a brokerage king. By 1987 he bossed 1,700 account executives nationwide, making his firm, by that measure, the United States' tenth-largest.[14]

Denver's economy, like the penny-stock business, resembled a meringue mountain of hyperbole sweetened with greed and blind faith. Much of the economic activity was circular. People came; people needed to eat, live in houses, borrow money to buy the houses; to heat the houses, buy clothes, travel, make telephone calls. Supermarkets, department stores, phone companies, home builders, refineries, utilities, and banks flourished. They hired people who needed to eat and live in houses, so the cycle continued. Among the region's major employers in the 1980s were its supermarkets, King Soopers and Safeway; its telephone company, US West; a home builder, MDC Incorporated; and Total Petroleum.

The prosperity, although overblown, was not without foundation. By continuing its traditional role as a regional service, processing, transportation, commercial, service, and governmental center, the city insured its postwar boom. Of Denver County's 244,838 civilian workers in 1980, nearly a quarter engaged in professional or related services; only 12.2 percent worked in manufacturing. That percentage was offset by manufacturing in Adams, Jefferson, and Boulder counties, each of which did more than Denver. Jefferson County, home to Rocky Flats, Coors, and Martin Marietta, derived almost a third of its payroll from manufacturing in 1980.

Defense expenditures, escalating as the United States became the world's policeman after World War II, also enriched Denver. Military installations such as Lowry Air Base and Fitzsimons Army Medical Center continued to bolster the economy. Despite Defense Department threats to close Lowry, a training school without air flights, it stayed open and in 1988 provided paychecks for 10,000 people. Civilian defense and aerospace contributed even more than did direct military employment. Martin Marietta, Honeywell, Rocky Flats, Ball Aerospace, and the Rocky Mountain Arsenal gave thousands of jobs to Front Range residents. Smaller companies by the hundreds also warmed to the cold war. In Littleton the American Coleman Company built tow tractors for the Air Force, and in Englewood, Creative Fabric Systems, originally a tent maker, stitched covers for MX and Titan missiles.[15]

416

Determining the local defense impact stumped even the experts. Officials at the University of Colorado estimated in 1982 that 23 percent of the school's research funds came from defense, energy, and space contracts. In 1983 the Department of Defense predicted that it would spend around $6 billion in Colorado, a figure more than four times greater than its 1976 expenditure of $1.3 billion. By 1988 nearly 8 percent of the Defense Department's research and development budget was being used in the Denver-Boulder area. Asked to comment on the river of defense funds flowing into Colorado, John H. Boyd, public relations director at Martin, said in 1983, "Good Lord, it's gigantic."[16]

Federal dollars also drifted in for less warlike purposes. In 1976 when Colorado ranked twenty-fifth among states in per capita federal spending with total expenditures of nearly $4.6 billion, the Department of Defense accounted for only about 28 percent of the largesse. The Department of Health, Education and Welfare spent nearly $1.2 billion in Colorado that year, much of it going for social security and welfare payments in the metropolitan area. By 1988 dozens of other federal agencies, ranging from the Veterans Administration to the Environmental Protection Agency, helped push Colorado to eleventh nationally in per capita federal expenditures. Denver's piece of the pie exceeded $2.3 billion. Aurora ate a $245 million wedge, and Englewood got a tasty $41 million sliver.[17]

As had been the case during the depression of the 1930s, Uncle Sam's spending provided jobs. Lakewood's Federal Center reported nearly 10,000 federal civilian employees in 1980, Boulder had 3,262, and Denver counted 11,612. State and local governments also employed thousands. In 1980 the City of Denver gave jobs to nearly 12,000. Aurora made do with 1,612, and Lakewood functioned with only 597, but those figures did not include people working for county governments and hundreds of special districts.[18]

Closely related to defense were advanced technology companies, which often secured Defense Department contracts.[19] Hewlett-Packard, one of the first electronics goliaths to locate in Colorado, did so in part because its chairman, David Packard, was Colorado-born and wished to return something to the state. Hewlett Packard's plant in Loveland (1962) foreshadowed widespread technological development from Fort Collins to Colorado Springs. By the early 1970s, IBM had set up shop in Niwot, Bell Labs were operating in Denver, and Ball Brothers had opened in Boulder. IBM spawned Storage Technology and the smaller McData Corporation of Broomfield.[20] StorageTek, in turn, gave birth to NBI (Nothing But Initials) Corporation of Boulder.[21] By far the biggest egg hatched in the area was US West, one of more than half a dozen ostrich-sized offspring of American Telephone and Telegraph.[22] In 1989, *Denver Business* estimated that 1,300 advanced technology companies, most of them along the Front Range, employed 140,000 Coloradans. Large firms included Hewlett Packard with 7,300 employees, IBM with 5,000, Storage Technology with 4,500, and MiniScribe with 3,300.[23] Communications companies generated additional jobs.

In 1974, Joyce Meskis started in a small bookshop, The Tattered Cover, that became one of Denver's biggest boomers. Successfully competing with both chain bookstores and television, The Tattered Cover grew during the 1980s to a $7 million-a-year business and, according to the *New York Times* of July 17, 1989, "the best general bookstore in the United States."

American Television and Communications Corporation, a cable TV firm, employed 9,000 and US West reckoned its work force in excess of 17,000, making it the metropolitan area's biggest single private employer.

Denver's cable TV industry grew from infancy in the 1960s to a $3 billion behemoth in the 1980s. By 1988 the city claimed 7 of the nation's top 20 cable companies including the largest, TeleCommunications Incorporated (TCI); American Television and Communications Corporation (ATC); United Cable Television Corporation (UTC); Paragon Communications; and Jones Intercable. Mergers and takeovers continually remade the map of cableland. For example, United Artists, itself largely owned by TCI, bought out Daniels and Associates in 1988 for $190 million and in 1989 combined with United Cable Television, thereby creating the third-ranked cable firm in the nation and the country's biggest theater chain.[24] Yet while the city landed one big fish, another darted away — in 1989 American Television and Communications moved its headquarters from Denver.

Some observers credited Denver's cable prowess to its location between Europe and Asia, which positioned it to contact satellites serving both those continents. But Wayne Bilby of *Denver Business* suggested that human factors outweighed technological considerations. "Colorado became the capital of cable simply because Bill Daniels, who pioneered the medium, chose to live in the Rockies."[25] Daniels first saw television in Denver in 1952. Anxious to get TV for Casper, Wyoming, where he lived, he set up a cable system for that city. That began a long career for Daniels, who pioneered the use of microwave relays to send signals into remote places. Besides building systems, Daniels created an investment

Denver's modern mining firms, far removed from the pick-and-pan pioneering days, include the sleek international headquarters of Cyprus Minerals. (Cyprus Minerals.)

banking operation that helped finance the industry. Over the years his associates set up their own operations, thus strengthening Denver's dominance. Thomas Southwick of *Multichannel News* explained: "These people are characteristically Western. A lot of guys who started cable or are most important to it live in Denver. You won't find a Bill Daniels in New York. He's willing to lose $100 million and it doesn't bother him. And he's enormously generous."[26]

Cable and computers augmented older mainstays of the economy. In fiscal year 1986–87, Swift Independent Packing Company posted revenues of $3.7 billion, a reminder that Denver's cow-town days had not passed. Manville Corporation, although hurt by bankruptcy triggered by suits against it for manufacturing cancer-causing asbestos products, reported more than $2 billion in revenues. In 1988, Adolph Coors posted a profit of $46 million, while Public Service made over $125 million.[27] Those who recalled Colorado's mining decades delighted in the success of such locally headquartered companies as Newmont Mining, which took in more than a third of a billion dollars in 1987, and Cyprus Mineral Company, reporting more than $1.3 billion in 1988 revenue. But few Denverites noticed; oil companies and oil kings attracted far more attention.

Petroleum had long been important to Denver. Alexander M. Cassidy made Colorado's first oil discovery near Florence in 1862, an easy strike since the black gold was oozing from the ground. Florence soon blossomed into a derrick-studded field — in 1892 producing 824,000 barrels. Most of it became kerosene for lamps; refiners in those days flushed gasoline away since it had no commercial value. Cars changed that. Florence was declining by the time gasoline became important, but an oil boomlet in Boulder County early in the twentieth century and subsequent discoveries north and east of Denver gave Colorado hope of participating in the gasoline bonanza of the automobile age. Yet, compared to Texas, Oklahoma, and Wyoming, Colorado's pre–WW II production was modest. Only 86,000 barrels flowed from the state's wells in 1923, then production surged to over 900,000 barrels at an average price of 56¢ each in 1933. By 1956 both price and production had risen — the 58,496,655 barrels pumped that year sold for more than $160 million.

Oil baron Henry M. Blackmer, at age 80, returned to the United States in 1949 to clean up legal problems hanging over him since the 1920s. Blackmer is pictured with his lawyer, Harold Roberts (left). (Denver Public Library.)

Local discoveries and even richer fields in nearby states made Denver a regional oil center. Colorado entrepreneurs such as Verner Z. Reed developed Salt Creek near Casper, a field that in 1924 yielded more than 30 million barrels. Salt Creek's profits flowed to Denver, where Henry Blackmer, president of Midwest Refining Company, located his offices. When another local oilman, Albert Humphreys, Sr., sold 33.3 million barrels of oil from his Texas field to a combine of which Blackmer was a part, Humphreys and his partners pocketed a check for $50 million. Blackmer and his associates diverted money from that deal to their own uses. Caught in the web surrounding the 1920s Teapot Dome scandal, Blackmer fled to France. His exit, however, left the Mile High City with a still-ample coterie of petroleum potentates including Thomas A. Dines, Arthur E. Johnson, and Harold D. Roberts, all associated with Midwest Oil.[28]

Salt Creek declined, but the slack was taken up by post–WW II discoveries in northwestern Colorado near Rangely and in northeastern Colorado near Sterling. Steady production from Wyoming, Nebraska, and Kansas also benefited Denver. By 1964 over a hundred exploration, service, and production companies were located in Denver — many independently owned. Among them were Philip F. Anschutz's Circle A Drilling Company, Marvin Davis's Davis Oil Company, and Jerome A. Lewis's Petro-Lewis Company. Although not a major oil center since the giant multinational corporations were feebly represented, Denver did have enough oilmen to support a club atop the Petroleum Club Building at Sixteenth and Broadway. The club reflected the boom and bust character of the oil industry. The prosperity of the 1950s waned in the 1960s, forcing the club to reduce initiation fees to a mere $360. Gushing petroprofits of the 1970s rejuvenated the organization. By 1981 it was asking $3,000 for memberships, and would-be joiners faced an 11-year waiting list. That backlog evaporated in the mid-1980s as membership dropped by 400 and the staff fell by a third.

External factors explained the club's shifting fortunes just as they explained petroleum's ups and downs. The 1973 Arab embargo, followed by OPEC price fixing, pushed oil from $2.25 a barrel to more than $12 by the late 1970s. The disruptive effects of the 1979 Iranian Revolution tripled prices, which briefly passed $40 a barrel in 1981. Oilmen responded by looking for more oil. Other Americans sought alternate fuels, considered solar power, and promoted energy conservation. Federal support for solar energy in the late 1970s brought the Solar Energy Research Institute (SERI) to Golden. Under President Jimmy Carter, SERI's budget rose from $3 million to $120 million and its staff peaked at 960. During Ronald Reagan's presidency SERI lost budget, employees, and its director, Denis Hayes, who was fired in 1981. Hayes, an environmental activist who had helped found Earth Day in 1970, condemned "the Reagan administration's attack" on SERI, but he hoped that "common sense here and elsewhere is going to get an increasing number of people to make the right decisions."[29]

Common sense at one time suggested that the United States could rely on nuclear power. But as clouds cast shadows on SERI in the 1980s, the sun slowly set on Fort St. Vrain, a facility originally touted as a thorium-uranium–powered answer to the region's rising electric-power needs. Supposed to cost $47 million, the plant north of Denver near Platteville had soaked up $80 million by 1974. Public Service hoped to generate 330,000 kilowatts of electricity there, but the company later reduced the estimate to 200,000. Even that guess proved optimistic. After two decades of cost overruns, bad publicity, and sporadic operation, Public Service decided in 1988 to close its atomic fiasco.

In terms of profits, oil outshone both the sun and Fort St. Vrain. As prices shot up in the 1970s, multinational corporations and independent producers searched for additional supplies. Some hoped to recover a portion of the estimated 500 trillion barrels of petroleum locked in shale on Colorado's Western Slope. Others saw fortunes to be made in the geologically complex Overthrust Belt in western Wyoming, eastern Utah, and Idaho, where optimists dreamed 15 billion barrels of oil lay hidden.[30] By 1982 an estimated 28,500 people worked in Denver's oil patch — many of them well-paid geologists and executives. Major companies, including Gulf, Mobil, Chevron, and Phillips, located regional offices in the Mile High City — Mobil, for example, ran operations in 33 states from its Denver base. To house these giants, nearly 20 million square feet of space was added to downtown between 1981 and 1983. At Seventeenth and Broadway, New York architects Kohn Pederson Fox built the 36-story Amoco Building with six sides, both for aesthetic effect and to make "more corner offices for executives."[31]

Oil moguls Marvin Davis, Philip Anschutz, and Jerome Lewis exemplified the industry's rewards and risks. Each of them, like many other Mile High petroleum princes, had started out at lower altitudes. Anschutz's and Lewis's fathers were Kansas oilmen; Davis's father a New York dress manufacturer.[32] None could claim rags to riches careers, although each greatly added to the legacies left by their parents. Anschutz's father, for example, built a solid foundation for his son's success by assembling large tracts in the overthurst belt.

Marvin Davis came to Denver in 1953 to supervise Ryan-Davis Oil, a company founded by his father and Ray Ryan in 1949. By convincing investors to risk their money in long-shot drilling ventures, Davis financed enough wells to assure that some would be productive. His independent status allowed him to make decisions quickly. "We'll make multimillion-dollar deals in a matter of minutes," one Davis employee reported.[33] The decisions paid off. When prices soared, the value of Davis's holdings, including hundreds of thousands of acres in Wyoming, skyrocketed. By 1977 his wealth was estimated at $100 million and by the early 1980s he was a billionaire. The six-foot, five-inch, 300-pound Davis could not avoid being noticed. Although he protected his privacy by hiring guards, he seemed to relish the social spotlight and the company of such luminaries as ex-president Gerald Ford and singer Frank Sinatra. His charities, especially the annual Carousel Ball that summoned celebrities from afar to raise money for the Children's Diabetes Foundation, brought him ample publicity, as did his lavish life-style.[34] His Cherry Hills mansion featured such amenities as its own movie theater, sauna, swimming pool, and tennis courts. His Rolls Royces, his private jet, and his penchant for entertaining Hollywood stars all gave him an air of splendor enjoyed by no Denverite before him.

Philip Anschutz appeared to be the antithesis of Marvin Davis. When Anschutz gave a party he was likely to invite his Cherry Hills neighbors; when he vacationed it was not to Palm Springs but to his Utah ranch in sight of the wells that had made him rich. Rarely did his picture appear in the papers; even more rarely did he grant an interview. While Davis prospered by putting together numerous partnership deals, Anschutz seemed to prefer quiet, closely held operations. Yet in other ways they were similar. Both invested heavily in Denver real estate: Davis in Miller-Klutznick-Davis-Gray Company; Anschutz as part of Oxford-AnsCo. Both rode the oil boom to become billionaires, and both sold big chunks of their energy empires at high prices in the early 1980s. Timing, they understood, was essential in the oil business.

Jerome Lewis learned the hard lesson of timing in 1987 when, after several shaky years, his once spectacularly successful Petro-Lewis Corporation was forced to liquidate. Founded in the 1960s with three employees, Petro-Lewis grew into a $2 billion marketer of oil and gas partnerships, the largest such enterprise in the nation.[35] Tumbling prices hobbled the company so badly that in 1984 it laid off nearly 80 percent of its 2,200 employees, and in 1987 it sold out for $770 million to Freeport-McMoran. Petro-Lewis, which had once occupied 13 floors of its own building, vanished. Even its art collection, some 850 items including a totem pole, was auctioned and the proceeds given to charity.[36]

As the roller coaster shot upward, few guessed when it would reach the summit. Optimists predicted that the good times would last for decades. Weakening oil prices in 1981 and 1982 did not shake general confidence, nor did many people see Davis's decision to sell a large part of his petroleum production in January 1981 as anything but a shrewd move by a wise billionaire. Far more alarming was Exxon's May 2, 1982, closure of western Colorado's Colony Oil Shale Project. That decision, to scuttle an investment of nearly a billion dollars, shook the petroleum industry and ended the oil orgy.[37]

Exxon gave its Colony Project workers at Parachute no notice and only two hours' severance pay. In Denver oil plunged less precipitously but with similar effect. The price slide that began in 1981 slowed between 1982 and 1984, but in 1985 prices collapsed. By 1986 a barrel of oil fetched less than $9 — a fourth of its 1980 cost. Many geologists and drillers stopped searching for oil, and firms trimmed or eliminated their operations. In an eight-week period beginning in late 1982 Rocky Mountain drilling declined by 20 percent — a drop described by one oilman as the sharpest he had seen in 33 years.[38] Chevron USA, which handled production and exploration for 41 states from its Englewood office, announced plans to cut its local work force by 350 in 1988. The same year Phillips eliminated nearly 300 workers. A year later Mobil slashed its staff by 340 people, leaving only 110 employees in the city. By 1988 more than 14,000 petroleum jobs had disappeared from Denver.

That was only part of the bad news. According to the United Bank of Denver, the Mile High City suffered a series of setbacks between 1982 and 1987. The first decline, linked to the oil bust and to a national economic slowdown, hit the state in 1982. But that pullback was short lived. Although oil workers, geologists, and executives lost jobs, the state's overall employment rose in 1982. Electronics companies, defense contracts, and tourist dollars helped balance the economy until a second, more serious downturn began in 1984 as high-technology companies laid off workers.

Just as oil proved to be less stable than most people had expected, electronics and computer firms turned out to be susceptible to sudden reversals. StorageTek went bankrupt and laid off thousands during the mid-1980s. MiniScribe, a Longmont maker of disk drives, reported record sales of $362 million in 1987. Three years later it declared bankruptcy amid reports that former executives had "cooked the books."[39] MiniScribe's decision to lay off 110 people in December 1989 came shortly after NBI of Boulder cut its work force by 266. By 1990 even the venerable Hewlett Packard was trying to shed 400 senior employees by offering them early retirement.

Layoffs in one sector inexorably led to losses in others. In 1982, Denver's First National Bancorporation reported that 316,000 jobs had been created in the metropolitan area between 1970 and 1980. Of those, 82,000 were credited to petroleum — 28,500 in direct employment and nearly 55,000 spin-off jobs.[40] In Boulder, economists estimated that each high-tech job produced 1.1 support positions. The reverse was also true. Jobs lost at StorageTek or Chevron meant jobs lost in construction, restaurants, barber shops, banks, and symphony orchestras. An avalanche of bankruptcies swept the state in 1988 with 17,926 business failures, a figure nearly matched by the 17,459 registered in 1989. In June 1989, Denver tallied nearly 4,000 insolvencies, helping make it the nation's 1988–89 bankruptcy champion.[41]

Many people, although they did not formally declare bankruptcy, lost savings and homes. In 1985 home prices declined after a 20-year upward spiral that had brought the average cost to $96,898 in 1984.[42] Marvin Davis, who left Denver for Beverly Hills, put a $4.5 million price tag on his 10,000-square-foot Cherry Hills mansion in 1987; he settled for $1.7 million in 1988.[43] Others, with smaller piggy banks, simply walked away from debts. In January 1987 alone, 324 foreclosures were filed in Denver County, 297 in Jefferson, and 354 in Arapahoe. Flooded with repossessed houses, the U.S. Department of Housing and Urban Development held multimillion-dollar auctions to get rid of unwanted properties.[44] Apartment dwellers, unable to meet monthly payments, faced deputy sheriffs who evicted more than 4,000 people in Denver County during 1988.[45]

Commercial real estate likewise plummeted. As early as April 1982 developers of the Reliance Center, fearing that Denver might be "slightly overbuilt" canceled their plans to build what would have been the city's tallest office tower.[46] Downtown land prices declined by as much as 80 percent in the mid-1980s, and between 1987 and mid-1989 more than "$140 million in downtown real estate" faced foreclosure.[47] Older buildings such as the Guaranty Bank at Seventeenth and Stout were vacated as tenants sought bargain rents in new structures. By 1987 the Equitable Building, one of the city's most prestigious, was 40 percent empty. With office vacancies exceeding 25 percent, construction ceased.

Bankruptcies and defaults left lenders with millions of dollars in bad debts. The failure of more than a dozen industrial banks in 1987 jolted the public into questioning the soundness of all banks. The answer came in 1988 when three large savings and loans — Key Savings, Columbia Savings, and Silverado Banking — reported massive losses. Silverado, the *Rocky Mountain News* revealed, suffered a negative net worth of more than $167 million on September 30, 1988. That prompted a federal takeover of the savings and loan that, it appeared by 1990, would cost the government a billion dollars.[48]

Miraculously, Denver did not plunge into a 1930s-style depression. Many businesses remained healthy. Cable and communication firms prospered, and occasionally an oil company, such as DeKalb Energy, moved to Denver. Oil prices briefly rose above $20 a barrel in the late 1980s, giving hope to producers. Federal money continued to pour into the region — welfare, social security, and retirement payments helped stabilize the economy. In the Denver-Boulder area, employment increased slightly between 1987 and 1988, rising from 800,000 to 808,000, and the unemployment rate dropped from 7.2 to 5.9 percent.

Good news competed with bad news. With heartbreaking repetitiveness the Denver Broncos won American Football League championships, only to be humiliated in superbowls. The air seemed to be getting better: In 1989–90 the city reported only six bad carbon monoxide days compared to 125 in 1972. But just as citizens breathed a little easier, they learned of more than 60 pounds of deadly plutonium contaminating the air ducts at Rocky Flats. Davis left Denver; Anschutz expanded his empire to include the Denver and Rio Grande Western Railroad, which he consolidated with the Southern Pacific (SP), and began spending much of his time at SP headquarters, in San Francisco. Savings and loans went broke, but, perhaps as a booby prize, Denver was made a regional headquarters for the Resolution Trust Corporation, the agency charged with liquidating failed thrifts.

Big-league hopes led to expansion of Mile High Stadium. Built in 1948, on a former dump as the Denver Bears Baseball Stadium, the stadium was enlarged to 76,000 seats after Denver captured one of the six original 1959 American Football League teams. McNichols Arena (in background) houses Denver's National Basketball Association team, the Nuggets. (Photo by Glenn Cuerden.)

As the 1990s dawned the metropolitan area seemed to be stuck in a nearly motionless car at a low point on the roller coaster. Despite an economy reminiscent of the 1860s, the 1890s, and the 1930s, Denverites hoped to resume their uphill climb. In the 1860s they built railroads to pull them out of their slump; in the 1890s they realized the importance of diversity; in the 1930s they looked to the federal government to bail them out. In the 1990s they dreamed old dreams on a grand scale: They hoped that the government would continue to spend; they expected that a new convention center would lure more tourists; and they started building a great airport.

CHAPTER 29

Air Age Aspirations

If you would measure the heartbeat of a city . . . take the pulse of her airport.

Brigadier General Billy Mitchell[1]

Like many Americans, Denverites had been fascinated with Orville and Wilbur Wright's 1903 flight at Kitty Hawk. Colorado's first recorded engine-powered flight came seven years later when Louis "Birdman" Paulhan brought his Farman biplane to Denver in a boxcar. Thousands thronged Overland Park to witness the arrival of the air age. This Frenchman, famous for his exhibitions in Paris, had performed at the first U.S. air show, the Los Angeles Aviation Meet, just two weeks earlier. After some tinkering, Paulhan left the ground in a big, boxy contraption wired together and sporting a yellow linen skin. He failed to circle Pikes Peak, as one promoter had promised, but spent three days making skilful, if short, flights — none lasted more than a few minutes. On his sixth flight, he crashed into the crowd, injuring three spectators.[2]

The pioneer, stunt-filled days of aviation ended with World War I, which promoted more-serious development of flying machines. The war also provided hundreds of trained pilots, mechanics, and technicians as well as surplus U.S. Air Service planes. The first commercial flights in Colorado were inaugurated in 1919. Ira B. Humphreys, son of a wealthy Denver oilman, formed the Curtiss-Humphreys Airplane Company and

U.S. Air Mail planes, like railroads before them, initially bypassed the Mile High City and its two-mile-high Rocky Mountain barrier.

built an aerodrome at East Twenty-sixth Avenue and Oneida Street. After acquiring five Curtiss Orioles and three Curtiss-Standard J-1 planes, Humphreys in 1920 began flying customers to Cheyenne, Estes Park, and the Broadmoor Hotel at Colorado Springs. Although 3,500 passengers paid $12.50 each for these open-cockpit flights, Humphreys abandoned Colorado's first passenger airline after his hangar and three planes burned in 1921.[3]

During the 1920s, U.S. aviation found its angel in the postal service. Just as it had subsidized stagecoach and rail service, the Post Office began underwriting experimental airmail routes as early as 1910. A decade later, it established its own transcontinental service. Pilots sometimes carried passengers as well as mail — if anyone would pay 10¢ to 15¢ a mile to face ferocious winds, roaring motors, and raw weather on open-cockpit flights. Competition for the routes resembled the nineteenth-century scramble for stage and rail routes. The first transcontinental airmail route, like the first nation-spanning railroad, bypassed Denver and its dangerous mountain barrier in favor of Cheyenne and the gentler hills of Wyoming.

Between 1920 and 1926, politicians and promoters worked frantically to plug the Mile High City into the national airways system. Colorado's Senator Lawrence Phipps helped arrange the city's deliverance on May 31, 1926, when, "on the crest of a zipping tailwind, a black-and-silver sky ship swung into Denver."[4] Its pilot, Denver's first air mailman, alighted at the Humphrey-Curtiss Aerodrome, which auto dealer Don Hogan had converted into the 40-acre Don Hogan Field. The plane, a modified biplane with a 150-horsepower Hispano-Suiza engine, had wide wings for high-altitude flying. Native Americans hired for the occasion danced around the flying machine, anointing it with magic medicine. As the D&RG Railroad band played stirring music, the dancers were upstaged by horsemen costumed as Pony Express riders, who tossed their mailbags into the biplane. Some 40,000 spectators whistled, clapped, and yee-hawed.

Colorado Airways had come to the rescue, just as the Denver Pacific Railroad had in 1870. This Denver-based airline was headed by Anthony

F. Joseph, whose wife, Angela, was the first Colorado aviatrix to win a commercial pilot's license. Colorado Airways carried the mail for 80 percent of the airmail stamp revenue — a dime for half-ounce local letters and 15¢ to 30¢ for out-of-state mail. Colorado Airways hoped to handle not only mail but also freight and passengers. Anthony and Angela, like General Palmer of the D&RG before them, envisioned a north-south line along the Front Range, stretching southward to Santa Fe, Albuquerque, El Paso, and Mexico. The Josephs' dream crashed less than five years after the firm's 1926 creation. Angela, a prominent official of the Woman's National Aero-

Like thousands of other women, this 1956 trainee in Frontier Airlines' Denver stewardesses' schoolroom found a glamorous new career in the skies. (Chick Stevens Collection.)

nautical Association, was killed in a 1930 accident while barnstorming at Holyoke, Colorado. Following this tragedy, Colorado Airways was grounded by sparse freight and passenger business, contract squabbles with the Post Office, and the Great Depression.[5] Its routes were picked up by Boeing Air Transport, Western Air Express, Varney Speed Lines, Wyoming Air Lines, and Monarch Airlines. Two new characters emerged as giants of Colorado aviation — Robert Foreman Six and Raymond M. "Pappy" Wilson.

Six took over Varney Speed Lines in 1938, reorganizing it as Denver's largest hometown line, Continental. Six, whose hobbies were ranching and perfecting his six-shooter fast draw, presided over Continental for 38 years. Although he moved the headquarters from Denver to Los Angeles in 1963, it remained Colorado's second-largest carrier. Six maintained a Cherry Hills mansion and a Montrose ranch — the Lazy 6 — where he horsed around with his actress wives — Ethel Merman, then Audrey Meadows. A hard-driving manager and a clever promoter, Six ran one of the most cost-efficient airlines, emphasizing passenger service and the memorable slogan, "the proud bird with a golden tail," while Audrey Meadows designed fashionable stewardess attire complete with pearl necklaces.[6] Although Six retired in 1966, Continental survived. Taking advantage of airline deregulation, the once-proud bird used a 1983 bank-

Jimmy Stewart and other Hollywood stars glamorized flying and, in this 1950 pose, a new Denver airline. (Jim Krebs Collection.)

ruptcy to break its union contract, lower labor costs, restructure its debt, and merge with Texas Air.[7]

Pappy Wilson is best known as the founder of Monarch Airlines, which acquired a Colorado airmail contract in 1946. Monarch established routes to many smaller towns, including Alamosa, Boulder, Cañon City, Colorado Springs, Cortez, Durango, Glenwood Springs, Grand Lake, Greeley, Monte Vista, and Trinidad.[8] Wilson opened the first federally approved air training school in the Rockies at Denver Municipal Airport. He also became a local celebrity known for his role as an airborne Santa Claus who attached a 20-by-30–foot neon cross to the fuselage of his plane every yuletide between 1929 and 1959.

In 1950, Monarch merged with Challenger Airlines of Salt Lake City and Arizona Airways of Phoenix to become Frontier Airlines. Frontier, like Colorado Airways, was essentially a north-south carrier. But it carved out, as no other transportation network has before or since, Denver's Rocky Mountain Empire — 11 states from Arizona to the Dakotas, from Texas to Idaho. Flying into tourist territory, Frontier served eight national parks and advertised itself as the "Dude Ranch Airline" and as the skiers' route to "Snow Shows." After acquiring Central Airlines in 1968, Frontier reigned in the Rockies. In 1980, its peak year, Frontier made $23.2 million, employed 5,800 workers, and flew to 86 cities, including several in Canada and Mexico. After Continental moved to Los Angeles, Frontier remained Denver's only major hometown airline until the 1980s, when it suffered bankruptcy, became a part of Continental Airlines in 1986, and witnessed the suicide of president Al L. Feldman.[9]

United Airlines Stratocruisers, deluxe, double-decker luxury planes introduced in 1950, carried vacationers as far as Hawaii. (Tom Noel Collection.)

Another major carrier for decades has been United Airlines. Although based in Chicago, United has made Denver its number-two hub and built many of its facilities, including the University of the Air flight-training school, in Denver. United was founded in Chicago in 1934 as a consolidation of various lines including Boeing Air Transport of Seattle, the Ford Motor Company Airlines of Detroit, and Varney Air Lines of San Francisco.[10]

Many other airlines have come and gone since the Kelly Act of February 2, 1925, privatized airmail in hopes of encouraging private aviation. Seven of the 12 airmail lines formed in 1926 operated west of the Mississippi. Uncle Sam continued to impose controls: The 1926 Air Commerce Act gave the Bureau of Air Commerce power to rate airfields and choose airmail terminals. After its creation in 1938, the Civil Aeronautics Board (CAB) pushed the consolidated airport concept, using federal regulations and funding to create "union stations of the sky." Archibald Black, in his 1929 *Civil Airports and Airways,* had proposed that scattered, competing private airports should be replaced by consolidated, municipally owned operations because the latter option "puts the city in control of the situation [and] offers the greatest possible inducement to air transport firms and to occasional flyers to make that city a stopping point on the way, if not indeed the end of their journey."[11]

Denver's handful of scattered terminals competed with the large, modern, consolidated airports of other cities. Charles A. Lindbergh had helped Kansas City open its municipal airport in 1927; Fort Worth opened its airport in 1927; Dallas acquired Love Field, a U.S. Army airfield, in 1928, while Los Angeles opened its municipal airport in 1930. To keep up with other cities, Mayor Benjamin Stapleton built an airport on the northeastern outskirts of the Mile High City. The mayor met opposition, shrilly led by the *Denver Post,* which ridiculed the idea as "Stapleton's Folly" and dubbed the proposed Sand Creek site "Simpleton's Sand Dunes."[12] Critics called the scheme a boondoggle, a way for the mayor to reward his crony H. Brown Cannon by buying his dairy farm. Opponents claimed the city could save money by acquiring and expanding one of the existing private airfields, such as Don Hogan Field. Some naysayers recalled the Greek myth of Icarus; others argued that if God wanted people to fly he would have given them wings. Rattlesnake Hollow, as some cynics dubbed the site, was also blasted as a taxpayer subsidy for a few rich kids who liked to play with airplanes. While the *Post* and the public balked, the city's power elite, whose offspring were taking up the sport of aviation, endorsed the plan. Denver's first families served on the dedication committee, planning a four-day gala, October 17–20, 1929 — one week before the stock market crashed.

The city spent $143,013 for the 640-acre site at 8100 East Thirty-second Avenue and another $287,000 to build the airport, which consisted of four gravel runways, one hangar, a tiny terminal, and a wind sock. The field was designed by Herbert S. Crocker, a Denver parks department engineer, to Bureau of Air Commerce standards. Dedication festivities attracted crowds estimated at 15,000 to 20,000, rubberneckers who craned to watch the climbs and dives, the loops and rolls of airplanes overhead. There were altitude and speed races, and precision flying contests. Sightseers thronged around Boeing's "Leviathan of the Air," a 14-passenger biplane equipped with Pullman sleepers, a kitchen, and a dining area. One of the most popular events was the bombing of a mock village by Army Air Corps pilots. In the evening thousands joined in the parade of automobiles around the field, which boasted a $30,000 lighting system. Denver celebrated "The West's Best Airport . . . one of the three best airports in America . . . a model for future airport development . . . a great center on America's aerial map."[13]

City planner Saco R. DeBoer realized that Denver Municipal Airport would replace Union Station as the city's gateway. He designed the airport's parkway entrance with exuberant flower beds.[14] The Denver Planning Commission pronounced the airport "large enough and level enough to meet all future needs of long distance passenger flying from the standpoint of speed" and "of sufficient size to take care of several thousand arrivals and departures daily."[15]

Like other U.S. airports, Denver Municipal grew in response to increased traffic, federal guidelines, and technical advances. The first great breakthrough in commercial aviation came in the 1930s with the introduction of the Douglas DC-3. These reliable, safe, fast, and roomy aircraft had stable tricycle landing gear and boasted elegant sky lounges and beds. As DC-3 travelers multiplied, Denver Municipal undertook extensive expansion with WPA financing. The east-west runway was extended to 5,200 feet and the north-south to 6,500 feet. Both were widened to 150 feet with 75-foot shoulders. A $1 million terminal, a control and five radio towers, and daily weather balloons made flying easier and safer.[16]

World War II transformed commercial aviation, speeding the United States into the jet age, with larger, faster, safer planes and radar-guided landing systems. In 1940, less than 1 percent of all intercity travel was aboard the 19 domestic carriers.[17] By 1960, almost half the intercity passengers using common carriers traveled by air.[18]

Denver Improvements and Parks Manager George Cranmer, an avid flyer and world traveler, had been impressed by the Templehof Airport in Berlin. He worked with Denver architect G. Meredith Musick, Sr., to give Denver a similar, semicircular terminal.[19] It sported an observation deck atop the second floor, a men's bar, a mixed cocktail lounge, and Helen "Mom" Williams's Skyline Buffet.

Mayor Stapleton, a penny-pincher, had Cranmer supervise airport design and construction and cut corners by using asphalt from the city plant to build runways. Catchpenny devices were installed wherever the city thought it could nab some spare change. Coin-operated turnstiles guarded the stairway to the observation deck. Pay toilets captured as much as $45,000 a year until 1974, when the Women's Coalition to End Pay Toilets sued the city. Feminist eyebrows had already been raised by the baggage bunnies — teenage girls attired in culottes and polka-dot ties — who replaced male baggage attendants. "Winsome lasses man their stations," reported the *Rocky Mountain News*, May 10, 1970, "with soft smiles and feminine finesse" to convince travelers that "Denver really does have something special about it." During the bathroom brouhaha, women pointed out that only 27 percent of the women's 116 fixtures were free compared to 73 percent of the the 121 toilets in the men's rooms. The feminists flushed out Mayor Bill McNichols, who sheepishly agreed to have the locks removed on half of the pay toilets.[20]

After World War II, Denver's airport began to fulfil the rosy expectations of its 1929 dedication. To honor the mayor who had braved considerable opposition to build it, Denver Municipal Airport was renamed Stapleton Airfield on August 25, 1944.[21] The name changed again in 1964, after the Denver Chamber of Commerce suggested that it be renamed Stapleton International Airport. Four years later it actually became international when Western Airlines inaugurated nonstop flights

A few years after Denver Municipal Airport was completed in 1929 for $430,000, "Mom" Williams opened her Skyline Buffet next door. (Photo by Ralph Morgan.)

to Calgary.[22]

Although Stapleton still had few international flights (one direct flight to London, one to Calgary, and two to Mexico as of 1989), domestic flights proliferated. Passengers, two-thirds of whom were merely switching planes, began to complain that one had to go through Stapleton even to get to heaven or hell. Stapleton soared from the twenty-first–busiest terminal in 1960 to the fifth-busiest in the world during the mid-1980s in terms of passengers boarding, disembarking, or changing planes:

1940	12,089	1970	7,429,150
1950	243,437	1980	20,848,864
1960	2,052,544	1986	34,685,944[23]

To accommodate growth, the airport was expanded northward onto Rocky Mountain Arsenal land in 1959 and again in 1969. The two north-south runways were extended over I-70, Sand Creek, and the UP tracks. When the army stopped using the Arsenal in the 1980s, Mayor McNichols and others suggested it be used once again for further expansion. Meanwhile, Concourse E opened in 1987 but was underused as the passenger count dipped from the 1986 high of 34 million to less than 32 million in 1988.

Mom Williams's 1930 airport eatery evolved by the 1960s into the Sky Chef, favored for some of the best meals in town. Noted for its shrimp-boat dinners and ice cream sundaes, the Sky Chef was a special place to go for birthday parties, live band music, and dancing.[24] Amenities proliferated over the years and by the 1980s Stapleton boasted an

aviation museum, a chapel, two
nurseries, and even a golf-driving-
practice area with videotape swing
critiques. Businesspersons could
brush up on their game before
boarding flights that put the Mile
High City within a few air hours of
either coast. This encouraged many
national firms to open branch of-

Dead or alive, passengers found
Frontier Airlines the fastest
way to get around Colorado.
This Gunnison resident came
home in 1955 to stay. (Chick
Stevens Collection.)

fices. A few, including Anaconda Minerals, Johns-Manville, and Newmont Mining, shifted their national headquarters to Denver. Although
other factors were involved, jet age connections made such moves much
easier.

Even the mortuary business was changed by aviation, according to a
funeral trade journal that claimed: "The funeral director, in shipping
human remains to distant points in the United States and abroad . . . will
find efficient and courteous service from the airlines . . . something which
has not been evidenced in numerous instances by persons and organizations representing highway transportation."[25]

At the turn of the century, 110
passenger trains a day made
Union Station the busiest
place in town. As late as 1950,
when this photo was taken,
Union Station still offered 37
daily arrivals and departures.
(*Denver Post.*)

436

Despite obituaries for train travel, Denver's last private sector passenger service, the D&RG Ski Train, renovated in 1989, has become a sellout on winter weekends. (Photo by Tom Noel.)

Aviation also reshaped life-styles, facilitating weekend escapes to California beaches and New York theaters, winter holidays in Hawaii, and summer vacations in Europe. Frequent, inexpensive flights also brought many vacationers to Colorado. By 1940 visitors constituted the state's third-largest source of income, after agriculture and manufacturing. Approximately 8,000 visitors arrived by air that year, and this elite tended to spend twice as much per day as travelers who arrived by auto, train, or bus. Such data led to a recommendation to construct "large airports at the tourist centers of the state [as] the airplane puts Colorado closer in travel time to the large population centers of the east. . . . Colorado has been selling her attractions to the small markets of the closer states. Air transportation will open the larger tourist market area to Colorado."[26]

Air age recreation was epitomized by the booming ski business, Colorado's steadiest growth industry. Unlike the nonrenewable riches of the earth, snow reappeared annually and could be increased by cloud seeding and artificial snowmakers. Of out-of-state skiers trying Colorado's fine powder, an estimated 65 percent arrived by air in 1987, when 9.4 million skier visits had created over 52,800 jobs and $1.8 billion in retail activity.[27] Colorado boasted 55 ski areas, and the number of skier days reached a 1990 estimate of 10 million. Aviation expedited this growth and led to the creation of Aspen Airways and Rocky Mountain Airways as well as jetports at Aspen, Avon, and Telluride. Like the mining towns they often replaced, ski towns made Denver their supply hub.

Denver's role as the regional metropolis was due in large part to its ability to make itself the travel and trade center of the Rockies, but the city's large ambitions have depended on government funding. In the 1990s, as in the 1860s, Denver hoped that improved transportation would perk up its stagnating economy. In the 1860s, the Denver Pacific Railroad was rescued by a generous federal land grant.[28] One hundred twenty-five years later, Denver also counted on the largesse of the federal government. As aviation historian Paul Barrett has shown, cities have long been at the mercy of federal administrators, who have been wary of overly ambitious airport proposals. As one CAB official put it during the 1940s, "A great number of our average sized cities sought to develop airports out of all proportion to the type and volume of air traffic they would generate. Thus it became a sort of competition between cities to see which could outbuild the other": a fair description of Denver's 1990s airport aspirations.[29]

Despite declining air-passenger traffic at Stapleton, Denver broke ground in 1989 on what boosters claimed would be the world's largest airport. The mayor and other civic and business officials announced that the airport would end Denver's downward economic roller coaster ride.

Throughout the twentieth century, Denver struggled to maintain its position among western cities but had been losing ground. Since 1900, the Mile High City has fallen behind Standard Metropolitan Statistical Areas in the West — Anaheim–Santa Ana, Dallas–Fort Worth, Houston, Los Angeles–Long Beach, Phoenix, San Diego, San Francisco, and Seattle-Everett. Other western cities of a million or more residents — Kansas City, Portland, Riverside-Ontario, Sacramento, San Antonio, and San Jose — were gaining on Denver during the 1980s.[30] Denver's air age dream was to become a "world-class city" — or at least to catch up with Dallas. Like Denver's slow-starting professional football team, Denver's new airport finally began to worry the Texans. A 1989 lead editorial in the *Dallas Times Herald*, "DFW vs. Denver Airport" warned:

> Now that Denver has voted to go ahead with its new $2.3 billion airport, Dallas–Fort Worth International Airport must move to get its own American Airlines expansion under way. The vote to build the Denver Airport — a huge project with 45 [53] square miles and five runways — emphasizes all the more that DFW must be vigilant in protecting its position. Currently DFW is expected to be the nation's

Stapleton International Airport traffic peaked during the mid-1980s, when it briefly reigned as the world's fifth-busiest air passenger hub. (Photo by Glenn Cuerden.)

second-busiest airport in the year 2000, behind Chicago's O'Hare. Denver is likely to be third.[31]

Ironically, it was Dallas–Fort Worth's 1973 airport, the last major one to be built in the United States, that inspired Denver's grandiose scheme. After its 1973 opening, DFW went from 9 to 43 carriers and soared ahead of Stapleton to become the world's fourth-busiest in terms of passengers served. This new airport — and the oil boom — were the two greatest factors in the mushrooming of the Dallas–Fort Worth region, which experienced 25 percent growth during the 1970s.[32] The DFW success story was not lost on Denver, which had become the national champion in empty office space and business bankruptcies.[33]

While Denver was envying Dallas, it got a poke in the backside from Salt Lake City. The Utah capital emerged as a rival after Delta Airlines acquired Western Airlines in 1986 and made Salt Lake its western hub. This new threat was underlined by full-page ads in the *New York Times* and other national publications in February 1986: A harried executive arriving late for a meeting apologizes, "Sorry I'm late but I had to fly through Denver." Next time he would fly through Salt Lake City. Mayor Federico Peña protested to the airlines and authorized a $200,000 campaign to sing Stapleton's praises.[34] Boosters of the Beehive State stung Coloradans again in 1987 by creating a new, snow-white license plate with a skier and the slogan "Utah! Greatest Snow on Earth."

Utah's stinging competition jolted new airport proponents. So did Las Vegas, Nevada's long-range strategy of "overbuilding" its airport "to promote economic growth."[35] A blue-ribbon panel of Colorado business and civic leaders championed the idea, arguing that "in Dallas–Fort Worth and Atlanta, cities whose economies are similar to Denver['s] as regional centers, new airports have been the key element in attracting new business." Proponents claimed the new skyport would pay for itself with revenue bonds to be paid from landing fees, concession rental, and other airport income. This was typical financing and had been used over the years at Stapleton. If the airport for any reason did not make enough money to pay off the bonds, Denver taxpayers would not be liable. Thus, supporters argued, Denver could build a new airport at no risk. And it would be a gold mine: "By 2010, the new airport can lead to over $200 million per year in state and local taxes and 230,000 jobs."[36]

Proponents claimed that Denver had to grow or wither, that it must erect a new regional airport or lose business to rivals. Opponents charged that Denver's new skyhub will generate more traffic and automobile pollution by moving the airport farther from the core city. Denver, they added, would be the first city ever to scrap a major, functioning airport. Others worried that the new airport, located 13 miles farther away from downtown, would take business, conventions, and tourists away from the urban core to eastern suburbs.

Denver International Airport was approved by Adams County voters in 1988 and by Denver residents in 1989, with considerable cheerleading from business and political figures. Adams County citizens had to say yes to allow Denver to annex the land, while opponents forced a special Denver election on the issue. In oratory reminiscent of past promises for transportation panaceas, Governor Roy Romer declared in 1989: "The airport is the single most important economic decision this state will make in the next 20 years. We have an opportunity to build an airport that will be second to none and will lead Colorado into the next century as the transportation hub of this nation."[37]

A study of Atlanta, Dallas–Fort Worth, and Kansas City airports found many advantages of new airports, including increased air freight operations that "triggered substantial industrial development in the . . . airport environs."[38] Air freight at Stapleton had doubled from 200 million pounds in 1977 to over 400 million in 1988. The report added that airport developments could include posh residential areas, such as the Las Colinas executive homes near Dallas–Fort Worth Airport.

Denver's 53-square-mile airport would be the largest in the world — larger than O'Hare and DFW combined. Preliminary architectural plans called for a Teflon-coated tented terminal that would glow at night atop a man-made mesa. Four vehicular approach levels would be connected underground to four concourses by "the most efficient ground transportation and people mover systems at any airport in the world."[39]

Careful attention to the natural environment characterized the plans. Nearby Rocky Mountain Arsenal would be converted to a wildlife preserve, allowing travelers to observe golden and bald eagles and to see the buffalo roam and the deer and the antelope play. Greenways would connect the air terminal with the 250-mile urban trail system. Wheat farming would continue, on a lease arrangement, around the five projected 12,000-foot runways and one 16,000-footer. It all sounded like a dream until September 1989, when Denverites watching the evening news saw ground broken in a wheat field and heard a beaming Mayor Peña declare that the world's largest airport would open there in May 1993.

Initially, Continental and United airlines threatened to sue to stop construction, which they claimed was unneeded and would force them — and their customers — to pay exorbitant landing fees. The airlines pointed out that two of the five concourses at Stapleton were practically empty, as passenger service had declined since 1986. Critics further charged the airport would cost much more than the $1.9 billion city estimate.[40] That figure, they pointed out, did not cover highways and light rail to the airport, airline equipment costs, and clean-up costs of the abandoned airport. Denver's claim that it could sell Stapleton for $100 million was also challenged.[41]

The Federal Aviation Administration (FAA) discredited the opposition, saying a new facility was necessary to end flight delays and hazardous congestion in the national air network. Noting that Denver was the only major U.S. city seriously contemplating a large new airport, the

FAA in 1989 endorsed the project. It approved the final Environmental Impact Statement and contributed $60 million for the ground breaking. Secretary of Transportation Sam Skinner and FAA Administrator James Busey promised that as much as $441 million more in federal aid would be forthcoming.[42]

Even if Uncle Sam did not come up with all $501 million, the city maintained that Denver International would be self-supporting. Stapleton had not only paid for itself but generated a net operating income of $13,405,335 in 1980, which grew to $17,512,684 by 1988.[43] Critics countered that both Continental and United, the two major carriers, were financially troubled. Both might shift hubbing flights from Denver's expensive new facility to other cheaper airports. Denver nevertheless charged ahead. In April 1990, the city sold $704 million in tax-free municipal revenue bonds paying 8.63 percent, although declining passenger numbers, the Denver-area depression, and the shakiness of both Continental and United led the Moody Investor Service to assign the bonds a lusterless rating.[44]

This did not daunt Denver's air age aspirations. Mayor Peña and the planning team promised that, in contrast to the hodgepodge at Stapleton, the new skyport would be a thoroughly planned, cutting-edge solution. A master plan, worked out among Denver, Aurora, Commerce City, and Adams County, clarified each community's sphere of interest in developing surrounding commercial, industrial, recreational, and residential possibilities. Once again the Mile High City was trying to boost itself higher. Whereas Denver once railroaded the Rockies, this time the high and haughty city's flight plans were global.

A glaring omission flawed the fantasy — it included a planned corridor for possible future light rail but no firm plans or flicker of financial hope for such a connection between the city and its new airport. While undertaking the world's largest skyport, Denver had not solved what some thought was its largest ground transport problem — lack of rail transit. The failure festered in some of the nation's worst smog problems, thickening traffic jams; and in fighting — finger fighting and even gunplay — among short-tempered motorists.

Indeed, while crews worked day and night on Denver International, other laborers were ripping out railroad track, bridges, and rail infrastructure in the Platte Valley, although some contended that future mass transit might use the rail facilities of yesteryear.[45]

With that possibility in mind, the Regional Transportation District (RTD) had been acquiring rail rights-of-way ever since it began operating

RTD's free Sixteenth Street Mall shuttle, captured here on its October 7, 1982, Grand Opening Day, has helped revive downtown. (Photo by William Larkin.)

in 1974. RTD took over remnants of what had been the Denver Tramway Company, which had gone out of business in 1970, selling its antiquated buses and facilities to the city for $6.2 million. The tramway had succumbed to the same mounting operating costs and declining ridership that killed mass transit in many other U.S. cities. City ownership of what was briefly renamed the Denver Metro Transit was only a temporary

bailout of bus service until the legislature authorized creation of RTD.

Initially, RTD aspired to be one of the largest transportation districts in the country, embracing Douglas and Weld counties as well as the five metropolitan counties. But residents of Douglas and Weld, as well as those in eastern Adams and Arapahoe counties, removed themselves from the RTD tax district. On September 7, 1973, voters in Adams, Arapahoe, Boulder, Denver, and Jefferson counties approved by a 57.2 percent vote a 0.5 percent sales tax to finance RTD.[46] Afterward, RTD strove to revitalize bus service and expand it to the suburbs, buying seven suburban bus lines. A free Sixteenth Street Mall shuttle, express buses, a temporary free-ride program, numerous new bus stop shelters, park-and-ride auto stations, and massive publicity helped RTD to double bus ridership during the 1970s.

An RTD light rail proposal, to be funded by additional sales taxes, was voted down in 1980. RTD and various metropolitan planning agencies also failed to convince the federal government; the Department of Transportation maintained that other, more densely settled cities needed mass transit more. Planners countered — unsuccessfully — that Denver could shape its future by using mass transit as a development tool. In

Frustrated by failure to get federal funding, RTD put mass-transit plans on a back track and focused on accelerating bus service with devices such as exclusive lanes for heavy-occupancy vehicles.

1990, RTD pondered a commuter train system using existing track and Union Station as a terminal. Possibilities included using a UP line to the old and new airports; the old C&S/Denver Interuban Line from Denver to Boulder and Fort Collins; the UP line connecting Denver with Brighton and Greeley; and a Denver, Littleton, and Castle Rock line along D&RG Western and Santa Fe tracks. Such passenger service would have to share existing freight trackage or build a second set of tracks next to them, a possibility permitted by generally wide existing rights-of-way.[47]

Meanwhile, an unlikely group of railroad and streetcar buffs proved that light rail could roll. The Denver Rail Heritage Society, a nonprofit corporation created in 1988 to preserve the historic Moffat Depot and C & S roundhouse and turn table, opened trolley service in 1989. Volunteer rail and traction buffs obtained a replica of the "Seeing Denver" trolleys. Instead of rerigging trolley lines, the Platte Valley Trolley used diesel-electric power. Daily excursions along unused track between Confluence Park and Sheridan Boulevard attracted tourists headed for the Children's Museum, the Forney Museum, and Mile High Stadium.

Put together on a shoestring by volunteers with the cooperation of the city, Elitch Gardens, RTD, and Burlington Northern, this rail resurrection hoped to extend service to Lakewood using the old Denver, Lakewood & Golden tracks along West Thirteenth Avenue. While Denver gave the trolley some support, it contributed much more — $3 million — to developer Andrew Schlenker's transformation of the Civic Center and nearby streets into a Grand Prix course for 180-mile-per-hour Formula One race cars. A well-greased lobbying effort sold the mayor and council on this August race. Then citizens would be barred from Civic Center and much of downtown by a 2.5-mile-long, six-foot-high fence to make sure that spectators paid to witness this boisterous tribute to automobility.

While preparing downtown streets for the Grand Prix, Denver's Public Works Department came across old streetcar tracks. Public officials announced they had no idea the tracks had been there and asked for more money to remove them. Just as the city forgot its streetcar past, it lacked any conception that the tracks might be useful again someday. Only a few cranks and visionaries pointed out that Denverites might ride out of the twentieth century in rail cars similar to those that had carried their grandparents into it. While metro-Denver leaped into the air age at Denver International, its ground transportation priorities and problems remained far from solved.

CHAPTER 30

Rocky Mountain Metropolis

Some form of metropolitan government is inevitable and desirable. The impetus will come, not from the politicians, but from the people. Local government will become so expensive, the people will rebel at the needless duplication of services.

Mayor William H. McNichols, Jr.
Rocky Mountain News, June 19, 1983

Warm, December sunshine smiled on the Mile High City. People in shorts and T-shirts swatted golf and tennis balls, jogged and bicycled under brilliant blue skies. Downtown office workers found it hard to anticipate the holidays despite the Sixteenth Street Mall decorations and Parade of Lights. Twinkly-eyed television weathermen began predicting on December 22, 1982, that Denver might, after all, have a white Christmas.

Snow started falling around midnight on the twenty-third and did not stop for 24 hours, dumping two feet in a single day. The great Blizzard of 1913 had left more snow — 47.5 inches — but took five days to do it. The 1982 Christmas blizzard paralyzed Stapleton International Airport and interstate highways, leaving thousands of holiday travelers stranded. The *Post* and the *News* both missed an edition. Some of Denver's 1.7 million residents lacked groceries as well as newspapers when supermarket shelves emptied. Mail carriers did not get through, nor did trash collectors. Governor Richard D. Lamm and Mayor William

The 1980s recession left thousands of Denverites homeless and helpless. (Photo by Glenn Cuerden.)

H. McNichols, Jr., declared a state of emergency. The Colorado National Guard mobilized to remove 10-foot snowdrifts that had buried cars, closed streets, and isolated homes.

Two months of bitter cold followed, deepening the nationwide economic chill that had left thousands of Coloradans unemployed, homeless, and hopeless. As subzero cold persisted into February, Father Charles "Woody" Woodrich, pastor of Holy Ghost church, opened his doors to street people. Over 400 squeezed into the rich travertine marble sanctuary to sleep on the golden oak pews. Their urine and filth distressed some parishioners, so Woodrich burned incense to cover the stench, declaring that "a city is more than soaring skyscrapers filled in the day and emptied by evening. It is people, a milling mix of diversity, that brings life to the architecture and commerce. The rich and the poor are all part of the cityscape although the poor are too often unfairly and summarily dismissed."[1]

PLANNING AND PRESERVATION

Despite the economic hardships and personal tragedies, the mid-1980s depression had a bright side. The city had time—as during the 1860s doldrums, during the Speer era following the 1893 depression, and during the New Deal decade following the 1929 crash—to think about its quality of life. "The flat economy," noted the *1989 Denver Comprehensive Plan*, "has reawakened an interest in planning for Denver's future."[2]

Federico Peña, Denver's young, ambitious mayor, took advantage of the lull to reshape the city. A former Chicano activist and state representative, he had advocated dramatic change. After his 1983 upset victory, he would make it happen. Former mayor Quigg Newton, who had played a similar role of sweeping out the old guard 35 years earlier, endorsed Peña, saying that Denver once again needed a shaking up. For his part, the suave, 36-year old candidate emphasized issues rather than ethnicity.[3] Eleven new planners were hired to "imagine a great city" — Peña's campaign theme — and, while wrestling with various new ideas, rediscovered Mayor Speer's City Beautiful dream. This secondhand reverie of public works, parks, and parkways became the inspiration for much of the Peña administration agenda.

Peña's populist approach to civic activism emphasized citizen and neighborhood participation. Responding to invitations from City Hall, 130 neighborhood organizations registered with the planning office. They were invited to planning sessions and public meetings. Such cumbersome, time-consuming empowerment of neighborhoods during the mayor's first term helped him gain reelection in 1987 and undertake massive construction projects during his second term.

Unable to annex land because of the Poundstone amendment, the city turned inward to preserve its old neighborhoods. Denver's historic preservation movement was born during the 1960s as a part of the environmental crusade. Although Charleston, San Antonio, Santa Fe, New Orleans, and a few other cities

Resurrecting City Beautiful–era monumentality, massive twin pylons adorned with a tablature showing downtown's street grid were installed in 1990, as a North Denver gateway on Speer Boulevard at Zuni Street. (Photo by Tom Noel.)

Historic Denver's Ninth Street Park project restored a block of homes for office use on the Auraria campus. Higher education administrators, who originally opposed saving the crumbling little houses, later fought to get out of bland new brick buildings into the restored Victorians. (Photo by Roger Whitacre.)

had pushed preservation for decades, Denverites mobilized in reaction to an epidemic of federally funded urban renewal demolitions. Between 1969 and 1974, DURA had leveled most of the city's oldest neighborhood, Auraria. In place of factories, shops, and a heavily Hispanic residential community, the Auraria Higher Education Center rose as an experiment in shared facilities for the Community College of Denver, Metropolitan State College of Denver, and the University of Colorado at Denver. "The legislature liked the Auraria idea," recalled the first chairman of the board, Philip Milstein. "It was low-cost education, with no frills such as stadiums or housing. We also sold them on the idea that Denver, and particularly its minorities, needed greater access to higher education."[4] The campus opened in January 1977. Its wide menu of courses and programs, reasonable tuition, and convenient downtown location soon made it the largest campus in the state, with over 30,000 students. The success of Auraria further eroded enrollments in private colleges, contributing to the deaths of Colorado Woman's and Loretto

449

Heights colleges during the 1980s. Regis College remained healthy, and the University of Denver, Colorado's oldest college, survived by pruning programs and raising tuition to more than $10,000 a year.

The Molly Brown House, an 1889 Queen Anne at 1340 Pennsylvania, is now a house museum. (Photo by Sandra Dallas.)

Across Cherry Creek from the Auraria campus, the Skyline urban renewal site remained bleak. Unlandscaped parking lots stood for a decade, a forlorn flat of seedy, weedy asphalt in the heart of the city. The last Skyline development — the Tabor Center — did not open until 1984. Although DURA had critics, Director J. Robert Cameron countered that the new towers gave Denver an impressive profile and that developers had to devote 40 percent of their sites to open space. "Think how gray, how hemmed in you'd feel with just those old buildings," said Donna McEncroe, a downtown resident compiling a history of DURA. "The new downtown is more spacious and gracious, with wonderful amenities like the Sixteenth Street Pedestrian Mall opened in 1982."[5]

The disappearance of old downtown jolted historical consciousness, giving rise to a private preservation group. Ann Love, wife of Governor John Love, and others, distressed about the proposed demolition of the Molly Brown House, incorporated Historic Denver on December 11, 1970. The property, at 1340 Pennsylvania Street, had become a home for wayward girls. In 1971 Historic Denver purchased the Brown House for $80,000. Restored as a house museum, it became one of the city's top tourist targets. Heartened, Historic Denver, Inc., led efforts to save other edifices and promoted the restoration of Curtis Park, one of the city's oldest neighborhoods.[6] Using revolving loan funds, tour proceeds, and volunteer time and money, Historic Denver helped residents restore aging houses, provide infill structures, and reinstall flagstone sidewalks. By the mid-1970s, Historic Denver claimed that with

The Curtis Park neighborhood, Denver's first streetcar suburb, has been partially restored to its former Victorian elegance. (Photo by Roger Whitacre.)

Redeveloper Dana Crawford and state Senator Dennis Gallagher inspect the Edbrooke Lofts, a 1990 reincarnation of a former Wynkoop Street warehouse. (Photo by Tom Noel.)

6,000 members it was the second-largest private preservation group in the United States.[7]

The movement was sparked by women. Dana Crawford, whom DURA Director Cameron dubbed the Dragon Lady of Larimer Square, recalled: "I first went down to Larimer Street looking for antiques. Goodwill, Salvation Army, the second-hand stores, and pawn shops were loaded then. Looking for old furniture to restore, I couldn't help but notice that some of the buildings themselves were fine antiques."[8] In 1963, Crawford formed Larimer Square Associates, whose members included future congresswoman Pat Schroeder, to rescue one block from the DURA bulldozers. Inspired by Ghirardelli Square in San Francisco, Gaslight Square in St. Louis, and Old Town in Chicago, Crawford revitalized the 1400 block of Larimer as shops, cafes, offices, and boutiques. With the help of her husband, oilman John Crawford, she made Larimer Square a success story that inspired similar projects on Market, Blake, Wazee, and Wynkoop streets. The Wynkoop Street warehouse strip opposite Union Station, which *New York Times* architectural critic Paul Goldberger called Denver's treasure, was recycled as the Wynkoop Brew Pub, offices, a design center, and lofts.

Another woman, Helen Millet Arndt, spearheaded creation of the Denver Landmark Preservation Commission. Educated at Denver's Kent School for Girls, Miss Porter's School in Connecticut, and Columbia University, she married a Denver physician. Besides her role as a wife and mother, Arndt plunged into civic activities, earning a place as the first woman on the Denver Planning Board. Denver, she told all who would listen, was not a "cow town." It had a City Beautiful tradition, "a great deal of education, judgment and balance. . . . People [felt] that their city was going to be beautiful and nothing but the best would do." But "after 1946 . . . metropolitan Denver had grown so fast that it had just lost . . . its sense of quality . . . its identity."[9] Following her 1959 appointment to the planning board, Arndt organized its Urban Environment Subcommittee, which probably did more to change Denver than did the board's comprehensive plans. Arndt and historian Louisa Arps, developer Dana

Crawford, preservationists Barbara Norgren and Barbara Sudler, and architects Alan Fisher, James Sudler, and Edward D. White, Jr., had social clout, keen commitment, and a talent for rallying the community.

Arndt's first step was a questionnaire asking residents what they thought was special about Denver. "We found," Arndt recalled in 1974, "that their image of Denver was indeed one of a mountain landscape." Denverites used mountains not only for a sense of geographical direction but also for spiritual inspiration. Being able to look up from city concerns to the snowcapped Rockies recharged the urban spirit.

Seeing the mountains was becoming more difficult. Not only smog but monstrous billboards darkened the horizon; according to Arndt, "signs extended far out from the pavements, things that disrupt a street without giving it identity — the exploited street instead of the helpful street . . . the spires of the Immaculate Conception cathedral on the crest of the Colfax Hill with the tremendous large, McDonald yellow arches beside it . . . and the tremendous Coca-Cola sign blocking out the Colorado Capitol."

Armed with testimony from concerned citizens, Arndt and her colleagues persuaded City Council to pass a Mountain View Preservation ordinance in 1968. This protected vistas from City, Cheesman, and Ruby Hill parks and the state capitol by restricting heights of new structures. While protecting the mountainous backdrop that is Denver's greatest landmark, Arndt also tried to save man-made landmarks: "What we needed was a landmark preservation commission that would serve as an agency to identify and press for the preservation of these structures . . . . Mayor Currigan was very leery, but . . . a remarkable lot of Denver citizens of all sexes and all ages from ninety to about ten . . . stood up and said they didn't like to see their city all torn apart."[10] The Denver Landmark Preservation Commission was established in 1967 to hold public hearings on whether to recommend proposed landmarks to City Council. If the council approved, any application for a building permit to change or demolish the structure was sent to the commission. It could put a 90-day hold on the permit, allowing time for negotiation and design review. Over the years the 1967 ordinance has been refined, making it possible to designate historic districts where demolition or building permits can be permanently denied. With individually designated landmarks, demolition permits may be delayed for a year and then granted only if the wrecker has a building permit for the site.

Aware of criticism that preservationists were impractical "little old ladies in tennis shoes" obstructing progress, Arndt replied: "It is wrong, I

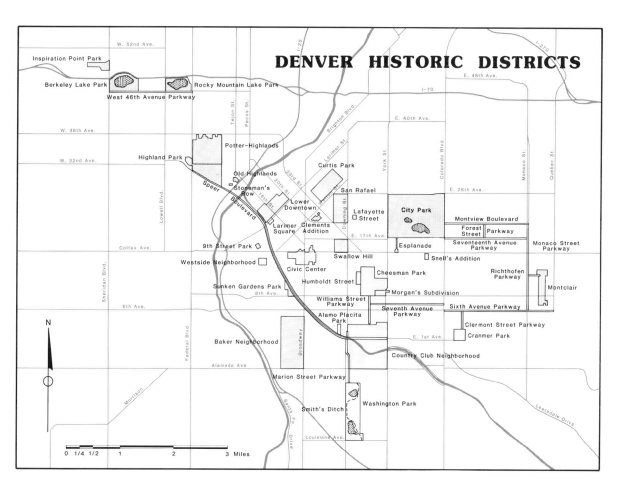

DENVER HISTORIC DISTRICTS

think, for us to try to judge what another generation wants to do. Where an older generation will see nothing but obsolete and worn-out buildings, a younger generation may see an opportunity for a new kind of space. . . . [Yet,] historic preservation concerns ought not to be a dead hand on the development of the city any more than the bulldozers should be." The Denver Landmark Preservation Commission has designated approximately 200 individual landmarks and 18 historic districts. Although most of Auraria and Capitol Hill and the Cheesman, City, and Washington parks neighborhoods still lack protection, parts of Country Club, Curtis Park, Highlands, Lower Downtown, and Montclair have used historic districts to protect their residential flavor.

The basic problem, according to Mayor Peña's first planning director, William Lamont, sprang from 1950s overzoning of the whole city. Anticipating a core city population of 1–2 million, Denver emphasized large-scale, high-rise construction. A few affluent neighborhoods were

protected, but large chunks of the city were turned into speculative playgrounds for potential commercial, industrial, and high-rise residential uses. Lamont noted in 1989 that over 13,000 single-family homes sat on land zoned for high rises.[11]

While protecting some neighborhoods with historic districts, Peña and the planners encouraged development in others, most notably Cherry Creek, the Central Business District, Platte Valley, and the new Airport Corridor. Pursuing these developments, the mayor brought business and booster communities together with labor and minorities, all of whom saw public works as a way to create jobs and jump start a stalled economy. Voters concurred. In spring 1989 they approved the new air-

Circular service ramps and bowed entries grace the boxy Colorado Convention Center, pictured shortly before its 1990 grand opening. (Tom Noel Collection.)

Gene Amole, a spokesman for Denverites concerned about soaring public expenditures such as $2.1 billion for the new airport, shares memories of the good old days with restaurateur Joe "Awful" Coffee. (Denver Public Library, Western History Department.)

port, on which construction began that September. Two months later, Denverites voted for a $242 million bond issue to rebuild streets, provide an infrastructure for Platte Valley developments, improve parks, plant 30,000 trees, expand the stock show grounds, improve Denver General Hospital, air condition the City and County Building, and enlarge the city jail. In 1990 the city completed the $126 million Colorado Convention Center, with almost a million square feet on a 25-acre site between Cherry Creek and the Central Business District.[12]

Voters in 1990 likewise approved $199 million in general obligation bonds for the Denver Public Schools, a $91.6 million general obligation bond issue for new or expanded libraries, and a 0.1 percent sales tax for a new stadium in hopes of attracting major league baseball. Many conservatives and old-timers were horrified as Denver's gross bonded indebtedness climbed over $1 billion. "Feddy and the dreamers," a few critics charged, were bankrupting the city and fantasizing that financially shaky airlines would pay for the proposed $2.1 billion airport. Veteran Rocky Mountain News columnist Gene Amole complained that the administration was "charging it on our credit card." Amole led a chorus of naysayers blasting the city for suffocating future generations with bond payments, rather than using a pay-as-you-go approach. A majority of voters, however, proved willing, as the mayor, City Council, and Chamber of Commerce put it, to "invest in Denver's future."[13]

Municipal millions were sunk into revitalizing the Platte Valley, the last major parcel of undeveloped land within the city limits. Excited about South Platte possibilities, Denver clung to its hope of keeping a high-rise core city as the nucleus of the metropolis rather than sanctioning the idea of village centers, as Los Angeles, Phoenix, and other cities have done.[14]

Beautification and recreation became key components of the core-city renaissance. Peña asked Don and Carolyn Etter, a husband and wife team, to head the Department of Parks and Recreation. He was an attorney and author, she a former Simmons College dean of students and civic activist. Through Historic Denver, Inc., they initiated restoration of Ninth Street Park, a block of middle-class Victorian houses restored for office use on the Auraria Campus. After taking charge of Parks and Recreation in 1987, the Etters began renovating Denver's parks and parkways, using the $59 million for parks in the 1989 bond issue.

Denver joined Adams, Arapahoe, and Jefferson counties to implement a regional greenway plan for a system of parks linked by paved bike-hike-walkways. The South Platte and its tributaries served as the core of this effort, which began with the creation of the Denver Greenway during the 1960s. As long ago as 1900, Jerome Smiley had pronounced the "neglected, unsightly and forlorn" South Platte River a municipal disgrace. A generation later, Saco DeBoer urged that the Platte and other "stream beds and frontage of mountain streams be brought back into the hands of the public step by step."[15]

Mayor McNichols began the transformation of Denver's trash-strewn waterfront by putting Republican state Senator Joe Shoemaker in charge of the Platte River Development Committee. Mayor Bill "turned over $1.9 million of revenue sharing funds," Shoemaker recalled later, "and fully supported our efforts."[16] Completion of Confluence Park at the junction of the South Platte and Cherry Creek in 1976 made believers of many skeptics. An industrial wasteland was reincarnated as a grassy amphitheater, river walk, and kayak run. Along the greenway trails radiating from Confluence Park, murals were used to enhance grimy factory walls. Waterfalls were created in the river to drown out the urban racket. Trails led upstream to Cherry Creek and Chatfield reservoirs, two flood control projects enhanced with recreational and wildlife areas. Along Denver's once-dumpy river, creeks, and gulches, paved paths greeted bicyclists, runners, walkers, roller-skaters, and skateboarders.

While Shoemaker and Mayor McNichols focused on the Greenway, the Etters suggested a broader look at "the importance of the cultural

In the wake of the disastrous 1965 Platte River flood, the Platte River Development Committee planned a riverside greenway to serve both as a park and a floodplain. (*Denver Post*.)

landscape . . . of landforms, parks and parkways, ranches and farmsteads, the design of urban open spaces, plant materials, gardens and the setting of buildings."[17] Such aspirations were soon tested. What should be done with Denver's 13,500 acres of mountain parks in Jefferson, Clear Creek, and Douglas counties? After Denver dropped the Denver Mountain Park property tax in 1955, funding to maintain, much less develop, this vast property vanished. By 1987, the mountain parks staff had been cut to seven with an annual budget of only $300,000. This allowed little more than trash pickup and picnic table repair. Despite suggestions that the mountain parks be sold or transferred to another government agency, the Etters and Peña disagreed. "Those mountain parks," the mayor declared, "are an inheritance for the next century."[18]

Denver's City Beautiful inheritance was threatened in town as well. Following the loss, in the 1960s and 1970s, of 40 percent of the city's street trees to disease and age, replanting was begun by the city forester, the Denver Board of Realtors, and the Park People, a group formed in

At Confluence Park, the cradle of the city, the South Platte River and Cherry Creek have been rejuvenated as the nucleus of a network of urban greenways. (Photo by Tom Noel.)

1969 to provide funding, ideas, and moral support for city parks. To further promote tree planting, the Etters cofounded the Denver Urban Forest Group in 1985. They contended that Denver's quality of life was partly due to the devotion that residents lavished on their lawns, gardens, and trees. Denver's city seal, as journalist Robert L. Perkin once suggested, should be a lawn sprinkler.

WATER

The green oasis in the Great American Desert was fostered by one of the state's most powerful agencies—the Denver Water Department (DWD). With single-minded purposefulness, the DWD redirected statewide water flow to the metropolis. As the South Platte carries only a tenth of the state's water while the Colorado carries 70 percent, diversions took from the latter river to increase the former. Western Slopers complained that the DWD made Colorado River water flow uphill, over the Continental Divide to Denver.

The first major transmontane diversion was the pioneer bore (used to probe geology and remove debris from the main tunnel) of the Moffat Railroad Tunnel. It was leased, enlarged, and concrete lined to carry headwaters of the Colorado River to Ralston (1937) and Gross (1954) reservoirs. The thirsty metropolis added the Williams Fork Collection

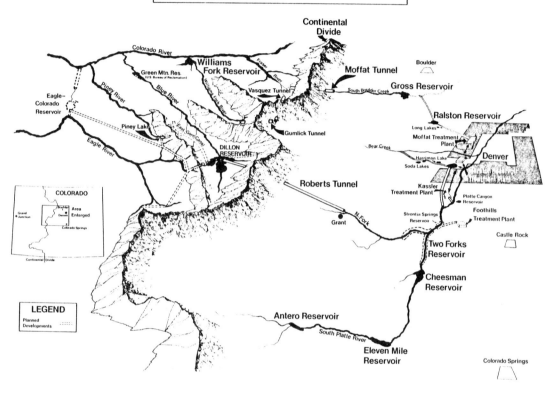

Water Supply System
DENVER WATER DEPARTMENT

Water, as the Denver Water Department's system map shows, flows uphill from the Western Slope over the Continental Divide to Denver. (Denver Water Department.)

System (1940) and Gumlick (1940) and Vasquez (1958) tunnels. Raw mountain water is purified at the Kassler (1890), Marston (1925), Moffat (1937), and Foothills (1983) water treatment plants for Denver drinkers. Dillon Reservoir and the Roberts Tunnel doubled Denver's water supply in 1964, enabling it to sell reserves to suburbs.

The Water Department has struggled to keep ahead of growth ever since Walter Cheesman constructed Cheesman Reservoir in 1905. Cheesman's Denver Union Water Company, a consolidation of what had been 11 private firms, was purchased by the city in 1918. The new municipal water department acquired Antero Reservoir (1924), built Eleven Mile Canyon Dam (1932), and aggressively collected water rights. However, the postwar boom and several 1950s droughts caused a shortage. The DWD responded with its Blue Line, beyond which it refused to supply water, despite pleas from burgeoning suburbs. These restrictions led some suburbs to establish their own water agencies, thus fragmenting metropolitan supplies. Faced with the threat not only of drought but of suburban competition, the DWD redoubled its efforts. More than 30 pumping stations and 1,900 miles of conduits and mains were constructed. The DWD serves two-thirds of the metropolitan population from a slick, three-story office building wrapped around an atrium waterfall. Completed in 1978, the $10 million facility occupies the site of the city's first water storage facility, Archer Reservoir.[19]

Independent of tax dollars, DWD supports itself through water fees and sales. Its board, appointed by the mayor for staggered six-year terms, determines where water flows in the metropolis and at what cost to users. As department Manager William Miller noted: "The Denver Water Department succeeded in maintaining its independence from the city administration and city council. Even though some mayors have been able to appoint a majority of board members, they have not found it possible to exercise any considerable control or direction over the decisions of the Board."[20]

Since the 1970s, this super agency has clashed with an increasingly strident environmental movement. The Colorado Mountain Club, the Colorado Open Space Council, the Sierra Club, Trout Unlimited, and their allies targeted water as a growth management tool. Environmentalists challenged the DWD's predictions that the metropolis would reach a population of 2.5 million by the year 2000. The board's ambitious plans for one of the West's largest dams and water storage facilities — Two Forks — was scuttled in 1989 when the Environmental Protection Agency denied a permit to begin construction in the South Platte Canyon.

The city had been eying Two Forks ever since 1898, when Denverites first proposed the dam site. Not only Denver but Metropolitan Water Providers had contributed to preliminary studies for Two Forks, encouraging many to feel that the project would lead to a metropolitan water authority promoting cooperation between Denver and the suburbs. The DWD and the Metropolitan Water Providers requested further review of the Environmental Impact Statement, although over $40 million had been spent on planning and the permit process since 1984. That $40 million might once have built the dam, groused Manager William Miller, who declared the Two Forks foot-dragging was "approaching a national scandal."[21]

CULTURAL FACILITIES

While water remained a hot topic, metropolitan cultural harmony triumphed in 1988 with passage of the scientific and cultural facilities tax. Adams, Arapahoe, Boulder, Denver, Douglas, and Jefferson counties voted for this 0.1 percent sales tax for cultural facilities throughout the metropolis. In 1989, this tax provided $13 million for the major cultural facilities, as well as many lesser ones. In 1990, this amounted to approximately $3 million for the Denver Museum of Natural History, $2.3 million for the Denver Art Museum, $2.3 million for the Denver Zoological Gardens, $1.3 million for the Performing Arts, $500,000 for the Arvada Center for the Arts and Humanities, $500,000 for the Children's Museum, $150,000 for the Colorado Ballet, $167,000 for Opera Colorado, and $164,000 for the Central City Opera.[22]

The largest, most illustrious, and most popular of Colorado's cultural facilities — the Denver Museum of Natural History — more than doubled its space during the 1980s. The museum added the Gates Planetarium (1968) and the IMAX large-screen theater while refurbishing its older attractions — life-sized wildlife and Native American dioramas and the dinosaur hall. After the museum began charging admission in 1982, attendance slipped but climbed back to 1,436,249 by 1989.[23]

The museum's neighbor in City Park, the Denver Zoological Gardens, grew even faster than the metropolis during the postwar era. Lean budgets crippled the zoo during the 1930s and 1940s, before the 1950 formation of the Denver Zoological Gardens Foundation. It funded restoration of Monkey Island (1950) and bankrolled the Pachyderm Habitat (1959), Feline House (1964), and Animal Hospital (1966). Bird World (1975) enabled visitors to walk through exotic environments of fluttering, strutting, and squawking specimens. Northern Shores (1987) allowed underwater views of harbor seals, polar bears, and sea lions from subterranean windows. Wolf Pack Woods (1988) and a 1989 restoration of the zoo's first wildlife environment, the famous 1918 Bear Mountain, kept people coming. Future plans call for a "Tropical Discovery" (1991) exhibit and "Primate Panorama" (1993), an encounter area between *Homo sapiens* and their hairier cousins.[24]

Like the zoo and the Museum of Natural History, the Denver Art Museum (DAM) flourished after 1950. Earlier, the museum had struggled to find gallery space, even using nooks and crannies of the City and County Building. In 1949, Director Otto Karl Bach oversaw creation of the museum's first permanent home on the south side of the Civic

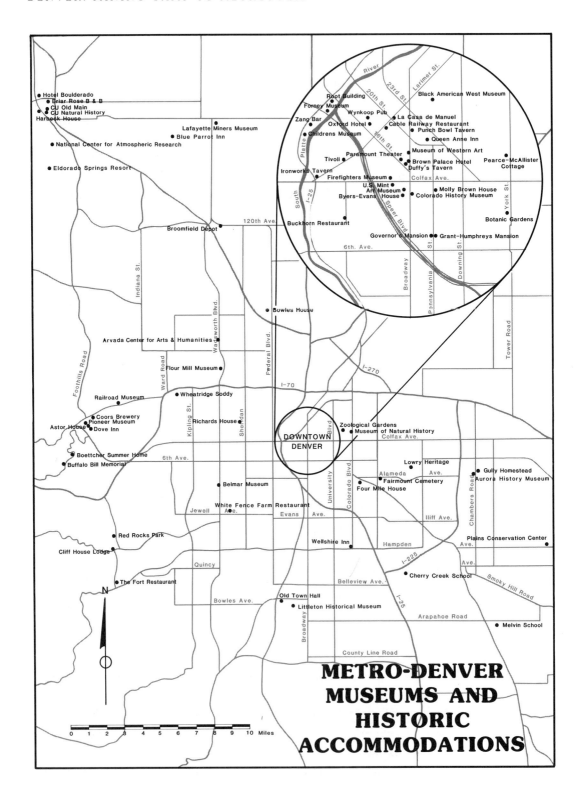

Hotel Boulderado
Briar Rose B & B
CU Old Main
CU Natural History
Harbeck House

Lafayette Miners Museum
Blue Parrot Inn

National Center for Atmospheric Research

Eldorado Springs Resort

Root Building
Forney Museum
Zang Bar
Oxford Hotel
Childrens Museum

Wynkoop Pub
La Casa de Manuel
Cable Railway Restaurant
Punch Bowl Tavern
Queen Anne Inn
Museum of Western Art

Black American West Museum

Paramount Theater
Tivoli

Ironworks Tavern
Firefighters Museum
U.S. Mint
Byers-Evans House

Brown Palace Hotel
Duffy's Tavern
Colfax Ave.
Art Museum
Molly Brown House
Colorado History Museum

Pearce-McAllister
Cottage

Botanic Gardens

Buckhorn Restaurant

Governor's Mansion
Grant-Humphreys Mansion

6th. Ave.

120th Ave.

Broomfield Depot

Bowles House

Arvada Center for Arts & Humanities

Flour Mill Museum

I-70

I-270

Railroad Museum
Coors Brewery
Pioneer Museum
Astor House
Dove Inn

Wheatridge Soddy

Richards House

Zoological Gardens
Museum of Natural History
Colfax Ave.

DOWNTOWN
DENVER

Boettcher Summer Home
Buffalo Bill Memorial

6th. Ave.

Lowry Heritage
Ave.

Gully Homestead
Aurora History Museum

Belmar Museum

Alameda
Fairmount Cemetery
Four Mile House

White Fence Farm Restaurant

Jewell Ave.

Evans Ave.

Iliff Ave.

Plains Conservation Center

Red Rocks Park

Wellshire Inn

Hampden

Cliff House Lodge

Quincy

Ave.

The Fort Restaurant

I-225

N

Belleview Ave.

Cherry Creek School

Smoky Hill Road

Bowles Ave.

Old Town Hall
Littleton Historical Museum

Arapahoe Road

Melvin School

County Line Road

METRO-DENVER
MUSEUMS AND
HISTORIC
ACCOMMODATIONS

0 1 2 3 4 5 6 7 8 9 10 Miles

Among both locals and out-of-towners, the most popular cultural attraction has been the Denver Museum of Natural History. (Photo by Glenn Cuerden.)

Center. Bach tended Renaissance paintings donated by the New York philanthropist Samuel Kress and built a good oriental collection. Some of the museum's many Native American art treasures were exhibited in Chappell House at 1300 Logan. In 1971, the DAM celebrated completion of its Civic Center castle, a seven-story, tile-faced structure designed by the Italian Gio Ponti with James Sudler as the local supervising architect. This edifice struck some observers as overbearing, but locals pointed to it as evidence that they were keeping up with Fort Worth and Kansas City, Missouri. Lewis Sharp, who moved from the Metropolitan Museum in New York to become director of DAM in 1989, planned a four-story wing along Acoma Street. Sharp, unlike some of his predecessors, promised to make regional and western art a major thrust of the museum.

This "Look-at-Me" structure in the Civic Center lures sightseers inside to the Denver Art Museum. (Photo by Tom Noel.)

The late 1970s and the 1980s, particularly when oil money flowed freely, saw a greater interest in art and architecture. Numerous small galleries opened in downtown Denver, and the old Navarre Restaurant and nightclub reemerged as the Museum of Western Art. Public art received enthusiastic support from the Peña administration, which committed 1 percent of all new construction projects for art, inventoried public art, and promoted various projects, including new airport art and a giant mural of Colorado characters to adorn the Colorado Convention Center.[25]

Architects also became more imaginative, reacting against functional glass-and-concrete flat-topped boxes. Curt Fentress, a young Denver architect, crafted several gleaming, rounded, distinctive high rises. After designing Amoco Tower at the southeast corner of Seventeenth and Broadway for Kohn Pederson Fox Associates of New York, he formed his own Denver firm. Fentress and Associates planned 1999 Broadway (which hovers over Holy Ghost church) and sensitive rehabilitations of older structures such as the Navarre/Museum of Western Art and the former University of Denver Law School, which was converted into the City Permit Center. Such work helped Fentress gain commissions for the Colorado Convention Center and Denver International Airport. Both the Denver and the Colorado chapters of the American Institute of Architects, despite a membership decline caused by the construction bust, took a more active interest in civic design traditions and preservation.

The most spectacular edifice on the cultural scene during the postwar era was the Denver Center for the Performing Arts. This multiblock complex, funded by the Boettcher, Bonfils, and Denver Post foundations, incorporated the 1907 Auditorium Theatre and old police building with a new Denver Center Theater Company complex, Boettcher Concert Hall, and an eight-story parking garage. The grand opening in 1980 attracted rave reviews from architectural critics for its brutal, functional concrete masses joined by a giant, clear plastic, arched atrium.[26] Concrete cracks and other shortcomings had emerged a decade later, when a $31 million renovation began, including plans for a new theater.

With a staff of more than 300 people and an annual budget of $13 million, the DCPA houses four theaters and employs its own repertory company. (Denver Center for the Performing Arts.)

The Denver Center for the Performing Arts (DCPA), with a peak season staff of over 300 and a $13 million budget by the late 1980s, mounted ambitious projects. Its Helen Bonfils Theater Company, for example, housed a nationally prominent Recording and Research Center, four stages, and its own repertory company as well as the old Auditorium Theater, where impresario Robert Garner staged national productions.

While the well-endowed DCPA survived the economic downturn of the late 1980s, the Denver Symphony Orchestra (DSO) hit some sour financial notes. Beginning in 1944, when Saul Caston became conductor, the DSO gradually climbed into the ranks of the nation's better orchestras. Prominent, if usually short-term, conductors — Vladimir Golschmann, Brian Priestman, Gaetano Delogu, and Philippe Entremont — added luster and increased the size and season of

465

In spite of innumerable "Save Our Symphony" crusades, Denverites allowed the DSO to disband in 1989. Musicians revived it as the Colorado Symphony Orchestra. Mayor Bill NcNichols, who on occasion sang opera with the DSO, championed this 1977 campaign. (Photo by Roger Whitacre.)

the DSO. Despite growing musical competence, the DSO suffered labor-management problems, strikes, canceled performances, and chronic financial woes exacerbated by the 1980s recession. A desperate board dissolved the orchestra in 1989, but the musicians reorganized as the Colorado Symphony Orchestra, declaring that they would travel across the state to reach larger audiences.

The Denver Botanic Gardens sprouted in the 1940s as the Colorado Forestry and Horticultural Association. Prime cultivators were Gladys Cheesman Evans, Saco DeBoer, and George Kelly. This group of socialites and plant lovers tended gardens in City Park until the 1950s, when the city acquired the Catholic portion of the old City Cemetery for $80,000, with the proviso that the city pay to remove the remaining 6,000 corpses to Mount Olivet Cemetery. Crews worked rapidly at night to transplant most of the bodies. Yet, expansions of the Botanic Gardens sometimes unearthed a corpse. Doctor and Mrs. James Waring bought the mansion next door at 909 York

Wellington Webb became Denver's first African-American mayor in 1991.

The Denver Botanic Gardens (Boettcher Conservatory in background) flourishes on the old City Cemetery site. (Photo by Tom Noel.)

Street and donated it as a headquarters. The well-fertilized gardens expanded to cover most of the former boneyard with Alpine, Aquatic, Cutting, Herb, Japanese, and High Plains gardens. Tropical plants within the large, domed conservatory provide exotic relief to the winter-weary.[27]

The overcrowded main library, forced to store most of its collection elsewhere, persuaded voters in 1990 to okay a $91.6 million bond issue for a major expansion. (Photo by Roger Whitacre.)

A lively newcomer on the cultural scene was the Children's Museum, started in 1975 in a rental storefront at 931 Bannock. In 1984, the popular museum moved to a vibrant green, postmodern, three-story structure on the Platte River Greenway, just across I-25 from Mile High Stadium. Inside, youngsters could don greasepaint and clown around in the circus tent, scramble through an automobile chassis, wade through a room of 80,000 plastic balls, or examine sex-education "Mom Dolls."

A long-unsung verse of the western saga found a voice in the Black American West Museum. Founder Paul Stewart started out as a barber who collected tales from his customers. "Sometimes when I was cutting hair I would reach back and secretly turn on the tape recorder," Stewart later confessed.[28] Impressed by his zeal to collect and preserve black history, folks dropped in with stories, artifacts, photos, and names of people for Stewart to interview. "I put up displays in the shop as conversation pieces," Stewart recalled, "but I got so much stuff that I ran out of room." By the 1970s, Stewart had given up barbering to devote full time to his museum, except for a night job at the airport. After outgrowing the storefront on Bruce Randolph Avenue and two other locations, Stewart and his tapes, artifacts, and documents landed in 1989 in the restored home of Doctor Justina Ford, the celebrated black physician, at 3091 California Street. As Stewart traveled around the city and the country lecturing, his wife, gospel singer Johnnie Mae Davis, refined his act: "Paul always liked to wear Western-style clothing. He just needed a wife to show him how to pull it all together. There aren't too many grown men who can walk around dressed like a cowboy and carry it off."

The Denver Public Library, which serves the entire state through its special collections and interlibrary loan program, suffered a jolt in the late 1970s. The legislature yanked its supplemental funding, forcing the library to close on Thursdays and Sundays and to begin charging non-Denver residents a user fee. Preparing for a bond issue election in 1990 to expand the main building and restore, expand, or build 19 branches, City Librarian Rick J. Ashton put the century-old institution in a strong position to go to the voters. Amicable, paying relations had been reestablished with the legislature. Over half of all Denverites had library cards, and the main library was open again every day of the week. A DPL Friends Foundation sponsored famous-author lectures, poetry readings, and an annual used-book–sale carnival. These popular events helped develop a 3.8 million item collection, making DPL the eighth-largest public library in the nation, second only to Boston in per capita circulation.[29]

SOCIAL SERVICES

Although the 1980s saw tremendous physical improvements, Denver struggled with the toughest test of a great city — care for its poorest residents. Health, education, and welfare for disadvantaged citizens became a lower priority for Denver and the nation as a whole. The gap between rich and poor expanded, and the percentage of people living below the poverty line has been growing since 1980, when it was 13.7 for Denver and 8.4 for the metropolitan area.[30] A *Profile of Poverty in Metropolitan Denver* concluded in 1987:

> The chronically poor offer the greatest challenge to the community —
> to develop and implement early intervention and prevention programs
> in order to slow down the growth of this group. . . . Poverty rates for the
> adult population in Denver are only slightly higher than in the metro-

politan area [but a Denver child] is more than twice as likely to be poor than a child living elsewhere in the metropolitan area. A surprisingly small proportion of the poor actually receive some kind of assistance.[31]

Education, the traditional path of upward economic mobility, did not always work. When youngsters disliked school, found it difficult, or became discipline problems, they often dropped out. Among Hispanics, only 43 percent completed high school. Even some graduates proved to be functionally illiterate.[32]

Homeless indigents haunted the core city, sleeping in cardboard and newspaper nests under bridges over Cherry Creek and the South Platte River. Others snuggled up in garbage dumpsters. The mentally ill, evicted from asylums because of federal guidelines prescribing deinstitutionalization, roamed the streets, muttering, yelling, or silently brooding. A small, ragtag army occupied "Hobo Hill" across from the Denver Rescue Mission and Samaritan House. Some young men peddled flowers on street corners or confronted passing motorists with homemade signs: "Will Work For Food." Others turned to crime and drug dealing. No significant assistance to the homeless came from the state or federal government, even after militants marched in 1989 on the office and on the million-dollar Cherry Hills home of Denver's regional HUD administrator.

Mayor Peña, in 1989, cut the ribbon for a city Homeless Resource Center offering assistance in seeking benefits, job training, job placement, and accommodations at the Sand and Sage Motel. The center is strategically located at Twenty-first and Stout streets next to the Volunteers of America Meal Line, Central Denver Community Services Food Bank, and the Stout Street Clinic, which provides free dental and medical care to the homeless. Goodwill Industries, the Salvation Army, the Volunteers of America, and others offered jobs, meals, and housing.

The Denver Rescue Mission, started by Galilee Baptist church in 1892, had ministered to victims of the 1893 and 1929 depressions. Evicted from 1818 Larimer Street by DURA, the mission moved its flock to the old Dieter Bookbindery at Twenty-third and Lawrence. After installing a large neon cross proclaiming that JESUS SAVES on the two-story brick building, Denver's oldest mission resumed feeding, sheltering, and providing spiritual refreshment for hundreds daily.[33]

Across the street from the mission, the Archdiocese of Denver constructed a $6.7 million, 250-bed shelter. Father William Kraus, the Capuchin monk in charge of Samaritan House since its 1986 opening, reported: "This time, for a change, the poor get to go first class. Usually shelters are recycled old buildings unwanted for anything else, so they become human warehouses."[34] During its first year of operation, the Samaritan House often overflowed and had to turn away applicants. Still it managed, during its first year, to bed 14,020 persons, serve 778,200 meals, enroll 1,165 in job training, and place 411 in full-time jobs.

Low-income housing vanished as both DURA and private owners demolished residence hotels and boarding houses. A 1986 survey of 29 subsidized housing complexes found that the most desirable places — Argonaut Apartments, Cathedral Plaza, Corona Residences, Sakura Square, Sunset Towers — had waiting lists. Many of the others had no vacancies.[35] Meanwhile, the price of the average house in the metropolitan area shot past $100,000 during the boom years. The bust stuck many marginal home owners with high interest rates and huge mortgages on residences whose value had dropped by as much as a third. Amid thousands of foreclosures and bankruptcies, the American dream of home ownership, previously realized by most Denverites, became a nightmare of $1,000-a-month house payments.

Some looked to the Denver Housing Authority (DHA), established in 1938 along guidelines set by the Federal Housing Act. The DHA was first chaired by James Newton, Sr., father of the mayor who constructed much public housing. Between 1940 and 1955, the city built 11 projects with approximately 3,000 units. From 1965 to 1976, the DHA shifted to high-rise public housing, erecting seven towers with 900 units. After 1976, the DHA, complying with federal policy, sought dispersed housing, leased or purchased from private builders.[36] A $10 million Housing Development Bond issue approved by Denver voters in 1972 enabled the DHA to sell some units to residents. After constructing painfully conspicuous, suburban-style ranch homes in nineteenth-century neighborhoods, the DHA learned to rehabilitate existing structures. Despite efforts to integrate dispersed units into southeast Denver and suburbia, public housing remains concentrated in north, west, and central Denver.[37]

During the 1960s and 1970s, thanks to generous support from Washington, Denver's Department of Health and Hospitals had aspired to provide not only health but dental, mental, and social service care to all. Denver pioneered a nationally innovative neighborhood health plan, offering preventive, ambulatory, and prenatal care. To direct municipal health care, Mayor McNichols recruited Dr. Abraham Kauvar, who had set up Denver's neighborhood health program in 1965, to head Health and Hospitals from 1974 until 1980, when he took the same post in New

York City. He worked with McNichols to persuade the State Legislature to contribute $20 million of a $90 million budget, of which $60 million came from Washington. The legislative support came despite objections from a lawmaker that "if Denver didn't have such a good system, it wouldn't attract so many sick people." Kauvar claimed in 1974 that Denver's "neighborhood health centers are the finest in the country . . . A third of all the people whom we see [have] never seen a doctor before in their lives. . . . We offer family planning, mental health, social service, food stamps."[38]

When federal funding for health care dwindled, Mayor Peña struggled to put Health and Hospitals on a paying basis by cutting a few services, such as the Denver Visiting Nurse Service. The service had been searching out patients since 1889, when, as the Denver Flower Mission, its staff took bouquets and nursing care to the sick. Their first written record instructed volunteers:

Go find the heart less blessed than thine,
And pour within his ear
Sweet words of peace and comfort too,
With sympathizing cheer.[39]

These uniformed angels have virtually vanished from flophouses and housing projects; the visiting nurses are now privatized and looking for paying patients. Denver Health and Hospitals' indebtedness has been reduced by Peña, who set an example for city employees by signing up as a paying customer of Denver General Hospital (DGH). Peña's solution was to drum up paying patients and collect bills more vigorously for what remained a first-rate hospital, nationally prominent for its emergency room and trauma care.

METROPOLITAN GOVERNMENT

A metropolitan health district to be funded by taxes on cigarettes and liquor was proposed to fund indigent health care in the region. It has not materialized. Aurora agreed, during the 1980s, to contribute $1 million a year for care of its poorer residents at DGH. Aurora's willingness to share services with Denver was one of the few bright spots in a fragmented metropolis. Aurora mayor Dennis Champine and City Manager James Griesemer worked with Peña on a path-breaking cooperative agreement in 1984 — the Galleria Shopping Center compromise. Rather than fight over the proposed shopping center and its immense projected sales taxes, Denver, which owned land on three sides of the site but could not annex because of the Poundstone amendment, cooperated with Aurora. In exchange, Aurora agreed not only to the $1 million a year for Denver General but also promised to donate $200,000 a year to Denver's cultural facilities and to give Denver a share of Galleria's sales tax revenues.

Next came the Fire Academy agreement. Instead of building its own badly needed facility for training fire fighters, Aurora pumped $1 million into the Denver Fire Academy, allowing it to make long-postponed improvements. The first-rate academy used by Denver and Aurora was also leased to other communities, including Lakewood. Harmony also prevailed in 1988 when Aurora, Brighton, Commerce City, Denver, and Adams County collaborated to define annexation spheres and infrastructure responsibilities for land surrounding Denver International Airport.[40] Aurora City Manager James Griesemer, a major promoter of this intergovernmental harmony, reflected in 1989: "It has taken a long time but we have made great strides toward metro cooperation. One successful negotiation has led to another since the 1984 Galleria agreement, replacing rivalry with a spirit of cooperation. In that respect metro-Denver has become a national model of intergovernmental cooperation."[41]

Metropolitanism was advanced not only by cooperative efforts to build a new airport and convention center but also by a transformation of the Denver Chamber of Commerce. Richard C. D. Fleming, the flamboyant chief of Downtown Denver, Incorporated, succeeded Rex Jennings in 1987 as president and chief executive officer of the restructured Greater Denver Chamber of Commerce. Fleming hoped to broaden the chamber's goals, as he explained in 1990:

> The world sees Denver as you see it from an airplane — without artificial boundaries. We should treat it that way and deal together on common problems of air pollution, economic development, transportation, and water. We need to market Denver as a five-county metropolis and let prospects see all the alternatives. That's a lot better than having each county try to build itself up by running down the others.[42]

The most successful and least controversial joint venture was the Metropolitan Sewage District, perhaps because local governments did not feel strong territorial interests in sewage. Organized by a state law in 1961, the district eventually encompassed 20 municipalities, serving a

473

population of 1.4 million. In 1988, voters approved a $97 million bond authorization to expand sewers and treatment plants in what environmentalists called a model program. Sewage was recycled as sludge used to enrich soil, but most bottles, cans, newspapers, and other solid waste were not recycled. Peña, who personally sorted his household trash for aluminum, glass, plastics, and newspapers, urged others to do likewise. Yet, Denver and most other metropolitan governments did not provide the curbside pickup offered by Boulder, Seattle, and other cities.

Although a few agencies pointed the way, cooperation remained an elusive mirage. Over 300 special districts existed in the five counties in 1990; a 50 percent increase since the 1970s. This governmental maze makes administration and planning difficult, confuses taxpayers about who taxes and who serves them, and leads to a wasteful duplication of services. Colorado ranked ninth nationally in the number of minigovernments, with over 1,000 special jurisdictions. In the metropolitan area alone, there were 213 fire protection districts.[43] To finance all these layers of bureaucracy, cities and other local government units generally rely on sales taxes, heightening the frantic competition to attract shopping centers. As the statewide chaos suggests, the legislature has not always promoted local government consolidation and reform. In 1961, lawmakers did authorize, besides the new sewage district, a proposed metropolitan capital improvement district — the pioneer plan thrown out by the Colorado Supreme Court after Adams County filed suit.

Frustrated officials tried to deal with the court's objections by creating an urban super county to consolidate services. This plan was submitted to the legislature, which rejected it in 1965, 1967 and, in modified form, 1968. In 1969, lawmakers approved the RTD, a metro–storm sewage district, and a Regional Service Authority, provided voters statewide concurred. They did, by a two-to-one margin. Even after this clear mandate, the legislature dawdled, finally passing the Service Authority Act of 1972. It allowed a broad range of consolidated services — if approved by voters in each county concerned. In her research, political scientist Susan W. Furniss concluded, "In essence, the arena in which the battle for metropolitan reform will be waged has now shifted to the electorate in the Denver Metropolitan Area. The legislative response during the last decade to proposals for metropolitan reform was a refusal to use the power of the state to encourage the restructuring of local government units."[44]

The agency charged with promoting regional government originated with the Inter-County Regional Planning Association created by Mayor

Quigg Newton in 1955. It changed its name to Denver Regional Council of Governments in 1968 and flourished with federal, state, and local funding; but by 1990, both funding and enthusiasm for DRCOG's studies, plans, and publications were shrinking. "For all the money we've put into DRCOG," former governor Lamm complained in 1989, "the returns are marginal. When you try to list the dynamic things DRCOG has done, nobody can think of anything."[45]

When the metropolis has a workable metropolitan agency, the legislature seems determined to undermine it. The RTD, for instance, found itself threatened by a rival metro–transit agency authorized by the General Assembly: the Transit Construction Authority with developer George Wallace at the steering wheel. The authority fatally crashed in 1989 but Governor Romer and the legislature, unhappy with RTD's failure to develop light rail, tried to create another rival in 1990. Besides promoting a Metropolitan Transportation District Commission, the state also strove to raid the RTD treasury of $10 million and replace its elected 15-member board with a 7-member board appointed by the governor. Still other legislators, led by Senator Terry Considine of Cherry Hills Village, suggested that RTD be privatized and that its funding be put into highway construction.[46]

This struggle between mass transit and private auto proponents epitomized the major issue throughout Denver's development: How can private freedoms and opportunities be reconciled with the need for collective action? The core city wanted more community involvement, but the suburbs were wary, often considering government the problem rather than a solution. This became apparent in the fall 1989 special elections. Denver voters turned out in record numbers to approve all of the proposals in the $241 million bond issue packet. On the same day, voters in Adams, Douglas, and Jefferson counties decisively defeated school bond issues and mill levies.

The maturing metropolis had graduated to big city problems of fragmented government, feuding ethnic groups, financial crises, congestion, crime, drugs, gangs, homelessness, and smog. Even the Mile High City's traditional assets, its rich hinterland and salubrious climate, were endangered. Rapid, reckless exploitation of gold and silver, coal and oil had diminished the riches of the earth, while automobiles darkened with smog a city that had once puffed itself as the nation's health spa.

Despite its problems, Denver fared better than many big cities. Its core remained vital, in part because of energetic leadership from strong mayors, in part because it is the nexus of the metropolis, a point of

In 1990, the Colorado Historical Society completed restoration of the Byers-Evans house at Thirteenth and Bannock. The building is now open as the first museum dedicated to Denver's history. (Photo by Roger Whitacre.)

convergence. Deteriorating residential neighborhoods used historic district zoning to check the usual ring of speculation, decay, demolition, and parking lots that blight many U.S. core cities. Even the air seemed to be clearing in the 1990s after Mayor Peña made Denver the first large U.S. city to impose a wood-burning ban on high-pollution days, to inspect diesel vehicles, to mandate the use of oxygenated auto fuels, and to declare all city facilities "smoke-free."

Metro-Denver ranked second, as of 1980, only to the Washington, D.C., area in the educational level of its residents (81 percent are high school graduates; 26 percent college graduates). Most are Denverites by choice rather than by accident of birth. With western optimism, Mayor Peña and many other Denverites feel that their city can improve upon the nation's troubled urban condition. Although ethnic tensions persist, Denver has escaped major race riots and has integrated city schools and some neighborhoods. Park Hill in northeast Denver claims to be one of the best-integrated neighborhoods in the Unites States. Unlike most cities, Denver offers most of its residents the American dream of home ownership, complete with a garage and front, back, and side yards. Many homes and neighborhoods are within reach of the growing metropolitan network of greenways linking urban parks and suburban greenbelts.

476

Perhaps Denver's greatest asset is easy escape from the urban scene. Within an hour's drive to the east lie prairie ghost towns, national grasslands, and the exquisite solitude of the High Plains. An hour's drive to the west leads to campgrounds, hiking trails, mountain lakes, ski resorts, and wilderness areas snuggled against the snowcapped crest of the continent. There, Denverites can look back upon the sprawling city to contemplate the problems and the possibilities of the mining camp that grew into the metropolis of the Rockies.

CONCLUSION

Historians, intellectuals, and planners have not been enamored of the western metropolis, although a few scholars, such as Sam Bass Warner, Kevin Starr, and Carl Abbott, have found much to recommend sunbelt cities. Minorities and the poor, for instance, have found better homes, opportunities, and integration in open cities such as Denver than in ghettoized eastern cities.

Given a choice between urban living and suburban tract homes, westerners have, by a large majority, taken freeways to suburbia. Los Angeles, despite its many problems, has become the prototype — a "fragmented metropolis" in the words of historian Robert Fogelson. Rather than pursue concentrated, mass transit–oriented, urbane eastern models, Denverites, too, have built an automobilized, privatized, sprawling city. Rambunctious individuals and communities scrambled, with minimal governmental control, for the riches of the earth. The exploitative legacy of mining days continues to haunt the city. After the oil bust of the 1980s, Colorado experienced its first major population exodus since the 1890s.

While creating a privatized society, Denverites did work together to construct ambitious transportation networks, from the Denver Pacific Railroad to Denver International Airport. Such achievements furthered the Mile High City's tendency to blanket its isolation, provincialism, and cultural inferiority complex with blatant boosterism. Mineral rushes were followed by a rush to respectability; the city exported pay dirt and imported eastern and European culture. Only belatedly did Denver come to appreciate its Native American and Hispanic cultural heritage.

To temper a boom-and-bust economy overly dependent on the riches of the earth, Denver pursued economic diversity and struggled for independence from eastern capital and decision-makers. The city made its greatest progress toward building a sense of community during its bust cycles, when the public sector had time to catch up with private developers. During the days of Mayors Speer and Peña, Denver departed from laissez-faire western ways to pursue the City Beautiful dream, to build a neoclassical oasis in a western desert. Following the 1980s bust, Denver undertook ambitious public works — massive refurbishing of its parks and parkways, completing an urban greenway, preserving historic districts, and spending billions on new public facilities.

While conforming to many national patterns, Denver displays differences stemming from its unusually spacious and isolated setting. A spread-out western city with a vast, sparsely settled hinterland, its land was plentiful and cheap. This is reflected in the prevalence of single-family, detached housing, as well as in uncontrolled growth that checkerboards the Front Range from Fort Collins to Colorado Springs.

As the crusade for a gigantic new airport indicates, Denver's isolation has led to an obsession with transportation. Railroads made the city and automobiles remade it. While promoting mobility, automobility created an asphalt town beneath a brown cloud. Following patterns set by streetcar suburbanization, the car paved the foothills and invaded the High Plains.

Unrestrained by physical barriers, the metro area sprawls over five counties and more than a thousand square miles. Almost 2 million people, well over half of all Coloradans, live in the Mile High Metropolis. Further growth may be constricted by a limited water supply, which Denver must share with Las Vegas, Los Angeles, Phoenix, San Diego, and other thirsty southwestern sunbelt cities. The struggle over water epitomizes the underlying dilemma. In the future, as in the past, Denver's basic challenge is to reconcile private goals with a search for community. Individuals must be persuaded to work collectively to promote the common good and quality of life. Not only individual citizens but many separate communities must together cope with economic development, health care, housing, mass transit, smog, social services, and water shortages.

"Suburbanization has become the quintessential physical achievement of the United States," Kenneth T. Jackson concluded in *Crabgrass Frontier: The Suburbanization of the United States*. Certainly this is true in Denver, where three out of four residents now live outside the core county. In suburbia, many of the hopes, dreams, and fears of the American West have come to roost, as the core city becomes an ever more challenging frontier of a fragmented metropolis.

Appendixes, Sources, and Notes

APPENDIX 1: Mayors of Denver

John C. Moore, 1859–1861
Charles A. Cook, 1861–1863
Amos Steck, 1863–1864
Hiram J. Brendlinger, 1864–1865
George T. Clark, 1865–1866
Milton M. Delano, 1866–1868
William M. Clayton, 1868–1869
Baxter B. Stiles, 1869–1871, 1877–1878
John Harper, 1871–1872
Joseph E. Bates, 1872–1873, 1885–1887
Francis M. Case, 1873–1874
William J. Barker, 1874–1876
Richard G. Buckingham, 1876–1877
Richard Sopris, 1878–1881
Robert Morris, 1881–1883
John L. Routt, 1883–1885
William Scott Lee, 1887–1889
Wolfe Londoner, 1889–1891
Platt Rogers, 1891–1893
Marion D. Van Horn, 1893–1895
Thomas S. McMurray, 1895–1899
Henry V. Johnson, 1899–1901
Robert R. Wright, Jr., 1901–1904
Robert W. Speer, 1904–1912, 1916–1918
Henry J. Arnold, 1912–1913
James M. Perkins, 1913–1915
William H. Sharpley, 1915–1916
William F. R. Mills, 1918–1919
Dewey C. Bailey, 1919–1923
Benjamin F. Stapleton, 1923–1931, 1935–1947
George D. Begole, 1931–1935
James Quigg Newton, 1947–1955
Will F. Nicholson, 1955–1959
Richard Y. Batterton, 1959–1963
Thomas G. Currigan, 1963–1968
William H. McNichols, Jr., 1968–1983
Federico F. Peña, 1983–1991
Wellington Webb, 1991–

APPENDIX 2: County Populations

	Adams	Arapahoe	Boulder	Denver	Jefferson
1870		6,829	1,939		2,390
1880		38,644	9,723		6,804
1890		132,135	14,082		8,450
1900		153,017	21,544		9,306
1910	8,892	10,263	30,330	213,381	14,231
1920	14,430	12,766	31,861	256,491	14,400
1930	20,245	22,647	32,456	287,861	21,810
1940	22,481	32,150	37,438	322,412	30,725
1950	40,234	52,125	48,296	415,786	55,687
1960	120,296	113,426	74,254	493,889	127,520
1970	185,789	162,142	131,889	514,678	235,368
1980	245,944	293,621	189,625	492,365	371,753
1990	265,038	391,511	225,339	467,610	438,430

Source: U.S. Census. Arapahoe, Boulder, and Jefferson counties were created in 1861. Adams and Denver counties were created in 1902. Before then, both were part of Arapahoe County; Denver City, the county seat, provided the bulk of Arapahoe's population.

Denver has long enjoyed contemplating its past. Its first biography, Junius E. Wharton's *History of the City of Denver from Its Earliest Times* (Denver: Byers and Dailey, 1866), appeared when the town was only eight years old. William B. Vickers wrote a weighty tome, *History of the City of Denver* (Chicago: O. L. Baskin, 1880); and in 1901 Jerome C. Smiley published his monumental *History of Denver* (Denver: Sun Publishing, 1901). For more than three-quarters of a century thereafter, no one published a comprehensive treatment of Denver. Then, in 1977, Lyle Dorsett produced his *The Queen City: A History of Denver* (revised edition, with co-author Michael McCarthy, Boulder, CO: Pruett Publishing, 1986), which placed Denver in the framework of scholarly urban studies.

The dearth of general works after 1901 does not indicate that Denverites had lost interest. Instead, amateur and professional historians examined the city's past slice by slice. This microscopic approach led to hundreds of books and articles, many characterized by boosterism, nostalgia, and antiquarianism. Sainthood came easily to empire builders and their sons. Women, with the exception of a few socialites and colorful personalities such as Maggie Brown and Baby Doe Tabor, were often slighted. So, too, were most "common people," men and women. African-Americans, Hispanics, Jews, workers, reformers, radicals, and prophets received little attention.

Until recently, historians also ignored Denver's suburbs, seemingly unaware that as early as the 1960s more than half of the metropolitan population lived outside the city's bounds. Historical societies in Arvada, Aurora, Boulder, Golden, Lakewood, Littleton, Longmont, and elsewhere have helped fill the gap as have a number of books published in the last decade.

The following sources, while not complete, include many items on Denver's neglected groups and on the five-county metropolitan area. Readers who want more information should visit their local historical societies, the Colorado Historical Society Library, and the Denver Public Library's Western History Department. Scholars should be aware that the WHD's card catalog has been published, and that the entire DPL catalog is available through the Colorado Academic Research Library's computer system. Many works on Denver are listed in Bohdan S. Wynar, ed., *Colorado Bibliography* (Littleton, CO: Libraries Unlimited, 1980).

We have followed certain conventions in sources and notes: The two most frequently cited newspapers are abbreviated as *RMN* (*Rocky Mountain News*) and *DP* (*Denver Post*); Denver Public Library Western History Department is abbreviated as DPLWHD. The first time a work is cited in each chapter it is given a full citation. Thereafter, we use the author's last name and a shortened title. Three common sources are cited only once in full: Jerome Smiley's *History of Denver*, LeRoy Hafen's *Colorado and Its People: Narrative and Topical History of the Centennial State*, 4 vols. (New York: Lewis Historical Publishing, 1948), and Robert Perkin, *The First Hundred Years: An Informal History of Denver and the Rocky Mountain News* (Garden City, NY: Doubleday, 1959).

CHAPTER 1: Gold!

Sources

Trappers, explorers, and prospectors have all been given considerable historical attention, both because Americans are fascinated with the Old West and because there is a wealth of early nineteenth-century material, often written by explorers, including Zebulon M. Pike, Stephen H. Long, and John C. Fremont. Long camped on the Denver site July 5, 1820; Fremont stopped in July 1843. Visitors such as Rufus Sage (at Denver site September 10, 1842), Francis Parkman (stopped on Cherry Creek August 14, 1846), and George Ruxton (1847) wrote books about the area. Some of the gold seekers of 1858–1859 kept diaries or later produced reminiscences, sensing that they had made history.

Thanks to LeRoy Hafen, editor of *The Colorado Magazine* from 1925 to 1954, and his wife, Ann, many of the primary sources have been published, including *The Mountain Men and the Fur Trade of the Far West*, 10 vols. (Glendale, CA: Arthur H. Clark, 1965–1972); *Colorado Gold Rush: Contemporary Letters and Reports, 1858–59* (Glendale, CA: Arthur H. Clark, 1941); *Pikes Peak Gold Rush Guidebooks of 1859 by Luke Tierney [and] William B. Parsons, and Summaries of the Other Fifteen* (Glendale, CA: Arthur H. Clark, 1941); and *Overland Routes to the Gold Fields, 1859, from Contemporary Diaries* (Glendale, CA: Arthur H. Clark, 1942). Hafen also worked with Nolie Mumey, a Denver physician, to produce facsimile reprints of 18 gold rush guides. See, for example, William Byers, *Handbook to the Gold Fields of Nebraska and Kansas* (Denver: Nolie Mumey, 1949).

Doris Monahan, *Destination, Denver City: The South Platte Trail* (Athens, OH: Sage Books, 1985), details the journey west. Newspapermen, including Horace Greeley, *Overland Journey from New York to San Francisco in the Summer of 1859* (New York: C. M. Sexton, Baker, 1860); Henry Villard, *The Past and Present of the Pikes Peak Gold Regions* (St. Louis, MO: Sutherland & McEvoy, 1860); and Albert D. Richardson, *Beyond the Mississippi* (Hartford, CT: American Publishing, 1867), provided eyewitness chronicles of the gold rush. Other primary accounts include Libeus Barney, *Letters of the Pikes Peak Gold Rush* (San Jose, CA: Talisman Press, 1959), and the recollections of William Henry Harrison Larimer, *Reminiscences of General William Larimer and His Son William H.H. Larimer* (Lancaster, PA: New Era Printing, 1918). Nolie Mumey, *History of the Early Settlements of Denver (1599–1860)* (Glendale, CA: Arthur H. Clark, 1942), provides many tidbits of Denver history, a list of firsts, and a bibliography.

Halka Chronic covers geology in *Roadside Geology of Colorado* (Missoula, MT: Mountain Press Publishing, 1980). Glenn R. Scott has created a map, clear to nongeologists: *Map Showing Some Points of Geologic Interest in the Morrison Quadrangle, Jefferson County, Colorado* (Washington, D.C.: U.S. Geological Survey, 1972).

Notes

1. LeRoy Hafen, *Colorado Gold Rush, Contemporary Letters and Reports, 1858–59* (Glendale, CA: Arthur H. Clark, 1941), p. 39.
2. Francis Parkman, *The Oregon Trail: Sketches of Prairie Life and Rocky Mountain Life* (New York: Dodd, Mead, 1964), pp. 251–56.
3. LeRoy Hafen, *Colorado and Its People*, vol. 1, pp. 64–81; Smiley, *Denver*, pp. 149–55; LeRoy Hafen, "Mountain Men — Louis Vasquez," *The Colorado Magazine* 10 (January 1933):14–22.
4. LeRoy Hafen, *Relations with the Indians of the Plains, 1857–1861* (Glendale, CA: Arthur H. Clark, 1959), p. 112. See Smiley, *Denver*, p. 229, on trails leading through Denver. Also see interview with George Tritch in the *Denver Times*, undated newspaper clipping in Dawson Scrapbook, in Colorado Historical Society Library, vol. 36, p. 21, in which he discusses trails and streets. John O. Maberry, *Map of Pioneer Trails, Stage Stops with a View in the Parker Quadrangle, Arapahoe and Douglas Counties, Colorado* (Washington, D.C.: U.S. Geological Survey, 1973), outlines trails in Denver's south suburban area.
5. LeRoy Hafen, "Cherokee Goldseekers in Colorado 1849–1850," *The Colorado Magazine* 15 (May 1938):108. The spelling and grammar of sources is erratic but has been faithfully given in all quotations. Arvadans argue about the proper way to mark the site — uncomfortably near a sewage treatment facility — of this first known gold discovery in the Denver area; see the *Arvada Sentinel*, June 23, 1983. There are reports of 1857 discoveries by Hispanos near the present intersection of Virginia Avenue and the South Platte; see Smiley, *Denver*, pp. 182, 188–89.
6. Quotation from T. C. Dickson, a member of the Russell party, in LeRoy Hafen, *Pikes Peak Gold Rush Guidebooks of 1859* (Glendale, CA: Arthur H. Clark, 1941), p. 108.
7. James H. Pierce, "With the Green Russell Party," *The Trail* 13 (May 1921):11.
8. Auraria, Georgia, which derived its name in 1833 from the Latin word for gold, was named, some sources say, by South Carolina's U.S. senator, John C. Calhoun. But E. Merton Coulter, *Auraria: The Story of a Georgia Gold-Mining Town* (Athens: University of Georgia Press, 1956), p. 8, credits John Powell, a resident of the town, with the name. After the consolidation of Denver and Auraria, Colorado, in 1860, the name was little used, although the West Denver–Auraria Historical Society helped keep it alive. It was revived in the mid-1970s as the designation for the Auraria Higher Education Complex.
9. Hafen, *Colorado and Its People* vol. 1, p. 156.
10. Pierce, "With Green Russell," p. 11.
11. Albert D. Richardson, *Beyond the Mississippi* (Hartford, CT: American Publishing, 1867), p. 185.
12. Denver (1817–1892), a captain in the Mexican War, a congressman from California, and a U.S. commissioner of Indian Affairs before becoming governor of Kansas, became a brigadier general in the Civil War and practiced law after the war. He was succeeded in Kansas by Samuel Medary, after whom Denver might have been named had the Larimer party known of the change. Smiley, *Denver*, pp. 226, 447–48, discusses street names. Benjamin P. Draper, "City Ordinance #57 Series of 1873 . . . Changing the Name of Certain Streets" (2 vols.; typescript in DPLWHD), is an excellent compilation of street names.
13. Smiley, *Denver*, p. 246.
14. Hafen, *Colorado and Its People*, vol. 1, p. 161.
15. Edith Eudora Kohl, *Denver's First Christmas* (Denver: A. B. Hirschfeld Press, 1944). Besides the Nolie Mumey biography, *James Pierson Beckwourth, 1856–1866, An Enigmatic Figure of the West: A History of the Later Years of His Life* (Denver: Fred A. Rosenstock, 1957), other treatments of Beckwourth include John E. Sunder, *Jim Beckwourth: Mountain Man* (Norman: University of Oklahoma Press, 1959). On Baker, see Nolie Mumey, *The Life of Jim Baker, 1818–1898* (Denver: World Press, 1931). Wootton is covered in LeRoy Hafen, *The Mountain Men and the Fur Trade of the Far West*, 10 vols. (Glendale, CA: Arthur H. Clark, 1965–1972), vol. 3, pp. 397–411; Baker in vol. 3, pp. 39–47; and Beckwourth in vol. 6, pp. 37–61. Wootton's autobiography appeared first in 1889. See Howard L. Conrad, *Uncle Dick Wootton* (Lincoln: University of Nebraska Press, 1980). Photographs of Baker provided the inspiration for the hunter at the base of the Pioneer Monument (Colfax and Broadway) sculpted by Frederick MacMonnies. Christopher "Kit" Carson, who stands atop the monument, had little to do with Denver, but citizens, rallied by the local artist John Dare "Jack" Howland, preferred Carson to the Native American statue that MacMonnies had proposed. The monument's dedication on June 24, 1911, was attended by Oliver P. Wiggins, a mountain man and pioneer of 1858. See Nolie Mumey, *The Pioneer Monument* (Denver: Denver Board of Realtors, 1955).
16. Mumey, *Baker*, p. 154.
17. Hafen, *Pikes Peak Guidebooks*, p. 121, from Tierney's guide.
18. For a contemporary observer's barbed comments on gold camp fever, see Philip S. Foner, *Mark Twain, Social Critic* (New York: International Publishers, 1966), p. 210.
19. Hafen, *Pikes Peak Guidebooks*, p. 169, from William B. Parsons's guide. See also James F. Willard, "Sidelights into the Pike's Peak Gold Rush, 1858–59," *The Colorado Magazine* 12 (January 1935):3–13.
20. *RMN*, June 11, 1859, quoted in Hafen, *Colorado Gold Rush*, p. 382.
21. Hafen, *Pikes Peak Guidebooks*, p. 121, from Tierney's guide.
22. William Byers, "History of Colorado, 1884" (manuscript in Bancroft Library, University of California, Berkeley), p. 4.
23. Lawrence N. Greenleaf, "Pikes Peakers of 59," in *King Sham and Other Atrocities in Verse* (New York: Hurd & Houghton, 1868), p. 61.

24. Horace Greeley, *Overland Journey from New York to San Francisco in the Summer of 1859* (New York: C. M. Sexton, Baker, 1860), p. 114.
25. Hafen, *Colorado and Its People*, vol. 1, p. 174.

CHAPTER 2: Native Americans

Sources

J. Donald Hughes, *American Indians in Colorado* (Boulder, CO: Pruett Publishing, 1976) provides a good overview and extensive bibliography. The most comprehensive work on Colorado's prehistoric peoples is E. Steve Cassells, *The Archaeology of Colorado* (Boulder, CO: Johnson Publishing, 1983). The Colorado Archaeological Society's magazine, *Southwestern Lore*, keeps readers abreast of area discoveries.

On the Arapahos, see Virginia C. Trenholm, *The Arapahoes, Our People* (Norman: University of Oklahoma Press, 1970), and Margaret Coel, *Chief Left Hand: Southern Arapaho* (Norman: University of Oklahoma Press, 1981). George Bird Grinnell, *The Fighting Cheyennes* (Norman: University of Oklahoma Press, 1956), attempts to provide the Native American point of view. Also see Donald J. Berthong's solid *The Southern Cheyennes* (Norman: University of Oklahoma Press, 1963). Extensive Sand Creek literature includes the massive treatment by Gary L. Roberts, "Sand Creek: Tragedy and Symbol" (Ph.D. diss., University of Oklahoma, Norman, 1984), and Stan Hoig's popular work, *The Sand Creek Massacre* (Norman: University of Oklahoma Press, 1961). Marshall Sprague has provided a readable account of the Utes in *Massacre: The Tragedy at White River* (New York: Little, Brown, 1957).

Notes

1. Patricia N. Limerick, *The Legacy of Conquest: The Unbroken Past of the American West* (New York: W. W. Norton, 1987), pp. 27–28.
2. Nolie Mumey, *James Pierson Beckwourth, 1856–1866, An Enigmatic Figure of the West: A History of the Later Years of His Life* (Denver: Fred A. Rosenstock, 1957), p. 151.
3. Helen Hunt Jackson, *A Century of Dishonor: A Sketch of the United States Government's Dealings with Some of the Indian Tribes* (Originally published 1881; reprint Boston: Little, Brown, 1905), p. 345; *Rocky Mountain Herald*, November 15, 1947.
4. *RMN*, December 17, 1864.
5. James Rancier, Gary Haynes, and Dennis Stanford report on Lamb Spring in "1981 Investigations of Lamb Spring," *Southwestern Lore* 48 (June 1982):1–17. For a list of sites see William P. Butler, "Eastern Colorado Radiocarbon Dates," *Southwestern Lore* 47 (September 1981):12–13. Digs near Denver are detailed by Cynthia and Henry J. Irwin-Williams in *Excavations at Magic Mountain* (Denver: Denver Museum of Natural History, 1966) and *Excavations at the Lo Dais Ka Site* (Denver: Denver Museum of Natural History, 1959). The Dent discoveries initially suggested a connection between people and mammoth in North America, but some archaeologists now doubt that Dent was a mammoth kill site. Projectile points from Dent are known as Clovis points, after similar weapons found near Clovis, New Mexico. They are older than the more famous Folsom points that were unearthed near Folsom, New Mexico, in 1926 by Jesse D. Figgins of the Denver Museum of Natural History.
6. LeRoy Hafen, *Colorado and Its People*, vol. 1, pp. 133–34, gives a short account of the 1851 Fort Laramie treaty. The fort, now a living museum and National Historical Monument, is in southeastern Wyoming. Ray Allen Billington, *Westward Expansion: A History of the American Frontier* (New York: Macmillan, 1974), p. 565, reveals the divide and conquer aspects of U.S. strategy. In "Who Have the Power," *The Colorado Magazine* 16 (January 1939):1–11, Robert Stearns, then dean of the University of Colorado Law School, argued that the Fort Laramie treaty was not ratified and hence not binding on the United States.
7. Hafen, *Colorado and Its People*, vol. 1, p. 133.
8. LeRoy Hafen, *Pikes Peak Gold Rush Guidebooks of 1859* (Glendale, CA: Arthur H. Clark, 1941), p. 325.
9. Albert D. Richardson, *Beyond the Mississippi* (Hartford, CT: American Publishing, 1867), p. 185.
10. *RMN*, April 18, 1860, quoted in Mumey, *Beckwourth*, pp. 150–51.
11. Horace Greeley, *An Overland Journey from New York to San Francisco in the Summer of 1859* (New York: C. M. Sexton, Baker, 1860), p. 15.
12. John Stands in Timber, et al., *Cheyenne Memories* (New Haven, CT: Yale University Press, 1967), p. 40. Peter Powell, *Sweet Medicine: The Continuing Role of the Sacred Arrow, the Sun Dance, and the Buffalo Hat in Northern Cheyenne History*, 2 vols. (Norman: University of Oklahoma Press, 1969), doubts that Sweet Medicine was a real person.
13. Smiley, *Denver*, p. 204, cites Frank Cobb: "Smith and McGaa were squaw men . . . we took them in on account of the land belonging to the Indians." For Smith's career see Stan Hoig, *The Western Odyssey of John Simpson Smith* (Glendale, CA: Arthur H. Clark, 1974).
14. William D. Unrau, "A Prelude to War," *The Colorado Magazine* 51 (October 1954):299–313, discusses the Treaty of Fort Wise. Albert G. Boone's papers (Colorado Historical Society) reveal that the federal government refused to reimburse him for the money he spent to get the treaty. George Bird Grinnell, *The Fighting Cheyennes* (Norman: University of Oklahoma Press, 1956), p. 126, says that Little Raven, an Arapaho chief, did not know what he was signing when he agreed to the Fort Wise Treaty. The validity of Denver property titles rests in part on this treaty, but there were also subsequent agreements — Little Arkansas (1865) and Medicine Lodge (1867).
15. "Interview with John Evans 1884" (manuscript in the Bancroft Library, University of California, Berkeley), p. 11 (hereafter Evans interview).

16. George Hyde, *Life of George Bent Written from His Letters*, ed. Savoie Lottinville (Norman: University of Oklahoma Press, 1983), p. 119.
17. Stan Hoig, *The Sand Creek Massacre* (Norman: University of Oklahoma Press, 1961), p. 35.
18. Jackson, *Century of Dishonor*, p. 348.
19. Susan Riley Ashley, "Reminiscences of Colorado in the Early Sixties," *The Colorado Magazine* 13 (November 1936):219–30.
20. Kassler to Stebbins, October 19, 1864, in Philip Alexander, "George W. Kassler: Colorado Pioneer" (2 vols.; typescript in DPLWHD), vol. 1, p. 43.
21. Donald F. Danker, ed., *Mollie: The Journal of Mollie Dorsey Sanford in Nebraska and Colorado Territories 1857–1866* (Lincoln: University of Nebraska Press, 1959), p. 189.
22. Reginald S. Craig, *The Fighting Parson, the Biography of Colonel John M. Chivington* (Los Angeles: Westernlore Press, 1959), takes a favorable view of Chivington. Dee Brown, *Bury My Heart at Wounded Knee* (New York: Holt, Rinehart & Winston, 1970), does not. Michael A. Siever's "Sands of Sand Creek Historiography," *The Colorado Magazine* 49 (Spring 1972):116–42, sorts through many of the conflicting interpretations. Raymond G. Carey, "The 'Bloodless Third' Regiment," *The Colorado Magazine* (October 1961):275–301, presents details not found elsewhere. The attribution of "muscular Christianity" is from Samuel Elbert, in Benjamin P. Draper, "Manuscripts in the Bancroft Library Relating to Colorado" (manuscript in DPLWHD reproducing interviews in the Bancroft Library, University of California, Berkeley), vol. 1, "John Chivington" (hereafter Draper, Bancroft manuscripts).
23. Hoig, *Sand Creek Massacre*, p. 112.
24. Ibid., p. 149.
25. *RMN*, December 12, 1864, quoted in Hoig, *Sand Creek Massacre*, p. 162. Estimates of the number killed are given in U.S. Congress, *Report of the Joint Committee on the Conduct of the War at the 2nd Session of the 38th Congress* (Washington, D.C.: GPO, 1865).
26. Hoig, *Sand Creek Massacre*, p. 161.
27. Ibid., p. 164.
28. Ibid., pp. 166–68.
29. C. A. Prentice's "Captain Silas S. Soule, A Pioneer Martyr," *The Colorado Magazine* 12 (November 1935):224–28, tells of Soule's association with abolitionist John Brown. One of the last soldiers to die during the Civil War in Colorado, Soule's name is inscribed on a plaque on the Civil War Monument (pedestal by Frank Edbrooke; statue of soldier, completed 1909, by Denver artist John Howland [1843–1914]) on the west side of the State Capitol).
30. Mumey, *Beckwourth*, p. 137.
31. Clara V. Witter, "Pioneer Life" (typescript in DPLWHD), p. 11.
32. Buffalo Bill died at 2932 Lafayette, Denver, on January 10, 1917, and is buried on Lookout Mountain overlooking the city. He has been the subject of numerous biographies, the best of which is Don Russell's *The Lives and Legends of Buffalo Bill* (Norman: University of Oklahoma Press, 1960). Richard Weingart, *Sound the Charge* (Englewood, CO: Jacqueline Enterprises, 1978) treats Summit Springs.
33. Marshall Sprague, *Massacre: The Tragedy at White River* (New York: Little, Brown, 1957), p. 96.
34. Chivington (1821–1894) left Denver in 1867, returning in 1883. He became an Arapahoe County undersheriff and, in 1891, county coroner. Denverites continued to debate Sand Creek. William Gilpin later said: "I never approved of [Sand Creek. Chivington] had a certain section of the people with him but it was a very extraordinary race of people congregated here at that particular time." See Bancroft manuscripts, vol. 2, "William Gilpin," p. 6. As late as 1941, the city considered naming an east Denver street after Chivington. Lee Casey of the *Rocky Mountain News* objected in an editorial titled "Honor Murder," *RMN*, January 26, 1941. Mayfair Drive was, instead, renamed Hale Parkway for General Irving Hale, another Denverite, who had helped take the Philippines from Spain in the Spanish-American War. On the objections raised by Native Americans to calling Sand Creek a "battle," see *DP*, March 10, 1985.
35. Evans interview, p. 20.

CHAPTER 3: Town Building

Sources

Visitors found frontier Denver an interesting place. James Rusling, *Across America* (New York: Sheldon, 1874), wrote favorably of Denver, but William Hepworth Dixon, *New America* (Philadelphia: J. P. Lippincott, 1867), did not. Smiley, *Denver*, p. 431, says that Dixon was hoodwinked into thinking badly of Denver by an acquaintance who told tall tales. However, Denver did have many saloons. See Thomas J. Noel, *The City and the Saloon: Denver 1858–1916* (Lincoln: University of Nebraska Press, 1982). A kinder account than Dixon's is presented by Bayard Taylor in *Colorado: A Summer Trip* (1867) edited by William W. Savage, Jr., and James H. Lazalier (Niwot: University Press of Colorado, 1989).

Denverites fondly remembered the 1860s. Samuel Kline, *Recollections and Comments* (Chicago: Tony Rubovits, 1924), devotes nearly 80 pages to Denver. Also meaty is Clara V. Witter, "Pioneer Life" (typescript in DPLWHD), and Philip Alexander, "George W. Kassler: Colorado Pioneer" (2 vols.; typescript in DPLWHD). *The Colorado Magazine*, for over 50 years the principal scholarly periodical covering Coloradan history, ran articles on pioneers, including recollections, as did its predecessor, *The Trail*. On Jefferson Territory, see J. L. Frazier, "Prologue to Colorado Territory," *The Colorado Magazine* 38 (July 1961):161–74. Frazier also compiled "Civil War Bibliography," *The Colorado Magazine* 38 (January 1961): 65–69. Colorado's minor part in the Civil War has been detailed in Ovando Hollister, *Boldly They Rode* (1863; Reprint Lakewood, CO: Golden Press, 1949), and in William C. Whitford, *Colorado Volunteers in the Civil War: The New Mexico Campaign in 1862* (Denver: State Historical & Natural History Society, 1908).

Religion is surveyed by Louisa Arps, ed., *Faith on the Frontier* (Denver: Colorado Council of Churches, 1963). Allen Breck tells of Episcopalians in *The Episcopal Church in Colorado, 1860–1963* (Denver: Big Mountain Press, 1963) and of Jews in *A Centennial History of the Jews in Colorado, 1859–1959* (Denver: A. B. Hirschfeld Press, 1961). William H. Jones, *The History of Catholic Education in the State of Colorado* (Washington, D.C.: Catholic University of America Press, 1955), details much Roman Catholic history as does Thomas J. Noel in *Colorado Catholicism: The Archdiocese of Denver* (Niwot: University Press of Colorado, 1989). A wealth of material is in the Iliff School of Theology's library, University of Denver.

Bill Brenneman, *Miracle on Cherry Creek* (Denver: World Press, 1973), takes a microscopic look, with emphasis on the 1860s, at a section of lower downtown Denver. Gunther Barth also highlights Denver's first decade in *Instant Cities: Urbanization and the Rise of Denver and San Francisco* (New York: Oxford University Press, 1975), one of the few works to put Denver in the larger context of urban history. Peter R. Decker, *Fortunes and Failures: White Collar Mobility in Nineteenth-Century San Francisco* (Cambridge, MA.: Harvard University Press, 1978), employs statistical analysis to fathom changes in San Francisco.

Notes
1. See William Hepworth Dixon, *New America* (Philadelphia: J. P. Lippincott, 1867), pp. 95–96, for this and subsequent Dixon quotations.
2. *RMN*, May 16, 1864, quoted in Nolie Mumey, *James Pierson Beckwourth, 1856–1866, An Enigmatic Figure of the West: A History of the Later Years of His Life* (Denver: Fred A. Rosenstock, 1957), p. 113.
3. *RMN*, November 24, 1859, quoted in Perkin, *First Hundred Years*, p. 174.
4. Bancroft manuscripts, vol. 2, "William Gilpin" (manuscript in DPLWHD), p. 7.
5. Colorado Territory, *General Laws . . . First Session of the Legislative Assembly* (Denver: Thomas Gibson, 1861), pp. 297–300.
6. The meager vote of 149 for merger and 36 against indicates both a small population and lack of civic interest in early 1860; see Smiley, *Denver*, p. 324.
7. Moore, Denver's mayor during part of the Jefferson Territory period, was elected December 19, 1859. Because he apparently did little, and since Jefferson Territory was of dubious legality, some prefer to count Charles A. Cook, elected November 18, 1861, under the authority of Colorado Territory, as Denver's first mayor. See Perkin, *First Hundred Years*, p. 225. Denver's pre-1876 mayors are covered by Richard Fusick, "A History of the Mayors of Denver, 1859–1876" (M.A. thesis, University of Denver, 1977). One early mayor has received special treatment by Richard Hong Fee Lee in "Milton Minor Delano: Denver Pioneer and United States Consul at Foochow, China, 1869–1880" (M.A. thesis, University of Colorado, Boulder, 1952).
8. Bancroft manuscripts, vol. 2, "William Gilpin," p. 5.
9. A marker at West Eighth Avenue and Vallejo Street designates what was the southwest corner of Camp Weld. After the 1864 flood the camp housed dislocated persons; perhaps this explains why another camp, Evans, was set up to shelter the Third Regiment. Weld was largely destroyed by fire in 1865.
10. As the Confederates retreated, they buried some of their cannons to keep them out of Union hands. Thirty-three years later, the guns were dug up and given to Colorado.
11. William Byers, "History of Colorado" (manuscript in the Bancroft Library, University of California, Berkeley), p. 20, said Gilpin was "a peculiar man." Gilpin (1813–1894), a graduate of West Point, visited Colorado as a member of Fremont's 1843–1844 expedition. After leaving the governorship, he stayed in Denver promoting his landholdings in southern Colorado and New Mexico and dreaming of a railroad from Alaska to Peru through Denver.
12. Harry Kelsey, *Frontier Capitalist: The Life of John Evans* (Boulder, CO: Pruett Press, 1969), p. 121.
13. Ibid., p. 121.
14. John Nicolay, "Notebook . . . Trip to the Rocky Mountains — Summer of 1863," Nicolay Papers, box 1, Library of Congress, Washington, D.C.
15. Smiley, *Denver*, p. 369. James Rusling, *Across America* (New York: Sheldon, 1874), p. 60, said that in 1866 Denver had "scarcely a tree or shrub." The dandelion story was told to the authors by Caroline Bancroft (1900–1986), journalist, historian, and granddaughter of Doctor Bancroft.
16. *RMN*, June 8, 1863.
17. Gunther Barth, *Instant Cities: Urbanization and the Rise of Denver and San Francisco* (New York: Oxford University Press, 1975), p. 129.
18. Quoted in Duane A. Smith, *The Birth of Colorado: A Civil War Perspective* (Norman: University of Oklahoma Press, 1989), p. 234.
19. Kassler to Stebbins, May 23, 1864, in Alexander, "George W. Kassler," vol. 1, p. 39.
20. Perkin, *First Hundred Years*, pp. 212–19, reprints Goldrick's description of the flood, which first appeared in Denver's *Daily Commonwealth and Republican*, a rival of the *News*. Perkin calls Goldrick's purple prose "the most famous news article in the annals of Denver journalism."
21. There was a special territorial census in 1866; see Smiley, *Denver*, p. 430.
22. Nolie Mumey, *The Life of Jim Baker, 1818–1898* (Denver: World Press, 1931), p. 159.
23. Smiley, *Denver*, p. 303.
24. *Thayer's Map of Denver 1872* (Denver: Thayer & Stubbs, 1872).
25. Bancroft manuscripts, "Wilbur F. Stone."

26. Credit rating for D. H. Moffat, Jr., in R. G. Dun & Company, "Credit Ratings for Colorado Territory," ledger in the Baker Business Library, Harvard University, Cambridge, MA.
27. Noting the prevalent but often ignored funding of westward expansion, Joe B. Frantz, *Aspects of the American West* (College Station: Texas A&M Press, 1976), p. 81, writes: "But the truth is that from start to finish [the Westerner] was subsidized from his brogans to his sombrero."
28. Witter, "Pioneer Life," p. 11. Colfax became vice-president of the United States in 1869 but, touched by scandal, did not run again. One of Denver's principal avenues was named for this politician who visited the town in 1865, when tickets for a ball in his honor went for $16 a person, and again in 1868 and 1873.
29. In his foreword to Barth's *Instant Cities* historian Richard C. Wade notes that between 1870 and 1890 Denver was the fastest-growing city in the United States.
30. Rusling, *Across America*, p. 61, was one of the first to recognize the power elite in Denver: "As gold had been first discovered here, it got the start, and bade fair to maintain its supremacy. The sharpest and the shrewdest men in Colorado, we found were all settled here."
31. Denverites celebrated the end of the Civil War by placing candles in their windows in homemade tin candle holders and by hanging an effigy of Confederate president Jefferson Davis "at which passerbys took shots." See Samuel Kline, *Recollections and Comments* (Chicago: Tony Rubovits, 1924), pp. 33–34.

CHAPTER 4: A Spiderweb of Steel

Sources

For a broad overview of western stagecoaching and railroading, see Oscar O. Winther, *The Transportation Frontier: Trans-Mississippi West, 1865–1890* (New York: Holt, Rinehart & Winston, 1964). There is no summary or definitive source on Denver, Colorado, or Rocky Mountain stagecoaching. Most useful for Denver is Margaret Long, *The Smoky Hill Trail: Following the Old Historic Trails on Modern Highways* (Denver: W. H. Kistler Stationery, 1947). She carefully traces not only the three branches of the Smoky Hill Trail but also the various stage routes into Denver, including the Leavenworth and Pike's Peak, Overland Trail, and Butterfield Overland Dispatch. Another valuable study is Frank A. Root, *Overland Stage to California* (Topeka, KS: Frank A. Root, 1901).

At least 200 books and booklets track Colorado railroads. For an overview see D&RG Chief Engineer Arthur Ridgway's erudite section on "Transportation," in James H. Baker and LeRoy R. Hafen, eds., *History of Colorado*, 5 vols. (Denver: Linderman, 1927), vol. 2; and Herbert O. Brayer, "History of Colorado Railroads," in Hafen, *Colorado and Its People*, vol. 2. Tivis E. Wilkins, *Colorado Railroads: Chronological Development* (Boulder, CO: Pruett Publishing, 1974), provides a most useful, year-by-year, line-by-line list of constructions and abandonments. Much railroad promotional literature survives and some has been reprinted. See, for example, the D&RG's monthly, *The Railroad Redbook*. For a stimulating look at how railroads shaped the environment, popular culture, and even childhood, see John R. Stilgoe, *Metropolitan Corridor* (New Haven, CT: Yale University Press, 1983).

Two dozen books on the D&RG range from Robert G. Athearn's scholarly, company-sponsored, *Rebel of the Rockies* (1962; Reprint Lincoln: University of Nebraska Press, 1977) to Lucius Beebe's raucous *Rio Grande: Mainline of the Rockies* (Berkeley, CA: Berkeley-Howell, 1962). On Denver's first railroads see George L. Anderson, *Kansas West* (San Marino, CA: Golden West Books, 1963) and Thomas J. Noel, "All Hail the Denver Pacific," *The Colorado Magazine* 50 (Spring 1973):91–116. Mac Poor's classic *Denver, South Park & Pacific* and its *Pictorial Supplement* (Denver: Rocky Mountain Railroad Club, 1949 and 1959) has become a model for rail biographers. Kenton Forest and Charles Albi provide detail and pictorial splendor in *Denver's Railroads: The Story of Union Station and the Railroads of Denver* (Golden, CO: Colorado Railroad Museum, 1981). Also see Richard C. Overton, *Gulf to the Rockies: The Heritage of the Fort Worth and Denver-Colorado [sic] and Southern Railways* (Austin: University of Texas Press, 1953).

Anyone wishing to spend a weekend following the old rail grades should consult Robert M. Ormes, *Tracking Ghost Railroads in Colorado* (Colorado Springs, CO: Century One Press, 1975). Rail buffs also enjoy the Colorado Railroad Museum, founded in Golden in 1949, a two-acre shrine of railroadiana that maintains an excellent research library, issues lavishly illustrated, diligently researched publications, and conducts steam train excursions.

Notes

1. Henry Adams, *The Education of Henry Adams* (Boston: Houghton Mifflin, 1918), p. 240.
2. LeRoy Hafen, *The Overland Mail* (Cleveland, OH: Arthur H. Clark, 1926), p. 153. Alexander Majors, one of the owners of the Leavenworth and Pike's Peak, forbade swearing and gave Bibles to each of his drivers, hoping to improve their image.
3. Henry P. Walker, *The Wagonmasters* (Norman: University of Oklahoma Press, 1969), p. 185.
4. Noel, *The City and the Saloon: Denver 1858–1916*, (Lincoln: University of Nebraska Press, 1982), p. 87. Residents of Market Street above Twenty-third and below (west) of Cherry Creek, wary of Market's red light reputation, had those portions renamed Walnut Street.
5. Fremont quoted in William H. Goetzman, *Exploration and Empire: The Explorer and Scientist in the Winning of the American West* (New York: Vintage Books, 1966), p. 270; Smiley, *Denver*, p. 582.
6. *Cheyenne Daily Leader*, September 24, 1867.
7. *RMN*, November 20, 1867.
8. Noel, "All Hail the Denver Pacific," *The Colorado Magazine* 50 (Spring 1973):106–7.
9. *RMN*, December 4, 1867, quoting the Central City *Colorado Times*.

10. Generous federal land grants to both the Kansas Pacific and the Denver Pacific explain why so many Denver-area property records begin with titles in the name of these railroads.
11. This account of the variously told silver spike story is from Helen S. Digerness, "Jesse Summers Randall and Pioneer Georgetown," *The Colorado Magazine* 22 (November 1945):263.
12. *RMN*, April 22, 1934.
13. Colorado Historical Society, *The Georgetown Loop: A Capsule History and Guide* (Denver: Colorado Historical Society, 1986). Scrapped during the 1940s for a few hundred dollars, the Georgetown Loop was reconstructed as a tourist attraction in 1984 by the Colorado Historical Society for $1 million.
14. Mac Poor, *Denver, South Park & Pacific* (Denver: Rocky Mountain Railroad Club, 1949), p. 121; Sam Arnold, *The View from Mt. Morrison: The Story of a Colorado Town* (Denver: Fur Press, 1974).
15. Poor, *Denver, South Park & Pacific*, p. 443.
16. Denver's far-reaching influence is reflected in the fact that founders of Grand Junction for a time called their town Denver West.
17. Denver Chamber of Commerce, *Seventh Annual Report* (Denver: News Printing, 1890), p. 33, shows that Denver's three smelting and refining companies accounted for $17,305,189 (slightly over half) of the city's 1889 manufacturing production.
18. See "Comparative Chart of Mineral Production in Colorado from 1858–1943," in Hafen, *Colorado and Its People*, vol. 2, p. 691; and Salma A. Waters, ed., *Colorado Year Book, 1962–1964* (Denver: Colorado State Planning Division, 1964), p. 550.
19. Denver Chamber of Commerce, *Seventh Annual Report*, p. 33, lists flour mills and breweries as the second- and third-largest manufacturers in Denver. Livestock, listed on p. 34, had the city's eighth-largest sales for an industry, $3,378,000 in 1889.
20. L. W. Canady, "On the Summit," *Great Divide* 10 (November 1893):61, cited in M. James Kedro, "Literary Boosterism," *The Colorado Magazine* 52 (Summer 1975):207. See also *Rhymes of the Rockies; or, What the Poets Have Found to Say of the Beautiful Scenery on the Denver & Rio Grande Railroad* (Chicago: Poole Brothers, 1899).
21. William C. Ferril, "Scrapbook" vol. 4, p. 62, in DPLWHD. Flies were another import, according to Wolfe Londoner, quoted in *DP*, November 24, 1911.

CHAPTER 5: The Braggart City

Sources

Denverites avidly promoted their city during the 1880s. Useful, if not always accurate, are the publications of the Denver Chamber of Commerce and Board of Trade. Books of photographs such as *Denver Illustrated* (Denver: Pictorial Bureau of the Press, 1887) graphically demonstrate that the boasts were not without substance.

Tourists, normally more candid than the promoters, were more impressed with Colorado's mountains than with Denver. Isabella Bird, a rare, lone woman traveler, wrote the perceptive *A Lady's Life in the Rocky Mountains* (1874; Reprint New York: Ballantine Books, 1973). Like Bird, Jules Leclercq, a Frenchman, offered critical appraisal in his *Une été en Amérique, de l'Atlantique aux Montagnes Rocheuses* (Paris: E. Plon, 1877). More substantial than most accounts is William H. Thayer, *Marvels of the New West* (Norwich, CT: Henry Bill Publishing, 1887). Also useful are John H. Tice, *Over the Plains and on the Mountains* (St. Louis, MO: Industrial Age Printing, 1872); Mary E. Blake, *On the Wing: Rambling Notes of a Trip to the Pacific* (Boston: Lee & Shepard, 1883); and William Bickman, *From Ohio to the Rocky Mountains* (Dayton: Journal Book & Job Printing House, 1879). Bickman corrected the notion held by some easterners that Denver was in the mountains.

Recollections include Joseph Emerson Smith, "Personal Recollections of Early Denver," *The Colorado Magazine* 20 (January 1943):1–16; John W. Horner, "Boyhood Recollections," *The Colorado Magazine* 20 (September 1943):168–175; and Eddie Foy and Alvin F. Harlow, *Clowning through Life* (New York: E. P. Dutton, 1928).

Historians Gene M. Gressley, Clark Spence, W. Turrentine Jackson, and Rodman Paul have published major studies treating eastern investment in the West. Focusing on Colorado are Joseph E. King, *A Mine to Make a Mine: Financing the Colorado Mining Industry, 1859–1902* (College Station: Texas A&M Press, 1972); Alfred P. Tischendorf, "British Investment in Colorado Mines," *The Colorado Magazine* 30 (October 1953):241–46; and Paul, "Colorado as a Pioneer of Science in the Mining West," *Mississippi Valley Historical Review* 47 (June 1960):34–50. The mining engineer Thomas Rickard wrote several books, including *Retrospect: An Autobiography* (New York: McGraw Hill, 1937). Ore processing and smelter kings are well covered by James E. Fell, Jr., in *Ores to Metals: The Rocky Mountain Smelting Industry* (Lincoln: University of Nebraska Press, 1979). The long-lived Henry Porter is covered in an as-yet-unpublished biography by Mark Foster, which he generously allowed us to read.

Louisa Arps dips into water in *Denver in Slices* (Denver: Sage Books, 1959), but for a complete inundation one should dive into Earl L. Moseley, "History of the Denver Water System" (2 vols.; typescript in DPLWHD). Gretchen Claman, "The Typhoid Fever Epidemic and the Power of the Press in Denver in 1879," *The Colorado Magazine* 56 (Summer–Fall 1979):143–60, considers the interplay among publicity, politics, and disease. Also see Robert M. Shikes, M.D., *Rocky Mountain Medicine: Doctors, Drugs and Disease in Early Colorado* (Boulder, CO: Johnson Publishing, 1986). For the history of gas and electric utilities see Ellen Fisher, *One Hundred Years of Energy: Public Service Company of Colorado and Its Predecessors, 1869–1969* (New York: Garland Press, 1989). The story of "Ma Bell" before she became part of US West in 1983 is told in Herbert J. Hackenburg, Jr.'s lavish tome, *Muttering Machines to Laser Beams: A History of Mountain Bell* (Denver: Mountain Bell, 1986).

Notes

1. Isabella Bird, *A Lady's Life in the Rocky Mountains* (1874; Reprint New York: Ballantine Books, 1973), p. 127
2. Woodbury (1841–1903) came to Colorado in 1866 after serving as a Union captain in the Civil War. He gained influence in the

1870s as owner of the Denver *Times*, in which he suggested that Colorado be called "the Centennial state." In the 1880s he helped develop north Denver. He was buried at Riverside Cemetery. Woodbury Branch Library at 3265 Federal recalls his support of the Denver Public Library.

3. See Denver Chamber of Commerce, "Chamber Record, 1884 to 1885" (manuscript in files of the Denver Chamber of Commerce), p. 261; Denver Chamber of Commerce, *Sixth Annual Report 1888*, p. 67, *Ninth Annual Report 1891*, pp. 75, 117, and *Eleventh Annual Report 1895*, p. 28 (Denver: News Printing, 1889).

4. S. A. Gardner, "A Trip to Colorado in 1878" (typescript copy of letters to the Peoria *Evening Call* in DPLWHD), pp. 5–6.

5. Lloyd Lewis and Henry Smith, *Oscar Wilde Discovers America* (New York: Harcourt Brace, 1936), p. 281.

6. Bird, *Lady's Life*, p. 128.

7. Gardner, "Trip," p. 5.

8. John H. Tice, *Over the Plains and on the Mountains* (St. Louis, MO: Industrial Age Printing, 1872), p. 59.

9. Denver Chamber of Commerce, "Record Annual Meetings: 1886–1891" (manuscript in files of the Denver Chamber of Commerce), p. 197.

10. Duane Smith, *Horace Tabor: His Life and Legend* (Boulder: Colorado Associated University Press, 1973), p. 316.

11. Mary E. Blake, *On the Wing: Rambling Notes of a Trip to the Pacific* (Boston: Lee & Shepard, 1883), p. 39.

12. Richard R. Brettell, *Historic Denver: The Architects and the Architecture, 1858–1893* (Denver: Historic Denver, 1973), p. 35.

13. *Denver Republican*, June 18, 1882.

14. Leopold H. Guldman's Golden Eagle was Denver's cut-rate department store. Guldman's papers are at the Norlin Library, University of Colorado, Boulder.

15. *RMN*, quoted in Gretchen Claman, "The Typhoid Fever Epidemic and the Power of the Press in Denver in 1879," *The Colorado Magazine* 56 (Summer–Fall 1979):143.

16. Denver has had telegraphic service since October 10, 1863; see Thomas C. Jepsen, "The Telegraph Comes to Colorado: A New Technology and Its Consequences," *Essays and Monographs in Colorado History* 7 (1987):1–26. By 1881 there were 200 telephone subscribers.

17. John W. Horner, "Boyhood Recollections" *The Colorado Magazine* 20 (September 1943):168, notes that the bright arc lamps attracted birds that smashed into the lights and their supporting towers. Men carted the feathery remains away in wheelbarrows. By 1890 city homes boasted 50,000 electric lights. Eddie Foy, the vaudeville comic, commented that Denver was a most up-to-date city in the 1880s: "It was there that I saw my first incandescent electric light, there that I first used the telephone." See Foy and Harlow, *Clowning Through Life*, pp. 149–150.

18. Bird, *Lady's Life*, p. 169.

19. Jules Leclercq, *Une été en Amérique, de l'Atlantique aux Montagnes Rocheuses* (Paris: E. Plon, 1877), p. 246.

20. Smith Lake is now the north lake in Washington Park; Grasmere Lake, the park's shallow south lake, was a later, artificial creation. The ditch was sold to the city in 1882. Over the years it was largely covered over, but a free-flowing portion may still be seen in Washington Park where signs warn against guzzling its untreated water. The ditch terminates in City Park Lake. See Earl L. Moseley, "History of the Denver Water System" (typescript in DPLWHD), vol. 1, p. 343. One of Denver's great fortunes, that of Henry Porter, was based in part on the City Ditch, for Porter married Smith's daughter. Thayer's 1872 Denver Real Estate Map shows that the ditch benefited both Smith and Porter, who owned parcels of land along it. Smith (1815–1895) was one of Denver's leaders in the 1860s and 1870s, but as Louisa Arps, *Denver in Slices* (Denver: Sage Books, 1959), p. 72, points out, he was "eclipsed by the silver kings of the 1880s."

21. The Highline Canal, beginning south of Denver near Waterton and ending east of the Rocky Mountain Arsenal, is now 71 miles long. Nearly 60 miles of its banks are open to bikers and hikers. See *RMN*, July 10, 1983; *DP*, May 23, 1976; *Denver Times*, May 26, 1902; and James E. Sherow, "Watering the Plains," *Colorado Heritage* 4 (1988):2–13.

22. *Denver Daily Times*, November 7, 1879, quoted in Claman, "Typhoid," p. 151.

23. *RMN*, November 16, 1879, quoted in Claman, "Typhoid," p. 154.

24. Suburban water was not necessarily better than Denver's. An 1889 correspondent of the *Denver Republican* complained about the Beaver Brook Company: "Their water is pure unadulterated concentrated death." Moseley, "History of Denver Water," vol. 1, p. 309.

CHAPTER 6: Streetcar Suburbs

Sources

The best brief account of Denver's streetcars is in Smiley's *Denver*, pp. 853–70. For another side of the story see Clyde L. King, *The History of the Government of Denver with Special Reference to Its Relations with Public Service Corporations* (Denver: Fisher Book, 1911). King, a reform-minded professor of political science, offers a critical account of the rise of the Denver Tramway Company's "monopoly." Less critical of the company is Allen D. Breck, who devotes a chapter in *William Gray Evans, 1855–1924: Portrait of a Western Executive* (Denver: University of Denver History Department, 1964) to the tramway. A pictorial account is provided by William C. Jones, et al. in *Mile High Trolleys* (Boulder: Pruett Publishing, 1965).

For helpful perspectives see the analytical work of Sam Bass Warner, Jr., *Streetcar Suburbs: The Process of Growth in Boston, 1870–1900* (Cambridge, MA: Harvard University Press, 1962); Richard Sennett, *Families Against the City: Middle Class Homes of Industrial Chicago, 1872–1890* (Cambridge, MA: Harvard University Press, 1970); and Kenneth T. Jackson, *Crabgrass Frontier: The Suburbanization of the United States* (New York: Oxford University Press, 1985).

The keen interest in neighborhood history during the 1970s and 1980s has resulted in several local studies strong on illustrations and architectural history. See Don D. Etter, *Denver University Park: Four Walking Tours, 1886–1910* (Denver: Graphic Impressions, 1974); Etter's *Auraria: Where Denver Began* (Boulder: Colorado Associated University Press, 1972); William A. West and Don D. Etter, *Curtis Park: A Denver Neighborhood* (Boulder: Colorado Associated University Press, 1980); and Thomas J. Noel, *Richthofen's Montclair: A Pioneer Denver Suburb* (Boulder, CO: Pruett Publishing, 1978). Ruth E. Wiberg, *Rediscovering Northwest Denver* (Boulder, CO: Pruett Publishing, 1978), offers 212 pages on the various towns and neighborhoods now constituting northwest Denver. For a more detailed discussion of the "moral geography" behind suburbanization, see Thomas J. Noel, *The City and the Saloon; Denver 1858–1916* (Lincoln: University of Nebraska Press, 1982), pp. 67–78.

Notes
1. Smiley, *Denver*, p. 870.
2. Ibid., p. 968.
3. Richard Harding Davis, "The Heart of the Great Divide," *Harper's Weekly* (June 11, 1892):571.
4. Smiley, *Denver*, p. 854; William B. Vickers, *History of the City of Denver* (Chicago: O. L. Baskin, 1880), p. 267. Ellsworth Avenue, the dividing line between north and south street addresses in Denver, is named for the Chicagoan who became a Colorado state senator and was active in railroad as well as streetcar promotion.
5. William C. Jones et al., *Mile High Trolleys* (Boulder, CO: Pruett Publishing, 1965), p. 8.
6. Smiley, *Denver*, p. 856.
7. Allen D. Breck, *William Gray Evans 1855–1924* (Denver: University of Denver History Department, 1964), p. 111.
8. Smiley, *Denver*, pp. 865–68. Another street railway technology used briefly in Denver was the steam dummy, a steam-powered streetcar designed to look like an electric trolley. Steam dummys operated on the Denver & Berkeley Park Rapid Transit routes to northwest Denver, on the Colfax Motor Line to Aurora, and on the Denver Circle Railway to South Denver and University Park.
9. Ibid., p. 860.
10. Ibid., p. 918.
11. Clyde L. King, *The History of the Government of Denver . . .* (Denver: Fisher Book, 1911), p. 196.
12. Larry Betz, *Globeville: Part of Colorado's History* (Denver: Larry Betz, 1972).
13. This and other quotations on Park Hill are from *The Road to Downington: Denver's Most Beautiful Residence Section* (Denver: n.p., c. 1907), pp. 5, 6, 13.
14. Thomas J. Noel, *Richthofen's Montclair* (Boulder, CO: Pruett Publishing, 1978), pp. 8, 7, 19.
15. J. O. Patterson, "History of South Denver," in the *Denver Eye* (undated; c. 1900).
16. *Denver Eye*, January 1, 1890.
17. *Town of Highlands: Its Progress, Prospects and Financial Condition: First Annual Report* (Highlands, CO: Highlands Chief Press, 1891), p. 10.
18. Ferril, "Scrapbook," vol. 1, p. 139.
19. Denver Tramway Company, *1923 Chart of Standard Colors*, in possession of Ed J. Haley, Denver.
20. David F. Halaas, *Fairmount and Historic Colorado* (Denver: Fairmount Cemetery Association, 1976), pp. 47–66.
21. Denver Planning Commission, *The Denver Plan*, vol. 3: *A Study for Mass Transportation* (Denver: Denver Planning Commission, 1932), p. 10.

CHAPTER 7: Growing Pains

Sources
Much material on Denver's late nineteenth-century problems is found in unpublished sources. The Police Department is exhaustively covered in Eugene Rider's "The Denver Police Department: An Administrative, Organizational, and Operational History, 1858–1905" (Ph.D. diss., University of Denver, 1971). Also see Richard Hogan, "Law and Order in Colorado, 1858–1888" (Ph.D. diss., University of Michigan, Ann Arbor, 1982); Anne Curtis Knapp, "Making an Orderly Society: Criminal Justice in Denver, Colorado, 1858–1900" (Ph.D. diss., University of California, San Diego, 1983). Mary M. Farley and Marcella E. Dillon cover the career of one of Denver's more successful police chiefs in "Farley Scrapbook: Biography of John F. Farley, 1849–1940" (typescript in DPLWHD). For a model study of city police see Roger Lane, *Policing the City: Boston, 1822–1885* (New York: Atheneum, 1971).

Edwina Fallis, *When Denver and I Were Young* (Denver: Big Mountain Press, 1956), recounts the life of a schoolgirl during the 1880s and 1890s. Fallis, who became a kindergarten teacher, has an elementary school at 6700 East Virginia Avenue named for her. Winona Graham looks at kindergartens and preschools in *First Encounters: A History of Early Childhood Education in Colorado* (Louisville, CO: Kedro Editing & Design, 1983). Martha A. Morrison, "The Denver High School, 1873–1880," *The Colorado Magazine* 15 (May 1938):109–12, tells about East High while it was still housed in the Arapahoe School. A history of West High is given by Gene E. Vervalin in *West Denver: The Story of an American High School* (Boulder, CO: EHV Publications, 1985). The massive compilation by the Denver Public Schools, "Histories of Denver Public Schools" (typescript in DPLWHD), contains accounts, varying in quality, of dozens of schools. Owen J. Goldrick's 1882 tale, "The First School in Denver," was reprinted in *The Colorado Magazine* 6 (March 1929):72–74. Additional light is shed by Thomas F. Dawson, "Colorado's First Woman School Teacher," *The Colorado Magazine* 6 (July 1929):126–31. Dexter Takesue provides information and insight in "Aaron E. Gove: Denver School Superintendent, 1874–1890" (M.A. thesis, University of Denver, 1967). Allen Zohn, "The Development of Public Education in

Denver, 1859–1902" (M.A. thesis, University of Denver, 1940), gives an overview.

On higher education see Michael McGiffert, *The Higher Learning in Colorado: An Historical Study, 1860–1940* (Denver: Sage Books, 1964); Harold Stansell, S.J., *Regis: On the Crest of the West* (Denver: Regis Educational Corporation, 1977); Frederick Allen, et al., *The University of Colorado, 1876–1976* (New York: Harcourt, Brace, Jovanovich, 1976).

Bernard Rosen, "Social Welfare in the History of Denver" (Ph.D. diss., University of Colorado, Boulder, 1976), looks at Denver's sporadic efforts to meet the needs of its poor. Also see Katherine L. Hill, "A History of Public Health in Denver" (Ph.D. diss., University of Denver, 1970); and Flora H. Hulburt, "History of the Federated Charities of Denver" (M.A. thesis, University of Denver, 1933). Harvey T. Sethman, ed., *A Century of Colorado Medicine* (Denver: Press-Monitor, 1971), delves into medical history difficult to find elsewhere.

Denver's governmental and political history is placed in a larger context by Jon C. Teaford in *The Unheralded Triumph: City Government in America, 1870–1900* (Baltimore, MD: Johns Hopkins University Press, 1984). Teaford argues that cities have been maligned, that they did many things well. Elliot West unveils Wolfe Londoner's turbulent political career in "Dirty Tricks in Denver," *The Colorado Magazine* 52 (Summer 1975):225–43. Forbes Parkhill, *The Wildness of the West* (New York: Henry Holt, 1951), gives much anecdotal information. At the opposite extreme in historical methodology is Robert Tank's statistical study, "Mobility and Occupational Structure on the Late Nineteenth Century Urban Frontier: The Case of Denver, Colorado," *Pacific Historical Review* 47 (May 1978):189–216, in which he demonstrates that many Denverites were birds of passage. Stephen J. Leonard, in "The Denver Chamber of Commerce and Board of Trade, 1884–1900" (M.A. thesis, University of Wyoming, Laramie, 1966), considers how businessmen dealt with their rapidly changing city.

Notes

1. *RMN*, July 15, 1890.
2. Ibid.
3. Daniel Pidgeon, *An Engineer's Holiday* (London: Kegan Paul, 1883), p. 127.
4. Robert Tank, "Mobility and Occupational Structure," *Pacific Historical Review* 47 (May 1978) reports that of a selected sample of Denverites taken from the 1870 census, only 37 percent were found in the city in 1880.
5. Samuel J. Kline, *Recollections and Comments* (Chicago: Tony Rubovits, 1924), p. 9.
6. Eugene Rider, "The Denver Police Department" (Ph.D. diss., University of Denver, 1971), pp. 523, 527.
7. *RMN*, February 20, 1886, quoted in ibid., p. 274.
8. Patrolman Thomas Stuck learned that the boxes could be dangerous when his prisoner overpowered him and stuck Stuck in one of the cages; see *RMN*, September 19, 1906.
9. *Denver Evening Post*, June 17, 1897, quoted in Rider, "Denver Police," pp. 455–56. Denver's newsmen were not above making up such a story.
10. Smiley, *Denver*, p. 642
11. Elsner's reminiscences are cited in Marjorie Hornbein, "Dr. John Elsner: A Colorado Pioneer," *Western States Jewish Historical Quarterly* 13 (June 1981):291–303.
12. *DP*, February 16, 1901.
13. Bernard Rosen, "Social Welfare in the History of Denver" (Ph.D. diss., University of Colorado, Boulder, 1976), p. 227.
14. *RMN*, August 11, 1884.
15. For the rhetoric of the 1889 campaign see *Denver Republican*, March 24, 26, 28, and April 1, 1889.
16. Londoner (1839–1912) believed in direct action. When councilmen disagreed with him, he urged citizens to make their wishes known. With ropes in hand they went to the City Hall, where, reputedly by threatening to lynch council members, they got their way. Londoner is buried at Fairmount Cemetery under a large boulder. See Dawson Scrapbook, Colorado Historical Society Library, vol. 59, p. 439.
17. *RMN*, April 3, 1889.
18. Rider, "Denver Police," p. 324.
19. *RMN*, February 2, 1891.
20. Denver Chamber of Commerce, "Directors' Record II, March 11, 1886" (manuscript in files of Denver Chamber of Commerce).
21. Isabella Bird, *A Lady's Life in the Rocky Mountains* (New York: Ballantine Books, 1973), p. 169.
22. Owen J. Goldrick, "The First School," *The Colorado Magazine* 6 (March 1929):72.
23. Dexter Takesue, "Aaron E. Gove" (M.A. thesis, University of Denver, 1967), p. 45.
24. Ibid., p. 99.
25. Loretto Academy, like St. Mary's run by the Sisters of Loretto, was initially a boarding high school for young ladies — many of whom came from outside Denver. It added college classes for four women in 1918. In the late 1980s the venerable institution, once known as "dollar bill hill" because of the affluence of some of its students, fell on lean times and was sold to Regis College, which in turn sold it to a Japanese college.
26. Denver Public Schools, "Histories of Denver Public Schools" (typescript in DPLWHD), Franklin High School section.
27. East High's most famous alumnus, Julius Ullman, became better known to film fans under his assumed name, Douglas Fairbanks. On his life in Denver consult Ralph Hancock and Letita Fairbanks, *Douglas Fairbanks* (New York: Henry Holt, 1953).
28. Takesue, "Aaron Gove," pp. 71, 75.
29. Edwina Fallis, *When Denver and I Were Young* (Denver: Big Mountain Press, 1956), pp. 52–53.
30. The University of Denver, founded as Colorado Seminary in 1864, faced financial problems from the start. It did not regularly operate until the 1880s. Regis, founded in 1877, was first located in Las Vegas, New Mexico. Then it moved to Morrison, a

hamlet southwest of Denver, and in 1889 completed its north Denver main building. Popularly known as the "Jesuit College," it combined high school and college operations. Colorado Woman's College, although chartered in 1888, ran into financial problems in the 1890s, so its campus was sold. It revived in the twentieth century, but in the early 1980s it again failed and was sold to the University of Denver, which transferred its Law School from downtown to CWC.

31. Harvey T. Sethman, *A Century of Colorado Medicine* (Denver: Press-Monitor, 1971), p. 156.
32. Mary M. Farley and Marcella E. Dillon, "Farley Scrapbook" (typescript in DPLWHD), p. 27.
33. L. Vernon Briggs, *Arizona and New Mexico* (Boston: n.p., 1932), p. 138.
34. *Denver Tribune-Republican*, July 28, 1886. William M. King's *Going to Meet a Man* (Niwot: University Press of Colorado, 1990) goes into detail on the Green execution.

CHAPTER 8: The Rush to Respectability

Sources

Much information on Denver society may be gleaned from biographies. Christine Whitacre, *Molly Brown: Denver's Unsinkable Lady* (Denver: Historic Denver, 1984), is the best work on the legendary social climber whose life was also popularized by Caroline Bancroft in *The Unsinkable Mrs. Brown* (Boulder, CO: Johnson Publishing, 1963). Bancroft, a keen observer of Denver's social scene, shares her knowledge in "Denver's Major Clubs," in John J. Lipsey, ed., *1962 Brand Book of the Denver Posse of the Westerners* (Boulder, CO: Johnson Publishing Co., 1963), and in *The Melodrama of Wolhurst* (Lakewood, CO: Golden Press, 1952). Bancroft's oral history interview of July 22, 1971 (OH 37, DPLWHD), is a valuable source on the Hill family.

Thomas J. Noel, *The Denver Athletic Club, 1884-1984* (Denver: Denver Athletic Club, 1983), tells of one of Denver's most durable clubs; Margaret Ekstrand and Thomas J. Noel, *The University Club of Denver, 1891–1991* (Denver: University Club, 1991), survey another venerable male bastion. Edward Ring in "Clubs of the Past," *The Colorado Magazine* 19 (July 1942):140–41, recalls lesser-known clubs, such as the Corkscrew and the Lotus. The history of the Colorado State Historical Society is carefully treated by Maxine Benson, "A Centennial Legacy," *The Colorado Magazine* 57 (1980 Annual):1–80. Frederick J. Younce catalogs the Denver Public Library's past in *The Denver Public Library: 100th Anniversary Celebration* (Denver: Denver Public Library, 1989). Denver's art scene is sketched in Mary L. Matriano's "Artists and Art Organizations in Colorado" (M.A. thesis, University of Denver, 1962).

Contemporary accounts of the elite can be found in the society columns of the newspapers, but researchers should remember that the *Denver Republican* was not always in a position to be objective because it was owned by Nathaniel Hill, Mrs. Crawford Hill's father-in-law. Agnes Leonard Hill, *The Colorado Blue Book 1892* (Denver: James R. Ives, 1892) and *Social Questions No. 2 What Makes Social Leadership* (Denver: Chain & Hardy, 1893), gives tips designed to make Denver's Maggie Browns into Louise Hills. (on women's clubs see Sources for Chapter 9).

Marshall Sprague looks at prominent tourists in *A Gallery of Dudes* (1966; reprint, Lincoln: University of Nebraska Press, 1979). Commentary on Denver's social scene is provided by Ernest Ingersoll, "The Metropolis of the Rocky Mountains," a reprint from *Scribners Magazine* (1880) in Skip Wilson, comp., *Colorado 100 Years Ago* (Albuquerque, NM: Sun Books, 1976); and by Beatrice Webb in David Shannon, ed., *Beatrice Webb's American Diary, 1898* (Madison: University of Wisconsin Press, 1963).

Edith Eudora Kohl made Denver aware of its mansions in her *Denver's Historic Mansions* (Denver: Sage Books, 1957; photographs by Orin Sealy), which appeared before developers pounded many of the proud houses into dust. Sally Davis and Betty Baldwin delve into the lives of the mansion dwellers in *Denver Dwellings and Descendants* (Denver: Sage Books, 1963). Sandra Dallas covers Denver society and architecture in *Gaslights and Gingerbread* (Denver: Sage Books, 1965) and *Cherry Creek Gothic: Victorian Architecture in Denver* (Norman: University of Oklahoma Press, 1971). Robert Roeschlaub has been given his due by Francine Haber, Kenneth R. Fuller, and David N. Wetzel in *Robert S. Roeschlaub: Artchitect of the Emerging West* (Denver: Colorado Historical Society, 1988), a well-written and beautifully illustrated book.

When Richard Brettell wrote *Historic Denver: The Architects and the Architecture, 1858–1893* (Denver: Historic Denver, Inc., 1973) many of the buildings he praised were gone. More had disappeared by the time Langdon Morris published *Denver Landmarks* (Denver: Charles W. Cleworth, 1979; photographs by Melvyn E. Schieltz), which provided a compilation of structures designated by the Denver Landmark Preservation Commission. That they had survived was due in large part to the efforts of Historic Denver, the Junior League of Denver, and the Landmark Preservation Commission, all of which helped create a massive inventory of Denver buildings; see Denver Planning Office, *Historic Building Inventory City and County of Denver* (Denver: Denver Planning Office, 1981).

Notes

1. David Shannon, ed., *Beatrice Webb's American Diary 1898* (Madison: University of Wisconsin Press, 1963), p. 110.
2. William W. Grant, *Such Is Life* (Denver: A. B. Hirschfeld Press, 1952), p. 52.
3. Albert D. Richardson, *Beyond the Mississippi* (Hartford, CT: American Publishing, 1867), p. 333.
4. Marshall Sprague, *A Gallery of Dudes* (1966; Reprint Lincoln: University of Nebraska Press, 1979), pp. 92–117.
5. Ernest Ingersoll, "The Metropolis of the Rocky Mountains," in Skip Wilson, comp., *Colorado 100 Years Ago* (Albuquerque, NM: Sun Books, 1976), p. 10.
6. Christine Whitacre, *Molly Brown* (Denver: Historic Denver, 1984), p. 22. Margaret Tobin Brown (1867–1932) was informally called Maggie during her life but is now remembered as Molly Brown because of a Broadway musical comedy, *The Unsinkable Molly Brown* (1960) starring Tammy Grimes, and a motion picture (1964) featuring Debbie Reynolds.
7. Anonymous, *Who's Who in Denver Society 1908* (Denver: W. H. Kistler, 1908), features a picture of Louise Hill as its frontispiece.

Mrs. Hill spent her declining years at the Brown Palace Hotel, dying at age 94 in 1955. Her colonial revival mansion at 969 Sherman (1906) was sold to the Town Club, which used it until 1989. In 1947 many of her treasures were auctioned including the 10-foot-long, raspberry-colored velvet cape in which she was presented to Edward VII; it brought $22.50. Nathaniel Hill died in 1900; his son Crawford in 1922. See *Denver Times*, May 24, 1900; *RMN*, June 1, 1955; Pueblo *Star Journal and Sunday Chieftain*, February 25, 1968.

8. Mark Twain [Samuel L. Clemens] and Charles Dudley Warner, *The Gilded Age: A Tale of Today*, 2 vols. (New York: Harper & Brothers, 1915), vol. 2, p. 9.
9. Caroline Bancroft, *The Melodrama of Wolhurst* (Lakewood, CO: Golden Press, 1952), pp. 7–15. For a more favorable view of Wolcott, see Lee Casey's comments in *RMN*, December 10, 1950. Wolhurst was designed by Theodore D. Boal, a flittering society architect who with his partner Frederick L. Harnois also did the Grant-Humphrey's mansion (1902) at 770 Pennsylvania and the Crawford Hill mansion. From 1906 to 1910 Wolhurst belonged to Thomas Francis Walsh, a gold king of the San Juan mountains in southwestern Colorado. His daughter, Evalyn Walsh McLean, once owner of the Hope diamond, told her family's story in *Father Struck It Rich* (Boston: Little, Brown, 1936). Walsh sold Wolhurst in 1910 to real estate tycoon Horace W. Bennett. In 1944 the Bennett family sold to Ova Elijah Stephens, also known as Smiling Charlie, who converted Wolhurst into a classy gambling casino. Many tribulations, the last a fire in 1976, destroyed the house.
10. Agnes Leonard Hill, *The Colorado Blue Book 1892* (Denver: James R. Ives, 1892), p. 28.
11. Because the Society of Colorado Pioneers would admit only those who had come to Colorado before 1861, latecomers founded the Sons of Colorado for those who arrived before 1871. In 1932 the two groups, their ranks depleted by deaths, merged. For many years Elizabeth Byers, who died at age 87 in 1920, was the cynosure of the remaining pioneers. Many of these were women such as Elizabeth Sopris, who died at 96 in 1911, and Maria Kassler, who passed away at 93 in 1932. Elizabeth Byers's son, Frank, rallied the old-timers until his death in 1937. When his sister, 83-year-old Mary Robinson, died after an automobile accident in 1940, the *Rocky Mountain News* reported her demise in detail, for she was not only William and Elizabeth Byers's daughter. She was also apparently the last of the '59ers.
12. Walt Whitman, *Specimen Days in America* (London: Walter Scott Publishing, 1887), p. 225.
13. The post office, also known as the Federal Building and the Old Customs House, was replaced in 1910 by a much more beautiful structure of Colorado yule marble at Eighteenth and Champa. The Denver Branch of the Federal Reserve Bank now occupies the site once shared by the old post office and the Tabor Opera House.
14. Richard R. Brettell, *Historic Denver* (Denver: Historic Denver, Inc., 1973), p. 180.
15. Other Edbrooke edifices include Joslin's Dry Goods at Sixteenth and Curtis, the Majestic Building at Sixteenth and Broadway, and the elegantly restored Oxford Hotel at Seventeenth and Wazee; see James Day, comp., *Our Architecture* (Denver: n.p., 1906).
16. Unidentified newspaper clipping dated August 1908 in Dawson Scrapbook (Colorado Historical Society Library), vol. 42, p. 109.
17. Maxine Benson, "A Centennial Legacy," *The Colorado Magazine* 57 (1980 Annual):3, 10.
18. Unidentified newspaper clippings in Dawson Scrapbook, vol. 42, pp. 119, 143. The Brown collection disappeared from the Denver Art Museum between 1943 and 1950, "allegedly . . . returned to his heirs"; see *Cervi's Rocky Mountain Journal*, January 27, 1972.
19. *RMN*, April 20, 1953.
20. Thomas J. Noel, *The Denver Athletic Club, 1884–1984* (Denver: Denver Athletic Club, 1983), p. 23.
21. Papers of the Fortnightly Club are at the DPLWHD.
22. *Polly Pry*, October 10, and December 5, 1903.
23. Paul de Rousiers, *American Life* (Paris: Furman-Didot, 1892), pp. 160–61.
24. Don Bloch, "The Saga of the Wandering Swede," in Erl H. Ellis, ed., *Brand Book of the Denver Posse of the Westerners for 1954* (Boulder, CO: Johnson Publishing, 1955), p. 277.
25. Shannon, *Webb's American Diary*, pp. 110–12, 121.
26. Ibid., pp. xiii–xiv.

CHAPTER 9: Women's Roles and Rights

Sources

The best starting place for women's history in Denver and Colorado is the excellent bibliographical essay by Joyce D. Goodfriend and Dona K. Flory, "Women in Colorado Before the First World War," *The Colorado Magazine* 53 (Summer 1976):201–29. The same issue includes articles on the WCTU's Cottage Home, Josephine Roche and Patience Stapleton. Minnie Reynolds Scalabrino is profiled by Dolores Plested in "Amazing Minnie: A Nineteenth Century Woman of Today," *Colorado Heritage* 1 (1984):18–27. Elinor Bluemel has written *One Hundred Years of Colorado Women* (Denver: Elinor Bluemel, 1973), and Mary DeMund looks at women doctors in *Women Physicians of Colorado* (Denver: Range Press, 1976). Also see Minnie Hall Krauser, "The Denver Women's Press Club," *The Colorado Magazine* 16 (March 1939):62–69. Wider treatments include Julie R. Jeffrey, *Frontier Women: The Trans-Mississippi West, 1840–1880* (New York: Hill & Wang, 1979); and Sandra L. Myres, *Westering Women and the Frontier Experience, 1800–1915* (Albuquerque: University of New Mexico Press, 1982). Recent scholarship is included in Susan Armitage and Elizabeth Jameson, eds., *The Women's West* (Norman: University of Oklahoma Press, 1987).

Increased interest in women's history in the 1970s and 1980s has led to at least four significant treatments of women's organizations: Carolyn J. Stefanco, "Pathways to Power: Women and Voluntary Associations in Denver, Colorado, 1876–1893" (Ph.D. diss., Duke University, Durham, NC, 1987), delves into the WCTU, the People's Tabernacle, and the suffrage movement. Other recent studies include: Mary L. Sinton's "A History of the Woman's Club of Denver: 1894–1915" (M.A. thesis, University of Denver, 1980); Gail Beaton's "The Literary and Philanthrophic Work of Six Women's Clubs in Denver, 1881–1945" (M.A. thesis, University of Colorado, Denver, 1987); and Lynda E. Dickson, "The Early Club Movement among Black Women in Denver, 1890–1925" (Ph.D. diss., University of Colorado, Boulder, 1982). This sophisticated scholarship contrasts sharply with such earlier popular works as Max Miller's *Holladay Street* (New York: New American Library, 1961), which focuses on prostitution. For a scholarly study of prostitution see Anne M. Butler, *Daughters of Joy, Sisters of Sorrow: Prostitutes in the American West, 1865–1890* (Urbana: Illinois University Press, 1985).

Anna W. Vaille and Ellis Meredith's "Women's Contribution," in James H. Baker and LeRoy Hafen, eds., *History of Colorado*, 5 vols. (Denver: Linderman, 1927), vol. 3, provides a useful summary that is updated to the 1940s by Eudochia Bell Smith, "Women," in Hafen, *Colorado and Its People*, vol. 2. Mollie Sanford's "Diary of a Pioneer Woman," in Erl H. Ellis, ed., *Brand Book of the Denver Posse for Westerners for 1954* (Boulder: Johnson Publishing, 1955), is a romanticized version of the diary that is carefully reproduced by editor Donald F. Danker in *Mollie: The Journal of Mollie Dorsey Sanford in Nebraska and Colorado* (Lincoln: University of Nebraska Press, 1959). Emily French has also enjoyed a good editor; see *Emily: The Diary of a Hard-Working Woman*, edited by Janet Lecompte (Lincoln: University of Nebraska Press, 1987). Rachel Wild Peterson remains unedited; her *The Long Lost Rachel Wild or Seeking Diamonds in the Rough* (Denver: Reed Publishing, 1905) is as rambling and as interesting as the day it was published.

Colorado's equal suffrage movement is treated by Billie Barnes Jensen in her 1959 M.A. thesis at the University of Colorado, Boulder, as well as in her "Colorado Woman Suffrage Campaigns of the 1870s," *Journal of the West* 12 (April 1973):254–71, and in her "Let the Women Vote," *The Colorado Magazine* 41 (Winter 1964):13–25. Also see John R. Morris, "The Women and Governor Waite," *The Colorado Magazine* 44 (Winter 1967):11–19. Joseph G. Brown gives a firsthand account of the struggle for women's voting rights in *The History of Equal Suffrage in Colorado, 1868–1898* (Denver: News Job Printing, 1898). The Meredith collection at the Colorado Historical Society is filled with material on women's suffrage.

More work needs to be done on childhood in early-day Colorado. Gene Fowler's *A Solo in Tom Toms* (New York: Viking Press, 1946) captures the flavor of growing up in Denver, as does Edwina Fallis in *When Denver and I Were Young* (Denver: Big Mountain Press, 1956). In a broader context the neglected role of youngsters has been illuminated in Elliott West's fine study, *Growing Up with the Country: Childhood on the Far Western Frontier* (Albuquerque: University of New Mexico Press, 1989).

Notes

1. Benjamin P. Draper, Manuscripts in the Bancroft Library Relating to Colorado (Manuscript in DPLWHD), vol. 3, p. 7, "Augusta Tabor" (hereafter "Augusta Tabor").
2. Kassler to Stebbins, March 19, 1863, in Alexander, "George W. Kassler: Colorado Pioneer," 2 vols. (typescript in DPLWHD), vol. 1 p. 25.
3. Lawrence N. Greenleaf, "Pikes Peakers of '59" in *King Sham and Other Atrocities in Verse* (New York: Hurd and Houghton, 1868), pp. 57–58.
4. Emily M. Raymond, "How I Went to Denver" (mimeograph in DPLWHD), p. 44.
5. *RMN*, August 1, 1918.
6. Clara V. Witter, "Pioneer Life" (typescript in DPLWHD), p. 9.
7. Ibid., p. 13.
8. Palmer, usually identified with Colorado Springs, was living in Denver in 1870. Data on servants is derived from U.S. Bureau of the Census, "1870 Census Arapahoe County, Colorado" (microfilm of manuscript census available from the U.S. National Archives).
9. "Augusta Tabor," vol. 3, p. 11.
10. Danker, *Mollie*, p. 137.
11. Ibid., pp. 153, 157, 192.
12. U.S. Bureau of the Census, *Special Reports: Marriage and Divorce, 1867–1906, Part II, General Tables* (Washington, D.C.: GPO, 1906), presents a wealth of data; see esp. p. 710.
13. Gene Fowler, *A Solo in Tom Toms* (New York: Viking Press, 1946), pp. 50–51.
14. Janet Lecompte, ed., *Emily: The Diary* (Lincoln: University of Nebraska Press, 1987), pp. 108–22.
15. Colorado, Bureau of Labor Statistics, *First Biennial Report* (Denver: Collier & Cleaveland, 1888), p. 335.
16. Ibid., pp. 313–69; *Second Biennial Report* (Denver: Collier & Cleaveland, 1890), pp. 29, 31; *Seventh Biennial Report* (Denver: Smith-Brooks, 1900), p. 78; *Fourteenth Biennial Report* (Denver: Smith-Brooks, 1914), pp. 142–43.
17. William C. Ferril, "Scrapbook," (in DPLWHD), vol. 1, pp. 112–14.
18. Thomas J. Noel, *The City and the Saloon: Denver 1858–1916* (Lincoln: University of Nebraska Press, 1982), p. 87.
19. Perkin, *First Hundred Years*, pp. 314–18. Byers sold his share in the *Rocky Mountain News* in 1878. Then it became a Democratic paper owned by the Golden entrepreneur William A.H. Loveland.
20. Doe to parents, March 29, 1880 (manuscript in DPLWHD). The letter is probably to Baby Doe's parents rather than to Harvey Doe's parents.
21. Elmer Ellis, *Henry Moore Teller: Defender of the West* (Caldwell, ID: Caxton Printers, 1941), p. 155.
22. *Denver Times*, August 2, 1900.
23. Edward Keating, *The Gentleman from Colorado* (Denver: Sage Books, 1964), p. 48.
24. *RMN*, January 23, 1983.

25. *Queen Bee*, January 13, 1892. At age 93, Churchill died on January 15, 1926, in Colorado Springs.
26. George Kassler to Maria Kassler, June 24 and 27, 1871, in Alexander, "Kassler," vol. 1, pp. 81–82.
27. Billie B. Jensen, "The Woman Suffrage Movement in Colorado" (M.A. thesis, University of Colorado, Boulder, 1959), p. 45.
28. Carolyn J. Stefanco, "Pathways to Power" (Ph.D. diss., Duke University, Durham, NC), pp. 95–134, details WCTU history. Stefanco notes that the WCTU was not organized as an effective group until 1880. Other sources give the year 1878.
29. See Mary L. Sinton, "A History of the Women's Club of Denver" (M.A. thesis, University of Denver, 1980), pp. 12–13, for a list of clubs.
30. *RMN*, April 15, 1894, quoted in ibid., p. 14.
31. Ibid., p. 28.
32. Stone to Meredith, June 12, 1893, in Meredith Papers, box 1, Colorado Historical Society Library.
33. *The Women's Tribune*, November 18, 1893, in ibid.
34. Anthony to Meredith, November 27, 1893, in ibid. Theater manager Peter McCourt, Baby Doe Tabor's brother, took immediate advantage of the vote. He asked women to take off their hats at the theater so that the men could see the stage. Grateful women did so.
35. Anthony to Conine, March 29, 1900, in Conine Scrapbook (in DPLWHD), p. 100.
36. *Interocean*, February 28, 1904, in Meredith Papers, box 2.
37. Unidentified clipping in Conine Scrapbook.
38. David Shannon, ed., *Beatrice Webb's American Diary, 1898* (Madison: University of Wisconsin Press, 1963), pp. 110, 120–23.

CHAPTER 10: The Depression of 1893

Sources

The Depression of 1893 in Colorado has received little attention from historians. Fortunately, there is a good treatment by Forest L. White, "Panic of 1893 in Colorado" (M.A. thesis, University of Colorado, Boulder, 1932). William A. Platt, "The Destitute in Denver," *Harper's Weekly* 27 (August 19, 1893):787–88, surveys the problems Denver faced in taking care of the unemployed. The *Commercial and Financial Chronicle* 57 (January 6, 1894):6–7, provides statistical data.

The politics of the era have been better explored than the economic and social aspects. Governor Waite is lambasted in Charles Hartzell's *A Short and Truthful History of Colorado During the Short Reign of "Davis the First"* (Denver: C. J. Kelly, 1894). Robert G. Dill's *Political Campaigns in Colorado* (Denver: Arapahoe Publishing, 1895) is another useful, contemporary view. Frank E. Day delves into the career of Lafe Pence, a one-term congressman, in "The Populist Congressman from Colorado, 1893–1895" (M.A. thesis, University of Colorado, Boulder, 1947). More recently, Colorado's Populists have received considerable attention: See James E. Wright, *The Politics of Populism: Dissent in Colorado* (New Haven, CT: Yale University Press, 1974); John R. Morris, "Davis Hanson Waite: The Ideology of a Western Populist" (Ph.D. diss., University of Colorado, Boulder, 1965), and his "Waite-Diaz Correspondence," *The Colorado Magazine* 38 (January 1961):49–53. Waite is also accorded a chapter in Richard Lamm and Duane Smith's *Pioneers and Politicians* (Boulder, CO: Pruett Publishing, 1984).

Donald L. Kinzer, *An Episode in Anti-Catholicism: The American Protective Association* (Seattle: University of Washington Press, 1964), looks at the APA on a national basis, while Carla J. Atchinson focuses on the local scene in "Nativism in Colorado Politics: The American Protective Association and the Ku Klux Klan" (M.A. thesis, University of Colorado, Boulder, 1972). The *Rocky Mountain News* provides good contemporary information on the APA, as does the Reverend Thomas Malone's paper, the *Colorado Catholic*.

Levette J. Davidson's "The Festival of Mountain and Plain," *The Colorado Magazine* 25 (July and September 1948):145–57, 203–211, covers the festival. Visitors' and boosters' literature of the 1890s includes George W. Steevens, *The Land of the Dollar* (London: William Blackwood & Sons, 1897); Emma A. Gage, *Western Wanderings and Summer Saunterings through Picturesque Colorado* (Baltimore, MD: Lord Baltimore Press, 1900); and Thomas Tonge, *Denver by Pen and Picture* (Denver: F. S. Thayer, 1898). The Tonge Collection at the Colorado Historical Society is filled with booster articles written by Tonge for English newspapers.

Notes

1. Dennis Sheedy, *The Autobiography of Dennis Sheedy* (n.p., 1922), p. 55.
2. *RMN*, June 11, 1892.
3. Robert S. Pulcipher, *We Propose to Make This One of the Permanent Institutions of Colorado . . . The First National Bank of Denver* (Denver, Robert S. Pulcipher, 1971), p. 124.
4. Samuel W. Johnson, *Autobiography of Samuel Wallace Johnson* (Denver: Big Mountain Press, 1960), p. 105.
5. Forest L. White, "Panic of 1893 in Colorado" (M.A. thesis, University of Colorado, Boulder, 1932), p. 79.
6. Ibid., p. 74; *Denver Republican*, June 13 and 15, 1894.
7. Eugene F. Rider, "The Denver Police Department: An Administrative, Organizational, and Operational History, 1858–1905" (Ph.D. diss., University of Denver, 1971), pp. 375–79; *Denver Times*, July 21, 1901.
8. Denver Trades and Labor Assembly, American Federation of Labor, *Souvenir American Federation of Labor . . . December 10, 1894* (Denver: n.p., 1894) contains Waite's "Bloody Bridles" speech.
9. *RMN*, March 16, 1894.
10. Rider, "Denver Police," p. 393.
11. Quotation from *Colorado Catholic*, March 8, 1894; see also ibid., August 18, October 8 and 20, 1894; *RMN*, October 10, 1894.

12. Unidentified article by Meredith in Meredith Papers, box 2 (in Colorado Historical Society Library).
13. *RMN*, February 12, 1899.
14. Myron W. Reed, *Temple Talks* (Indianapolis: Bowen & Merrill, 1898), p. 19.
15. *The Coloradoan*, April 1, 1893.
16. Reed, *Temple Talks*, p. 18.
17. Upton Sinclair, *The Metropolis* (New York: Moffat, Yard, 1908), p. 175.
18. "Miscellaneous Items Concerning Myron Reed," (E. A. Burton Collection, DPLWHD).
19. Clipping in Pliny F. Sharp Scrapbook (in DPLWHD), vol. 3, p. 11.
20. Rachel Wild Peterson, *The Long Lost Rachel Wild or Seeking Diamonds in the Rough* (Denver: Reed Publishing, 1905), pp. 129–30.
21. Unidentified clipping in Uzzell clippings at DPLWHD.
22. The Tabernacle, which moved to a new building at Twentieth and Lawrence in 1900, ceased operations in 1969. There have been numerous newspaper articles on Uzzell, filed under his name in the clipping collection in DPLWHD. See especially *RMN*, August 23, 1932; *The Greeley Sunday Journal*, October 16, 1966.
23. Among the good newspaper articles on Schlatter are those appearing in the *Denver Catholic Register*, August 7, 1941; in *DP* September 30, 1951; and Frances Melrose's treatment in *RMN*, April 25, 1982. Francis X. Hogan wrote a play about Schlatter titled *Denver Messiah*.
24. *Denver Times*, September 24, 1899. The festival included a rodeo until 1905.
25. Ibid., September 28, 1899.
26. Denver Chamber of Commerce and Board of Trade, *The Denver Chamber of Commerce and Board of Trade . . . 1898 Report* (Denver: Carson-Harper, 1898), p. 17.

CHAPTER 11: Economic Diversity

Sources

Data on Denver's economic progress can be found in Denver Chamber of Commerce minutes, and annual reports, and in other chamber publications such as *Home Industry Catalog 1914* (Denver: n.p., 1914) and *Survey of Denver and Colorado* (bound collection of chamber pamphlets in DPLWHD). Year-end editions of newspapers sometimes provided statistical information. See, for example, the *Rocky Mountain News* for December 31, 1899, and the *Denver Post* for December 31, 1900. Local publications often derived their data from U.S. government reports such as Bureau of the Census, *Abstract of the Census of Manufacturers, 1914* (Washington, D.C.: GPO, 1917).

Allen D. Breck's *William Gray Evans: 1855–1924: Portrait of a Western Executive* (Denver: University of Denver, History Department, 1964) and Geraldine Bean's *Charles Boettcher: A Study in Pioneer Western Enterprise* (Boulder: Westview Press, 1976) are valuable for understanding Denver's commercial development. David Moffat's career is tracked in Harold A. Boner, *The Giant's Ladder: David H. Moffat and His Railroad* (Golden: Colorado Railroad Museum, 1979), and in Steven Mehls, "David H. Moffat, Jr., Early Colorado Business Leader" (Ph.D. diss., University of Colorado, Boulder, 1982). Some of Mehls's research is published in "An Area the Size of Pennsylvania: David H. Moffat and the Opening of Northwest Colorado," *The Midwest Review*, 2nd Series, 7 (Spring 1985):15–30. On the Moffat tunnel see Charles Albi and Kenton Forrest, *The Moffat Tunnel: A Brief History* (Golden: Colorado Railroad Museum, 1978). Much information on Moffat and general Denver economic development can be found in Eugene Adams, Lyle W. Dorsett, and Robert S. Pulcipher, *The Pioneer Western Bank — First of Denver: 1860–1980* (Denver: First Interstate Bank and Colorado Historical Society, 1984). Moffat's papers are in the DPLWHD, as are the business-oriented scrapbooks of Charles A. Johnson.

James E. Fell, Jr., *Ores to Metals: The Rocky Mountain Smelting Industry* (Lincoln: University of Nebraska Press, 1979), illuminates a vital but often neglected part of Colorado history. Jay E. Niebur looks at a successful Denver businessman in *Arthur Redman Wilfley: Miner, Inventor, Entrepreneur* (Denver: Colorado Historical Society, 1982). Ellsworth Mittick, "The Development of Mining Machinery Manufacture in Colorado" (M.A. thesis, University of Denver, 1947), demonstrates the importance of this industry to Denver. John K. Mullen has been briefly treated in Charles W. Hurd, "J. K. Mullen: Milling Magnate of Colorado," *The Colorado Magazine* 29 (April 1952):104–18. The Henry Porter papers at the Colorado Historical Society, made accessible by Paul Ton's excellent calendar, contain much primary information. Ton's "Henry Miller Porter: Merchant, Private Banker and Cattleman, 1858–1917" (Ph.D. diss., University of Denver, 1969) is supplemented by Mark Foster's yet-unpublished biography. For Jesse Shwayder see Walter B. Lovelace, *Jesse Shwayder and the Golden Rule* (Denver: n.p., 1960).

Denver's colonial position is discussed by Roscoe Fleming in his "Denver Civic Schizophrenic," in Robert Allen, ed., *Our Fair City* (New York: Vanguard Press, 1947). Gene M. Gressley, *The Twentieth Century American West: A Potpourri* (Columbia: University of Missouri Press, 1977), intelligently delves into the importance of outside capital in development. The theme was earlier treated by such historians as Earl Pomeroy and Walter Prescott Webb. Historians, in turn, learned from Davis Waite and other nineteenth-century Populists who well knew that the West was dominated by the East.

Books such as Charles Denison's *Rocky Mountain Health Resorts* (Boston: Houghton, Osgood, 1880) advertised Colorado's climate as a potential cure for tuberculosis. Thomas C. Galbreath, *Chasing the Cure in Colorado* (Denver: Thomas C. Galbreath, 1908), shows that all was not as the boosters said. The horrible conditions under which many TB sufferers lived is detailed by the Denver Tuberculosis Society in *A Limited Investigation of Housing Conditions for the Tuberculous in Denver* (typescript in DPLWHD). James R. Giese looks at the impact of TB on one group in "Tuberculosis and the Growth of Denver's Eastern European Jewish Community . . . 1900–1920" (Ph.D. diss., University of Colorado, Boulder, 1982). Jeanne L. Abrams focuses on one institution in

"Chasing the Cure: A History of the Jewish Consumptive Relief Society of Denver" (Ph.D. diss., University of Colorado, Boulder, 1983). An overview is provided by Billy M. Jones, *Health Seekers in the Southwest, 1817–1900* (Norman: University of Oklahoma Press, 1967). Earl Pomeroy concentrates on healthier visitors in *In Search of the Golden West: The Tourist in Western America* (New York: Alfred A. Knopf, 1957).

Notes

1. Denver Chamber of Commerce, *Annual Report 1903* (Denver: Carson-Harper, 1904), p. 23.
2. *DP*, March 25, 1909.
3. Roscoe Fleming, "Denver Civic Schizophrenic," in Robert Allen, ed., *Our Fair City* (New York: Vanguard Press, 1947), p. 291.
4. Ibid., p. 290.
5. Ibid., p. 284. In the mid-1940s, Fleming estimated that one in every three Denverites owed her or his presence in the city directly or indirectly to TB. The impact of the disease can be seen in the history of George J. Krakow's family. Captain Krakow, grandfather of co-author S. J. Leonard, evidently contracted TB in France during World War I. After the war he came to Denver for treatment at Fitzsimons, bringing with him his wife Katherine (née Halley) and their two daughters, Mary and Violet. Eventually, they were joined by Katherine's sister Josephine and their mother, Katherine (née Whalen), as well as George's father, Christian. The Krakow migration, without taking into account descendants, added seven people to Denver's population.
6. Thomas C. Galbreath, *Chasing the Cure in Colorado* (Denver: Thomas C. Galbreath, 1908), pp. 29–32.
7. Ibid., p. 31.
8. The JCRS complex, with its old synagogue serving as a mini-museum, has been maintained as a National Historic District.
9. Walt Whitman, *Specimen Days in America* (London: Walter Scott Publishing, 1887), p. 227.
10. *RMN*, December 31, 1899.
11. William C. Ferril, "Scrapbook," (in DPLWHD), vol. 1, p. 50.
12. An estimated 150,000 tourists visited Colorado in 1907, according to the Denver Chamber of Commerce, *Potential Facts Regarding Denver* (n.p., c 1908). In 1941, 2.079 million visitors came by car, 1.025 million by train, and 263,000 by bus. See Chamber of Commerce, *Survey of Denver and Colorado* (in DPLWHD), p. 144.
13. Newspaper clipping dated November 25, 1919, in Pliny Fisk Sharp Scrapbook (in DPLWHD), vol. 8, p. 63; Steven Mehls, "David H. Moffat, Jr." (Ph.D. diss., University of Colorado, Boulder, 1982), p. 248, says that Mrs. Moffat did not die poor. In 1921 the Denver Post launched a campaign to properly mark Moffat's grave. The paper received only $1,282, so it donated the rest of the money itself. See *DP*, March 15, 1921.
14. Polly Pry, *DP*, September 1903, quoted in Allen D. Breck, *William Gray Evans, 1855–1924* (Denver: University of Denver History Department, 1964), p. 101.
15. Edward Keating, *The Gentleman from Colorado* (Denver: Sage Books, 1964), p. 128.
16. Geraldine Bean, *Charles Boettcher* (Boulder, CO: Westview Press, 1976), p. 159.

CHAPTER 12: Reformers Versus the Beast

Sources

Roland DeLorme sets the stage for Denver's reform years in "Turn-of-the-Century-Denver: An Invitation to Reform," *The Colorado Magazine* 45 (Winter 1968):1–15. Marjorie Hornbein, whose father, Philip, participated in many of the reform crusades, carefully looks at one battle in "Denver's Struggle for Home Rule," *The Colorado Magazine* 48 (Fall 1971):337–54. J. Richard Snyder, "The Election of 1904: An Attempt at Reform," *The Colorado Magazine* 45 (Winter 1968):16–26; Fred Greenbaum, "The Colorado Progressives in 1906," *Arizona and the West* 7 (Spring 1965):21–32; Harlan Knautz, "The Colorado Progressive Party of 1912" (M.A. thesis, University of Denver, 1964); and J. Paul Mitchell, "Boss Speer and the City Functional: Boosters and Businessmen Versus Commission Government," *Pacific Northwest Quarterly* 63 (October 1972):156–74, all consider aspects of the progressive movement. For an even fuller treatment see Mitchell's "Progressivism in Denver: The Municipal Reform Movement, 1904–1916" (Ph.D. diss., University of Denver, 1966).

Speer has been accorded two book-length biographies: Edgar C. MacMechen's *Robert W. Speer: A City Builder* (Denver: Smith-Brooks Printing, 1919) is orderly, laudatory, and short; while Charles Johnson's *Denver's Mayor Speer* (Denver: Green Mountain Press, 1969) is longer. A thoughtful interpretation is given by Walter Garnsey in "Robert W. Speer and Ben Lindsey" (honors thesis, Yale University, New Haven, CT, 1967). Garnsey argues that Speer and Lindsey represented different strains of progressive reform. John R. Pickering, "Blueprint of Power: The Public Career of Robert Speer in Denver 1878–1918" (Ph.D. diss., University of Denver, 1978), is the most detailed treatment of Speer available. A skimpy file of Speer's papers is in DPLWHD, which also owns the desk from which he governed.

Published works on Speer's supporters are sparse. Allen D. Breck's *William Gray Evans, 1855–1924: Portrait of a Western Executive* (Denver: University of Denver History Department, 1964) praises Evans and takes a dim view of the reformers. Eulogies on Charles J. Hughes, Jr., published at his death by the U.S. Senate as *Charles J. Hughes, Jr., Memorial Addresses* (Washington, D.C.: GPO, 1911), are naturally kind. Edgar MacMechen's short work, *Walter Scott Cheesman: A Pioneer Builder of Colorado* (n.p., n.d.), praises Cheesman. Thomas J. Noel, in *The City and the Saloon: Denver, 1858–1916* (Lincoln: University of Nebraska Press, 1982), pokes into bars, bosses, and the seamy side of politics.

Robert E. Smith's "Thomas M. Patterson: Colorado Crusader" (Ph.D. diss., University of Missouri, Columbia, 1973) helped save Patterson from oblivion, as have Smith's articles, "Senator T. M. Patterson, The Colorado Supreme Court, and Freedom of the Press," *The Colorado Magazine* 54 (Winter 1977):58–71, and "Thomas M. Patterson: Counsel for the Defense," *Essays and Monographs in Colorado History* 2 (1983):166–74. John Shafroth has been the subject of two University of Denver M.A. theses: one by Lloyd K. Musselman (1961); the other by Gerald D. Welch (1962). Also see E. K. MacColl, "John Franklin Shafroth, Reform Governor, 1909–1913," *The Colorado Magazine* 29 (January 1952):37–52.

On Edward Costigan see Fred Greenbaum's overview, *Fighting Progressive: A Biography of Edward P. Costigan* (Washington, D.C.: Public Affairs Press, 1971). Roland DeLorme looks at Costigan in Denver in "The Shaping of a Progressive: Edward P. Costigan and Urban Reform in Denver, 1900–1911" (Ph.D. diss., University of Colorado, Boulder, 1965), and Ronald Brockway, "Edward P. Costigan: A Study of a Progressive and the New Deal" (Ph.D. diss., University of Colorado, Boulder, 1974), focuses on Costigan's later career. Costigan's papers are at the University of Colorado, Boulder, and some have been published; see Colin B. Goodykoontz, ed., *Papers of Edward P. Costigan Relating to the Progressive Movement, 1902–1917* (Boulder: University of Colorado, 1941). Walter W. Wilder pays tribute to Justice Robert Steele in *Robert Wilbur Steele: Defender of Liberty* (Denver: Carson-Harper, 1913). Marjorie Hornbein considers Josephine Roche's long career in "Josephine Roche: Social Worker and Coal Operator," *The Colorado Magazine* 53 (Summer 1976): 243–60.

Benjamin Lindsey's 95,000-item collection in the Library of Congress has helped assure that he is remembered. Local historians generally have shunned him, the exception being Marjorie Hornbein, whose "The Story of Judge Ben Lindsey," *Southern California Quarterly* 55 (Winter 1973):469–82, summarizes his career. Charles Larsen's *The Good Fight: The Life and Times of Ben B. Lindsey* (Chicago: Quadrangle Books, 1972) is a favorable, readable account. The most detailed work is by Francis Huber, "The Progressive Career of Ben B. Lindsey" (Ph.D. diss., University of Michigan, Ann Arbor, 1963). Lindsey wrote much himself. His *The Rule of Plutocracy in Colorado* (Denver: Hicks Printing House, 1908) was followed by his most famous muckraking piece, written with Harvey J. O'Higgins, *The Beast* (New York: Doubleday Page, 1910). Lindsey looks back on his career in *The Dangerous Life* (New York: Horace Liveright, 1931), which he wrote with Rube Borough.

George Creel's autobiography, *Rebel at Large: Recollections of Fifty Crowded Years* (New York: G. P. Putnam's, 1947), and Edward Keating's *The Gentleman from Colorado* (Denver: Sage Books, 1964) are important accounts of the period. Also useful are Samuel W. Johnson, *Autobiography of Samuel Wallace Johnson* (Denver: Big Mountain Press, 1960) and Frank Johnson, *Autobiography of a Centenarian* (Denver: Big Mountain Press, 1961). Jared Warner Mills wrote a series on Denver that appeared in *The Arena*, a national magazine, starting in July 1905 and, after some interruptions, ending in October 1906. Additional firsthand information is provided by John Rush in *The City-County Consolidated* (Los Angeles: John Rush, 1941) and by Clyde L. King, *The History of the Government of Denver* (Denver: Fisher Book, 1911).

Notes

1. Benjamin B. Lindsey and Harvey J. O'Higgins, *The Beast* (New York: Doubleday Page, 1910), p. 337.
2. John Rush, *The City-County Consolidated* (Los Angeles: John Rush, 1941), pp. 329–30. The legislative session that took control of the Board of Public Works away from Denver in 1889 went down in Colorado history as the "Robber Seventh" because of its corruption.
3. Until 1902 Denver had been the seat of Arapahoe County. When Denver became a consolidated city and county, Littleton became Arapahoe County seat. All school districts in the new City and County of Denver were merged into School District One in 1902. Denver annexed no more territory until 1941.
4. Eugene Rider, "The Denver Police Department" (Ph.D. diss., University of Denver, 1971), p. 543. Marjorie Hornbein, "Denver's Struggle for Home Rule" *The Colorado Magazine* 48 (Fall 1971):348–54, tells of the court cases that grew out of the Rush amendment. Also see RMN, September 4, 10, and 23, 1903; *Denver Republican*, September 19, 1903; *Denver Times*, September 21, 1903. The *News, Republican*, and *Times* supported the reform charter; the *Post* did not. See DP, September 21, 1903.
5. Shafroth (1854–1922) also served in the U.S. House of Representatives, 1895–1903. His son John became a vice-admiral in the United States Navy; another son, Morrison (1888–1978), was a Denver attorney and Democratic party stalwart. Morrison's son-in-law, James Quigg Newton, Jr., became mayor of Denver in 1947. Keating (1875–1965) was elected to the U.S. House of Representatives in 1913, where he remained until 1919. He is remembered for co-authoring the Keating-Owen Child Labor Act (1916) and for his opposition to World War I. Creel (1876–1953) became nationally known as WW I director of propaganda.
6. Edward Keating, *The Gentleman from Colorado* (Denver: Sage Books, 1964), p. 113.
7. Lindsey, *Beast*, p. 16.
8. Ibid., p. 81.
9. RMN, September 3, 1903.
10. Ibid., September 4, 1903.
11. J. Paul Mitchell, "Progressivism in Denver" (Ph.D. diss., University of Denver, 1966), p. 84, quoting Thomas, "Autobiography" (typescript at Colorado Historical Society Library).
12. J. Warner Mills, "The Economic Struggle in Colorado," series of articles in *The Arena* (1905–1906) (bound as a book in DPLWHD), p. 248.
13. Perkin, *First Hundred Years*, p. 409. Lindsey boasted to Theodore Roosevelt: "Doherty is a Wall Street banker in New York and said to be the only trust president in America who ever was in jail, and I sent him there, and he stayed there until the Supreme Court let him out. Of course, they are bitter against me." Lindsey to Roosevelt, May 12, 1912, Lindsey Papers, box 37, Library of Congress.
14. Keating, *Gentleman from Colorado*, p. 173.
15. Lindsey to Addams, June 1, 1908, Lindsey Papers, box 15.

16. McLaughlin, letter to supporters of the Anti-Saloon League, May 14, 1908, Lindsey Papers, box 15.
17. Keating, *Gentleman from Colorado*, pp. 173–75; *RMN*, May 17, 1908.
18. Fred Greenbaum, "The Colorado Progressives in 1906," *Arizona and the West* 7 (Spring 1965):22, quoting Edward Costigan in *RMN*, March 10, 1906.
19. George Creel, *Rebel at Large* (New York: G. P. Putnam's, 1947), p. 104.
20. Charles Johnson, *Denver's Mayor Speer* (Denver: Green Mountain Press, 1969), pp. 1–2.
21. Lindsey, *Beast*, p. 191.
22. Ibid., pp. xii–xiii.
23. Edgar C. MacMechen, *Robert W. Speer* (Denver: Smith-Brooks Printing, 1919), p. 53, says that Collins used a small rubber rod to break the glass in Arnold's door. Still, the nickname "Crowbar" stuck to Collins, who remained a political power behind the scenes until his death in 1946. See *DP*, February 15, 1946.
24. Lindsey to Scripps, May 28, 1912, Lindsey Papers, box 37.
25. Charles Lindsey to Benjamin Lindsey, June 6, 1913, Lindsey Papers, box 135.
26. Lindsey to Creel, May 1, 1916, Lindsey Papers, box 52.

CHAPTER 13: Mayor Speer's City Beautiful

Sources

For a national overview with a chapter on Denver see William H. Wilson, *The City Beautiful Movement* (Baltimore, MD: Johns Hopkins University Press, 1989). The movement shaped Denver until the 1940s, according to Thomas J. Noel and Barbara S. Norgren, *Denver: The City Beautiful and Its Architects, 1893–1941* (Denver: Historic Denver, 1987). Treatments of Denver's parks include Ben Draper's 1934 Civil Works Administration compilations, "History of Denver Parks" and "History of the Mountain Parks" (typescripts in the Colorado Historical Society Library); and Bette D. Peter, *Denver's City Park* (Boulder: Johnson Publishing, 1985). Louisa Arps's "Cemetery to Conservatory," *Green Thumb* 33 (Summer 1976):34–40, is a splendid history of Cheesman Park. Phil Goodstein covers Cheesman, the Botanic Gardens, the Country Club, and City Park in his meticulously researched and socially conscious book *Denver's Capitol Hill* (Denver: Life Publications, 1988). David K. Ballast, *Denver's Civic Center: A Walking Tour* (Denver: City Publishing, 1977), helps walkers enjoy the Civic Center complex. The evolution of the city's parks and parkways is detailed by Don Etter in *The Denver Park and Parkway System* (Denver: Colorado Historical Society, 1986). The Saco DeBoer collection at the DPLWHD is a rich primary source for material on Denver parks, and the Sopris Collection at the Colorado Historical Society contains material on Denver's first park commissioner.

Denver's role in World War I has not received much attention. LeRoy Hafen's *Colorado and Its People*, for example, gives only a few pages (vol. 1, pp. 537–41) to the war effort. More helpful is John H. Nankivell, *History of the Military Organizations of the State of Colorado, 1860–1935* (Denver: W. H. Kistler Stationery, 1935). Phil Goodstein, "Convention City," *Colorado Heritage* 4 (1984):2–10, tells of the 1908 Democratic convention.

Notes

1. Edgar C. MacMechen, *Robert W. Speer* (Denver: Smith-Brooks, 1919), p. 47.
2. Ibid., p. 75.
3. *Municipal Facts*, March 13, 1909; *RMN*, September 10, 1903.
4. Smiley, *Denver*, p. 646; Louisa Arps, "Cemetery to Conservatory," *Green Thumb* 33 (Summer 1976):39.
5. Unidentified clipping in Florence Burton Scrapbook (in DPLWHD), vol. 2, p. 9.
6. George W. Steevens, *The Land of the Dollar* (London: William Blackwood & Sons, 1897), p. 199.
7. Emma A. Gage, *Western Wanderings and Summer Saunterings Through Picturesque Colorado* (Baltimore, MD: The Lord Baltimore Press, 1900), p. 48.
8. *Municipal Facts*, February 27, 1909. *Municipal Facts* was published weekly by the City of Denver and is an excellent source on Denver in the early twentieth century.
9. Smiley, *Denver*, p. 975.
10. Anonymous, *That Snow Storm: Its Flakes, Its Flurries, Its Freaks* (Denver: W. E. Heatley, 1914). The storm lasted for several days: December 4, 1913, brought 20.4 inches; December 5, 1913, 16.5 inches.
11. Cheesman Park was first named Congress Park because Congress sold Denver the land for $1.25 an acre. When the park was renamed, the name Congress was given to a park along Eighth Avenue east of Josephine Street.
12. *RMN*, August 1, 1905.
13. MacMechen, *Speer*, p. 78.
14. Lowry, a 1913 graduate of Manual High School, was the son of Walter B. Lowry, manager of parks and improvements under Mayors Speer, Bailey, and Begole. Lowry Field was named after him in 1937. With many other WW I fatalities, Lowry is buried at Fairmount Cemetery. See *DP*, December 22, 1937, and November 23, 1958.
15. MacMechen, *Speer*, p. 71.
16. *Denver Republican*, August 31, 1911.
17. *DP*, May 6, 1917.
18. Ibid., May 15, 1918.

CHAPTER 14: Denver at Leisure

Sources

Although Denver's general social, leisure, and recreational history has not received much attention from historians, individual institutions have. See, for example, Thomas J. Noel, *The Denver Athletic Club, 1884–1984* (Denver: The Denver Athletic Club, 1983). For the Denver Bears professional baseball team (renamed the Denver Zephyrs in 1985), consult Mark S. Foster, *The Denver Bears: From Sandlots to Sellouts* (Boulder, CO: Pruett Publishing, 1983). *Trail and Timberline*, published monthly since 1918 by the Colorado Mountain Club, is a treasury of information on outdoor recreation and conservation, as is Hugh Kingery's *The Colorado Mountain Club* (Evergreen, CO: Cordillera Press, 1988). For skiing see Abbott Fay, *Ski Tracks in the Rockies: A Century of Colorado Skiing* (Evergreen, CO: Cordillera Press, 1984). On bicycling, see Andrew W. Gillette, "The Bicycle Era in Colorado," *The Colorado Magazine* 10 (November 1933):213–17; and *Cycling West* magazine, which was published in Denver, 1892–1899.

Elitch Gardens is covered by Caroline L. Dier, *The Lady of the Gardens: Mary Elitch Long* (Hollywood, CA: Hollycrofters, 1932); Jack Gurtler and Corinne Hunt, *The Elitch Gardens Story* (Boulder, CO: Rocky Mountain Writers Guild, 1982); and Edwin L. Levy, "Elitch Gardens, Denver, Colorado: A History of the Oldest Summer Theater in the U.S." (Ph.D. diss., Columbia University, New York, 1960). Downtown Denver's completely demolished theater district comes back to life in Forrest H. Johnson's *Denver's Old Theater Row* (Denver: Bill Lay, 1970).

Music is surveyed in the Denver Public Library's *Music in Denver and Colorado* (Denver: DPL, 1927) and by Stanford Linscome, "A History of Musical Development in Denver, Colorado, 1858–1908" (Ph.D. diss., University of Texas, Austin, 1970). Joan Reese's excellent article, "Two Gentlemen of Note: George Morrison, Paul Whiteman, and Their Jazz," *Colorado Heritage* 2 (1986):2–13, gives insights into Denver's African-American community. Movie theaters are treated in Don Bloch's "Flickorama for Denver," in Dabney Otis Collins, ed., *The 1948 Brand Book of the Denver Posse of the Westerners* (Denver: Artcraft, 1948), and in Paul O'Malley's "Neighborhood Nickelodeons," *Colorado Heritage* 3 (1984):49–58. Ralph J. Batschelet, a longtime theater manager, gives firsthand reminiscences in *The Flick and I* (Smithtown, NY: Exposition Press, 1981). James E. Hansen II tells of the war against demon rum in "A Study of Prohibition in Denver" (M.A. thesis, University of Denver, 1965). Denver needs a radio history. Helpful raw sources include the DPLWHD clipping file and the Freeman Talbot scrapbooks, and the Reynolds Broadcasting Company collection at the Colorado Historical Society Library, which includes 1920s scripts. Ben Bezoff and Wallis Reef, both at times radio executives, have deposited their papers with the DPLWHD.

Local newspaper wars are reported extensively in Gene Fowler's *Timber Line: A Story of Bonfils and Tammen* (New York: Covici, Friede, 1933), and more accurately and thoroughly by Bill Hosokowa in *Thunder in the Rockies: The Incredible Denver Post* (New York: William Morrow, 1976). Robert L. Perkin provides a thorough, lively history of Denver's oldest paper, the *Rocky Mountain News*, in *The First Hundred Years*. Pat Paton writes affectionately of Ruth Underhill in "Ruth Underhill Remembered," *Colorado Heritage* 1 (1985):14–21.

Notes

1. Edward Hungerford, *The Personality of American Cities* (New York: McBride, Nast, 1913), p. 268. Hungerford calls Denver the "American Paris" and "a mecca for American tourists." He says that it is "clean," "green," and "solidly and substantially built, but short on theater possibilities."
2. Colorado Historical Society, "National Register of Historic Places Nomination for the Denver Country Club" (typescript in Colorado Historical Society Library).
3. *Denver Republican*, June 15, 1912.
4. Thomas J. Noel, *The Denver Athletic Club, 1884–1984* (Denver: Denver Athletic Club, 1983), p. 30.
5. *RMN*, June 17, 1895.
6. As of 1973, 392 species of birds had been officially spotted within a 50-mile radius of downtown Denver, according to James A. Lane and Harold Holt, *A Birder's Guide to Denver and Eastern Colorado* (Sacramento, CA: L & L Photography, 1973), p. 99.
7. Colorado State Planning Commission, *Colorado Year Book, 1939–1940* (Denver: Bradford-Robinson, 1940), p. 72.
8. Hungerford, *Personality of Cities*, p. 269.
9. *Denver Republican*, May 31, 1908.
10. *Polly Pry*, December 19, 1903, p. 14.
11. See Joan Reese, "Two Gentlemen of Note" *Colorado Heritage* 2 (1986):2–13. see *DP*, November 6, 1974, for Morrison's obituary.
12. James R. Noland (Secretary of the Fire and Police Board) to a theater license applicant, September 15, 1911, in Denver Fire and Police Board, Letters, Denver Fire and Police Department Museum, Denver.
13. Philip S. Van Cise, *Fighting the Underworld* (Cambridge, MA: Riverside Press, 1936), p. 21.
14. Lindsey, testimony before Denver Grand Jury, October 17, 1921, in Lindsey Papers, box 65, Library of Congress.
15. *DP*, October 5, 1921.
16. *RMN*, February 8, 1931.
17. *DP*, February 19, 1933.
18. George Cranmer, "The Social Economics of Good Taste," *The Art Register* 1 (November 1931):43.
19. Tureman, a graduate of Denver's West High and later a pupil of the French composer Claude Debussy, conducted the Denver Philharmonic Orchestra from 1911 until it folded in 1917. In 1922 he took charge of the newly formed Denver Civic Symphony, an unpaid group from which professional members split in 1934 to form the Denver Symphony Orchestra. Tureman conducted that orchestra until 1944 when he retired and was replaced by Saul Caston.

20. "History of KOA and KOA-TV, Denver" (typescript in DPLWHD clipping file).
21. *RMN*, February 7, 1930.
22. Ibid., October 31, 1946; *DP*, March 8, 1954. KTLN began operating in 1948 under the ownership of Alf Landon, ex-governor of Kansas. Later it was sold to a group that included ex-senator Edwin Johnson of Colorado and his son-in-law, Robert Howsam. See radio logs in *RMN*, February 23, 1927; February 21, 1937; and February 26, 1947. Denver's religious station, KPOF, is not included in these radio logs. Taking its call letters from the religion it represented, the Pillar of Fire, KPOF began broadcasting in 1928 under the direction of the church's founder, Bishop Alma White (1862–1946), whose Alma Temple was completed at 1340 Sherman in 1937. See *RMN*, October 24, 1937, and June 27, 1946.
23. Malcolm G. Wyer, *Of Books and People* (Denver: Old West Publishing, 1964).
24. The creature, Dowd explained, while it looked like a giant rabbit, was in fact a *pooka* — an animal that appears to Irish drunkards. The plot of *Me Third* was loosely based on a 1934 Denver scandal involving a "love market" at 1145 Marion; see *RMN*, June 28, 1934.
25. The Eugene Field Library occupied Field's small frame cottage for many years; it eventually moved to Ohio Avenue and University Boulevard. The Field house remains in the park.
26. Benjamin B. Lindsey and Harvey J. O'Higgins, *The Beast* (New York: Doubleday, 1910), p. 226.
27. *DP*, November 1, 1925.
28. On military and other official documents, Packer spelled his name Alfred. Fred M. Mazzulla and some others have used the spelling Alferd.
29. Bill Hosokawa, *Thunder in the Rockies* (New York: William Morrow, 1976), pp. 16, 138–47, 156.
30. Samuel W. Johnson, *Autobiography of Samuel Wallace Johnson* (Denver: Big Mountain Press, 1960), p. 189.
31. Charles McCabe to Roy Howard, June 3, 1935, in Roy Howard Papers, box 100, Library of Congress.

CHAPTER 15: Working People

Sources

Although Colorado's stormy labor history, particularly between 1880 and 1920, has received some attention, few historians have focused on Denver. As a result, more is known about the 1914 Ludlow Massacre than about day-to-day union history in Denver for the last 80 years. Harold V. Knight's *Working in Colorado: A Brief History of the Colorado Labor Movement* (Denver: World Press, 1971) provides a starting place. Henry Seligson and George E. Bardwell, *Labor-Management Relations in Colorado* (Denver: Sage Books, 1961), emphasize the period 1940 to 1960. Elizabeth Jameson, *Building Colorado: The United Brotherhood of Carpenters and Joiners of America in the Centennial State* (Denver: Egan Printing, 1984), concentrates on carpenters but also unearths much general local labor history. Still useful is Carroll D. Wright's *A Report on Labor Disturbances of Colorado from 1880 to 1904* (Washington, D.C.: GPO, 1905).

George G. Suggs, Jr., *Colorado's War on Militant Unionism* (Detroit, MI: Wayne State University Press, 1972), provides a scholarly view of the WFM. Also see Vernon Jensen, *Heritage of Conflict: Labor Relations in the Non Ferrous Metals Industry* (Ithaca, NY: Cornell University Press, 1950). Two articles of interest are David Lonsdale's "The Fight for an Eight Hour Day," *The Colorado Magazine* 43 (Fall 1966):339–53, and Thomas J. Noel, "William D. Haywood," *Colorado Heritage* 2 (1984):2–12.

Lonsdale's and Suggs's published works grew out of Ph.D. dissertations on Colorado labor. David T. Brundage also offers excellent scholarship in "The Making of Working-Class Radicalism in the Mountain West, Denver Colorado, 1880–1903" (Ph.D. diss., University of California, Los Angeles, 1982). Gene Marlatt considers one of Denver's most colorful labor leaders in "Joseph R. Buchanan: Spokesman for Labor during the Populist and Progressive Eras" (Ph.D. diss., University of Colorado, Boulder, 1975); see also Robert Brown, "The Denver Tramway Strike of 1920" (M.S. thesis, University of Colorado, Boulder, 1967). Ellen A. Slatkin, "A History of the Response of the Colorado State Federation of Labor to the Great Depression, 1929–1940" (M.A. thesis, University of Denver, 1984), sheds much-needed light on Colorado's labor history in the 1930s. Also illuminating is Richard Gould's "The CIO Comes to Denver's Packinghouse Row," *University of Colorado-Denver Historical Studies* 1 (1983–1984):1–17.

Primary sources include Joseph Buchanan, *The Story of a Labor Agitator* (New York: Outlook, 1903), which Buchanan dedicated "to the little band of Denver men and women whose faith in me, and whose sacrifices for 'The Cause' saved me many times from failures and despair." William D. Haywood, in *The Autobiography of Big Bill Haywood* (1929; Reprint New York: International Press, 1974), tells of his exciting life. Two books by Alfred E. Horsley — *The Confessions and Autobiography of Harry Orchard* (New York: McClure, 1907) and *Harry Orchard: The Man Who God Made Again* (Nashville, TN: Southern Publishing Association, 1952) — are, some historians think, more colorful than true. The much drier biennial reports of the Colorado Bureau of Labor Statistics are also valuable.

Notes

1. *Miners' Magazine*, January 1, 1900, pp. 16–17.
2. *DP*, April 26, 1919.
3. Gene Fowler, *Timberline: A Story of Bonfils and Tammen* (New York: Covici, Friede, 1933), p. 326.
4. George Creel, *Rebel at Large* (New York: G. P. Putnam's, 1947), p. 85.
5. William D. Haywood, *The Autobiography of Big Bill Haywood* (1929; Reprint New York: International Press, 1974), p. 71.
6. *John Swinton's Paper*, May 19, 1887, quoted in David T. Brundage, "The Making of Working-Class Radicalism" (Ph.D. diss., University of California, Los Angeles, 1982), p. 154.

7. Charles Larsen, *The Good Fight: The Life and Times of Ben B. Lindsey* (Chicago: Quadrangle Books, 1972), p. 70.
8. Colorado Bureau of Labor Statistics, *Twelfth Biennial Report, 1909–1910* (Denver: Smith-Brooks, 1911), p. 249.
9. Colorado Bureau of Labor Statistics, *Fourteenth Biennial Report* (Denver: Smith-Brooks, 1914), p. 60.
10. Carroll D. Wright, *A Report on Labor Disturbances* (Washington, D.C.: GPO, 1905), p. 137.
11. Colorado Bureau of Labor Statistics, *Seventh Biennial Report, 1899–1900* (Denver: Smith-Brooks, 1900), p. 103.
12. Haywood, *Autobiography*, p. 101. Governor Grant's mansion at 777 Pennsylvania, later owned by oilman Albert Humphreys, Sr., is now a house museum and offices operated by the Colorado Historical Society.
13. Ibid., p. 101.
14. Thomas J. Noel, "William D. Haywood," *Colorado Heritage* 2 (1984):6.
15. Vernon Jensen, *Heritage of Conflict*, (Ithaca, NY: Cornell University Press, 1950), p. 93.
16. Both quotations from *Polly Pry*, November 28, 1903.
17. *DP*, "Contemporary," February 18, 1968.
18. Alfred E. Horsley, *Harry Orchard* (Nashville, TN: Southern Publishing Association, 1952), p. 66.
19. Jensen, *Heritage of Conflict*, p. 93.
20. All quotations from *RMN*, August 3, 1920.
21. *DP*, August 3, 1920.
22. *Denver Catholic Register*, August 12, 1920.
23. Elizabeth Jameson, *Building Colorado* (Denver: Egan Printing, 1984), p. 48.
24. Ellen A. Slatkin, "A History of Response of the Colorado State Federation of Labor" (M.A. thesis, University of Denver, 1984), p. 133.
25. Jameson, *Building Colorado*, p. 63.
26. John Gunther, *Inside USA* (New York: Harper and Brothers, 1947), p. 222.

CHAPTER 16: Ethnic Diversity

Sources

Denver's ethnic history is scattered among many different sources. A starting place for bibliographical information is Carl Abbott et al., *Colorado: A History of the Centennial State* (Boulder: Colorado Associated University Press, 1982), pp. 369–73. Although individual groups have received some attention, there are few broad studies on Denver's immigrants. Thomas J. Noel synthesizes in "The Immigrant Saloon in Denver," *The Colorado Magazine* 54 (Summer 1977):201–19, as does Stephen J. Leonard in "The Irish, English and Germans in Denver, 1860–1890," *The Colorado Magazine* 54 (Spring 1977):126–54. Daniel Doeppers, "The Globeville Neighborhood in Denver," *The Geographic Review* 47 (October 1967):506–22, provides a model study of a multiethnic neighborhood. Stanley Cuba tells of one ethnic parish in "A Polish Community in the Urban West: St. Joseph's Parish in Denver, Colorado," *Polish American Studies* 36 (Spring 1979):33–74. Stephen J. Leonard covers major groups in "Denver's Foreign-Born Immigrants, 1859–1900" (Ph.D. diss., Claremont Graduate School, Claremont, CA, 1971).

Gerald Rudolph, "The Chinese in Colorado, 1869–1911" (M.A. thesis, University of Denver, 1964), presents much material on Denver, and Roy T. Wortman treats an ugly event in "Denver's Anti-Chinese Riot, 1880," *The Colorado Magazine* 42 (Fall 1965):275–91. Fumio Ozawa's thesis, "Japanese in Colorado, 1900–1910" (M.A. thesis, University of Denver, 1954), with additional material, appears in *Japanese American Who's Who* (Denver: Colorado Times, 1959).

Articles on specific groups, although not necessarily focusing on Denver, often contain information on the city's ethnics. See M. James Kedro, "Czechs and Slovaks in Colorado, 1860–1920," *The Colorado Magazine* 54 (Spring 1977):93–125, and, in the same issue, Kenneth W. Rock, " 'Unsere Leute': The Germans from Russia in Colorado," pp. 155–83. Several older works are still useful. See Giovanni Perilli, *Colorado and the Italians of Colorado* (Denver: n.p., c 1922); and Mildred S. MacArthur, *History of the German Element in Colorado* (Chicago: German-American Historical Society, 1917). Modern treatments of the Italians and Germans include Christine DeRose's "Inside 'Little Italy': Italian Immigrants in Denver," *The Colorado Magazine* 54 (Summer 1977):277–93, and Lyle Dorsett's "The Ordeal of Colorado's Germans during World War I," *The Colorado Magazine* 51 (Fall 1974):277–93. On the Red scare see Philip L. Cook's informative "Red Scare in Denver," *The Colorado Magazine* 43 (Fall 1966):309–26. Bibliographical information on Denver's African-Americans, Hispanics, and Jews is given in the Sources section of Chapters 17, 26, and 27.

Notes

1. Oscar Handlin, *The Uprooted: The Epic Story of the Great Migrations That Made the American People* (New York: Grossett & Dunlap, 1951), p. 7. Handlin's Pulitzer Prize–winning history has been criticized but is still among the most readable of immigration histories.
2. Interview with S. J. Leonard, July 20, 1970.
3. R. G. Dun and Company, "Credit Ratings," entries for Adolph Coors dated September 27, 1873, and May 2, 1874, in R. G. Dun Collection, Baker Business Library, Harvard University.
4. Edward Keating, *The Gentleman from Colorado* (Denver: Sage Books, 1964), p. 46.
5. Anonymous, *Our Lady of Mount Carmel* (Hackensack, NJ: Custom Book, 1975), pp. 5–6.
6. Rudolph Mapelli, "Herman and Rudolph Mapelli and Cousin Salvatore Iacobucci from Year 1900" (typescript in Metropolitan State College [Denver] History Department Files), p. 3.
7. Ibid., p. 3.

8. Ibid., p. 2.
9. Ibid., p. 5.
10. Wysowatcky interview with Turner, November 30, 1938, in Federal Writer's Program: Colorado, "Racial Groups" (mimeograph copy in Colorado Historical Society Library), p. 2.
11. All quotations from Chopyak interview with Lucy Turner, November 28, 1938, in Federal Writers Program: Colorado, "Racial Groups," pp. 1–4.
12. Eddie Foy and Alvin F. Harlow, *Clowning through Life* (New York: E. P. Dutton, 1928), p. 157.
13. Colorado Bureau of Labor Statistics, *Second Biennial Report, 1889–1890* (Denver: Collier & Cleavland, 1890), p. 57.
14. *RMN*, February 3, 1908.
15. *Denver Express*, January 8, 1920, quoted in Philip L. Cook, "Red Scare," *The Colorado Magazine* 43 (Fall 1966):320.
16. Colorado Bureau of Labor Statistics, *Seventh Biennial Report* (Denver: Smith-Brooks Printing, 1900), p. 61.
17. *RMN*, July 5, 1920.

CHAPTER 17: The Ku Klux Klan

Sources

Robert A. Goldberg's superb, scholarly, and well-written *Hooded Empire: The Ku Klux Klan in Colorado* (Urbana: University of Illinois Press, 1981) ranks high among the few books on Denver that command national attention. Earlier treatments of the Klan include James Davis, "Colorado Under the Klan," *The Colorado Magazine* 42 (Spring 1965):93–108; Gerald L. Marriner, "Klan Politics in Colorado," *Journal of the West* 15 (January 1976):76–101; and Carol J. Carter, *Adams and the Ku Klux Klan* (Alamosa, CO: Adams State College, 1980). A good survey of the Denver Klan compared to the movement in other cities is provided by Kenneth Jackson in *The Ku Klux Klan in the City: 1915–1930* (New York: Oxford University Press, 1967).

Philip S. Van Cise tells of his struggle to defeat Denver's bunco men in *Fighting the Underworld* (Cambridge, MA: Riverside Press, 1936). James E. Hansen II considers another aspect of crime in the 1920s in "Moonshine and Murder: Prohibition in Denver," *The Colorado Magazine* 50 (Winter 1973):1–23. Lowell E. Jarratt's *The Incredible Politician* (New York: Carlton Press, 1981) presents the reminiscences of Adolph Hecker, a Denverite who operated on the fringe of the law.

Articles on Denver blacks before 1940 include Harmon Motherstead, "Negro Rights in Colorado Territory," *The Colorado Magazine* 40 (July 1963):212–36; Eugene H. Berwanger, "Reconstruction on the Frontier: The Equal-Rights Struggle in Colorado, 1865–1867," *Pacific Historical Review* 44 (August 1975):313–29; and George H. Wayne, "Negro Migration and Colonization in Colorado: 1870–1930," *Journal of the West* 15 (January 1976):102–20. Among popular book-length treatments are Forbes Parkhill, *Mister Barney Ford: A Portrait in Bistre* (Denver: Sage Books, 1963); Marion Talmage and Iris Gilmore, *Barney Ford: Black Baron* (New York: Dodd, Mead, 1973); and Kathleen Bruyn, *Aunt Clara Brown: Story of a Black Pioneer* (Boulder, CO: Pruett Publishing, 1970). Paul Stewart's Black American West Museum is a treasure trove of exhibits, artifacts, and research materials. Many recent treatments of local blacks are indebted to such early works as Ira De A. Reid, *The Negro Population of Denver, Colorado: A Survey of Its Economic and Social Status* (Denver: Lincoln Press, 1929), and James Rose Harvey, "Negroes in Colorado" (M.A. thesis, University of Denver, 1941). Much statistical information is given in U.S. Department of Commerce, Bureau of the Census, *Negroes in the United States, 1920–1932* (Washington, D.C.: GPO, 1935). Lionel D. Lyles, "An Historical-Urban Geographical Analysis of Black Neighborhood Development in Denver" (Ph.D. diss., University of Colorado, Boulder, 1977), updates earlier studies with material on the 1940–1970 period. The papers of the NAACP are at the Library of Congress, as are the Benjamin Lindsey papers. The papers of Klansman Gano Senter are at DPLWHD.

Ida Uchill's *Pioneers, Peddlers and Tsadikim* (Denver: Sage Books, 1957) is a model study. Also see Allen Breck, *A Centennial History of the Jews of Colorado, 1859–1959* (Denver: A. B. Hirschfeld Press, 1961), and Marjorie Hornbein, *Temple Emanuel of Denver: A Centennial History* (Denver: A. B. Hirschfeld Press, 1974). Roman Catholics are extensively covered in Thomas J. Noel's *Colorado Catholicism: The Archdiocese of Denver* (Niwot: University Press of Colorado, 1989), which acknowledges its debt to such earlier works as William H. Jones, *The History of Catholic Education in the State of Colorado* (Washington, D.C.: Catholic University of America Press, 1955), and Thomas Feely's "Leadership in the Early Colorado Catholic Church" (Ph.D. diss., University of Denver, 1972). Harold Stansell, S.J., looks at one Catholic college in *Regis: On the Crest of the West* (Denver: Regis Educational Corporation, 1977).

Notes

1. Robert A. Goldberg, *Hooded Empire* (Urbana: University of Illinois Press, 1981), p. 1.
2. *DP*, August 8, 1924, quoted in ibid., p. 34.
3. *DP*, August 13, 1924.
4. Ibid., August 14, 1924.
5. George P. Rawick, ed., *The American Slave: A Composite Autobiography* (Westport, CT: Greenwood Press, 1977), pp. 30–31.
6. *DP*, "Empire," September 7, 1969.
7. At Fairmount Cemetery, many African-Americans were buried in the northeastern corner, known as the Ten Commandments section because that was the only major marker there.
8. Ibid., May 28, 1920.
9. Ibid., May 19, 1920.
10. *RMN*, July 8, 1921.
11. *Denver Express*, January 17, 1925.

12. *Jewish Outlook*, February 2, 1909, quoted in Ida Uchill, *Pioneers, Peddlers, and Tsadikim* (Denver, Sage Books, 1957), p. 191.
13. *Denver Catholic Register*, March 9, 1922.
14. Cited in ibid., February 17, 1921.
15. *DP*, July 25, 1921, quoted in Goldberg, *Hooded Empire*, p. 4.
16. Ibid., p. 15.
17. Ibid., p. 18.
18. Untermeyer to Lindsey, September 15, 1924, in Lindsey Papers, box 68, Library of Congress.
19. Lowell E. Jarratt, *The Incredible Politician* (New York: Carlton Press, 1981), p. 22.
20. *DP*, February 23, 1923, quoted in Goldberg, *Hooded Empire*, p. 30.
21. Shafroth to Bryan, November 15, 1924 (papers in DPLWHD, box 24).
22. Goldberg, *Hooded Empire*, p. 86.
23. *Denver Catholic Register*, January 25, 1925.
24. Carol J. Carter, *Adams and the Ku Klux Klan* (Alamosa, CO: Adams State College, 1980), p. 13.
25. *DP*, January 8, 1925.
26. Lindsey to Boyd Gurley, October 3, 1927, Roy Howard Papers, box 13, Library of Congress.
27. *Denver Express*, May 16, 1923.
28. Jarratt, *Incredible Politician*, p. 21.
29. Lindsey to Wainwright Evans, November 3, 1924, Lindsey Papers, box 152.
30. Lindsey to Roche, August 15, 1924, Lindsey Papers, box 68.
31. Benjamin Lindsey to Sweet, September 13, 1924, Lindsey Papers, box 68.
32. Howard to Lindsey, March 28, 1927, Howard Papers, box 13.
33. Shaw to Lindsey, December 14, 1924, Lindsey Papers, box 152.
34. Gene Fowler, *A Solo in Tom-Toms* (New York: Viking Press, 1946), p. 167.

CHAPTER 18: Depression Denver

Sources

Richard Lowitt, *The New Deal and the West* (Bloomington: Indiana University Press, 1984), provides perspective and an excellent overview. James F. Wickens, *Colorado in the Great Depression* (New York: Garland Press, 1979), is the indispensable starting point for studying the Depression in Denver. Wickens has also published "Tightening the Colorado Purse Strings," *The Colorado Magazine* 46 (Fall 1969):271–86. See also Bernard Mergen's "Denver and the War on Unemployment," *The Colorado Magazine* 47 (Fall 1970):326–37. Marjorie Hornbein gives a good account of Denver's leading woman New Dealer in "Josephine Roche: Social Worker and Coal Operator," *The Colorado Magazine* 53 (Summer 1976):243–60. She has also written about the planting of a microphone in Governor Ammons's office in "For the Public Good: The Strange Case of Colorado's Eavesdroppers," *Colorado Heritage* 3, (1985):33–38. The entire issue of *Journal of the West* for October 1985 was devoted to studies of the depression in the West.

O. Otto Moore discusses the Colorado pension movement in *Mile High Harbor* (Denver: Associated Publishers, 1947). Edgar M. Wahlberg, in *Voices in the Darkness: A Memoir* (Boulder, CO: Roberts Rinehart, 1983), presents a firsthand account of depression Denver. On Reds in Denver see Manuel L. Chait, "The Development of American Communism with Particular Emphasis on Colorado" (M.A. thesis, University of Denver, 1959). On Red Rocks near Denver see Milton E. Bernet, "The Incomparable Red Rocks, from Depression to Rock n' Roll," in Edwin A. Bathke, ed., *Denver Westerners Brand Book 1972* (Boulder: Johnson Publishing, 1973). Useful in understanding political change is Leah M. Bird's "The History of Third Parties in Colorado" (M.A. thesis, University of Denver, 1942).

Much information on the depression remains locked in unpublished theses and dissertations. Robert C. Sims, "Colorado and the Great Depression: Business Thought in a Time of Crisis" (Ph.D. diss., University of Colorado, Boulder, 1970), notes the resistance of business leaders to taxes and relief programs. Helpful for understanding relief are three University of Denver M.A. theses: Leonard J. Bisbing, "Family Relief in Denver, 1928–1939" (1939); Grace E. Wilson, "The History of the Development of the Denver Bureau of Public Welfare" (1938); and Dorothy D. Hutchinson, "History of Colorado's Private Relief Programs" (1944). Patrick F. McCarthy, in "Big Ed Johnson — A Political Portrait" (M.A. thesis, University of Colorado, Boulder, 1958), looked at one of Colorado's most popular leaders. Theater during the 1920s is extensively treated in Hebron C. Kline's three-volume "A History of the Denver Theater during the Depression" (Ph.D. diss., University of Denver, 1963).

The DPLWHD oral history collection, particularly the interviews done in the late 1970s with persons connected with New Deal art projects, are a rich mine of primary material. On artists also see Ronald Bruner, "New Deal Art Works in Colorado, Kansas, and Nebraska" (M.F.A. thesis, University of Denver, 1980). Cile M. Bach, *Frank Mechau: Artist of Colorado* (Aspen, CO: Aspen Center for the Visual Arts, 1981), looks into the short career (1904–1946) of an artist whose work gained national attention. The Denver Emergency Relief Committee Papers in DPLWHD provide untapped accounts of the early 1930s in Denver. The Wahlberg Papers and the John A. Carroll Collection at the Auraria Library are moderately useful. The Rocky Mountain Fuel Company Collection (Josephine Roche Papers) is at the University of Colorado, Boulder, as are the Edward Costigan Papers. Publisher Roy Howard's Papers at the Library of Congress contain correspondence between Howard and the various editors of the *Rocky Mountain News* in the late 1920s and the 1930s. Much material on the Federal Theater Project and Colorado relief operations may be found in the collections of the National Archives in Washington, D.C.

Notes

1. Edgar M. Wahlberg, *Voices in the Darkness* (Boulder, CO: Roberts Rinehart, 1983), p. 54.
2. Fred A. Rosenstock, "The Denver I Remember," in Robert W. Mutchler, ed., *The Denver Westerners 1973 Brand Book* (Boulder: Johnson Publishing, 1974), p. 418.
3. Interview with Helen Christy, September 24, 1979 (oral history in DPLWHD; hereafter Tribble interview).
4. Wahlberg, *Voices*, p. 53.
5. Ibid., pp. 57–58.
6. Perkin, *First Hundred Years*, p. 534.
7. Wahlberg, *Voices*, p. 61.
8. Ibid., p. 55.
9. E. B. Lawrence to George Begole, February 28, 1933, Denver Emergency Relief Committee Papers (in DPLWHD).
10. *The Taxpayer's Review*, May 13, 1933. This piece of campaign literature is in DPLWHD.
11. Denver Emergency Relief Committee, January 20, 1933, "Report of the Visiting Committee," DERC Papers at DPLWHD.
12. Denver Civil Works Commission, "Minutes," December 26, 1933, pp. 4–8, in DPLWHD.
13. Frank Cross, "Revolution in Colorado," *The Nation* (February 7, 1934):153.
14. Tribble interview.
15. Danks to Carl Milliken, June 7, 1934, quoted in James F. Wickens, *Colorado in the Great Depression* (New York: Garland, 1979), p. 79.
16. Cross, "Revolution," p. 153.
17. Costigan, untitled typescript of radio speech on KOA Radio (Denver), September 9, 1930, in John A. Carroll Papers, Metropolitan State College, Auraria Library, Denver.
18. Ibid.
19. *DP*, August 12, 1957.
20. Radio speech, February 16, 1932, quoted in Hornbein, "Josephine Roche," p. 243.
21. *DP*, September 8, 1934.
22. *RMN*, September 7, 1934.
23. *DP*, September 12, 1934.
24. "Colorado National Bank Confidential Reports," manuscript files in U.S. Department of the Treasury, Comptroller of the Currency, Washington, D.C.
25. Interview with Helen Christy, October 1, 1979 (oral history in DPLWHD).
26. Ibid.
27. Tribble interview.
28. Wickens, *Colorado in Depression*, p. 283.
29. *DP*, December 26, 1938 quoted in Helen C. Kline, "A History of the Denver Theater during the Depression" (Ph.D. diss., University of Denver, 1963), vol. 1, p. 249.
30. Boettcher to Howard, August 24, 1936, Roy Howard Papers, box 111, Library of Congress.
31. Howard to Boettcher, August 25, 1936, in ibid.
32. Quotations from Davis to Howard, October 2, 1936, in ibid.
33. *RMN*, July 2, 1938.
34. Tribble interview.
35. Chris Dobbins, interview with Nancy Whistler, April 22, 1977 (oral history in DPLWHD).
36. *Congressional Record*, 76th Congress, 1st session, 1939, 84, Part 5, 5074, quoted in Robert C. Sims, "Colorado and the Great Depression" (Ph.D. diss., University of Colorado, Boulder, 1970), pp. 73–74.

CHAPTER 19: Denver Goes to War

Sources

Gerald D. Nash, *The American West Transformed: The Impact of the Second World War* (Bloomington: Indiana University Press, 1985), shows how the war spurred economic growth in Denver and other western cities. Harvey S. Perloff, et al., *Regions, Resources and Economic Growth* (Lincoln: University of Nebraska Press, 1960), demonstrates the strengths and weaknesses of Colorado's economy compared to other states; see esp. the table on pages 469–71. For a succinct account of the home front see A. Russell Buchanan, *The United States and World War II*, 2 vols. (New York: Harper & Row, 1964), vol. 1. Mark J. Harris, et al., in *The Homefront: America during World War II* (New York: G. P. Putnam's Sons, 1984), pieces together interviews with ordinary citizens to create an impressionistic picture.

After the war, Colorado historian LeRoy Hafen asked local war agencies to provide histories of their activities. Much of the information he collected is now at the Colorado Historical Society Library in collection 657, "War Records Survey, World War II." The papers of Representative Lawrence Lewis, also at the Colorado Historical Society, are useful for material on the period before the United States entered the war.

One of the best short accounts of Colorado in World War II is given by the Colorado State Planning Commission in *Year Book of the State of Colorado, 1945–1947* (Denver: Bradford-Robinson, c 1947), which includes a list of casualties. Stephen F. Mehls, "A

History of the Denver Federal Center" (M.A. thesis, University of Colorado, Boulder, 1975), details the development of the federal office complex that took over the Remington Arms plant. Joan Reese recounts the barriers faced by Denver's African-Americans in both world wars in "Two Enemies to Fight," *Colorado Heritage* 1 (1990):2–17. Two student papers done at the University of Colorado, Denver, focus on aspects of World War II in Denver: Mark T. Gallagher chronicles the economic impact of the war in "Denver Goes to War: World War II and War Production," and Gail M. Beaton explores societal changes in "Denver Welcomes the Military: CivilianM-ilitary Relations during World War II" (unpublished typescripts in possession of Thomas J. Noel). We are indebted to *Colorado Heritage* for permission to reprint material appearing in Stephen J. Leonard's "Denver at War," *Colorado Heritage* 4, (1987):30–41.

Notes

1. *Rocky Mountain Herald*, July 24, 1943. Ferril's *Herald* can be found in DPLWHD.
2. *DP*, December 30, 1940.
3. Ibid., October 7, 1937.
4. Ibid., December 30, 1940.
5. Ibid., December 8, 1941.
6. Ibid., December 7, 1941. Denver shut the Civic Center lights off in 1942 and they remained off until 1945. Outdoor home lighting was not possible in late 1945 because of the shortage of electric wire. See ibid., December 23, 1945.
7. Anonymous, *Buckley Field* (n.p., n.d.), p. 13. Internal evidence suggests that this booklet in DPLWHD was published c 1943. Buckley was named for a Longmont, Colorado, flyer, John Harold Buckley, killed as he flew over France, September 17, 1918.
8. Henry W. Hough, comp., *Americans with Spanish Surnames* (Denver: WPA Workers Service Program, 1942), p. 17.
9. *RMN*, February 26, 1944.
10. *Salida Daily Mail*, August 22, 1942, quoting Lowry *Rev-Meter*.
11. *DP*, July 9, 20, September 29, 1942, and February 21, 1944.
12. Ibid., March 22, 1954. See *RMN*, December 31, 1942, for an article on the arsenal that reported that 700 buildings, including 154 houses, had been cleared from the site where, the *News* suggested, poison gas was to be manufactured.
13. The *USS Denver*, a light cruiser, was put into service in 1942. Kamikaze pilots and torpedos were not able to destroy the vessel. Wreckers broke the *Denver* up in 1959. See *RMN*, August 22, 1987.
14. *DP*, August 7, 1944.
15. Cranmer, interview with David McComb, May 22, 1974 (typescript in Colorado Historical Society Library), p. 39.
16. *DP*, December 31, 1940.
17. *RMN*, December 29, 1942.
18. *Littleton Independent*, July 31, 1942.
19. Interview with S. J. Leonard, July 10, 1989.
20. *Fort Collins Coloradan*, August 14, 1969.
21. *Colorado Salvage Newsletter*, July 19, 1943.
22. Denver Defense Council, Advisory Board, "Minutes, July 19, 1945," p. 4, in Colorado Historical Society Library.
23. Allen Moore, "History of the Office of Price Administration in Colorado" (typescript in Collection 657, Colorado Historical Society Library), p. 114.
24. *RMN*, December 21, 1942.
25. Ibid., February 19, 1944.
26. *Littleton Independent*, July 31, 1942.
27. Moore, "Office of Price Administration," p. 35.
28. *DP*, October 27, 1942.
29. James Grafton Rogers, "The Trend of Modern History," *The Colorado Magazine* 11 (January 1934):16.
30. *DP*, April 28, 1935. George Meredith Musick, Sr.'s autobiography, *Wayfarer in Architecture* (Denver: privately printed, 1976), tells of many large federal projects, both military and civilian, that he and other architects undertook during the war.
31. Colorado State Federation of Labor, *Official Colorado Victory Edition 1942 Yearbook* (n.p., n.d,), p. 17.
32. Ibid., p.21.
33. Unidentified newspaper clipping, probably *DP*, dated August 19, 1952, in clipping collection of DPLWHD.
34. Denver Bureau of Public Welfare, "A Study of the Japanese Population of the City and County of Denver" (n.p., n.d.), p. 55. Also see feature article on "Little Japan" in *RMN*, November 18, 1944.
35. *RMN*, April 30, 1945. On alien land legislation see ibid., February 3, 1944; and *DP*, February 17 and November 9, 1944.
36. *RMN*, March 26, 1949; *DP*, March 22, 1950. Both discrimination cases involved restrictive covenants aimed at keeping nonwhites out. Gow, it appears, did purchase the house, for he is listed at that address in 1950s Denver city directories.
37. *RMN*, August 15, 1945.
38. *DP*, June 3, 1948. The first cemetery at Fort Logan, a small, base burial ground established in 1889, had fewer than 400 graves in 1946. On Miller see *DP*, October 31 and November 2, 1950. An average of nearly 1,000 persons a year were buried at Fort Logan between 1951 and 1984. Among them was John Carroll, who had served as a private in World War I and, after resigning his OPA post, as a major in World War II.
39. Denver Defense Council, Advisory Board, "Minutes, July 19, 1945," p. 2.
40. Ibid., April 20, 1944, p. 5.
41. Ibid., February 6, 1945, p. 3.

42. *DP*, December 31, 1946.

CHAPTER 20: The Postwar Awakening

Sources

For an overview and the thesis that World War II was the "greatest single influence" shaping the modern West see Gerald D. Nash, *The American West Transformed: The Impact of the Second World War* (Bloomington: Indiana University Press, 1985). George V. Kelly, a onetime Director of Publications and Public Information for Mayor Newton, gives an insider's look at the administrations of Stapleton, Newton, Nicholson, Batterton, Currigan, and McNichols in *The Old Gray Mayors of Denver* (Boulder, CO: Pruett Publishing, 1974). Another useful guide is Kenneth Gray's *Report on Politics in Denver* (Cambridge, MA: Harvard-MIT Joint Center for Urban Studies, 1959). William Zeckendorf's autobiography, *Zeckendorf* (New York: Holt, Rinehart & Winston, 1970), offers three amusing chapters on Denver from 1945 to the 1960s.

Allen D. Breck, longtime professor of history at the University of Denver, provides one of the few published biographies on a mid-twentieth-century Denver business leader in *John Evans of Denver: Portrait of a Twentieth Century Banker* (Boulder, CO: Pruett Publishing, 1972). Margaret Pilcher has looked at Gene Cervi in "Eugene Cervi and *Cervi's Rocky Mountain Journal*" (Ph.D. diss., University of Denver, 1986). Architecture and public improvements during the Speer and Stapleton eras are covered by Thomas J. Noel and Barbara S. Norgren in *Denver: The City Beautiful and Its Architects, 1893–1941* (Denver: Historic Denver, 1987).

Much of the scattered information on postwar Denver has not yet been digested by historians and put into books. In the mid-1970s, David McComb, a Colorado State University professor financed by a Boettcher Foundation grant, conducted numerous interviews with Denver's movers and shakers. In addition to those cited in the notes, the McComb interviews with Helen Black, George Cavender, Vincent Dwyer, and Alan Fisher offer insights into the power structure. Transcripts are at the Colorado Historical Society Library. The DPLWHD also has an excellent oral history collection that includes interviews with various Denver leaders including George Cranmer. The authors of this book have also interviewed many of the figures involved, including Hugh Catherwood, George Cranmer, Montgomery Dorsey, Maxine Kurtz, Quigg Newton, and Bruce Rockwell.

Notes

1. John Gunther, *Inside USA.* (New York: Harper & Brothers, 1947), p. 224.
2. Robert L. Perkin's chapter on Denver in Ray B. West, Jr., ed., *Rocky Mountain Cities* (New York: W. W. Norton, 1949), p. 281.
3. Gunther, *Inside USA*, p. 22.
4. Eugene H. Adams, Lyle W. Dorsett, and Robert S. Pulcipher, *The Pioneer Western Bank-First of Denver, 1860–1980* (Denver: First Bank and Colorado Historical Society, 1984), p. 139.
5. William Merriam Bart Berger, interview with T. J. Noel, July 10, 1985. Also see Thomas J. Noel, *Growing Through History with Colorado: The Colorado National Banks, The First 125 Years* (Denver: Colorado National Banks and the Colorado Studies Center, University of Colorado at Denver, 1987).
6. Neil L. King, *History of Banking in Denver, Colorado, 1858–1950* (Rutgers, NJ: Rutgers Graduate School of Banking, 1952), p. 88, reports that the deposits of Denver's 10 leading banks climbed from $205,392,000 in 1939 to $604,839,000 in 1945 while loans went from $50 million to $78,744,000.
7. West, *Rocky Mountain Cities*, p. 286. For information on Kaiser we are indebted to our colleague Mark S. Foster for his *Henry J. Kaiser: Builder of the Modern American West* (Austin: University of Texas Press, 1989).
8. By marriage or by blood, the Coors brewing family was connected with the Cranmers and the Porters; the Phipps were intertwined with the Garretts, the Bromfields, and the Van Schaacks (real estate). The Grants (smelters and banking) were allied with the Mitchells (banking), who were in turn related to, among others, the Kountzes, the Van Schaacks and the Phipps. For a genealogy of Denver's inbred power elite, see *Westword*, January 27, 1983.
9. Gunther, *Inside USA*, pp. 215–16.
10. Interview with S. J. Leonard, February 28, 1975 (hereafter Dorsey interview).
11. E. Warren Willard, interview with David McComb, February 20, 1975, in Colorado Historical Society Library, p. 39.
12. Ibid., p. 20.
13. John Clark Mitchell II, interview with David McComb, April 8, 1975, p. 4, in Colorado Historical Society Library.
14. Dorsey interview.
15. George Cranmer, interview with David McComb, May 22, 1974, in Colorado Historical Society Library, p. 5 (hereafter Cranmer interview).
16. Remarks of Stapleton in Denver Defense Council Advisory Board Meeting, November 16, 1944, p. 4 (typescript in World War II Historic Records Collection 657 in Colorado Historical Society).
17. Cranmer interview, p. 33; *RMN*, March 9, 1947.
18. *Life*, May 10, 1947. The picture is reprinted in George V. Kelly, *The Old Gray Mayors of Denver* (Boulder, CO: Pruett Publishing, 1974), p. 22.
19. Newton, interview with T. J. Noel, October 1, 1987.
20. Hugh Catherwood, interviews with T. J. Noel, May 28 and August 26, 1986 (hereafter Catherwood interview).
21. Ibid.
22. Cranmer interview, p. 33.
23. Catherwood interview.
24. Bruce M. Rockwell, interviews with T. J. Noel, February 1, 4, 27, 1985.
25. Ibid.

26. *RMN*, June 14, 1972.
27. Cranmer interview, p. 32.
28. Maxine Kurtz, interviews with T. J. Noel, June 12, July 14, and December 2, 1986.
29. All quotations from William Zeckendorf, *Zeckendorf* (New York: Holt, Rinehart & Winston, 1970), pp. 107–8, passim.
30. Interview with David McComb, February 26, 1974, p. 14.
31. Temple Buell interview with David McComb, p. 29 (hereafter Buell interview).
32. Gunther, *Inside USA*, p. 224.
33. Alan Phipps, interview with David McComb, January 28, 1974, in Colorado State Historical Society Library, p. 32.
34. Buell interview, p. 30.

CHAPTER 21: Automobility

Sources

Coloradans have been far more enthusiastic about owning automobiles than about compiling the history of automobility. Although local studies are sparse, a growing national literature exists. Good background overviews are provided by James J. Flink, *The Car Culture* (Cambridge, MA: MIT Press, 1975); John Keats, *The Insolent Chariots* (Philadelphia: Lippincott, 1958); and John B. Rae, *The Road and the Car in American Life* (Cambridge, MA: MIT Press, 1971).

Mark S. Foster, *From Streetcar to Superhighway* (Philadelphia, PA: Temple University Press, 1981), uses Denver as one of seven case-study cities; see, too, LeRoy R. Hafen, "The Coming of the Automobile and Improved Roads to Colorado," *The Colorado Magazine* 7 (January 1931):1–16. Steven L. Beaghler, "The Automobile in Denver," *University of Colorado at Denver Historical Studies Journal* 5 (1988):47–60; and Thomas J. Noel, "Paving the Way to Colorado: The Evolution of Auto Tourism in Denver," *Journal of the West* 26, no. 3 (July 1987):42–49.

Notes

1. Neal Cassidy, Denver's most celebrated car thief, appears as Dean Moriarity, the hero of Jack Kerouac's novel of the beat generation, *On the Road* (New York: Viking, 1957).
2. David W. Brunton's unpublished diary, in Colorado Historical Society Library.
3. *Polly Pry* magazine, September 5 and October 10, 1903.
4. *Colorado Highways* (September 1928):6.
5. Interview with T. J. Noel, Denver, May 24, 1979.
6. City Club of Denver, *Art in Denver* (Denver: Denver Public Library, 1928), p. 40. Since the 1930s, autos have generally outshone uninspired showrooms. The Cullen-Thompson showroom has been remodeled by Gart Brothers, Colorado's leading sporting goods dealer, as a "sports castle," complete with an indoor ski slope and rooftop tennis court.
7. *DP*, July 22, 1899.
8. *Fritchle Electric Sales Catalogue, 1914–15*, a part of the Oliver Parker Fritchle Collection at the Colorado Historical Society that includes the only known working Fritchle.
9. James J. Flink, *Car Culture* (Cambridge, MA: MIT Press, 1975), p. 149.
10. *Denver Republican*, September 10, 1903.
11. State expenditures for 1923–1927 in the *Year Book of the State of Colorado 1930* (Denver: State Board of Immigration, 1931), p. 183.
12. Arthur H. Carhart, "Denver's Greatest Manufacturing Plant," *Denver Municipal Facts* (September–October 1921):3–7.
13. March 13, 1914, letter, Olmsted to the Denver Park Commissioners, in "The Records of Olmsted Associates," job file 5582, box B 305, Library of Congress.
14. August 10, 1914, letter, Letts to Olmsted Associates, in ibid.
15. August 14, 1914, letter, Olmsted to Letts, in ibid.
16. Undated *DP* clipping, in Anne Louis Johnson Collection, Colorado Historical Society Library.
17. Denver Chamber of Commerce, "Minutes, 1912–1915," Chamber of Commerce Building, Denver.
18. United States, National Park Service, *Annual Report for 1917* (Washington: GPO, 1918).
19. *DP*, April 18, 1922. Such complaints led Mayor Ben Stapleton to ban public dances at Overland Park in 1923.
20. *Colorado Highways* (October 24, 1924):8. Denver's courtship of automobile tourists was consistent with the national patterns traced in Warren J. Blasco, *Americans on the Road: From Autocamp to Motel, 1910–1945* (Cambridge, MA: MIT Press, 1979).
21. *Denver Times*, April 7, 1902.
22. Ibid., July 30, 1902.
23. Denver Planning Commission, *The Denver Plan*, vol. 3: *A Study for Mass Transportation* (Denver: Denver Planning Commission, 1932), pp. 13–22.
24. Quoted in Mark S. Foster, *From Streetcar to Superhighway* (Philadelphia, PA: Temple University Press, 1981). Foster argues that "contemporary critics of the automobile culture have been guilty of presentism in condemning early planners and traffic engineers" (p. 177) and defends automobile proponents as sincere reformers who found automobility a welcome escape from wretched turn-of-the-century urban congestion.
25. *RMN*, July 19, 1987; *DP*, *Empire Magazine*, July 26, 1970.
26. Benjamin B. Lindsey and Wainwright Evans, *The Revolt of Modern Youth* (New York: Boni & Liveright, 1925), p. 161. After 25 years of dealing with troubled youths as Denver's first juvenile court judge, Lindsey estimated that among the high school set who

"ride together in automobiles, more than 90 percent indulge in hugging and kissing" (p. 56).

27. Louis E. Ballast's "Application for Registration of Trademark," January 1, 1932, in the "Cheeseburger" ephemera file, Colorado Historical Society Library.

28. Denver's most notable hometown hamburger chain, Rockybilt, was not a drive-in operation but a collection of inexpensive restaurants. Roy Chesney, a journalism graduate of Kansas State University, opened the first Mr. Rockybilt in 1936 at 960 East Colfax. His nickel hamburgers with spicy mustard-onion sauce sold well during the depression era, so he expanded the menu (milk shakes, grilled cheese sandwiches, and chili cost a dime each) and added 11 more restaurants. These sanitary, service-oriented eateries behind glistening white terra cotta façades thrived until after Chesney sold out in 1972.

29. *Drive In Management* magazine (December 1966):8; Jerry Anderson, interview with Kelley Wensing, April 2, 1986 (in Tom Noel Collection).

30. Ralph J. Batschelet, *The Flick and I* (Smithtown, NY: Exposition Press, 1981), pp. 97–98; DP, *Empire Magazine*, September 29, 1984.

31. RMN, August 31, 1946.

32. Denver Planning Commission, *The Denver Plan*, vol. 7: *The Problem of Decentralization and Disintegration in Cities as Discussed in the Conference Held . . . at the Massachusetts Institute of Technology, Oct. 15–17, 1941* (Denver: Denver Planning Commission, 1941), pp. 5–6.

33. Henry A. Barnes, *The Man with the Red and Green Eyes* (New York: E. P. Dutton, 1965), pp. 125–26.

34. Ibid., p. 126

35. Ibid., p. 109.

36. DP, May 24, 1953.

37. *The New York Times*, September 18, 1968.

38. S. R. DeBoer, "Auto Roads," in Denver Planning Commission, *The Denver Plan* vol. 4. (Denver: Denver Planning Commission, 1933).

39. Marion C. Wiley, *The High Road* (Denver: Colorado Department of Highways, 1976), pp. 31–32.

40. *Commemorating the Opening of the Denver Valley Highway, November 23, 1958* (Denver: Colorado Department of Highways, 1958).

41. George V. Kelly, *The Old Gray Mayors of Denver* (Boulder, CO: Pruett Publishing, 1974), pp. 84–85.

42. RMN, July 24, 1988.

43. DP, February 18, 1972.

44. Lamm, quoted in Jane Simonton, *Vail* (Dallas, TX: Taylor Publishing, 1987), p. 115. For an overview of the voter rebellion against funding the Olympics, see Mark S. Foster, "Colorado's Defeat of the 1976 Winter Olympics," *Colorado Magazine* 53 (Spring 1976):163–86.

45. *Rocky Mountain Motorist* (September 1989):12.

46. Suburban growth was neither uniform nor guaranteed; social and economic conditions within suburbia vary as much as they do within the core city. Poorer residents, including many blacks, moved to northwest Aurora; while low-income residents, including Hispanics, moved northwest to Northglenn, Thornton, and Westminster. The dangers of oversimplifying urban-suburban growth are pointed out by Carl Abbott in "The Suburban Sunbelt," *Journal of Urban History* 14 (May 1987):275–301.

CHAPTER 22: Arapahoe County

Sources

The *Colorado Year Book*, published between 1918 and 1964 by the state, provides encyclopedic information, including brief histories of counties and towns. For the somewhat arbitrary dates of a town's birth and death we have used the post office as the vital sign, a task made easy by W. J. Bauer, J. L. Ozment, and J. H. Willard, *Colorado Post Offices, 1859–1989* (Golden: Colorado Railroad Museum, 1990). Public libraries and historical societies of the communities discussed generally have local history sections that are helpful. All population figures, unless otherwise noted, are from the official U.S. Census. Vickers's and Smiley's histories provide helpful coverage of Denver suburbs.

Notes

1. For the history of Littleton we relied heavily on the staff, exhibits, publications, and files of the Littleton History Museum. See also Edwin A. Bemis's unpublished autobiography, "So I Took an Apple," in the Littleton Public Library and his article, "Littleton: Dynamic Town of Colorado," in the Denver Posse of the Westerners, *The Denver Westerners Brand Book*, ed. Francis B. Rizzari, vol. 20 (Boulder, CO: Johnson Publishing, 1964), pp. 25–58; Dave Hicks, *Littleton from the Beginning* (Denver: Egan Printing, 1975); and Smiley's *Denver*, as well as Robert J. McQuarie and Curt W. Buchholtz, *Littleton, Colorado: Settlement to Centennial* (Littleton, CO: Littleton Historical Museum, 1990).

2. Credit Ratings for Colorado Territory, 1867, 1873, and 1874 entries for Richard Sullivan Little, R. G. Dun Collection, Baker Business Library, Harvard University.

3. William B. Vickers, *History of Denver* (Chicago: O. O. Baskin, 1880), pp. 178–80, 264, 504.

4. Houston Waring, *Hous's Littleton: A Historical Miscellany* (Littleton, CO: Independent Printing, 1981), p. 5.

5. Ibid., p. 19.

6. Ibid., p. 22.

7. *Littleton Independent*, July 29, 1960.
8. Based on corporate sketch in Thomas J. Noel, *Denver: Rocky Mountain Gold* (Tulsa, OK: Continental Heritage, 1980), pp. 215–16 and DP, April 8, 1989.
9. C. A. Norgren Company, which the family sold to English investors in 1972, became a major metropolitan success story, chronicled in the 1976 booklet, issued on the firm's fiftieth anniversary, *The History of C. A. Norgren Co.*, and in the corporate histories section of Noel, *Denver: Rocky Mountain Gold*, pp. 222–23. Carl A. Norgren's *As I Was Saying* (Boulder, CO: Johnson Publishing, 1965), while containing his reflections on everything from "My Son" to "Insidious Socialism," serves as neither an autobiography nor a corporate biography.
10. Interview with T. J. Noel, April 26, 1988.
11. Pete Smythe, *Big-City Dropout* (Boulder, CO: Pruett Press, 1968), p. 5.
12. Two brief, illustrated histories are *Englewood, Colorado, 1903–1978* (Englewood, CO: Englewood Public Library, 1978); and Dave Hicks, *Englewood from the Beginning* (Denver: A-T-P Publishing, 1971). See also Shellie Clark's 1923 University of Denver M.A. thesis, "History of the City of Englewood." Nancy Bunker, local history specialist at the Englewood Public Library, has been a generous and knowledgeable resource.
13. Property Records for Orchard Place, Local History Collection, Englewood Public Library; *Denver Republican*, October 2, 1903.
14. Alvin T. Steinel, *History of Agriculture in Colorado* (Fort Collins, CO: State Agricultural College, 1926), pp. 282–83.
15. John A. deVries, *Alexander Eaglerock: A History of Alexander Aircraft Company* (Colorado Springs, CO: Century One Press, 1985).
16. For a history of Colorado's once-flourishing carnation industry, see Dick Kingman, *A History: Colorado Flower Growers* (Denver: Colorado Greenhouse Growers Association, 1986).
17. Interview with T. J. Noel, April 5, 1989.
18. Bette D. Peters, *Denver's Four Mile House* (Denver: Golden Bell Press, 1980), traces the evolution of the oldest structure in metropolitan Denver, while Jack and Patricia Fletcher, *Colorado's Cowtown* (Yuma, AZ: J. and P. Fletcher, 1981), sketch Glendale's history.
19. RMN, August 7 and 8, 1977, features Bob's Place in a two-part series on Glendale.
20. Steinel, *History of Agriculture in Colorado*, pp. 462–63.
21. DP, March 26, 1984.
22. David and Holly Franke, *Safe Places for the 80s* (Garden City, NY: Doubleday, 1984), pp. 58–61.
23. DP, March 17, 1983.
24. Ibid.
25. Ibid., October 25, 1975.
26. RMN, April 29, 1975.
27. DP, March 13, 1989.
28. See RMN, March 30, 1986, for this and following quotations.

CHAPTER 23: Jefferson County

Sources

For overviews, see Edward L. Berthoud, "History of Jefferson County," in *History of Clear Creek and Boulder Valleys* (Chicago: O. L. Baskin, 1880); Georgina Brown, *The Shining Mountains* (Gunnison, CO: B&B Printers, 1976); *From Scratch: A History of Jefferson County Colorado* (Golden, CO: Jefferson County Historical Commission, 1985); and Ethel Dark's fine "The History of Jefferson County, Colorado" (M.A. thesis, Colorado State College of Education, Greeley, 1939). Golden's early history has been well covered, but its twentieth century is barely touched by historians. *Golden: The 19th Century* (Littleton, CO: Harbinger House, 1987) by Lorraine Wagenback and Jo Ann E. Thistlewood is a good start. Charles S. Ryland, "Chrysopolis . . . The Golden City," in *The Denver Posse of the Westerners Roundup* 16 (November 1960):4–14, argues that Golden is not a suburb of Denver, "whose tentacles reach out hungrily promising the civic blessings of abundant water and the privilege of connecting to an overloaded sewer system." For the Adolph Coors Company sketch, we relied on R. G. Dun and Company credit ledgers at Baker Business Library, Harvard University; William Kostka, *The Pre-Prohibition History of Adolph Coors Company, 1873–1933* (Denver: Adolph Coors Company, 1973); newspapers; and Charles S. Ryland, "Adolph Coors of Golden," in *The Denver Westerners Brand Book*, vol. 23, ed. Richard A. Ronzio (Boulder, CO: Johnson Publishing, 1968).

Lakewood's Belmar Museum is a repository of historical documents as well as artifacts. See also the "Lakewood History Scrapbooks" in the city clerk's office; *The Lakewood Sentinel*; and a rewarding anthology: Patricia K. Wilcox, ed., *76 Centennial Stories of Lakewood* (Boulder, CO: Johnson Publishing and the Lakewood Historical Society, 1976). Arvada's history is unusually well surveyed up to the 1940s in publications of the Arvada Historical Society: *Waters of Gold, 1850–1904; More Than Gold, 1870–1904*; and *Arvada, Just Between You and Me, 1904–1941*. Wheat Ridge's early history is covered in the booklets *History of Pioneer Wheat Ridge* (Wheat Ridge: City Historical Committee, 1971) and in *Biographical Sketches of Early Settlers of Wheat Ridge* (Wheat Ridge, CO: Wheat Ridge Bicentennial-Centennial Committee, 1976).

Evergreen is portrayed in Mary Helen Crain's *Evergreen, Colorado* (Boulder, CO: Pruett Publishing, 1969). Crain and her husband Willard have published since 1958 Evergreen's *Canyon Courier*, chronicling the town's boom and subsequent antigrowth sentiments. Noted architect Gene Sternberg and his sociologist wife Barbara have focused on the search for community in *Evergreen: Our Mountain Community* (Boulder, CO: Johnson Publishing, 1987). Although smaller Jefferson County towns have been grossly neglected here, readers will find some of them well surveyed in studies such as Helen N. Brush and Catherine P. Dittman's elegant *Indian Hills* (Denver: Graphic Impressions, 1976). Judith Allison, *Edgewater: Fourscore* (Edgewater, CO: Edgewater Historical Commission, 1979), has captured the colorful past of the town where her mother served as mayor and state representative. For Morrison see Lorene Horton and Mary Helen Crain, *Memory Album: Morrison, Colorado* (Evergreen, CO: Canyon Courier Press, 1976); and Sam Arnold, *The View from Mt. Morrison* (Denver: Fur Press, 1974). The county's many private clubs and semiprivate summer communities have eluded historical treatment, with a few exceptions such as Nolie Mumey, *Wigwam: The Oldest Fishing Club in the State of Colorado. . . .* (Boulder, CO: Johnson Publishing Company, 1969).

The Jefferson County Historical Commission, established in 1973, has created a Hall of Fame and a biennial publication called *Historically Jeffco*, and is erecting roadside historical markers and compiling a county place-names directory, commission president Marcetta Lutz reported in 1989.

Notes

1. Ralph Moody, *Little Britches: Father and I Were Ranchers* (New York: W. W. Norton, 1950), pp. 121–22.
2. *RMN*, December 28, 1859; more-recent county oppositon to governmental forces is covered by Laura Misch, "This Land Is My Land," *Westword*, January 31–February 6, 1990.
3. *Jefferson County Record Book* cited in Ethel Dark, "The History of Jefferson County" (M.A. thesis, Colorado State College of Education, Greeley, 1939), p. 9–11; see also Francis B. Rizzari, "Notes on a Few Early Towns of Jefferson County," in Arthur L. Campa, ed., *Brand Book of the Denver Westerners* (Boulder, CO: Johnson Publishing, 1965), pp. 236–55.
4. Quoted in "George West," an article by his grandson Neil W. Kimball, in *The Colorado Magazine* 27 (July 1950):198–208.
5. *Commonwealth* (Denver), January 25, 1864, quoted in Georgina Brown, *The Shining Mountains* (Gunnison, CO: B&B Printers, 1976), p. 29.
6. Robert C. Black III, *Railroad Pathfinder: The Life and Times of Edward L. Berthoud* (Evergreen, CO: Cordillera Press, 1988), p. 91. Berthoud, a scholar of encyclopedic interests, wrote reports on biological and archaeological specimens that he collected while surveying wagon and railroad routes, including Berthoud Pass, and later donated to the Smithsonian and to the Colorado School of Mines.
7. Quoted in James E. Le Rossignol, *History of Higher Education in Colorado* (Washington D.C.: GPO, 1903), p. 45. Discipline remained a problem among students described by churchmen as "the most difficult problem in higher educational circles in the state," as quoted in Michael McGiffert, *The Higher Learning in Colorado* (Denver: Sage Books, 1964), pp. 110–16, 191.
8. Frank Hall, *History of Colorado*, vol. 3 (Chicago: Blakeley Printing, 1891), p. 509.
9. *The Golden Transcript*, November 16, 1989; and R. Laurie Simmons and Christine Whitacre, *The 1989 Survey of Historic Buildings in Downtown Golden* (Denver: Front Range Research Associates, 1989).
10. Bob Richardson is the subject of the cover story of *Trains: The Magazine of Railroading* (February 1988):24–29.
11. See *Golden Cemetery, Jefferson County, Colorado Cemetery Series* (Lakewood, CO: Foothills Genealogical Society of Colorado, 1989), a history and guide.
12. Gail L. Paulsen, "What's Happening in Golden?" *Straight Creek Journal*, April 10, 1975.
13. *For Your Information: Jefferson County Colorado* (Golden, CO: Jefferson County Planning Department, 198[ ]), p. 53.
14. Patricia K. Wilcox, ed., *76 Centennial Stories of Lakewood* (Boulder, CO: Johnson Publishing, and Lakewood Historical Society, 1976), pp. 20–22. The Loveland home, an undesignated landmark, survives.
15. Ibid., pp. 139–42; for a detailed study see Jeanne L. Abrams, "Chasing the Cure" (Ph.D. diss., University of Colorado, Boulder, History Dept., 1983).
16. John Bailey, "The Federal Center," in Wilcox, *76 Centennial Stories*, pp. 66–69.
17. Ibid.; *Willits Farm Map for Parts of Weld, Boulder, Arapahoe and Jefferson Counties.* (Denver: W. C. Willits, 1899).
18. The Ladies Grange Club program for Friday, January 11, 1929, reproduced in Wilcox, *76 Centennial Stories*, p. 145.
19. Stanley W. Zamonski, *The Westernaires on the Gallop* (Denver: Stanza-Harp, 1967).
20. *Jefferson County Republican*, January 15, 1947.
21. David Nelson, "Finally a City," in Wilcox, *76 Centennial Stories*, pp. 160–67.
22. James J. Richey, "Lakewood Celebrates 20 Years!" *Looking at Lakewood* 5, no. 5 (September 1989):2–3.
23. Arthur J. Gude, letter to the editor, *DP*, April 16, 1973.
24. Wilcox, *76 Centennial Stories*, pp. 80–82.
25. *DP*, April 7, 1982.
26. Interview with Thomas J. Noel, November 10, 1989.
27. Arvada Historical Society, *More Than Gold, 1870–1904*, pp. 1–4.
28. Lois C. Lindstrom, *The Old Mill: Arvada Flour Mills, 1925–1980* (Arvada: Arvada Historical Society, 1980).
29. *Arvada, Just Between You and Me*, pp. 179–80.
30. *Arvada Enterprise*, September 9, 1976.
31. *DP*, May 2, 1962.
32. *Other Voices: An Oral History of Arvada* (Arvada: Arvada Center for the Arts & Humanities, 1985), p. 6.
33. *City of Arvada Comprehensive Plan* (Arvada: Arvada Planning Commission, 1985), p. 52.
34. *DP*, October 17, 1985.
35. W. W. Wilmore, "Wheat Ridge as I Knew It in 1880," in *History of Pioneer Wheat Ridge* (Wheat Ridge: Historical Committee, 1971), pp. 3–5.
36. Financier Victor Sayyah's 476-acre estate, with a 13,500-square-foot house, 500-bottle wine cellar, nine full bathrooms, and

five-car garage, went on the market for $16 million in 1988, according to *DP*, October 10, 1988.

37. Barbara and Gene Sternberg, *Evergreen: Our Mountain Community* (Boulder, CO: Johnson Publishing, 1987), p. 216.
38. Ibid., p. 219.
39. *Jefferson County Open Space Master Plan* (Lakewood, CO: B.R.W. Urban Edges, 1988).
40. Interview with T. J. Noel, December 9, 1989; facts and figures are from the department's annual reports and *Open Space News*, its quarterly newsletter.
41. An obituary for Johnson in the *RMN*, December 30, 1988, reported that his lawsuit against the county led to a $150,000 settlement in 1985. For his Rocky Flats research, see *The American Journal of Epidemiology* 26 (1987):153–55, and other articles indexed in the *Index Medicus*.
42. *RMN*, December 11, 1988.
43. Marcia Klotz, *A Citizen's Guide to Rocky Flats: Environmental and Safety Issues at the Nuclear Weapons Plant* (Boulder, CO: Rocky Mountain Peace Center, 1988), p. 4. This is a lucid, conscientious, footnoted overview.
44. Carl J. Johnson, "Cancer Incidence in an Area Contaminated with Radionuclides Near a Nuclear Installation," *Ambio* 10 (1981):176–82.
45. Joseph Daniel and Keith Pope, *A Year of Disobedience . . . Demonstration, Civil Disobedience, Arrests and Trials of Thousands of People Against the Rocky Flats Nuclear Weapons Plant* (Boulder, CO: Daniel Production, 1979), p. 92.
46. *DP*, June 21, 1989.
47. *RMN*, December 3, 1989.
48. Jefferson County Planning Department, *For Your Information*, pp. 35, 36, 41, 53.
49. *City & State*, a biweekly national magazine assessing local government, in the August 28, 1989, issue reported that Jefferson County Schools achieved the fourth-best SAT scores and the second-best ACT scores among the nation's largest school districts; *RMN*, December 12, 1989.
50. *RMN*, February 5, 1990.

CHAPTER 24: Boulder County

Sources
Among a dozen urban biographies of Boulder, a readable, footnoted book oriented toward the twentieth century is Phyllis Smith, *A Look at Boulder from Settlement to City* (Boulder, CO: Pruett Publishing, 1981). Academic studies covering every imaginable angle, from Boulder's insect life to its notoriously high winds, are available in the various CU libraries. Boulder's downtown Carnegie Library has been made into a branch specializing in local history; the City Planning Department is also a valuable source of information. Historians have given the county and most towns outside Boulder little attention, with exceptions of histories and guides to the western mining towns by Boulder author and book dealer Sylvia Pettem; Isabel M. Becker's elegant book, *Nederland: A Trip to Cloudland* (Denver: Scott Becker Press, 1989); and Duane A. Smith's *Silver Saga: The Story of Caribou, Colorado* (Boulder, CO: Pruett Publishing, 1974). For a fine overview of coal miners, their towns and labor troubles see Phyllis Smith, *Once a Coal Miner: The Story of Colorado's Northern Coal Field* (Boulder, CO: Pruett Publishing, 1989).

Notes
1. Carson Reed, "Boulder County . . . has a Business Climate as Rock-Solid as the Flatirons," *Colorado Business Magazine* (September 1989):33–54.
2. *RMN*, August 16, 1976; *Straight Creek Journal*, September 10, 1979; telephone interview with Paul Danish by T. J. Noel, July 8, 1989. Danish was the most notorious of Boulder's "greennecks" pursuing radical environmental controls. A former CU history student and editor of *The Colorado Daily*, he served on the Boulder City Council from 1976 to 1982, crusading to keep Boulder from becoming "an indistinguishable piece of the Front Range Megalopolis." The Danish Plan passed in 1976 but was not renewed five years later when it expired, after capping growth during the boom years. After leaving the council, Danish shocked many of his former allies by joining the staff of Boulder's right-wing *Soldier of Fortune* magazine and crusading against gun control.
3. Neal Peirce, "Despite its 'whacky' image, Boulder is a Model for Urban Planning," *DP*, May 28, 1989; interview with John C. Buechner, former mayor and councilperson, by T. J. Noel, April 28, 1989; "Boulder Planning Milestones," 1987 mimeograph, Boulder Planning Department; American Society of Planning Officials, *Urban Growth Management Systems* (Chicago: ASPO, 1975, Reports nos. 309, 310), pp. 10–12; interview with Denver Planning Director William Lamont by T. J. Noel, July 10, 1989.
4. Memoirs of Thomas Aikins in the *Boulder County News*, July 14, 1876; and in Amos Bixby, "History of Boulder Canyon," in *History of Clear Creek and Boulder Valleys, Colorado* (Chicago: O. L. Baskin & Co., 1880), p. 379.
5. Bixby, "History of Boulder Canyon," pp. 378–80. Niwot's relations with the whites are explored in detail in Margaret Coel, *Chief Left Hand: Southern Arapaho* (Norman: University of Oklahoma Press, 1981), pp. 63–70. Today Chief Niwot is memorialized by Left Hand Creek, by the town of Niwot, by a bust on the county courthouse lawn, and by a ruddy, squatting statue sculpted by Thomas Meagher Miller, which graces the Charles S. Heartling Sculpture Gardens on Boulder Creek, where Niwot warily welcomed the whites in 1858.
6. Article 4 of *The Articles of Organization of the Boulder City Town Company*, Daybook Minutes for February 10, 1859, p. 13, Boulder City Town Company Records, Western Historical Collections, Norlin Library, University of Colorado, Boulder.
7. Bixby, *History of Clear Creek and Boulder Valleys*, p. 401.

8. See mineral production by county charts in *Colorado Year Book, 1962–1964* (Denver: Colorado State Planning Division, 1964).

9. Laurence T. Paddock, "The Peripatetic Press or How the Good News Came to Boulder," in *The Denver Westerners Roundup* 40 (May–June 1984):3–14.

10. Although Boulder was an early leader in petroleum production, it has not been among the top 20 producers in recent decades. A. H. Scanlon, *Oil and Gas Fields of Colorado: Statistical Data Through 1981* (Denver: Colorado Geological Survey, Department of Natural Resources, 1982), pp. 12, 57–61.

11. Frederick Stetson Allen, Ernest Andrade, Jr., Mark S. Foster, et al., *The University of Colorado, 1876–1976* (New York: Harcourt Brace Jovanovich, 1976), p. 17.

12. Ibid., p. 33.

13. Jane Sewall, *Jane, Dear Child* (Boulder: University of Colorado Press, 1957), p. 41; See also William E. Davis, *Glory Colorado! A History of the University of Colorado, 1858–1963* (Boulder, CO: Pruett Press, 1965), p.57.

14. James H. Baker, *Of Himself and Other Things* (Denver: Bradford Robinson, 1922), pp. 90–91.

15. Mabel Downer Durning, *The Chicago-Colorado Colony Founding of Longmont* (Longmont, CO: Career Development Center, 1976); James F. Willard and Colin B. Goodykoontz, *Experiments in Colorado Colonization* (Boulder: University of Colorado Historical Collections, 1926).

16. William C. Jones and Noel T. Holley, *The Kite Route: The Story of the Denver & Interurban Railroad* (Boulder, CO: Pruett Publishing, 1986), p. 98.

17. Ibid., p. 20.

18. *RMN*, July 24, 1966.

19. Interview with T. J. Noel, March 21, 1983.

20. Carolyn Conaroe, *The Louisville Story* (Louisville: Louisville Times, 1978).

21. The *Colorado Labor Advocate*, January 6, 1989; *DP*, June 11, 1989. Perry Eberhart provides a detailed account, "Trouble in Serene," in his *Ghosts of the Colorado Plains* (Athens, OH: Swallow Press, 1986), pp. 222–34.

22. All 1989 employment statistics are from *The Boulder County Answer Book*, p. 30, a Sunday Magazine Supplement to the *Boulder Daily Camera*, June 25, 1989. See also the annual *Directory of Colorado Manufacturers* published by the CU College of Business and Administration, Research Division, Boulder.

23. *DP*, March 22, 1984; *RMN*, December 8, 1989.

24. *The Boulder County Answer Book* (1989), p. 30.

25. Frederick Law Olmsted, Jr., *The Improvement of Boulder, Colorado* (1910; reprint, Boulder, CO: Thorne Ecological Foundation, 1967).

26. Letter to the *Boulder Daily Camera*, October 12, 1947, quoted in Phyllis Smith, *A Look at Boulder* (Boulder, CO: Pruett Publishing, 1981), p. 186.

27. Samuel Bowles, *Our New West* (Hartford, CT: Hartford Publishing, 1869), p. 127.

28. *DP*, April 24, 1989; Diane Johnson, "Baring the Coot Lake Controversy," *Westword*, February 10, 1983, detailed efforts to transform nude swimmers into topless swimmers.

29. Josephine Robertson, *Highlights of PLAN: Boulder County 1959–1968* (Boulder: PLAN, 1986); *This Is Boulder* (Boulder, CO: League of Women Voters, 1984); *Boulder Daily Camera*, March 6, 1989.

30. Stan Zemler, "How One City Works to Reduce Its Solid Waste with Recycling," *Colorado Municipalities* (monthly magazine of the Colorado Municipal League) 45 (July–August 1989):10–15.

31. *Newsweek*, July 28, 1980, pp. 69–70.

32. *Boulder Daily Camera*, May 8, 1974. In 1988 Boulder did pass a gay rights ordinance. For an overview of the Denver gay rights movement, see Thomas J. Noel, "Gay Bars and the Emergence of the Denver Homosexual Community," *The Social Science Journal* 15 (April 1978):59–74.

33. The Colorado average, as of 1983, was 6,610 crimes per 100,000, with metropolitan crime greatest in Adams (11,127) and Denver (11,066) counties, followed by Boulder (6,198), Jefferson (5,033), and Arapahoe (3,152), according to the *Statistical Abstract of Colorado, 1987* (Boulder: University of Colorado College of Business Administration, Research Division, 1987).

34. Peter Pollock, Boulder City Planning Department planner, interview with T. J. Noel, June 27, 1989.

35. Claire Martin, "Boulder: Sports Town, U.S.A.," *DP*, August 6, 1989, *Contemporary Magazine*, pp. 8–16. *Outside Magazine* (May 1989), also profiled Boulder as the United States' number-one sports town.

36. CU Geography Professor Richard E. Stevens, interview with T. J. Noel, June 29, 1989.

37. Joni Teter, "Highlights of the Boulder Valley Comprehensive Plan" (Boulder, CO: Boulder Planning Board, 1987); *The Boulder County Answer Book* (1989), p. 16.

38. *DP*, April 6, 1989.

39. H. A. Waldrop, *Arapahoe Glacier: A Sixty-Year Record*, University of Colorado Studies, Series in Geology no. 3, November 1964.

40. Olmsted, to Sierra Club activist Duncan McDuffie of Berkeley, California, April 9, 1939, Rocky Mountain National Park file, folder 5589, Olmsted Associates Collection, Library of Congress.

41. Olmsted, *Improvement of Boulder*, p. vi.

SOURCES AND NOTES

CHAPTER 25: Adams County

Sources

Albin Wagner's two-volume booklet, *Adams County: Crossroads of the West* (Brighton, CO: Adams County Board of Commissioners, 1977), is a starting point for county history. As Wagner notes in his preface, "Adams County has always had 'bad press'. . . . One of the reasons for this is because the authors . . . must depend on local histories and other published material for their information. Until recently, almost none of the necessary basic research had been done on the Adams County area and no local histories had been published beyond a few accounts in newspapers."

Wagner's brief sketches are the only attempt at a county history other than W. Carl Dorr's booklet, *History of Adams County, Brighton and Fort Lupton, Colorado* (Brighton, CO: n.p., 1959). The Brighton Genealogical Society tome, *Brighton, Colorado and Surrounding Area* (Dallas, TX: Curtis Media, 1987), includes 302 pages of brief articles on special topics, places and institutions, as well as genealogies. *The Forgotten Past of Adams County*, written by the students of Thornton High School and edited and introduced by Richard Marcy and William O'Connor, is a valuable look at selected sites and institutions.

Individual communities have received more attention, as in W. Carl Dorr's *Looking Back: A Historical Account of the Development of Brighton and Surrounding Community* (Brighton, CO: Centennial-BiCentennial Committee, 1976); Marion Smith's *Westminster Then and Now* (Westminster, CO: City of Westminster, 1976) and his *History of Westminster, Colorado, 1911–1961* (Westminster: Citizens Advisory Committee, 1961); and publications of Westminster's Chamber of Commerce and its League of Women Voters, as well as in the city's fiftieth anniversary history.

Marjorie Christiansen, ed., *Commerce City Reminisces* (Commerce City, CO: Department of Community Development, 1976), is a 23-page booklet on that young, unheralded community; and Emma Michell of Strasburg, who spearheaded the construction of the extensive Comanche Crossing Museum complex, has written *Our Side of the Mountain* (Strasburg, CO: Eastern Colorado News, 1968) and *Comanche Crossing Centennial, 1870–1970* (Strasburg, CO: Comanche Crossing Historical Society, 1970).

Aurora has received a detailed examination by Steven F. Mehls, Carol J. Drake, and James E. Fell, Jr., *Aurora: Gateway to the Rockies* (Evergreen: Cordillera Press, 1985), which contains an extensive bibliography. Carl Vincent McFadden's lengthy, profusely illustrated, anecdotal book, *Early Aurora* (Aurora, CO: Aurora Technical Center, 1978), covers selected topics in exhaustive detail. The Aurora History Society has published various booklets, including walking tours, and the Aurora History Museum, repository for local manuscript collections, has also produced a historic building inventory.

Notes

1. *Adams County Population* (Brighton: Adams County Planning Department, 1969), p. 6.
2. *RMN*, April 16, May 29, and June 1, 1978; Thomas J. Noel, *Colorado Catholicism* (Niwot: University Press of Colorado, 1989), p. 431.
3. *RMN*, February 7, 1984.
4. For documentation of these charges and many others see the Adams County listings in the general index, DPLWHD; *RMN*, February 3, 1979, and February 12, 1985.
5. Brighton Genealogical Society, Brighton, *Colorado and Surrounding Area* (Dallas, TX: Curtis Media, 1987), pp. 33–42.
6. *The Brighton Blade*, February 28, 1908; W. Carl Dorr, *Looking Back* (Brighton, CO: Brighton Centennial-BiCentennial Committee, 1976), pp. 42–44.
7. See *Report on Mexican Welfare* (Denver: Denver Diocesan Council of Catholic Women, 1929) in the Archdiocese of Denver Archives.
8. "Spanish Origin [individuals] in Group Homes," 1980 U.S. Census figures for Adams County.
9. *DP* and *RMN* June 22, 1989, obituaries for Representative Younglund; Senator Dennis Gallagher, interview with T. J. Noel, July 7, 1989.
10. Colorado Legislative Council, *Migrant Labor Problems in the 1970s*, Research Pub. No. 157 (Denver: Colorado Legislative Council Staff Report, 1970).
11. *The Colorado Migrant Health Program* (Denver: Colorado Health Department, 1989), p. 23.
12. *RMN*, November 18, 1977.
13. Dorr, *Looking Back*, pp. 44–45.
14. 1989 Adams County Parks Packet; and Crystal Gray, Adams County Department of Parks and Community Relations, interview with T. J. Noel, July 28, 1989.
15. Steven F. Mehls, Carol J. Drake, and James E. Fell, Jr., *Aurora: Gateway to the Rockies* (Evergreen, CO: Cordillera Press, 1985), p. 22.
16. Michael H. Levy and Patrick M. Scanlan, *Pursuit of Excellence: A History of Lowry Air Force Base, 1937–1987* (Denver: Lowry Air Force Base, 1987), pp. 4–12. Buckley Air National Guard Base is covered in Charles Whitley's lavish *Colorado Pride: A Commemorative History of the Colorado Air National Guard, 1923–1988* (Dallas: Taylor Publishing, 1989).
17. *DP*, November 27, 1988.
18. General Charles S. Shadle, interview with T. J. Noel, June 2, 1983.
19. See U.S. Army, *History of Rocky Mountain Arsenal* (Commerce City, CO: Rocky Mountain Arsenal, 1980).
20. Rachel Carson, *Silent Spring* (Boston: Houghton Mifflin, 1962), pp. 42–43.
21. *DP*, November 27, 1988.
22. U.S. Army, *History of Rocky Mountain Arsenal*, p. 7.
23. *DP*, February 2, 1988.

514

24. Tour of Rocky Mountain Arsenal, February 18, 1989, and interviews with Colorado Division of Wildlife and Denver field ornithologists, by T. J. Noel.
25. See Charles A. Wemlinger, *The Development of Aurora's Water Supply* (Aurora, CO: Aurora Water Department, 1982).
26. *Aurora Sentinel*, September 28, 1977.
27. *RMN*, February 9, 1989.
28. Interview with T. J. Noel, August 21, 1989.
29. *RMN*, July 1, 1984.
30. Ibid., September 14, 1987.
31. Interview with T. J. Noel, August 10, 1989.
32. See Marion Smith, *History of Westminster, Colorado, 1911–1961* (Westminster, CO: Westminster Citizens Advisory Committee, 1961).
33. Ibid., p. 17; and Marion Smith, *Westminster Then and Now* (Westminster, CO: City of Westminster, 1976).
34. Richard Marcy and William O'Connor, eds., *The Forgotten Past of Adams County* (mimeo, n.d.), pp. 13-16.
35. *Priorities in Print, 1982–83* (Westminster, CO: Westminster Chamber of Commerce, 1983).
36. *DP*, January 8, 1988.
37. Marjorie Christiansen, ed., *Commerce City Reminisces* (Commerce City, CO: Department of Community Development, 1976), p. 2.
38. *Cervi's Rocky Mountain Journal*, January 25, 1961; Woody Paige, "Town Without Pity," in *DP*, February 9, 1989.
39. *RMN*, May 25, 1986.
40. Ibid., February 9, 1989, and December 18, 1980.
41. This poem and other information on Northglenn are from "North Glenn to Northglenn," a 1986, 14-page typescript history compiled by Northglenn City Clerk Joan M. Baker and edited by Northglenn City Historian Dorothy Bollman.
42. "Thornton Was First Planned Community," in Albin Wagner, *Adams County: Crossroads of the West* (Brighton, CO: Adams County Board of County Commissioners, 1977), vol. 2, pp. 44–45.
43. *RMN*, October 1, 1983.
44. Ibid., January 22, 1989.
45. Steve Wing, "Thornton Town Center," *Denver Business* (October 1988):16–17.
46. Thornton Senior City Planner Martin Landers, interview with T. J. Noel, August 22, 1989.
47. Jim Griesemer, interview with T. J. Noel, August 21, 1989. *The Intergovernmental Agreement on a New Airport* (Denver: Mayor's Office, April 21, 1988) was the pioneer effort to specify annexation spheres.
48. Interview with T. J. Noel, February 18, 1990.
49. United States Department of Census, Bureau of the Census, "Summary of Economic Characteristics," in *1980 Census* (Washington, D.C.: GPO, 1981), Colorado 7-15, Table 57.

CHAPTER 26: Ethnic Relations

Sources

A starting place for research on African-Americans, Hispanics, Japanese, and Jews is James A. Atkins; *Human Relations in Colorado: 1858–1959* (Denver: Colorado State Department of Education, 1961), which contains bibliographical references. Also valuable is Mayor Newton's Committee on Human Relations's 1947 study, *A Report of Minorities in Denver, with Recommendations by the Mayor's Interim Survey Committee on Human Relations*. The killing of Alan Berg is detailed by Stephen Singular in *Talked to Death: The Life and Murder of Alan Berg* (New York: Beech Tree Books, 1987). For bibliographical information on ethnic groups before World War II see Chapters 16 and 17 above; for material on Hispanics see Chapter 27.

James Rose Harvey's "Negroes in Colorado" (M.A. thesis, University of Denver, 1941) is still useful. James P. Thogmorton looks at the Urban League in "The Urban League of Denver, a Study in the Techniques of Accommodation" (M.A. thesis, University of Denver, 1951). Susan B. Baumunk, et al. delve into prejudices in "The Problem of Racism: An Attitudinal Study of Southwest Denver Residents" (M.S.W. thesis, University of Denver, 1970); on the same topic is Jane C. Hays's "Attitudes of Denver Area Suburbanites toward Ethnic Minorities" (M.A. thesis, University of Denver, 1969). Lionel D. Lyles tells of black neighborhoods in "An Historical–Urban Geographical Analysis of Black Neighborhood Development in Denver, 1860–1970" (Ph.D. diss., University of Colorado, Boulder, 1977). George E. Bardwell considers geography in *Characteristics of Negro Residences in Park Hill Area of Denver, Colorado* (Denver: Commission on Community Relations, 1966).

Much biographical material on blacks, assembled by Juanita Gray, is in the manuscript collection of the DPLWHD. The African-American newspapers *Colorado Statesman* and *Denver Star* provide much information that is being made accessible through indexing being done by Joan Reese at the DPLWHD. James Atkins's papers are at the Colorado Historical Society. Minoru Yasui's extensive collection, rich in material on the Commission on Community Relations and the Japanese, is in the Auraria Library archives, which also house the Judge William Doyle collection.

Among the more significant newspaper articles on Denver's blacks are the September 1951 *Denver Post* series by George Brown and the May 1988 *Rocky Mountain News* week-long retrospective on the "tarnished dream." Joan Reese's "Two Enemies to Fight: Blacks Battle for Equality in Two World Wars," *Colorado Heritage* 1 (1990):2–17, well covers much previously unreported African-American history. An extensive review of busing is provided by James Meadows in "Busing: A Cervi's Rocky Mountain Journal Special Report," *Cervi's Rocky Mountain Journal*, May 8, 1974. Calvin Trillin's "U.S. Journal: Denver, Doing the Right Thing Isn't

Always Easy," *The New Yorker* (May 31, 1969):85–89; Richard A. Shafer's "Showdown in Denver," *Wall Street Journal*, June 15, 1972; Richard E. Price's "Test of Northern Integration," *The Washington Post*, September 21, 1972; and Joseph Alsop's "Denver Holds Key in School Busing," *San Francisco Chronicle*, March 13, 1972, demonstrate the national attention paid to Denver's rocky road to school integration. Patricia A. Shikes treats much school history in "Denver Public School Superintendents: A Historical Study of Educational Leadership" (Ph.D. diss., University of Denver, 1987).

Notes

1. *RMN*, August 18, 1932. The *News* covered the riot on page one; the *Post* relegated it to page four.
2. *DP*, August 18, 1932.
3. *RMN*, August 18, 1932.
4. Shriver quotation from *Colorado Statesman*, March 7, 1941. See also Juanita Gray, "Denver Negro Leaders — Jerome Biffle"; (manuscript in DPLWHD) and *RMN*, February 18, 1964.
5. Anonymous, "A City Looks at Its Minorities: An Abridgment of a Report on Minorities in Denver," *Foothills* (Winter 1948):18 (the abridged of Mayor's Interim Committee report in DPLWHD).
6. Ibid., p. 64.
7. By the 1960s, as prejudice dwindled and Japanese-American income grew, many began moving to various parts of the metropolis. A few, including Minoru Yasui and Larry Tajiri, lived in other areas of the city. Tri-State Buddhist church, poetically rendered in Japanese *Santoo Sanshu Bukkyo Kai* (Three States East of Mountain), was the moving force in making Sakura Square. The church, which had early in its history occupied the former brothel of Mattie Silks at 1942 Market Street, bought the Sakura Square site from Denver Urban Renewal in 1970 for $188,000. The $4 million project, including a 20-story high rise for senior citizens, was dedicated in May 1973.
8. Allen D. Breck, *The Centennial History of the Jews of Colorado, 1859–1959* (Denver: A. B. Hirschfeld Press, 1960), p. 196.
9. Kenneth Goff, *The Scarlet Woman of Revelation* (n.p., n.d.), p. 19; See also Goff's *Hitler and the 20th Century Hoax* (n.p., n.d.), p. 38, in DPLWHD. Goff, sometimes associated with the Englewood evangelist Harvey Springer, claimed to have once been a Communist. Rejecting his Marxist ties, he spent much of the rest of his life fighting communism and water fluoridation while preaching fundamental Christianity in his tabernacle at 125 South Sherman. See his obituary in *RMN*, April 13, 1972.
10. Interview with David McComb, January 29, 1975, p. 19, in the oral history collection of the Colorado Historical Society. See also *Straight Creek Journal*, January 21–27, 1975.
11. Louis E. Sidman, "The High Cost of Prejudice," reprint from *Rocky Mountain Life*, February 1948, in Minoru Yasui Papers, Auraria Library Archives, Denver.
12. *RMN*, May 17, 1964.
13. Ibid., September 9, 1949.
14. *DP*, September 28, 1951.
15. Ibid., September 30, 1951.
16. Ibid., February 7, 1952.
17. In 1966, George E. Bardwell, *Characteristics of Negro Residences in Park Hill Area of Denver, Colorado* (Denver: Commission on Community Relations, 1966), defined Park Hill as the 491-block area bounded by Colorado Boulevard on the west, Quebec Street on the east, East Thirty-eighth Avenue on the north, and Colfax on the south. Lionel D. Lyles, "An Historical–Urban Geographical Analysis of Black Neighborhood Development in Denver, 1860–1960" (Ph.D. diss., University of Colorado, Boulder, 1977), notes that Five Points did not become the center of the Denver black community until the twentieth century; earlier, blacks had been more dispersed in the city's lower-downtown sections.
18. *RMN*, May 18, 1949.
19. *DP*, March 29, 1954.
20. In 1949 the median annual income for Denver's Hispanics was $1,840. For blacks it was $1,930. See Denver Area Welfare Council, *The Spanish-American Population of Denver: An Exploratory Survey* (Denver: Denver Area Welfare Council, 1950), p. 34.
21. Northeast Park Hill Civic Association and the Park Hill Action Committee, "How Can We Get an Open City?"; flyer dated July–August 1965, in DPLWHD.
22. *DP*, October 30, 1963.
23. Ibid., December 5, 1968.
24. *RMN*, August 8, 1965.
25. Phil Goodstein, interview with S. J. Leonard, January 12, 1988 (hereafter Goodstein interview). Park Hill Elementary reintegrated as more blacks moved into the area. By the 1968/1969 school year it had 684 Anglos and 223 blacks; Barrett that year enrolled 410 blacks and only one Anglo.
26. *RMN*, March 24, 1963; *DP*, September 8, 1968. Noel served on the school board from 1965 to 1971. Later she was a regent of the University of Colorado.
27. *DP*, January 22, 1969, called Benton "the most luminous intellect on the school board."
28. Ibid. Pascoe was seeking a seat being vacated by Allegra Saunders, an integration supporter.
29. Calvin Trillin, "U.S. Journal: Denver," *The New Yorker*, May 31, 1969, p. 85.
30. See *RMN*, February 27, 1987, for retrospective article on Keyes. Other plaintiffs were Christine A. Colley, Irma J. Jennings, Roberta R. Wade, Edward J. Starks, Jr., Josephine Pérez, Maxine N. Becker, and Eugene R. Weiner. See also *DP*, October 10, 1971. The Supreme Court case was *Keyes v. School District No. 1*, Denver, Colorado, 413 U.S. 189. Paradoxically, the antibusing

school board, by rejecting the limited busing proposed by Noel and Benton, triggered extensive busing and court control of Denver's schools.

31. *RMN*, March 22, 1970. The *News* for May 22, 1970, contains the text of the ruling. The *Straight Creek Journal* did extensive reporting on the schools; see issues of June 18–25 and July 23–30, 1974, June 5 and December 16, 1975. Doyle died in 1986 at age 75. Election to the Colorado Supreme Court gave him a stepping stone to the federal judiciary, where he served first as a district court judge appointed by President John F. Kennedy and then as a circuit court judge appointed by President Richard Nixon. That, however, did not indicate political compatibility between Doyle and Nixon, for the judge traced his political roots back to Edward Costigan and was allied with his brother-in-law, U.S. Senator (1957–1963) John Carroll.

32. *RMN*, September 30, 1970.

33. *Cervi's Rocky Mountain Journal*, May 8, 1974. The *Straight Creek Journal* did a profile on Southworth in its October 22–28, 1974, issue.

34. William E. Doyle, "In the United States District Court for the District of Colorado Civil Action No. C-1499 Memorandum Opinion and Order" (typescript in the William E. Doyle Papers, Auraria Library), p. 5. The text of the "Final Judgment and Decree" of April 17, 1974, is given in *RMN*, April 28, 1974.

35. *Cervi's Rocky Mountain Journal*, May 8, 1974, quoting the *New York Times*, December 28, 1973.

36. *RMN*, April 19, 1974.

37. Ibid., September 30, 1970.

38. Between December 1983 and April 1985, nearly a decade after the appeal process began, the school board spent $1.27 million on legal and consultant fees. Ibid., May 12, 1985. Frustration over court control of Denver's schools and over busing continued into the 1990s; see, for example, Gene Amole's comments, ibid., February 4, 1990.

39. Goodstein interview, October 1, 1988.

40. The Poundstone amendment was to Article XX, Section 1. At the same election in November 1974, voters expressed their dislike of busing by amending Article IX, Section 8, to forbid "the assignment or transportation of any pupil to any public educational institution for the purpose of achieving racial balance." That provision apparently put Denver in the awkward position of violating the state constitution in order to comply with the federal court mandate to integrate. See James C. Wilson, ed., *Colorado Revised Statutes 1973*, vol. 1A, *1980 Supplement* (Denver: Bradford Robinson, 1980), pp. 316, 433. On the enrollment decline see *RMN*, September 14, 1983. The Anglo percentage began dropping in the mid-1960s before busing was seriously suggested. See ibid., November 17, 1972.

41. Interview with S. J. Leonard, November 5, 1986.

42. *RMN*, October 28, 1973.

43. Ibid., October 13, 1970. Congressman Wayne Hayes, who investigated the Barnes-Rogers contest concluded: "I don't think God himself knows who won that primary." Rogers (1900–1983) succeeded Carroll as Denver's congressman in 1950 by defeating Richard Luxford, 70,165 to 67,436. His victory was also narrow in 1952 when he beat Mason Knuckles. After that he easily beat Republicans including Ellen Harris (1954), William Chenoweth (1962), and Glenn Jones (1964). Greg Pearson provided more competition in 1966, but Rogers still won. In 1968, Republican Frank Kemp came within 9,000 votes of beating Rogers.

44. *RMN*, June 14, 1971.

45. Clarence Holmes to Oswald Garrison Villard, undated letter, c. June 1915, NAACP collection, in branch files, group I, box G27, Library of Congress.

46. Kenneth Gray, "A Report on Politics in Denver, Colorado," (M.A. thesis, Joint Center for Urban Studies, MIT-Harvard, 1959), ch. 5, p. 4. Also see *RMN*, November 3, 1950. Besides Mann, Caldwell, and Brown, other black legislators in the 1940s, 1950s, and early 1960s included Oswald C. Abernathy, Robert C. Rhone, Jr., and Isaac E. Moore. Rhone died in 1964 after a short stint in the the legislature. His family, who wished him to rest at Crown Hill Cemetery, complained of being steered into a black section of the burial ground. Crown Hill said it was bound to honor restrictive covenants written into plot contracts; see *DP*, November 5, 1964.

47. *DP*, September 9, 1969.

48. Ibid., September 10, 1969.

49. *RMN*, November 24, 1968.

50. Unsigned flyer in DPLWHD clipping collection.

51. In 1968, Denver police spent 25,000 man hours preventing riots. In 1969 the number rose to 65,000 and in both 1970 and 1971 it was 75,000. See Research for Progress 1776–1976, Inc., *Denver Leaders Said . . .* (n.p., 1972), pp. viii–xii.

52. *DP*, November 23, 1972, and June 23, 1983.

CHAPTER 27: Fractured City

Sources

Denver's Hispanics deserve more attention than they have received. General histories such as Julian Samora and Patricia V. Simon, *A History of the Mexican American People* (Notre Dame, IN: University of Notre Dame Press, 1977), and L. H. Gann and Peter Duggan, *The Hispanics in the United States: A History* (Boulder, CO: Westview Press, 1986), give little attention to Denver. Early studies include Robert McLean and Charles A. Thompson's *Spanish and Mexican in Colorado* (New York: Board of National Missions of the Presbyterian Church, 1924), and Paul S. Taylor, *Mexican Labor in the United States*, 2 vols. (New York: Arno Press, 1970).

Post–WW II treatments include Thomas W. Ewing, *A Report on Minorities in Denver: The Spanish-speaking People in Denver*

(Denver: Mayor's Interim Survey Committee on Human Relations, 1947); Denver Unity Council, *The Spanish-speaking Population of Denver: Housing, Employment, Health, Recreation, Education* (Denver: University of Denver, 1946); Denver Area Welfare Council, *The Spanish-American Population of Denver: An Exploratory Survey* (Denver: Denver Area Welfare Council, 1950; with a 1952 supplement). Full of data is the Colorado Commission on Spanish Surnamed Citizens, *Report to the Colorado General Assembly: The Status of Spanish Surnamed Citizens in Colorado . . . 1967* (n.p., n.d.). Also helpful is the Colorado Legislative Council's *Report to the Colorado General Assembly: Migratory Labor in Colorado*, Publication no. 72 (Denver: n.p., 1962). Kenneth Keller's "Denver's Westside: Patterns of Social Interaction and Decay" (Ph.D. diss., University of Colorado, Boulder, 1979) covers an area with a heavy Hispanic concentration. Also useful is City and County of Denver, Planning Office, Community Renewal Program, *Denver: Condition of the City, March, 1973* (Denver: Denver Planning Office, 1973).

Lino M. López's *Colorado Latin American Personalities* (Denver: López, 1959) provides brief biographies of leading Hispanics. Christine Marín *A Spokesman of the Mexican-American Movement: Rodolfo "Corky" Gonzales and the Fight for Chicano Liberation, 1966–1972* (San Francisco: R&E Research Associates, 1977), tells of the founding and early years of the Crusade for Justice. Rodolfo Gonzales's epic poem, "I am Joaquím," published by the author in 1967, became an early literary touchstone for the Chicano movement. Thomas J. Noel provides a taste of the ethnic flavors of Larimer Street in *Denver's Larimer Street: Main Street, Skid Row, and Urban Renaissance* (Denver: Historic Denver, 1981). Magdelena Gallegos gives insights into Hispanic life in "The Forgotten Community: Hispanic Auraria in the Twentieth Century" and in "The Swallowtail Butterfly," both in *Colorado Heritage 2* (1985):5–26.

Both the *DP* and the *RMN* have done in-depth stories on Hispanics. See, for example, the *DP* for July 20, 1965; August 19, 1968; May 13, 1969; and the *RMN* for May 4, 1966; February 19, 1979; September 21, 1986, and May 1, 1988. For an inside view see issues of the Crusade's newspaper *El Gallo*. Hispanic collections at the Colorado State Historical Society include material from the League of Latin American Citizens, the Latin American Research and Service Agency, and the Latin American Student Clubs.

Kenneth Gray's "A Report on Politics in Denver, Colorado" (M.A. thesis, Joint Center for Urban Studies, MIT-Harvard, 1959) provides an intelligent overview of Denver politics in the 1950s. The best source on postwar politics is George V. Kelly's *The Old Gray Mayors of Denver* (Boulder: Pruett Publishing, 1974). Since Kelly's account stops in the early 1970s one needs to look at the newspapers during May and June of mayoral election years to bring the story up to date. Also helpful is Dale Tooley's autobiography, *I'd Rather Be in Denver* (Denver: Colorado Legal Publishing, 1985).

Notes
1. *RMN*, April 1, 1973; *DP*, April 1, 1973. For accounts more sympathetic to the Crusade see articles by Stephen Gascoyne in *Straight Creek Journal*, March 20–27, and March 27–April 3, 1973. Gascoyne notes that the battle began at 12:44 A.M. The city razed the shattered building within 24 hours; see also ibid., April 4, 1973, and March 12–19, 1974.
2. *El Gallo*, July 1973. In English, "Goodbye, Brother! You have not died. WE WILL OVERCOME!!!!!!"
3. *RMN*, April 1, 1973.
4. *DP*, April 1, 1973.
5. *Cervi's Rocky Mountain Journal*, August 30, 1971. See also *Straight Creek Journal*, November 28, 1972, on police-Chicano relations.
6. United States Supreme Court, No. 71-507, "Wilfred Keyes et al. v. School District No. 1, Denver Colorado, et al." June 21, 1973, p. 6.
7. United States Bureau of the Census, *1970 Census of the Population: Detailed Characteristics, Colorado* (Washington, D.C.: GPO 1972), p. 359. Most linguistic groups tallied roughly half their members living in Denver and the other half living in the greater metropolitan area. Spanish speakers were more heavily concentrated, with two of every three residing within the city limits.
8. Supreme Court, "Keyes v. School District 1," p. 8.
9. James Michener, *Centennial* (Greenwich, CT: Fawcett, 1975), p. 979.
10. Ibid., p. 979.
11. Anonymous, student paper dated December 10, 1983, in S. J. Leonard's possession.
12. *DP*, September 12, 1974.
13. Paul S. Taylor, *Mexican Labor in the United States* (New York: Arno, 1970), vol. 1, p. 155.
14. *Englewood Monitor*, April 3, 1935.
15. *RMN*, April 3, 1945.
16. *Western Voice*, May 9, 1946. Springer, "who built the Independent First Baptist Church and Tabernacle of Englewood into one of the largest congregations in Colorado" died in 1966; see his obituary in *RMN*, July 10, 1966. Springer was associated with such Christian fundamentalists as Gerald L.K. Smith and Gerald B. Winrod. Winrod praised him: "Brother Springer is a builder, possessed of a great creative spirit"; see "Pray for Brother Springer" (mimeographed fund-raising letter dated November 24, 1954, in the files of the DPLWHD).
17. Denver Mayor's Interim Survey Committee on Human Relations, *A Report of Minorities in Denver with Recommendations* (Denver: n.p., 1947), pp. 32, 35; Anonymous, "A City Looks at Its Minorities," p. 19.
18. *DP*, May 14, 1950.
19. Ibid., May 13, 1969.
20. *RMN*, May 5, 1966.
21. *DP*, September 2, 1965.
22. *RMN*, September 24, 1965.

23. Currigan raised $90,000 for the May 1967 election. Nicholson spent less than $16,000. In 1987 the candidates had spent $1.7 million by the May election. Mike Licht spent $330,000 to get 6,109 votes — more than $50 a vote; see *RMN*, May 20, 1987.
24. *El Gallo*, April 1972; see also *RMN*, May 1, 1988.
25. *El Gallo*, July 1973; *RMN*, October 16, 1977. On the Newton Center incident see *RMN*, August 25, 1973, which reported that juveniles between the ages of 10 and 14 entered the building and threw furniture around. An extensive two-part article by Ron Wolf in the *Straight Creek Journal*, July 16–20 and 23–30, 1974, treats Betty and Waldo Benavídez and divisions within the west side community.
26. *RMN*, June 6, 1988, told of the alleged murder of a Chicano suspected of being an FBI informant by members of the Brown Berets, a group affiliated with the Crusade.
27. Ibid., September 11, 1977, provides a retrospective look at the Crusade.
28. George V. Kelly, *The Old Gray Mayors of Denver* (Boulder, CO: Pruett Publishing, 1974), pp. 59–63. Ironically, Nicholson had been raised a Roman Catholic and, after he became mayor, returned to his childhood faith.
29. *RMN*, August 12, 1946.
30. Many of Denver's police officers had been around a long time. August Hanebuth, chief from 1938 to 1947, joined the department in 1906. He weathered the 1946 grand jury investigations, but on May 22, 1947, the day after Newton defeated Stapleton, he announced his resignation as chief. Deputy Chief H. Rugg Williams outdid Hanebuth. Williams became a policeman in March 1890, served as chief in Stapleton's first administration and in 1949 was still boss of uniformed patrolmen. On Hanebuth see *RMN*, May 23, 1947; on Williams, *DP*, March 3, 1949.
31. Bobbie G. Whaley as told to Robert L. Whearley, "I Was a Burglar with a Badge," *Saturday Evening Post* (February 10, 1962):86. Kelly, *Old Gray Mayors*, pp. 124–39, provides a detailed account of the scandal. *Denver Police Department Pictorial Review and History, 1859–1985* (n.p., n.d.) gives much information about the police department.
32. Whaley, "I Was a Burglar," p. 88.
33. Ibid., p. 86.
34. Kelly, *Old Gray Mayors*, p. 128.
35. *RMN*, May 16, 1979.
36. The first woman on the Denver City Council was Elisa Palladino, daughter of prominent north Denver contractor Frank Damascio. Palladino, a Republican, was appointed to the council in 1935 by Mayor George Begole to fill the remaining two months in the term of Eugene Veraldi, who had resigned. See ibid., March 1, 1935.
37. Pomponio's father, Felice, a founder of the Potenza Lodge, had been market master at the City Market. Pomponio's brother Frank served as Denver's postmaster in the late 1940s.
38. Eugene J. Veraldi represented District Nine in the early 1930s. Later, Michael Marranzino became the district's councilman. On his death in 1946 his son Ernest took over, but at times in the 1950s Joe Ciancio, Jr., also served on the council. Marranzino prevailed in the 1960s. When district boundaries were redrawn, he unsuccessfully ran for an at-large council position. On Veraldi see *DP*, March 5, 1936; on Ernest Marranzino see ibid., March 15, 1947.
39. Sandos died in 1987; see *RMN*, November 4, 1987. Indicative of the changing ethnic character of north-central Denver was the purchase in 1983 of Carbone's, a popular Italian restaurant, by Carpio and school board member Paul Sandoval; see ibid., December 22, 1983.
40. Ibid., December 31, 1982; see the special section on the storm that buried much of Denver under two feet of snow and dumped up to four feet on some parts of the metropolitan area. That snow was matched by storms in early November 1946 and exceeded by the 45.7 inches of snow that accumulated during a five-day blizzard in early December 1913.
41. Dale Tooley, *I'd Rather Be in Denver* (Denver: Colorado Legal Publishing, 1985), p. 56.
42. Ibid., p. 56.
43. *RMN*, May 18, 1983.
44. Ibid., June 17, 1987.
45. Ibid., December 21, 1986.
46. Ibid., June 17, 1987.

CHAPTER 28: An Economic Roller Coaster

Sources

Few historians have yet atttempted to make sense out of Denver's or Colorado's recent past, but Andrew Gulliford, *Boomtown Blues: Colorado Oil Shale 1885–1985* (Niwot: University Press of Colorado, 1989), presents a study that will likely guide future researchers. Much statistical data may be found in U.S. Department of Commerce, Bureau of the Census publications such as *County and City Data Book 1983* (Washington, D.C., GPO, 1983). Denver Regional Council of Goverment publications including *Regional Data Series: 1982 Population and Housing Estimates* (Denver: Denver Regional Council of Governments, 1982) are also filled with mountains of numbers. City budgets such as the *Annual Budget for the City and County of Denver for 1988* (Denver: Denver Management & Budget Office, 1987) also go into great detail. Similarly helpful are Colorado Municipal League and state agency publications.

Without the help of the *Colorado Year Book*, which ceased publication in the mid-1960s, researchers must rely on scattered sources. Colorado State University's Cooperative Education Service loose-leaf county data books, updated from time to time, can be found at major libraries. One of the most useful compilations is the University of Colorado, Business Research Division's *Statistical*

Abstract of Colorado (Boulder: University of Colorado, 1987). Concise statistical material is provided by Woods and Poole Economics, Inc., in *1989 Colorado State Profile* (Washington, D.C.: Woods & Poole, 1989).

Summaries and interpretations of economic data are given by area banks. See, for example, First Interstate Bank, *The Colorado Economy in 1990* (Denver: First Interstate Bank, 1989), and United Banks of Colorado, *1989 Economic Forecast* (Denver: United Banks of Colorado, 1988). Jim Manire compiles much of this difficult-to-find material in *What's Published About Colorado* (Boulder: University of Colorado, Business Research Division, 1985). Newspapers and periodicals, among them *Colorado/Business, Colorado Business, Colorado Business Magazine, Denver Business, Denver Business Journal, Denver Business World, Straight Creek Journal,* and *Westword,* have charted the metropolitan area's economy during the recent past. The Boulder Public Library has done scholars a favor by publishing the annual *Colorado Business: An Index to Articles in Colorado Magazines* (Boulder, CO: Boulder Public Library, 1983–).

Notes

1. *RMN,* October 20, 1973.
2. *Historic Denver News* (February–March 1990) gives a short history of Denver's air pollution. Also see *RMN,* January 15, 1990.
3. *Denver Business World,* January 22, 1979.
4. Ibid., August 1, 1983; *Colorado/Business* (June 1978):22–33.
5. Denver Urban Renewal Authority, untitled typescript history and summary of activities, in files of Colorado Information Resource Center, Auraria Library, Denver.
6. J. Robert Cameron and Galen G. McFadyen, "New College Facilities, New In-Town Vitality," *Journal of Housing* (March 1977):124–27.
7. *Denver Business Journal,* November 27, 1989.
8. *Denver Business World,* July 11, 1983; *RMN,* August 31, 1980, and January 6, 1990.
9. *Denver Business Journal,* November 20, 1989. Phil Goodstein, *Denver's Capitol Hill* (Denver: Life Publications, 1988), p. 73, claims that Chaffee Park (1947–1949) at Forty-eighth and Pecos was Denver's first shopping center.
10. *Denver Business* (December 1986):45. In 1986 a British company, Peninsular and Oriental Steam Navigation, bought controlling interest in the Tech Center. Also see *RMN,* January 28, 1990.
11. *Denver Business World,* February 19, 1979.
12. See Bill Brenneman, *Miracle on Cherry Creek* (Denver: World Press, 1973), pp. 1–11.
13. *Denver Business World,* February 19, 1979.
14. Matthew Schifrin, "Blinder, Robinson — Blind 'em and rob 'em," *Forbes* (April 20, 1987):33–38, questioned Blinder's tactics. In February 1990, Blinder and others were indicted for "an alleged stock swindle and international money laundering scheme"; see *RMN,* March 1, 1990. For an overview of the city's turbulent penny stock history see *Denver Business* (April 1988):14–17.
15. *Westword,* May 14, 1983; *RMN,* October 7, November 26, and December 24, 1989, and March 18, 1990.
16. *Westword,* May 19, 1983. Despite the large defense expenditures, Employment Research Associates of Lansing, Michigan, estimated in 1986 that by diverting funds from civilian use the military buildup of 1981–1985 had cost Colorado 66,210 jobs; see *RMN,* October 27, 1986.
17. *RMN,* December 24, 1989.
18. United States Bureau of the Census, *County and City Data Book 1983* (Washington, D.C.: GPO, 1983), p. 687.
19. *RMN,* March 18, 1990.
20. Ibid., February 9, 1990.
21. See *Denver Business* (April 1989):38–41 and (September 1989):16–17.
22. Ibid. (May 1989):15–17; *RMN,* January 14, 1990.
23. *Denver Business* (April 1989):38–41.
24. Ibid. (April 1988):19–24; *RMN,* May 3, 1988.
25. *Denver Business* (April 1988):20.
26. Ibid., p. 21.
27. Ibid. (July 1988):12–13.
28. Harold Roberts, *Salt Creek: The Story of a Great Oil Field* (Denver: Midwest Oil Company, 1956). On Teapot Dome and a hint at the scandal surrounding Salt Creek see Burl Noggle, *Teapot Dome: Oil and Politics in the 1920's* (New York: W. W. Norton, 1962).
29. *Westword,* August 10, 1983.
30. *Colorado/Business* devoted much of its September 1979 issue to oil in the West.
31. *Denver Business World,* October 9, 1978.
32. *RMN,* January 11, 1981.
33. Quotation from ibid.; see also *DP,* August 21, 1981; and February 12, 1984.
34. *DP,* November 23, 1977; *Westword,* October 17, 1984.
35. *Colorado/Business* (September 1978):40.
36. *RMN,* August 30, 1985; and May 6, 1988.
37. Andrew Gulliford, *Boomtown Blues* (Niwot: University Press of Colorado, 1989), pp. 151–94.
38. *Denver Business World,* February 2, 1983.
39. *RMN,* December 19, 1989; and March 17, 1990.
40. *Denver Business World,* May 31, 1982.

41. *RMN*, January 5, 1990.
42. *RMN*, June 29, 1985.
43. Ibid., December 30, 1988.
44. Ibid., November 15, 1987.
45. Ibid., November 20, 1988.
46. Ibid., April 22, 1982.
47. *Colorado Business Magazine* (July 1989):22.
48. *RMN*, January 15, February 7, and August 23, 1989; January 20, January 27, February 4, May 18, and July 10, 1990.

CHAPTER 29: Air Age Aspirations

Sources

Local historians continue to be more interested in horseback, stagecoach, railroad, and automobile history than in airplanes. Aviation has received little attention, with the exception of Jeff Miller's *Stapleton International Airport: The First Fifty Years* (Boulder, CO: Pruett Publishing, 1983) and Nolie Mumey's *Colorado Airmail* (Denver: Range Press, 1977). Howard Lee Scamehorn, one of the few western historians to focus on aviation, published two monographs on Colorado aviation in the University of Colorado Studies, history series (cited below). See also Scamehorn's article, "Pioneer Heroes in the Age of Aviation," in Francis B. Rizzari, ed., *The Denver Westerners Brand Book*, vol. 20 (Boulder, CO: Johnson Publishing, 1964), and his "The Development of Air Transportation in the West," in Robert G. Ferris, ed., *The American West: An Appraisal* (Albuquerque: Museum of New Mexico, 1963). Paul Barrett, "Cities and Their Airports: Policy Formation, 1926–52," *Journal of Urban History* 14 (November 1987):112–37, argues that planners have treated airports narrowly as transportation facilities, not as part of the total urban milieu.

Notes

1. Quoted in *Stapleton International Airport* (Denver: City and County of Denver, 1967), p. 1.
2. Howard L. Scamehorn, *The First Fifty Years of Flight in Colorado*, University of Colorado Studies, Series in History no. 2 (Boulder: University of Colorado Press, 1961), p. 102.
3. Scamehorn, *First Fifty Years*, p. 120.
4. Howard L. Scamehorn, *Colorado's First Airline*, University of Colorado Studies, Series in History no. 3 (Boulder: University of Colorado Press, 1964), pp. 26–27; Emerson N. Baker, "Colorado Mail Takes Wings," *The Colorado Magazine* 20 (March 1943):95–99; Nolie Mumey, *Colorado Airmail* (Denver: The Range Press, 1977), p. 43.
5. Scamehorn, *Colorado's First Airline*, pp. 34–37.
6. Robert J. Sterling, *Maverick: The Story of Robert Six and Continental Airlines* (New York: Doubleday, 1974), pp. 160–61, 238; and Robert F. Six, *Continental Air Lines: A Story of Growth* (New York: Newcomen Society in North America, 1959).
7. Myron J. Smith, Jr., *The Airline Bibliography: The Salem College Guide to Sources on Commercial Aviation*, vol. 1: *The United States* (West Cornwall, CT: Lowell Hill Press, 1986):141–42 (includes short sketches of individual passenger airlines).
8. Mumey, *Colorado Airmail*, pp. 135–46.
9. Smith, *Airline Bibliography*, vol. 1, pp. 155–56; Olga Curtis, "The Man Who Saved Frontier," *DP, Empire Magazine*, August 18, 1974, pp. 10–14.
10. Smith, *Airline Bibliography*, vol. 1, pp. 205–10.
11. Black, *Civil Airports and Airways*, p. 3.
12. Jeff Miller, *Stapleton International Airport* (Boulder, CO: Pruett Publishing, 1983), p. 18.
13. Denver Municipal Airport, "Dedication of the Denver Municipal Airport Program," in DPLWHD; Miller, *Stapleton International*, pp. 18–29.
14. Sketch of airport and landscaping in the Saco R. DeBoer Collection, DPLWHD.
15. A. W. Newberry, "Airways and the Denver Region," in Denver Planning Commission, *The Denver Plan*, vol. 4, (Denver: Denver Planning Commission, 1933), pp. 31–34.
16. Miller, *Stapleton International*, pp. 44–47.
17. Howard Lee Scamehorn, "Development of Air Transportation in the West," in Robert G. Ferris, ed., *The American West* (Albuquerque: Museum of New Mexico, 1963), p. 76.
18. Federal Aviation Agency, *Air Commerce Traffic Pattern (Scheduled Carriers), June 1961* (Washington, D.C.: GPO, 1961), p. 1.
19. G. Meredith Musick, Sr., *Wayfarer in Architecture* (Denver: privately printed, 1976), pp. 76–78. Additional details are provided in G. Meredith Musick, "Stapleton Airfield, Denver, Colorado," in *Architectural Record* (January 1951):126–30.
20. *DP*, December 20, 1974, and January 16, 1975.
21. *RMN*, August 26, 1944.
22. Miller, *Stapleton International*, p. 101.
23. The 1940 and 1950 figures are from James Buckley, Inc., *Air Service Requirements of Denver Colorado* (New York: J. C. Buckley Research Report prepared for the City of Denver, 1954); Stapleton International Airport, *Summary of Activity, 1955–1988* (one page of annual statistics available from Stapleton International Airport). The 1970–1971 figure from the Federal Aviation Administration's *Airport Activity Statistics of Certificated Route Air Carriers, 12 Months Ended June 30, 1971* (Washington, D.C.: GPO, 1971), p. 15, lists Denver as the nation's eleventh-busiest airport with 3,748,521 enplanements. By 1989, Stapleton had slipped from fifth- to seventh-busiest.

24. *RMN*, April 12, 1963.
25. Editorial in *Casket & Sunnyside, Voice of the Funeral Service/Cemetery Industry* 104 (March 1974):6.
26. University of Colorado Bureau of Business Research and Engineering Experiment Station, *Colorado Aviation Development Survey* (Boulder: University of Colorado, 1946), pp. 71–74.
27. "Executive Summary: The Contribution of Skiing to the Colorado Economy, 1987," prepared for Colorado Ski Country USA by Browne, Brotz, and Coddington, Inc., December 1987, p. 1.
28. Thomas J. Noel, "All Hail the Denver Pacific: Denver's First Railroad," in *The Colorado Magazine* 50 (Spring 1973):91–116.
29. CBA Administrator D. W. Nyberg, quoted in "American Airports: Federal Standards and Urban Change," paper delivered by Paul Barrett at the Western History Association Conference, Tacoma, Washington, October 14, 1989, p. 2, from MIT, *Proceedings, Conference on Ground Facilities for Air Transportation, September 12 to 14, 1950* (n.p., n.d.; mimeograph in Library of Congress), pp. 82–83.
30. United States, Department of Commerce, Bureau of the Census, *Number of Inhabitants: U.S. Summary* (Washington, D.C.: GPO, 1983).
31. *Dallas Times Herald*, May 22, 1989.
32. Roger Bilstein and Jay Miller, *Aviation in Texas* (Austin: Texas Monthly Press, 1985), Elliot J. Feldman and Jerome Milch, *Technology Versus Democracy: The Comparative Politics of International Airports* (Boston: Auburn House, 1982), p. 252.
33. *DP*, March 6, 1987, and June 9, 1988; Tom Simmons, *Metro Denver Population [estimated]* (Denver: Denver Regional Council of Governments, 1988).
34. *DP*, February 22, 1986.
35. Eugene P. Moehring, *Resort City in the Sunbelt: Las Vegas, 1930–1970* (Reno: University of Nevada Press, 1989), p. 264.
36. "The Regional Economic Impact of Stapleton International Airport and the Future Airport Development." (Denver: Colorado Forum, 1986); 13-page mimeograph at DPLWHD).
37. *Partners in Progress for a New Airport Bulletin*, 1988.
38. *Ready for Takeoff: The Business Impact of Three Recent Airport Developments in the U.S.* (Denver: Colorado National Banks, 1989), p. 34.
39. "The Denver International Airport Report II" (1988; a four-color news sheet issued by the Aviation Division of the Department of Public Works, City & County of Denver), p. 1.
40. *RMN*, September 24, 1989.
41. Abandonment of Stapleton within 24 hours of the opening of the new Denver International Airport was one of the terms of the *Intergovernmental Agreement on a New Airport*, p. 3. For various articles discussing the proposed airport see *Wings West: The Western Aviation Community Magazine* (Spring 1987).
42. Laurie McGinley, "FAA Seeks More Airports to Lessen Congestion, But Its Chances Amount to a Wing and a Prayer," *The Wall Street Journal*, August 26, 1987; *RMN*, September 28, 1989.
43. *Financial Statements and Auditors' Report Stapleton International Airport December 31, 1980* (Denver: Alexander Grant, 1981), p. 4; City and County of Denver, *Stapleton International Airport Report on Audit of Financial Statements for the Year Ended December 31, 1988* (Denver: Coopers & Lybrand, 1989), p. 5.
44. *RMN*, April 30 and May 9, 1990.
45. *Transportation in Denver: Issues and Alternatives* (Denver: City Club of Denver, 1984), pp. 5–13.
46. *The History of the Regional Transportation District* (Denver: RTD, 1985).
47. RTD Systems Planning, *Commuter Rail Feasibility Study* (Denver: RTD, 1990).

CHAPTER 30: Rocky Mountain Metropolis

Sources

Newspapers and oral history collections, particularly at the Colorado Historical Society and the Denver Public Library, cover the modern metropolis. Since September 1977, some of the best muckraking has been done by Patricia Calhoun's feisty free weekly, *Westword*. *The Colorado Magazine*, a publication of the Colorado Historical Society since 1923, was renamed *Colorado Heritage* in 1981 but continues to be the major source for publishing metro-Denver, as well as statewide, historical research. *Denver Magazine*, a slick, commercial monthly published by various firms since 1970, includes articles of interest as does its sister publication, *Denver Business*.

The *Historic Building Inventory* (Denver: Denver Planning Office, 1977; revised 1981) lists for each of Denver's 73 neighborhoods architecturally and historically significant pre-1910 structures by address, and, if known, the architect, date of construction, and style. Several suburban communities have undertaken similar surveys. The computerized files of the National Register of Historic Places at the Colorado Historical Society Preservation Office also yield a wealth of material on the built environment of the metropolitan area. Joanne Dittmer, in her "Raising the Roof" column in the *Denver Post*, has covered environmental, historic preservation, and urban design issues since 1962.

As the Denver Broncos have been so exhaustively covered by the media and in a half-dozen books since their first Super Bowl debacle, we have given them a rest here. For a lavishly illustrated, rosy view of other metropolitan businesses, see Jerry Richmond, *Denver: America's Mile High Center of Enterprise* (Denver: Denver Chamber of Commerce and Windsor Publications, 1983).

For insight into Denver's underworld, ethnic communities, and Police Department, consult the detective novels of Rex Burns. For a detailed political overview, see Lyle W. Dorsett and Michael McCarthy, *The Queen City: A History of Denver* (Boulder, CO:

Pruett Publishing, 1986). *The Queen City* and Thomas J. Noel's *Denver: Rocky Mountain Gold* (Tulsa, OK: Continental Heritage, 1980) are surveys focusing primarily on the City and County of Denver. For overviews putting the Mile High City into a national perspective, see Carl Abbott, *The New Urban America: Growth and Politics in Sunbelt Cities* (Chapel Hill: University of North Carolina Press, 1981), and Bernard J. Frieden and Lynne B. Sagalyn, *Downtown, Inc.: How America Rebuilds Cities* (Cambridge, MA: MIT Press, 1990).

Notes

1. *DP*, November 14, 1984.
2. *1989 Denver Comprehensive Plan* (Denver: Denver Planning and Community Development Office, 1989), summary report, p. 1.
3. Rodney E. Hero and Kathleen M. Bailey, "The Election of Federico Peña as Mayor of Denver: Analysis and Implications," *Social Science Quarterly* 70 (June 1989):300–10.
4. Interview with T. J. Noel, April 10, 1990. See also Philip Milstein, "The Auraria Higher Education Center" (Ph.D. diss., University of Colorado, Denver, 1990).
5. Interview with T. J. Noel, April 16, 1990. McEncroe hopes her manuscript, "The Urban Renewal Movement," will be published in 1991.
6. Sandra Dallas, *Cherry Creek Gothic: Victorian Architecture in Denver* (Norman: University of Oklahoma Press, 1971), first pointed out that Curtis Park escaped the attention of developers, urban renewal, and highway builders to remain a neighborhood of handsome Victorian homes.
7. *DP*, May 9, 1976. For a detailed sketch of Historic Denver's origins and achievements see *Historic Denver News* (December 1980).
8. Quoted in Thomas J. Noel, *Denver's Larimer Street: Main Street, Skid Row and Urban Renaissance* (Denver: Historic Denver, 1981), p. 38.
9. All Arndt quotations are from interview of February 20, 1974, with David McComb, in the Colorado Historical Society Library.
10. Boston, New York, and other cities created landmark commissions two years before Denver did. By 1990 over 1,500 preservation commissions had been established across the country, according to the National Trust for Historic Preservation's *Preservation News* (June 1990):5.
11. Interview by T. J. Noel, October 2, 1989.
12. *Denver Planning News* (a quarterly in-house newspaper published by City and County of Denver; Spring 1990).
13. *RMN*, April 12, 1990.
14. Bradford Luckingham, *Phoenix: The History of a Southwestern Metropolis* (Phoenix: University of Arizona Press, 1989), p. 236.
15. Smiley, *Denver*, p. 976; Saco R. DeBoer, "Scenic and Recreational Resources," in Denver Planning Commission, *The Denver Plan*, vol. 4 (Denver: Denver Planning Commission, 1933).
16. Joe Shoemaker, *Returning the Platte to the People* (Denver: The Greenway Foundation, 1981), p. v.
17. Carolyn and Don Etter, "Denver's Landscape Legacy," *Historic Denver News* (April 1986):5.
18. *DP*, October 24, 1988.
19. *Features of the Denver Water System* (Denver: Denver Water Department, Office of Public Affairs, 1976).
20. James L. Cox, *Metropolitan Water Supply: The Denver Experiment* (Boulder: n.p., 1967), p. 96, quoted in William H. Miller, "The Denver Water Department" (typescript, dated November 18, 1971, in the library of the Denver Water Department).
21. Alex Shoumatoff, "The Skipper and the Dam," *The New Yorker* (December 1, 1986):71–99. Two Forks as a dam site is mentioned in the *Denver Times*, October 22, 1898.
22. *DP*, March 22, 1990.
23. *Denver Museum of Natural History, 1989 Annual Report*, p. 2.
24. Denver Zoological Foundation, *The Zoo Review*, August 1, 1986, discusses the zoo's 25-year master plan. See also Richard Johnson, "Life's a Zoo," *DP*, *Contemporary Magazine*, September 18, 1988, pp. 12–15; and Earl Pomeroy, *Zoo, City Park, Denver, Colorado* (Denver: Denver Zoological Foundation, 1953).
25. *Inventory of and Condition Assessment of Public Art Collection* (Denver: Commission on Cultural Affairs, 1987); see also Phil Goodstein, "Monumental Denver," *Colorado Heritage* 3, (1987):34–43.
26. *AIA Journal* (May 1980):144–55; William Kostka and Associates, *Boettcher Concert Hall* (Denver: Denver Center for the Performing Arts, 1980).
27. Louisa Ward Arps and Bernice E. Petersen, *Cemetery to Conservatory* (Denver: Denver Botanic Gardens, 1980).
28. All quotes are from Evelyn C. White, "Paul Stewart's Romance with the West," *Smithsonian Magazine* 20 (August 1989):58–68.
29. *The Denver Public Library: 100th Anniversary Celebration* (Denver: Denver Public Library, 1989); Suzanne Weiss, "Library Issue Going to the Voters," *RMN*, January 12, 1990.
30. *A Profile of Poverty in the Denver Metropolitan Area* (Denver: Piton Foundation, 1987), p. 111.
31. Ibid., pp. 103–4.
32. Ibid., pp. 35–49.
33. Lyle W. Dorsett, *Denver Rescue Mission: A Brief History* (Denver: Denver Rescue Mission, 1983).
34. Quoted in Thomas J. Noel, *Colorado Catholicism* (Niwot: University Press of Colorado, 1989), p. 215.
35. *Downtown Denver Housing: The Subsidy Dilemma* (Denver: City Club of Denver, 1986), pp. 21–24.
36. William J. Ratzlaff, *Historical Perspective on the Denver Housing Authority* (Denver: Denver Housing Authority, 1975).
37. *Denver Housing Authority's 40th Anniversary Report* (Denver: Housing Authority of the City of Denver, 1977), pp. 21, 23.

38. Quotation from interview with David McComb, January 29, 1976, in Colorado Historical Society Library; see also interview with T. J. Noel, April 20, 1990.
39. *A History of the Visiting Nurse Association of Denver, Colorado, 1889–1939* (Denver: n.p., 1939), p. 11.
40. See *Intergovernmental Agreement on a New Airport* (Denver: Mayor's Office, April 21, 1988).
41. Griesemer, interview with T. J. Noel, August 21, 1989. Marshall Kaplan, who facilitated Denver-Aurora negotiations, has elaborated on the process in "Mediation of Public Disputes: The Wave of the Future?" *National Civic Review* 77 (July–August 1988):285–97; see also Neal Pierce, "Denver: Model of Metro Unity," *DP*, March 8, 1987. Ironically, the Galleria Shopping Center never materialized after developer Bill Walters declared bankruptcy and moved to California. The 100-acre, $27-million site was returned to its natural state — a wildlife wetlands.
42. Interview with T. J. Noel, April 20, 1990.
43. *RMN*, March 18, 1984.
44. Susan W. Furniss, "The Response of the Colorado General Assembly to Proposals for Metropolitan Reform," *The Western Political Quarterly* 26 (December 1973):747–65.
45. Quoted in Mike O'Keefe, "Doctor No: Is the Denver Regional Council of Governments a Prescription for Metro Mediocrity?" *Westword*, November 8–14, 1989.
46. *RMN*, April 16, 1990; *DP*, April 22, 1990.